UNM
GALLUP

Zollinger Library

THE ENCYCLOPEDIA OF
CRIME SCENE INVESTIGATION

THE ENCYCLOPEDIA OF
CRIME SCENE
INVESTIGATION

Michael Newton

Foreword by John L. French
Crime Scene Supervisor, Baltimore Police Crime Laboratory

Facts On File
An imprint of Infobase Publishing

The Encyclopedia of Crime Scene Investigation

Facts On File, Inc.
An imprint of Infobase Publishing, Inc.
132 West 31st Street
New York NY 10001

Library of Congress Cataloging-in-Publication Data

Newton, Michael.
The encyclopedia of crime scene investigation / Michael Newton.
p. cm.
Includes bibliographical references and index.
ISBN-13: 978-0-8160-6814-2 (hardcover)
ISBN-10: 0-8160-6814-3 (hardcover)
1. Crime scene searches—Encyclopedias. 2. Criminal investigation—Encyclopedias.
3. Evidence, Criminal—Encyclopedias. I. Title.
HV8073.N49 2007
363.25'2—dc22   2007004406

Facts On File books are available at special discounts when purchased in bulk quantities for businesses, associations, institutions, or sales promotions. Please call our Special Sales Department in New York at (212) 967-8800 or (800) 322-8755.

You can find Facts On File on the World Wide Web at http://www.factsonfile.com

Text design by Cathy Rincon
Cover design by Salvatore Luongo

Printed in the United States of America

VB CGI 10 9 8 7 6 5 4 3 2 1

This book is printed on acid-free paper.

Inventor, n. A person who makes an ingenious arrangement of
wheels, levers and springs, and believes it civilization.

—Ambrose Bierce
The Devil's Dictionary

If the human race wants to go to hell in a basket,
technology can help it get there by jet. It won't change the desire or
the direction, but it can greatly speed the passage.

—Charles M. Allen
"Unity in a University,"
speech at Wake Forest
University, 25 April 1967

Contents

Foreword

A BIT OF HISTORY

As long as one man has and another wants, there will be always be crime. The second story of the Bible is that of people breaking established rules. It is followed by an account of the first murder. And not much has changed since then. Murder, robbery, theft, and rape are part of mankind's history.

To maintain order, most societies establish laws, rules of behavior that people are expected to obey. Those who do not are punished as an example and a warning to the rest. Laws that go unenforced soon cease to be effective. So when a crime is committed, it is vital to society to quickly identify the lawbreaker. Only by the swift detection, capture, and punishment of the criminal can order be maintained.

That is society's interest. Those who would break the law have another, mainly to cover up their crimes and elude detection for as long as possible, preferably forever.

For a long time, the advantage was with the criminal. If he could commit his crime and leave the scene undetected, he stood a good chance of escaping justice. Those charged with law enforcement had to rely on luck, witnesses, and any obvious clues that the criminal may have left behind. Luck was often with the careful criminal, who made sure not to leave behind any incriminating personal effects.

A larger danger in these times was that the wrong man could be arrested and convicted for a crime. Victim and witness identification is not 100 percent reliable. Suspects developed by police through witnesses, analysis of past behavior of known felons, and the interpretation of whatever evidence was found on scenes had little chance of proving their innocence once accused of a crime. The real criminal was not likely to confess, nor was law enforcement likely to admit the possibility of mistakes. Justice was swift, punishment brutal, and mistakes were doubtless made.

It was not until the latter part of the 19th century that matters began to improve. Advances in science aided both law enforcement officials and those who stood falsely accused of crimes.

One concern of the justice system was the identification of repeat offenders. Until the late 1800s, police relied upon their memories to identify those who had been previously arrested. Then, in 1878 the development of the dry-plate photographic process made it possible to record images of people taken into custody. Police, however, were slow to make use of this new technology.

In 1879, while working for the French prefect of police, Alphonse Bertillon proposed that a series of 14 different measurements taken of a prisoner would positively identify him. In November 1882, his system was adopted on a trial basis and in February 1883, a prisoner calling himself Dupont was identified as one who had been previously arrested under the name "Martin." By the end of 1884, Bertillon's method had led to the identification of more than 300 repeat offenders. By then, Bertillon had embraced the new technology of photography, establishing a rogues' gallery of felons, their images preserved in what is now the traditional full face and profile "mugshots."

The Bertillonage system was universally accepted until the turn of the last century when two cases, one in England and the other in the United States, pointed out its deficiencies. In England in 1901, one of a pair of identical twins, Albert and Ebenezer Fox, stood accused of theft. But which one? Their Bertillon measurements identical, they could be identified only through fingerprints. Once their identities were established, Ebenezer went to jail and Albert was set free.

Two years later, a prisoner named Will West arrived in Fort Leavenworth Prison. However, based on his Bertillon measurements, "Will West" was already incarcerated there. As it turned out, there were two men, one William West, the other Will—with the same features and the same Bertillon measurements. Only through fingerprints could the men be separately identified.

At the same time, the use of fingerprints to solve crime was growing. The earliest known case was in Tokyo in 1879 where Scottish doctor and missionary Henry Faulds used a sooty handprint left on the scene of a theft to exonerate the man police had arrested for the crime. A second man arrested a few days later confessed, his handprint matching that found on the scene.

In 1892, Juan Vucetich of the Argentine police solved the double murder of two children, using a bloody print found on a door post to show that their mother had committed the deed. Scotland Yard had its first arrest and conviction using fingerprints in 1902. This was for a burglary. Its first murder conviction from prints came in 1905.

Other methods of identification were also being developed. In 1902 came the first attempts to employ ABO blood typing to solve crimes. In 1916, Dr. Leone Lattes of the University of Turin's Institute of Forensic Medicine used ABO grouping to exonerate a suspect in an assault.

Some years later, the growing science of forensic ballistics was beginning to allow investigators to match bullets and expended cartridge cases to the weapons that had fired them. In 1915, a man named Charlie Stielow was arrested for a murder committed in Orleans County, New York, the murder weapon a .22 pistol. Stielow was tried, convicted, and sentenced to be executed in Sing Sing. Those convinced of his innocence persevered. Finally, his life was spared and he was set free when it was demonstrated that the pistol recovered from him could not have fired the fatal shot. Further developments in the 1920s and '30s by such experts as Calvin Goddard of the U.S. Army's Ordnance Reserve and Sir Sydney

Smith, medicolegal adviser for the British government in Egypt, led to the methods of firearms identification that are being used to the present day.

Of course, just as law enforcement used technology to combat crime, the criminal class was not slow to employ it for their own ends.

To cite one example, fingerprints have long been a bane to the criminal, especially those who do not wear gloves on crime scenes. Efforts to disguise or alter prints have been made throughout the years. Most were unsuccessful. The only known case of a man succeeding in fully and permanently eliminating his prints was that of Robert Phillips, aka Roscoe Pitts. In 1941, Dr. Leopold Brandenburg grafted skin from Phillips's abdomen onto his fingertips, successfully obscuring his fingerprints. Unfortunately for Phillips, when he was next arrested, police used his palmprints to identify him.

THESE DAYS

In 1977, I began my career with the Baltimore Police Department's crime laboratory. As a crime laboratory technician and later as a supervisor, my job was (and still is) to document crime scenes and the evidence found on them. My job was also to search for and find that evidence with the goal of identifying those involved in the crime. In doing so, I found myself using much the same techniques described above. Fingerprinting on the scene was still being done with brushes and powders. Once a latent print was found, it could only be identified if there was a suspect, or else after a long and tedious search through arrest records and open case files. Likewise, while spent cartridge cases and fired bullets could be matched to recovered weapons, linking them to other crimes in which the weapon had been used again required the long process of manually sifting through evidence from past cases.

Blood found on the scene was matched to suspects and victims through ABO grouping and similar genetic markers. Semen and other bodily fluids were useless unless the person from whom they came secreted these markers. And all too often, more than one of the people involved in the crime had identical marker profiles, making a positive identification impossible.

Gradually, though, the technology we employed caught up with our needs. By the early 1980s, the BPD Crime Lab began using cyanoacrylate (Super Glue) fumes to develop prints on surfaces that were previously considered unsuitable for processing. Lasers gave us another tool with which to find still more latent prints. And then our evidence gathering capability again increased with the use deoxyribonucleic acid (DNA) analysis. Not only could we better compare blood and semen from victims and scenes to those suspected of committing the crimes, but such items as the mouths of soda bottles, the handles of weapons, and the triggers of handguns now bore invisible traces that, if properly recovered, could positively identify a suspect.

If I were asked to pick the one recent scientific advance that changed law enforcement most radically, I would have to choose the computer. Its effect on crime and crime fighting, and the satisfaction one gets from doing the job, has been amazing. Computers are used in the analysis of crime patterns: reports, crime scene diagrams, and facial composites by witnesses of suspects—back in 1977 all of these were prepared by hand, and not always done as accurately or presented as neatly as we would have liked. Computers now allow us to do these jobs more thoroughly and professionally.

This, however, is office work, administrative matters that, while important, are secondary to the main goal: putting the criminals in jail. And it is in this area where the computer best serves law enforcement.

Police departments on the local, state, and federal levels have established massive databases—databases that hold digital records of inked prints of those arrested, latent prints recovered from crime scenes, lands and grooves from fired bullets, firing pin impressions from spent cartridge cases, and DNA patterns from body fluids recovered on crime scenes and taken from sex offenders.

The use of these computer databases gives law enforcement a powerful weapon. No longer do police need to develop a suspect to have a recovered print matched to one. Entering the print into an AFIS (Automated Fingerprint Identification System), a fingerprint examiner can sometimes make a match in a case without witnesses or suspects within 24 hours of the crime's being committed. Similar databases exist to match recovered bullets and cartridge cases from one scene to those on another and to the gun that fired them. Still another does the same for the DNA patterns from recovered evidence and known offenders. Thanks to these tools, law enforcement

no longer need rely on luck, witnesses, and obvious clues to identify participants in crimes.

These databases also turn back time. Investigations of crimes that occurred five, 10, even 20 years ago are given new life as more and more information is gathered and criminals who walked free for far too long are being identified and arrested for their past misdeeds.

More important, with the ability to make faster and more accurate identifications comes the opportunity to free those falsely accused of or unjustly imprisoned for crimes they did not commit. Just as the beginnings of fingerprint, firearms, and ABO comparisons lead to the exoneration of innocent men, so too is DNA comparison freeing or clearing those wrongly suspected or convicted.

BEYOND THE CRIME SCENE

In addition to the mainstays of forensic investigation—the fingerprints, bullets, blood, and similar evidence recovered from crime scenes—other areas of science are having their effect on the war against crime. Medical technology used to diagnose illnesses is employed in airport security. Disciplines such as anthropometry and entomology are helping in identifying human remains and times of death. Forensic engineers investigate the causes of structural collapses while forensic accountants trace stolen money back to its source. There is hardly an established field of science that does not have a forensic application.

Just how much modern science and technology affects the world of crime and crime fighting is explored in the following work. Just as he did in his previous volumes on kidnappings and serial killers, Michael Newton ably uses the encyclopedia format to discuss the history and advances of forensic investigation, giving the reader a look at the science involved, the techniques used and the people who developed and promoted the science, and made it work.

The reader should be warned. Mr. Newton's work may challenge some dearly held ideas and concepts. Who can read about the number of people exonerated by DNA and other evidence and not question the validity of past convictions and executions? Who can feel absolutely certain that what has long been regarded as historical fact will stand up to scientific scrutiny? Who can continue to enjoy certain cop shows knowing how things are done in the real world?

On the other hand, knowledge that this technology exists also may provide its own sense of security. No longer will the stranger in the dark preying on women be anonymous. The means are there to track him by the traces he leaves behind. And the public confidence in our legal system may grow as unjust convictions become fewer and fewer as the means to identify the true criminal improve.

In this regard, Michael Newton's *Encyclopedia of Crime Scene Investigation* serves us well, discussing how pioneering investigators found the way to make science work for the law and how technology today continues to improve on their work.

John L. French,
Crime Scene Supervisor,
Baltimore Police Crime Laboratory

REFERENCES:

Barnes-Svarney, Patricia, et al. *The New York Public Library Science Desk Reference.* New York: Stonesong Press/MacMillan, 1995.

National Criminal Justice Reference Service. "What Every Law Enforcement Officer Should Know About DNA Evidence." Available online. URL: http://www.ncjrs.gov/nij/DNAbro/id.html. Accessed March 9, 2007.

Onin.com. "The History of Fingerprints" (author not credited). Latent print examination. Available online. URL: http://onin.com/fp/fphistory.html. Accessed March 25, 2003.

Ragle, Larry. *Crime Scene.* New York: Avon Books, 2002.

Russo, Gus, *The Outfit.* New York: Bloomsbury, 2001.

Siegel, Jay, Pekka J. Saukko, and Geoffrey C. Knuper, eds. *The Encyclopedia of Forensic Sciences.* London: Academic Press, 2000.

Smith, Sydney. *Mostly Murder.* New York: Dorset Press, 1988.

Smyth, Frank. *Cause of Death, The Story of Forensic Science.* New York: Van Nostrand Reinhold, 1980.

Thorwald, Jurgen. *Crime and Science.* New York: Harcourt, Brace and World, 1967.

Author's Note

Entries in *The Encyclopedia of Crime Scene Investigation* are alphabetically arranged. SMALL CAPITALS within the text denote a subject with its own discrete entry elsewhere in the book. "Blind" entries provide further cross-referencing for certain topics, as where one or more individuals are treated collectively—e.g., HERNANDEZ, Alejandro. See CRUZ, ROLANDO.

Introduction

"May you live in interesting times."

Robert F. Kennedy, visiting South Africa in July 1966, invoked that phrase in a globally publicized speech, describing it as an ancient Chinese curse. Linguists and historians in the past four decades have found nothing to support Kennedy's claim, which appears to be pure invention, but his instincts were true. Interesting times are those marked by conflict and courage, peril and progress, fear and fascination.

For good or ill, we live in interesting times.

Children of the post–World War II "baby boom," now middle-aged, were ill prepared for the 21st century. Their generation was raised on novels, films, and Saturday morning cartoons that predicted an era of intergalactic travel and adventure, hover cars and ray guns, global peace and harmony. Reality is rather different, with nonstop wars and terrorism, the AIDS pandemic, deforestation and global warming, and fossil fuel crises. Space exploration has languished, for the most part, with manned flight halted at the Moon and our neighbor Mars inviolate outside of sci-fi fantasies. At the same time, however, even as humanity gave up on colonizing outer space, technicians labored to invent a new dimension: cyberspace.

It is the new frontier, a virtual realm where reality itself is fluid, and rules—if they exist at all—seem made to be broken. And like every other frontier in the long parade of human history, the new domain has outlaws.

It seems to be a law of nature that criminals always outpace law enforcement in adopting and adapting new technology. From six-guns to automatic weapons, Model-T Fords to Lear jets, adding machines to the Internet, lawbreakers always get there first, while law-abiding servants of the people lag behind.

The reasons for this law-and-order gap are twofold. First, law enforcement and the related private security industry are by nature both reactive and conservative. Both *respond* to threats of criminal activity as they arise. "Pro-active" law enforcement is, in fact, no more than an aggressive drive against crimes recognized from past experience. Investigators and technicians in the field do not anticipate new problems on a daily basis, much less when the crimes defy pedestrian imagination.

Second, the police are forced to work within a framework of established laws, which always lag behind criminal trends, mending fences after the fact. Offenses must be legally defined, parameters and penalties debated, guidelines for investigation clarified, budgets approved. The process may take months or years, and even when it is accelerated—as in the congressional response to terrorist attacks of September 11, 2001—implementation of new legislation still takes time.

The "9/11" crisis, in fact, provides a perfect case in point for how criminals run circles around sedentary law enforcement agencies. Slipping through loopholes in the extant security and immigration statutes, terrorist leader Osama bin Laden used American flight schools to train his suicide pilots for airline hijackings that would level the World Trade Center and gravely damage the Pentagon. Rather than risk his men by sending them aboard those planes with firearms, he armed them with simple knives permitted under short-sighted airline security regulations. In the wake of September 11, new regulations were enacted pertaining to screening of luggage—which played no part whatever in the 9/11 attacks—and even when those statutes were passed in record time, airline and airport spokesmen reported that installation of the newly mandated security devices might take three years or more to complete.

Criminals, for their part, are bound by none of the restrictions that hamper law enforcement. The most notorious of them are innovators, always thinking of new ways to victimize the public. As the Reno gang "invented" train robbery in 1866, and Jesse James pioneered daylight bank robbery a few years later, so modern felons labor nonstop to take full advantage of new technology, seeking more efficient ways to beat the system and avoid detection in the process. "High-tech" crimes are defined by their era. When bank robber Henry Starr abandoned horses and made his first getaway by automobile, in 1914, he was on the cutting edge of outlaw technology, and it served him well for the next seven years. Today a computerized thief in Moscow can steal millions from a New York bank without leaving his apartment—and he stands a better chance than Starr ever did of escaping with the loot, unrecognized.

A thread of inevitability runs throughout recorded human history. The discovery of electricity paved the way, albeit unpredictably, for the invention of modern computers. Before the invention of transistors, glass vacuum tubes regulated the flow of electricity inside computers—the largest and most powerful of its day being the Electronic Numerical Integrator and Computer (ENIAC) built at the University of Pennsylvania in 1946. ENIAC weighed almost 60,000 pounds, filled a 30-by-50-foot room, and cost more than $3.2 million to build. Transistors were invented in 1958, and the first case of American computer crime was recorded the same year. By 1976, U.S. authorities had logged 374 cases of "computer abuse"—including four cases of frustrated owners who shot their own computers in fits of rage.

The rest is history.

Some high-tech crimes are simply variations on familiar themes, their ancient motives—greed, desire, revenge, religious and political fanaticism—coupled with new technology to become at once more profitable and more threatening to organized society. Such crimes as theft, fraud, stalking and harassment, espionage, sabotage, and terrorism are as old as *Homo sapiens,* but new advances in communications, data storage and retrieval elevate common felons to new levels of achievement.

At the same time, certain modern crimes are truly that: without computers and associated hard- or software they would not exist. "Phreaking"—the art of defrauding long-distance telephone carriers with computers or other devices—has existed only since the final quarter of the 20th century. Computer "hacking," likewise, is a product of the 1960s, turned to crime (for sport or profit) even as aging pioneers in the field volubly defend an illusory "hacker ethic." Child pornography may be as old as the first camera, but its present global proliferation—complete with "morphing" of victims' bodies and faces to confound investigators—is a product of our interesting times. Drug dealers and addicts have existed throughout history, but only in the past three decades have synthetic "designer drugs" been manufactured with an eye toward societal demographics. Embezzlers have always plagued financial institutions, but before the cyberage they were unable to grow rich by "data diddling" and "salami slicing." (See the CYBERCRIME entry for definitions.)

Progress always has a price. No advance in technology comes without corresponding changes in society, both good and bad. It is the challenge of a free society to use modern technology for the greatest benefit, while restraining those who would corrupt new inventions and use them for personal gain, to the detriment of their neighbors and in violation of the law. It remains for future historians to judge how well that task has been achieved, or whether cyberspace shall prove to be an ungovernable Wild Frontier.

Entries A–Z

ABRAHAMSEN, David (1903–2002)

A native of Trondheim, Norway, born in 1903, Abrahamsen earned his doctorate from the Royal Frederick University in 1929, practicing neurology and psychiatry in Oslo until 1940. He left Norway shortly before the Nazi invasion, working for a time in London before he immigrated to the United States. From 1948 to 1952, he served as director of scientific research at New York's Sing Sing Prison. In 1966, he was appointed to serve as medical and psychiatric director of the Foundation for the Prevention of Addictive Diseases. Abrahamsen also taught at several New York universities while publishing 15 books and founding the Forum for the Study and Prevention of Crime at Columbia University. In 1977, his interviews with serial killer David "Son of Sam" Berkowitz influenced a New York court to find Berkowitz sane and fit for trial. Abrahamsen's publications in the field of forensic psychiatry include *Crime and the Human Mind* (1945), *Who Are the Guilty?* (1952), *The Psychology of Crime* (1960), *Our Violent Society* (1970), *The Murdering Mind* (1973), *Nixon vs. Nixon* (1977), *The Mind of the Accused* (1983), and *Confessions of Son of Sam* (1985). His last book, *Murder and Madness: The Secret Life of Jack the Ripper* (1992), raised a storm of controversy when critics highlighted numerous factual errors and Scotland Yard spokesmen denied Abrahamsen's claim that it was based on previously unpublished data from their files. Abrahamsen died in 2002.

ACCIDENT Reconstruction

Accident reconstruction is a relatively new field of forensic science, pioneered in the 1940 New York City case of *People vs. Herman*. That case concerned an automobile crash allegedly caused by excessive speed. The driver, defendant Herman, denied exceeding the posted speed limits, but professors of CHEMISTRY and physics from a local university appeared as expert witnesses for the prosecution, demonstrating from measurement of skid marks that Herman must have been speeding before he applied his brakes. Today, experts in accident reconstruction investigate thousands of cases each year, involving cars and trucks, bicycles and motorcycles, buses, boats, trains, and all kinds of aircraft. Many police academies offer courses in accident reconstruction, while various private consulting firms offer expert services for a fee. The NATIONAL TRANSPORTATION SAFETY BOARD devotes itself full time to investigation and reconstruction of mass-transit accidents and certain serious automobile crashes.

In 1985, the U.S. National Highway Traffic Safety Administration provided a grant to develop national guidelines for standardized training in auto accident reconstruction. A task force composed of experts in the field produced a report titled *Minimum Training Criteria for Police Traffic Accident Reconstructionists,* which addressed the issue of accreditation for accident reconstructionists, recommending formation of a national certification board. Action on that recommendation was still pending in 1990 when representatives of 12 international accident reconstruction agencies met to form the Accreditation Commission for Traffic Accident Reconstruction (ACTAR). ACTAR's board of directors included one spokesman from each of the 12 founding agencies, including police officers, forensic engineers, educators and private consultants active in the field throughout the United States and Canada. Incorporated in 1992, ACTAR has worked since that time to promote recognition of minimum standards in accident reconstruction and to compile a list of accredited experts. Those accredited must continue their education in the field, earning a minimum number of educational units during successive five-year periods in order to retain their ACTAR certification.

Much of the actual work in accident reconstruction is today performed by various computer software programs such as those produced by Eos Systems under the PhotoModeler trade name. Such programs generate three-dimensional images of various automobiles or other vehicles, then proceed to map skid marks and calculate crush measurements for different speeds on impact. Meanwhile, laboratory examination of damaged vehicles or their remains provides further evidence toward the determination of an accident's cause, be it mechanical failure, metal fatigue, sabotage, other external forces (weather, etc.), or some human error. Such calculations are vital to establishing responsibility, with an eye toward both potential civil litigation and/or criminal prosecution.

ACCOUNTING, Forensic

Forensic accounting is the application of accounting (or bookkeeping) to matters considered by civil or criminal courts. Forensic accountants use their auditing and investigative skills to investigate cases of suspected financial malfeasance and in support of litigation (where they calculate and quantify prospective damages). The field includes but is not limited to investigations of embezzlement, FRAUD, MONEY LAUNDERING, WHITE-COLLAR CRIME, and various aspects of organized (or syndicated) crime. Forensic accountants perform both *internal* and *external* audits. Internal

audits are conducted on behalf of the accountant's employer to determine whether various laws and prescribed operational guidelines have been observed by other employees. External audits are performed at the behest of law enforcement or regulatory agencies, court-appointed referees, and others, to determine whether individuals or organizations under scrutiny have conducted business in a lawful and ethical manner. When an investigation is completed, forensic accountants also assist prosecutors or civil attorneys with preparation of exhibits for presentation at trial.

ADAMS, Kenneth   See "FORD HEIGHTS FOUR."

ADMISSIBILITY of Evidence

Regardless of its relevance to guilt or innocence, before any piece of forensic evidence may be revealed and explained to a jury, it must first be ruled admissible in court. Specific guidelines must be observed in regard to search warrants (required by law in many but not all circumstances) and in documenting the *chain of custody* from original collection of the evidence through any testing and storage to its final presentation in court. Any failure to abide by relevant statutes and guidelines may result in vital evidence being thrown out of court, with potentially catastrophic results for the prosecution. Even when evidence *is* admitted, defense attorneys may raise questions concerning its treatment and handling that raise doubts in the minds of jurors and result in unexpected acquittals. The ORENTHAL JAMES (O. J.) SIMPSON murder trial is a case in point, where attorney BARRY C. SCHECK and others cast doubt on the handling of BLOODSTAIN and DNA EVIDENCE by members of the Los Angeles Police Department and their expert witnesses. Despite apparently conclusive evidence of guilt, jurors acquitted Simpson on all charges and later voiced suspicions that he was the victim of a police FRAME-UP. (A second jury subsequently disagreed, holding Simpson liable for the wrongful deaths of his ex-wife and her male companion in a civil suit.)

AIRPORT Security

In the wake of airborne terrorist attacks that claimed some 3,000 American lives on September 11, 2001, airport and airline security is a matter of paramount importance both to government officials and to the millions of travelers who fly each day around the world. It remains to be seen whether new security devices and techniques, coupled with stricter legislation passed since 9/11, will in fact make air travel safer, or simply cause increased delays and aggravation for commercial passengers.

The world's first airline hijackings (or "skyjackings") occurred in Peru, with two planes commandeered by political dissidents on February 21 and 23, 1931. Sporadic incidents were recorded over the next 30 years, mostly involving defectors from communist nations, but the United States did not experience its first skyjacking until May 1, 1961, when a Korean War veteran of Puerto Rican extraction diverted a National Airlines flight to Havana. Skyjackings proliferated through the 1960s and became a standard terrorist tactic in the early 1970s, compelling airports worldwide to install metal detectors (for passengers) and X-ray devices (for carry-on luggage). The United States, Israel, and a few other nations also stationed armed "sky marshals" on selected flights, particularly those scheduled for high-risk areas. Although sky marshals frustrated a handful of skyjackings and killed or wounded several terrorists, their numbers were never sufficient to end the threat. Rather, skyjacking seemed to run its course and taper off as U.S. relations with Cuba, and Middle East peace initiatives, sapped support from major radical groups. Still, occasional skyjackings and bombings of commercial aircraft continued into the 21st century, capped by the tragic events of September 2001.

Modern guidelines for U.S. airport security are established by Civil Aviations Security (CAS), a division of the Federal Aviation Administration (FAA). FAA/CAS agents are found in every American airport, prepared for immediate threat response, and most major U.S. airports have their own police forces (or officers assigned from the local metropolitan police department). Since September 11, uniformed troops of the National Guard are also found in airports nationwide, generally stationed near security checkpoints barring access from the airport concourse to departure and arrival gates. CAS guidelines have three main goals in terms of security: (1) to prevent attacks on airports or aircraft; (2) to prevent accidents or injuries due to transport of dangerous materials; and (3) to ensure the safety of passengers.

Step one in the airport security chain is identity confirmation on both passengers and airport employees. Upon check-in, all passengers are required to present a photo ID (and a passport, if traveling internationally). The ID must be presented a second time, with the passenger's ticket and boarding pass, before he or she boards an aircraft at the departure gate. Travelers are also briefly questioned on check-in, specifically asked whether they personally packed their luggage, if the bags have been in their possession at all times, and whether any third party has asked them to carry objects aboard the plane. Those questions are designed to prevent terrorists from slipping explosive devices onto a flight without risk to themselves (as happened in at least one incident during the 1980s, when a young woman unwittingly carried a disguised bomb in her luggage as a favor for a new "boyfriend").

Airport and airline employees, from janitors to pilots and flight attendants, are also required to carry photo ID clearly stating the subject's name, position, and access privileges. Ten-year background checks were supposedly required for airport/airline personnel even before September 2001, but the system remains deeply flawed. On December 14, 2001—three months after the worst terrorist attacks in U.S. history—officials at San Francisco International Airport revealed that 29 employees with full access to aircraft and runways were convicted felons (including sex offenders, kidnappers, and individuals convicted of firearms violations). The ex-convicts were discovered after airport officials belatedly screened fingerprints for 3,000 of their 13,000 employees. (The other 10,000 background checks were still in progress.) Apparently relieved that "only" 1 percent of their employees thus far had turned out to be felons, airport officials declared that those ex-convicts discovered on staff had "lost their access to secure areas"—but they would not be fired.

Access to airport departure and arrival gates has been restricted since September 2001 to passengers with valid tickets. Prior to reaching the terminal gates, all passengers are required to pass through metal detectors, while their carry-on baggage is x-rayed. Federal legislation passed since 9/11 mandates installation of new equipment to x-ray check-through baggage as well, but airports around the country have predicted that they will miss the mandatory installation deadline by several years, due to shortages of equipment and funding. In addition to weapons—now including knives of any size, formerly those with blades of four inches and longer—airline passengers and personnel are forbidden from transporting the following items without specific authorization:

Explosives including fireworks, ammunition, sparklers, matches, gunpowder, or signal flares

Pressurized containers including hair spray, oxygen tanks, propane tanks, spray paint, or aerosol insect repellent

Poisons including arsenic, cyanide, or any pesticides and insecticides

Corrosives including acids, lye, drain cleaner, mercury, and automobile batteries

Household items including any solvents, bleach, pool chemicals, flammable liquids, or flammable perfume in bottles of 16 ounces or larger

Liquids, gels, and aerosols must be in three-ounce or smaller containers with the exception of baby formula and medication, which must be presented at the security gate

Failure to declare weapons or any of the items listed above when boarding an aircraft may result in criminal prosecution, with penalties including prison time and stiff fines. It is furthermore illegal even to joke about weapons, explosives, hijacking, or other such threats in an airport or on board an airplane, pranksters being liable to arrest and criminal prosecution even when they are unarmed and have no criminal intent.

The majority of airport metal detectors operate on the pulse induction (PI) principle. PI systems typically employ a coil of wire on one side of an arch as a transmitter and receiver. Short, powerful pulses of electric current pass through that coil, each generating a momentary magnetic field. As each pulse ends, the magnetic field reverses polarity and collapses,

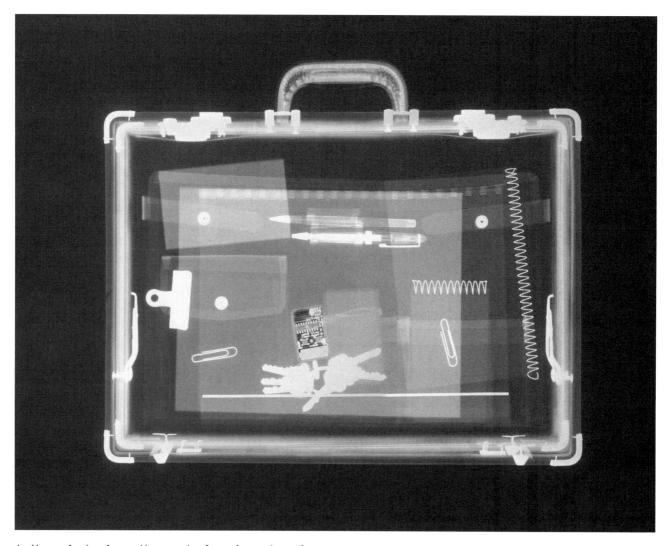

An X-ray of a briefcase. X-ray technology plays a key role in airport security. (Lester Lefkowitz/CORBIS)

thereby sending another burst of current (called the "reflected pulse") through the coiled wire. Common PI metal detectors send out anywhere from 25 to 1,000 pulses per second, depending on the model, with each reflected pulse lasting some 30 microseconds (millionths of a second). When a metal object passes through the arch, the electric pulse creates an opposite magnetic field around the object, thereby triggering a longer-than-normal reflected pulse, detected by a built-in "sampling circuit," which notes discrepancies in the length of any reflected pulse and sounds an audible alarm. Many newer metal detectors are "multi-zone" models, equipped with multiple transmit-receive coils at different heights, to increase their sensitivity.

Prior to September 2001, passengers who triggered alarms from airport metal detectors after emptying their pockets (and sometimes removing jewelry and other items) might be double-checked with hand-held metal detectors, frisked for hidden weapons, or asked to disrobe in private examination rooms. Since 9/11, random frisks and double-scans of passengers have become routine, including requests that some travelers remove their shoes for inspection prior to boarding. One security firm, Adams Electronics, offers special "HF-1 Detector Gloves" with built-in, battery-powered metal detectors, thereby leaving both of an inspector's hands free in the event hand-to-hand self-defense is required. The HF-1 gloves are made from Kevlar and Nomex, protecting the wearer's hands from being cut, punctured, or burned (in the event that an incendiary device is uncovered).

While passengers are individually screened, their carry-on luggage passes through an X-ray system that typically divides objects scanned into three categories: organic, inorganic, and metal. Most airport units operate on a dual-energy X-ray system, generating X-rays in the range of 140 to 160 kilovolt peaks (KVP)—a reference to the X-ray's penetrating power. (Higher KVP means greater penetration.) In dual-energy systems, X-rays pass through the object being examined, then strike a detector that passes the X-rays to a filter, which in turn blocks out lower-energy rays. The remaining high-energy X-rays then strike a second detector, whereupon computer technology compares the images from both detectors to present the clearest possible picture. Items are usually displayed in color on the viewing monitor, with organic materials always depicted in orange,

while the colors for inorganic material and metal varies depending on the unit's manufacturer. Most explosives are organic, and would thus be among the objects highlighted in orange. Airport security personnel are (theoretically) trained to identify weapons, ranging from obvious handguns and knives to improvised explosive devices (IEDs), but once again, human negligence and faulty equipment make the system far from perfect. One example: on December 30, 2001 (11 weeks after 9/11, with strict new procedures in place), passenger Barry Brunstein was arrested in Memphis, Tennessee, for attempting to carry a loaded pistol on board an airliner. Prior to arrival in Memphis that day, he had carried the gun aboard two other flights, departing Tampa and Atlanta, without being stopped.

X-ray scanning systems are admittedly imperfect, even with the best technicians in charge. Electronic devices, such as laptop computers, contain so many intricate components that an intelligent bomber could easily hide explosive devices within. Requiring travelers to remove their computers from cases and turn the computers on still fails to guarantee that a small explosive charge is not concealed inside. To that end, chemical "sniffers" are employed—essentially "an automated chemistry lab in a box." Security personnel rub a cloth over the suspect device or article of baggage, then "read" the cloth with the sniffer, detecting any trace residue of chemicals commonly used to build bombs.

Examination of checked luggage, in airports where it presently occurs at all, is carried out by one of three different methods. *Medium* X-ray systems are fixed devices that scan whole pallets of cargo or luggage for contraband items. *Mobile* X-ray units are contained within large trucks, capable of scanning loaded luggage carts or vans as they drive slowly past a stationary target. *Fixed-site* X-ray systems are whole buildings constructed as massive scanners, examining tractor-trailers of luggage parked inside. Legislation passed since September 2001 mandates X-ray screening of all checked luggage in every American airport, but purchase and installation of large units at ticket check-in counters remains problematic. (When all else fails, bomb-sniffing dogs are sometimes used to check luggage before it is loaded aboard an aircraft.)

An alternative method to standard X-ray inspection is found in computer tomography (CT) scanner systems. The CT scanner is a hollow tube that surrounds luggage, slowly revolving while bombarding it with X-rays, recording the data and creating a highly detailed "slice" (tomogram) of the bag. From there, the CT scanner calculates mass and density of objects inside the bag, reporting on any items that fall within the normal range of dangerous materials. Most European airports run all checked baggage through CT scanners, and while many American airports possess the technology, it has not been used consistently because its slow rate of operation plays havoc with tight airline schedules. Before 9/11 only overtly suspect bags were subjected to CT scans. Even today, the devices are not universally available or consistently employed in the United States.

How effective are the latest airport security regulations in America? On September 28, 2001, President George W. Bush called for installation of two reinforced cockpit doors on commercial airliners, each door with a separate key. He further suggested increasing the number of armed sky marshals to cover "most" domestic flights and increased federal control of airport security measures, though he stopped short of requiring that screeners be made federal employees. Bush announced his plan to work with Congress and pass new security regulations "in an expeditious way," but some accused the president of paying mere lip service to heightened security. On December 30, 2001, Bush's Department of Transportation discarded new rules that would have required airport screeners to be high school graduates—a regulation that would have dismissed one-fourth of the nation's 28,000 airport security agents.

Bush's strange reversal brought heated criticism from experts in the field of airline security. James Hall, former chairman of the National Transportation Safety Board, told reporters, "We're dealing with very sophisticated and trained individuals who are trying to blow up our commercial aircraft. These screeners are going to be an important line of defense, and it seems to me we should have higher educational standards for them." Meanwhile, a federal investigator sneaked three knives past airport screeners in Miami, while similar experiments defeated X-ray devices in Fort Lauderdale and Philadelphia. Billie Vincent, former FAA security director, angrily dismissed Bush's improvements as "more of the half-assed measures that got us into the September 11 hijackings and will produce the same half-assed results."

"AIRSNORT" wireless password decryption program

Introduced in August 2001, AirSnort is a wireless local area network (WLAN) surveillance tool that passively monitors transmissions, computing encryption keys upon collection of sufficient data. After collecting 100MB to 1GB of data, AirSnort is reportedly able to produce a target password in less than one second.

Local area networks are theoretically protected by a built-in security, the Wired Equivalent Privacy (WEP) system—also labeled the "802.11b standard"—which automatically encrypts data as it is transmitted. But system analysts agree that WEP leaves much to be desired in terms of real security. In fact, AirSnort designers Blake Hegerle and Jeremy Bruestle insist they went public with their creation in hopes of spurring WLAN technicians to install better security systems. As Bruestle told *Wired News*, "We felt that the only proper thing to do was to release the project. It is not obvious to the layman or the average administrator how vulnerable 802.11b is to attack. It's too easy to trust WEP. . . . It's easy to be complacent. AirSnort is all about opening people's eyes."

Or opening their networks to pernicious hackers, as the case may be. The AirSnort Web site maintained by Hegerle and Bruestle includes detailed instructions on downloading their program and the hardware required to use it effectively. Mark Denon, a freelance technology writer, found it "very easy" to access networks using AirSnort. "I've been able to connect to networks when standing outside of businesses, hospitals, or Internet cafés that offer the service," he told *Wired News*. "You can jump in and use the network to send e-mail or surf the Net, and often it's quite possible to access whatever information is moving across the network."

One benefit for hackers using AirSnort is the program's virtual untraceability. As inventor Hegerle explains, AirSnort does not communicate in any way with other computers on the target network. As a passive eavesdropper, it simply listens to the network's flow of traffic, capturing sufficient data to decode a busy network's password in three or four hours. Low-traffic networks take longer to crack, but Bruestle notes that data collection need not be continuous. AirSnort can revisit a network over several days of intermittent snooping, until sufficient data is collected to decrypt the password.

ALEJANDRO, Gilbert exonerated by DNA evidence

On the night of April 27, 1990, a woman in Uvalde County, Texas, was attacked in her home by a stranger who forced a pillowcase over her head, then raped her. Unable to describe her assailant's face, the victim recalled his general build and his clothing, including a cap, gray T-shirt, and dark shorts. Police canvassed the neighborhood and questioned three men, one of whom wore clothes matching the rapist's description. None were detained for a lineup, but the victim later identified suspect Gilbert Alejandro via mug shots from a previous arrest.

At trial, Alejandro's only defense was an alibi provided by his mother, testifying under oath that he was at home when the rape occurred. Against that testimony, prosecutors offered the victim's shaky identification, buttressed by testimony from FRED ZAIN, chief medical examiner of nearby Bexar County. Zain told the court that a DNA test of semen found on the victim's clothing matched Alejandro's DNA "and could only have originated from him." Jurors convicted Alejandro, and he was sentenced to a 30-year prison term.

On appeal it was discovered that Fred Zain had grossly misrepresented results of the Bexar County DNA tests in Alejandro's case. The first test performed, in July 1990, had produced inconclusive results, while a second test performed three months later actually excluded the defendant as a source of the semen on file. Alejandro's lawyers filed a writ of habeas corpus and he was released to his parents' custody, his movements tracked by an electronic monitor. A Uvalde County judge reviewed Alejandro's case on July 26, 1994, receiving testimony that the 1990 DNA test had excluded Alejandro as a suspect. Two members of the original trial jury also testified that their guilty verdicts were based solely on Fred Zain's false testimony. As a result of that hearing, Alejandro's conviction was overturned, and Uvalde County prosecutors dismissed all charges on September 21, 1994. Alejandro later sued Uvalde County for false imprisonment and was awarded $250,000 in damages for his four-year incarceration.

Fred Zain, meanwhile, was fired by Bexar County in 1993, and later charged with aggravated perjury, evidence tampering, and fabrication for his part in Alejandro's wrongful conviction. Jurors acquitted him at trial, in 1998, but 100 more convictions based upon his testimony are under review across Texas.

Despite his cash award, Gilbert Alejandro remains understandably bitter toward Zain. "He should be put away for a long time," Alejandro told reporters, "like I was put away in prison doing hard labor."

ALEXANDER, Richard exonerated by DNA evidence

In 1996, a sexual predator known only as the River Park Rapist terrorized female residents of South Bend, Indiana. Police arrested 30-year-old Richard Alexander that August, charging him with four of the attacks on the basis of eyewitness statements from victims. DNA testing excluded him as a suspect in one of those rapes, and some investigators were skeptical of the other three cases, Detective Sergeant Cindy Eastman telling reporters, "We had a gut feeling that Alexander was not the guy." Supporting that belief, at least three more similar rapes were reported after Alexander's arrest. Still, task force officers and prosecutors forged ahead with their case. Alexander's first trial ended with a hung jury in June 1997. At his second trial, in March 1998, jurors acquitted him of one rape but convicted him of two others. Alexander received a 70-year prison term for those crimes.

He caught a break five years later, when alleged burglar and child-molester Michael Murphy confessed to one of the rapes for which Alexander stood convicted. New DNA tests were ordered, and their findings conclusively exonerated Alexander of an attack committed on August 7, 1996. Four days later, on December 12, 2001, he was released from custody by order of the St. Joseph County Superior Court. Authorities now say two rapists are suspected in the River Park attacks, and that five of those crimes remain under active investigation.

AMERICAN Academy of Forensic Sciences

Established in 1949, the AAFS is a professional society "dedicated to the application of science to the law [and] committed to the promotion of education and the elevation of accuracy, precision, and specificity in the forensic sciences." At press time for this volume it had more than 5,600 members including attorneys, criminalists, dentists, document examiners, educators, engineers, physical anthropologists, physicians, psychiatrists, toxicologists and other professionals in the field of forensic science. With headquarters in Colorado Springs, Colorado, the AAFS has members in all 50 states, plus Canada and some 50 other nations around the globe. Each February, the AAFS holds an annual scientific conference, where more than 500 papers are presented for consideration. Its *Journal of Forensic Sciences* is published by the affiliated American Society for Testing and Materials.

AMERICAN Board of Criminalistics

Founded in 1989, to develop a national certification program for criminalists, the American Board of Criminalistics consists of various regional and national organizations representing forensic scientists. Each affiliated group contributes one member to the ABC Board of Directors and one member on the ABC Examination Committee. The ABC's three stated goals include: (1) establishment of professional levels of knowledge, skills, and abilities; (2) recognition of those who have the requisite levels; and (3) promotion of growth within the profession. Certification, as defined by the ABC, is "a voluntary process of peer review by which a practitioner is recognized as having attained the professional qualifications necessary to practice in one or more disciplines of criminalistics." To that end, the organization administers a periodic General Knowledge Examination and various specialty tests in the fields of forensic biology, drug chemistry, fire debris analysis, and trace evidence.

AMERICAN Board of Forensic Anthropology

Created in 1977, the ABFA was formed with five goals in mind. As stated on the group's Web site, those aims were: (1) to encourage the study of, improve the practice of, establish and enhance standards for, and advance the science of forensic anthropology; (2) to encourage and promote adherence to high standards of ethics, conduct, and professional practice in forensic anthropology; (3) to grant and issue certificates, and/or other recognition, in cognizance of special qualification in forensic anthropology to voluntary applicants who conform to the standards established by the board and who have established their fitness and competence thereof; (4) to inform the appropriate branches of federal and state governments and private agencies of the existence and nature of the ABFA and the professional quality of its diplomates for the practice of forensic anthropology; and (5) to maintain and furnish lists of individuals who have

been granted certificates by the board. Three decades later, fewer than 70 forensic anthropologists had achieved ABFA certification.

AMERICAN Society of Crime Laboratory Directors

In autumn 1973, FBI director Clarence Kelley—acting at the behest of FBI LABORATORY director Briggs White—sponsored a meeting of 30 American crime laboratory directors at the FBI Academy in Quantico, Virginia. At that gathering, a steering committee was created to organize the ASCLD, accomplished in Kansas City during spring 1974. The new organization held its first formal meeting in autumn 1974, again at Quantico (with Briggs White as chairman). The ASCLD is a nonprofit organization dedicated, in its own words, "to providing excellence in forensic science through leadership and innovation." The group pursues those goals primarily by means of a yearly symposium on leadership and management techniques, together with an Internet Web site providing weekly updates on current news from the world of forensic science. Membership is presently restricted to past or present crime lab director/managers and educators in the field of forensic science.

ANDERSON, Marvin Lamont wrongly convicted; cleared by DNA

A Virginia resident, convicted of rape in 1982 on the basis of a victim's eyewitness testimony, Marvin Anderson received a 210-year prison sentence at his trial. He was paroled in 1997, after serving 15 years, but the stigma of his rape conviction followed Anderson as he attempted to rebuild his life. New legislation signed by Governor Jim Gilmore in May 2001 allowed Anderson's lawyers to petition for DNA testing of semen recovered from the original crime scene. "I knew once they did the testing it would exonerate me," Anderson told reporters. "I knew because I didn't do this."

His longstanding assertion of innocence was vindicated in December 2001, when results of DNA testing excluded Anderson as a possible suspect in the rape. The test results partially matched DNA from two convicted sex offenders in Virginia's data bank, but the evidence samples were too degraded for a positive match to be made on either suspect. Anderson, for his part, was the 99th convicted felon cleared by

Marvin Anderson clutches his absolute pardon from Virginia governor Mark Warner as he and his sister walk out of the capitol in Richmond on Wednesday, August 21, 2002. Anderson was pardoned after being exonerated of rape charges by DNA evidence. (AP)

DNA testing in the United States since the procedure was discovered. "I'm not bitter," he told interviewers. "There's no anger. What happened to me was a mistake by many people, not just any one individual."

Prior requests for DNA testing in Anderson's case had been stalled when authorities reported semen evidence missing from their files. The crucial evidence was rediscovered in 2001, in time for Virginia's new statute to waive the existing deadline on submission of exculpatory scientific evidence. Anderson announced his intent to seek a pardon from the governor. In 2002 Anderson was pardoned by the governor and received $1.2 million as compensation, while another suspect in the crime was charged and convicted.

ANTHROPOLOGICAL Research Facility

Commonly known as the "body farm," the ARF was established by Dr. William Bass in 1972, at the University of Tennessee in Knoxville. It serves as an outdoor field laboratory for study of human decomposition and the various factors that are critical to estimates of time elapsed since death. Donated cadavers provide the raw material for exposure to insects and the elements in varied conditions. As an adjunct to the body farm, the William Bass Skeletal Collection includes more than 400 sets of human skeletal remains collected since 1981, ranging in age from unborn fetuses to 101 years. A forensic data bank launched by Dr. Richard Jantz also serves the facility, providing forensic anthropologists nationwide with current data from some 2,000 individuals to assist in estimations of stature, gender, and ancestry.

ANTHROPOLOGY, Forensic identifying skeletal remains

Anthropology—literally the study of human beings—is broadly divided into three subfields: cultural anthropology (the study of cultures, societies, lifestyles, beliefs, etc.); archaeology (the study of past cultures, via dwellings and relics left behind); and physical (or biological) anthropology (involving all physical and/or biological aspects of the primate order from prehistoric times to the present). A broad field in its own right, physical anthropology is further subdivided into various specialties, including osteology (study of bones). Within the field of osteology we find another subspecialty: forensic anthropology—the study of skeletal remains as they are relevant to legal cases.

In essence, forensic anthropologists examine skeletal remains (a) to identify the subject, where feasible; and (b) to determine cause of death, where evidence exists. Incomplete or badly damaged remains make the task more difficult—sometimes impossible—but

some facts are discernible even from incomplete skeletons. A skull may reveal the subject's race (though interracial marriages confuse the issue) and sex (with a 25 percent margin of error when the skull alone is found). In adult subjects the pelvis identifies gender (with a 10 percent margin of error), but no difference is seen in prepubescent males or females. Long bones of the arms and legs give a fair indication of height and may help suggest age. Bones may also be dated with fair accuracy, to determine if a skeleton is "new" (and thus of concern to police) or a relic from earlier times (as when aboriginal graves are disturbed). Old injuries or abnormalities become definitive in cases where detailed X-rays of missing persons are available. While evidence of soft-tissue injury is wiped out by decomposition, skeletal remains may still reveal cause of death if they display unhealed fractures, knife or bullet wounds, a broken hyoid bone (from strangulation), and so forth.

The most dramatic task performed by forensic anthropologists is facial reconstruction from skulls or their fragments. Work in this field dates from the early 1940s. Pioneers included FBI technician Wilton Krogman and I. A. Gerasimov, in Russia. Once sex

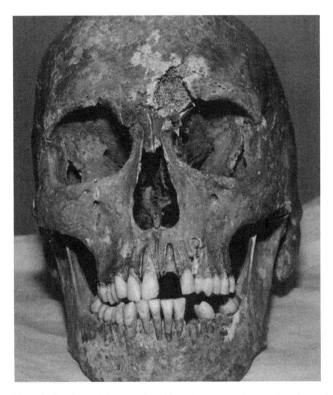

The skull of a soldier in the War of 1812 is cleaned and ready for the anthropologist to make a facial approximation. The skull is covered in Latex and gauze to make a mold. (Kathleen O. Arries)

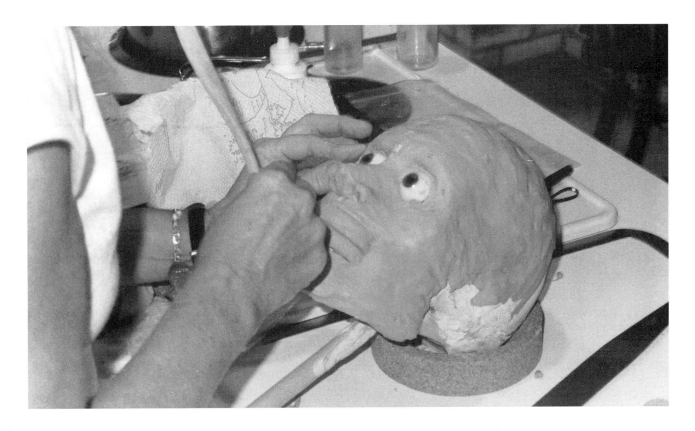

Strips of clay are placed on the mold and smoothed to the desired tissue depths. Applying the nose, lips, and ears takes an artist's touch. The finished approximation of the soldier is as he might have looked after his death. (Kathleen O. Arries)

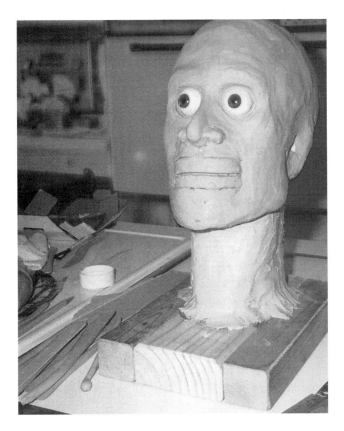

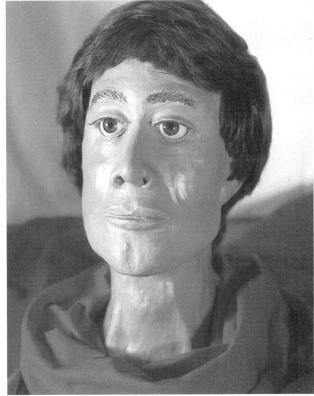

A police officer kneels at the edge of a shallow grave where the dirt has been removed to reveal the image of a woman. Her polyester clothes are still intact after nine years in the ground. (Kathleen O. Arries)

and race are determined, science yields to art as modeling clay is applied to the skull, reconstructing the subject's face in part from careful measurements and partly from the sculptor's imagination. Race helps determine the shape of eyes, nose, and lips, but much of the rest remains guesswork. Without photographs or eyewitness descriptions, forensic anthropologists cannot determine whether a subject was fat or thin in real life, scarred or tattooed, bearded or balding. Hair styles, created with wigs, generally spring from pure speculation. Still, in some cases the models may jog memories, leading authorities to witnesses who may have known the anonymous subject in life.

The same technique may be used to "age" images of missing persons, whether they be runaways, kidnap victims, or fugitives from justice. Modern computer technology makes aging of photographs simple, and such photos are often seen on posters of missing children or fugitive felons, including members of the FBI's "Ten Most Wanted" list. While photos dominate the "aging" field, clay models are also sometimes used. One such model, sculpted in Philadelphia by Frank Bender, led directly to the arrest of longtime fugitive John Emil List. In New Jersey, List had shot and killed five members of his family on November 9, 1971, then disappeared, starting a new life as "Robert Peter Clark." He was still at large on May 21, 1989, when Bender's "aged" bust of List appeared on the TV show *America's Most Wanted*. Recognition by neighbors led the FBI to List's Virginia workplace 10 days later; he was convicted on five murder counts in April 1990 and sentenced to life imprisonment.

Various professional organizations exist to promote understanding and proper application of forensic anthropology. The Canadian Association of Physical Anthropology was founded at Banff in 1972, so that practitioners from Canada "should not have to travel to Kansas in order to meet each other professionally." Five years later, the AMERICAN BOARD OF FORENSIC ANTHROPOLOGY was created "to provide, in the interest of the public and the advancement of the science, a program of certification in forensic anthropology." The board's Web site lists numerous certified members who are available for consultation with law enforcement agencies, attorneys, and the like. The 300-member Midwest Bioarchaeology and Forensic Anthropology Association was created in 1994, "in an effort to support communication on both formal and informal levels." Members of these organizations (and others abroad) regularly share information on major cases, including investigation of mass graves discovered around the world, from Central America to Bosnia-Herzegovina and the Far East.

ANTHROPOMETRY

Anthropometry uses detailed body measurements to identify specific individuals. Before the general acceptance of FINGERPRINTS and DNA profiling as a standard means of identification, anthropometry was widely used under a system pioneered by ALPHONSE BERTILLON ("Bertillonage"), combining 11 specific bodily measurements with photographs and written descriptions to identify known criminals. While anthropometry is no longer used to identify living subjects, it occasionally still proves useful in forensic ANTHROPOLOGY, for examination of skeletal remains where DNA and fingerprints are unavailable. In those cases, bodily measurements determine the size of unknown decedents, while other skeletal factors reveal race and gender. No precise identification is possible from measurements alone, but forensic anthropologists can determine whether the skeleton belonged to a Caucasian female, Negroid child, and so on.

ARCHAEOLOGY, Forensic

Archaeology is the scientific study of historical or prehistoric peoples and their cultures by analysis of their artifacts, inscriptions, and monuments. While archaeologists also sometimes uncover human physical remains, study of those remains (to determine cause of death, etc.) belongs more properly to the fields of ANTHROPOLOGY and/or PATHOLOGY. The disciplines overlap in cases where archaeologists and anthropologists mutually study burial customs, weapons, and warfare, archaic medical technology, rituals involving cannibalism or human sacrifice, and so on. Forensic archaeology focuses primarily on the location and delicate excavation of human remains, rather than medical analysis of injuries and wounds.

ARMORED Vehicles

Armored or "bulletproof" vehicles have long been a staple of crime and crime-fighting, as well as military action. Prohibition-era gangsters like Chicago's Al Capone protected themselves from bootleg rivals with armored limousines, and the 1930s Barker-Karpis gang used similar vehicles (some equipped with smokescreen generators) to escape from police after their daylight bank holdups. Private security firms, in turn, initiated use of armored vehicles for shipping cash and other valuable merchandise, a practice that continues to the present day. Increasingly, as the threat of TERRORISM or ransom kidnapping spreads throughout the world at large, high-ranking government and business figures seek advanced security in transit for themselves, their families, and their associates.

Civilian armored vehicles typically rely on steel plating, shatter-resistant glass, and special "run-flat" bulletproof tires to protect their drivers and passengers. Weapons and gun ports are also frequently included, to give the targets of attack a fighting chance at self-defense. Drawbacks of heavily armored vehicles include reduced speed and increased fuel consumption, all of which comes with a greatly inflated price tag. Manufacturers are typically close-mouthed about specifics of their armor plating, but

multiple layers of tempered steel and occasional lighter materials such as Kevlar are standard for civilian vehicles. Military and police vehicles often employ more expensive, bulkier armor, including the following types:

Composite armor, true to its name, incorporates layers of different substances, each with different protective properties against specific kinds of attack. One system employs steel armor inlaid and reinforced with a network of titanium rods; another sandwiches heat-absorbing chemical layers between steel plates; yet another provides layers of rubber between armor plates to absorb the shock waves of explosive rounds on impact.

Explosive reactive armor (ERA) actually employs a layer of explosive material between thick steel plates, attached like shingles to the existing armor of a military vehicle, but spaced somewhat away from it. On impact of an armor-piercing round, the explosive layer detonates, flinging the steel plates apart and absorbing most of the incoming round's destructive force before it reaches the primary target.

It is presently illegal for American civilians to purchase or possess armor-piercing ammunition, either in the form of small arms "cop-killer" rounds or larger military ordnance, but black-market sources make most forms of weaponry available to terrorists, revolutionaries, and well-financed criminal gangs. Three common antiarmor rounds designed specifically for military use are:

1. Armor-piercing, fin-stabilized, discarding sabot (APFSDS) rounds. The projectile in one of these shells is a long, small-diameter dart with tail fins, made of some extremely hard and dense material such as tungsten carbide or depleted uranium. Because it is much smaller than the bore of the weapon that fires it, the dart is encased in a light alloy sleeve (the "sabot"), which disintegrates and falls away upon firing. The dart—or "penetrator"—itself is designed to pierce armor and shatter inside the vehicle, spraying any occupants with white-hot shrapnel and fragments of the vehicle's own ruptured plating.

2. High-explosive antitank (HEAT) ammunition. These shells penetrate armor by using the

Brinks armored truck in front of City National Bank in Miami Beach, Florida. (Jeff Greenberg/The Image Works)

"Monroe effect" of detonating explosives at a critical distance from the target. HEAT projectiles are cylindrical full-bore shells containing several pounds of high explosives. The front of each round is a hollow cone lined with copper or some other dense material, its extended nose bearing a piezoelectric crystal at the tip. The crystal is crushed on impact, generating an electric pulse that passes to a detonator at the base of the round's explosive payload. When the charge explodes, a detonation wave passes around the cone and collapses it in a "focusing" action, converting it to a fast-moving (16,000 mph) jet of molten material and high-explosive gas. Heat and velocity combine to penetrate the armor, incinerating the vehicle's occupants on contact and detonating any live ammunition in the round's path.

3. High-explosive squash-head (HESH) ammunition. These rounds premiered in World War II and have been constantly refined over the past half-

century. Each HESH round is a blunt-nosed projectile filed with plastic explosive that "squashes" against its target on impact, then detonates from a fuse in the base of the charge. Rather than piercing the armor, the HESH round's massive shock wave dislodges a large steel "scab" from the vehicle's interior plating, which then ricochets around inside the vehicle with killing force.

Use of such destructive ammunition would be excessive and counterproductive for bandits intent on robbing an armored truck of cash—and it would hardly be necessary. When neo-Nazi members of The Order robbed a Brink's truck at Ukiah, California, of $3.8 million on July 19, 1984, three shots from a .308-caliber semiautomatic rifle pierced the armored truck's windows and persuaded the guards to surrender. The bandits scarcely needed the harmless cardboard tube, which they had painted to resemble a bazooka rocket-launcher.

ARMSTRONG, Ralph exonerated by DNA

In 1980, 19-year-old Charise Kamps was raped and murdered at her apartment in Madison, Wisconsin. Suspicion quickly focused on a friend of the victim, 27-year-old Ralph Armstrong, who was then on parole from rape and sodomy convictions in New Mexico. Armstrong admitted visiting Kamps's flat on the night she died, but claimed that he left several hours before she was murdered. At trial, expert witnesses testified that two hairs found on Kamps's bathrobe were consistent with Armstrong's, while his blood type matched that of semen from the crime scene. Jurors convicted Armstrong of the slaying, and he received a lifelong prison term. A quarter-century later, DNA testing—unknown at the time of Armstrong's original trial—proved beyond doubt that the hair and semen were not his. Wisconsin's Supreme Court dismissed Armstrong's murder conviction on July 13, 2005, and ordered a new trial. Dane County district attorney Brian Blanchard announced plans to retry the case, but no trial date had been set at press time for this volume.

ARSON Investigation

According to the U.S. Fire Administration, part of the Federal Emergency Management Administration (FEMA), there were 31,500 intentionally set fires in 2005, which resulted in 315 deaths and $664,000,000 in property loss. The FBI's *Crime Classification Manual* (1992) lists seven motives for deliberate fire-setting. They include:

VANDALISM

Subcategories of this motive include willful and malicious mischief (wherein motive may be determined by choice of targets) and peer-group pressure (most commonly seen in juvenile offenders).

EXCITEMENT

Variants of this motive include fire-setting by thrill-seekers, by arsonists craving attention, by those seeking recognition as "heroes" (firefighters sometimes fall into this category), or sexual deviants who achieve satisfaction from the act of setting fires.

REVENGE

A more "rational" form of fire-setting, this form may target individuals, specific groups or institutions, or society in general. It may also include acts of intimidation, as in the case of fires set to discourage particular activities (e.g., the testimony of a witness, purchase of specific property, etc.).

CRIME CONCEALMENT

Fire destroys evidence, and various arsonists have used it to conceal acts of murder, suicide, burglary, theft, or embezzlement, and to destroy crucial records pertaining to disputed property or activities.

PROFIT

These fires are normally set to obtain an insurance payoff, to liquidate property, to dissolve a failing business, to eliminate unwanted inventory, or to eradicate competition.

EXTREMISM

Fires in this category include acts of TERRORISM and discrimination (if indeed there is any discernible difference between the two acts), and arson incidents committed during riots. Religious fanaticism may be a factor, in addition to political or racial concerns. (In 1999 a self-styled Satanist confessed to burning more than 30 Christian churches across the Midwest.)

SERIAL ARSON

Defined as compulsive, repetitive fire-setting. Indeed, repetition alone seems to distinguish this category from the "excitement" motive listed above. FBI taxonomists confuse the issue by creating a subcategory for *spree* arsonists (who set multiple fires without an emotional "cooling-off" period between incidents), and by adding a *mass* arson category for offenders who set multiple simultaneous fires at one location. (The latter, clearly, has nothing to do with "serial" arson, which by definition involves successive and separate incidents.)

Arson investigators begin their task by studying the complex chemical process that is fire. Each fire consists of three basic elements: fuel, oxygen, and heat. The physical state and shape of the fuel, available oxygen, and the transmission of heat all play critical roles in development of a specific fire. Investigators must also understand the basics of building construction, including materials used and the nature of any fire-protection systems in place, which determine the course of a fire's development and progress.

The first step in any fire investigation is determining a blaze's point of origin. Only when the point of origin has been determined can authorities discover how and why a blaze began. This "backwards" investigation must be fully documented via field notes, diagrams and sketches, photographs, and collection of fire scene evidence. If investigators can eliminate accidental causes—faulty equipment, careless smoking, flammable liquids, lightning, electrical failures, and spontaneous combustion—they are ready to proceed in search of a deliberate incendiary cause for the fire. That evidence may include traces of accelerants (gasoline, kerosene, etc.) or the remnants of an incendiary/explosive device recovered from the fire scene. Various mechanical sensors and specially trained dogs assist investigators in the discovery of accelerants and other clues at a fire scene. That evidence, in turn, may prove vital in tracing the arsonist (or, in the alternative, for use in attempts at PSYCHOLOGICAL PROFILING of an unknown fire-setter).

Collection of evidence at any crime scene must conform to rigorous forensic standards if that evidence is to withstand legal challenges in court. Photographs and fire-scene sketches document the points where evidentiary items were initially discovered, and each fire department or law enforcement agency follows established procedures to document the chain of custody between discovery and trial. Modern computer software, such as the FireFiles system, provides arson investigators with case-management tools to organize various details of the case, track evidence from collection through analysis, and to help in preparation of technical reports.

ART, Forensic

Forensic art is the application of artistic skills—drawing, painting, or sculpting—to the needs of law enforcement, commonly employed to help identify unknown persons, apprehend fugitives from justice, or assist in reconstruction of events. The field encompasses subdisciplines including age progression, composite art, demonstrative evidence, image modification, and postmortem reconstruction.

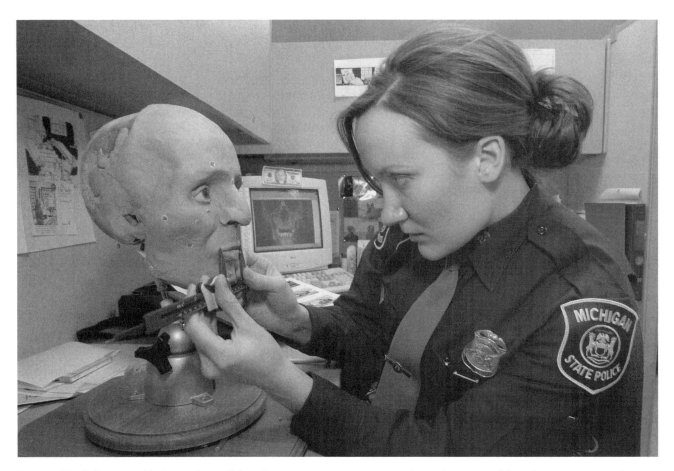

Trooper Sarah Foster, a Michigan State Police forensic artist, measures a three-dimensional facial reconstruction from an unidentified human skull. (Paul Sancya/AP)

ASCHAFFENBURG, Gustav (1866–1944)

A pioneer of forensic PSYCHIATRY, Gustav Aschaffenburg was born in Germany on May 23, 1866. After completing psychiatric studies in his homeland and in Austria, Aschaffenburg entered private practice and secured many high-profile European patients. At various times, he also taught neurology and psychiatry at universities in Cologne, Halle, and Heidelberg. Four days after his 40th birthday, Aschaffenburg delivered a stinging attack on Sigmund Freud to the Congress of Neurologists and Alienists from South-Western Germany, in Baden-Baden, in a speech titled "The Relations between Sexual Life and the Occurrence of Nervous and Mental Diseases."

Meanwhile, he pursued his true passion in the field of criminology, publishing his masterwork *Crime and Its Repression* in 1903. As editor of the *Monthly for Criminal Psychology and Reform of Criminal Law* between 1904 and 1935, Aschaffenburg also used that journal to expound his views on criminal psychology. While linking alcoholism to criminal behavior and asserting that environment played a more significant role than heredity in creating felons, Aschaffenburg expounded a theory of "multiple causation" that listed seven classes of offenders. They were: criminals by affection, by chance, by consideration, by occasion, habitual criminals, professional criminals, and recidivist criminals. In broad terms, Aschaffenburg believed that criminal behavior is not a mental pathology but, rather, a form of socially adaptive behavior.

Aschaffenburg immigrated to the United States two years after Adolph Hitler's rise to power in Germany, but he never recovered from the move emotionally or professionally. Largely forgotten at his death in 1944, Aschaffenburg enjoyed a posthumous renaissance in 1968, with the translation and reprinting of *Crime and Its Repression* in America.

ASSOCIATION of Firearm and Tool Mark Examiners

In 1969, a group of 35 specialists in firearms and toolmark analysis gathered at the Chicago Police Department Crime Laboratory to organize a professional association. Founding members included both civilian and police technicians from various parts of the United States and Canada. As stated in the minutes of that first conference, "this meeting is being held to determine the advisability of forming an organization of Firearms and Tool Mark Examiners. It is hoped that the organization will consider future meetings that could be devoted to the presentation of scientific and technical papers, descriptions of new techniques and procedures, review of instrumentation and the solution of common problems encountered in these scientific fields." Since 1970 the AFTE has hosted annual training seminars at various locations throughout North America. In 1979, 149 delegates from seven nations attended the group's 10th convention. A year later, the organization published a 291-page *AFTE Glossary*, produced by a five-member standardization committee. An official AFTE training manual followed in 1992, with new editions of the glossary published in that year and in 1994. At press time for this work, AFTE membership included 850 specialists from 40 countries worldwide.

ASTM International

Founded in 1898 as the American Society for Testing and Materials and subsequently renamed, ASTM International ranks among the world's largest organizations devoted to development of voluntary standards for materials, products, systems, and services. Its founders were engineers and scientists concerned by frequent breaks in 19th-century railroad lines, whose work vastly improved the safety of rail travel in the United States and abroad. With passage of time and expansion of industry, new technology demanded improved standardization requirements making products better, safer, and more cost-effective. A subsidiary Committee on Forensic Sciences, organized in 1970, includes subcommittees concerned with behavioral science, biology, criminalistics, engineering, jurisprudence, odontology, pathology, psychiatry, questioned documents, toxicology and interdisciplinary forensic science standards. At press time for this work, ASTM International boasted more than 30,000 members in more than 100 nations worldwide.

ATKINS, Herman exonerated by DNA evidence

On April 8, 1986, a female shoe-store clerk was confronted by an unmasked gunman who stole $130 from the store's cash register, then raped her twice and forced her to fellate him, all the while threatening to "blow [her] brains out." While giving her statement at the Riverside County, California, sheriff's office, the victim saw a wanted poster on fugitive

Herman Atkins, sought for assaulting two Los Angeles policemen, and she identified him as her attacker. Atkins was arrested in Phoenix seven months later, held over for trial on charges of rape and armed robbery. At trial in 1988, his wife testified that Atkins was at home (in Los Angeles) with no car on the day of the rape. Jurors convicted him on all counts, and he received a 45-year prison term; a second trial in Los Angeles County added two years and eight months for the assault on the patrolmen.

In 1993, encouraged by reports of other inmates freed from custody when DNA testing exonerated them of rape and other crimes, Atkins contacted the New York–based CARDOZO INNOCENCE PROJECT. California authorities resisted petitions for a new DNA test in Atkins's case, but an appellate court ordered the test in August 2000. A report filed on January 15, 2001, excluded Atkins as a suspect in the rape, and he was freed in February 2001, the 64th inmate cleared by DNA evidence since American courts first admitted its use for appeals in 1993. Greeting reporters with a smile, Atkins proclaimed, "Now God, me and the people of California and the United States know I am an innocent man."

AUSTRALIAN Society of Forensic Dentistry

As its name suggests, the Australian Society of Forensic Dentistry (ASFD) is a professional organization devoted to the promotion of forensic ODONTOLOGY in the nation of Australia, to facilitate identification of murder, accident, and disaster victims. The ASFD's 48 identified members in 2001 reportedly included all practicing dentists in Australia, but membership is open (at a price of $45 per year) to "any professional who has an interest in the application of dental techniques for forensic purposes." The sole member listed from outside Australia for 2001 was Dr. Hirofumi Aboshi, a professor of dentistry at Nikon University in Tokyo. The ASFD's Web site includes links to similar organizations around the world and provides contact information for members available to consult on a contract or emergency basis.

AUTOMATED Fingerprint Identification System (AFIS)

AFIS is a computerized system designed to match and identify FINGERPRINTS by searching various connected databases. The name was initially applied only to criminal justice automated fingerprint identification systems (CJAFIS), but it is currently used more broadly to include civil identification as well as law enforcement applications. AFIS uses digital imaging technology to obtain, store, and analyze fingerprint data. It was pioneered by the FBI to identify criminal suspects, but today finds a much wider application in the fields of general identification and fraud prevention. Civil applications include screening of job applicants and participants in various public benefits programs (welfare, Aid to Families with Dependent Children, Social Security, etc.). Recent AFIS advances include plain-impression live scanning of fingerprints (versus use of digitized prints on file), and the FBI LABORATORY's Integrated AFIS (IAFIS) system, allowing access to fingerprints of some 35 million people from various federal, state, regional, and local databases. As this work went to press, an increasing number of private sector administrators were involved in "transactional" AFIS programs, applied in such fields as health care and personnel management.

AVERY, Steven exonerated by DNA

On the afternoon of July 29, 1985, a 36-year-old woman was brutally attacked, sexually assaulted, and nearly killed on the shore of Lake Michigan, in Manitowoc County, Wisconsin. Statements from a lone eyewitness led police to Steven Avery, a Green Bay resident who claimed that he had spent the day and evening shopping with his family. Avery presented 16 alibi witnesses, including his wife, five children, and various store clerks, but police nonetheless pressed rape charges. At trial, a forensic expert testified that a single hair found on Avery at the time of his arrest was "consistent" with the victim's. Jurors convicted Avery on December 14, 1985, and he received a 32-year prison term in March 1986.

In 1995, Avery requested DNA tests of fingernail scrapings retrieved from the victim on the day she was attacked. Those tests revealed genetic markers consistent both with Avery and the victim, plus DNA from an unknown subject. Despite that evidence, Wisconsin's courts rejected Avery's appeal on grounds that the DNA evidence was insufficient to warrant a retrial. In April 2002, the WISCONSIN INNOCENCE PROJECT obtained a court order for retesting with new technology. The state crime lab then examined a foreign pubic hair retrieved from the victim after she was raped, excluding Avery as a suspect and naming the actual assailant as one Gregory Allen (currently serving 60 years in prison for rapes committed after the Manitowoc attack). Avery's prosecutor stipulated his innocence on September 10, 2003, and Avery was freed the following day, after serving 18 years for a crime he did not commit. On October 12, 2004, Avery filed a federal lawsuit against Manitowoc County for wrongful conviction.

The story might have ended there, but Avery's troubles with the law were not all behind him. Even before he filed his lawsuit, Avery was arrested for disorderly conduct in Manitowoc County, pleading no contest on March 2, 2005. Seven months later, on October 31, 25-year-old Theresa Halbach van-ished from her home in Hilbert, Wisconsin. Police soon learned that Halbach—a professional pho-tographer—had visited Avery's home on the day she vanished, to take pictures of a car that he had advertised for sale. Officers found Halbach's car abandoned at a nearby junkyard on November 6 and searched Avery's home the next day, recover-ing a pistol. On November 9, they charged Avery with illegal possession of a firearm by a convicted felon. November 10 brought the announcement that human bone fragments were found on Avery's property, and he was subsequently charged with Halmbach's murder. Trials in that case and Avery's federal lawsuit were pending when this volume went to press.

B

BALTHAZARD, Victor (1872–1950)

A native of Paris, born in 1872, Victor Balthazard was a child prodigy in MATHEMATICS who stunned his family by abandoning his studies to join the French army in 1893. While serving as an artillery officer, he also found time to pursue medical training, specializing in the new field of RADIOLOGY. On leaving the army in 1904, Balthazard changed careers yet again and applied himself with equal zeal to forensic science, soon winning appointment as the chief MEDICAL EXAMINER for Paris, doubling as a professor of forensic medicine at the Sorbonne.

In 1909, reviewing evidence in a local murder case, Balthazard determined that hair found beneath the fingernails of victim Germaine Bichon belonged to a woman. He subsequently matched those samples to suspect Rosella Rousseau and thereby secured her conviction, afterward teaming with Dr. Marcelle Lambert to publish the first comprehensive study of human hair, *Le poil de l'homme et des animaux* (The hair of man and animals), in 1910. Two years later, Balthazard used photographs to demonstrate that each gun barrel leaves unique markings on bullets fired through it. His groundbreaking article on individualized bullet markings was published in 1913, including observations on the unique IMPRESSION EVIDENCE left on ejected cartridge casings by automatic and semiautomatic FIREARMS. In 1939, Balthazard presented his first lecture on the value of bloodstain patterns as forensic evidence. At his death in 1950,

Dr. Balthazard was recognized as an extraordinary pioneer in multiple areas of forensic science.

BAYLE, Gaston Edmond (1879–1929)

French criminologist Gaston Bayle was born in 1879 and pursued a university education in CHEMISTRY. First employed at the Pasteur Institute in Paris, he subsequently served in the French government's railroad service, then joined the Parisian police as a forensic chemist and physicist in January 1915. Another nine years elapsed before a murder case allowed Bayle to reveal his true skill. Examination of the crime scene left authorities with no apparent useful evidence, but Bayle found two particles of an unknown red substance that demonstrated fluorescence under ultraviolet light. Further examination by means of SPECTROSCOPY identified the substance as rhodamine, which police also found in the prime suspect's basement, thus earning him a date with the guillotine.

One of Bayle's most puzzling cases, ultimately unresolved, was the notorious "Glozel affair." On March 1, 1924, 17-year-old Emile Fradin was plowing a field at Glozel when one of his cows stepped into a hole, revealing an underground chamber lined with clay bricks and tiles, containing a skull and other human bones with various crude ceramic vases and fragments. Further excavation revealed a small stone axe, three bricks bearing handprints, stones engraved with cryptic symbols, and a needle made from bone.

Various scholars and amateur archaeologists reviewed the artifacts over the next three years, before members of a self-styled "international commission" undertook further excavation, exposing two bone awls, a pebble engraved with a reindeer head and six Glozelian letters, a "bisexual idol," two bone pendants, a schist ring, a clasp made from a deer's antler, and an engraved tablet. Soon, accusations of FRAUD and FORGERY hit the headlines, and police became involved after yet another dig revealed more artifacts (including another tablet) in April 1928. Bayle produced a 500-page report on the Glozel artifacts in May 1929, demonstrating that far from being ancient relics, they were in fact no more than 15 years old.

While the Glozel fraud first brought Bayle international acclaim, another swindle ended his career only four months later. In mid-September 1929, Bayle examined a document used by traveling salesman Joseph Emile Philipponet to procure money from his landlord. Bayle quickly proved the paper fraudulent, and Philipponet took the news badly. Days later, he invaded Bayle's laboratory and shot Bayle three times, inflicting fatal wounds. In custody, Philipponet told jailers, "Monsieur Bayle committed an act of bad faith! My document was genuine! What I have done was worth the death of a father of five children!"

BEHAVIORAL Science

Behavioral science is the study of human behavior, including all aspects of PSYCHIATRY and psychology with various other medical and sociological disciplines. Forensic applications include the controversial fields of DECEPTION ANALYSIS ("lie detecting") and PSYCHOLOGICAL PROFILING, in which behavioral clues from crime scenes are used in an effort to identify unknown offenders. As discussed elsewhere in this volume, profiling rarely (if ever) solves crimes, though certain profiles of subjects at large have proved uncannily accurate after the offenders were caught via traditional police procedures. In broader terms, behavioral studies may suggest an offender's motive, while recognition of "signature" behavior sometimes permits investigators to link serial crimes before the offender is identified. Unlike the MODUS OPERANDI, which commonly evolves and improves as criminals gain experience and become more skilled, signature elements—use of a favorite weapon, selection of particular victim types, infliction of specific ritualized trauma, etc.—rarely changes over

time. That knowledge may provide insight into an unknown subject's psyche, but it rarely leads police to the offender's door.

BELL, Corethian   exonerated by DNA evidence

A resident of Cook County, Illinois, 23-year-old Corethian Bell telephoned police one night in July 2000, reporting that he had found his mother shot to death in her Calumet City apartment. In fact, she had been stabbed and sexually assaulted, the struggle leaving BLOODSTAINS from a second party on the walls, while semen traces were recovered from the victim's clothing. Authorities suspected Bell, and he obliged them with a videotaped confession to the crime, thus ensuring his indictment on capital murder charges. A second woman was raped and stabbed in December 2000, five blocks from the first crime scene, but police were confident they had their man in custody and drew no link between the attacks.

A suspect was later booked for the second crime, while Bell sat in jail awaiting trial, and DNA tests were ordered to confirm the new suspect's guilt in that case when he refused to confess. Police were startled when the second suspect's DNA also matched blood and semen samples lifted from the apartment where Bell's mother was slain in July 2000. Bell's case was one of several profiled by the *Chicago Tribune* in 2001, detailing incidents of negligence and worse on the part of Cook County authorities, including multiple wrongful convictions and several apparent cases of deliberate "FRAME-UPS" over the past decade. From his cell, Bell confirmed that he had confessed only after 50 hours of near-constant interrogation, allegedly including physical abuse by relays of detectives. On January 4, 2002, Bell was released from custody, all charges dismissed by the state at a hearing before Circuit Court Judge Daniel Darcy. Even with conclusive evidence of another suspect's guilt, some local police remained stubbornly fixated on Bell. "He gave us a statement," Sergeant Stan Salura told reporters. "I believe that is factual." As for Bell, he dismissed the incident as a "crazy thing" and sought to get on with his life. "I feel so good," he told the press upon release. "Let's go. I'm hungry."

BERTILLON, Alphonse   (1853–1914)

French criminologist Alphonse Bertillon was born in Paris on April 23, 1853, the son and younger brother of renowned 19th-century statisticians. Beginning his law enforcement career as a records clerk for the Parisian police force, Bertillon soon grew dissatisfied with the haphazard methods of criminal identification and in 1882 invented the science of ANTHROPOM-ETRY, wherein individuals are identified by precise head and body measurements, coupled with records of scars, tattoos, and other unique features. In 1884 alone, Bertillon used his method—also called Bertil-lonage—to identify 241 multiple offenders. In February 1888, Bertillon was promoted to serve as chief of the Paris police department's Service of Judicial Identity. A year later, he published an article on use of contact PHOTOGRAPHY to reveal erasures in QUESTIONED DOCUMENTS.

British and American police soon adopted anthropometry, singing its praises until 1903, when two inmates with identical measurements were located at Leavenworth Prison in Kansas. Defendant Will West had been wrongfully imprisoned based on Bertillon's system, FINGERPRINTS belatedly proving him innocent. Bertillon's loss of prestige was also accelerated by the Dreyfuss case, wherein he testified as a handwriting expert despite total lack of experience in that field. Bertillon's "expert" opinion, naming Capt. Alfred Dreyfuss as the author of a document revealing French military secrets to Germany, helped convict Dreyfuss of treason and sent him to Devil's Island, but the case was later exposed as a FRAME-UP by anti-Semitic officers who resented serving with a Jew. By the time crusading author Emile Zola exposed the document in question as a FORGERY, anthropometry had largely been supplanted by fingerprinting as a means of criminal identification. Bertillon spent his declining years in Switzerland and died at Münsterlingen on February 13, 1914.

BIOLOGY, Forensic

Biology is the scientific study of living things, whether plants or animals. Its forensic applications include any examination or analysis of biological evidence whatsoever, including but not limited to the sub-disciplines of biochemistry, BIOMECHANICS, BOTANY, DNA profiling, ENTOMOLOGY, immunology, LIMNOLOGY, ODONTOLOGY, PATHOLOGY, PHARMACOLOGY, serology (BLOODSTAINS and other body fluids), and TOXICOLOGY. While not commonly ranked among the forensic sciences, zoology (the study of animal life) also proves relevant in many cases—e.g., animal attacks

or scavenging on human remains, venomous bites or stings, smuggling or slaughter of endangered species, and instances where trace evidence includes animal remnants or remains.

BIOMECHANICS, Forensic

Biomechanics is the study of movement in biological organisms ranging from amoebas to whales and elephants. It focuses primarily but not exclusively on muscle-driven movements such as walking, running, and lifting. Forensic biometrics applies that science to legal matters, either criminal or civil. Its range includes such diverse elements as calculation of a suspect's stride, documentation of injuries and determination of their causes, inspection of crime scenes or accident sites, and evaluation of safety equipment, among other functions. Courtroom applications may include demonstrations that particular injuries were inflicted by a right- or left-handed assailant, re-creation of injuries caused by falls or vehicular collisions, extrapolation of a subject's size from stride or footprints, and determinations as to whether a suspect of specific size and weight is physically capable of certain actions.

BIOMETRICS high-tech security techniques

Biometrics is, broadly, the use of automated technology to identify individual persons via specific physiological or behavioral characteristics. *Physiological* biometrics employs various devices to define identity from data gathered by direct measurement of the human body. Examples include fingerprint scanning, hand geometry, iris or retina scanning, and facial geometry. *Behavioral* biometrics tracks a subject's specific actions—speech patterns, handwriting, or even something as seemingly neutral as typing on a computer keyboard.

In addition to those broad categories, biometrics is further defined as passive or active techniques. *Passive* biometrics, including voice and facial scans, may be employed without the subject's knowledge or cooperation. (In the case of vocal scans, recordings obviate even the need for a subject's physical presence.) *Active* biometrics, by contrast, demands personal cooperation for scanning of hands, eyes, or signatures with various computerized devices. Manufacturers of those devices describe their respective systems as "fail-safe," while Hollywood depicts a

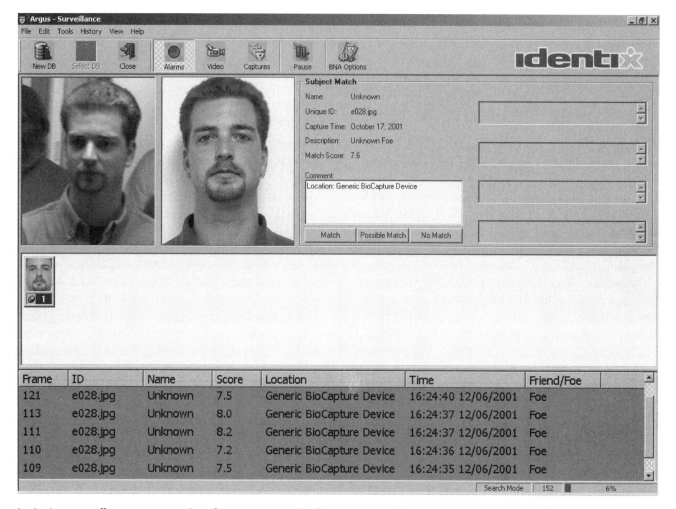

Linked to surveillance cameras, facial recognition technology can match faces with images from a database. (Identix Inc.)

steady stream of super-villains defeating biometric scanners with false eyes, counterfeit FINGERPRINTS— even amputated body parts removed from legitimate users. A more likely approach to defeating biometric scanners would involve computer hackers or physical interference with the hardware.

Biometrics has a number of diverse applications for modern law enforcement, government, and private security. The most obvious, *personal identification,* employs a "one-to-many" search to discover an individual's identity. As a case in point, security cameras at an airport or other facilities may photograph suspect individuals and use a biometric system to compare the suspect's likeness with a large database of known lawbreakers, foreign agents, and so forth. The related process of identity *verification* executes a "one-to-one" search, comparing the claimant of a particular identity with recorded characteristics of

the known individual. Thus, a thief using a stolen credit card to withdraw funds from an automatic teller machine (ATM) might be photographed, examined, and denied the cash—or stalled with automated delaying tactics while police are summoned to the scene.

Physiological biometric verification devices, particularly those employing fingerprint scans or hand geometry, may be employed for many purposes, incorporated in a wide variety of everyday objects. Some companies use biometrics to monitor employee time and attendance, thereby eliminating time cards and improving payroll accuracy by eradication of "buddy-punching" scams. Access control in secure areas is critical to many governmental, law enforcement, correctional, and corporate operations. Devices currently designed with built-in biometric scanners include vaults and safes, custom vehicles, home security systems, personal computers, and various weapons—including "SMART" GUNS designed to fire only if held in particular registered hands.

Interest in biometric security devices increased dramatically after the terrorist attacks of September 11, 2001. Manufacturers were naturally pleased with the rash of new orders, but they noted certain problems with the existing technology. Among them:

1. The performance of biometric devices in daily real-world situations does not match test results obtained in vendor-controlled laboratories. Advertising claims aside, no system provides 100 percent security and some can be defeated more easily than others. Even the best scanners sometimes reject authorized users or fail to catch imposters, and a small percentage of the population (for reasons unexplained) cannot be reliably registered in current biometric systems. In short, while installation of biometrics at airports and other "hot spots" would clearly improve security standards, breaches would still be recorded.

2. Employee-facing systems are significantly cheaper and easier to operate than passenger-facing systems designed to scan large numbers of unknown subjects around the clock. Employees

may be subject to background checks and punitive action (including dismissal and/or prosecution) for attempting to defeat security systems. The general public—airline customers, for example—may scheme to frustrate the scanners in a variety of ways, ranging from simple disguises to plastic surgery. Passengers who travel rarely may undergo natural changes with time, from aging, injury, or disease. Finally, the sheer number of subjects—millions of travelers, versus hundreds or thousands of employees—vastly increases the scope and expense of security systems.

3. Biometric systems are limited by the integrity of the initial enrollment process. Individuals who create a false identity before enrolling in a biometric system—as by presenting a counterfeit passport or driver's license—will normally be deemed legitimate unless they duplicate another name enrolled in the system. Biometrics cannot prevent individuals from assuming false identities, only from impersonating subjects previously catalogued.

4. Biometric *identification* and *verification* address separate issues, with the latter generally much simpler and less expensive. Subjects seeking verification, as noted above, are compared to a known exemplar and accepted or rejected on that

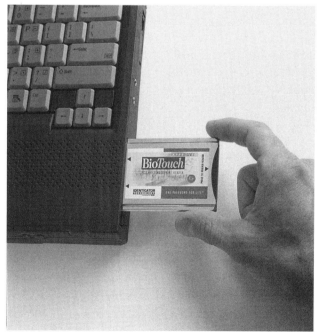

The BioTouch PC Card features an optical fingerprint reader, allowing secure access for laptop users. (Identix Inc.)

basis. In broader identification scans, the subject may claim no particular identity at all, requiring comparison of his or her facial scan with known subjects numbering in the tens of thousands. The further a search extends, including external data-bases like the FBI's, the more expensive and time-consuming it becomes.

5. Biometric scanners use templates, rather than raw images, to perform their comparisons. Each template is a small computer file based on distinctive individual characteristics—and like any other computer file, it is vulnerable to damage or tampering. Even without interference, each personal interaction with the scanner varies slightly—even microscopically. No two fingerprints are applied in precisely the same manner, for instance, thus insuring that air-tight 100-percent accuracy is unattainable by any mechanical system.

As of early 2002, biometric scanning devices employed at most major American airports—including Chicago's O'Hare Airport, San Francisco International, Charlotte/Douglas (in North Carolina) and Reagan National (in Washington, D.C.)—were restricted to access screening of employees. Eight U.S. and Canadian airports have experimented with use of biometric scanners to let citizens circumvent immigration lines, but enrollment of the population at large is a daunting prospect, if not impossible. Iceland's Keflavik International Airport uses facial scans to check passengers against a surveillance "hot list," facilitated by the airport's relatively low volume of traffic. While 9/11 increased demands for facial-scan technology as a cure-all for future terrorist attacks, various problems remain. They include:

1. Variance between enrollment and surveillance devices. Enrollment in facial-scan systems normally involves use of a clear photograph, including passport photos, drivers' licenses, or mug shots. Surveillance is maintained by video cameras, with significantly lower resolution than the original images, making it possible for subjects to slip through the net unrecognized.

2. Environmental changes at the surveillance point. Anything from altered lighting to a change in angle of the surveillance camera's wall mount may result in poor resolution and the failure of a system to identify enrolled subjects.

Fingerprint scanners provide physical access to secure areas. (Identix Inc.)

3. Changes in a subject's appearance. Alterations sufficient to confuse surveillance systems may include a gain or loss of weight, a change of hairstyle, aging, application of cosmetics or prosthetics, even the wearing or removal of eyeglasses.

Despite its present limitations, biometric scanning will clearly expand in the future, finding new applications in both law enforcement and private industry. Hand and fingerprint scans have traditionally been used for access control to secure areas, but iris and retinal scans offer a new level of security, while making deception more difficult. Airline passengers may in future be required to provide some biometric data prior to traveling, in the interest of greater security. Similar enrollment may be required upon issuance of passports for international travel. Integration of existing FBI and other criminal databases would potentially apprehend hundreds of fugitives each year. Finally, surveillance systems will certainly expand, presumably becoming more effective and reliable.

At the same time, wide-scale implementation of biometric surveillance raises legal and ethical questions yet unanswered. Is it physically and/or economically feasible to make biometric enrollment mandatory for all travelers (much less all residents) of America or any other nation? What safeguards can be imposed to guarantee that biometric systems do not violate individual rights to privacy? How will human agencies respond to the inevitable errors every technological system produces from time to time? Will use of biometrics alone create a dangerous sense of false security? Until those questions are satisfactorily answered, full-scale biometric surveillance remains poised on the line between established fact and science fiction.

BLOODSTAIN Evidence

Every bloodstain tells a story. Aside from DNA testing, which may identify the donor of a particular stain—and thus distinguish between offenders and victims—the shape, number, and placement of bloodstains may chart the course of a crime for experts trained to interpret such evidence. The very presence of blood (or its lack) at a crime scene tells investigators whether a murder victim was killed on the spot, or perhaps slain elsewhere and transported to a separate dump site. If the latter, authorities may later seek warrants for the search of prospective murder scenes, in hopes of discovering where the crime actually occurred.

A murder scene with body and bloodstains intact is more useful to detectives and technicians in their search for answers to an unsolved crime. Scientific analysis of bloodstain patterns is a relatively new phenomenon, dating approximately from the 1950s. In 1955, during trial of Ohio's controversial Sam Sheppard case, Dr. Paul Kirk testified that blood-spatter evidence enabled him "to establish the relative position of the attacker and victim at the time of the . . . beating. He was able to determine that the attacker administered blows with a left hand, which was significant in that Dr. Sheppard was right-handed." (Sheppard was initially convicted, nonetheless.) By 1983 an International Association of Bloodstain Pattern Analysts was organized, its studies documenting the fact that bloodstain evidence at crime scenes may reveal:

- The source of particular stains
- The relative position of persons and objects at the time of impact

- The number of separate impacts
- Whether impact was inflicted with a blunt or sharp object
- The distance blood traveled, and its velocity
- The elapsed time between impact and examination by authorities
- The movement of persons and objects after impact (including blood smears, drag marks, footprints, etc.)

A blood-spatter pattern is determined by multiple factors, including the distance a drop of blood falls, the force with which it falls (arterial spray versus dripping from a vein, oozing from wounds or flung from an upraised bludgeon, etc.), whether it falls vertically or diagonally, and the type of surface it strikes. In addition to charting the course of an attack, bloodstains may also preserve contact marks from other objects: footprints, fingerprints, tool marks, fabric patterns, tire marks, and so forth. In the case of the army doctor JEFFREY MACDONALD—a case as controversial in its time as that of Dr. Sheppard 30 years earlier—crime lab technicians used blood-spatter evidence to demonstrate that the defendant bludgeoned his wife and young daughters to death, then stabbed himself in the chest to simulate an assault by third parties. (As in the Sheppard case before it, substantial evidence today suggests that MacDonald may, in fact, be innocent.) Similar evidence may be gleaned from shootings, stabbings, explosions, or hit-and-run accidents.

Some bloodstains are invisible to authorities by the time they begin to process a crime scene. Perpetrators may exert great energy to clean up a scene, but blood evidence is very difficult to eradicate. Even when stains are expunged beyond visibility to the naked eye, traces may be found by using luminol, a chemical spray that causes covert bloodstains to fluoresce. In such instances, blood evidence may be found beneath carpets and floorboards, concealed in the pattern of fabric or wallpaper, or hidden in sink traps and plumbing. Wherever it lies, bloodstain evidence may prove guilt by placing an absent victim at the scene (through DNA), thus challenging a suspect's alibi. In these days when science allows identification of one individual to the exclusion of all others on earth (except an identical twin), blood evidence is more important than ever to prosecutors and police.

BLOODSWORTH, Kirk exonerated by DNA evidence

On July 25, 1984, a nine-year-old girl was found dead in a wooded area of Baltimore County, Maryland. She had been raped, strangled, and beaten with a rock found at the murder scene. Five witnesses claimed to have seen the child walking with a man on the day she was killed, and they collaborated with police to produce a sketch of the unknown suspect. Soon, an anonymous telephone call directed authorities to Baltimore resident Kirk Bloodsworth. The five alleged eyewitnesses identified him as the man last seen with the victim, while a neighbor of Bloodsworth's recalled his confession of doing "a terrible thing" on the day of the crime. On March 8, 1985, Bloodsworth was convicted of rape, sexual assault, and first-degree premeditated murder, drawing a sentence of death.

Bloodsworth's attorney appealed the conviction, contending that police illegally withheld evidence pointing to another suspect and that the "terrible thing" Bloodsworth confessed to his neighbor was a failure to buy his wife a taco salad as promised. The Maryland Court of Appeals overturned his conviction in July 1986 and remanded the case for a new trial. Convicted a second time, Bloodsworth was spared but received two consecutive life sentences. An appeal of the second conviction was denied, but Bloodsworth had been busy in the meantime, studying the British case of serial killer COLIN PITCH-FORK, convicted on the basis of DNA evidence. Bloodsworth's attorney petitioned for release of the state's evidence for more sophisticated testing and the prosecution finally agreed, delivering the victim's clothing in April 1992. Semen from the underpants was compared with Bloodsworth's DNA, excluding him as a possible suspect in June 1993. The FBI Crime Laboratory repeated the test on June 25, 1993, with identical results.

Although Maryland statutes forbid presentation of new evidence more than one year after a defendant's final appeal, Baltimore County prosecutors joined Bloodsworth's attorney in petitioning for a pardon. Bloodsworth was released from prison on June 28, 1993, and the governor granted his pardon six months later. No other suspects have yet been charged in the case.

"BLUE Box" device used in telephone fraud

Invented sometime in the late 1960s, the "blue box" is a tone-generating device that signals telephone company equipment that a call has been terminated, while in fact the conversation continues without being billed for additional time. Refinements on the original device include a "black box" that emits an electronic signal that a call did not go through (when in fact it did), and a "red box" that simulates the sound of coins being loaded into a pay telephone. Such devices are employed by hackers—commonly dubbed "phreakers"—to cheat phone companies throughout the world, with yearly losses estimated in the millions of dollars. Employment of any device to suppress billing information is a federal crime in the United States, placing the "phreaker" at risk of prosecution for interstate wire fraud.

BODY Armor

Written history does not record the first use of protective body armor by fighting men (or women), but shields, helmets, and injury-resistant clothing certainly date from the earliest days of armed human conflict. Leather and wood were used extensively before technology allowed the manipulation of various metals, and steel remained the epitome of armor for generations thereafter. Bandits and G-men fought their epic battles of the 1930s wearing crude steel plates in fabric vests that slipped over their heads like sandwich signs, and such cumbersome gear remained the norm until bullet-resistant fabrics like DuPont's Kevlar, Honeywell's GoldFlex and Zylon, or the European firm Akzo's Twaron were developed in the 1960s and 1970s.

The NATIONAL INSTITUTE OF JUSTICE (NIJ) rates body armor on a scale of ballistic protection levels. The armor is tested not only for resistance to actual penetration, but also for minimization of blunt force trauma (either from projectile impact or direct blows from a hand-to-hand assailant). Blunt trauma is measured by the dent inflicted on a soft clay pad behind the armor, with a maximum depth of 1.7 inches permitted for physical safety. The NIJ's armor rankings are:

I—Blocks .38 Special round-nose lead projectiles traveling at 850 feet per second (fps) and .22-caliber Long Rifle ammunition at 1,050 fps. This armor, also protects the wearer against birdshot charges from a shotgun but is not recommended for use against any higher-velocity ammunition.

This body armor is specially designed for tactical operations where total protection is necessary. (Courtesy of Point Blank Body Armor, Inc.)

IIA—Consisting of 16 to 18 layers of Kevlar, this armor is designed to cope with most threats encountered in urban shooting situations. It will stop various rounds including 9-mm full metal jacket (FMJ) projectiles traveling at 1,090 fps and .357 Magnum jacketed, hollow-point (JHP) projectiles traveling at 1,250 fps.

II—With 22 to 24 layers of Kevlar, this thickness should stop bullets including 9-mm FMJ rounds traveling at 1,175 fps and .357 Magnum jacketed, soft-point (JSP) projectiles traveling at 1,395 fps. Most shotgun pellets are also deflected.

IIIA—Offering 30 to 32 layers of Kevlar, IIIA level armor stops numerous rounds including 9-mm FMJ projectiles traveling at 1,400 fps (the usual muzzle velocity for most 9-mm submachine guns) and .44 Magnum rounds at the same velocity. Its blunt-trauma protection rating is the highest offered by soft armor, thus allowing for more effective return fire in a gunfight.

III—To repel most rifle bullets, this armor abandons soft fabrics to employ 1/4-inch specially treated steel, 1/2-inch ceramic armor plates, or 1-inch polyethylene plates. Blunt trauma should

be minimized, but the armor is heavier and is not concealable.

IV—Finally, to protect against armor-piercing rifle bullets, this armor is crafted from 3/4-inch ceramic plates.

Special circumstances require special armor, beyond those listed above. Bomb-disposal personnel require full-body coverage in the event of an explosion, typically combining both ballistic-resistant and fire-retardant fabrics, some of which protect the wearer from projectiles traveling up to 2,250 fps. A typical bomb-disposal suit would include an armored coat (sleeves included), removable collar and groin protector, armored trousers (often open at the rear for comfort, providing front-coverage only), a helmet with fragment-resistant face shield, an armored chest plate, with special boots and gloves (available for cases where an explosive device must be disarmed, rather than simply transported). "Bomb blankets" are also available to screen personnel or to shroud small devices and contain shrapnel in the event of a blast.

Manufacturers are quick to stress that no body armor is ever 100 percent bulletproof. Likewise, special stab-resistant fabrics or fabric combinations may be needed to deflect blades, in the event of an assault with knife or sword. Armor-piercing ammunition has been banned from civilian sales in the United States for many years, but sufficient quantities of "cop-killer" bullets are still available to render many forms of concealable armor superfluous. Factors to consider in selecting body armor include:

Threat assessment The type of protection required obviously varies from person to person. A motorcycle racer needs less (or different) protective clothing than a bomb-disposal technician. If an assailant's weapons are known, armor may be adjusted accordingly.

Comfort Uncomfortable armor is more likely to be removed and abandoned, thus making it useless when a crisis finally arrives. A compromise between comfort and coverage must be attained in order for the gear to be effective.

Concealability If an assailant knows his target is wearing a protective vest, he may fire at the head or lower body and inflict fatal wounds without regard to the armor. Various situations, such as diplomatic functions or corporate gatherings, may also require discretion on the part of those wearing protective gear.

Cost The better the armor, the higher its price. Urban patrolmen forced to purchase their own Kevlar vests have more limited options (and consequent greater exposure) than wealthy corporate CEOs or military personnel whose equipment is funded by taxpayers.

Coverage Some vests offer only front-and-back protection, while others wrap around the wearer's torso to include side coverage. Various other garments, including entire business suits, may be crafted from thin layers of bullet-resistant fabric, albeit with some sacrifice of fashion points. Tactical vests, worn outside the clothing by officers on SWAT teams and other assault units, offer 50 percent more protection on average than vests designed to be worn under shirts or jackets.

Mobility Armor becomes a handicap if it retards the wearer's movement, making him or her a proverbial "sitting duck." Whether fleeing an attack or fighting back, a certain amount of mobility is required for survival.

Temperature A primary concern for wearers of protective clothing, heat buildup may prove uncomfortable in some situations, or debilitating (even lethal) in others. Whenever possible, armor intended for long-term use should be tailored to the environment where it will be worn. Some modern (more expensive) vests include built-in cooling systems for extra comfort.

Weight Heavy armor induces fatigue with prolonged wear, and it also reduces mobility. In most cases, this issue arises most often with Class III or IV armor, and in bomb-disposal suits. Ceramic and polyethylene plates weigh less than steel and may be preferred if they provide equivalent protection from rifle bullets.

In addition to "bulletproof" clothing, various tactical shields are also available. Special canine "vests" are sold for police dogs in firefight situations, and projectile-resistant fabric may be crafted into a variety of other shapes. Some of the more common forms include use as upholstery (for office furniture or car seats), and in backpacks or briefcases (which may be used to shield an otherwise unprotected person).

"BOSTON Strangler" renewed scientific investigation

Ten years before the term *serial killer* entered popular usage, Boston was terrorized by an elusive predator who raped and strangled women in their homes, slaying 11 between June 1962 and July 1964. According to conventional wisdom, the case broke in November 1964, when 33-year-old Albert DeSalvo was jailed on rape charges, subsequently confessing to the "Boston Strangler" crimes and adding two more victims police had failed to count on their official list. A plea bargain engineered by lawyer F. Lee Bailey sent DeSalvo to prison for life on unrelated charges. He was murdered there in November 1973, and while DeSalvo never stood trial for the Boston murders, the case was officially "solved."

Or was it?

The case against DeSalvo has been widely criticized for more than 30 years. Deviations in MODUS OPERANDI led some critics to suggest multiple stranglers at large in Boston, while Mafia hit man Vincent Barbosa confided to a journalist that DeSalvo had been paid to "take a fall" for the actual (still unidentified) killer. An alternative suspect, convicted two-

Recent DNA tests have cast doubt on the guilt of confessed serial murderer Albert DeSalvo. (Author's collection)

time killer George Nassar, was accused in one theory of feeding DeSalvo vital details on the murders while they shared a ward at Bridgewater State Hospital.

Finally, more than a quarter-century after DeSalvo was murdered in prison, forensic scientists revisited the Boston Strangler case in an effort to determine whether or not DeSalvo committed the murders to which he confessed. His body was exhumed in October 2001, for extraction of DNA material unknown to pathologists at the time of the original murders. The material was slated for comparison with evidence collected in the case of 19-year-old Mary Sullivan, the strangler's last victim, found dead on January 4, 1964.

Announcements of "new evidence" in the Boston case were made on December 6, 2001, with James Starrs—a professor of law and forensic science at George Washington University—promising "blockbuster results." Another GWU spokesman, Paul Fucito, said of the DNA findings: "Whether they announce one way or another whether [DeSalvo] did it or not, I think that will be a fairly conclusive announcement." He added that the DNA report would "be revealing enough that it will give the Boston authorities the incentive to look at their evidence and their findings and maybe compare notes and maybe bring the investigation forward."

In fact, by December 2001, neither DeSalvo's family nor Mary Sullivan's believed DeSalvo was the Boston Strangler. That opinion was apparently supported on December 6 by reports that Prof. Starrs's "All-Star Forensic Science Team" had discovered foreign DNA from *two* individuals on Sullivan's body and clothing, neither of the samples linked to DeSalvo. As Professor Starrs told the press, "It's indicative, strongly indicative, of the fact that Albert DeSalvo was not the rape-murderer of Mary Sullivan. If I was a juror, I would acquit him with no questions asked." Sullivan's nephew, Casey Sherman, had an even more emphatic statement for the press. "If he didn't kill Mary Sullivan, yet he confessed to it in glaring detail, he didn't kill any of these women."

Retired Massachusetts prosecutor Julian Soshnick disagreed, retorting, "It doesn't prove anything except that they found another person's DNA on a part of Miss Sullivan's body." Seeming to ignore that neither donor was DeSalvo, Soshnick stood firm: "I believe that Albert was the Boston Strangler." Another retired investigator, former Boston homicide detective Jack Barry, cited DeSalvo's detailed confes-

sions. "He just knew so much," Barry said, "things that were never in the paper. He could describe the wallpaper in their rooms." Dr. Ames Robey, Bridgewater's supervisor in the 1960s and the chief psychiatrist who evaluated DeSalvo, found the confessions less persuasive. "He was a boaster," Dr. Robey told reporters. "I never believed it for a minute."

In any case, the DNA discovery still stopped short of solving Boston's most famous murder case. Professor Starrs believes at least one of the DNA samples recovered from Sullivan's body belongs to her killer, but as he admitted in December 2001, "We cannot tell you the $64,000 question as to whose it is."

BOTANY, Forensic

Botany is the scientific study of plants. Its broad forensic applications are manifold, including study of (a) drug-producing plants such as coca, hashish, marijuana, opium poppies, and others; (b) plants that produce various poisons; (c) analysis of vegetable matter from a decedent's stomach to determine approximate time of death; (d) botanical evidence found during criminal investigations, which may link persons and objects to a particular physical scene; and (e) examination of plant life in the wild as a means of discovering clandestine graves. Examination of algae may determine whether a corpse or other object was submerged in a particular body of water. Discovery of diatoms (microscopic organisms) in various internal organs (or lack thereof) may determine if a supposed drowning victim was alive or dead when he/she entered the water. Palynology—a botanical subdiscipline involving the study of pollen and spores—is also useful in linking suspects and victims to particular crime scenes and/or determining the season when a body was placed in its final resting place.

BRAVO, Mark Diaz exonerated by DNA evidence

On February 20, 1990, a female patient of a Los Angeles psychiatric hospital complained to staff members that she had been sexually assaulted. During successive police interviews, she named several different assailants, one of them Mark Bravo, a hospital orderly. Bravo was ultimately charged with rape after the victim told police she was "sure" of his guilt. Semen recovered from a blanket at the alleged crime scene matched Bravo's blood type, found in only 3 percent of the American population. Jurors later convicted Bravo of rape, and he was sentenced to an eight-year prison term.

Bravo's appeal of the conviction was denied in 1992. A year later, he filed a post-conviction motion for DNA testing on the blanket, a semen-stained sheet, and the victim's underpants. The motion was granted, and a subsequent report, dated December 24, 1993, revealed that none of the semen stains matched Bravo's DNA. His lawyer filed a writ of habeas corpus on January 4, 1994, and Bravo was released from prison three days later. By that time, the victim had also recanted her testimony accusing Bravo of rape.

BRIL, Jacques L. (1906–1981)

A native of New York City, born on September 17, 1906, Jacques Bril earned his B.A. from the University of Michigan and his Ph.D. from Washington and Lee University, in Lexington, Virginia. Long fascinated by primitive techniques of DECEPTION ANALYSIS, in 1931 Bril organized his own Jacques L. Bril Criminology Consultants and Investigators, specializing in "lie detection" for New York prosecutors and police. His first device, invented in collaboration with Rev. Walter Summers, was the pathometer, a forerunner of the modern-day polygraph. By the time New York's courts declared the pathometer unreliable, in 1954, Bril had produced a new device—the eponymous Brilograph—to measure changes in skin resistance allegedly produced by lying. Despite Bril's best efforts, the field of deception analysis remains fraught with peril, and no American state allowed admission of "lie detector" evidence at the time of Bril's death, in 1981.

BRISON, Dale exonerated by DNA evidence

On the night of July 14, 1990, while walking home from a neighborhood convenience store, a female resident of Chester County, Pennsylvania, was grabbed from behind by a man who seized her throat and pressed a knife into her back, commanding that she walk in front of him. Stabbed moments later, she lost consciousness briefly, waking as the attacker dragged her into some bushes near an apartment complex. There, she was raped repeatedly before the man fled. The victim subsequently identified Dale Brison as her attacker, and he was arrested. At trial, the prosecution introduced a hair "consistent" with Brison's,

found by police at the crime scene. Brison requested a DNA test, but the court denied his motion. Brison's mother corroborated his alibi—that he had been sleeping at home when the rape occurred—but jurors disbelieved the testimony, convicting him of rape, kidnapping, aggravated assault, carrying a prohibited offensive weapon, and three counts of involuntary deviate sexual intercourse. He received an aggregate sentence of 18 to 42 years in state prison on the various charges.

On appeal, in 1992, the Pennsylvania Superior Court ordered DNA testing performed on the semen stains from the victim's clothing, and Brison was excluded absolutely as a suspect in the case. County prosecutors next insisted on performing their own tests and produced identical results. Dale Brison was released from custody in January 1994, after serving three and a half years of his undeserved sentence.

BROCA, Paul (Pierre-Paul Broca) (1824–1880)

Born at Sainte-Foy-la-Grande, France, on June 28, 1824, Paul Broca was a child prodigy who held bachelor's degrees in literature, MATHEMATICS, and physics by the time he entered medical school at age 17. Completing his studies in three years, Broca soon became a professor of surgical PATHOLOGY at the University of Paris, where he was renowned for his research in various fields. His diverse fields of study included aneurysms, cancer, the histology of bone and cartilage, infant mortality, and neuroanatomy. Best known in medicine for his study of human speech, Broca located a speech-production center in the brain's frontal lobes, known today as "Broca's area." Forensic science also owes a debt to Broca for his pioneering work in physical ANTHROPOLOGY, leading successively to his foundation of the Anthropological Society (in 1859), the *Revue d'Anthropologie* (1872), and the School of Anthropology in Paris (1876). Broca advanced the science of cranial ANTHROPOMETRY by inventing new measuring instruments (craniometers) and some 26 other devices, while publishing 223 works on physical anthropology. Despite his many contributions to science, some prominent Europeans denounced Broca's support of Charles Darwin's evolutionary theory as "subversive." Late in life, Broca won election as a lifetime member of the French senate. He died in Paris during 1880.

BROUARDEL, Paul Camille Hippolyte (1837–1906)

A French scientist, born in 1837, Paul Brouardel was recognized during the latter 19th century as a pioneer in forensic PATHOLOGY whose extensive work with corpses helped examiners distinguish strangulation HOMICIDES from suicides by hanging. With Jean Charcot, mentor of Sigmund Freud, Brouardel also published *Les attentets aux moeurs,* a detailed study of rapes committed against children by adults. In fact, Freud himself wrote of Brouardel's influence on his own research: "I abandoned my occasional attempts at attending other lectures after I have become convinced that all they had to offer were for the most part well constructed rhetorical performances. The only exceptions were Professor Brouardel's forensic autopsies and lectures at the morgue, which I rarely missed." Another aspect of Brouardel's work, conducted in collaboration with Bergeret d'Arbois, broadened the scope of forensic ENTOMOLOGY by using insects to determine time and place of death. Brouardel died in 1906, at age 69.

BROWN, Albert exonerated by DNA evidence

At age 19, in 1981, Oklahoma resident Albert Brown was convicted of murdering a retired Tulsa firefighter, Earl Taylor, found gagged and drowned in Lake Fort Gibson. Conviction hinged on testimony regarding human hairs—specifically, that hairs found on the gag in Taylor's mouth matched Brown's, and that hairs from Taylor's head were found in the trunk of Brown's car. Brown was sentenced to life and served 20 years before DNA testing revealed that hairs lifted from the gag were not, in fact, his.

A hearing on Brown's case was held in Tulsa on October 2, 2001, whereupon the court scheduled his release for October 16. Prosecutors initially agreed, saying a retrial was "possible but not likely." When Brown's release date arrived, however, authorities "discovered" his history of 44 prison disciplinary infractions, including allegations that Brown had conspired with others in the stabbing of a fellow prisoner. Prosecutor Dianne Barker Harold found, not surprisingly, that after being falsely imprisoned for two decades Brown had "some anger issues and authoritative issues." She also reversed the prior decision of her office, requesting six months to decide if enough evidence existed for a retrial on the Taylor homicide. Freedom remains elusive for Albert Brown, as the state seeks ways to keep him imprisoned despite the scientific evidence that apparently exonerates him.

BROWN, Danny exonerated by DNA

In 1981, 28-year-old Bobbie Russell was raped and strangled at her apartment in Toledo, Ohio, left with an electrical extension cord wrapped around her neck. Two of Russell's three children, a two-year-old daughter and six-year-old son, were present when she died but were not physically assaulted. Russell's son told police that two men, one known as "Danny," visited his mother at different times on the night she died. Detectives suspected 25-year-old Danny Brown, who had dated Russell for several months, and her son picked Brown from a lineup, claiming that he had engaged in a heated argument with Russell. Frightened, the child had gone to bed and fell asleep, waking to find his mother dead the next morning. Brown passed a polygraph test and presented numerous alibi witnesses, but prosecutors pressed charges of murder and robbery. Jurors convicted him in 1982, whereupon Brown received a life sentence. Nearly two decades later, DNA testing on semen found at the crime scene exonerated Brown and implicated suspect Sherman Preston, convicted in 1983 for the similar rape-slaying of victim Denise Howell. Brown was released from prison in April 2001, despite claims from Toledo prosecutors that he may have accompanied Preston to the crime scene. (That allegation contradicted statements from Russell's son, that his mother's killer was alone.) In May 2001 District Attorney Julia Bates announced that her office would retry Brown if further investigation linked him to the crime, but no additional charges were filed. Sherman Preston, likewise, has not been charged with Russell's murder. Today the case remains officially unsolved.

BROWN, Dennis exonerated by DNA

In September 1984, a masked intruder invaded a home in Covington, Louisiana, and raped its female occupant at knifepoint. The victim described her attacker as a black man, assisting in preparation of a police sketch despite her admission that she only saw the rapist's eyes. Seventeen-year-old Dennis Brown was not suspected in that case when he volunteered to stand as "filler" in a police lineup. He was astounded when the victim picked him out, and while he later confessed to the rape, Brown recanted at trial, insisting that policemen threatened him with knives to extract his confession. Semen recovered from the crime scene identified the rapist as a type O secretor—a trait shared by Brown and 40 percent of America's black population. At trial in 1985, jurors discounted Brown's claim of coercion and accepted the victim's revised claim that she saw her rapist "clearly" for a period of 20 minutes. Convicted of aggravated rape, aggravated burglary, and aggravated crimes against nature, Brown received a sentence of life imprisonment. Louisiana state law denied Brown the right to a lawyer during his subsequent appeals, forcing the barely literate teenager to represent himself as best he could.

In 2003, members of the INNOCENCE PROJECT NEW ORLEANS agreed to review Brown's case. Since DNA testing was unknown at the time of his original trial, IPNO attorneys petitioned for tests on the semen collected in 1984. Those tests excluded Brown as a donor of the semen, thus exonerating him of rape. He was released with all charges dropped in September 2004, after serving 19 years in prison for a crime he did not commit. At press time for this volume, Brown had received no compensation for his wrongful conviction and incarceration. The rape remains officially unsolved today.

BRUSSEL, James Arnold (1905–1982)

Born in New York City on April 22, 1905, James Brussel received his bachelor's degree from the University of Pennsylvania in 1926 and earned his M.D. from the same institution three years later. After completing his internship and residency in PSYCHIA-TRY, Dr. Brussel found employment with New York's Department of Mental Hygiene. That work heightened his interest in criminal psychology and helped Brussel develop his theory of PSYCHOLOGICAL PRO-FILING for unknown offenders. The first test of his method came in 1956, when Brussel volunteered to help catch New York City's "Mad Bomber."

The unknown serial terrorist planted his first pipe bomb—which failed to explode—at a Consolidated Edison office in November 1940, with a note reading "CON EDISON CROOKS—THIS IS FOR YOU." One year later, another dud surfaced in Manhattan with a note signed "F.P." (later explained as an abbreviation for "fair play"), which promised police a hiatus in bombings for the duration of World War

II. The bomber's third device was found in Grand Central Terminal on March 29, 1950, and defused before it could explode. His fourth bomb—and the first to detonate—demolished a telephone booth at the New York Public Library several weeks later. Sporadic threats and bombings continued over the next three years, wounding the bomber's first casualty in 1953. Dr. Brussel entered the case on December 2, 1956, after a blast injured six victims in a Brooklyn movie theater.

Brussel's profile described the Mad Bomber as a middle-aged European immigrant, unmarried, and a Catholic, living with a female relative in Connecticut. At his arrest, Brussel predicted, the bomber would be dressed in a double-breasted suit with the jacket buttoned. Unlike most modern profilers, Brussel also suggested a means of catching the bomber, inviting correspondence to a local newspaper, the *Journal-American*. While that plea resulted in scores of false confessions, it also brought one anonymous letter railing against Con Edison executives for some unspecified injustice. A search of company files soon led police to 53-year-old George Metesky, an immigrant living in Connecticut with his two unmarried sisters. Employed by Con Ed during 1929–31, Metesky had been injured on the job and later complained of headaches without apparent medical cause. Con Ed had fired Metesky and denied his bid for a disability pension in 1932, prompting an unsuccessful lawsuit and a series of threatening letters. At his arrest in January 1957 while wearing a double-breasted suit with the jacket buttoned, Metesky admitted his guilt in the bombings. A judge deemed him insane and committed Metesky to a state hospital, where he remained until 1973.

Brussel's performance in the Mad Bomber case won him accolades as "a psychic seer" and "the Sherlock Holmes of the couch." Thereafter, he profiled many unknown subjects for police—including the "BOSTON STRANGLER"—but never again scored a hit to compare with his triumph in the Metesky case. Brussel's experiments with what he called "Blitz Electric Shock Therapy," inflicting 40 to 50 electro-convulsive shock treatments on various female patients within two-day time spans, were followed by experiments using methamphetamine hydrochloride on patients suffering from depression. Some critics questioned the value and safety of such treatments, but Dr. Brussel's reputation suffered most from his involvement as a prosecution witness in the JEFFREY MACDONALD murder case. In that instance, where defendant MacDonald claimed his wife and daughters had been murdered by a gang of "hippie" home invaders, Brussel branded the story a lie. His reasoning: Since MacDonald said the perpetrators had mentioned "acid" (LSD), Brussel presumed all involved would be drugged and thus too "lethargic" to commit homicide. Furthermore, such killers would not use weapons found in the home, Brussel said, but would carry "daggers or similar ceremonial type weapons." Finally, in Brussel's opinion, hippies would not have "entered the house by walking only on the sidewalk. They would 'stroll' and not care where they walked." Brussel delivered that verdict in 1971, eight years before meeting MacDonald for a brief psychiatric interview. He was not called as a witness at MacDonald's trial, and died in October 1982.

BULLOCK, Ronnie exonerated by DNA evidence

On March 18, 1983, in Chicago, a nine-year-old girl on her way to school was accosted by a man wearing a police uniform, who forced her into his car and drove to a nearby alley, where he raped her. A second case was reported on April 18, 1983, the rapist flashing a badge at a 12-year-old before he abducted and raped her. The victims described their attacker to police, and a sketch was prepared, later used to identify suspect Ronnie Bullock. Both victims selected Bullock from a lineup and later identified him in court. Convicted at trial in May 1984, Bullock received a 60-year sentence for deviate sexual assault and a concurrent 15-year sentence for aggravated kidnapping.

An appellate court upheld Bullock's conviction in March 1987, but his motion to have the rape evidence impounded for future study was granted. Prosecutors agreed to his motion for DNA testing in June 1993, presumably confident that the results would confirm Bullock's verdict. Following a delay, in which the victim's underpants "disappeared" and were then rediscovered, testing proceeded in October 1994. The lab's report excluded Bullock as a suspect in the case, and he was released from prison on October 14, 1994, confined to his parents' home while prosecution experts duplicated the DNA tests. The secondary tests again excluded Bullock, and the charges were dismissed, liberating Bullock after he had served 10 and one-half years of his sentence. The actual rapist has not been apprehended.

BURGLARY

British common law defined burglary as unlawfully entering a dwelling place at night. Modern statutes generally do not specify an hour of the day or night and most do not specify a residential setting. The general offense thus involves gaining entry to some dwelling or commercial building where the offender has no legal right to be. (Incursion on private grounds *outside* the building in question constitutes the lesser offense of trespass.) Some laws and jurisdictions classify "breaking and entering" as a separate offense, while reserving burglary for cases where theft occurs or the occupants of a building are assaulted. Any violence or use of weapons during a break-in is generally considered an aggravating factor and increases the convicted offender's penalty.

While burglary is most often a profit-motivated crime involving theft of money or other valuables, intruders commit break-ins for a variety of reasons. Illegal entry may precede a variety of other crimes, including vandalism, ARSON, SEX CRIMES, or HOMICIDE. Law enforcement officers may also be guilty of burglary, when they enter homes or other buildings to install surveillance devices without the necessary warrants. In FBI parlance, such illegal entries are called "black-bag jobs," based on the fiction that agents performed the break-ins on their own initiative—in a "black bag" of secrecy—without their superiors' knowledge or consent.

Depending on their choice of targets, modern burglars may require special knowledge and training to defeat various locks, alarms, and other security systems. Most professionals perform advance surveillance on a target, sketching floor plans or obtaining original blueprints, schematic designs and other details of the facility. Except in cases of an "inside job," where codes and combinations are provided, safecrackers commonly require special tools and EXPLOSIVES to penetrate vaults, safe-deposit boxes, and the like. Forensic processing of a burglary scene involves collection of FINGERPRINTS, IMPRESSION EVIDENCE, and any TRACE EVIDENCE that the intruder(s) may have left behind. In those cases where burglars stop at the scene to eat, drink, masturbate, or relieve themselves—a common occurrence in cases of sexually motivated fetish burglary—DNA evidence may be collected from various bodily fluids. Impressions found at a crime scene may be matched to a suspect's tools, footwear, or automobile tires, while many stolen objects may be traced and identified by their serial numbers.

BUTLER, Sabrina exonerated by medical evidence

Mississippi resident Sabrina Butler, an 18-year-old unwed mother, was charged with murder in 1990 after her nine-month-old son was pronounced dead at a community hospital. Butler told physicians and police that she had found the boy unconscious in his crib, attempting to revive him with CPR techniques before rushing to the hospital. Police noted contradictions in her statement, discounting grief and Butler's diagnosis as borderline mentally retarded when they filed the murder charge. At trial, prosecutors sought the death penalty on grounds that Walter Butler had been killed during commission of another felony—specifically, child abuse. Butler's defense attorneys presented the CPR story but offered no supporting evidence. (One of the lawyers was later described by a local newspaper as an "incompetent drunk.") Butler was convicted of first-degree murder and sentenced to die.

Mississippi's Supreme Court overturned the conviction in 1992, on grounds that Butler's prosecutor had improperly urged jurors to infer guilt from the fact that Butler did not testify in her own defense. Retried in 1995, Butler had the advantage of a skilled defense attorney and belated testimony from a neighbor who confirmed her original account of attempted CPR. New medical evidence also revealed that Walter Butler suffered from cystic kidney disease and may have died from Sudden Infant Death Syndrome. His abdominal injuries were diagnosed as posthumous results of a failed attempt to revive him. Butler was acquitted after brief deliberation and released from custody.

BYRD, Kevin exonerated by DNA evidence

In 1985, a Houston woman was attacked and raped in her home by an unknown intruder. In statements to police, she repeatedly described her rapist as a white man, adding that "he had an unusual color of skin . . . a honey-brown color, but he was not black." Four months later, while shopping in a neighborhood grocery store, she glimpsed Kevin Byrd—a dark-skinned African American—and reported him to the authorities as her attacker. At trial, prosecutors convinced a jury that the victim's repeated descriptions of her assailant as "white" were in fact a "mistake" by one of the detectives assigned to her case. Byrd was convicted in August 1985 and sentenced to life in prison.

Twelve years later, in early 1997, DNA testing of semen collected in the case proved beyond doubt that Byrd was innocent. The Texas Board of Pardons and Paroles recommended to Governor George W. Bush that Byrd be pardoned immediately on grounds of actual innocence, but Bush refused until October 1997, finally compelled by adverse publicity to grant the belated pardon. Critics accused Bush of racism, noting that Byrd was the first black recipient of clemency among 15 inmates pardoned by Bush, but the reaction of Harris County authorities was even more troubling. In the wake of Byrd's pardon, the county clerk ordered "rape kit" evidence destroyed in 50 other cases, thereby making DNA tests impossible—and presumably sparing county prosecutors from further embarrassment.

C

CALDWELL, Charles (1771–1853)

A son of Irish immigrants, Charles Caldwell was born in Newark, Delaware, on May 14, 1771. His family soon moved to North Carolina, there determining that Charles should be a minister, but he ignored their expectations and enrolled at the University of Pennsylvania's medical school at age 21. Upon obtaining his M.D., Caldwell briefly joined the fledgling U.S. Army as a medical officer, then migrated to Lexington, Kentucky, where a new medical school was under construction. Over the next two decades, Caldwell spent most of his time and much of his money in pursuit of excellence for that institution, then moved on to found a new medical school in Kentucky (which subsequently became the University of Louisville).

By the time of his last move, Caldwell's attention had strayed into the pseudoscience of phrenology, wherein the shape of a subject's skull is thought to determine intelligence and moral character. Those studies led to publication of his magnum opus, *Elements of Phrenology*, in 1824. That work in turn established Caldwell as a preeminent criminologist of the early 19th century, although phrenology and all its tenets have long since been discredited. Caldwell died in 1853, before the reputation of his "science" suffered greatly, and his autobiography was posthumously published in 1855.

CALIFORNIA Association of Criminalists

The CAC was founded in 1954 by 16 members from various California law enforcement agencies, meeting to exchange case histories, ideas, and new testing procedures. While maintaining its original title, the group has since expanded to include members throughout the United States and Europe. Present-day members of the CAC include chemists, criminalists, document examiners, educators in forensic science, firearm and tool mark examiners, molecular biologists, serologists, and toxicologists. CAC members also participate in many other professional organizations.

CALLACE, Leonard exonerated by DNA evidence

In January 1985, a teenage resident of White Plains, New York, was accosted by two strangers as she approached her car in a mall parking lot. The men brandished knives and forced her into the backseat of a nearby sedan, where one sexually assaulted her while his companion watched. Police arrested Leonard Callace on the basis of a suspect sketch; the victim later picked his likeness from a photo lineup and identified him in court as her rapist. (The second man was never found.) Adamant in his protestation of innocence, Callace rejected a plea bargain offered by the state, which would have freed him after four months in jail. At trial, prosecutors demonstrated that Callace's blood type matched semen collected from the victim, and his alibi was uncorroborated. Jurors deliberated less than an hour before convicting Callace on four counts of sodomy, three counts of sexual abuse, one count of wrongful imprisonment, and criminal possession of a weapon. On March 24, 1987, Callace received a prison term of 25 to 50 years.

The verdict was affirmed on appeal, and Callace was denied leave to pursue further action before the state court of appeals. While serving his time, Callace learned the basic details of DNA testing from the case of another New York defendant, CHARLES DABBS. On June 27, 1991, a Suffolk County judge approved DNA testing of semen stains from the victim's clothing, which eliminated Leonard Callace as a source. He was released from prison on October 5, 1992, after serving nearly six years of his sentence. Prosecutors dismissed all charges and declined to pursue a new trial based on the victim's testimony alone.

CANTER, David Victor (1944–)

A native of Liverpool, England, born in 1944, David Canter received his B.A. (1964) and Ph.D. (1969) in psychology from the University of Liverpool. He subsequently taught psychology at his alma mater and at Strathclyde University, then joined the University of Surrey's faculty, chairing that institution's psychology department in 1987 and founding its master's course in investigative psychology five years later. As the author of 20 books and some 150 scholarly articles, Canter is a recognized expert in the field of forensic psychology. At last report, he had participated in more than 150 police investigations and is credited with helping British authorities capture serial rape-slayer John Duffy in 1986 (although Duffy's accomplice, David Mulcahy, remained at large until 2000). Dr. Canter is a fellow of the British Psychological Society and the American Psychological Association.

CARDOZO Innocence Project defenders of the falsely accused

Operating from the Benjamin N. Cardozo School of Law in New York City, the Innocence Project was founded in 1992 by lawyers BARRY SCHECK (best known for his role in the defense of ORENTHAL JAMES (O. J.) SIMPSON) and Peter Neufeld. A clinical law program for students, supervised by law professors and university administrators, the project offers pro bono (free) legal assistance to prison inmates challenging their convictions on the basis of DNA evidence. (The inmates are required, however, to obtain private funding for the actual tests, which may cost as much as $10,000.) Limited funding and personnel currently force the Innocence Project to decline any cases where DNA is not the primary issue. In addition to legal defense for imprisoned clients, the project also lobbies state legislatures for passage of laws authorizing compensation of wrongly convicted and incarcerated persons. To date, those efforts have enjoyed limited success (only Illinois and New York have passed such laws to date), but defense of wrongly convicted prisoners has achieved more dramatic results. As of April 2007, 200 American inmates had been exonerated and freed on the basis of DNA testing, 38 of those thanks to members of the Innocence Project. Those represented directly by the Cardozo Innocence Project include HERMAN ATKINS, TERRY CHALMERS, EDWARD HONAKER, and CALVIN JOHNSON JR.

CASPER, Johann Ludwig (1789–1864)

Johann Casper was born on March 11, 1789, but published accounts differ on the location, some naming him as a native of Berlin, while others claim he was born at Breslau, in the Prussian province of Silesia (later part of Poland). He studied medicine in Berlin and earned his M.D. in 1819, becoming a full professor at the local university six years later. Over the next 35 years he dedicated himself to forensic PATHOLOGY, publishing *A Handbook of the Practice of Forensic Medicine* in 1861. He was also outspoken on the subject of SEX CRIMES, warning in one publication against the "outright lies" of women who filed rape charges. Modern gay activists also hail Casper as the first medical authority to assert (in 1850 or 1852, reports differ) that homosexuality might be an inborn trait. Today, Casper is best known for his insistence on meticulous documentation of autopsies. He died in Berlin on February 24, 1864.

CELL Phone Cloning wireless fraud technique

Every cell phone is designed to have a unique factory-set electronic serial number (ESN) and mobile identification number (MIN). "Cloned" cell phones are those reprogrammed to transmit the ESN and MIN of another (legitimate) telephone when calls are made. Swindlers obtain those numbers by monitoring radio wave transmissions and intercepting calls in progress. After "cloning," the legitimate phone shares its ESN/MIN combination with one or more additional phones—but all charges are billed to the registered owner. In a variation of the theme, called "tumbling," some bootleg cell phones are programmed to use a different stolen ESN/MIN combination for each call, running through a list of multiple numbers. This technique prevents a single legitimate user from noting a sudden rash of bogus calls on his or her monthly bill and thus delays exposure of the fraud in progress.

Profits from a cloning operation are limited only by the swindler's nerve and imagination. Small-timers simply use the phones themselves or share with friends until the fraud is discovered and the ESN/MIN combination is deactivated. Others sell cloned telephones, individually or in bulk lots. Finally, in larger cities, it is not unusual to find "customers" lined up on sidewalks or in shopping malls,

"Cloned" cell phones are used to run up millions of dollars in fraudulent calls each year.

waiting their turns to make long-distance calls on a "vendor's" cloned telephone for a fraction of the normal cost. Nationwide, by 2000, cell phone cloning cost the industry an estimated $650 million. Cloned cell phones are also extremely popular with drug dealers and other felons who have a vested interest in keeping their telephone records untraced.

Experiments with new forms of cell phone security are constantly ongoing, but wily thieves seem to crack each new system within months of its development. Meanwhile, the U.S. government took action in April 1998, with the Cellular Telephone Protection Act, making it a federal crime to possess, use, or traffic in any hardware or software configured to alter or modify a cell phone without proper authorization. Enforcement of the act fell to the U.S. Secret Service, which reports a doubling in the number of arrests for wireless telecommunications fraud each year since 1991.

While the industry strives to outwit high-tech swindlers on the drawing board, legitimate cell phone users can still take certain basic steps to protect themselves from fraud. Experts recommend the following precautions:

1. Whenever possible, disable any "roaming" functions built into a cell phone. Roaming permits use of a telephone via analog systems when the caller is outside a server's normal digital range, but it also frequently defeats the purpose of secure personal identification numbers (PINs). Cloners love roaming phones for that reason and often target areas surrounding airports or interstate highways, to capture signals (and ESN/MIN combinations) from callers in transit.
2. Turn off telephones when they are not in use. Cell phones left on poll the cellular base station with the strongest signal every few seconds, thus allowing the system to route calls through the appropriate base station. At the same time, however, polling leaves a phone vulnerable to interception and cloning, even when a call is not in progress.
3. Review all bills in detail and report any fraudulent calls to the service provider. A cursory glance may not reveal the occasional bogus call generated by "tumbling," but many cloning victims are billed for dozens—or thousands—of illegitimate calls in a single month.

CENTRAL Identification Laboratory

During the Vietnam War, two U.S. Army mortuaries operated at Danang and at Tan Soo Nhut Air Force Base outside Saigon. Both closed in 1972, with the end of overt American involvement in Vietnam, with their equipment and personnel consolidated at a single facility in Thailand. That operation, christened the U.S. Army Central Identification Laboratory in January 1973, was designed to seek, recover, and identify remains of American servicemen lost between 1965 and 1972. In 1976, as a result of U.S. troop reductions in Thailand, the lab was relocated to Hickam Air Force Base in Hawaii. Since August 12, 1985, its orders include location and recovery of U.S. service personnel lost in World War II, the Korean War, the Vietnam War, "and other conflicts and contingencies." No comprehensive statistics are presently available, but the CIL has been favored with various decorations, including a meritorious unit commendation (February 1976) and two superior unit awards (December 1988 and September 1995). Methods employed by the CIL staff to identify remains include DNA typing and forensic ANTHROPOLOGY.

CENTRAL Park Rape Case DNA exonerations

On the night of April 19, 1989, a 28-year-old female jogger was attacked, beaten, and raped in New York City's Central Park. Passersby found her near death, with 75 percent of the blood drained from her body and her temperature at 84 degrees. Upon recovery, the victim had no memory of the assault, but police swiftly focused their attention on a group of black and Hispanic youths arrested for other attacks committed in Central Park the same night. Prolonged interrogation produced contradictory confessions from five suspects—Anton McCray, Kevin Richardson, Yusef Salaam, Raymond Santana, and Kharey Wise—who ranged in age from 11 to 14 years. Prosecutors sought to resolve their divergent claims as to when and where the rape took place by presenting forensic evidence. In 1990, at two separate trials, jurors heard that a hair found on one defendant "matched and resembled" the victim's; that a hair found on the victim "matched" one defendant's; and that blood and hair found on a rock at the crime scene belonged to the victim. All five defendants were convicted and sentenced to prison.

In early 2002, convicted murderer and rapist Matias Reyes confessed that he alone was responsible for the attack in Central Park. At the time of his confession, Reyes was already serving life in prison for similar attacks, committed near the same location in 1989. Although police had his name and MODUS OPERANDI on file, they failed to link him with the second attack and initially refused to accept his belated confession. Evidence collected from the crime scene was later subjected to DNA testing, whereupon authorities admitted that the hair found on one convicted defendant did not match the Central Park victim, but hairs found on the victim *did* match Reyes. On December 19, 2002, Manhattan's district attorney recommended that the convictions of McCray, Richardson, Salaam, Santana, and Wise should be overturned. By the time they were finally released from prison, McCray had served six years, Richardson and Salaam had served six and a half years each, Santana had served eight years, and Wise had served 11.5 years.

CENTURION Ministries defenders of the wrongfully accused

America's first Innocence Project, Centurion Ministries was organized in 1983 by James McCloskey, a corporate executive-turned-minister who earned his master of divinity degree from Princeton University. Operating from Princeton since its foundation, Centurion Ministries describes its singular mission as a campaign "to liberate from prison and vindicate individuals who are completely innocent of crimes for which they have been convicted and imprisoned." More than a dozen inmates have been freed to date through the efforts of McCloskey and his staff, including EDWARD HONAKER and CLARENCE MOORE, cleared on the basis of DNA evidence.

In a 1989 article, "Convicting the Innocent," McCloskey maintained that wrongful convictions occur primarily from one or more of seven causes: (1) a widespread "presumption of guilt" against those charged with crimes; (2) perjury by police officers; (3) false testimony by prosecution witnesses; (4) illegal manipulation or suppression of evidence by prosecutors; (5) shoddy police work (as opposed to deliberate FRAME-UPS); (6) incompetent defense counsel; and (7) misconceptions by jurors concerning evidence and testimony.

Because of its small staff and meager resources, Centurion Ministries holds potential clients to a stringent standard. As described on the group's Web

Jim McCloskey poses near a board listing cases being worked on by his organization, Centurion Ministries. (AP)

site, cases are accepted only if the inmate has been sentenced to death or life imprisonment, with no parole for at least 15 years; the inmate is "100% innocent," with no involvement in the crime (thereby excluding cases of accidental death or self-defense); the inmate must be indigent and have exhausted all standard legal appeals; and the case does not involve child molestation, since such cases "require a special expertise that CM does not possess." Inmates who meet those strict criteria are invited to contact Centurion Ministries for a review of their cases.

CHALMERS, Terry Leon exonerated by DNA evidence

Defendant Terry Chalmers was arrested following the rape and robbery of a young woman in White Plains, New York, on August 18, 1986. The victim

first identified his photo from an array of police mug shots, then twice selected him as her attacker from police lineups. At trial, Chalmers's alibi remained uncorroborated, and the victim identified him again. On June 9, 1987, he was convicted of rape, sodomy, robbery, and two counts of grand larceny, drawing a prison term of 12 to 24 years.

Chalmers first appealed his conviction on grounds that the police lineups were improperly conducted. On July 18, 1990, the New York Supreme Court's appellate division rejected that argument, finding that police conduct was proper in the case, and that the victim's courtroom identification of Chalmers made the lineups superfluous. Chalmers next applied to the CARDOZO INNOCENCE PROJECT for aid, and its lawyers obtained physical evidence from the case for DNA testing. On July 26, 1994, those tests eliminated

Chalmers as a possible donor for the semen traces recovered by authorities in August 1986. Chalmers's conviction was vacated, with the rape and sodomy charges dismissed on January 31, 1995. Authorities stalled for three months before dropping the larceny charges. Terry Chalmers was released after serving eight years of his undeserved sentence.

CHANAL, Pierre serial murder suspect indicted by DNA

Between 1980 and 1987, eight young men either vanished or were found brutally murdered in the Marne region of France, northeast of Paris. Several of the victims were soldiers, based at one or another of three army camps located in what soon became known as the "Triangle of Death." Pierre Chanal, himself a senior warrant sergeant with the crack 4th Dragoons commando regiment, fell under suspicion in 1988, after he kidnapped and raped a Hungarian hitchhiker in the same region. Convicted and sentenced for that crime, Chanal was free again by August 2001, when French authorities announced their intent to charge him with multiple murders.

DNA testing, unavailable to French authorities in 1988, had recently been applied to several human hairs discovered in Chanal's van—the same vehicle in which he was earlier caught red-handed, his male victim trussed up in a parachute harness, while Chanal videotaped his rape and torture. Results of those DNA tests indicated a "very strong probability" that Chanal murdered three of the previous victims, including 19-year-old Trevor O'Keefe, an Irish tourist found strangled and buried in a shallow grave during August 1987. Five counts of murder were dismissed on August 14, 2001, since the victims have never been found, but Chanal was ordered to stand trial for the deaths of O'Keefe and two others. At this writing, no trial date has been set. Unlike America's legal system, the French Napoleonic Code presumes a suspect's guilt until innocence is proved in court.

CHEILOSCOPY, Forensic

In forensic science, cheiloscopy is the study of patterns formed by wrinkles, scars, and other features of the human lips that may leave impressions on objects such as drinking glasses. French criminologist EDMOND LOCARD first recommended use of lip prints as a means of identification in 1932, subsequently supported by author LeMoyne Snyder in his book

Homicide Investigation (1950). Snyder specifically cited the case of a woman struck by a hit-and-run driver, who initially denied the event but confessed after the victim's lip print was lifted from the left-front fender of his car. That result notwithstanding, no American court presently recognizes cheiloscopy as a positive means of identification. Still, the science has its vocal supporters, including Dr. Anil Aggrawal. In various Internet articles, Dr. Aggrawal cites the work of one "Santos," who reportedly classified eight groups of lip prints in 1967; a "Dr. Suzuki," who in 1970 divided the lip prints of 107 Japanese females aged 20–36 into five classifications; and one "Tsuchihashi," who surveyed the lips of 1,364 subjects in 1974, emerging "convinced of their value in identification." Students of cheiloscopy suggest that hereditary factors influence lip-print patterns, while the aforementioned Dr. Suzuki reportedly found "striking similarities" between lips in 18 pairs of identical twins.

CHEMICAL & Biological Weapons (CBW)

Between September 18 and October 9, 2001, an unknown person or persons mailed several letters from New Jersey, addressed to the U.S. Senate office building in Washington, D.C., and to media outlets in New York and Florida. The envelopes contained anthrax spores, which infected some two dozen victims, six fatally. White House spokesmen linked the mailings to the TERRORISM attacks of September 11, 2001, but no proof of that charge was forthcoming. FBI agents mounted a massive coast-to-coast search for the killer(s), but at this writing (in mid-October 2002) the G-men have not taken legal action against any or released any trial-worthy evidence.

On the one-year anniversary of the anthrax murders, President George W. Bush called for war with Iraq, alleging that Iraqi dictator Saddam Hussein had illegally stockpiled "weapons of mass destruction" while scheming to launch new attacks against the United States. Bush's own CIA chief disagreed, reporting that Hussein was more likely to retaliate for an invasion than to launch a unilateral assault, but the real irony of the war-hawk position was revealed on October 9, 2002, when the Associated Press published documents proving that U.S. military forces had conducted secret testing of chemical and biological weapons (CBW) on some 3,000 soldiers in the 1960s. While belatedly couched in terms of "an effort to develop defenses against such weapons," the illegal tests prompted critics to ask whether U.S. leaders were any more responsible or trustworthy than Iraq's Hussein.

As suggested by its name, CBW involves two distinct and separate groups of elements. *Chemical* agents are manmade, including a wide variety of drugs and poisons, hallucinogens, defoliants, toxic metals, and nerve agents (often called "nerve gases," though they may not be in gaseous form). Some applications of chemical warfare verge on slapstick comedy, as when the Central Intelligence Agency planned to spike Fidel Castro's cigars with LSD (to cause him to make erratic, nonsensical speeches) or to dust his clothes with a depilatory (thereby causing fallout from his famous beard). At the other end of the scale are deadly serious applications, such as the September 1957 assassination of Soviet defector Nikolai Khokhlov in Frankfurt. The assassin sprinkled Kokhlov's food with thallium, a rare toxic metal. The result is described by author John Barron in *KGB* (1974).

Hideous brown stripes, dark splotches, and black-and-blue swellings disfigured his face and body. A sticky secretion oozed from his eyelids, and blood seeped through his pores; his skin felt dry, shrunken, and aflame. At the mere touch of his hand, great tufts of hair fell out.... Tests on September 22 showed that Kokhlov's white corpuscles were being swiftly and fatally destroyed, his bones decaying, his blood turned to plasma, and his saliva glands atrophying.

Biological agents, by contrast, are destructive organisms found in nature—bacteria, viruses, spores, parasites—though some may be genetically altered in labs to enhance their offensive application. Unlike chemical weapons, biological warfare has been used at least since the Middle Ages, when rotting livestock carcasses were catapulted over castle walls to spread death and disease under siege. Some modern scholars also believe the "Black Death," which claimed one-third of the known world's population between 1347 and 1351, may have begun as a primitive form of "germ warfare." A century later, European diseases began decimating aboriginal people in the Western Hemisphere, and not always by accident. Cruel settlers in the United States and Mexico sometimes resolved their local "Indian problem" by offering Native Americans treacherous gifts of poisoned food or smallpox-infected blankets.

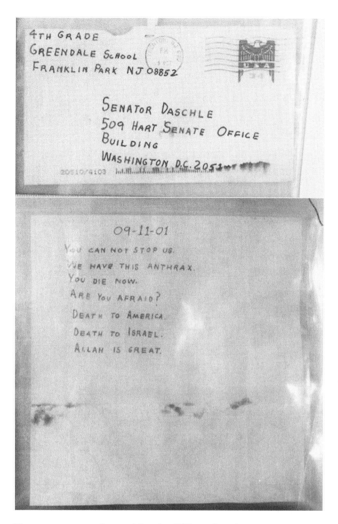

These images released by the FBI on October 23, 2001, show the envelope and letter sent to the office of former Senate Majority Leader Tom Daschle containing anthrax. (Getty Images)

Modern chemical warfare left its mark on Europe during World War I, with the use of toxic gas by both sides producing results so horrific that it was banned by the subsequent Geneva Convention. Suspicion of CBW research by Japan and Nazi Germany prompted the U.S. military to begin its own production of chemical and biological weapons in 1942 and to continue for nearly three decades beyond V-J Day (victory over Japan, 1945). American diplomats leveled charges of CBW violations against North Korea in the early 1950s and later made similar accusations against the Soviet Union and the People's Republic of China. In the United States, meanwhile, military researchers conducted a series of covert tests that are only now coming to light, in the first decade of the 21st century. The tests revealed in October 2002 included:

"Devil Hole I"—Designed to test dispersal patterns of the nerve agent sarin after release from rockets and artillery shells in aspen and spruce forests similar to those in the USSR, this experiment was carried out in the summer of 1965 at the Gerstle River test site near Fort Greeley, Alaska.

"Devil Hole II"—Another test at the Gerstle River site, this time involving the nerve agent VX, deployed against mannequins dressed in military uniforms, seated in U.S. Army trucks.

"Big Tom"—A 1965 test that involved spraying bacteria over the Hawaiian island of Oahu to simulate a biological attack on an island compound. Researchers used *Bacillus globigii,* a bacterium believed harmless at the time (later found to cause serious infections in persons with weakened immune systems).

Those acknowledged tests do not include the deliberate exposure of some 3,000 U.S. soldiers to CBW agents in the name of national defense, and rumors persist of other tests still concealed from the public at large. Author Ed Regis reports, in *The Biology of Doom* (1999), that the U.S. program employed 4,036 persons at its peak and tested various agents on 2,000 human volunteers before "its abrupt cancellation in 1969." After decades of government lies and evasions, however—beginning with the Vietnam "credibility gap" and proceeding through Watergate, the Church Committee hearings on intelligence abuses (1975–76), and the Reagan era's Iran-Contra scandal—some critics contend that the testing never really stopped at all. Indeed, a report published in the *New York Times* one week before the terrorist attacks of September 11, 2001, revealed that the Pentagon had conducted recent CBW experiments and that its scientists had "further plans to genetically engineer a more virulent form of the bacterium that causes anthrax, a deadly disease ideal for germ warfare." When the anthrax mailings began two weeks later, FBI agents initially blamed Muslim extremists but later suggested the infected letters may have been sent by someone employed at a covert U.S. laboratory. Critics took no solace from claims issued by the Bush White House, that all American CBW experi-

ments were "completely consistent" with international treaties.

Another nation with an unsavory record of CBW experimentation was South Africa under the fallen apartheid regime. According to reports aired in 1998, that country's white-supremacist government employed a renowned cardiologist, 50-year-old Dr. Wouter Basson, to develop and deploy CBW agents against opponents of the repressive apartheid regime. Dubbed "Dr. Death" by his critics, Basson allegedly sought to produce bacteria that would kill only blacks, along with "vaccines" to sterilize black women. Testimony before the nation's Truth and Reconciliation Commission also suggested that Dr. Basson, operating after 1983 from South Africa's Roodeplaat Research Laboratories, cultivated strains of anthrax, cholera, and botulinum, while studying the use of illegal drugs like Ecstasy, THC, and LSD for "crowd control." Basson's team, dubbed "Project Coast," reportedly developed covert assassination tools (including a syringe disguised as a screwdriver), concocted plans to distribute T-shirts poisoned with hallucinogenic drugs in black townships, and schemed to poison imprisoned black leader Nelson Mandela with thallium (the same toxic metal used by the Soviets to kill Nikolai Khokhlov in 1957). Project Coast additionally is said to have produced poisoned beer, chocolate, cigarettes, and envelope glue. Mandela disbanded the unit upon becoming president in 1993.

The only known criminal use of CBW agents to date occurred in Japan, in the case of the cult known as Aum Shinrikyo ("Supreme Truth"). The sect's "venerable master," Shoko Asahara, prophesied an imminent apocalypse, predicting that 90 percent of the earth's population would die in poison gas attacks by 1997, but he was finally unable to wait for his own deadline. Seven residents of Matsumoto were killed in June 1994, with another 200 injured, after cultists released sarin nerve gas in a residential neighborhood. Nine months later, on March 20, 1995, the incident was repeated on a Tokyo subway train, leaving 12 persons dead and 5,500 in treatment for nonfatal injuries. Several cultists were in custody, captured with $7 million in cash and enough sarin to kill 4 million people, when other sect members released phosgene gas at Yokohama's main railroad terminal on April 19, 1995, injuring 300 persons. Two days later, another 25 persons were hospitalized after a gas attack on a Yokohama shopping mall. Cyanide canisters were retrieved from a Tokyo train station on July 4, 1995, disarmed before they could release their deadly contents. By that time, Shoko Asahara and more than a dozen of his disciples were in custody, awaiting trial on multiple murder charges. Several were convicted at trial, and the cult was officially disbanded by court order on October 30, 1995.

CHEMICAL Castration medical control of sex offenders

In an age when sexual assault—and particularly sexual abuse of minors—has become a high-profile crime and a hot-button issue in political debates, new methods of prevention are constantly under debate. Convicted offenders are subject to increasingly severe prison sentences, ranging literally into thousands of years for some multivictim child molesters, and experimental statutes in several American jurisdictions now permit detention of inmates judged "sexually dangerous" to society beyond completion of their statutory terms. While those laws—and corresponding statutes mandating public broadcast of a paroled sex offender's home address—remain under heated attack by defense attorneys and civil libertarians, all concerned agree that prison time and subsequent registration of known sex offenders with police do little or nothing to prevent recidivism.

Sex criminals repeat their crimes—against adult or minor victims, male or female—because of deep-seated urges and desires. Sterilization of repeat offenders, believed to be a "cure" as late as the 1930s in Germany, in fact does nothing but eliminate the criminal's ability to procreate. Surgical castration, likewise, has proved ineffective in those cases where the sexual assaults stem from rage, sadism, or any other cause unrelated to production of testosterone. In recent years, a less invasive but equally controversial method has been mandated in several states, involving "chemical castration" by means of medication that lowers the testosterone level, thereby reducing a subject's sex drive.

The drugs of choice for chemical castration are Depo-Provera and Depo-Lupron (medroxyprogesterone acetate), which operate by lowering the blood serum testosterone levels in males who receive the injections. Sexual drive is reduced by influencing the hypothalamus portion of the brain that stimulates the pituitary gland to release hormones that in turn control sperm production. The drugs are alleged to

reduce recidivism among serial sex offenders from 87 percent to a mere 2 percent, but medical researchers question those statistics, noting that men subjected to the drugs can still obtain an erection, engage in sexual intercourse, and ejaculate.

California was the first state to impose chemical castration as a legal penalty (or remedy) through a statute passed by the state legislature on August 28, 1996, and signed by Governor Pete Wilson on September 18. The law provides that any person convicted of specified sex offenses against a victim under 13 years of age may be required to undergo medroxyprogesterone acetate treatment during parole for a first offense, and all repeat offenders must receive the treatment during their parole. Those treatments would in fact begin prior to an inmate's release from prison and would continue through the term of that parole unless the state department of corrections demonstrates to the board of prison terms that the treatments are no longer necessary.

Immediate objections were raised by the American Civil Liberties Union and its California affiliate. ACLU spokesperson Valerie Navarro told reporters, "There are problems regarding the right to privacy, the right to procreate, the right to exercise control over one's body." The ACLU termed chemical castration "barbaric, unconstitutional and ultimately ineffective in protecting our children," predicting that the new law would be challenged in court. "Society has an overwhelmingly important interest in keeping children safe," Navarro said. "But this is a simplistic and ultimately ineffective response to the problem of child abuse. As medical and psychiatric experts have testified, the complex reasons that impel people to assault children cannot be eliminated by giving people shots. This measure is nothing more than an election year bill that won't do anything to make it safer for our children."

Dr. Michael Meek and the California Psychiatric Association raised concerns of greater import to most Californians than the civil rights of convicted child molesters. "It's a bad law as written," Dr. Meek told the press. "The classic example would be someone who molests children because voices tell him to molest children. Well, they're doing it from a psychotic point of view because voices tell them. Progesterone is not going to help them at all." Dr. Fred Berlin of Johns Hopkins Hospital also derided the notion that progesterone is a cure-all for SEX CRIMES. "The notion we can give someone a shot once a week, and walk away from them and feel comfortable," Berlin said, "I think is a very naïve point of view."

Naïve or not, the notion of a quick fix instantly appealed to lawmakers in other states. Over the next three years, similar statutes were enacted in Georgia, Iowa, Louisiana, Montana, Oregon, and Wisconsin. Alabama governor Don Siegelman sponsored legislation offering a choice of chemical or surgical castration to any male defendant who sought probation on a first-time conviction for rape, sodomy, sexual torture, or first-degree sexual abuse of a victim under 13 years of age. (Female offenders, as in all other states so far, would be exempt and unaffected by the law.) As of March 2000, the costs for progesterone treatment of paroled sex offenders averaged $2,400 per subject, per year.

Aside from potential failure, medical experts point out that use of progesterone-related drugs poses a potentially lethal health risk for subjects who suffer from obesity, diabetes, pulmonary disease, or high blood pressure—issues ignored in the statutes passed to date. Known side effects of the treatment in males include breast enlargement, tumors, and edema. Women who have used the medication to correct menstrual irregularity for two months or more, meanwhile, report a history of malignant breast tumors, venous thromboses, and an increased tendency toward hemorrhage. Prevailing medical (as opposed to public and political) opinion suggests that use of progesterone should be evaluated on an individual basis, rather than on mandatory terms as specified by existing state legislation. A 1991 research report that recommended Depo-Provera chiefly for use with serial rapists and homosexual pedophiles also added the following cautionary notes:

1. Antitestosterone agents should be employed only if there is
   a. substantial risk of repeated offenses in the period during which behavior therapy has been initiated but has not yet been effective or
   b. a risk that any single offense will produce substantial harm to a victim as, for example, an act of child molestation as opposed to an act of exhibitionism.
2. Such agents should be employed for as short a time as possible. Their use should be tapered once evidence is gained that behavior therapy is becoming effective.

3. Such agents should be given at the lowest dose necessary to produce the required reduction in sexual drive.
4. Such agents should be employed in cases in which continued monitoring of plethysmograph recordings and plasma testosterone levels can occur.
5. Such agents should not be employed as the sole therapeutic approach.
6. Such agents should only be employed in cases in which competent consent can be obtained or in which a guardian can approve their administration.

The latter point is of particular concern with regard to juvenile offenders, as new research continues to report disturbing side effects of chemical castration. In addition to those already noted, recent studies now report extreme weight gain (up to 50 percent of body weight) in some subjects; hyperinsulinemic response to glucose load; compromise of gastrointestinal or gall bladder functions; chills; phlebitis; nausea and vomiting; headaches; hypoglycemia; leg cramps; and sleep disturbances (including bizarre nightmares).

A report on chemical castration in the *New England Journal of Medicine* (February 12, 1998) added support to arguments of those who believe the treatment benefits society via control of sexual offenders. Citing a study of 30 male subjects' recurring deviant sexual behavior, including 25 convicted pedophiles, the article found treatment with a new drug—triptorelin—more effective than Depo-Provera in curbing recidivism (and less risky in terms of medical side effects) when used in combination with traditional psychotherapy. Used primarily in Europe at the present time, triptorelin has yet to gain widespread acceptance in the United States, but the news encouraged proponents of chemical castration in their long-running effort to defeat skeptical challenges. Medical effectiveness, however, still does not address the constitutional issues raised by civil libertarians, and the controversy will doubtless continue until finally settled before the U.S. Supreme Court at some future date.

CHEMISTRY, Forensic

Chemistry is broadly defined as the study of matter dealing with its composition, structure, the properties of substances and the changes that they undergo in interaction with themselves, with other substances, or with applied energy. Forensic chemistry applies that study and its principles to subjects involving the civil or criminal law. Whole volumes and university curricula are devoted to the various details of forensic chemistry. The tasks performed by forensic chemists on a daily basis include quantification and identification of drugs and other CONTROLLED SUBSTANCES, EXPLOSIVES, poisons, gunshot residue, blood and other body fluids, ORGANIC and INORGANIC COMPOUNDS, and any other TRACE EVIDENCE such as PAINT, GLASS, FIBERS, and so forth. Methods employed by forensic chemists, covered elsewhere in this volume, include CHROMATOGRAPHY, DNA profiling, ELECTROPHORESIS, ELEMENTAL ANALYSIS, and SPECTROSCOPY.

CHERRILL, Frederick R. (1892–1964)

A British subject, born in 1892, Frederick Cherrill never abandoned his childhood desire to become a policeman. His parents disapproved, insisting that he study art at Oxford, but illness forced him to withdraw from the university. While recovering from surgery, he shared his hospital room with a retired police officer whose tales of crime-fighting reaffirmed Cherrill's wish to pursue a career in law enforcement. He joined the London Metropolitan Police Force in 1914 and studied FINGERPRINT techniques in his spare time. Cherrill's superiors granted his request for a transfer to the Fingerprint Bureau at Scotland Yard six years later, thereby launching him on a remarkable career. Before his retirement in 1953, as chief of the Fingerprint Bureau, Cherrill would be credited with solving more murder cases than any other British detective of his era.

His breakthrough technique, developed in 1930 with colleague Harry Batley, was a method of identifying suspects from a single fingerprint, rather than a full set of 10. That complex system, which requires extensive training, involves precise measurements of arches, tented arches, loops, and whorls within a given fingerprint, defining common points that Cherrill and Batley called *cores* and *deltas*. In greatly simplified terms, a line drawn through a fingerprint between the core and delta crosses friction ridges ranging in number from one to 30 or more. When prints are indexed by the number of those ridges—e.g., 5, 12, or 19—it then becomes possible to scan only fingerprints with similar characteristics, thus limiting the number of files to be searched for any

single print. Cherrill also worked extensively with palm prints, and submitted England's first such evidence to a criminal court in 1931 (although the defendant's guilty plea excused Cherrill from testifying in that case).

Cherrill's most famous case began on June 1, 1948, when a milkman in Maidenhead delivered a bottle of milk to the home of a 94-year-old widow, Mrs. Freeman Lee. Finding bottles from the past two days still sitting on her porch, the milkman summoned a neighbor, who peered through the letter drop and saw one of Mrs. Lee's shoes with a key ring she habitually carried, lying on the floor next to a large steamer trunk. Police were summoned and found Mrs. Lee's corpse crammed inside the trunk. She had been bound and gagged, then bludgeoned with a hammer, though evidence collected by the coroner named suffocation as the cause of death. Detective Inspector Cherrill visited the scene and found a small cardboard box in Mrs. Lee's bedroom, bearing partial fingerprints of an unknown subject's right thumb and ring finger. A 10-minute search through Cherrill's single-print files linked the fingerprints to convicted burglar George Russell, who was subsequently convicted of murder and hanged. Cherrill called the case "one of the greatest triumphs in the realms of fingerprint detection."

One year after retiring from the London force, Cherrill published his book *The Fingerprint System at Scotland Yard* (1954), which achieved global recognition as a standard text on the subject. Frederick Cherrill died in 1964, at age 72.

CHILD Pornography and Solicitation Online

Pornography is big business on the World Wide Web. According to one Nielsen NetRatings report, 17.5 million Americans visited Internet porn sites from their homes in January 2001 alone, a 40 percent increase over the next most recent survey, from September 2000. The Web's premier porn site—PornCity.net—scored more hits than ESPN.com or the Internet book vendor barnesandnoble.com. Since most porn sites charge visitors for any view beyond a brief "free sample," the profit potential is enormous—$970 million in 1998, according to the research firm Datamonitor. A report from Forrester Research estimates that cyber porn sales (including videos and other merchandise purchased online for home delivery) matched overall Internet book sales

The logo for "Crimes Against Children," a unit of the FBI that incorporates "Operation Candyman," an operation that broke up a computer-based pornography ring that targeted children. (AP Photo/Kenneth Lambert)

advertisement of child porn, without regard to interstate operations. The Child Protection and Obscenity Act of 1988 made it illegal to use computers for transmission or advertisement of child pornography; it also criminalized the buying, selling, or otherwise obtaining custody of children for the purpose of producing porn. Interstate or foreign shipment of three or more child porn images by any means (including computers) became a federal crime in November 1990. The Telecommunications Act of 1996 bans use of any interstate or international communications medium to solicit sexual acts from minors. Finally and most controversially, the Child Pornography Prevention Act of 1996 amends definition of the term to include any simulated depiction of children having sex—even if the models are themselves legal adults or the images include only nonexistent "virtual" children. (Artists and civil libertarians continue to battle the latter provision in court.)

Despite the seeming glut of legislation and increasing international cooperation between law enforcement agencies (at least in North America and western Europe), the lucrative trade in "kiddy" porn still thrives. Frustration over inability to capture foreign dealers and producers has prompted certain U.S. agencies—notably the FBI and Customs Service— to initiate covert domestic "sting" operations that sometimes smack of entrapment. In such cases, the agency generates its own advertisements for child pornography, then arrests all those who attempt to purchase the items (generally material confiscated in previous raids). Since some of those arrested have no prior police records, the agencies involved have been accused of "creating crime" to inflate their own lagging arrest and conviction statistics. At the very least, it can be argued that their time and money would be better spent pursuing producers and vendors of child pornography, rather than soliciting private individuals to break the law by purchasing a magazine or videotape.

And to be sure, there are enough legitimate targets at large to keep any agency busy, without attempting to seduce others. A sampling of recent cases includes:

August 2001 Three members of a Houston, Texas, team that searches for missing children were indicted on federal child pornography charges following an FBI investigation. Defendants Henry Gerdes, Jason Krieg, and Thomas

in 1999 ($1.3 million) and far exceeded the $800 million spent on airline tickets. By a very conservative estimate, 70,000 sex-oriented Web sites existed in March 2007, and the number was steadily rising.

Those figures, however, refer only to "legitimate" porn sites, wherein the models (and presumably the visiting "surfers") are certified adults. Despite poorly documented complaints from church groups that some 200,000 Americans suffer from Internet porn addiction, legislative efforts to impose "decency" standards on the Web have thus far been defeated in the courts. Only in the area of child pornography has legislation been approved to punish vendors and recipients.

It was not always so. While child molestation is a crime in every American state (with the age of consent varying from one jurisdiction to another), no federal ban on child pornography existed until 1977, when the Sexual Exploitation of Children Act banned the production, interstate shipment, and advertisement of such items. Seven years later, settling a point of persistent uncertainty, the Child Protection Act of 1984 defined as "children" any person below the age of 18 years. The Child Sexual Abuse and Pornography Act of 1986 tightened bans on production and

McBarron were all members of the South Texas Advanced Tactical Search and Rescue unit, a missing-person recovery unit for which Krieg served as the official spokesman. Police in Dickinson, Texas, received a tip in July 2001 that the suspects intended to create a child porn Internet site. FBI agents joined the investigation and raided the suspects' homes on August 28, seizing computers, disks, tapes, and two vehicles. All three defendants were charged with sexual exploitation of a child and conspiracy to produce child pornography; Krieg faced an additional charge of sexually assaulting a juvenile. Authorities say the trio taped two teenage boys having sex and that Krieg taped himself having sex with an underage girl. At that, police seemed satisfied that "We got them early on in this project."

November 2001 Ronald C. Kline, a 61-year-old judge of the Orange County (California) Superior Court, surrendered to federal agents at the courthouse on November 9 and was charged with possessing child pornography, his bail set at $50,000. Authorities targeted Judge Kline after receiving tips from a private group that surfs the Internet seeking child-pornography traders. Apparently, an unnamed member of the group hacked into Kline's computer and reported his findings to police. According to Kline's attorney, "The photos were discovered when a hacker in a remote location infected [Kline's] computer with a virus and made an unauthorized copy of the entire contents of his hard drive." Those contents included child porn images and a private diary in which Kline allegedly confessed his preoccupation with adolescent boys. Trial on the charge was still pending in March 2002, when Judge Kline stood unopposed for reelection in Orange County. Meanwhile, an alleged victim has contacted police, claiming that Kline molested him between 1976 and 1978, when the witness was a child and Kline was a lawyer in private practice.

December 2001 Authorities in Winnipeg, Manitoba, vowed to "leave no stone unturned" in their investigation of what they called the province's "largest and most sadistic Internet child-abuse case" to date. Bryan William Larsen, a 41-year-old computer programmer and member of Manitoba's Crocus Grove Nudist Resort was

arrested on December 13, following investigation of what police spokesmen termed a "pedophile ring." The owners of Crocus Grove called the arrest "very disturbing" and "a total shock." Raiders seized 100,000 computer images from the suspect's home, allegedly posted to eight different Web sites that the defendant operated from his apartment. Also seized were a camera, binoculars, 40 pairs of young girls' panties, and assorted other evidence. The alleged pedophile ring was uncovered through an international law enforcement effort dubbed "Project Snowball," intended to crack down on Internet pornography worldwide. Participants included local Canadian officers, as well as members of the Royal Canadian Mounted Police. Aside from Larsen, Canadian authorities report that Project Snowball has thus far identified 406 suspects in British Columbia, 946 in Ontario, 436 in Quebec, 232 in Alberta, 82 in Manitoba, 61 in Nova Scotia, 52 in Saskatchewan, 35 in New Brunswick, 20 in the Northwest Territories, eight in Newfoundland, six on Prince Edward Island, and four in the sparsely settled Yukon.

January 2002 Responding to an "epidemic" of child pornography—which they dubbed "our hidden crime, our hidden shame"—police in Toronto, Ontario, announced the arrest of three suspects, with 200 more still at large. Suspect Blair Evans, a 51-year-old physicist formerly involved in national defense work, was arrested on January 18, charged with making, possessing, and distributing child pornography. Police raiders confiscated some 200,000 "horrendous" computer images at his home, said to depict the sexual abuse of "tens of thousands of innocent children, some as young as six months old." At the time of his arrest, Evans was on probation for a 1999 child-porn conviction, involving 6,000 illicit photographs. The arrest in that case, dating from 1996, had cost Evans his government job and prompted his wife to divorce him before he was sentenced to eight months in jail. Toronto authorities declared their city a major hub in the global child-porn trade, noting that the number of cases with international links had nearly doubled—to 500—between 2000 and 2001. "It's not an expansion," said Corporal François Dore of the Ottawa Provincial Police, "it's an explosion."

January 2002 In Vancouver, British Columbia, 67-year-old retired city planner John Robin Sharpe faced trial on two counts of possessing child pornography and two more of possession with intent to distribute. Initially charged in May 1996, when police and customs officials raided his home to seize books and computer disks, Sharpe had challenged Canada's child pornography possession statute before the British Columbia Supreme Court, arguing that the law was too broad and therefore violated free-speech provisions of the Canadian constitution. He won that case in January 1999, with the decision upheld by the B.C. Court of Appeal, but the Supreme Court of Canada reversed that finding and affirmed the statute's constitutionality in January 2001, thus allowing Sharpe's trial to proceed.

March 2002 Patrick Quigley, a 47-year-old former social worker in Charlottesville, Virginia, pleaded guilty to distributing child pornography he downloaded from the Internet. At the time of his arrest, Quigley was an investigator for Child Protective Services.

January 2003 British police arrested rock star Pete Townshend on child pornography charges. Charges filed included possessing indecent images of children, making indecent images of children, and incitement to distribute indecent images of children. Townshend, a 57-year-old guitarist with The Who, admitted viewing kiddy porn "two or three times for research purposes," but told reporters, "I am not a pedophile." Two months later, London's *Daily Mail* announced official plans to "caution" Townshend without formally prosecuting him. Townshend's arrest was part of Operation Ore, Britain's broadest child pornography investigation to date, which produced dozens of arrests. Most charges were dismissed in July 2005, when an appellate court ruled the investigation "a shambles from the word go."

January 2004 U.S. Immigration and Customs Enforcement (ICE) agents jailed John Maxwell, a substitute teacher and Boy Scout volunteer, on child porn charges in Clifton, New Jersey. Prosecutors charged that Maxwell downloaded and printed more than 100 illegal images obtained from Regpay, a company based in Belarus that allegedly provided credit card billing services

for 50-plus child pornography Web sites worldwide and operated at least four child pornography Web sites of its own. By the time of Maxwell's arrest, global investigations of Regpay had produced arrests of three corporate officers in Europe, guilty pleas from two officers of Connections USA (a Florida firm that processed Regpay's American transactions), and seizure of $800,000 in kiddy porn proceeds. During the course of their investigation, ICE agents seized records listing 270,000 credit card transactions from child porn Web sites. The pursuit of individual purchasers from those records continues.

May 2004 Testimony before the U.S. House Energy and Commerce Subcommittee in Washington, D.C., indicated that federal investigation of Internet peer-to-peer (P2P) file-sharing technology had produced "1,000 cases and 65 arrests" involving child pornography. The hearings presaged introduction of new federal legislation designed to regulate P2P technology.

March 2005 Authorities in Princeton, Minnesota, charged 34-year-old Kevin Scott Patterson with possession of pornographic work involving minors and child neglect/endangerment. The case emerged from a St. Paul Police Department investigation of child-porn Web sites, which included the tracing of e-mail addresses. During a search of Patterson's home, police seized two computers, computer disks, three rolls of film, and a photo of a 14-year-old boy identified only as "SMC." Detectives told reporters that SMC occasionally spent the night at Patterson's home.

May 2006 Virginia state attorney general Bob McDonnell announced the re-arrest of convicted child pornographer Thomas Taveggia for violating his suspended sentence in a June 2005 criminal case. On that occasion, Taveggia's trial judge sentenced him to 100 years in prison, then suspended 99 years of the jail term on condition that Taveggia refrain from "access [to] a computer with Internet access." While serving his one-year sentence in a state work-release program, Taveggia allegedly accessed the Internet and viewed illegal child-sex images, which were traced by the Richmond Police Department's Computer Crime Unit.

October 2006 Federal agents based in New Jersey reported the nationwide arrests of 125 persons linked to an Internet child pornography ring. Those jailed in 22 different states included a Bible camp counselor from Vancouver, Washington; a Boy Scout leader from Mission, Texas; and a pharmaceutical researcher in New Jersey. Several of those arrested had prior police records of child molestation. One suspect captured in San Diego, California, confessed to sexually abusing at least eight children over a 30-year period. Another, arrested in Sacramento, California, owned a video camera with tapes depicting his rape of an eight-year-old girl.

November 2006 A four-month investigation climaxed with the arrest of a Sheboygan, Wisconsin, man on 14 charges of possessing Internet child pornography. Suspect Kenneth Karsnick posted $10,000 bond in that case. Each charge carries a maximum penalty of 25 years in prison and a $100,000 fine.

February 2007 ICE "Operation Emissary" resulted in the federal indictments of three Massachusetts defendants for receipt and possession of child pornography. Defendant Philip Herzberg faced six counts of receipt and one of possession; Donald Banker was charged with two counts of possession; and Matthew Wilson faced one count of possession. The ICE operation targeted a Web site that offered hardcore images and films to Internet subscribers. U.S. Attorney Michael Sullivan told reporters, "Those who think that they are safe behind the perceived anonymity of the Internet should be put on notice that there is no safe haven for child sex predators. We will continue to aggressively pursue those who traffic in child pornography."

March 2007 In three separate raids, Spanish police arrested 12 persons accused of distributing child pornography via the Internet. Spokesmen for Interpol reported that the illicit material originated in Russia and was broadcast via a German Internet server.

March 2007 One of Australia's oldest private academies, the Armidale School, suffered its worst-ever scandal when Jeremy Roberts, a house master, cricket coach, and English teacher, resigned following arrest for production of Internet child pornography. Police charged Roberts with two counts of producing child pornography and 10 counts of disseminating forbidden images. Arresting officers seized two computers, digital cameras, and various data storage devices after Roberts allegedly sent child porn to a police officer masquerading as a pedophile.

Supporters of a tough crackdown on child-porn purveyors and their customers note that children injured by the traffic are not only those compelled to perform for the cameras. Increasingly, it appears that some predatory pedophiles draw inspiration from Internet porn, then go on to abuse children themselves, either for personal pleasure or as part of some perverse commercial enterprise. Some cases in point:

June 2001 Rev. William Cabell, a graduate of Yale Divinity School and Princeton Theological Seminary—serving since 1990 as pastor of Faith United Church of Christ in State College, Pennsylvania—was jailed for crossing state lines to have sex with a minor. The arrest followed a protracted Internet chat-room correspondence with a 14-year-old boy in New Jersey. After eight months of on-line flirtation, Cabell drove to meet his adolescent paramour at a restaurant in Piscataway, New Jersey, and found himself confronted with an undercover FBI agent. Cabell was released on $100,000 bond pending trial, confined to house arrest, and barred from using a computer. Critics of such sting operations denounce law enforcement for translating "harmless" fantasies into criminal action, which might otherwise never occur.

August 2001 Authorities in Nassau County, New York, arrested three suspects—identified as James Warren, Beth Loschin, and Michael Montez—on charges of kidnapping and sexually abusing a 15-year-old girl from Wrentham, Massachusetts. The child disappeared from her home on August 3, allegedly abducted after she struck up a friendship with defendant Warren on the Internet. Warren and Loschin then allegedly held the girl for a week as their sex slave, on Long Island, and "loaned" her to Montez for two days of abuse. They were jailed after the child escaped and telephoned police, directing officers to her kidnappers. Warren faced one count of kidnapping, 10 counts of sodomy, six counts of rape and one count of sexual abuse; Loschin was charged with eight counts of sodomy, six counts of rape and one count of sexual abuse; Montez faced three counts of kidnapping, plus five counts each of rape, sodomy, and endangering the welfare of a child. The two male defendants were held without bond, while Loschin was unable to raise her $80,000 bail. Queens prosecutor Richard Brown ranked the crime "among the most despicable cases of sexual assault on a minor that I have seen in my ten years as district attorney. In addition to the utter depravity of this crime and the lasting damage such an ordeal inflicts on a child, the fact that the victim and the Nassau defendants met in an online chat room is terrifying to us all, especially those of us who are parents." Resolution of the case was postponed indefinitely on August 15, 2001, when defendants Warren and Loschin waived their constitutional right to a speedy trial.

August 2001 While the Long Island case was still making national headlines, 43-year-old Darrell Crawford was arrested in Charlestown, Rhode Island, charged with transporting a 16-year-old Rhode Island girl across state lines for purposes of prostitution. FBI agents who captured Crawford say the case may also involve at least three other juvenile victims. According to charges filed against him, Crawford met the victim in July 2001, on a telephone chat-line, and persuaded her to work for him as a prostitute. Running away from home, the girl allegedly met Crawford and a still-unidentified female accomplice, joining them on a trip to Boston, where she serviced an average of five men per night until July 15, earning $100 for intercourse and $50 for oral sex, giving all the money to Crawford. After briefly returning home on July 16, the girl allegedly returned to Boston with Crawford 10 days later, continuing work for the pimp until her mother tracked her down and took the girl to police on August 13, 2001.

July 2003 Judge David Davis upheld the constitutionality of Ohio's controversial "importuning" (urgent solicitation) law in the case of Otis Ketron, a Procter & Gamble employee who admitted using his workplace computer to solicit sex from a sheriff's deputy posing as an underage girl. Defense attorney James Perry challenged the law and his client's arrest, on grounds that Ketron neither met nor attempted to have sex with a minor victim. "There is no danger to a child's physical or psychological well-being," Perry told the court, "because there is no child." Judge Davis disagreed, ruling that "the importuning law is designated to protect children on the Internet." Stings conducted under the Ohio statute resulted in 23 arrests between January 2002 and March 2003. Fifteen defendants were convicted and one suspect killed himself prior to trial.

November 2004 Wisconsin police jailed 24-year-old university student Nathan Zillges on charges of using the Internet to solicit sex from a 14-year-old girl. In custody, Zillges admitted seeking sexual relations with an underage partner but denied that he intended to have intercourse "on the first date." Police monitored a series of chat room discussions between Zillges and his intended partner, making the arrest when Zillges arrived (condom in hand) for their first rendezvous at a Milwaukee restaurant.

April 2005 Another child-sex sting operation ended with the arrest of three Pennsylvania men on charges of "attempting to contact a minor unlawfully and criminal use of a communication facility." Authorities claim that Omar Bakth, Dale Catley Jr., and Harry Danhart Jr. engaged in Internet chats with a subject they believed to be a 13-year-old girl. In fact, the "child" was a female member of the state attorney general's Child Sexual Exploitation Task Force. When the three men gathered to meet their intended playmate, police made the arrests.

June 2005 Police in Uniontown, Pennsylvania, arrested 54-year-old Joseph Nicholson as part of "an interstate child-luring net," after Nicholson sent sexual e-mail messages to a Florida police officer posing as a 14-year-old girl. Held in lieu of $250,000 bail, Nicholson faced extradition to Florida for trial.

May 2006 Carlos Rivera, a 35-year-old pedophile convicted of sexually assaulting an 11-year-old boy in 1996, was arrested by Connecticut authorities for producing child pornography. At the time of that arrest, Rivera was free on bond pending trial in a 2005 case, alleging that he used the Internet to meet two other boys, age 13 and 15, for sexual encounters. Prosecutors announced their intention to try Rivera under

Connecticut's "Protect Act," which mandates life imprisonment for repeat sexual offenders.

August 2006 Robert Lott, a 54-year-old special education teacher in Luzerne County, Pennsylvania, was arrested in an Internet child-sex sting after requesting sex from a police officer posing as a 12-year-old child. School administrators suspended Lott with pay, pending disposition of his case.

January 2007 Australian police jailed two Brisbane residents, Damian Geyer and his fiancée, Ashlea Rutherford, on charges of using the Internet to procure a child for sex and producing "child exploitation material." As in so many American cases, the "child" whom they solicited for sex was, in fact, an undercover policeman. The arrests came at a restaurant where Geyer had scheduled a meeting with his intended victim.

February 2007 Police in North Little Rock, Arkansas, arrested Colonel Donald Wodash, deputy chief of staff for the 153rd Brigade of Arizona's National Guard, on charges of soliciting child sex over the Internet. Once again, the "child" in question was a police officer posing as a minor. The trap closed when Wodash drove to Arkansas from Arizona to keep a date with his mythical underage paramour. While Wodash posted bond and returned to Arizona, Major Paul Aguirre of the Arizona Guard told reporters, "Leadership is taking a look at whatever's happening, and will take whatever the appropriate action is for a situation like this."

April 2007 Australian police struck again, this time in East Perth, where the Police Cyber-Predator Team arrested a 26-year-old suspect for sending pornographic photos of himself via the Internet, to a supposed child. The strike force boasts 30 arrests and 100-plus criminal charges filed since its creation in April 2006.

How common are such cases? According to a media report published the same month as the Boston and Long Island arrests, 19 percent of underage Internet users surveyed had received unwanted sexual solicitations within the past year; 5 percent received solicitations that frightened or upset them; 3 percent received "aggressive" solicitations involving off-line contact or attempts to stage a personal meeting; 70 percent of those solicited were using home computers at the time; and 49 percent of those solicited

kept the fact a secret. In an era when thousands of children run away from home every year, and suspect JOHN ROBINSON, a.k.a. "Slavemaster," faces trial as the first Internet serial killer, online predators seem to qualify as a serious and growing threat.

CHROMATOGRAPHY

The term *chromatography* covers a wide range of scientific methods used to separate and analyze complex mixtures. By one means or another, the components of a sample are separated and distributed between two phases, termed *mobile* and *stationary*. Various components of a mixture pass through a chromatograph at different rates and are thus identified by their specific, known *retention times*. Different chromatographic techniques employ a gas or liquid mobile medium, while the stationary medium includes substances such as paper, gelatin, or magnesium silicate gel. *Analytical* chromatography—the kind employed in forensic science—determines both the identity and concentration of various molecules within a sample mixture, while *preparative* chromatography purifies specific molecules.

Russian botanist Mikhail Tsvet invented the first chromatograph in 1901, to separate pigments found in plants. Tsvet published his results two years later, in the *Proceedings of the Warsaw Society of Naturalists*, but used the term *chromatography*—from the Greek *chroma* (color) and *graphikós* (drawing or writing)—for the first time only in 1906. (Curiously, Tsvet's surname also means "color" in Russian.) Chromatography devices and techniques proliferated during the remainder of the 20th century, until the following techniques were recognized:

Adsorption chromatography, one of the older methods, wherein a mobile liquid or gaseous phase is adsorbed (condensed) upon the surface of the stationary solid phase. Different solutes are separated according to the balance of the mobile and stationary phases.

Affinity chromatography, recognized as the most selective method presently available, based on the interaction between specific solute molecules (primarily biological compounds). The device's stationary phase packing material—dubbed the *affinity matrix*—is typically composed of agarose, which includes antibodies to specific proteins. As the various proteins pass by in the mobile phase, they adhere to their specific antibodies and are thus identified.

Column chromatography, using a vertical glass column filled with stationary material, through which the mobile phase sample passes from top to bottom under the influence of gravity. This is the method employed by Mikhail Tsvet in his original tests, but W. C. Stills developed a new method of *flash column chromatography* in 1978, which involves application of positive pressure to the mobile phase solvent from the top of the column. The "flash" method reduces time involved in testing to 20 minutes or less, whereas standard column chromatography may take much longer.

Countercurrent chromatography (CCC) is a method employing liquid media for both mobile and stationary phases. The process occurs in a column, with three stages generally known as *mixing, settling,* and *separation.* The elimination of solid supports avoids permanent adsorption of analytes onto the column, and thus permits nearly 100 percent of the sample to be retrieved after testing. The oldest form of countercurrent chromatography is *droplet CCC,* which relies on gravity alone to move the mobile phase and thus results in relatively slow completion of a test, as in basic column chromatography. *High-speed CCC,* developed by Dr. Yoichiro Ito at Japan's National Institutes of Health, uses a centrifuge to accelerate the process.

Gas chromatography employs a pressurized gas cylinder and a *carrier gas* (often helium) to move the solute past flame ionization detectors or thermal conductors. Three variants of gas chromatography include: *capillary gas chromatography,* the most common method, using slender glass or fused silica capillary tubes lined with some adsorbent substance; *gas adsorption chromatography,* using a packed bed of adsorbents such as activated alumina, silica gel, or zeolite; and *gas-liquid chromatography,* using an inert porous solid (usually diatomaceous earth) coated with a viscous liquid for the stationary phase.

Gel permeation chromatography (GPC)—also known as *filtration chromatography, Sephadex gel chromatography, molecular exclusion chromatography,* and *size exclusion chromatography*—separates molecules on the basis of their size within a porous medium, where larger molecules exit the column sooner than smaller molecules. This technique is used primarily to determine molecular weight distribution in polymers.

High performance liquid chromatography (HPLC) is another form of column chromatography, often used in both analytical CHEMISTRY and biochemistry. In this method, analytes are forced into a column by a liquid at high pressure, thereby reducing the time involved in testing. The method is easy to learn and may also be used to purify various compounds.

Immobilized metal ion affinity chromatography (IMAC), used chiefly to purify various proteins, is based on the specific covalent binding between amino acids and various immobilized metal ions (commonly including copper, iron, nickel, and zinc).

Ion exchange chromatography employs a charged stationary phase within the usual column, used to separate various charged compounds such as amino acids, peptides, and proteins. The stationary phase is typically a resin that carries charged particles designed to bond with specific molecules. Positively charged exchangers attract *anions* (negatively charged ions), while negatively charged exchangers attract *cations* (positively charged ions).

Paper chromatography, as suggested by its name, used paper as the stationary phase. A small spot of solute is applied to a strip of paper near its base, after which the paper is dipped into a solvent (typically water or ethanol and placed inside a sealed container. As the solvent permeates the paper, it slowly distributes the solute, with different compounds in the mixture traveling various distances.

Partition chromatography employs a thin film of liquid stationary phase on a solid support, which interacts with samples in the mobile phase. Invention of this process earned a Nobel Prize for Archer Martin and Richard Synge in 1952. *Centrifugal partition chromatography* accelerates the process, as with high-speed CCC above.

Reverse phase liquid chromatography used a hydrophobic, low polarity stationary base that is chemically bonded to silica or some other inert solid. Strong aqueous bases such as alkali cannot be tested, however, since they destroy silica, and exposure to aqueous acid must also be of limited duration.

Thin layer chromatography used a thin layer of adsorbent (such as alumina, cellulose or silica gel) on a flat carrier (such as a glass plate or plastic sheet), but otherwise performs in a manner similar to paper chromatography, albeit with faster runs and clearer separations. Small amounts of fluorescent dye may be added to the adsorbent to permit visualization under ultraviolet light.

CHURCHILL, Robert (1886–1958)

Born in 1886, British ballistics expert Robert Churchill acquired his knowledge of FIREARMS as an apprentice, then a partner, of his uncle, renowned London gunsmith Edwin John Churchill. His first experience with a police investigation came at age 17, when officers found the skeletal remains of 56-year-old Camille Holland in a drainage ditch near Clavering, Essex. Holland had been dead for four years by the time police recovered those remains, then filed murder charges against gigolo and swindler Samuel Dougal. Churchill examined Holland's remains, skull shattered by a gunshot, and also studied ammunition found at a nearby farm. Experiments conducted with a sheep's head convinced Churchill that Holland had been shot with a revolver, at a range of six to 12 inches. Based on his testimony and recovery of a pistol from Dougal's effects, jurors convicted Dougal of murder and he was hanged in July 1903.

Seven years later, Churchill inherited the family business and continued manufacturing custom firearms, while participating in police investigations. His most famous case began on September 27, 1927, when Constable George Gutteridge was murdered in Essex, shot four times in the head (including bullets fired through both eyes).

Investigators linked the slaying to a local auto theft, in which the car was found abandoned in London. Blood stained the running board, while inside the car a spent .45-caliber cartridge case marked "RVIV" lay on the floorboard. Using a newly purchased comparison microscope, Churchill determined that the four slugs recovered from Gutteridge had been fired from a Webley .45-caliber revolver. One such weapon was found when police arrested suspect Frederick Browne, a London hoodlum, in Janu-

ary 1928. Churchill quickly matched the cartridge case and four bullets to Browne's weapon, whereupon Browne claimed that he had received the pistol from a friend, William Kennedy, after Gutteridge was killed. Kennedy subsequently confessed a role in the murder, while jurors convicted Browne and both men were hanged. Churchill remained active in gun making and ballistics investigations until his death in 1958.

COAKLEY, Marion exonerated by forensic evidence

A native of Beaufort, South Carolina, who later moved to New York City, Marion Coakley was an African-American day laborer with a tested IQ of 70. On the night of October 13, 1983, while Coakley attended a church prayer meeting, one of his neighbors was raped and robbed in her home. The victim subsequently accused Coakley and he was arrested, lab tests allegedly demonstrating that his blood type matched the rapist's. At trial, jurors ignored Coakley's alibi witnesses and convicted him of rape and robbery, whereupon he received a 15-year prison term.

Two years later, Coakley convinced attorneys BARRY SCHECK and Peter Neufeld of his innocence, prompting them to launch a renewed investigation of the case. Students from the Cardozo criminal law clinic joined in the project, attempting to arrange for DNA tests, but the court blocked testing on grounds that the "DNA fingerprint" results were still (in 1986) an unproven form of personal identification. Instead, the defense team retested semen samples from the crime scene and proved that Coakley's blood type did not, after all, match the rapist's. Coakley was released from prison, and the rape remains officially unsolved. Their experience in this case prompted Scheck and Neufeld to found the CARDOZO INNOCENCE PROJECT, which now serves as the last line of defense for wrongfully convicted prisoners in cases where scientific evidence is decisive.

COHEN, Earl convicted by DNA evidence

A repeat sex offender in Kentucky, born in 1964, Earl Cohen logged his first rape conviction in the late 1980s. Blood samples were secured from Cohen for the state's DNA database.

That evidence sent him back to prison for another rape in 2001. Cohen's second known victim was attacked in Louisville, in April 2001. Forensic evidence from the backseat of the victim's car was compared against samples on file. Cohen was duly arrested and convicted by a jury on October 21, 2001.

COLDEN, Cadwallader (1688–1776)

A Scotsman born on February 17, 1688, while his mother was touring Ireland, Cadwallader Colden earned his B.A. from the University of Edinburgh at age 17, then studied medicine in London. Convinced that his prospects would improve in the American colonies, he immigrated to Philadelphia in 1708 or 1710 (reports differ), then moved on to New York in 1718 and won appointment as that colony's surveyor general in 1720. A year later, he was picked to serve Governor George Clinton as a councilor. By the time Clinton left office in 1761, Colden was the colony's lieutenant governor, a post that he held until shortly before his death.

Aside from politics, Colden was widely recognized as one of the best-educated British colonists in America. From 1710 until his death, Colden corresponded with the most learned scientists of the 18th century—including taxonomist Carl Linnaeus, whom Colden furnished with descriptions of more than 300 American plant species. While in Philadelphia, he performed multiple postmortem examinations, which helped gain approval for the practice of forensic PATHOLOGY long before autopsies in suspicious deaths were mandated by law. His wide-ranging publications include a *History of the Five Indian Nations depending upon New York* (1727), *Cause of Gravitation* (1745), *Principles of Action in Matter* (1752), and *Observations on Exidemical Sore Throat* (1753). At the end of his life, Colden remained a loyal supporter of the British crown. He retired as lieutenant governor with the outbreak of the American Revolution and died at his Long Island estate on September 28, 1776.

COLEMAN, Roger Keith   controversial DNA case

On March 10, 1981, 19-year-old Wanda McCoy was raped and fatally stabbed at her home in Buchanan County, Virginia. Police found the victim with wounds in her chest and throat, plus cuts on her hands, broken fingernails, and a bruise on her arm. A dark, dusty substance also clung to parts of her body.

For reasons still unclear, the autopsy report omitted mention of McCoy's defensive wounds and only limited forensic tests were run. Police likewise failed to identify a FINGERPRINT found on McCoy's screen door, near pry marks on the door frame. Instead, based on statements from McCoy's husband, authorities focused on brother-in-law Roger Keith Coleman, who had previously served two years for attempted rape. Coleman maintained his innocence in that case and had presented alibi witnesses at trial, but jurors convicted him on the victim's testimony.

Now, with rape and murder charges filed against him, Coleman once again produced a well-documented time line for his movements on the night in question, including affidavits from several alibi witnesses. Ignoring the pry marks and evidence of struggle, detectives theorized that McCoy had admitted Coleman to her home and died as a result, without fighting back. Semen from the CRIME SCENE matched Coleman's blood type, and a prosecution expert witness deemed hairs found on McCoy's body "consistent" with Coleman's. A jailhouse informant also claimed that Coleman had confessed the rape-murder to him while awaiting trial (and thereby obtained early release from custody). Jurors convicted Coleman of first-degree murder, whereupon he was sentenced to die. During the appellate process, an alternative suspect with a history of violent sex crimes privately admitted murdering McCoy, but prosecutors ignored his statement and took no biological samples from him for study. DNA testing—unavailable when Coleman was tried—suggested the possibility of an alternative suspect, but Coleman's lawyers miscalculated the cut-off date for their final appeal and missed the state's 30-day deadline for filing. That seeming injustice prompted a plea for mercy from Pope John Paul II, which landed Coleman on the cover of *Time* magazine. Governor Douglas Wilder agreed to grant clemency if Coleman passed an 11th-hour polygraph test, but authorities claimed that he failed, and Coleman died in the electric chair on May 20, 1992.

Still, ardent supporters continued to plead his case. In 2000, his advocates asked for new DNA testing on crime scene evidence, and while permission for those tests was reluctantly granted, Coleman's defenders suffered another setback with reports that all relevant biological evidence had been routinely destroyed after the rejection of his last appeal. In January 2006, investigators learned that such was not the case, reporting that a now-retired Virginia

State Police investigator had retained critical samples in his private files. Governor Mark Warner then ordered new tests to resolve the controversy over Coleman's case once and for all. On January 12, 2006, a spokesman for Warner's office announced that the new tests had confirmed Coleman's guilt in the rape and murder of Wanda McCoy.

COMBINED DNA Index System (CODIS)

CODIS is a national DNA database coordinated by the FBI LABORATORY which enables federal, state, and local crime labs to exchange and compare DNA profiles electronically, thereby linking crimes to each other and to convicted offenders, or identifying corpses and missing persons. Launched in 1990 as a pilot program serving 14 state and local crime labs, CODIS was formalized under FBI control by the federal DNA Identification Act of 1994. The bureau's National DNA Index System (NDIS) began operations in October 1998, and survives today as the highest (federal) level of a three-tiered CODIS hierarchy (above state and local levels). All DNA profile submissions begin at the local level, then proceed to state or federal levels in their search for "hits." CODIS presently operates with two separate indexes, a Forensic Index (containing DNA profiles from crime scene evidence) and an Offender Index (containing DNA profiles of convicted felons). Matches from the Forensic Index link unsolved crimes and may depict a pattern of serial offenses in progress, while matches from the Offender Index identify specific perpetrators. By October 1988, all 50 states participated in CODIS, together with Puerto Rico, the FBI and the U.S. Army. At press time for this volume, CODIS contained 4,760,386 profiles, subdivided into 177,870 forensic profiles and 4,582,516 offender profiles.

COMPUTING, Forensic

The field of forensic computing includes any and all conceivable applications of computer science and technology to criminal investigation, correctional institutions or any other aspect of jurisprudence (whether criminal or civil). The most obvious application lies

Rebecca Schuler, left, an applications scientist at ChemIcon Inc.; company president Patrick Treado; and forensic scientist David Exline, right, look over the computer data of a latent fingerprint from a piece of paper captured on a digital camera at their Pittsburgh lab. (Keith Srakocic/AP)

in the detection and solution of CYBERCRIMES, ranging from petty harassment to CHILD PORNOGRAPHY, FRAUD, THEFT, MONEY LAUNDERING, WHITE-COLLAR CRIMES and TERRORISM. Still, those diverse and often dramatic investigations barely scratch the surface of forensic computing. Other applications include but are not limited to GEOGRAPHIC PROFILING of unsolved crimes; generation of computer models used in ACCIDENT RECONSTRUCTION and re-creation of crimes; communication between patrol officers and police headquarters; daily administration of law enforcement agencies, forensic laboratories and correctional institutions; tracing and identification of fugitives and other MISSING PERSONS; code-breaking and decryption; comparative analysis of evidence collected from crime scenes; and maintenance of legal records at all levels. Only modern computer technology permits the operation of such national (or international) databases as AUTOMATED FINGERPRINT IDENTIFICATION SYSTEM, COMBINED DNA INDEX SYSTEM, Drugfire, INTEGRATED BALLISTICS IDENTIFICATION SYSTEM, VICAP, VICLAS and the National Crime Information Center, used by police and criminalists around the world to coordinate investigations and prosecutions.

CONFIDENCE Games

Confidence games—so called because they require offenders to gain the confidence or trust of their intended victims—rank among the oldest and most common types of FRAUD. No threats or violence are involved in "cons"; rather, the victims are persuaded to part voluntarily with cash or other valuables, usually in pursuit of some fanciful get-rich-quick scheme. Typical con games include the following:

Bank cons: Banks may be swindled in various ways, but the most common involves con artists who present a large (fraudulent) check to open a new account, depositing part of the (nonexistent) money while asking for the remainder in cash. Since many banks now place a hold on personal checks, allowing them time to clear before cash is withdrawn, wily operators may steal or forge commercial checks and thereby circumvent the security procedure with well-known corporate names.

Bank examiner cons: Unrelated to the bank cons described above, this scam involves recruitment of gullible citizens to participate in alleged police audits of a "corrupt" financial institution. The con artist poses as a law enforcement agent, asking potential victims to withdraw specified funds from their bank accounts and bring the money home, where it will be collected by the "bank examiners" as "evidence" in exchange for a worthless deposit slip. Neither the money nor the "officers" are seen again.

Faith-healing cons: A wide variety of self-styled healers or ministers dupe sickly and disabled victims by pretending to heal their infirmities in return for cash donations or "love offerings." Some, like discredited televangelist Robert Tilton of Texas, accomplish this feat long distance, selling prayers or "healing cloths" and similar objects to members of their TV or radio audience. Others use accomplices to feign disability, dropping crutches and leaping from wheelchairs at the touch of a hand. Variations on the theme involve "magic" surgery, lifting of curses or hexes for a price, and so on.

Free inspection cons: This time-honored fraud involves an offer of free inspection to some mechanical appliance or vehicle already owned by the victim. During the inspection, the con artist "finds" numerous mythical problems in need of repair, often at staggering cost to the consumer. A variation on the theme finds swindlers disassembling the appliance—commonly a furnace or air-conditioner—then refusing to reassemble it without payment. (In a comical scene from Mario Puzo's novel The Godfather, two con artists play the furnace trick on Don Vito Corleone, to their ultimate sorrow.)

Obituary cons: Some con artists watch newspaper death notices and spring into action against the bereaved, delivering worthless COD packages allegedly ordered by the deceased or promising hefty insurance pay-offs in return for one final premium. Victims unrelated to the lately dead are also sometimes targeted, as when a wealthy public figure dies and swindlers send out scores of letters to prospective "heirs," promising a share of the inheritance in return for a nominal "filing fee."

Pigeon drop con: This street con involves a "lost" wallet or purse filled with money, "found" on the street by a con artist in the presence of a potential victim. As swindler and prey discuss what should be done with the money, an accomplice arrives in the guise of an innocent passerby, suggesting that the victim hold the money until its true owner is found. If it remains unclaimed after a period of time, they agree to split the cash three ways. As a show of "good faith," the victim agrees to present an equal amount of his own money, which the satisfied con artists bundle up with the "found" cash, handing it all to their "pigeon." Later, when the con men fail to return for their shares, the victim opens the package to find that a bundle of worthless paper has replaced the cash.

Ponzi/pyramid schemes: Named for American swindler Charles Ponzi, who launched the first known "pyramid" con in December 1919, this scam solicits investors for some nonexistent project, using money collected from later investors to pay a high rate of "interest" to initial investors while con artists pocket the profits. Early victims near the pyramid's pinnacle see some return on their original investment (though few ever make a profit), while later investors are simply cleaned out. In variant forms of the con involving chain letters, "investors" may never even meet the swindlers who pocket their money. In one notorious case, the Tulsa-based Home Sales Production Company sold phony shares in nonexistent oil fields to various wealthy investors, including celebrities Jack Benny, Candice Bergen, Bob Dylan, Mia Farrow, Liza Minelli, Walter Matthau, Barbra Streisand, and Andy Williams (who personally lost $538,000).

Quick change/short change scams: These tricks normally involve a sleight-of-hand "flimflam" wherein clerks or cashiers in various business establishments are cheated out of cash. Confusing patter—or a flash of cleavage, if the con artist is female and her victim male—result in the swindler walking off with a tidy profit, while the duped employee discovers his loss hours later, when tallying receipts at day's end.

Shell games: Documented in America since the mid-19th century, these games typically involve a street hustler equipped with a pea or similar object and three walnut shells or similar hollow half-spheres. Using a "booster" or "shill" to make it look simple, the light-fingered operator convinces passersby to bet on which shell hides the pea as he rapidly shifts them around. Again, sleight-of-hand ensures that only selected players have a chance to win the game, while "suckers" lose their money betting against "the house."

Three-Card Monte: A variation of the shell game using playing cards, Three-Card Monte invites players to locate a particular card as three are whisked around the table at lightning speeds. Again, a "winning" shill is often used to lure a victim audience into the con man's web.

CONTROLLED Substances

The Controlled Substances Act (CSA)—otherwise known as Title II of the Comprehensive Drug Abuse Prevention and Control Act of 1970, is the foundation of the U.S. government's "war" against abuse of drugs and other substances. The law places all substances that are regulated under existing federal law into one of five schedules, based upon the substance's medicinal value, harmfulness, and potential for abuse or addiction. *Schedule I* is reserved for the most dangerous drugs that have no recognized medical use. *Schedule II* includes drugs defined as having some (often marginal) recognized medical use, but with a high potential for abuse and high incidence of physical or psychological dependence. They are legally available only by prescription, with distribution closely monitored by the Drug Enforcement Administration. *Schedule III* includes drugs with recognized medical uses and less potential for abuse than those in Schedules I or II, with moderate to low incidence of physical or psychological dependence. Again, prescriptions are required for legal sales, but DEA control of wholesale distribution is somewhat less stringent than for Schedule II drugs. *Schedule IV* continues the procedure by listing prescription drugs with even less potential for abuse and lower levels of dependency than those in Schedules I through III. Finally, *Schedule V* includes drugs with recognized medical uses and minor incidence of physical or psychological dependence, sometimes available without prescription. Specific drugs listed in the CSA and policed by the DEA include the following:

SCHEDULE I

acetorphine
acetyldihydrocodeine
acetylmethadol
allylprodine
alphacetylmathadol

alphameprodine
alphamethadol
benzethidine
benzylmorphine
betacetylmethadol
betameprodine
betamethadol
betaprodine
bufotenine
clonitazene
codeine methylbromide
codeine-n-oxide
cyprenorphine
desomorphine
dextromoramide
dextrorphan
diampromide
diethylthiambutene
diethyltryptamine
dihydromorphine
dimenoxadol
dimepheptanol
dimethylthiambutene
dimethyltryptamine
dioxaphetyl butyrate
dipipanone
ethylmethylthiambutene
etonitazene
etorphine
etoxeridine
5-methoxy-3,4-methylenedioxy amphetamine
4-methyl-2,5-dimethoxyamphetamine
furethidine
heroin
hydromorphinol
hydroxypethidine
ibogaine
ketobemidone
levomoramide
levophenacylmorphan
lysergic acid diethylamide
marijuana
mescaline
methyldesorphine
methylhydromorphine
morpheridine
morphine methylbromide
morphine methylsulfonate
morphine-n-oxide
myrophine

n-ethyl-3-piperidyl benzilate
n-methyl-3-piperidyl benzilate
nicocodeine
nicomorphine
noracymethadol
norlevorphanol
normethadone
normorphine
norpipanone
peyote
phenadoxone
phenampromide
phenomorphan
phenoperidine
pholcodine
piritramide
proheptazine
properidine
psilocybin
psilocyn
racemoramide
tetrahydrocannabinols
thebacon
3,4-methylenedioxy amphetamine
3,4,5-trimethoxy amphetamine
trimeperidine

SCHEDULE II

adderall
adolphine
alphaprodine
amphetamine
anileridine
bezitramide
cocaine
dextroamphetamine
dihydrocodeine
diphenoxylate
glutethimide
fentanyl
isomethadone
levomethorphan
levorphanol
metazocine
methadone
methadone-intermediate
methamphetamine
methylphenidate
moramide-intermediate

opium
oxycodone
pethidine
pethidine-intermediate-A
pethidine-intermediate-B
pethidine-intermediate-C
phenazocine
phencyclidine
racemethorphan
racemorphan
thebaine
tuinal

SCHEDULE III

amphetamine
barbituric acid or derivatives
chorhexadol
codeine
glutethimide
hydrocodone
ketamine
lysergic acid
lysergic acid amide
marinol
methylphenidate
methyprylon
nalorphine
phencyclidine
phenmetrazine
sulfondiethylmethane
sulfonethylmethane
sulfonmethane
tiletamine

SCHEDULE IV

armodafinil
barbital
bromazepam
chloral betaine
chloral hydrate
diazepam
diethylpropion
eszopiclone
ethchlorvynol
ethinamate
methohexital
meprobamate
methylphenobarbital

modafinil
paraldehyde
petrichloral
phenobarbital
phentermine
sibutramine
temazepam
zolpidem
zopiclone

SCHEDULE V

Any compound, mixture, or preparation containing any of the following limited quantities of narcotic drugs, which shall include one or more nonnarcotic active medicinal ingredients in sufficient proportion to confer upon the compound, mixture, or preparation valuable medicinal qualities other than those possessed by the narcotic drug alone:

1. Not more than 200 milligrams of codeine per 100 milliliters or per 100 grams;
2. Not more than 100 milligrams of dihydrocodeine per 100 milliliters or per 100 grams;
3. Not more than 100 milligrams of ethylmorphine per 100 milliliters or per 100 grams;
4. Not more than 2.5 milligrams of diphenoxylate and not less than 25 micrograms of atropine sulfate per dosage unit;
5. Not more than 100 milligrams of opium per 100 milliliters or per 100 grams.

In addition to the CSA's five schedules for drugs, federal law also regulates various chemicals, identified as List I and List II, commonly used in the manufacture of controlled substances. As defined in federal law, they include:

LIST I

anthranilic acid
benzaldehyde
benzyl cyanide
ephedrine
ergonovine
ergotamine
ethylamine
hydriotic acid
insosafrole
methylamine
n-acetylanthranilic acid

nitroethane
n-methylepherdrine
n-methylpseudoephedrine
norpseudoephedrine
phenylacetic acid
phenylpropanolamine
piperidine
piperonal
propionic anhydride
pseudoephedrine
safrole
3,4-methylenedioxyphenyl-2-propanone

List II

acetic anhydride
acetone
benzyl chloride
ethyl ether
potassium permanganate
toluene
2-butanone

In 1991, Congress added anabolic steroids to the list of controlled substances, defined as "any drug or hormonal substance, chemically and pharmacologically related to testosterone (other than estrogens, progestins, and corticosteroids) that promotes muscle growth." Steroids listed in the statute include boldenone, chlorotestosterone, clostebol, dehydrochlormethyltestosterone, dihydrotestosterone, drostanolone, ethylestrenol, fluoxymesterone, formebulone, mesterolone, methandienone, methandranone, methandriol, methandrostenolone, methenolone, methyltestosterone, mibolerone, nandrolone, norethandrolone, oxandrolone, oxymesterone, oxymetholone, stanolone, stanozolol, testolactone, testosterone, and "any salt, ester, or isomer of a drug or substance described or listed in this paragraph, if that salt, ester, or isomer promotes muscle growth."

While federal law recognizes only five schedules of controlled substances, some states add their own Schedule VI to the list, including various common chemicals that are not generally considered drugs but which are frequently abused for "recreational" purposes. Those most commonly banned or regulated under state law include alkyl nitrites, amyl nitrite, butyl nitrite, cyclohexyl nitrite, ethyl nitrite, isobutyl nitrite, isoppropyl nitrite, methyl nitrite, nitrous oxide ("laughing gas"), and toluene.

The CSA applies strict federal penalties to illegal distribution, importation, manufacture, possession, and use of controlled substances. Those penalties include the following prison terms and fines:

1. Five to 40 years in prison, with fines of $2 million to $5 million, for importation, manufacture or sale of 100 grams or more of heroin; 500 grams or more of coca leaves, cocaine or ecgonine; five grams or more of cocaine base; 10 grams of phencyclidine; one gram or more of LSD; 40 grams or more of N-phenyl-N-[1-(2-phenylethyl)-4-piperidinyl] propanamide; 100 kilos or more of marijuana; or 10 grams or more of methamphetamine. If death results from the drug dealing, prison terms increase to 20 years to life. Second offenses in the amounts listed here mandate prison terms of 10 years to life (with eight years' supervised parole), plus fines of $4 million to $10 million.

2. 10 years to life, with fines of $4 million to $10 million for importation, manufacture, or sale of one kilogram of heroin; five kilos of coca leaves, cocaine or ecgonine; 50 grams or more of cocaine base; 100 grams or more of phencyclidine; 10 grams or more of LSD; 400 grams of more of N-phenyl-N-[1-(2-phenylethyl)-4-piperidinyl] propanamide; 1,000 kilos or more of marijuana; or 100 grams or more of methamphetamine. If death results from the drug-dealing activity, prison terms increase to 20 years to life, while the fines also double.

3. Five years maximum, with fines of $250,000 to $1 million, for illegally importing, manufacturing, or selling less than 50 kilos of marijuana (except in cases of 50 or more marijuana plants, regardless of weight), 10 kilos of hashish, one kilo of hashish oil, or any controlled substance from Schedule III. A second offense doubles the maximum term to 10 years, while also doubling the minimum and maximum fines. Two years' supervised parole is required for a first offense, four years for a second offense.

4. Three years maximum, plus fines of $250,000 to $1 million, for illegally importing, manufacturing or selling any controlled substance from Schedule IV. A second offense doubles the maximum prison term and the fines. One year of supervised parole is required for a first offense, two years for a second.

5. One year maximum, with fines of $100,000 to $250,000, for any violations of CSA Schedule V, with penalties doubled for a second offense.

6. Prison terms as specified above by schedule, plus fines of $500,000 to $1 million, for cultivating controlled substances on federal property.

7. Ten years maximum and a $10,000 fine for placing booby traps on federal land where controlled substances are cultivated. A second offense doubles both penalties.

8. Ten years maximum for possessing or distributing listed chemicals with intent to manufacture controlled substances, and/or participating in evasion of mandatory record-keeping for such chemicals.

Lesser penalties, including civil fines and loss of professional licenses apply to individuals convicted of tampering with or defacing seals on controlled substances and similar relatively minor offenses detailed under the CSA.

COOLEY Innocence Project

On January 1, 2002, Michigan enacted a statute providing postconviction remedies for wrongfully convicted persons whose innocence can be established by DNA testing of evidence collected from crime scenes. Five months later, the Thomas M. Cooley Law School in Lansing, Michigan, launched the Cooley Innocence Project, to investigate cases falling within the statutory guidelines. Each term, the project accepts between six and 10 "especially qualified" students to collaborate with faculty members in case evaluations, singling out those cases where DNA evidence seems to offer proof of actual innocence (as opposed to reasonable doubt). Statewide, a network of 160 criminal defense attorneys work with members of the Cooley Innocence Project to appeal selected cases on a pro bono basis. At press time for this work, the project had reviewed more than 2,500 cases and secured the release of wrongfully convicted inmate KENNETH WYNIEMKO in June 2003.

COTTON, Ronald exonerated by DNA evidence

In July 1984, two female residents of Burlington, North Carolina, were attacked in separate incidents by a serial rapist who invaded their apartments, cut telephone lines, and afterward looted their homes

of cash and other valuables. Suspect Ronald Cotton was arrested on August 1, 1984, after one victim identified his photograph, then picked him from a police lineup. Charged with one of the rapes, Cotton was tried in January 1985. Prosecutors noted that a flashlight found in his home "resembled" one carried by the rapist, and that rubber from his tennis shoes was "consistent" with evidence found at the crime scene. Jurors convicted him on one count each of rape and burglary.

North Carolina's Supreme Court overturned that conviction on appeal, because the trial judge had excluded testimony that the rapist's second victim had selected a different suspect from a police lineup. Prior to Cotton's second trial, the alternative suspect—already imprisoned for similar crimes—admitted to a cellmate that he was guilty of the Burlington attacks. Cotton's new trial judge refused to admit the convict's statement into evidence, and Cotton was convicted again—of both rapes, this time—in November 1987. Cotton received a sentence of life for the rapes, plus 54 years on two counts of burglary. The verdict was affirmed on appeal in 1988.

New lawyers took over Cotton's case six years later, filing a motion for DNA testing that was granted in October 1994. Semen samples from one victim had deteriorated beyond the point of testing, but samples from the second excluded Ronald Cotton as a suspect in May 1995, while matching samples from the imprisoned alternative suspect found in the State Bureau of Investigation's DNA database. Cotton was released from prison on June 30, 1995, and pardoned by the governor in July. The pardon made him eligible for $5,000 in state compensation, based on a 1948 statute granting $500 for each year of wrongful incarceration up to a maximum of 10 years. His attorneys thus far have been unsuccessful in their efforts to secure passage of new legislation granting increased compensation.

COUNCIL on Forensic Science Education

Active since the late 1970s, the CFSE was founded by professors teaching forensic science courses at various public and private colleges and universities. Its stated goals were as follows:

1. To encourage the exchange of ideas and information regarding academic programs in the laboratory-

based forensic sciences and the discussion of problems of common interest.

2. To work collectively toward the coordination and upgrading of academic forensic science programs.
3. To promote constructive integration of formal academic training with postgraduate preparation for professional practice.
4. To foster friendship, cooperation, and synergism among academic forensic scientists, practicing professionals, and laboratory management.
5. To encourage research and the advancement of knowledge benefiting forensic science.
6. To pursue other objectives appropriate to the advancement of forensic science education.

With those goals in mind, the CFSE has labored to establish academic standards for education in forensic science, forced to cope at times with institutions where courses have been launched without adequate funding, lab space, or fully qualified instructors. The popularity of various *CSI*-type television programs ensures that demand for such courses surpasses the supply of adequate facilities and personnel.

COUNTERFEITING

Counterfeiting is a type of FORGERY involving duplication or simulation of valuable items, with intent to sell or pass them off as genuine. Paper currency is a frequent object of counterfeiters, but others include coins, credit and debit cards, negotiable instruments (stocks, bonds, money orders, etc.), legal documents (passports, driver's licenses, visas, etc.), collectible items, and manufacturer's labels on an infinite variety of marketable goods. In the latter case, items stolen or cheaply manufactured and sold with counterfeit labels are often described as *bootleg* merchandise.

The U.S. Secret Service has pursued counterfeiters of American currency since the 1860s, when Con-

Counterfeit dollars seized by the police in Medellín, 185 miles northwest of Bogotá, Colombia, in April 2005. Police arrested 27 people and seized $1.3 million in counterfeit bills. (Luis Benavides/AP)

federate partisans used "funny money" in efforts to destabilize the Union economy. Since then, the government has spared no effort or expense to defeat counterfeiters. All U.S. currency is printed on special paper (a 100-percent cotton rag formula with a uniquely textured surface), using particular ink—both closely guarded so that private acquisition of either is deemed "nearly impossible." Nonetheless, counterfeiters hold their own with a variety of tricks, including use of bleach to remove the markings from one-dollar bills, thus freeing the unique paper for use in printing more valuable 20-dollar notes (the most commonly forged currency on earth). Where hand-engraved plates were once required to duplicate currency, high-tech photocopiers and laser printers now enable relative novices to duplicate bills. Each new change made by the government to currency is quickly matched by clever criminals with new equipment at their fingertips, while overworked cashiers and some vending machines fail to recognize the false notes.

Counterfeit credit cards also reap millions of dollars per year for those who manufacture and use them. Criminals start with blank cards—generically dubbed "white plastic," although they may be any color—and use a variety of expensive machines to emboss the cards, apply magnetic stripes and labels, produce signature panels with adequate texture, and so on. Warning signs of a forged credit card include jagged edges to letters and numbers when viewed through a magnifying glass, air bubbles visible in a card's plastic coating, *lack* of plastic coating which allows a user to feel the card's paint with his/her fingertips, a PIN code that appears too smooth or even, and signature panels that flake or peel away when scratched.

Counterfeit manufacturer's labels are used primarily for two reasons: first, to permit sale of stolen or shoddy, cheaply manufactured products at the full price of original high-ticket items; and second, to avoid paying state or federal taxes on certain regulated items such as alcoholic beverages and tobacco products. No final estimate is available for the revenue lost through sale of bootleg clothing, computer software, music, movies, and similar items. The same technique is used in *drug dumping,* a process wherein diluted, outdated, or outlawed prescription medications are exported for sale in foreign markets without warning to physicians or patients.

CRIME Scene Investigation

Every criminal investigation begins with a report of some unlawful activity, usually telephoned to some law enforcement agency by a civilian witness or complainant. If the crime is still in progress, officers may be lucky enough to catch the offenders red-handed with irrefutable evidence of guilt. Otherwise, some measure of investigation is required, its nature and extent depending on the severity of the offense (and, realistically, the status of the victim). In broad terms, the investigation of a crime proceeds through the following stages:

1. Dispatch operators for a given law enforcement agency receive the initial report or complaint of a crime and pass details on to the department's patrol division (except in the case of federal agencies, where no such division exists).

2. Patrol officers visit the alleged crime scene, determine the nature of the offense (if any), and report their findings to Dispatch. If further investigation is required, the patrol officers request that detectives be sent to the scene. While waiting, patrol officers control the scene, containing any relevant witnesses and securing physical evidence against removal or tampering. If injured persons are present, the patrol officers may request an ambulance.

3. Detectives next visit the scene and decide what kind of support is required, be it forensic examiners, a MEDICAL EXAMINER, or special units such as bomb disposal teams, experts in handling hazardous materials, or tracking dogs to locate suspects. While criminalists and others go to work at the scene, detectives question all known witnesses and canvass the vicinity for any others yet unrecognized.

4. Criminalists and other forensic experts respond to the scene when summoned by detectives, sketching, photographing and/or videotaping evidence *in situ* before it is collected for further examination in a laboratory setting. Any and all objects related to the crime should be collected and preserved. Specialists also assist in discovery of evidence detectives may have missed, as when methane probes are employed to reveal clandestine graves. Unlike some Hollywood portrayals, care must be taken with all evidentiary items to prevent contamination and

Crime scene investigators examine a shooting scene at Western High School in Las Vegas in January 2007. (Isaac Brekken/AP)

preserve the legal chain of custody. PRESUMPTIVE TESTS may be performed at the crime scene, but more conclusive specific tests will generally await transportation of evidence to the nearest crime lab. When all tests are completed, evidence is delivered to the law enforcement agency's property department for storage pending presentation at trial.

5. Where local detectives or criminalists lack facilities to perform certain tests, evidentiary samples may be passed on to outside experts for testing. Various computer databases such as AUTOMATED FINGERPRINT IDENTIFICATION SYSTEM, COMBINED DNA INDEX SYSTEM, Drugfire, and INTEGRATED BALLISTICS IDENTIFICATION SYSTEM often permit

comparison of FINGERPRINTS, ballistics evidence and DNA to known samples without surrendering custody of the items themselves.

CRIMINALISTICS Certification Study Committee

Organized with a grant from the National Institute of Justice in 1975, the CCSC labored through 1979 to develop a certification program in the field of forensic science. A survey conducted in 1980 revealed that only 38 percent of active criminalists in the United States endorsed the program's outline as presented, while 69 percent indicated interest in applying for certification if it was offered. The CCSC thus failed to achieve its objective, but it laid groundwork for

the later, more successful AMERICAN BOARD OF CRIMI-
NALISTICS.

CRINER, Roy Wayne exonerated by DNA evidence

On September 27, 1986, 16-year-old Deanna Ogg
was raped, then beaten and stabbed to death in
Montgomery County, Texas. Police initially described
the missing murder weapon as a tire tool, but the
implement was never found. An informer's statement
led detectives to Roy Criner, a 21-year-old logger
from New Caney. Murder charges were filed, then
dismissed in the absence of a weapon, leaving Criner
to face a lesser charge of aggravated sexual assault.

At trial in 1990, three witnesses claimed Criner
had boasted of raping a hitchhiker whom he threatened with a screwdriver. Police now changed their
description of the murder weapon, deeming Ogg's
wounds "consistent with" a screwdriver—but no
blood was found on a screwdriver confiscated from
Criner's pickup truck in 1986. Tire tracks from the
crime scene failed to match Criner's vehicle, and a
pubic hair found on Ogg's body matched neither
the victim nor Criner. Still, jurors were convinced by
testimony that Criner's blood type matched semen
samples lifted from Ogg's corpse. Upon conviction,
Criner received a 99-year prison sentence.

DNA testing, performed by a private laboratory
in 1997, determined that Criner was not the source
of semen found on Ogg's body in 1986. Montgomery County prosecutors requested a second test by
the Texas Department of Public Safety's crime lab
and obtained the same result. District Judge Michael
Mayes sent Criner's case to the Texas Court of Criminal Appeals with recommendations for a new trial,
but appellate judge Sharon Keller rejected the motion
in May 1998, ruling that "overwhelming direct evidence" proved Criner's guilt. Keller cited no such
evidence to support her judgment, but suggested that
the semen evidence was meaningless, since Criner
might have worn a condom and Ogg was "known to
be promiscuous," presumably engaging in sex with
several partners each day.

That strange decision touched off a firestorm of
media criticism, spearheaded by the *Houston Press*.
Another DNA test was performed in 2001, on saliva
recovered from a cigarette butt at the crime scene.
(Criner was a nonsmoker.) DNA from the saliva
matched the semen found on Ogg's corpse, thereby
eliminating any theory of consensual sex at some

Roy Criner, left, embraces his father after his release
from the Montgomery County jail in Conroe, Texas. After
he had spent a decade behind bars, his conviction was
overturned as a result of DNA evidence. He was released
in advance of an expected pardon by then-governor
Rick Perry. (AP)

earlier time. Montgomery County District Attorney
Mike McDougal recommended clemency to the Texas
Board of Pardons and Paroles on July 28, 2001. The
18-member board voted unanimously to approve
the petition, and Governor Rick Perry announced
his intent to pardon Criner on August 14, 2001. As
for Ogg's murderer, her brother James suggested to
reporters, "They ought to pull in everybody [who
knew Deanna] and say, 'DNA test on everyone.'
They will find the person." To date, no such effort
has been undertaken in Montgomery County and the
case remains unsolved.

CROTZER, Alan J. exonerated by DNA

On the night of July 8, 1981, three black men armed
with shotguns trailed two families home from a
steakhouse in Tampa, Florida, robbing the victims of
cash and other valuables, then kidnapping one of the
women and her 12-year-old daughter, both of whom
were subsequently raped in the getaway car. Police
traced the car to brothers Corlenzo and Douglas

James, but their accomplice, the alleged ringleader, remained at large. Officers prepared a photo lineup of potential suspects, including a mug shot of 21-year-old Alan Crotzer, whose police record included one prior conviction of ROBBERY. Witnesses described the gang's leader as six feet tall and weighing 130 pounds, while Crotzer was five inches shorter and five pounds heavier. Four of the five victims initially rejected Crotzer's mug shot, but the fifth selected him after a deputy sheriff falsely informed her that Crotzer was linked to the getaway car. The other four victims then changed their statements to confirm Crotzer's identity as the third bandit-rapist.

At trial in 1982, Crotzer denied any role in the crime and presented four alibi witnesses to establish his movements on the night in question. Nonetheless, an all-white jury convicted him after less than an hour of deliberation, and Crotzer received a 130-year prison term for sexual assault (two counts), armed robbery, BURGLARY, aggravated assault, and false imprisonment. The James brothers also received long sentences without naming their accomplice in the crime. Crotzer's various appeals were rejected until members of the CARDOZO INNOCENCE PROJECT accepted his case for review in 2002 and filed petitions for DNA testing of semen collected from the victims in 1981 (before such tests were possible). After various legal delays, those tests were finally performed in 2005 and the results, published in January 2006, excluded Crotzer as a participant in the gang rape. Upon hearing that news, Douglas James also belatedly cleared Crotzer, naming his accomplice from 1981 as a longtime family friend. Crotzer was released on January 23, 2006, after spending a quarter-century in prison for crimes that he did not commit.

CRUZ, Rolando exonerated by DNA evidence

Sometime after 1:00 P.M. on February 25, 1983, 10-year-old Jeanine Nicario was kidnapped from her home in Naperville, Illinois. Authorities found her two days later, raped and bludgeoned to death in a wooded area of DuPage County, four miles from her home. On May 8, 1983, 19-year-old Rolando Cruz approached homicide detectives to report alleged "dream visions" of the murder, thereby presenting himself as a suspect. Cruz later claimed his statements—which incriminated two acquaintances—were motivated by a $10,000 reward offered for information on the case. The plan backfired on

March 8, 1984, when he was arrested along with 21-year-old Stephen Buckley and 20-year-old Alejandro Hernandez. Held in lieu of $3 million bond, each of the trio faced 12 charges, including multiple counts of murder, rape, deviate sexual assault, aggravated liberties with a child, aggravated KIDNAPPING, home invasion, and residential BURGLARY.

Detective John Sam resigned from the DuPage County Sheriff's Department in December 1984, voicing doubts about the three defendants' guilt, but his superiors remained confident. Prosecutors illegally withheld Cruz's "dream vision" statement from defense attorneys, but introduced it as evidence at trial, in January 1985. Several witnesses were called to testify that Cruz and Hernandez had admitted intimate knowledge of the crime, while defense attorneys failed to pursue their alibis. Jurors convicted Cruz and Hernandez on February 22, 1985, but failed to reach a verdict on Buckley. On March 15, 1985, Judge Edward Koval sentenced Cruz and Hernandez to die.

Authorities were surprised on November 8, 1985, when confessed serial killer Brian Dugan, already charged in two other Illinois murders, admitted killing Jeanine Nicario himself, without accomplices. Eleven days later, Dugan received two consecutive life sentences for the slayings of a seven-year-old girl and a 27-year-old nurse. On March 28, 1986, the *Chicago Lawyer* published an article claiming that DuPage County authorities believed Dugan guilty of Nicario's murder, but the state attorney's office denied the report, calling Dugan's confession a hoax. Judge Robert Nolan, presiding over Stephen Buckley's retrial, officially ruled Dugan's story fictitious and inadmissible on September 5, 1986—but prosecutors dismissed all charges against Buckley six months later, releasing him on March 5, 1987.

On January 19, 1988, the Illinois Supreme Court overturned the convictions of Cruz and Hernandez, ordering new and separate trials for the pair. On September 2, 1989, over prosecution objections, Judge Edward Koval ruled the Dugan confessions admissible at retrials of Cruz and Hernandez, but it made no difference. Cruz was convicted a second time, on February 1, 1990, and again sentenced to death. Jurors failed to reach a verdict on Hernandez in May 1990, but his third trial resulted in conviction on May 11, 1991. Instead of death, this time Judge John Nelligan sentenced Hernandez to 80 years for murder, 20 years for kidnapping and 12 years for residential burglary, making the terms concurrent.

The Illinois Supreme Court upheld Cruz's second conviction on December 4, 1992, then reversed itself and ordered a new trial on July 14, 1994, finding that the second trial court made errors in the admission and exclusion of evidence. An appellate court granted Hernandez a new trial on January 30, 1995, citing jury misconduct and Judge Nelligan's failure to disclose the problem. New evidence was revealed on September 24, 1995, when results from a DNA test excluded Rolando Cruz as Jeanine Nicario's rapist. The same test found that Brian Dugan "shared DNA traits" with semen samples from the prosecution's rape kit. Cruz was acquitted on November 3, 1995, after police lieutenant James Montesano recanted his prior testimony and admitted lying under oath about Cruz's "dream vision" statement. Charges against Hernandez were dropped on November 17, 1995, while a special prosecutor was appointed to investigate official misconduct in the case.

DuPage County Sheriff Richard Doria announced in June 1996 that an internal investigation revealed no evidence of perjury by any of his officers, Lt. Montesano's sworn admission notwithstanding. A grand jury was convened to study the case, and in December 1996 it returned a 47-count indictment against Montesano and three other detectives, along with three former prosecutors. The so-called "DuPage Seven" were acquitted on all counts in 1999, prompting critics to describe the verdict as a "whitewash." The Nicario murder remains officially unsolved today.

CULLIFORD, Brian (1929–)

Born in 1929, forensic serologist Brian Culliford was employed at London's Metropolitan Police Laboratory in 1967, when he developed a procedure for detecting enzyme phosphoglucomutase (PGM) in dried bloodstains. PGM is a hereditary polymorphic enzyme—i.e., found in multiple, distinct forms. Culliford published his findings in 1971, as *The Examination and Typing of Bloodstains in the Crime Laboratory*. Until the development of DNA profiling in the 1980s, Culliford's system of PGM analysis remained the primary forensic tool for classifying blood and determining possible sources for stains found at crime scenes (see BLOODSTAIN EVIDENCE).

CURPHEY, Theodore (1897–1986)

Born on October 25, 1897, New York native Theodore Curphey obtained his M.D. before joining the coroner's office in Nassau County, Long Island. He served as Nassau County's chief forensic pathologist from 1938 to 1957, when he moved to California as the first MEDICAL EXAMINER for Los Angeles County. A year later, frustrated by inconclusive findings in numerous drug-related deaths, Curphey pioneered the technique of "psychological autopsy" to determine whether certain overdose cases were accidents or deliberate suicides. One such case—Curphey's most famous—was the death of actress Marilyn Monroe on August 4, 1962. Suspicion still surrounds that case, with published allegations of murder involving mobsters, CIA agents, and prominent politicians, but Dr. Curphey concluded his 11-day investigation with a verdict of suicide. Critics of that finding note that no formal inquest was held, that various key witnesses were largely ignored, and that those interviewed by Curphey's panel did not testify under oath. Curphey retired on his 70th birthday and died on November 27, 1986.

CYBERCRIME computer-related crime and punishment

Rapid advances in computers since the 1980s, coupled with the advent of the Internet, have created new frontiers for lawbreakers and law enforcement alike. Computer-related or -assisted crimes vary widely, from personal intimidation and petty vandalism to multimillion-dollar thefts affecting giant corporations and espionage on a global scale. Even murder, the ultimate crime, may be facilitated by the World Wide Web—as demonstrated in 2001 by the case of JOHN EDWARD ROBINSON, a.k.a. "Slavemaster," billed in media reports as the first Internet serial killer.

Computer crime is not a new phenomenon, by any means. The first record of a computer-related crime dates from 1958, and 374 cases of "computer abuse" were logged by 1976 (including four instances of frustrated owners shooting their own computers, two "fatally"). The first federal prosecution of a computer crime occurred in 1966. Today, law enforcement agencies and civilian watchdog groups in the United States alone receive yearly complaints numbering in the tens of thousands. Cybercrimes evolve as rapidly as new technology, spurred on by the dark side of the human imagination, but a representative sampling would include the following offenses:

Hacking Whether performed by bored, precocious teenage "nerds" or sophisticated gangs akin to organized crime, the illicit penetration of corporate or government computer systems by unauthorized outsiders today is viewed as a significant threat to national and global communications infrastructures. "Idealistic" hackers deny any interest in monetary gain and insist their penetrations are designed to preserve "freedom of information," but purely mercenary hackers—sometimes dubbed *crackers* to emphasize their criminal motives—dedicate themselves to large-scale theft of cash, confidential information, and the like. Another problem area, described by computer aficionados as "darkside hacking," involves deliberate cybervandalism by such perpetrators as the "Legion of Doom" and its rivals from the "Masters of Deception."

Theft of cash In 1994 a Russian hacker named VLADIMIR LEVIN stole more than $10 million from Citibank Corporation without ever setting foot in the United States. Internet transfers of cash and securities between banks and other financial institutions are routine today, subject to interference and diversion by cyberbandits who invade corporate systems, steal passwords and bank account numbers, and divert huge sums to accounts under their own control. Techniques such as "lapping" (employee diversion of incoming cash to a bogus account) and "kiting" (use of normal delays in processing financial transactions to create the appearance of assets where none exist) victimize financial institutions from within. Another form of internal theft, nicknamed "salami slicing," occurs when employees shave small sums from numerous sources (as in the case of a computer operator for a New York garment-making firm, who stole two cents from the federal income tax withheld on each coworker's weekly paycheck). Automatic teller machines (ATMs), meanwhile, lose an estimated $200 million per year to various frauds. At the same time, Internet credit card fraud, involving theft or counterfeiting of credit and debit card numbers by the hundreds of thousands, levies a staggering toll against various financial institutions. The problem's gravity may be judged by Visa Corporation's report for 1997, listing losses of $490 million as an improvement over previous years.

An investigator for the Florida Attorney General's Child Predator Cybercrime Unit logs on to his computer and poses as a teenage girl in a chat room. (Oscar Sosa/AP)

"Phreaking" Akin to hackers, both in spirit and technique, "phreakers" are those who employ various devices (such as the classic "BLUE BOX") to cheat telephone companies on long-distance calls. Once again, some "purists" profess to regard their efforts as a blow for freedom of communication, while others unapologetically turn a profit on sale of charge-evasion devices and stolen calling numbers. Precise figures for losses from telephone fraud are unavailable, but industry spokespersons suggest that long-distance fraud costs the industry between $4 billion and $8 billion yearly; all forms of telecommunications fraud combined may top $15 billion per year, with wireless fraud alone exceeding $1 billion.

"Data diddling" Employed in a variety of settings, this technique involves manipulation or falsification of computer data for personal profit or other illegal motives. One case, reported in 1997, involved crackers who penetrated the computers of maritime insurance companies, inserting registration data for nonexistent ships and purchasing large insurance policies on the mythical vessels, then "sinking" them to collect the payoffs.

Extortion and/or blackmail As before the invention of computers and the Internet, these crimes involve coercion of tribute payments to prevent some threatened action by the extortionist or blackmailer. As early 20th-century racketeers sold "protection" (from themselves) to frightened neighborhood merchants, so cyberthugs victimize individuals or corporations via e-mail and the World Wide Web. On June 2, 1996, the *Times* (London) reported that various banks and investment firms in the United States and Britain had "secretly paid ransom to prevent costly computer meltdown and a collapse in confidence among the customers." None of the threats—said to emanate from cyberterrorists in America and Russia—or the payoffs (up to £13 million per incident) had been reported to authorities. Florida resident Michael Pitelis was arrested in August 2000 for attempting to extort $1 million from a Massachusetts corporation, threatening to expose software secrets. The same month, Kazakhstan native Oleg Zezov was charged with blackmailing the Bloomberg financial news company for $200,000. In May 2001 Russian operator Alexei Ivanov faced charges of victimizing firms across the United States with similar threats.

Bootlegging and piracy Lumped together by U.S. prosecutors as "intellectual property theft," these offenses include any unauthorized duplication and/or distribution of copyrighted material. The items most often bootlegged include computer software, motion pictures, and music, but any material covered by U.S. or international copyrights and patents is likewise subject to misappropriation. Profit motives were once considered essential for prosecution of such cases, but enactment of the No Electronic Theft (NET) Act on December 16, 1997, criminalized software piracy and other forms of bootlegging whether the items were sold or given away as a "public service."

Malicious programming Since the 1980s, thousands of computer viruses and worms have been unleashed upon the Internet by programmers around the world. Some are benign, with no more impact on their host computers than a brief, amusing video display, while others—like "Melissa" and the "Code Red" virus—cause global damage to corporate and personal computers estimated in the billions of dollars. Certain nations seem to spawn a disproportionate number of virus writers—160 separate viruses were traced to Bulgaria alone between 1989 and 1993—but no part of the world is presently immune. Almost as numerous are hoaxes, circulated on the Web by pranksters with too much free time on their hands. While most malicious programs are broadcast at random, often in the form of infected e-mail attachments, some are written with more specific targets in mind. Corporate victims fall prey most often to disgruntled past or present employees, while government computer systems may be targeted by foreign agents or domestic activists. "Logic bombs"—destructive codes that lie dormant within a computer until triggered by a specific signal—have been found within the systems of several U.S. agencies. (At that, federal spokesmen estimate that they detect no more than 10 percent of all attempted intrusions per year.)

Espionage Whether corporate or political, spying has been facilitated by the Internet. In 1986, a systems administrator at the Lawrence Berkeley Laboratory in California discovered that crackers from "Chaos," a West German group, had hijacked the computer account of a former employee and used it to steal U.S. military data for sale to the Soviet KGB intelligence agency. Three members of "Chaos" were indicted on espionage charges, while a fourth died mysteriously. The survivors were convicted at trial in 1990, receiving prison terms of 20 months to five years, with fines totaling $9,000. Eight years later, a group calling itself the "Masters of Downloading/2016216" claimed to have cracked the Pentagon's communications system, stealing software for a military satellite system and threatening its sale to terrorists, but the threat was never realized. Worldwide, various corporations are constantly on guard against attempts to penetrate computer systems and steal financial records, lists of customers, proprietary software, or other valuable secrets.

Cyberstalking Most of the crimes discussed so far are financially or politically motivated, targeting government or commercial institutions, but cyberstalking is uniquely personal. As malicious individuals in daily life stalk celebrities, family members, ex-lovers, and former friends, harassing their targets with phone calls and letters or worse, so their counterparts in cyberspace spew venom on-line. E-mail bombing is one common harassment technique, the target inundated with hundreds or thousands of unwanted messages, sometimes including personal threats. Other forms of cyberstalking may include posting of personal data or photos at large on the Web (as in the Wanted posters utilized by some antiabortion groups to intimidate physicians) or hacking of personal computers with malicious intent. Cyber Angels, a civilian volunteer group committed to opposing on-line stalkers, reports an average of 650 complaints per day on its Web site year-round.

Child pornography and solicitation While child molestation is a crime in every U.S. jurisdiction, no federal law banned production or sale of child pornography prior to 1977, with "children" legally defined in 1984 as any person below the age of 18 years. Further U.S. legislation has since been enacted to ban advertisement of child pornography (1986); use of computers to transmit, sell, or receive child pornography (1988); possession of three or more images depicting sex with children (1990); inducement of minors to participate in child pornography (1996); and possession of any image that *appears* to depict sex with children, even when the models are adults "morphed" with computer graphics to resemble children or where "virtual children" are depicted without use of live models (1996). The latter provision is especially controversial facing determined legal attacks from artists and civil libertarians who maintain that nonexistent children have no rights and cannot suffer harm. To date, despite prosecution of some notorious defendants—including teachers, ministers, judges, and other public officials—legislation seems largely ineffective at curbing child por-

nography, particularly that which is produced outside the United States.

"Mousetrapping" Designed to create a literal captive audience for otherwise unwelcome advertising, "mousetrapping" involves the creation of alluring Web sites with built-in snares that prevent online visitors from escaping once they log on to the site. While any type of advertisement may be used in mousetrapping, the more objectionable forms—especially on sites that lure minors with promised images of rock stars or other celebrities—are those for gambling, lotteries, pornography and psychics. The undisputed king of American mousetrapping, Pennsylvania operator John Zuccarini, has reportedly earned millions from his many Web sites, while logging more than 60 lawsuits from the Federal Trade Commission. Visitors to Zuccarini's Web sites (and their many copycats), unable to escape by any normal combination of keystrokes, are bombarded meanwhile by a rapid-fire barrage of advertisements displayed as individual "windows."

Identity theft This offense differs from simple credit card theft in both its scope and potential damage to the victim. Felons who obtain sufficient personal data about an intended target, whether from online sources or primitive "dumpster diving," are often able to create their own persona with someone else's name, Social Security number, and other vital information. While certain bizarre cases of celebrity impersonators rank among the most notorious incidents of identity theft—a West Indian immigrant spent years posing as the son of comedian Bill Cosby—middle-class victims suffer the greatest damage. In one egregious case, the ex-convict impostor ran up more than $100,000 in credit card debts, obtained a federal home loan, and purchased high-ticket items ranging from guns and motorcycles to houses before filing bankruptcy, all in his victim's name. The offender also tormented his victim with mocking telephone calls, immune from federal prosecution since no statute then penalized identity theft. The victim and his wife spent more than $15,000 to restore their credit and good names, while the thief escaped with a brief jail term (for giving a false name when purchasing a firearm) and paid no restitution. The case, and others like it, inspired Congress to pass new legislation on identity theft in 1998.

Internet fraud These crimes occur so frequently and evolve so rapidly that no detailed accounting is feasible, but certain broad categories are worthy of note. *Online auctions* generate more fraud complaints than any other Internet activity, most commonly when buyers bid on some valuable piece of merchandise and receive a counterfeit item or nothing at all. (Losing bidders are also sometimes approached to buy "surplus" items that never arrive.) Shills are also frequently employed to create a false impression of interest in some item and artificially inflate its price. *Retail fraud* involves the same basic scams, including nondelivery or bait-and-switch techniques. *Business opportunity fraud* advertises spurious "work at home" schemes, generating millions of "spam" e-mail messages daily, bilking thousands of gullible respondents for wasted "processing fees." *Money laundering*, while not a fraud upon the average consumer, uses financial institutions (and sometimes charities) to "wash" vast sums including profits from organized crime and forbidden political contributions. *Investment fraud* includes manipulation of securities via the "pump-and-dump" technique (inflating the prices of worthless stocks before they are sold) and "cybersmear" campaigns that deflate stock prices by attacking a company's reputation. In extreme cases, such activities not only defraud traders and damage individual companies, but may also affect the stock market as a whole. Cyberfraud allegations are heard by the Internet Fraud Complaint Center, a joint operation of the FBI and the Justice Department's National White Collar Crime Center (NW3C).

Because all law enforcement is reactive, the U.S. federal response to cybercrime has naturally lagged behind illicit innovations in the field. Today, most cases are handled by the Justice Department's Computer Crime and Intellectual Property Section (CCIPS), consisting of some two dozen U.S. attorneys who concentrate solely on cybercrime issues. Founded in 1991 as the Computer Crime Unit, elevated to "section" status five years later, CCIPS employs prosecutors with expertise in such diverse subject areas as encryption, electronic privacy laws,

copyrights, e-commerce, and hacking. Addressing the U.S. Senate on February 16, 2000, Attorney General Janet Reno called CCIPS "the cornerstone of our prosecutor cybercrime program." Current CCIPS responsibilities include:

Litigating cases This involves not only prosecuting felons charged with violation of relevant federal statutes, but also filing lawsuits against corporations and organizations deemed liable to civil penalties under prevailing federal law. Those penalties may include fines, reimbursement of parties damaged by some illegal action, and injunctions barring further proscribed activities.

Training CCIPS spearheads efforts to train local, state, and federal agents or prosecutors in the legal aspects of combating cybercrime. It does not provide technical training in use of computers or other high-tech devices, however, although such courses are offered to agents in training at the FBI Academy.

International liaison Confronted with the global Internet, CCIPS cannot afford a parochial approach to crime-fighting. Its leaders chair the G-8 Subgroup on High-tech Crime, which maintains a round-the-clock contact point for mutual assistance of investigators fighting cybercrime in 15 collaborating nations. CCIPS also plays a leading role in the Council of Europe Experts' Committee on Cybercrime and participates in a similar unit for the Organization of American States in Latin America. On November 23, 2001, in Budapest, the United States and 29 other nations signed the Council of Europe Cybercrime Convention, drafted during a four-year period to facilitate international cooperation among diverse law enforcement agencies.

Policy and legislation While it does not have the final word, CCIPS is tasked with proposing federal policy and legislation in the field of cybercrime, accommodating needs of the private sector where possible, and closing loopholes in extant legislation, to prevent today's felons from avoiding prosecution tomorrow.

One area of heated debate on cybercrime policy involves the handling of juvenile cases. Proliferation of personal computers gives millions of children free access to the Internet, supervised only by parents or guardians who are sometimes overworked, preoccupied, or simply negligent. The result may include minors being exposed to sexually explicit material and gambling Web sites, or it may go further, spawning criminal activity on the part of precocious young felons. Stripped of face-to-face interaction with merchants and other business persons, juveniles find themselves on a level playing field where Internet fraud is concerned. Armed with stolen or counterfeit credit card numbers, available today at bargain rates, minors can run up huge bills for merchandise. Telephone fraud also appeals to young "phreakers," and many notorious hackers have launched their careers during adolescence. Federal investigators note that "juveniles appear to have an ethical 'deficit' when it comes to computer crimes," citing studies that reveal 34 percent of university undergraduates freely admitting to software piracy, while 16 percent admit illegal hacking of computer systems to gain desired information.

Prosecution in such cases is frequently hampered by statutes limiting the liability and punishment of minors for their crimes. While each state maintains its own juvenile code, federal regulations are embodied in the Juvenile Justice and Delinquency Prevention Act. Justice spokesmen note that "As a threshold matter, it is important to note that a juvenile proceeding is not the same as a criminal prosecution. Rather it is a proceeding in which the issue to be determined is whether the minor is a 'juvenile delinquent' as a matter of status, not whether he or she is guilty of committing a crime." A finding of "delinquency" is therefore not a criminal conviction, although it may result in confinement, mandatory counseling, and other remedial action. Banning access to computers for a fixed amount of time is common punishment for underage cybercriminals.

As cybercrime has spawned new regulatory agencies, so it has also produced a new breed of defenders for those accused. The online Hacker's Defense Foundation solicits contributions for those accused of computer penetrations, and at least a handful of attorneys now profess to specialize in defending indicted cyberoutlaws. Oscar Figueroa, a San Francisco lawyer, promotes himself online as "a semantic warrior committed to the liberation of information," specifically inviting clients who are "charged with committing a computer-related criminal offense, such as hacking, cracking, phreaking, identity theft, copyright infringement or trade of theft secrets [sic]." Given the government's increasing preoccupation with computer-related crimes, it seems unlikely that Figueroa and other champions of the accused will suffer from a shortage of clients in the foreseeable future.

D

DABBS, Charles exonerated by DNA evidence

In the predawn hours of August 12, 1982, a female resident of Westchester County, New York, was attacked while walking near her home. A man grabbed her from behind, dragged her into a nearby alley, and shoved her down a flight of stairs. Upon regaining consciousness, the victim found herself confronted by three men, two of whom held her down while the third raped her. She identified the rapist as Charles Dabbs, a distant cousin. The other two assailants were never apprehended.

At trial, prosecutors relied on the victim's identification of Dabbs, including references to his "distinctive laugh," and noted that the blood type of semen stains found on the victim's clothing matched Dabbs's Type O blood. Jurors convicted him of first-degree rape on April 10, 1984, and Dabbs received a prison term of 12 to 20 years. His conviction was upheld on appeal, but the Westchester County Supreme Court granted Dabbs's request for DNA testing of the evidence on November 21, 1990. A private laboratory concluded that Dabbs was not the source of semen found on the victim's clothing, and the court acknowledged his innocence on July 31, 1991. The charges were officially dismissed three weeks later, on August 22, 1991. Dabbs was released after serving seven years of his sentence.

DAVIS, Gerald Wayne exonerated by DNA evidence

Police in Kanawha County, West Virginia, received a rape complaint on February 18, 1986. The alleged victim claimed she had taken some laundry to be washed at the home of Gerald Davis, a family friend, who attacked and raped her when she returned for the items hours later. According to her statement, Davis's father—Dewey Davis—was also present in the house but made no effort to assist her during the attack. Searching the Davis home, authorities found a shoe and jacket belonging to the victim. While both Davis and his father claimed innocence of any wrongdoing, they were jailed on charges of kidnapping and sexual assault.

At trial, in May 1986, state police chemist FRED ZAIN testified that DNA tests could not exclude Gerald Davis as a possible source of semen found on the victim's underwear. Both defendants maintained that they had done nothing while the victim washed her clothing, but jurors disbelieved their story. Gerald Davis was convicted of KIDNAPPING and two counts of sexual assault, while his father was found guilty of abduction, first-degree sexual abuse and second-degree sexual assault. Both defendants received prison terms of 14 to 35 years, reduced to a flat 10 years on appeal.

The defendants gained new hope in 1993, following revelations that Zain, the police chemist, excluded Gerald Davis as a semen donor. Prosecutors demanded a second test, this time on Davis's sheets and underpants, contending that Davis could have raped the victim without ejaculating. The new tests revealed no trace of the alleged victim's DNA, and Gerald Davis was released to home confinement on March 16, 1994, pending retrial. Jurors acquitted him on December 4, 1995, and charges against his father were subsequently dismissed.

DAYE, Frederick Rene exonerated by DNA evidence

On the evening of January 10, 1984, a young woman was attacked by two men while leaving a San Diego, California, drugstore. One assailant forced the victim into her own car from the driver's side, then opened the back door for his accomplice. Inside the car, the men rifled her purse and stole six dollars, then removed several articles of jewelry before they ripped off the victim's clothes and raped her. Afterward the two men dumped their victim on a nearby residential street and fled in her car. A witness to the crime identified the men as Frederick Daye and David Pringle, both soon arrested on charges of KIDNAPPING, robbery, rape, and auto theft. The victim identified Daye's mug shot as a likeness of her rapist and picked him out of a lineup at police headquarters.

The defendants were tried separately, with Pringle pleading the Fifth Amendment from the witness stand at Daye's trial. Blood typing on a semen stain from the victim's clothing matched Daye's Type B blood, and prosecutors noted that he had given police a false name at the time of his arrest. Jurors convicted him on August 14, 1984, after deliberating for nearly eight hours. Daye was sentenced to life imprisonment with possible parole on the kidnapping charge, plus 14 years and eight months on various other counts. David Pringle was convicted in a later trial and likewise sentenced to prison. An appellate court affirmed Daye's conviction on February 29, 1986, and California's Supreme Court declined to review the case.

David Pringle surprised authorities with a confession to the rape and kidnapping on February 1, 1990, his statement exonerating Daye and naming another man as his accomplice. The San Diego County Superior Court appointed an attorney to investigate the claim, and while a writ of habeas corpus was denied on August 11, 1992, the court ruled that Daye was entitled to new representation. Destruction of the original trial evidence was scheduled for October 1992, but last-minute motions preserved it for DNA testing, with a $2,000 grant to complete the procedure. Those tests, completed on April 21, 1994, excluded Daye as a source of semen collected from the victim's clothing following the rape. Daye's conviction was overturned on September 27, 1994, after he had served 10 years of his sentence.

DECEPTION Analysis

Much of an investigator's work on any legal case involves discrimination between truth and falsehood. Some inaccurate reports to the police are inadvertent, the product of honest mistakes, while others are deliberate lies. Much time and effort has thus been applied throughout history to deception analysis, both in forensic matters and within the private sector. In ancient times, conflicting witnesses were often judged through trial by ordeal, with "truth" determined by a particular subject's ability to withstand pain or perform difficult tasks. More scientific techniques evolved during the 20th century, with research equally divided between chemical and mechanical "lie-detectors."

Narcoanalysis—the use of various chemical "truth serums," commonly barbiturates such as scopolamine and sodium pentothal—enjoyed a vogue in the first half of the 20th century and remains a staple tactic of some intelligence agencies today, although results are universally inadmissible in American courts. A classic case was that of William Heirens, a teenage sex offender who confessed to three Chicago murders in 1946, while under the influence of "truth serum." Public opinion is still divided on the subject of Heirens's guilt in the crimes he confessed, including the stabbing deaths of two adult women and the kidnap-dismemberment of a six-year-old girl. Spared from execution by his tender age, Heirens remained in prison at press time for this volume, ranked as the longest-serving inmate in Illinois history. A new generation of supporters describe his incarceration as a FRAME-UP, while others point to details in his psychiatric interviews clearly suggesting guilty knowledge of the crimes.

The best-known mechanical "lie-detector" is the polygraph, a device refined over time and through various generations, which measures a subject's pulse, blood pressure, respiration rate and volume,

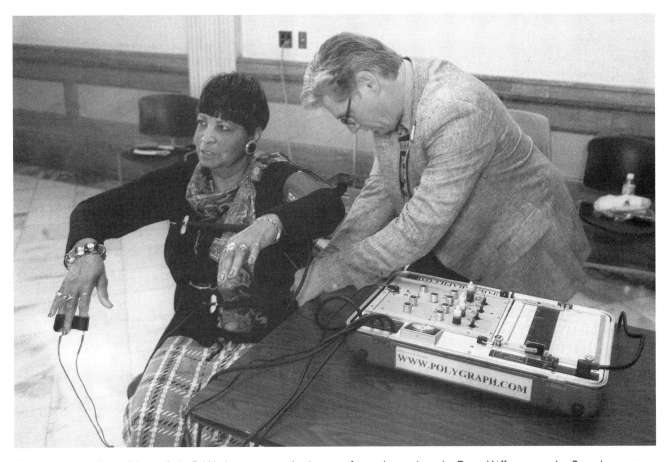

Representative Ruby Gilbert, left, D-Wichita, is attached to a polygraph machine by Doug Williams at the Statehouse in Topeka, Kansas, as part of a polygraph demonstration for legislators. (Chris Ochsner/AP)

and galvanic skin response (perspiration) during interrogation. Unlike the grillings portrayed in many films and television programs, expert polygraphers discuss all questions with their subjects in advance and accept only "yes" or "no" answers. Any surprise questions or questions requiring explanations automatically invalidate the test. Results may also be influenced by a subject's physical or mental health, medications consumed, external distractions, and errors on the part of the examiner. And while some professional polygraphers make extravagant claims of success in unmasking liars, an ideal polygraph test measures only the subject's physical reactions, *not* his or her veracity. For that reason, and based on various studies claiming accuracy rates of 50 percent or less, American courts do not admit polygraphy results as evidence. Nonetheless, most U.S. law enforcement agencies still use the devices when questioning criminal suspects and in screening potential employees.

A variation on polygraphy is *voice stress analysis*, in which recordings of a subject's voice are processed through a sound spectrograph to detect presumed evidence of stress in particular words or phrases. Heated debate continues as to whether stress can thus be measured—or, if so, whether signs of stress prove deception. As with the polygraph and various methods of "voiceprint" identification, American courts universally reject voice stress analysis as evidence, though it reportedly remains in use by the CIA and various other government agencies.

Deception analysis may apply not only to a subject's oral or written statements, but to his/her behavior in general. A particularly sensitive area is that of insanity pleas, widely viewed by the American public as a "scam" used by criminals to escape punishment. In fact, such pleas are filed in only a tiny minority of cases, but they often generate such sensational headlines—like those surrounding would-be presidential assassin John Hinckley—that they dominate legal news nationwide. One interesting case of faked insanity was that of Mafia boss Vincent "The Chin" Gigante, who spent years roaming the streets of New York City in slippers and a bathrobe, seeming to mutter incoherently while under surveillance by police and federal agents. Jurors at his racketeering trial saw through the ruse, with help from testimony by informants and psychiatrists, convicting Gigante on multiple felony charges that sent him to prison for life.

DESIGNER Drugs

Also widely known as "club" drugs for their prevalence at trendy nightclubs and teenage "rave" parties, designer drugs are synthetic substances created by changing the molecular structure of existing drugs—normally amphetamines or methamphetamines, PCP,

and fentanyl—to create new drugs with similar or enhanced pharmacological effects. Designer drugs initially came into vogue as an attempt to circumvent the Controlled Substance Act of 1970, which strictly regulated various psychoactive drugs (including LSD, amphetamines, and methamphetamines). A 1986 amendment to that law banned all existing designer drugs *and* all possible variations of any controlled substance, whether or not those variations had yet been imagined or manufactured.

As with other outlawed drugs, of course, a legislative ban has done no more than whet the public appetite while raising prices on the street. The effects of designer drugs vary widely, depending on potency and the latest recipe employed by their illicit manufacturers. Club drugs derived from methylenedioxymethamphetamine (MDMA), frequently sold as "Ecstasy," produce feelings of euphoria, but increased dosages may also generate paranoia,

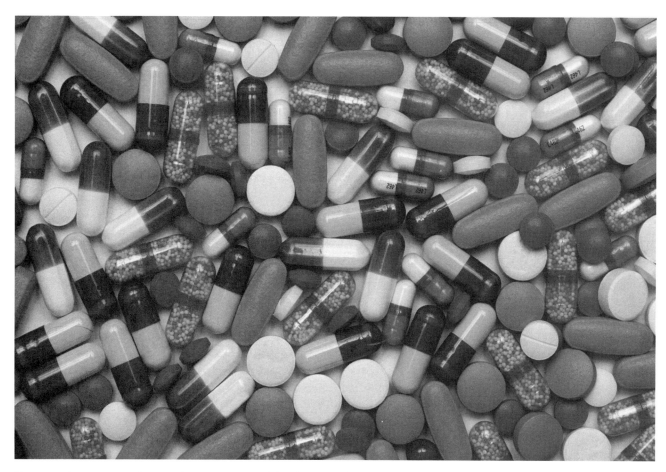

Designer drugs are synthetic substances created by changing the molecular structure of existing drugs—normally amphetamines or methamphetamines, PCP, and fantanyl—to create new drugs with similar or enhanced pharmacological effects.

depression, irrational violence, and hallucinations similar to those produced by LSD. Gamma hydroxybutyrate (GHB), once sold in health food stores as a performance-enhancer for body builders, is a central nervous system (CNS) depressant abused for its intoxicating effects. When taken in large doses or combined with other CNS depressants such as alcohol or sedatives, GHB can produce fatal respiratory depression. Undesirable side effects common to many club drug users include hypertension, increased heart rate, blurred vision, tremors and seizures, impaired speech, dehydration, and progressive brain damage. Psychological symptoms of designer drug abuse include confusion, irritability, amnesia, insomnia, and severe anxiety. The confusion was evident among four thieves at Noblesville, Indiana, on August 24, 2001. Intent on stealing the heroin-mimic OxyContin from a local pharmacy, the raiders instead escaped with oxytocin, a drug used to induce labor in pregnant women. "I don't know if they used any," Detective Todd Uhrick told reporters. "They were all pretty dumb."

As with any other deviant subculture, designer drug users apply various street names to their chemicals of choice. Among them are the following:

MDMA Adam, B-bombs, Bean, Blue kisses, Blue lips, Crystal, Clarity, Cloud nine, Dead road, Debs, Decadence, Dex, Diamonds, Disco biscuits, Doctor, Dolls, Driver, Ecstasy, Essence, Eve, ExitICity, Gaggler, Go, Greenies, Gum opium, Happy drug, Herbal bliss, Kleenex, Love drug, Mini beans, Morning shot, Nineteen, Rave energy, Ritual spirit, Scooby snacks, Speed for lovers, Strawberry shortcake, Sweeties, Ultimate Xphoria, Wafers, West Coast turnarounds, Wheels, Whiffledust

Fentanyl Apache, China girl, China town, Dance fever, Friend, Goodfellas, Great bear, He-man, Jackpot, King ivory, Murder 8, Poison, Tango & Cash, TNT

Dimethyltryptamine AMT, Businessman's LSD, Businessman's special, Businessman's trip, DET, DMT, Fantasia, 45-minute psychosis

Alpha-ethyltryptamine Alpha-ET, ET, Love pearls, Love pills, Trip

Methcathinone Bathtub speed, Cadillac express, Cat, Gaggers, Go-fast, Goob, Qat, Slick superspeed, Somali tea, Star, Stat, The C, Tweeker, Wild cat, Wonder star

Ketamine Cat valium, Honey oil, Jet, Ket, Kit kat, Purple, Special "K," Super acid, Super C, Vitamin K

GHB Georgia home boy, Grievous bodily harm, Liquid ecstasy, Scoop

Nexus (4-bromo-2, 5-dimethoxyphenethylamine) Bromo, MFT, Spectrum, Toonies, Venus

Rohypnol Forget me drug, La rocha, Lunch money drug, Mexican Valium, Pingus, R-2, Reynolds, Roaches, Roachies, Roofies, Rope, Row-shay, Ruffies, Ruffles, Wolfies

DIAZ, Luis exonerated by DNA

During 1977–79, a serial rapist kidnapped and sexually assaulted at least 25 women in the vicinity of Bird Road, outside Coral Gables, Florida. In 1979, police arrested 41-year-old Luis Diaz, charging him with eight of those cases. At trial in 1980, the eight victims identified Diaz as their attacker, prompting jurors to convict him on four counts of rape, three counts of attempted rape, five KIDNAPPING charges, plus various firearms and robbery counts. At sentencing, Diaz received 13 life terms plus 55 years, virtually ensuring that he would die in prison. Two of the victim-witnesses recanted their identifications of Diaz in 2002, under questioning by private investigator Virginia Snyner, and Florida authorities agreed to void the sentences in those two cases if Diaz would drop his remaining appeals. The bargain's net result was one life prison term.

Despite that agreement, members of the CARDOZO INNOCENCE PROJECT obtained permission for DNA testing on semen recovered from one Bird Road victim—the only biological evidence presented against Diaz in 1980—plus samples from two other women not listed among Diaz's alleged victims at trial when he was suspected of attacking. Testing of all three samples exonerated Diaz as a suspect, and he was released from prison on August 4, 2005, after serving 26 years for crimes he did not commit. The Bird Road rapes remain unsolved today.

DISASTER Mortuary Operational Response Team (DMORT)

DMORTs are federal teams of professionals including forensic anthropologists, odontologists, and pathologists, that respond to mass death scenes such as airplane crashes, earthquakes, and terrorist attacks.

DMORTs were the brainchild of New York funeral director Thomas Shepardson (1943-2003), who launched Onondaga County's disaster response team in the early 1980s. While that team never saw action locally, Shepardson was later recruited to lead a team for New York State, later expanding nationwide under the auspices of FEMA (the Federal Emergency Management Agency) and the U.S. Department of Health and Human Services. By the time Shepardson died in February 2003, there were 10 DMORT teams with an estimated 5,000 support personnel across the United States. Classic DMORT cases include the first World Trade Center bombing (1993), the bombing of Oklahoma City's Alfred P. Murrah Federal Building (1995), the "9/11" terrorist attacks (2001), and the recovery of 339 jumbled bodies from a crematory in Noble, Georgia (2002).

DNA Evidence

Often described as the basic building block of life on earth, deoxyribonucleic acid (DNA) is the substance that transmits genetic traits. Discovered by scientists James Watson and Francis Crick, DNA was admitted as legal evidence for the first time in 1985 and sent a criminal suspect—British serial killer COLIN PITCH-FORK—to prison for the first time in January 1988. Since then, the science of DNA analysis and comparison—sometimes dubbed "DNA fingerprinting"—has assumed strategic importance in many criminal trials where conviction or acquittal hinges on traces of blood, semen, hair, or other evidence containing genetic material.

To the best of modern scientific knowledge, only identical twins display precisely the same DNA, but all human DNA has certain traits in common and a relatively small percentage of it is used to determine identity. In fact, while human beings have 23 million pairs of chromosomes containing DNA, only 3 million pairs—13 percent of a subject's entire genome—varies from person to person. (Half of each pair is drawn from the subject's father and half from the mother.) The key to analyzing DNA evidence lies in comparison of genetic material found at a crime scene with a suspect's DNA in those segments that differ.

Two different kinds of "polymorphic regions"—areas with great diversity in DNA—are found within each genome, respectively dubbed sequence polymorphisms and length polymorphisms. *Sequence polymorphisms,* or simple substitutions of bases within genes, are generally of little value in criminal cases. *Length polymorphisms,* by contrast, are variations in the physical length of a DNA molecule. Forensic DNA evidence uses length polymorphism found in "non-coding" DNA (the portions that do not transmit genetic codes) by examining unique variations in repeat sequences of DNA. Because a specific sequence may be repeated from one to 30 times in a row, those regions are dubbed "variable number tandem repeats" (VNTRs). The number of VNTRs determines a DNA fragment's length, and the number found at specific places in the DNA chain (loci) is unique to a specific individual (again, excluding identical twins).

The scientific procedure used to isolate a subject's DNA profile is called *restriction fragment length polymorphism* (RFLP) analysis, developed in the 1980s by Britain's Dr. Alec Jeffreys. In essence, it simply means that analysts count the number of VNTR repeats at various distinctive loci to determine a subject's statistically unique DNA "fingerprint." Microscopic comparison of a known subject's DNA profile with the same information from an anonymous evidence sample should reveal if the genetic material lifted from a crime scene was produced by the suspect in custody. Comparison proceeds through several steps, including:

1. *Isolation of the DNA.* Genetic material found at crime scenes is frequently contaminated by contact with soil or other extraneous materials, commingling of bodily fluids from two or more subjects, and so forth. Thus, before analysis can proceed, the DNA must be cleaned and isolated for study. Failure to perform this step correctly leaves the evidence open to serious challenge by a suspect's defense team.

2. *Reduction of the large genome to manageable fragments.* This step is accomplished by application of "restriction enzymes"—bacterial enzymes that recognize specific four-to-six-base sequences and cut the DNA at predictable base pairs. Human DNA is thus broken down into millions of fragments ranging from 100 base pairs to longer segments in the tens of thousands. Distinctive VNTR loci may then be more conveniently examined.

3. *Arrangement of the DNA fragments by size via gel electrophoresis.* In this step, DNA is placed into a slab of agarose (a gel derived from sea-

Model of DNA double helix structure. (PhotoDisc)

weed, used to solidify various culture media) and exposed to an electric field. Since DNA is negatively charged, it will be drawn toward the field's positive electrode, with smaller fragments moving through the agarose more quickly than larger ones. The relative size of each fragment is determined by how far it moves through the agarose within a specific time frame.

4. *Isolation of specific DNA strands.* DNA fragments separated by gel electrophoresis begin to disintegrate within a day or two. Permanent preservation is achieved via the "Southern Blot" technique, which isolates single strands for more detailed examination. To accomplish this end, DNA is first denatured from its original double helix into a single strand, thus freeing nucleotides to base-pair with DNA probes in the final step (described below). A positively charged nylon membrane is used to lift negatively charged DNA from the agarose gel (the "blot"). Since DNA

remains invisible at this stage, one more step is required to permit visual comparison.

5. *Imprinting of the DNA on film.* Specific VNTR sequences on a DNA strand are located by means of a "DNA probe," created from a sequence complementary to that of a known VNTR locus, which binds to matching sequences on the nylon membrane. The probe includes a radioactive compound that allows it to be located and to produce a picture of the DNA strand via direct contact with special X-ray film. The final DNA photograph displays dark bands at each point where the DNA probe has bound itself to the suspect sample.

Mathematics finally determines identity when DNA strands are compared. A match on one VNTR locus is no more significant than a single digit lifted from a suspect's street address, where millions of addresses may contain, for example, the number 3.

DNA Evidence

Comparison of many loci found on different chromosomes, however, tell a very different story. Each VNTR locus has about 30 length variants (alleles), each of which occurs at a known frequency within the human population. When these are multiplied, using four loci, the odds of replicating a particular allele combination are approximately one in 5 million. The FBI typically tests 13 loci, with 26 different DNA bands, pegging the odds of two unrelated individuals matching the same profile at more than one in 100 *billion*. Since the entire population of Earth is less than 7 billion (in 2002), DNA "fingerprint" identification may fairly be labeled conclusive.

As a new form of evidence in the 1980s and early 1990s, DNA faced challenges from courts and attorneys who questioned the value of the testing as positive evidence. Most jurors still have only a vague understanding of DNA analysis and require a crash course in the testing procedure at trial, before they can reach an informed verdict. Even then, prosecu-

tors and defense attorneys have no recourse against jurors who misunderstand the evidence or simply refuse to consider it. A prime example was the case of ORENTHAL JAMES (O. J.) SIMPSON, acquitted of double murder in 1995 despite damning DNA evidence from the crime scene. In the wake of Simpson's acquittal, one juror told reporters: "I didn't understand the DNA stuff at all. To me it was just a waste of time. It was way out there and carried absolutely no weight with me."

Various improvements in DNA analysis have made the identification of subjects more streamlined and more precise since testing was initiated. RFLP analysis requires large amounts of relatively high-quality DNA, so that small or contaminated samples often yield inconclusive results. In 1983, California scientist Kary Mullins developed an alternative, the *polymerase chain reaction* (PCR) system, which permits amplification of very small DNA samples. (The procedure earned a Nobel Prize in chemistry for Mullins

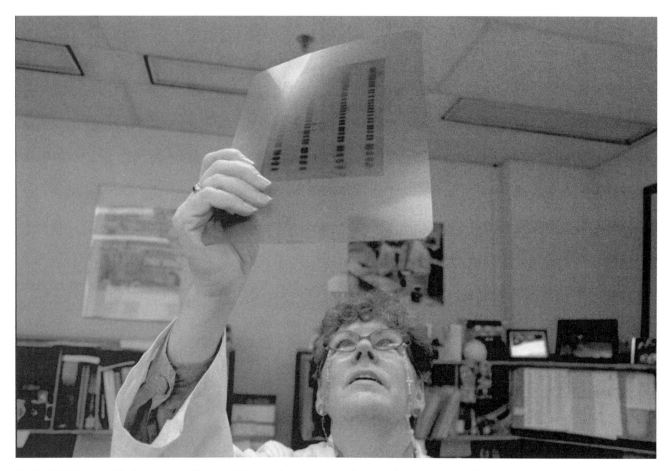

At the FBI National Laboratory in Boston, DNA analysis is carried out to find evidence related to certain criminal cases. (Amy Toensing/CORBIS SYGMA)

in 1993.) With the PCR system, a tiny amount of specific DNA can be replicated exponentially within hours, thus making the test sample virtually unlimited.

Aside from capability of testing smaller samples, science has also devised new ways of extracting DNA from sources formerly too difficult or too contaminated for use as evidence. Several nations, including Britain and the United States, have built extensive DNA databases, collecting unique profiles by the hundreds of thousands from military personnel, convicted felons, government employees, and voluntary submissions from the general public at large. Crime labs have improved training of technicians and have established formal protocols for handling DNA evidence, thus reducing contamination of samples. The most common forensic uses of DNA evidence today are proving guilt, exonerating innocent suspects, establishing paternity, and identifying anonymous human remains.

Conviction of criminals who leave genetic material at a crime scene is vastly simpler today than 20 years ago, when blood type and hairs were merely deemed "consistent" between a suspect and recovered crime scene evidence. A suspect with a common blood type might be convicted of rape or some other serious crime, when the only other evidence against him is a mistaken eyewitness identification—and indeed, many U.S. prison inmates convicted on precisely such evidence have been exonerated since the advent of DNA testing. Comparison of suspect samples with a database of known offenders often surprises investigators. British police, for example, report that their database of 360,000 DNA profiles from repeat offenders scores more than 500 positive matches in outstanding cases per week. The United States lags behind that impressive total, with Virginia authorities reporting 10 cases solved per week by DNA, while detectives in Washington state cleared five "cold" cases with the new technology in July 2001 (including three old rape cases solved in one day). A disturbing case in point from the United States is that of DENNIS FRITZ, where belated DNA testing identified the perpetrator of an Oklahoma rape-murder as one of the chief prosecution witnesses used to convict an innocent defendant at trial.

Even DNA from pets may be useful in solving a criminal case. The men who murdered Elizabeth Ballard in 1998, planting her corpse in the New Mexico desert, were captured after police recovered a single dog hair from the victim's body, and later matched it via DNA testing to a pit bull owned by one of the killers. Blood from a Seattle dog helped convict the gang members who murdered its owners. Traces of dog feces on another suspect's shoe sent him to prison for an Indiana triple murder. Dog urine sprayed on a truck tire in Iowa identified the pickup's driver as a prime suspect in the dog owner's death. Beth Davis, speaking for a veterinary genetics lab in Davis, California, told the press in 2001: "A lot of the technology is a fallout from the human genome project. We just applied that to animals."

Encouraged by such cases, police have eagerly applied DNA technology to their backlog of unsolved crimes. Texas became the first state to indict an unknown rapist solely on the basis of DNA evidence, in August 2001. The offender remains unknown today, but his "John Doe" indictment prevents a five-year statute of limitations from protecting him in the event that he is ultimately captured. New Hampshire police used DNA to convict 40-year-old Joseph Whittey of murder in 2001, 20 years after he killed and sexually assaulted an elderly widow, and they now hope DNA may help them solve 26 more slayings from the 1990s.

DNA evidence is especially helpful in linking serial offenses, when rapists or killers often travel widely to avoid detection, counting on a lack of communication between police departments to cover their tracks. In Fort Collins, Colorado, analysis of DNA samples from an unknown subject who raped five women between May and September 2001 linked the offender to six more rapes and a murder committed in Pennsylvania between July 1997 and August 1999. Without DNA profiles, police departments separated by some 1,750 miles would have no clue that they were seeking the same predator. August 2001 saw authorities in Michigan use DNA to link crimes committed between 1986 and 1990, though the killer still remains at large. Washington state detectives believed one serial killer was responsible for 11 murders of women on the Yakima Indian reservation, until DNA evidence linked imprisoned convict John Bill Fletcher Jr. with two of the slayings, while clearing him of nine others. In Vancouver, British Columbia, where 50 prostitutes are missing and presumed murdered since the 1980s, detectives scoured a farm for evidence in February 2002 and used DNA samples from kin of the victims to indict suspect Robert William Pickton on two counts of first-degree murder.

Exoneration of those falsely accused or imprisoned is perhaps the greatest public service performed by DNA analysts, since it remedies injustice *and* informs authorities (if they were not already conscious of the fact) that unknown criminals remain at large. DNA cleared its first innocent suspect, a British citizen accused of two rape-murders, in 1985. Since the late 1980s, more than 100 U.S. prison inmates have been liberated after DNA analysis proved they were innocent of murder, rape, or other heinous crimes. Ten have been freed from death row, condemned for the crimes of others, and those cases—including several deliberate FRAME-UPS by corrupt authorities—have sparked new debates over capital punishment in America. Illinois governor George Ryan declared a moratorium on executions in January 2000, after learning that 13 inmates had been wrongfully sentenced to death. Nationwide, FBI analysts report, DNA analysis of crime scene evidence exonerates primary suspects in 30 percent of all cases examined. That statistic alone offers cause for concern, with its implication that nearly one-third of all inmates convicted on less precise evidence—blood type alone, "consistent" hairs, etc.—may indeed be innocent.

Exoneration of the innocent—or confirmation of guilt, in some cases—is not inexpensive. In July 2000, San Diego, California, authorities began a review of 560 convictions obtained prior to 1992, when DNA testing became routine. The tab: $5,000 per case. Prosecutors in other jurisdictions refuse to perform the tests themselves, leaving defendants to raise the money by any means available. Organizations like the CARDOZO INNOCENCE PROJECT do their part, but they are perpetually short of funds, fighting time and official intransigence on behalf of penniless defendants.

State opposition to DNA review is particularly strident in cases where inmates have already been executed, while maintaining their innocence to the bitter end. A case in point, now under review, is that of Ellis Wayne Felker, in Georgia. Felker was condemned for the 1981 rape slaying of 19-year-old Evelyn Ludlam. His case made national headlines when the U.S. Supreme Court agreed to review it on an expedited basis, examining his challenge of a new statute curtailing federal appeals. The court refused to delay Felker's execution on grounds that new evidence of his innocence had not been discovered, and

he was electrocuted on November 15, 1996. Today, though private attorneys pursue posthumous DNA testing in Felker's case, his prosecutors scorn the effort as "a total waste of time."

The new vogue in DNA testing has created a vast backlog of cases awaiting disposition. By July 2000, evidence from 180,000 American rape cases was stored in various labs around the country, each item waiting its turn while trials are placed on hold, justice delayed for victims and defendants alike. Aside from cases still awaiting trial, more than 1 million American convicts have petitioned for DNA tests in their various cases. If only 5 percent are truly innocent—versus the FBI's prevailing 30 percent—it means some 50,000 innocent persons are caged in the United States for crimes they did not commit.

Thousands of persons—some sources say *hundreds* of thousands—disappear without a trace each year in the United States. At the same time, authorities discover the remains of *hundreds* who may never be identified. Decomposition may obscure not only a corpse's identity, but also cause of death, leaving the question of natural death versus accident or homicide forever unanswered. Nationwide, thousands of families seek closure, mourning the unexplained loss of their children, siblings, parents, or spouses.

Prior to the advent of DNA testing, "John Doe" or "Jane Doe" remains were sometimes identified via dental records, skeletal abnormalities, or (if flesh remained) by means of scars, tattoos, and birthmarks. Today, bone fragments or a single strand of hair may be sufficient for identification, provided that DNA is found within the sample. Where known DNA from a missing person is available—as from blood or tissue samples—a positive match can normally be made. If no samples exist from the subject himself, technicians can still use the methods applied in paternity testing to see if the deceased was related to members of a particular family, thereby resolving the issue in most cases.

In September 2001, after several nationally publicized cases of babies switched at birth in hospital maternity wards, a Wisconsin company called Innovative Control Systems announced development of a new "Surelink" DNA kit, designed to prevent such mistakes. The kit screens DNA from blood found in the infant's umbilical cord and a sample from the mother, both collected in the delivery room. The samples are placed in a tamper-proof pouch and filed in a secure location, where the DNA material allegedly remains intact and testable for at least a decade. If questions of maternity arise within that time, the genetic evidence is available to resolve all doubts.

More common by far than switched infants is the threat of child abduction in America. Authorities disagree on the frequency of such incidents, but recent FBI estimates claim an average of 300 "stranger abductions" per year, for an average of one kidnapping every 29 hours. Some of those victims are recovered without injury; others are molested or murdered; some are never seen again. In a few bizarre cases, pedophiles or other mentally unstable individuals have held children captive for years on end, imposing new identities that override a child's initial memories of home and family. When children are found dead, as in the notorious Lindbergh case from 1932, decomposition may retard identification or obscure cause of death.

Authorities in various states hope DNA testing may remedy some of those problems. Science cannot protect children from predators, but at least it can attempt to verify identity when they are found at last, alive or dead. In August 2001, Indiana State Police officers began distributing kits that allow parents to collect and store DNA samples from their children, with 1,000 kits passed out in Evansville alone by January 2002. Presumably the kits would replace more traditional fingerprint cards, especially for children under seven years of age, whose FINGER-PRINTS are often indistinct and difficult to read. The kits require no blood samples, instead relying on swabs taken from a child's mouth. Commercial kits typically cost between $25 and $75, but authorities note that parents can achieve the same result by keeping a child's used toothbrush, along with hair samples (roots included), and storing the items in a freezer against future need.

DNA testing is sometimes useful in famous criminal cases, as well as the obscure. Following the East Coast terrorist attacks of September 11, 2001, many victims killed in the explosion and collapse of New York's World Trade Center were too badly damaged for simple identification by visual means. DNA testing was employed in the worst cases, using samples obtained from toothbrushes, hairbrushes, and other known belongings of those trapped in the rubble. By October 24, 2001, eight victims had been identified using DNA evidence exclusively. As Marion DeBlase told reporters, following identification of her husband, James, "You have to come to some

kind of closure somehow, as each day goes by, but it's very difficult to come to terms with it when you have nothing to hold on to." With initial estimates of 4,339 missing (later reduced to less than 3,000), police had collected some 2,600 DNA samples from family members by late October.

On the very day of the New York terrorist attacks, media reports noted the emergence of DNA evidence in another famous case. In 1975, ex-convict James Riddle Hoffa was fighting to regain control of the Teamsters Union, lost when he was imprisoned for bribery and jury-tampering in the 1960s. Although granted clemency by President Richard Nixon in 1972, Hoffa was barred for a decade from participating in union affairs—a ruling he bitterly contested, described by some reporters as part of a corrupt bargain between Nixon and reigning Teamster president Frank Fitzsimmons. Hoffa disappeared on July 30, 1975, when he left home to keep a lunch date with union and underworld acquaintances at a Michigan restaurant. The presumed victim of a gangland murder "contract," Hoffa remains missing today, while theories abound as to where and how his remains were concealed.

On September 11, 2001, FBI spokesmen announced that DNA tests had identified samples of Hoffa's hair recovered from a car driven by Charles ("Chuckie") O'Brien on the day of Hoffa's disappearance. O'Brien, 66 years old in 2001 and retired to Florida, was raised in Hoffa's home but never formally adopted by the family. For more than a quarter-century he denied Hoffa's presence in the vehicle the day he disappeared, but federal agents now refute that claim. No charges have been filed to date, and Hoffa's daughter, St. Louis municipal judge Barbara Crancer, remains skeptical that the murder will ever be solved. "Unless they can break Chuckie down," she told *USA Today,* "I don't see it moving forward." Crancer's brother, James P. Hoffa, is the current Teamsters Union president and has urged investigators to pursue the case aggressively. The "new" evidence was revealed only after the *Detroit Free Press* filed a lawsuit under the Freedom of Information Act, forcing the FBI to open its files on the Hoffa case. Assistant U.S. Attorney Keith Corbett told reporters the obvious: "This is a 26-year-old case. There are a lot of hurdles to get over in bringing a case after this long."

With the advance of DNA testing, new legislation has evolved to control its application in criminal cases.

Congress, on October 2, 2000, passed a law to provide individual states with federal grants to expedite testing of evidence collected from crime scenes and from convicted offenders. The money was expected to benefit states like Michigan, where 15,000 blood samples from known sex offenders had been collected since 1991, with barely 500 samples analyzed and catalogued during the next nine years. The bill was introduced by Rep. Bart Stupak, who told reporters, "Right now, state and local police departments cannot deal with the number of DNA samples from convicted offenders and unsolved crimes. States simply do not have enough time, money or resources to test and record these samples."

At the same time, juvenile offenders in Kentucky were exempted from providing DNA samples for a newly established database on sexual offenders. That decision was announced on August 21, 2001, by the Kentucky Court of Appeals. Acting in the case of a juvenile sex offender identified only as "J.D.K.," convicted of molesting and sodomizing his nine-year-old sister and an eight-year-old friend, the court unanimously ruled that juveniles could not be required to contribute DNA samples for state police files, where DNA profiles of 3,200 adult sex offenders already reside. Critics of the decision noted that many repeat offenders (including serial killers) commit their first sexual assaults in adolescence, thus granting opportunity for swift identification in later cases if samples are preserved, but the Kentucky judges felt themselves constrained by state law. As Judge Sara Combs declared from the bench, "By employing the words 'convicted' and 'felony'—words which the legislature itself has expressly defined and to which it has given technical meaning—it is plainly intended that juveniles adjudicated in district court not be included in the DNA database." (In Kentucky and most other jurisdictions, felonies are those offenses punishable by confinement for one year or more in state prison.)

States have adopted various methods in their efforts to compile useful DNA databases. Some states make sample contribution mandatory for convicted criminals, with jailers in Maine and New York empowered to place reluctant donors in solitary confinement, there extracting the samples by force if necessary. California's legislature adopted a different approach, assigning misdemeanor penalties to inmates who withhold DNA samples, but requiring prison officials to obtain separate court orders for each sample forcibly obtained. About 40 percent of California's prison inmates are presently "required" to donate DNA samples, but the misdemeanor statute carries no weight with those serving long terms—particularly inmates jailed for life or condemned to death row. Compared to the risk of indictment for additional SEX CRIMES or murders, the threat of misdemeanor punishment—a maximum of one year's confinement in county jail—is no threat at all. To date, California has collected DNA profiles on 200,000 inmates convicted of qualifying felonies, but hundreds more resist and fight costly delaying actions in the courts. Inmate Fred Clark, serving 20 years at Vacaville's state medical facility, spoke for many other California inmates when he challenged authorities, saying, "If I don't submit, what are you going to do? Put me in jail? I tell you what. When I die, you can have all the DNA you want."

The reaction of local prosecutors to DNA testing varies from one location to the next. All are happy to use the new technology in pursuing convictions, but many resist application of testing to cases already resolved. San Diego provides a welcome change from official obstructionism, prosecutors volunteering in July 2000 to offer free DNA testing for any inmates claiming the results would set them free. Texas, by contrast, leads all other states in executions and in fighting to the last ditch against reviews of evidence in old cases. A state law enacted in April 2001 permits Texas inmates to seek post-conviction DNA analysis, but prosecutors in some jurisdictions seek to undermine the law by disposing of evidence before it can be tested. In December 2001, eight months after the statute took effect, the *Houston Press* reported that Harris County prosecutors were busily destroying rape kits, bloody clothing, semen swabs and other items of biological evidence from sexual assault cases. A prior statute permits county clerks to destroy trial evidence two years after conviction in noncapital felonies where a defendant is sentenced to more than five years, thus rendering DNA tests impossible in many cases. A spokesperson for the Harris County district attorney reported that 2,740 pounds of evidence had been destroyed in October and December 2001.

Under President Bill Clinton, the U.S. Justice Department set aside $750,000 for DNA testing of convicted felons, to resolve doubt in dubious cases, but Republican attorney general John Ashcroft scuttled the program in December 2001, announcing that the money would be used instead for identification of World Trade Center victims killed in the September 11 terrorist attacks. Justice spokesman Charles Miller assured reporters that "there's nothing sinister here," but some defense attorneys claimed to see a pattern in the new administration's disregard for civil rights (and President George W. Bush's record of excusing slipshod prosecution tactics during his stint as governor of Texas). John Pray, a professor at the University of Wisconsin Law School in Madison, opined, "It's safe to say that if you take away $750,000 that was earmarked, there's going to be some people who would have taken the test that would have proved them innocent." Virginia defense attorney Jerry Lyell was more direct, telling the press in response to Ashcroft's announcement, "It sounds a little fishy. To hear them cutting back, especially such a small amount comparatively . . . might suggest that their hearts weren't in the right place in the first place."

DONDERO, John A. (1900–1957)

A New York native, born November 11, 1900, John Dondero graduated from the City College of New York in 1923, with a degree in chemical engineering. His career took a surprising turn at a Manhattan dinner party in the early 1930s, where he shared a table with pioneer FINGERPRINT expert John Faurot. They discussed the problems caused by inks that smeared when fingerprints were taken, and Dondero—inspired by the hospital footprints of his infant daughter—soon developed a new inkless fingerprinting pad. Dondero soon quit his job and teamed with Faurot to create the Faurot Forensic Company, manufacturing crime-detection equipment with an emphasis on fingerprinting. In 1944, Dondero helped identify all but one of 168 victims killed in a tragic circus-tent fire at Hartford, Connecticut. After World War II, collaborating with the New York City Police Department, he founded a school to teach fingerprinting techniques.

Dondero died in August 1957, but his contributions to forensic science are posthumously honored via the INTERNATIONAL ASSOCIATION OF IDENTIFICATION's John A. Dondero Memorial Award. The award, bestowed for a year's most significant contribution to identification and related sciences, has been granted to only 18 recipients since its creation in 1958. The first honoree was FBI director J. Edgar Hoover.

DOSWELL, Thomas exonerated by DNA

In March 1986, a 48-year-old white female employee of a Pittsburgh, Pennsylvania, hospital was raped in the hospital's cafeteria by a black assailant armed with a knife. Another hospital employee interrupted the attack, prompting the rapist to flee. Yet another employee chased the attacker for three blocks before losing him in traffic. Police transported the victim to a second hospital, where an examination produced semen traces but no other physical evidence. Detectives subsequently showed the victim several photographs of potential suspects, whereupon she selected a photo of 25-year-old Thomas Doswell. At trial in November 1986, the victim and one coworker identified Doswell as the attacker. Although a forensic serologist found A, B, and H antigens in the rapist's semen, the test proved nothing, since the victim was an AB secretor whose blood type masked the offender's. Based on eyewitness testimony alone, jurors convicted Doswell of rape, criminal attempt, simple assault, terroristic threats, and unlawful restraint. He received an aggregate sentence of 13 to 26 years in prison.

Doswell's appeals of his conviction stressed the unreliability of eyewitness identification, noting that of all the photographs displayed to the victim in March 1986, his alone was marked with a letter "R" denoting a previous rape charge. (Doswell was not convicted in that case, and Philadelphia police no longer mark suspects' mug shots.) His various appeals were rejected, but Doswell persisted. In 1996, he contacted the CARDOZO INNOCENCE PROJECT. Two years later, he requested DNA testing of the semen collected in 1986, but another court rejected that appeal on grounds that it was filed too late. Finally, in 2004, Innocence Project staffers and attorney James DePasquale traced the evidence to a police property room and filed a new motion for DNA testing. That motion was granted in March 2005, and the test exonerated Doswell as a suspect in the case. He was released from prison on August 1, 2005, after serving 19 years for a crime he did not commit. The case remains unsolved today.

DOTSON, Gary exonerated by DNA evidence

On the night of July 9, 1977, a Chicago woman told police she had been kidnapped and raped by two men while walking near her home. The attackers allegedly forced her into a car and assaulted her there, one man afterward trying to scratch words on her stomach with a broken beer bottle. Composite sketches of the two men were prepared, and the woman later identified suspect Gary Dotson from a police mug book, then picked him out of a lineup. Semen stains from the woman's underpants matched Dotson's blood type, and a pubic hair recovered from her clothing was deemed "similar" to Dotson's. Convicted of rape and aggravated KIDNAPPING in July 1979, Gary Dotson received a prison term of 25 to 50 years.

The case began to unravel in March 1985, when the alleged victim recanted her testimony, reporting that she had lied to conceal a consensual act of sex with her boyfriend. Dotson's judge refused to order a new trial, insisting that the "victim's" original testimony was more believable than her new statement, eight years after the fact. The governor of Illinois likewise refused to accept the woman's revised statement and denied Dotson's petition for a pardon, but on March 12, 1985, he did commute Dotson's sentence to time served, pending good behavior. That parole was revoked in 1987, after Dotson's wife accused him of domestic violence, and the Appellate Court of Illinois affirmed Dotson's rape conviction on November 12, 1987. The governor granted Dotson a "last chance parole" on December 24, 1987, but an arrest for barroom brawling two days later sent Dotson back to prison once more.

In 1988, Dotson's new lawyer submitted the original trial evidence for DNA testing, unknown at the time of conviction nine years earlier. Those tests excluded Dotson as a donor of semen samples from the victim's clothing, and a new trial was ordered by the Cook County Criminal Court. In light of the DNA evidence and their "victim's" shaky credibility, prosecutors declined to retry the case. Dotson's conviction was overturned on August 14, 1989, after he had served a total of eight years in prison.

DOUGLAS, John Edward (1945–)

A Brooklyn native, born in 1945, Douglas is the first to admit that he was "no academic standout" in high school. Rejected by Cornell University, he enrolled at Montana State, in Bozeman, where he struggled to maintain a D average. In 1966, with the war in Vietnam heating up, Douglas joined the U.S. Air Force to avoid an army draft and was stationed in New Mexico, where he finished work for his B.A. He

also became fast friends with a local FBI agent, who urged him to join the bureau after his discharge from military service in 1970.

The FBI accepted Douglas, and he spent his first year as an agent in Detroit, assigned to the Reactive Crimes Unit, which investigated bank robberies, KIDNAPPINGS, and similar federal offenses. A year later, transferred to Milwaukee, he filled a similar position while doubling as a member of the FBI's SWAT team. Recalled to the FBI Academy for training as a hostage negotiator in 1975, Douglas met instructor and fellow agent ROBERT RESSLER, assigned to the Behavioral Science Unit. They became friends, and Ressler recommended Douglas for a job with the unit in July 1977. Together and separately, they conducted many prison interviews with convicted killers over the next six years as part of the BSU's Criminal Personality Research Project, leading to creation of the Violent Criminal Apprehension Program (VICAP) in 1985. Ressler retired five years later, whereupon Douglas replaced him as chief of the BSU—renamed Investigative Support Services—and held that post until his own retirement in 1995.

Although involved at the periphery of many infamous serial murder cases and often described as the model for fictional G-man Jack Crawford in the novels *Red Dragon* and *The Silence of the Lambs*, Douglas did not personally track and arrest serial killers. Still, the job had its dangers, including a schedule so hectic and stressful that it drove Douglas to a near-fatal brain hemorrhage in December 1983, while visiting Seattle to consult on the case of the "GREEN RIVER KILLER."

Although he was interviewed frequently and gave countless lectures while serving with the FBI, true fame found Douglas only in retirement, with several best-selling books, countless TV talk-show appearances, and a lucrative sideline in private consultation on criminal cases such as the infamous JonBenét Ramsey murder in Boulder, Colorado. Books coauthored by Douglas include *Sexual Homicide* (1988), the FBI's *Crime Classification Manual* (1992), *Mind Hunter* (1995), *Unabomber* (1996), *Journey into Darkness* (1997), *Obsession* (1998), *The Anatomy of Motive* (1999), *The Cases That Haunt Us* (2000), and *Anyone You Want Me to Be* (2003).

Ironically, Douglas's celebrity has evoked public hostility from his one-time mentor, Robert Ressler, who has criticized Douglas for his "flamboyance" and denounced claims that Douglas "went face-to-face" with serial killer John Gacy, when prison records prove Douglas and Gacy never met. (In fairness to Douglas, the claim was apparently made by a press agent, rather than Douglas himself; it appears nowhere in any of his published books.) When Douglas joined the Ramsey defense team in Boulder, announcing his "gut instinct" that the victim's parents were innocent of her murder, Ressler publicly questioned his judgment, describing Douglas in one interview as "a Hollywood type of guy." Douglas, for his part, has thus far declined to participate in public squabbling with his former boss.

DUNCAN, Andrew, Sr. (1744–1828)

A native of Scotland, born in 1744, Andrew Duncan studied medicine and joined the staff of Edinburgh University in his late 20s. Personal observation convinced him that forensic science—still unnamed in the 18th century—was not applied consistently or effectively to legal cases in his homeland. Duncan's personal prestige, including service as physician to the king of England and the Prince of Wales upon their visits to Scotland, aided Duncan in his efforts to advance forensic medicine. As a prolific author and editor of the pioneering journal *Medical Com-* *mentaries,* Duncan promoted forensic medicine at every opportunity. He chaired the Institutes of Medicine at Edinburgh University from 1790 to 1821 and also served as the university's first professor of medical jurisprudence, establishing a formal department for such studies (with his son, Andrew Jr., as chairman) in 1807. Additionally, Dr. Duncan founded the Edinburgh Royal Public Dispensary and the Royal Edinburgh Asylum, while serving at various times as president of the Royal Medical Society and the Royal College of Physicians of Edinburgh. He died in 1828, leaving his son to carry on the family's work.

DURHAM, Timothy Edward exonerated by DNA evidence

An Oklahoma college student, Timothy Durham was accused of molesting an 11-year-old Tulsa County girl in 1991. At trial in 1993, 11 alibi witnesses testified that Durham was 300 miles away from Tulsa when the crime occurred, but jurors convicted him regardless, and the court imposed a stunning sentence of 3,120 years in prison. DNA tests performed in 1997 proved Durham innocent, and he was subsequently released from prison. The crime remains unsolved today.

E

EASTMAN, Richard Mark indicted on DNA evidence
Police in Peel, Ontario, were baffled by the murder of 63-year-old Muriel Holland, raped and strangled to death at a local senior's home on August 27, 1991. Eleven years and four months elapsed before they finally broke the case, as a result of Canadian legislation requiring all defendants convicted of serious offenses to provide blood samples for a national DNA data bank. Richard Eastman was serving time for an unrelated felony when lab technicians matched his DNA to semen samples lifted from the Holland crime scene in 1991. Authorities charged him with first-degree murder in January 2002, evoking public expressions of gratitude from Holland's family. Eastman denies involvement in the murder, and his trial has not been held thus far. He is presumed innocent until convicted by a jury of his peers.

ECOLOGY, Forensic
Ecology is the branch of BIOLOGY dealing with the relations between organisms and their environment. Forensic ecology applies that study to the legal matters, chiefly (but not exclusively) in the field of locating bodies and charting time of death. Its subdisciplines include forensic BOTANY, ENTOMOLOGY, GEOLOGY, and LIMNOLOGY.

As an example, the discovery of a decomposed corpse without specific documents or other clues to its identity may baffle police at the onset of their investigation. Nonetheless, a survey of the body reveals much about when and where the person died. Knowledge of fly and other insect infestation give the forensic entomologist a good idea of when the corpse was first exposed. Analysis of other trace evidence found on the body—including soil, pollen, and other plant material—helps determine whether death occurred at the place where the body was found or if the corpse has been transported. Furthermore, the same materials can link the body to a primary crime scene, facilitated by the forensic ecologist's knowledge of where various plants and soils are normally found. Thus, a body found in the woods, bearing sand from a particular beach, silently directs investigators to a new location—and may bring them one step closer to finding the killer.

ELECTROPHORESIS
Electrophoresis is a method of separating macro molecules—chiefly proteins or nucleic acids (DNA and RNA)—and analyzing their molecular structure based on rate of movement through a colloidal suspension while they are subjected to an electric field. That movement, also called *cataphoresis,* proceeds through a buffer solution at different speeds based on the size of the respective molecules, small molecules traveling farther than larger ones. The various types of electrophoresis include:

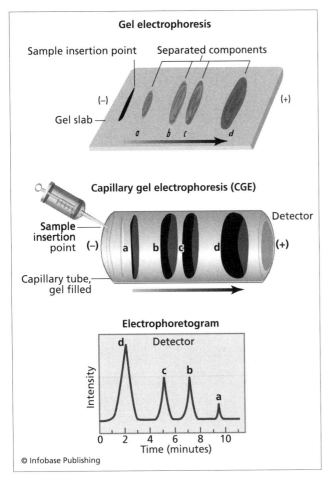

Gel electrophoresis

Sample insertion point
Separated components
(–)
Gel slab
a   b   c   d
(+)

Capillary gel electrophoresis (CGE)

Sample insertion point
(–)
a   b   c   d
(+)
Detector
Capillary tube, gel filled

Electrophoretogram

d
Detector
c   b
a
Intensity
0   2   4   6   8   10
Time (minutes)

© Infobase Publishing

Performance of capillary electrophoresis relative to slab gel electrophoresis. In the slab, an electrical field causes proteins to migrate, their speed dependent on their size. This process occurs analogously inside the capillary tube, and a detector signal is used to create the electropherogram, which registers the results.

Gel electrophoresis, pioneered in the 1950s, involves suspending a sample in buffer solution which is then applied to a flat slab of gel—typically agarose (or agar, made from seaweed) or polyacrylamide. With the application of electricity, the gel serves as a "molecular sieve," separating various molecules by size. After staining, the separated macromolecules appear as a series of bands spread from one end of the gel to the other. Limiting factors in gel electrophoresis include a limitation to low voltage (thus avoiding destructive heat) and occasional problems detecting the macromolecules with stain.

Capillary electrophoresis solves both of those problems by replacing the flat gel slab with a glass capillary tube, filled with buffer solution, whose surface radiates and thus reduces heat while permitting use of higher voltages. Detection of migrating molecules is achieved by shining light through a part of the tube, producing an *electropherogram* that reveals the relative speed of different molecules proceeding through the tubes in *electroosmotic flow.* Various types of capillary electrophoresis exist, with those most commonly used in forensic science including *capillary gel electrophoresis,* wherein samples are injected by syringe and "sieved" through gel; *capillary zone electrophoresis,* used primarily for drugs, inks, and gunshot residue; and *micellar capillary electrophoresis,* incorporating elements of CHROMATOGRAPHY and a special medium to isolate neutral (uncharged) molecules.

Crossed-over electrophoresis is used exclusively to identify the species of origin for BLOODSTAINS. After a PRESUMPTIVE TEST for blood is performed at a crime scene and samples are collected, sample extracts are placed into gel near the cathode (negative electrode), while known antibodies for various species are placed near the anode (positive electrode). Application of electricity drives the known antibodies and the questioned sample's antigens toward one another and produces a milk-white precipitate if the suspect antigen meets antibodies from its species of origin. Thus, human blood tested against antibodies from a dog or monkey produces no result. Crossed-over electrophoresis permits simultaneous testing of a suspect sample against multiple species for rapid elimination and/or identification.

ELEMENTAL Analysis

Elemental analysis of unknown substances involves testing to identify a sample's chemical elements. Objects of elemental analysis may include (but are not limited to) CONTROLLED SUBSTANCES, gunshot residue, PAINT, and other items of TRACE EVIDENCE collected during the course of an investigation. Various techniques of elemental analysis include:

Atomic absorption SPECTROSCOPY, also called *flame absorption spectrophotometry,* wherein solid or liquid samples are vaporized in a flame or graphite furnace and exposed to monochromatic light. Atomic composition is determined by the light-absorption rate of the various atoms, but problems may result with inconsistent vaporization of some analytes.

Atomic emission spectroscopy, a technique that measures the light emitted by samples subjected to high-temperature atomization. Some analysts consider this method superior to atomic absorption, but the sample spectra may be congested, requiring a high-resolution spectrometer for successful interpretation.

Mass spectrometry, a system used to perform both ORGANIC and INORGANIC COMPOUND ANALYSIS, wherein samples are ionized by various means to determine the unique atomic weight of their elemental components.

X-ray diffraction, also called *X-ray crystallography,* wherein crystalline samples are exposed to X-rays that bend (diffract) at different angles depending on the atomic structure of the crystals. As in mass spectrometry, X-ray diffraction may be used to identify both organic and inorganic structures.

ELKINS, Clarence controversial DNA case

In 1998, an intruder raped and murdered 58-year-old Judith Johnson at her home in Barberton, Ohio. Johnson's six-year-old granddaughter was also raped and beaten unconscious in the same attack. Police soon focused their attention on Clarence Elkins, Johnson's son-in-law and uncle of the younger victim. The young survivor told police that the attacker "resembled" her uncle, although she only glimpsed him briefly in the dark. Jurors accepted that shaky identification at trial, convicting Elkins of murder, rape, and other charges that sent him to prison for life. Appeals courts were unmoved by the victim's subsequent recantation of her identification, leaving Elkins to stake his hopes for freedom on DNA testing and the OHIO INNOCENCE PROJECT. Testing performed in early 2005 revealed that Elkins's DNA did not match semen samples from the 1998 crime scene. Despite that finding, the Summit County Court of Common Pleas denied a bid for a new trial. In September 2005, further DNA testing matched the crime scene samples to Earl Mann, a convicted child

molester who resembled Elkins and who was known to be present in Barberton at the time of the assaults. A new motion was filed for a retrial, supported by the region's largest daily newspaper, the Akron *Beacon-Journal.* No decision on that motion had been rendered at the time this volume went to press.

ENGINEERING, Forensic

Engineering combines art and science while making practical applications of pure science (CHEMISTRY, MATHEMATICS, METALLURGY, physics, etc.) to the construction of objects as diverse as buildings, bridges and highways, engines and vehicles, tunnels, and mines. Forensic engineers investigate and reconstruct traffic accidents and transportation disasters, explosions, and structural collapses. Their analysis may determine whether specific events were accidental, caused by material failure such as metal fatigue, or resulted from criminal action. In the realm of bridge and building collapses, investigation may reveal the use of shoddy or substandard materials in violation of prevailing law, thereby leading to criminal charges or civil sanctions. Analysis of factors such as static and dynamic loads (constant or variable weight borne by a structure) may reveal whether a building collapsed from its own weight or from external stress exerted by a storm, earthquake, or other force of nature. While many forensic scientists are summoned only to the scenes of crimes, forensic engineers deal also with a broad range of natural events that may result in litigation or affect insurance pay-offs.

ENTOMOLOGY, Forensic

Entomology is the scientific study of arthropods—invertebrates with jointed legs, including insects, arachnids (spiders and scorpions), centipedes, millipedes, and crustaceans (crabs, lobsters, etc.). Forensic entomology applies that study to legal proceedings, chiefly by using insects to determine time of death. Flies are most useful in that respect, since the progression of their life cycle is subject to fairly precise calculation. Based on long study of various flies, including their deliberate exposure to cadavers in natural settings, forensic entomologists know how long it normally takes for eggs to hatch and release wormlike larvae (or *maggots*), for the larvae to feed and develop into pupae (the intermediate stage), then

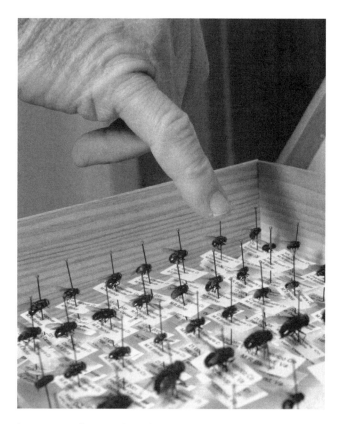

Insect samples used to identify and match bugs found on corpses. The type of bugs found on corpses can help determine how long a person has been deceased. (Andrew Shurtleff/AP)

digestive tracts. Consumption of flesh or fluids from a drugged or poisoned body may also affect the rate of larval and pupal development, thereby altering calculation of the death interval.

ENVIRONMENTAL Forensics

A distinct and separate field from forensic ECOLOGY, environmental forensics involves the detection of illegal pollution and similar actions banned by laws designed to protect Earth's environment. The U.S. Environmental Protection Agency is responsible for enforcing federal statutes in this field, while various state agencies across the country supervise compliance with state laws and regulations. Periodic testing determines whether specific factories, waste disposal plants, and similar facilities comply with all pertinent rules and procedures, where violations may result in fines or punishment. In cases of illegal dumping, analysts seek to identify the firms or individuals responsible and to compile sufficient evidence for a successful prosecution. Sadly, while pollution of the environment with toxic waste may sicken or kill thousands over time, the punishment is commonly restricted to fines that represent only a fraction of a large firm's yearly profits. Prison sentences are rare, and some firms with multiple citations on their records are still favored with lucrative U.S. government contracts—a situation that clearly sends mixed messages (and, some say, smacks of corruption in high places).

to emerge as adults. From those known factors, flies and certain species of beetles allow entomologists to determine how long a corpse has been exposed to insect activity. Naturally, that calculation may not coincide with time of death if the corpse has been frozen, sealed in some kind of airtight container, or otherwise removed from contact with insects.

A scientific field related to forensic entomology is that of *entomotoxicology*. In cases where decomposition or mummification of a corpse is too advanced to permit normal examination of the flesh and fluids for TOXICOLOGY, insects may help determine whether the deceased consumed drugs or poisons. Entomotoxicological examination requires that insects be collected from the corpse or its vicinity and chemically tested in the same way a toxicologist would normally test the body's tissue, hair, or fingernails for traces of lethal substances. Chemicals consumed in human flesh may or may not kill the scavenging insects, but in either case the evidence may still be found in their

ERDMANN, Ralph pathologist who falsified medical evidence

In Texas, where he plied his trade as a circuit-riding medical examiner, Dr. Ralph Erdmann was nicknamed "Dr. Death." He won the moniker from prison inmates and defense attorneys, based on the consistency with which Erdmann provided testimony in felony cases, sending dozens of accused murderers to death row. Apparently a tireless civil servant, Dr. Erdmann operated in 40 of the Lone Star State's 47 counties, once charging prosecutors $171,000 for 400 autopsies in a single year. His medical verdicts invariably supported police theories in the cases he examined—so dependably, in fact, that one investigator later told reporters, "If the prosecution theory was that death was caused by a Martian death ray, then that was what Dr. Erdmann reported."

And therein lay the problem.

Erdmann's reputation began to unravel in 1992, when relatives of one deceased man obtained a copy of Erdmann's autopsy report, noting the weight of a spleen surgically removed years earlier. The body was exhumed, revealing that no autopsy had been performed. Lubbock attorney Tommy Turner was appointed as a special prosecutor to review Erdmann's work. In the process, he examined 100 autopsies and found "good reason to believe at least 30 were false." In fact, as one judge noted, police sometimes refrained from sending bodies to Erdmann because "he wouldn't do the work. He would ask what was the police theory and recite results to coincide with their theories."

When Erdmann did operate, he made bizarre and disturbing mistakes which prosecutors managed to conceal from jurors. In one case, Odessa prosecutors were forced to dismiss murder charges after Erdmann lost the victim's head, including with it the fatal bullet wound. In another he claimed to have examined a victim's brain, but exhumation revealed no cranial incisions. Yet another case found Erdmann mixing organs from two bodies in the same container and offering false testimony on the cause of death. Turner's investigation disclosed that Erdmann sometimes allowed his 13-year-old son to probe wounds during autopsies, and on several occasions his wife sold bones removed from murder victims.

It should not be supposed that Erdmann always ruled defendants guilty, though: if police believed a death was accidental, he could skew the evidence in that direction just as well. One such case involved 14-month-old Anthony Culifer, smothered with a pillow by his mother's live-in boyfriend. Erdmann blamed the child's death on pneumonia, his finding reversed by a second autopsy nine years later. In a similar case, a woman found by Erdmann to have choked on her own vomit was in fact murdered by a violent ex-boyfriend. The killer was eventually sentenced to life imprisonment, while Erdmann was ordered to pay the victim's family $250,000. It was Erdmann's testimony in capital cases that made him most dangerous, though, with at least four defendants executed on his word alone. At least 20 more condemned inmates in Texas have appealed their verdicts since Erdmann's misconduct was revealed.

In 1992, Dr. Erdmann appeared before a judge in Randall County, pleading guilty to seven felony counts of perjury and falsifying autopsy results. It was merely the tip of the iceberg, as civil suits began to multiply across Texas, but authorities seemed satisfied. As part of the plea bargain, Erdmann was stripped of his medical license, sentenced to 10 years' probation with 200 hours of community service, and ordered to repay $17,000 in autopsy fees. He moved to Seattle, Washington, where police found him with a cache of weapons in June 1995, thereby violating terms of his probation. Texas hauled Erdmann back to serve his time, and while he was eligible for parole after serving 30 months, public protests scuttled his first parole bid in March 1997.

(See also: GILCHRIST, JOYCE; ZAIN, FRED).

EUROPEAN Institute for Computer Anti-Virus Research

An unofficial organization devoted to combating computer viruses in Europe and beyond, the European Institute for Computer Anti-Virus Research (EICAR) recruits members from leading universities, industry, government, the military, and law enforcement, while cooperating with the media and privacy advocates "to unite efforts against writing and proliferation of malicious code like computer viruses or Trojan Horses, and, against computer crime, fraud and the misuse of computers or networks, inclusive [of] malicious exploitation of privacy data."

With that broad mission in mind, members of EICAR are pledged to uphold a particular code of conduct that includes the following strictures:

1. "Total abstinence" from any publications or other activity that could promote panic at large—"i.e., no 'trading on people's fears'."
2. "Abstaining from the loud and vociferous superlatives and factually untenable statements in advertising, e.g., 'all known and unknown viruses will be recognised'."
3. Withholding any information suited to development of viruses from unauthorized third parties. Exchange of data between serious researchers and/or research institutions is permitted when all have passed inspection and accept the EICAR code of conduct.

In action, EICAR seeks to operate as a "Cyber Defense Alliance" (CDA), defined by organization spokesmen as "a framework of support that endeavours to create a 'User Friendly Information Society.'"

Reaching beyond the bounds of Europe, the CDA is envisioned as "a global initiative that includes legal frameworks, research, technical measures, and organisational co-operations in support of the objective." More specifically, that objective includes:

- Global cooperation with other security and anti-virus organizations
- Support for the European Commission's Convention on Cyber Crime
- Support for the EC's Research Technology Development Information Security Technology Program
- Warning, verification, and reporting of new computer viruses
- Compilation of a central database on malicious codes
- Establishment of a unified convention for naming new viruses
- Certification and licensing of antivirus researchers with standard recognized requirements
- Support for antivirus research and enhancement of defense mechanisms
- Improved public education and awareness of the problem

By 2001, various EICAR task forces were involved in debate on the issues listed here, developing policy statements while actively continuing research on computer viruses at a more practical level. Constant networking is maintained with similar groups, such as the Asian Anti-Virus Research Association.

EXPLOSIVES

Explosives are energetically unstable chemical compounds or mixtures capable of causing an *explosion*—defined as "a sudden increase in volume and release of energy in a violent manner, usually with the generation of high temperatures and the release of gases." Explosions produce pressure waves and are classified either as *deflagrations* (if those waves are subsonic) or as *detonations* (if the waves are supersonic, also called shock waves). Explosives deflagrate or detonate with application of heat or shock (as in a sudden impact) to a small part of the explosive material, yielding gas and heat as they decompose and rearrange with extreme speed. Otherwise flammable compounds are not deemed "explosive"

unless that reaction can be produced on demand, sometimes assisted by addition of "sanitizers" to the original compound.

Explosives are broadly classified as *low* or *high*, depending on their performance. Low explosives are generally mixtures rather than compounds. They burn at a maximum rate of some 400 meters per second but produce an explosion only if packed into a confined space. Common examples such as black powder and smokeless powder are used chiefly as propellants (in firearms ammunition), or in fireworks, flares, and illumination devices, while other mixtures have been features in various homemade bombs. Two infamous examples of the latter include the car bomb that damaged the World Trade Center in 1993 (composed of urea nitrate and other materials) and the mixture of ammonium nitrate with 6-percent fuel oil that demolished Oklahoma City's Alfred P. Murrah Federal Building on April 19, 1995. Simple pipe bombs also frequently contain low explosives.

High explosives, by contrast, are chemical compounds that detonate at rates of 1,000 to 8,500 meters per second, used primarily in demolition, mining, and in military applications. High explosives are subdivided, based on sensitivity, into *primary* and *secondary* explosives. Primary explosives are extremely sensitive to friction, heat, or shock, burning rapidly or detonating if ignited. They are often used in blasting caps or as primers in firearms cartridges, to ignite larger explosions. Secondary (or base) explosives—including dynamite, HMX, PETN, RDX, SEMTEX, and TNT—are relatively impervious to friction, heat, and shock, commonly requiring a primary explosive charge to produce detonation. Some definitions of high explosives add a *tertiary* class, also called blasting compounds, including the ammonium nitrate/fuel oil mixture (ANFO) mentioned above and classified in other definitions as a low explosive.

Adoption of explosives for military or law enforcement applications requires detailed study of a compound's properties and performance. Factors considered in any such decision include availability and cost; sensitivity to friction, heat, and shock; stability, including chemical composition, safe temperatures for storage, and vulnerability to electrical discharge; and power or performance. The latter is determined by performance of cylinder expansion and fragmentation tests, involving detonation of test charges inside copper cylinders to determine the rate of radial expansion, maximum cylinder wall velocity and maximum distribution of shrapnel.

Explosive warning signs used in the United States and other members of the United Nations display a standard set of numbers and letters used to identify the explosive substance and rate its danger. Numerical rankings are defined as follows:

1.1 – Mass Explosion Hazard
1.2 – Nonmass explosion, fragment-producing
1.3 – Mass fire, minor blast or fragment hazard
1.4 – Moderate fire, no blast or fragment
1.5 – Explosive substance, very insensitive (with a mass explosion hazard)
1.6 – Explosive article, extremely insensitive

Letters are also affixed to the warning signs—as 1.1A, 1.6G, etc.—to further clarify the hazard. Those letters are defined as follows:

A – Primary explosive substance.
B – Articles containing a primary explosive substance and not containing two or more effective protective features (including some primers and detonator assemblies, but excluding blasting caps).
C – Propellant explosive substances and other deflagrating explosive substances or articles containing such explosive substances.
D – Secondary detonating explosive substances, black powder, or articles containing a secondary detonating explosive substance, without means of initiation and without a propelling charge, or articles containing a primary explosive substance and containing two or more effective protective features.
E – Articles containing a secondary detonating explosive substance without means of initiation, with a propelling charge (other than one containing flammable liquid, gel, or hypergolic liquid).
F – Articles containing a secondary detonating explosive substance with its means of initiation, with a propelling charge (other than one containing flammable liquid, gel, or hypergolic liquid) or without a propelling charge.
G – Pyrotechnic substances, articles containing a pyrotechnic substance, or articles containing both an explosive substance and an illuminating, incendiary, tear- or smoke-producing substance (other than a water-activated article or one containing white phosphorus, phosphide or flammable liquid or gel or hypergolic liquid). Consumer fireworks are often classified 1.4G.
H – Articles containing both an explosive substance and white phosphorus.
J – Articles containing both an explosive substance and flammable liquid or gel.
K – Articles containing both an explosive substance and a toxic chemical agent.
L – Explosive substances or articles containing an explosive substance and presenting a special risk (e.g., due to water activation or presence of hypergolic liquids, phosphides, or pyrophoric substances) needing isolation of each type.
N – Articles containing only extremely insensitive detonating substances.
S – Substances or articles so packed or designed that any hazardous effects arising from accidental functioning are limited, to the extent that they do not significantly hinder or prohibit firefighting or other emergency response efforts in the immediate vicinity of the package. Commercial fireworks are sometimes labeled 1.4S.

Forensic scientists may be called upon to examine the scenes of either accidental or deliberate explosions. While explosions and their commonly resultant fires destroy much evidence, vital traces may still remain. Explosives commercially manufactured in the United States and some other nations contain internal *taggants*, materials designed to survive detonation and identify the compound's manufacturer. Vehicles used in both the World Trade Center and Oklahoma City bombings were traced by their vehicle identification numbers (VIN) to guilty parties who had rented them before the attacks. A bomber's FINGERPRINTS rarely survive an explosion. More hopeful evidence is found in fragments of wire, bomb casings, detonators and/or timing devices that may be traceable to manufacturers or vendors. Examination of those objects, coupled with chemical analysis of explosive mixtures or compounds, may link successive bombings and support charges against a suspect found with similar components in his/her possession.

FAIN, Charles exonerated by DNA evidence

Nine-year-old Daralyn Johnson was kidnapped on February 24, 1982, while walking to school in Nampa, Idaho. School administrators assumed she was absent due to illness, and Daralyn's parents knew nothing of her disappearance until she failed to return home that afternoon. Police soon learned that she had never reached the school. Her corpse was found three days later, in a ditch near the Snake River. Autopsy results showed that Daralyn had been raped, then drowned. Pubic hairs from an unknown subject were retrieved from her underpants and one stocking.

Seven months after the murder, an informant directed police to sanitation worker Charles Fain. Detectives noted that his light-brown hair appeared to match the hairs recovered from Daralyn's body. Fain also resided one block from Daralyn's home in September 1982, but at the time of the murder he had lived 360 miles away, in Redmond, Oregon. At his second interrogation, in October 1982, Fain agreed to a polygraph examination and passed it, the examiner reporting that Fain told the truth when he denied participation in Daralyn's rape and murder.

Still, local prosecutors charged him with the crime and held Fain for trial in 1983. The polygraph results were inadmissible in court, and while an Oregon librarian testified on Fain's behalf, describing him as a regular customer around the time of the Idaho murder, jurors chose to believe an FBI technician who described the crime scene hairs as "similar" and "consistent" to Fain's. Convicted of first-degree murder, KIDNAPPING and rape, Fain was sentenced to death in February 1984. Still maintaining his innocence, he converted to Christianity in prison and joined fellow inmates in a legal contest for the right to hold religious services on death row (victorious in 1989).

DNA analysis was unknown at the time of Fain's conviction and death sentence, but science caught up with his case in 2001, after he had served more than 17 years in prison. "Overall," he told reporters, "I believed I was going to get out because I was innocent. When this DNA stuff started coming on the news, something just told me it was going to be part of this case." Indeed, testing proved beyond doubt that the pubic hairs found on Daralyn Johnson's body in 1984 were not Fain's, a result confirmed by independent prosecution testing on June 28, 2001. One week later, Idaho attorney general Al Lance joined defense attorneys in petitioning a federal court to grant Fain a writ of habeas corpus. U.S. District Judge B. Lynn Winmill voided Fain's conviction on July 6, 2001, and remanded his case to the original trial court for further action.

Attorney General Lance, while cooperative to a point, still declared, "It is important to the interests of justice that there be no misunderstanding as to the meaning of this announcement. DNA testing was not available at the time of Fain's trial and conviction.

It is available today and, appropriately, has been used in this case. While this new evidence does show the need for further review, it would be wrong to say that it proves Fain's innocence. The DNA testing proves only one thing. It proves that the pubic hairs found on the victim's clothing did not belong to Charles Fain. That fact in itself does not mean that Fain did not commit these crimes. This evidence does not exonerate Mr. Fain."

And yet, despite such face-saving pronouncements, it did precisely that. Fain was released from custody on August 24, 2001, after prosecutors declined to retry the case against him, formally dismissing the charges. Fain expressed no bitterness at the system that had falsely imprisoned him, telling journalists, "I gave that up a long time ago. That is the one thing I know I can do: forgive." To date, the murder of Daralyn Johnson remains unsolved.

FALSE and Inconclusive Evidence

While collection of evidence is vital in every criminal case, examination and interpretation of that evidence may produce misleading or obscure results. Some test results are inconclusive, failing to provide the necessary information to resolve a case—as when a blood drop is too small for reliable typing, when a broken hair lacks the follicle required for DNA testing to match a particular suspect, or when fragments of a shattered bullet frustrate ballistics examiners. In such cases, ethical guidelines demand that expert witnesses refrain from overstating their conclusions to assist one side or the other at trial. When those ethics are breached—as by criminalists JOYCE GILCHRIST and FRED ZAIN—innocent defendants suffer unjust punishment, while the guilty escape and scandal ensues.

False test results need not be the result of some sinister FRAME-UP, however. Evidence may be contaminated at a crime scene (as where blood and other body fluids mingle), or inadvertently after collection (in cases of negligent handling). Testing of contaminated evidence may produce either false positive or false negative results. False positive or negative results are also common in PRESUMPTIVE TESTS, as when various chemical reagents produce the same color changes in samples of horseradish and human blood. Such errors and acceptance of presumptive test results (versus *specific* tests) may result in *false inclusion* or *false exclusion* of individuals from a suspect

pool based on inaccurate data. Likewise, careless collection techniques may result in false analysis of *spurious minutiae,* as when dust or other detritus from a crime scene is collected with FINGERPRINTS, then mistaken for pores and ridges during comparison. Despite its convenience for investigators, computerization of fingerprint records also introduces further opportunities for error. Systems like the AUTOMATED FINGERPRINT IDENTIFICATION SYSTEM (AFIS), for all their speed and technical efficiency, sometimes make mistakes. Expert criminalists recognize a *false classification rate* with such programs, including cases of *false acceptance* and *false rejection* for specific fingerprints. Repeat examinations may be necessary for purposes of quality assurance, particularly where independent evidence tends to incriminate or exonerate a particular suspect. Miscarriages of justice, whether deliberate or inadvertent, victimize the innocent and may discredit the bona fide majority of work performed by respected law enforcement institutions.

FAULDS, Henry (1843–1930)

Born at Beith, Scotland, on June 1, 1843, Henry Faulds left home at age 13 to work as a clerk in Glasgow. Eight years later he enrolled at Glasgow University, where he studied MATHEMATICS, logic, and the classics, later expanding to include medical studies at Anderson College. After obtaining his M.D., Faulds traveled to Japan as a missionary, there becoming superintendent of Tuskiji Hospital and subsequently founding the Tokyo Institute for the Blind. In his spare time, Faulds visited archaeological digs and observed the FINGERPRINTS left by ancient potters in clay. Intrigued, Faulds examined his own fingertips and those of his friends, soon convincing himself that no two were alike. His theory was tested following a BURGLARY at the hospital, when police jailed an employee whom Faulds believed to be innocent. Faulds secured the prisoner's release by comparing his fingerprints with those found at the crime scene. (Curiously, Faulds did not believe each single print was necessarily unique, but rather insisted on a full set of 10 prints to confirm identity.)

Faulds next sought to collaborate on fingerprint study with naturalist Charles Darwin. Darwin refused to participate but passed the notion on to FRANCIS GALTON, a relative, who in turn passed it on to the Royal Anthropological Society. While Galton's research was delayed for a further eight years, Faulds published the first article on forensic fingerprinting in *Nature,* in October 1880. One month later, Sir WILLIAM HERSCHEL wrote to *Nature,* asserting that he had used fingerprints to identify criminals since 1860. Faulds demanded proof and a bitter controversy ensued between the two men. Faulds returned to England in 1886 and offered his fingerprinting system to Scotland Yard, whose leaders rebuffed him in favor of the BERTILLON identification system. A decade later, with fingerprinting in widespread use, Faulds published the first in a series of books and pamphlets claiming that he had been cheated of credit for making the grand discovery. He died in 1930, before his role in the development of fingerprinting was publicly acknowledged.

FAUROT, Joseph A. (1872–1942)

A native of New York City, born on October 14, 1872, Joseph Faurot joined the municipal police department and rose to the rank of detective sergeant by 1904. In that year, while visiting the Louisiana Purchase Exhibition, Faurot observed a display touting forensic use of FINGERPRINTS and found himself intrigued. NYPD Commissioner William McAdoo granted Faurot's request for a leave of absence to study fingerprinting in London, with officers of Scotland Yard, but Faurot returned from England to find his patron sacked, replaced by a conservative commissioner who had no faith in newfangled theories and gadgets. Two years elapsed before Faurot had a chance to prove his technique, following a series of thefts from Manhattan's up-scale hotels. Faurot collared a suspect who identified himself as "James Jones," but fingerprints soon proved the man was one Daniel Nolan, sought by British police for a string of similar crimes.

Thus vindicated, Faurot proceeded to collect a large file of felons' fingerprints. In 1908, NYPD detectives solved their first murder case using fingerprint technology, and three years later career burglar Caesar Cellar became the first U.S. defendant convicted on fingerprint evidence alone. Faurot's successes brought promotion, ultimately boosting him to the rank of deputy commissioner for the NYPD. He participated with FBI agents in the scandalous "Red Raids" of December 1919 and retired from the force seven years later. Ironically, the year of his retirement (1926) also saw Faurot embroiled in a

case of mistaken fingerprint identification. New Jersey's notorious Hall-Mills murder case of 1922 was still unsolved—as it remains today—with rampant speculation surrounding the lover's lane slaying of a prominent minister and his apparent mistress. When three suspects faced trial in 1926, Faurot appeared for the prosecution, testifying that a fingerprint found at the murder scene belonged to defendant William Stevens. Other experts proved Faurot wrong, and all three suspects won acquittal. Faurot died on November 20, 1942.

FBI Computer Crimes Unit

Although the Federal Bureau of Investigation (FBI) has used computers for decades, for all manner of tasks including data storage and FINGERPRINT identification, no concerted effort toward tracking criminals in cyberspace was made in Washington before the late 1990s. The first such unit was apparently based in the Cleveland field office, spawned by an executive order from President Bill Clinton that created a new Infrastructure Protection Task Force. By year's end, similar units were operating from FBI field offices in New York City, San Francisco, and Washington, D.C. On February 25, 1997, the bureau announced that a similar unit would soon be operational in its Los Angeles field office, coordinating efforts across the country. Supervisory special agent John McClurg told reporters, "A number of other cities are actually on the verge of reaching that point in which they have the expertise [in tracking cybercriminals] that is certifiable. Los Angeles is very close. Teams are being formed across the U.S. in the field offices."

As described in FBI press releases, the computer crime unit was designed to bridge a gap between domestic criminal investigations and the bureau's national security function, operating internationally if evidence led investigators beyond the continental United States. Still, it was July 1999 before the FBI formally announced its "war" on computer criminals, in a press release from the Seattle field office. There, 10 agents were assigned to CYBERCRIME full-time, assisted by two assistant U.S. attorneys. Cases specifically earmarked for handling by the unit included CHILD PORNOGRAPHY, drug dealing, or financial crime, and intrusion into computer networks by disgruntled employees or recreational "hackers." In April 2000, Washington spokesmen felt confident enough to announce creation of a new InfraGuard program, described as "just one portion of a larger plan to tackle computer crimes as networks become more valuable to international commerce and carry more important information." By that time, FBI computer squads were collaborating full time with other agencies, via the Justice Department's National Infrastructure Protection Center and its Internet Fraud Complaint Center.

Ted Jackson, special agent in charge of the Atlanta field office, told reporters that the FBI considers computer crime "the new form of terrorism. Someone involved in attacking your system can cause more problems than bombs." The bureau was determined to root out cybercriminals, Jackson insisted. "When you're at your computer and do something illegal, and you affect commerce or government, we're going to do everything in our power to bring you before the bars of justice."

FBI investigators recognize two basic kinds of computer crime: (1) crimes facilitated by computers, as money laundering, transmission of pornography, or different kinds of fraud; and (2) crimes where a computer itself is the target of intrusion, data theft, or sabotage. Federal investigators derive their authority from computer crimes legislation passed by Congress, including some statutes—wire fraud, interstate transmission of threats or ransom demands, and so forth—enacted long before the first computer was invented. In theory, the FBI investigates a case only when federal statutes have been violated, and the U.S. attorney's office supports investigation with an agreement to prosecute if federal violations are substantiated. Under prevailing law, unless a subject voluntarily discloses information, FBI agents may only gather evidence pursuant to a search warrant, court order, or a federal grand jury subpoena.

Those are the rules, but civil libertarians remind us of the FBI's history, including numerous illegal break-ins, wiretaps, and all manner of criminal harassment against minority groups spanning the better part of a century, from the bureau's creation in 1908 through (at least) the early 1990s. Voices of concern were raised with the unveiling of the FBI's Carnivore program, a software tool designed to scan the Internet at large (some say illegally, at random) for evidence of crime in cyberspace, and bureau explanations of the software's "surgical" precision did little to pacify outspoken critics. Likewise, the passage of sweeping new search-and-surveillance legislation in the wake of September 2001's terrorist attacks on New York

City and the Pentagon suggested broad potential for abuse. It remains to be seen how federal agents and prosecutors will use their new powers, or whether they will once more exceed their authority in the name of "national security."

FBI Laboratory

No aspect of the FBI is more famous than its laboratory, globally renowned for solving some of history's most notorious criminal cases. In any given year the bureau's lab conducts an average of 15,000 forensic examinations, involving 200,000 individual pieces of evidence including blood and semen samples, PAINT chips and body parts, photographs and documents, guns and bullets, tire tracks and footprints, arson traces and suspected murder weapons of all kinds. Even critics of the FBI almost invariably list its lab among the proud achievements of Director J. Edgar Hoover's "clean-up" during 1924.

In fact, the FBI lab would not debut for another eight years, until November 1932, and its beginnings were hardly auspicious. The original laboratory's equipment consisted of a fluorescent light and a borrowed microscope, housed in the Southern Railway Building that doubled as the bureau's smoking lounge. The FBI's FINGERPRINT reference collection was launched in October 1933, with a Photographic Operations Unit added in 1935. One of the lab's first headline cases, that same year, was the LINDBERGH KIDNAPPING (now widely regarded as a classic miscarriage of justice). The FBI lab hired its first full-time chemist, William Magee, in 1937—the same year that bureau headquarters began offering free services to state and local law enforcement agencies with no labs of their own. A polygraph was added in 1938, then discarded by Hoover after a Florida "lie detector" implicated an innocent kidnapping suspect while exonerating the guilty party. The crime lab achieved division status in 1943, under Assistant Director Edmund Coffey.

The bureau's crime lab has evolved with the times, though not always for the better. President Richard Nixon, obsessed with White House news leaks, demanded resumption of polygraph tests in 1971, and a new Polygraph Unit was formally established in 1978 (although the tests remain highly controversial and are inadmissible in most U.S. courts). In 1979, a Special Photography Unit began adapting digital images developed by the National Aeronautics and Space Administration for use in criminal cases. Three years later, the FBI's Forensic Science Research and Training Center opened at Quantico, Virginia, as a subdivision of the Scientific Analysis Section. The FBI lab began accepting DNA EVIDENCE for analysis on December 1, 1988, producing the first DNA identification in a U.S. courtroom nine years later. In August 1991, the Laboratory Division created a Computer Analysis and Response Team to support FBI investigations. Eleven months later, a new Drugfire data base was established to examine ballistics evidence from unsolved shootings (mainly related to the narcotics trade). By the mid-1990s, the Laboratory Division included five major sections: Investigative Operations (formerly Documents), Special Projects, Latent Fingerprints, Scientific Analysis, and Forensic Science Research and Training.

Despite its reputation, the FBI lab has not been immune to criticism. In 1996, employee FREDERIC WHITEHURST, a chemist in the explosives unit, went public with complaints of nonscientists dictating laboratory policies. He also alleged that evidence was frequently mishandled and occasionally altered for the benefit of prosecutors. While FBI administrators hounded Whitehurst from his job, an 18-month investigation of his charges was initiated by the Justice Department's Office of the Inspector General. The results of that survey, published in April 1977, validated most of Whitehurst's claims and proved so damaging to FBI prestige that prosecutors in the case of Oklahoma City bomber Timothy McVeigh declined to put bureau lab technicians on the witness stand. Criticism of the lab soon spread to Congress, showcased in Senate hearings where Gerald Lefcourt (president of the National Association of Criminal Defense Lawyers) declared, "We are left to the conclusion that justice could be perverted by [FBI] alignment with the prosecution."

Clearly, matters had degenerated from the days when Hoover required that any state or local police department submitting evidence for evaluation should promise to accept FBI lab results as final, even if they proved a suspect innocent. Now, NACDL spokesmen charged that all but one of the bureau's blood technicians had failed a 1989 proficiency test (those results were suppressed at headquarters); that one DNA specialist (later fired) had manipulated test results to convict innocent black defendants; and that DNA samples were routinely mishandled, sometimes

deliberately altered to ensure convictions. The FBI denied all such claims while refusing to open its files for review, but on October 22, 1997, Director Louis Freeh named an outsider—Donald Kerr Jr.—to head the embattled Laboratory Division. At age 58, Kerr was a physicist and engineer who once directed the Los Alamos nuclear testing facility (1979–85), and became the first nonagent to supervise the bureau's lab.

As dust from the latest scandal began to settle, in February 1998, the FBI paid Frederic Whitehurst $1.1 million to settle his claim of harassment and illegal retaliation. Four lab supervisors facing censure for negligence or worse were allowed to resign without disciplinary action in June 1998, while two others received mild letters of censure. Former lab unit chief Roger Martz was officially chastised for "negligence, inadequate documentation and overstated trial testimony" in the ORENTHAL JAMES (O. J.) SIMPSON murder case, while former lab examiner David Williams was reprimanded for providing "overstated, inaccurate and unsupported expert opinions" in the 1993 World Trade Center bombing and the 1995 Oklahoma City bombing cases. Both men appealed their wrist-slap punishments, while Assistant Attorney General Stephen Colgate told reporters, "The fact that the discipline is minimal should not be viewed as an exoneration of the behavior of these individuals." Senator Charles Grassley countered that view with an observation that "FBI management has succeeded in protecting its rogues in the lab scandal." G-men, for their part, retaliated by spreading tales that "Senator Grassley is an old Soviet mole still trying to impede the efficiency of the FBI."

FEDELE, Fortunato (1550–1630)

Born in Palermo, Sicily, in 1550, Dr. Fortunato Fedele was a preeminent Italian physician of the late 16th and early 17th centuries. His volume *De Relationes Medicorum*, published in 1602, ranks among the earliest works on forensic medicine, including a review of material previously published in Arabic, Greek, and Latin. Fedele personally conducted hundreds of autopsies and advocated routine postmortem examinations in cases of suspicious death. He also contributed to early TOXICOLOGY, establishing the link between lead plumbing and chronic lead poisoning. Dr. Fedele died in 1630.

FIBER and Hair Evidence

Fibers rank among the most common pieces of TRACE EVIDENCE found at crime scenes. They are broadly classified as *natural* or *artificial*. Natural fibers include all those of mineral origin (e.g., asbestos or glass), vegetable origin (e.g., cotton, hemp, or linen), and animal origin (e.g., hair or wool). Artificial fibers includes any derived from natural fibers by some human process and those that are completely synthetic. Both natural and artificial fibers have countless uses in modern society, including manufacture of bedding, BODY ARMOR, carpets, clothing, tents, towels, toys, upholstery, and myriad other articles found in all walks of life around the world. Hairs and fibers are readily shed, all the more so during violent contact, guaranteeing that most crime scenes will have numerous specimens of varying relevance for experts to examine.

Fibers and hairs are relatively easy to identify via MICROSCOPY, as different types have unique individual structures, but matching to a common source is often problematic. Because artificial fibers are mass-produced and used in huge quantities, it is generally impossible to make a positive match between a fiber from a crime scene and another collected from a suspect's home. Both may contain the same materials and dyes, they may even be traced to the same manufacturer, but with identical carpet installed in thousands of homes or millions of automobiles, fibers alone only *suggest* a link between two separate locations. Further evidence—such as BLOODSTAINS or unique damage to specific fibers—is required to prove a case in court.

One case often cited as a victory for fiber evidence is that of Wayne Bertram Williams, convicted in February 1982 for two of Atlanta's 30 notorious "child murders." (In fact, Williams was convicted of killing two adult ex-convicts, after which prosecutors unilaterally declared him guilty murdering 21 children in crimes never charged against him. Several of the latter cases were officially reopened by a local district attorney in 2005.) Jurors later stated that the prosecution's most impressive evidence involved various synthetic fibers found on the corpses of children murdered during 1979–81. Specifically, bodies of five victims bore fibers from carpeting widely used in certain 1979 Ford automobiles, including one owned by Williams's parents. One victim's body also bore fibers common to various 1970 Chevrolets, one model of which also belonged to Williams's

parents. Prosecutors failed to inform the jury that neither car was physically available to Williams on the dates when those victims were slain. Admission of that evidence was all the more suspect since no such fibers appeared on the remains of the two adult victims Williams stands convicted of killing.

Hairs offer a better likelihood of positive identification, but only if they are found with the follicle intact, containing samples of the donor's DNA. Without the follicle and its genetic material, hairs may only reveal the donor's species, race, and blood type. Specific dyes or damage may suggest a donor, but since hair dyes are also mass-produced, DNA profiling remains the sole method of positive identification.

The U.S. Federal Trade Commission has developed a list of synthetic fibers classified by generic (family) names and subclasses, with common trade names. Fibers included on that list are:

ACETATE

Celanese
Celstar
Chromspun
Estron
MicroSafe

ACRYLIC

Acrilan
BioFresh
Bounce-Back
CFF Fibrillated Fiber
Conductrol
Creslan
Creslite
Cresloft
Duraspun
Evolutia
Ginny
MicroSupreme
Pil-Trol
The Smart Yarns
Wear-Dated
WeatherBloc

ANIDEX

ARAMID

Kevlar
Nomex

AZLON

BICOMPONENT
Fossfibre
No-Shock

ELASTOESTER

FLUORO
Tefaire
Teflon

GLASS

LYOCELL
Tencel

MELAMINE
Basofil

METALLIC

MODACRYLIC
SEF

NYLON 6
Anso
Anso AllSport
Anso Caress
Anso Choice!
Anso Color Solutions
Anso CrushResister III
Anso CrushResister III ACT
Anso CrushResister TLC
Anso DuroTwist
Anso f(x)
Anso HTX
Anso Infinty
Anso Premium
Anso Replacement Plus
Anso Soft
Anso Solution
Anso Total Comfort
Anso Vibrance
Caprolan
Caprolan-RC
Dry Step
Nylon 6ix
Permasoft
Royalbrite

Shimmereen
Silky Touch
Stay Gard
Trilene
Tru-Ballistic
Ultra Micro Touch
Ultra Touch
Zefsport
Zeftron Contex
Zeftron Savant
Zeftron Select
Zeftron Solure

NYLON 6.6
Antron
Antron Advantage
Antron II
Antron Legacy
Antron Lumena
Cordura
DSDN
DuPont XTI
DyeNAMIX
Enka
FiberLoc
Micro Supplex
Natrelle BCF
SolarMax
Stainmaster
Stainmaster Luxura
Stainmaster XTRA Life
Supplex
Tactasse
TACTEL
Ultron
Ultron 3D
Ultron VIP
Wear-Dated
Wear-Dated Assurance
Wear-Dated Freedom
Wear-Dated II
Wear-Dated ThermaSealed

NYLON 6 OR 6.6
Meryl Mattesse
Meryl
Meryl Microfibre
Meryl Nexten
Meryl Satiné
Meryl Skinlife

Meryl Souple
Meryl Spring
Meryl Techno
Wellon
Wellstrand

NYTRIL

OLEFIN

Amco
American
Angel Hair
Biobarrier
Bondtie
Crowelon
Crown Fiber
Duron
Dyneema
E-B Meshr
Elustra
Essera
Fibermesh
Floterope
Herculon
HY – Colour
HY – Comfort
HY – Medical
HY – Repeat
HY – Soft
HY – Strength
Impressa
Innova
Marqesa
Marquesa Lana
Microblocker
Mirafi
Nouvelle
Patlon III
Poly Tying
Polylasting
Polyloom
Polypro 6
Polystar
Prolan
Pur-Ty
Salus
Soft 71
Spectra 1000
Spectra 900
Spectra Fusion

Spectra Guard
Spectra Shield
Spectra Shield Plus
SpectraFlex
Tekton
Telar
Tensylon
Trace
Trustite
Typar
Typelle
Tyrite
Tyvec
Ultraline
Welltite

PBI

PELCO

Securus

PEN

Pentex

PLA

POLYESTER

A.C.E.
Accepta
Avora FR
Avora Plus
Barricaut
Beltec
Celbond
Colorbrite
ColorGuard
Comforel
ComFortrel
ComFortrel Plus
ComFortrel XP
Coolmax
Dacron
Delcron
Diolen
DSP
ESP
Fillwell
Fillwell II
Fillwell Plus
Fortrel

Fortrel BactiShield
Fortrel EcoSpun
Fortrel MicroSpun
HardCut
Holofiber
Hydrotec
Imbue
Loftguard
Loftguard Xtra
Microdenier Sensura
Microlux
Microtherm
Orel
Pentec
Polarguard 3D
Polarguard Classic
Polarguard Delta
Polarguard HV
QualiFlo
Reemay
Retrieve
Sensura
Serelle
Serene
Spunnaire
Steripur
Stretch-aire
Substraight
Tairilin
UltraFlo
Ultura

POLYPROPYLENE

RAYON

SARAN

SPANDEX

Dorlastan
Glospan
Lycra

SULFAR

TRIACETATE

VINAL

VINYON

FINGERPRINTS

Fingerprints have been used as a form of identification for at least 4,000 years, the first known record dating from ancient Babylon, where several captured army deserters were forced to leave marks of their fingers and thumbs as a permanent record. Two thousand years ago, the Chinese used thumbprints as seals for official documents, and the next millennium saw Chinese river pirates compelled to provide ink prints of their thumbs. Fingerprints made their first appearance in a criminal trial in pre-Christian Rome, after a senator was murdered and his killer left bloody handprints on the wall. Shape and size, rather than ridge detail, acquitted the prime suspect in that case and later convicted the senator's wife.

"Modern" fingerprint identification dates from 1788, when German analyst J. C. A. Mayer declared for the first time that each fingerprint is unique. Mark Twain and Sir Arthur Conan Doyle made fictional references to fingerprint identification in the 19th century, but practical identification waited for the near-simultaneous work (in 1892) of WILLIAM HERSCHEL in India, HENRY FAULDS in Japan, and FRANCIS GALTON in England. It was Galton who first proposed a practical system of fingerprint classification and filing, improved and expanded by Sir EDWARD HENRY in 1899–1900. Meanwhile, in Argentina during 1891, a competing classification system was developed by JUAN VUCETICH, still used in most Spanish-speaking countries. Official fingerprinting made its way to the United States in 1902, when New York State adopted the technique to eliminate fraud on civil service tests. By 1908 the U.S. armed forces had adopted universal fingerprinting of all personnel, and America witnessed its first criminal conviction based on fingerprints three years later. J. Edgar Hoover often boasted of the FBI's vast fingerprint collection, including not only convicted criminals and military personnel, but also persons printed for a wide variety of government positions, driver's licenses, and so forth. (Even casual tourists visiting FBI Headquarters were invited to donate fingerprints, purportedly to help identify victims of future natural disasters.)

With billions of fingerprints from millions of persons on file, each subject with his or her separate fingerprint card, identifying anonymous prints from a specific crime scene might require weeks of eye-straining effort. Even reducing the field to a smaller subset—e.g., convicted burglars or kidnappers—still left technicians with thousands of cards to examine, each bearing 10 fingerprints. Today, the process is greatly streamlined by an AUTOMATED FINGERPRINT IDENTIFICATION SYSTEM (AFIS), capable of scanning and rejecting hundreds of prints per hour. Recent improvements in software also "clean up" smudged prints and facilitate identification of partials.

Ironically, just when fingerprint scanning became nearly effortless, the very use of fingerprints themselves was called into question at a murder trial in Philadelphia. Defendants Carlos Llera-Plaza, Wilfredo Acosta, and Victor Rodriguez faced possible execution if convicted of running a Pennsylvania narcotics syndicate that committed at least four murders between 1996 and 1998. Defense attorneys for the trio challenged the scientific validity of fingerprint evidence, winning a decision from U.S. District Judge Louis Pollak on January 7, 2002, that barred fingerprint experts from linking crime scene prints to specific defendants. Acting in response to a 1993 U.S. Supreme Court decision requiring federal judges to take a more active role in weighing the admissibility of scientific evidence, Pollak ruled that experts may testify about similarities between "latent" crime scene prints and "rolled" fingerprints on file, but they may not claim specific latent prints positively match a criminal suspect. Judge Pollak found that, unlike DNA EVIDENCE, the error rate of fingerprint data has never been calculated, that the evidence itself has never been scientifically tested, and that no universal standards exist for a "match."

Prosecutors filed an immediate appeal of Judge Pollak's decision, noting that his ruling "would deprive the government of vital evidence in this case, in which latent fingerprints directly linked defendants to heinous murders. If carried to its logical conclusion, the court's reasoning would virtually eliminate any expert opinion on the myriad subjects on which subjective expert opinion has always been welcomed in the federal courts."

At a February hearing on Judge Pollak's decision, FBI fingerprint analyst Stephen Meagher cited the bureau's proficiency test as sufficient grounds for Pollak to trust expert testimony. British fingerprint expert Allan Bayle, appearing for the defense, noted that FBI tests used the same sample prints for three years in a row and branded the bureau's six-week training program "a joke." Of the final proficiency test, Bayle said, "They're not testing their ability, and they're not testing their expertise. If I gave my experts this test they would fall about laughing." Further-

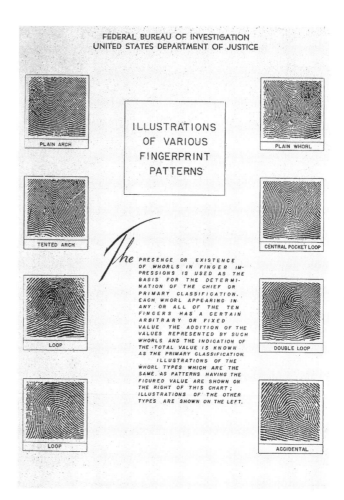

Fingerprints are classified based on eight basic patterns. (Kathleen O. Arries)

more, Bayle noted, there were no international standards for fingerprint comparison and identification: British courts required 16 specific "Galton points" of identity, Australian authorities demanded 12, and FBI experts often made do with 10 matching points. Meagher, recalled to the stand by Judge Pollack, reluctantly acknowledged that "there certainly have been erroneous [fingerprint] identifications testified to in the United States," but denied that the FBI had ever made such a mistake. Coming hard on the heels of sweeping scandals in the FBI's crime laboratory and reports that G-men had framed various innocent persons on murder charges across the United States, leaving three to sit in prison for 25 to 30 years each, Meagher's blanket endorsement of FBI methods was less than compelling.

Another embarrassment for the FBI surfaced on January 5, 2006, when bureau headquarters announced sweeping reviews of all state and federal cases wherein FBI fingerprint evidence resulted in convictions with death sentences. According to Joseph DiZinno, the FBI's assistant director for forensic analysis, the survey had begun 18 months earlier (in June 2004), after G-men matched prints found at the site of a terrorist bombing in Spain to Brandon Mayfield, an attorney from Portland, Oregon. Agents held Mayfield in custody for two weeks, as a "material witness" to the bombing, before Spanish police reexamined the print and identified its true owner—an Algerian linked to Muslim extremist groups. That snafu prompted a wholesale review of cases involving some 3,000 condemned inmates throughout the United States. By the time DiZinno revealed the program, technicians at the FBI LABORATORY had already reviewed 92 capital cases, pinpointing 10 in which the bureau had analyzed fingerprints. According to DiZinno, no mistakes were found, but the review process continued, with a vow from FBI headquarters that each capital case in America would be reviewed at least 30 days before a condemned inmate's scheduled execution.

The Mayfield glitch apparently involved some unknown problem with AFIS, which had "flagged" the lawyer's prints (and those of 20 other persons) as "possible matches" to fingerprints found at the Madrid bombing scene. Three FBI examiners and one consultant had confirmed Mayfield's "match" to the prints found in Spain, retracting their mistaken identification only after Spanish authorities publicly named the real suspect. Bruce Budowle, identified by *USA Today* on January 12, 2006, as the FBI's "chief scientist," called for more scientific "validation" to improve fingerprint ID techniques, but otherwise the bureau's faith in itself was unshaken. Assistant Director DiZinno told reporters, "There is no doubt in our minds about the scientific basis or validity of fingerprint identification."

FIREARMS and Ballistics

The use of gunpowder in China has been documented from A.D. 1000, and some sources suggest that it may have been invented even earlier. From the development of that EXPLOSIVE it was a relatively short step to the use of gunpowder as a *propellant*, hurling various *projectiles* at distant targets from a tube (or *barrel*) that became the first *firearm*. Firearms have evolved over time, and while many reference sources

are available on antique weapons—including the author's own *Armed and Dangerous* (1990)—our discussion here shall be limited for reasons of economy to modern guns.

Broadly speaking, the firearms legally available to civilian purchasers in North America are either *handguns* or *long guns*. Handguns—or *pistols*—are short guns designed to be fired with one hand. While some pistols are single-shot weapons and others have multiple barrels, the majority are either *revolvers*, named for the revolving cylinder that holds their ammunition, or *semiautomatic* weapons (also called *self-loading*), which hold ammunition in a spring-loaded *magazine* and fire one shot with each pull of the trigger until the ammunition supply is exhausted. Some "purists" insist that only semiautomatic handguns should be called "pistols," but the long history of firearms nomenclature—from muzzle-loading flintlocks to the present day—defeats their argument.

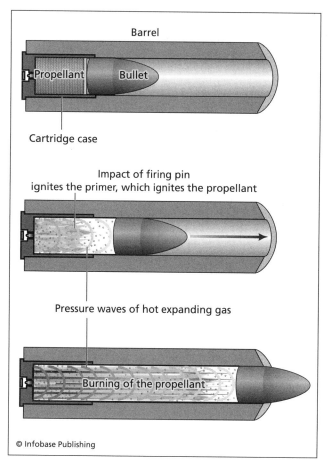

When the firing pin ignites the propellant within the barrel of a firearm, the pressure from expanding gas fires the bullet or other projectile.

Long guns are those designed to be fired from the shoulder, generally understood to mean *rifles, carbines* and *shotguns.* Rifles are names for the spiral "rifling" (grooves) inside their barrels, developed around 1476, which increases both the accuracy and velocity of bullets. Carbines are simply short rifles, initially designed for the convenience of mounted troops in the 19th century. Shotguns, originally designed for hunting birds, have no rifling inside their barrels and generally fire clusters of lead or steel pellets ("shot") in various sizes, which spread upon leaving the barrel. Shortening the barrel (as in sawed-off shotguns) causes the pellets to spread more rapidly, increasing the odds of a hit at close range.

Both pistols and long guns are *small arms,* firearms designed to be held and fired with one or both hands. In modern times the "small arms" designation has been broadened to include various *machine guns, submachine guns* and *assault weapons.* Machine guns are *automatic* weapons (as opposed to *semi*automatic), meaning that they fire continuously at high rates of speed until the trigger is released or ammunition is exhausted. Traditionally, most nations have designed machine guns to fire the same ammunition used by their standard-issue military rifles, although *heavy machine guns* require special ammo. Submachine guns (or *machine pistols*) generally fire pistol ammunition in automatic mode, though some are capable of *selective fire* (including semiautomatic fire or short preset bursts). Assault weapons (or *automatic rifles*) properly include only military rifles capable of automatic or selective fire, though many journalists and politicians wrongly apply the term to semiautomatic weapons manufactured to resemble military arms.

With the exception of some muzzle-loading antique replicas, all modern firearms use ammunition consisting of individual *cartridges.* The components of a standard cartridge include the *case* (called "brass," regardless of its composition), a propellant charge (usually in powder or granulated form), a *primer* to ignite the propellant (when struck by the gun's *firing pin*), and one or more projectiles (made of various materials including metals, rubber, wood, or ceramics, depending on the ammunition's purpose). The velocity, range, and *penetration* of a projectile depends variously on its weight, the size and composition of its propellant charge, the firearm's barrel length, the range of a particular shot, and the composition of its target.

Modern firearms leave IMPRESSION EVIDENCE on their ammunition in three ways. Rifled barrels mark each bullet fired with longitudinal striations from the *lands* and *grooves* inside the barrel. While all weapons manufactured with the same lathe may have rifling of the same dimensions, unique imperfections inside each barrel produce ballistic markings as distinctive as human FINGERPRINTS. Smooth-bore shotguns leave no such impressions on pellets fired through their barrels, but like all other firearms, they mark each cartridge's primer (with an impression of the firing pin) and each case (with toolmarks from the weapon's *ejector* or *extractor*). Thus, even when bullets are lost or deformed beyond recognition on impact, cartridge cases may still be linked positively to a specific firearm.

Identification of a shooter may be more problematical. Traces of burnt propellant escape from all guns upon firing, and various PRESUMPTIVE TESTS for gunshot residue (GSR) may suggest that a suspect has recently fired or handled a weapon, but false positive results may also be obtained from traces of PAINT and other substances containing the same chemicals found in gunpowder. Likewise, fingerprints found on a weapon may prove that a suspect has handled the gun, but may not prove that he/she fired the weapon at a particular victim. All modern firearms bear unique serial numbers, through which they may be tracked from manufacture to their last point of sale by a licensed gun dealer, and while this permits authorities to trace discarded weapons, private sales or THEFT of guns breaks that chain of custody. However, firearms may also bear trace evidence unique to a particular owner or shooter, including (but not limited to) BLOODSTAINS or tissue samples including unique DNA, FIBERS or hairs, and traces of dust, soil, or various chemicals that may be matched to samples found in a suspect's residence, vehicle, or place of business.

At last count, approximately 20,000 different local, state, and federal gun-control laws existed throughout the United States, none of which significantly limit the availability of weapons or their use in violent crimes. Federal statutes include the following:

National Firearms Act (1934): Prompted by Prohibition-era gang wars and holdups committed by the likes of John Dillinger and "Baby Face" Nelson, this law banned nothing but imposed a $200 federal transfer tax on sale of "gangster weapons" (machine guns, silencers, and sawed-off shotguns or rifles) and "gadget-type" firearms (guns disguised as walking sticks, etc.).

Federal Firearms Act (1938): Congress required all persons professionally engaged in selling or shipping firearms to obtain a Federal Firearms License (FFL) at the initial cost of one dollar per year (now $200 yearly).

Gun Control Act (1968): The public assassinations of President John Kennedy, brother Robert Kennedy, and Dr. Martin Luther King Jr. inspired this ban on mail-order sales of firearms, except to licensed dealers. Other provisions of the law restricted handgun sales to buyers aged 21 or older, with sale of long guns banned to persons under age 18; applied federal transfer taxes to various "destructive devices" (including most military weapons, such as flamethrowers and bazookas), and banned importation of foreign "Saturday Night specials," defined as any firearms not "generally recognized as particularly suitable for, or readily adaptable to sporting purposes."

Law Enforcement Officers Protection Act (1986): This law banned civilian sales of armor-piercing "cop killer" bullets or any automatic weapons manufactured after 1986.

Crime Control Act (1990): Escalating gang violence encouraged passage of this law, banning possession or discharge of firearms in a school zone and penalizing the assembly of illegal automatic weapons from legally imported parts.

Brady Handgun Violence Act (1994): Named for White House aide James Brady, brain-damaged in the 1981 attempted murder of President Ronald Reagan, this law imposed a mandatory background check and five-day "cooling off" period on handgun sales.

Violent Crime Control and Law Enforcement Act (1994): This statute included a misnamed "assault weapons ban," outlawing for 10 years the importation, manufacture, or civilian possession of various military-style semiautomatic weapons (defined by their cosmetic appearance) and/or large-capacity ammunition magazines manufactured after 1994. The ban was not renewed in 2004.

FLETCHER, John Bill, Jr. indicted by DNA evidence

Convicted of multiple felony charges in 1987, 45-year-old John Bill Fletcher Jr. was serving a 43-year sentence at the Washington State Penitentiary in Walla Walla when he received some bad news in December 2001. While DNA test results were being used to free wrongfully convicted inmates all over the country, more than 100 at last count, the same tests had a dramatically different effect on Fletcher's case. Far from liberating Fletcher, DNA profiling had linked him to an unsolved murder that would keep him in prison for the rest of his life.

Fletcher was on parole from Texas, after serving seven years of a 20-year aggravated rape conviction, when he moved to Washington's Yakima County in October 1986. Old habits die hard for a sociopath, and Fletcher was jailed in August 1987, after his latest rape victim identified him. Fletcher had kidnapped the woman, raped her, and stabbed her 16 times before she escaped, after disarming Fletcher and stabbing him in the leg with his own knife. A second victim came forward after Fletcher's arrest, leading to his ultimate conviction on two counts of first-degree rape, plus one count each of robbery and assault. At the time, he was also suspected in the rape-slayings of Theresa Branscomb (stabbed to death in February 1987) and Bertha Cantu (killed the same way, five months later), but scientific evidence was inconclusive.

"It was extremely frustrating at the time," investigator Jim Hall told the press. "It was one of those things where you knew what was going on but couldn't prove it. Technology has finally caught up with him." BLOODSTAINS from Fletcher's station wagon matched Branscomb's DNA, and Fletcher confessed to both slayings after he received assurances that prosecutors would not seek the death penalty. He was formally charged with two counts of first-degree murder on December 10, 2001.

FODÉRÉ, François-Emmanuel (1764–1835)

Born at St. Jean de Maurienne in 1764, French physician François-Emmanuel Fodéré was an early advocate of "state medicine"—official concern for public health—and an 18th-century pioneer in forensic PATHOLOGY. His paper "Essai sur le goitre et le cretinisme," published in 1791, proposed that exposure to high humidity and certain gases caused cretinism and goiters among residents of some mountainous regions in France. Fodéré's *Treatise on Legal Medicine and Public Hygiene* (1798) became the standard source for close to half a century. Fodéré also traveled widely throughout Europe, reporting on deplorable conditions in lunatic asylums like the one in Strasbourg, where he found that "for troublesome madmen and those who dirtied themselves, a kind of cage, or wooden closet, which could at the most contain one man of middle height, had been devised at the ends of the great wards." Those elevated cages had gratings instead of floors, covered with straw "upon which the madman lay, naked or nearly so, took his meals, and deposited his excrement." By the time Fodéré died in 1835, major universities in Prague and Vienna offered curricula in public hygiene based upon his work.

FOOD and Drug Administration

The Food and Drug Administration (FDA) is a federal scientific, regulatory, and public health agency responsible for assuring the safety, efficacy, and security of human and veterinary drugs, biological products, medical devices, cosmetics, products that emit radiation, and the U.S. food supply. In theory, it is also responsible for advancing public health by facilitating innovations that make medicines and foods more effective, safer, and more affordable. Predictably, some critics charge that partisan politics corrupts that process, delaying release of some products badly needed while allowing pharmaceutical concerns and others to reap fabulous profits at public expense. Given the climate in Washington, D.C., and in the United States at large, that debate is unlikely to fade.

Some historians date the FDA's history from 1862, with a single chemist serving as the U.S. Department of Agriculture's Bureau of Chemistry, while others cite passage of the federal Food and Drugs Act of 1906. In July 1927, the Bureau of Chemistry became the Food, Drug, and Insecticide Administration. The name was shortened to its present version three years later, and the FDA remained with the agriculture department until June 1940, when it was transferred to the newly created Federal Security Agency. In April 1953, it moved again, this time to the Department of Health, Education and Welfare (HEW). In 1968, it became part of HEW's Public Health Service. Finally, in May 1980, the education function was removed from HEW to create a new Department of Health and Human Services, which remains FDA's

current home. At press time for this volume, the former one-man agency boasted some 9,100 employees and a budget exceeding $1.3 billion. FDA staffers include attorneys, chemists, microbiologists, pharmacists, pharmacologists, physicians, veterinarians, and various other professionals. Two-thirds of those employees work in the nation's capital, while the remainder staff 150 field offices and laboratories across the United States.

FDA jurisdiction includes most food products (excluding meat and poultry), drugs intended for use on humans or animals, medical devices, cosmetics, animal feeds, and any products that emit radiation. FDA scientists evaluate applications for new drugs, medical devices, food additives, infant formulas, and so forth (sparking further controversy as some critics claim the process is unnecessarily protracted, while others accuse the FDA of hastily green-lighting various products from well-connected companies). The FDA also monitors the manufacture, importation, storage, and transportation of various products valued at around $1 trillion per year. Agency inspectors visit an average of 16,000 facilities each year, presumably ensuring compliance with all pertinent federal statutes and regulations. Since the notorious Tylenol murders in Chicago (1982), the FDA has overseen efforts to prevent deadly product tampering. The agency's Forensic Chemistry Center, based in Cincinnati since 1989, has developed various high-speed screening techniques for contaminants that may be added after manufacture to food and pharmaceutical supplies.

"FORD Heights Four" inmates exonerated by DNA evidence

Described in a *Chicago Tribune* report as "almost certainly the largest single, proven miscarriage of justice in Illinois history," the case of the "Ford Heights Four" began at 2:15 A.M. on May 11, 1978, when 28-year-old Larry Lionberg and his fiancée, 23-year-old Carol Schmal, were kidnapped from a Homewood gas station. Police later discovered them in an abandoned Ford Heights townhouse: Schmal had been raped and both victims were killed with close-range gunshots to the head.

Authorities had no leads in the case until an anonymous telephone call sent them looking for five young blacks on May 17. Those arrested were Kenneth Adams, Paula Gray, Verneal Jimerson, William Rainge, and Dennis Williams. On the day of his arrest, Williams recalls, a white officer warned him, "Nigger, you're gonna fry." While investigators juggled evidence—and buried testimony pointing to four other suspects—the sole female defendant was offered a bargain she could not refuse. In exchange for testimony against her supposed accomplices, Paula Gray would receive immunity from prosecution. Fearing for her life, Gray readily agreed.

In light of local sentiment and official malfeasance, the result was predictable. Adams, Jimerson, Rainge, and Williams were convicted on all charges: Jimerson and Williams were sentenced to die for the murders; Rainge was sentenced to life imprisonment; Adams received a 75-year prison term. The four maintained their innocence, and their convictions were overturned on appeal in 1983, but all four were convicted again in a 1985 retrial, with Williams once again sentenced to die. There the matter rested until May 1995, when condemned killer Girvies Davis—hours away from his own execution—urged a friend, journalism professor David Protess, to investigate the Ford Heights case. Preliminary research showed gaping holes in the prosecution's case, and Protess assigned some of his students from Northwestern University to find the truth. What they uncovered was a FRAME-UP fueled in equal parts by racism and the desire to clear a shocking case at any cost.

Paula Gray, the state's "star" witness with a tested IQ of 55, freely admitted lying under oath to save herself from prison. Worse yet, the students discovered that another informant had named four other suspects on May 17, 1978—suspects ignored by the police in their single-minded zeal to convict the "Ford Heights Four" already charged. One of those suspects, Ira Johnson, was serving 74 years for a separate murder when Protess found him in prison. Johnson signed an affidavit naming his deceased brother Dennis as Carol Schmal's killer, further admitting that he and two other gunmen—Arthur Robinson and Juan Rodriguez—killed Larry Lionberg.

Police and prosecutors dismissed the new evidence as fraudulent, but the Illinois Supreme Court felt otherwise, overturning Verneal Jimerson's conviction and death sentence on grounds that Paula Gray had lied under oath at his trial. Freed on bond pending retrial, Jimerson worked with the journalistic team to free his friends. That freedom came in June 1996, when DNA test results positively excluded all four defendants as participants in Carol Schmal's rape. Ira

Johnson, Arthur Robinson, and Juan Rodriguez were indicted on July 3, 1996, subsequently convicted and sentenced for the Ford Heights double slaying.

No police officers were charged with any crime in the Ford Heights frame-up, but state authorities offered to pay the four exonerated inmates $35,000 each for their 18 years in prison. Understandably reluctant to accept that low-ball offer, the Ford Heights Four sued Cook County, its sheriff's department, and various individual officers for false imprisonment. In March 1999, the case was settled out of court for a reported $36 million. A gag order was imposed to suppress details of the settlement. Dennis Williams, still embittered and distrustful, reportedly still telephones a friend or relative each time he leaves his home, to have an iron-clad alibi prepared in case authorities come after him again with more false charges.

FORENSIC Science Service

Established in 1991 as an executive agency of the British Home Office, the FSS is the primary provider of forensic services for the United Kingdom, assisting 43 police agencies in England and Wales. It established Britain's National DNA Database with 1.7 million samples, administered by FSS staffers for the Association of Chief Police Officers, and handles more than 100,000 criminal investigations each year. In addition to DNA screening, the FSS staff of some 2,800 employees also work ballistics cases and survey other evidence recovered from British crime scenes. London's Metropolitan Police Laboratory formally merged with the FSS in 1996.

FORGERY

In British common law, forgery was defined as the act of making or altering a written instrument for the purpose of FRAUD or deceit, as in the case of fraudulent checks or a false signature affixed to a will. In today's cyberage, forgeries are not restricted to written or printed documents, but may include a wide range of physical objects. For purposes of clarity, forged items such as currency, coins, collectibles, and similar objects are separately considered in this volume's entry on COUNTERFEITING, while this entry considers documents, works of art, and historical or archaeological relics.

Documents may be forged in a variety of ways, including: (1) fabrication of any document in the name of another with fraudulent intent; (2) application of a false signature to any true document; (3) application of a true signature to a false document or any other document for which it was not intended; (4) production of documents in a fictitious name, with fraudulent intent (as opposed to pen names used by novelists); (5) fraudulent alteration of true documents (contracts, receipts, etc.); and (6) fraudulent omission of any significant provisions from true documents under preparation (contracts, wills, etc.) that adversely affects one or more parties. Generally speaking, simple copies, replicas, or studio reproductions are not considered forgeries unless they are promoted as genuine originals.

Forgery may spring from a variety of motives. Financial gain is the most obvious and common motive, but others are also recognized. Scholars occasionally forge historical documents or fabricate relics in a bid to advance their reputations. Known archaeological forgeries include the spurious fossil remains of *Archaeoraptor* (a supposed "missing link" between ancient reptiles and birds), the mummy of a supposed Persian princess, Etruscan terra-cotta warriors (displayed in the Metropolitan Museum of Art), the ossuary of James (alleged brother of Jesus), the tiara of Saitaphernes (displayed in the Louvre), and the fragmentary skeletal remains of "Piltdown Man" (supposedly excavated from Sussex, England, by Charles Dawson in 1912, exposed as a hoax in 1953).

Political forgeries are generally contrived as propaganda items, to promote the agenda of a specific individual or faction. A prime example is *The Protocols of the Learned Elders of Zion,* a supposed blueprint for Jewish world domination fabricated by czarist secret police around 1903 to justify anti-Semitic pogroms, still widely circulated by neo-Nazi propagandists to the present day (and occasionally misattributed to Freemasons). Another such document, the *Zinoviev letter,* was allegedly sent by Soviet Comintern leader Grigori Zinoviev to members of the British Communist Party in September 1924, demanding increased political agitation in England. Exposure of the letter—actually forged by British secret agents, as revealed three decades later—toppled the Labour government of Prime Minister Ramsay MacDonald and derailed his efforts to normalize diplomatic relations with the Soviet Union. A 19th-century example, the *Ems telegram,* actually sparked the Franco-Prussian War of 1870. Ems was a part of

Prussia at the time, its ownership disputed by France (which feared a Prussian alliance with Spain). On July 13, 1870, King Wilhelm of Prussia met with French ambassador Count Vincent Benedetti, then sent a report of the meeting to Otto von Bismarck for publication. Bismarck drastically edited the king's message before releasing it, with the avowed intent "of waving a red cape in front of the face of the [French] bull." Properly outraged, France declared war six days later.

In a similar fashion, religious zealots have forged documents and artifacts throughout history, either with intent to profit from their frauds or to validate and legitimize particular doctrines. Notorious examples include countless splinters of "the true cross," alleged skeletal remains of John the Baptist or various martyred saints, and the still-controversial Shroud of Turin (advanced as proof of Christ's resurrection, claimed by some to contain "the DNA of God"). Supporters of Old Testament creationism (lately recycled as "intelligent design") fraudulently altered fossilized dinosaur tracks found near Paluxy, Texas, in 1908, to support their belief that modern humans coexisted with dinosaurs on an Earth no more than 6,000 years old. Antiquities dealer Moses Shapira (1830–84) made a career out of peddling forged biblical artifacts from his shop in Jerusalem, including a virtual flood of fake Moabite artifacts (including busts, clay pots, and erotic figurines). Shapira's final coup, in the year before his death, was his revelation of the "Shapira strips," 15 scraps of parchment allegedly found near the Dead Sea, whose inscriptions offered variations on the Ten Commandments and the text of Deuteronomy. Before they were proved fraudulent, Shapira offered his latest "find" to the British Museum for a mere £1 million.

Literary forgery is a potentially lucrative field. Asa Earl Carter, an Alabama Ku Klux Klan leader in the 1950s, adopted the pseudonym "Forrest Carter" (in honor of original KKK Grand Wizard Nathan Bedford Forrest) to write a fraudulent "oral history" of the Apaches, *Look for Me on the Mountain,* in 1978, while his most famous work, *The Education of Little Tree* (1986), was falsely advertised as the autobiography of a Cherokee orphan. In March 1972, hoaxer Clifford Irving faced charges of conspiracy, forgery, and perjury for selling a spurious autobiography of reclusive billionaire Howard Hughes to the McGraw-Hill publishing house. In April 1983, publishers of the German magazine *Der*

Stern announced that they had purchased Adolf Hitler's previously unknown diaries for the sum of 9.9 million marks ($6.13 million). Allegedly recovered from an airplane that crashed near Dresden during World War II, the "diary" proved to be a collection of Hitler's speeches and proclamations lifted from Nazi archives and forged by memorabilia purveyor Konrad Kujau in handwriting resembling Hitler's. Kujau and an accomplice in the fraud each received four-year prison terms. Equally notorious was the case of the "Salamander Letter," challenging certain scriptural foundations of the Mormon Church and providing new insights into the life of Mormon patriarch Joseph Smith. Allegedly penned by one Martin Harris in 1830, the letter was actually fabricated by 20th-century swindler Mark Hofmann, who claimed that he discovered it in the early 1980s. Aroused by Hofmann's frequent "discovery" of unique Mormon documents, church leaders submitted the letter to the FBI LABORATORY for analysis in 1985, whereupon Hofmann murdered two persons linked to the case with homemade bombs. A third bomb injured Hofmann himself and led to his imprisonment for murder.

Recognized cases of art forgery date from ancient times, when Roman sculptors crafted copies of Greek statues for sale to elite clientele. In medieval times, copying the work of a master was sometimes considered an homage rather than a criminal offense, but that changed with expansion of the commercial art market. Since the known works of master artists chiefly reside in museums or recognized private collections, forgeries today most often represent "new" works by famous artists, created (often clumsily) by melding elements from various genuine works. Techniques for "aging" new fraudulent works include concoction of PAINT using archaic methods and ingredients, application of various chemicals, and use of small drills to simulate worm holes in picture frames or statuary.

Art experts and forensic scientists detect forgeries in a variety of ways. The absence of a "paper trail" establishing the provenance of any classic master's work is widely viewed as a PRESUMPTIVE TEST of forgery. (British art dealer John Drewe overcame that hurdle by forging false documents of provenance and surreptitiously inserting photos of various forged works into the archives of prominent art institutions.) Carbon dating helps establish the true age of very old items, while infrared analysis and X-ray flu-

orescence help establish the age of more recent paints and canvases, also determining the relative purity of pigments or metals used in sculpture. FINGERPRINTS are occasionally useful, if the original artist—master or forger—inadvertently left his mark in wet paint. Digital images of suspect paintings, employed in an analytical technique called *wavelet decomposition,* permit detailed examination of brush and pen strokes in paintings and drawings (which may be compared to genuine exemplars).

FRAME-UPS

A frame-up is the malicious wrongful prosecution of any defendant for crimes that he or she did not commit. Many wrongful convictions have resulted from honest mistakes on the part of eyewitnesses or misinterpretation of forensic evidence (particularly in the years before DNA profiling revolutionized analysis of BLOODSTAINS and other biological matter). It is the element of malice that distinguishes a true frame-up, generally accomplished by (a) official fabrication of false evidence and subornation of perjured testimony, or (b) more rarely, fabrication by civilian third parties of false evidence that prosecutors carelessly accept in good faith. While frame-ups are thankfully less common in real life than in Hollywood fiction, they have occurred throughout history and into modern times. A few well-known examples include:

1920: The SACCO-VANZETTI CASE, wherein two Italian anarchists were convicted and executed for a Massachusetts holdup-murder actually committed by a gang of professional criminals (who escaped punishment). Dubious ballistics evidence and perjured eyewitness testimony sent both defendants to the electric chair.

1933: The Jake Factor kidnapping case. After failing to convict bootlegger Roger Touhy and several associates in the ransom kidnapping of brewer William Hamm (actually abducted by members of the Barker-Karpis gang, later convicted), FBI agents prosecuted and imprisoned the same defendants for kidnapping Chicago underworld figure Jake "The Barber" Factor. Marathon beatings failed to extract confessions, but Factor identified the defendants, who were bootlegging rivals of Factor's good friend "Scarface Al" Capone. G-men obtained corroborating testimony from several convicted felons, while defense witnesses were threatened with arrest or death if they testified on Touhy's behalf. In 1959, a federal judge declared that Factor had never been kidnapped at all, rather staging a disappearance to avoid extradition on FRAUD charges to his native England. Touhy was released from prison—and promptly murdered by Capone syndicate gunmen.

1935: Richard Bruno Hauptmann, a German immigrant, was convicted of murder by New Jersey jurors in the 1932 LINDBERGH KIDNAPPING. Evidence submitted against him in court, resulting in his ultimate execution, included perjured testimony from several alleged eyewitnesses, forensic evidence described as "fabricated" in classified FBI memos, and a telephone number written inside Hauptmann's closet by a journalist in search of a "scoop."

1965: The Edward Deegan murder. Deegan was a small-time Boston gangster, murdered by contract killers Joseph "The Animal" Barboza and Vincent Flemmi. Local FBI agents, who employed both killers as "top level" informants, participated in the frame-up of innocent defendants Luis Greco, Peter Limone, Joseph Salvati, and Henry Tameleo. Jurors convicted all four, based on perjured testimony from Barboza. Greco and Tameleo subsequently died in prison, while Limone and Salvati were formally exonerated in 2000. FBI agent John Connolly Jr., instrumental in framing the false charges, was convicted of bribery in September 2002 and received a 10-year prison term.

1970: Elmer "Geronimo" Pratt. A leader of the radical Black Panther Party in Los Angeles, California, Pratt was targeted for elimination by local police and agents of the FBI. Authorities first charged Pratt with stockpiling illegal weapons, but jurors acquitted him of those counts in July 1970. Five months later, LAPD charged Pratt with the holdup-murder of a woman robbed and shot in Santa Monica, in December 1968. The victim's husband, wounded in the same attack, "positively" identified one gunman and "tentatively" identified three others— none of them Pratt—before finally changing his story under intense police pressure. Pratt served 25 years in prison before an appellate court exonerated him of all charges. In April 2000, FBI headquarters paid Pratt $1.75 million for the wrongful prosecution, while LAPD kicked in another $2.75 million.

1971: Daniel and Philip Berrigan. Late in 1970, while seeking inflated appropriations for his agency, FBI Director J. Edgar Hoover regaled members of the U.S. Senate with baseless claims of an "incipient plot" by leftist radicals to bomb federal facilities in Washington, D.C., and to kidnap White House aide (later secretary of state) Henry Kissinger. Those named as conspirators included brothers Daniel and Philip Berrigan (both Catholic priests and convicted draft obstructers), plus several nuns and other associates of the Berrigans. Attorney General John Mitchell—later imprisoned for his role in the Watergate scandal—reluctantly indicted the "plotters" in what he described as a bid "to get Hoover off the hook" for lying to Congress. Daniel Berrigan and one female defendant were subsequently convicted of smuggling love letters in and out of a federal jail, while all other charges were dismissed.

FRAUD

Broadly speaking, fraud includes any act of deception committed with criminal intent, which results in damage to another party. Financial motives are common but not required, as in cases of election fraud where ballots are falsified or destroyed to assist a particular candidate. False advertising is a common form of fraud, wherein the quality or quantity of merchandise offered for sale is deliberately misrepresented. Many CYBERCRIMES incorporate elements of fraud, including Internet adoption rackets, identity theft, credit card swindles, offers of shabby or nonexistent merchandise for sale, sight-unseen. CONFIDENCE GAMES are as old as mankind, taking advantage of human gullibility with countless get-rich-quick schemes. International syndicates earn billions every year from telecommunications fraud, while pyramid (or Ponzi) schemes fleece other victims of their savings. WHITE-COLLAR CRIMES often include the fraudulent sale of worthless or stolen stocks, bonds, and securities. Another lucrative form of fraud, COUNTERFEITING, has expanded over time from the printing of "funny money" to include false labels placed on stolen or bootlegged merchandise ranging from designer clothes to movies, recorded music, computer software, and prescription medicines. Tax fraud involves the unlawful avoidance or underpayment of taxes owed to various levels of government. Fraud may also involve other crimes, such as ARSON, HOMICIDE, and THEFT, committed to wrongfully obtain an inheritance or insurance payments.

Legal investigators use various techniques to detect and prove fraud. Sundry methods of DECEPTION ANALYSIS are employed to catch liars at work, and while those test results may result in dismissal from various jobs, they are not generally admissible as evidence in American courts of law. Analysis of QUESTIONED DOCUMENTS—such as bonds, contracts, deeds, diaries, historical records, letters, promissory notes, stocks, and wills—is another field where frauds are commonly encountered. In such cases, prosecutors must prove (a) that the documents in question are fraudulent, and (b) that the person(s) promoting said documents for adjudication or sale were conscious participants in the fraud. It may not be a crime, for instance, to sell a bogus treasure map in good faith, but hoaxers have been imprisoned for selling false diaries or letters allegedly penned by historical figures such as Adolf Hitler, Thomas Jefferson, and Brigham Young.

FRITZ, Dennis, and Williamson, Ronald exonerated by DNA

Authorities in Ada, Oklahoma, labored for five years to solve the 1982 rape-murder of 21-year-old Debra Sue Carter. In May 1987, they arrested two suspects: 34-year-old Ronald Williamson and 37-year-old Dennis Fritz, a respected junior high school teacher and neighbor of the victim. Both men denied involvement in the crime, but they were charged and held for trial on the basis of forensic evidence including hairs and semen, deemed "consistent" with their own by methods common prior to the advent of DNA testing. At trial, in April 1988, the prosecution also relied heavily on testimony from jailhouse "snitches," including one Glen Gore, who claimed the defendants had confessed the crime in private conversations. Upon conviction, Williamson was sentenced to die, while Fritz received a life prison term. Williamson successfully appealed his conviction and won a new trial, but he was convicted again and once more sentenced to die. At one point

in his death row odyssey, Williamson came within nine days of execution, summoned to the warden's office to discuss disposal of his corpse.

A stay of execution saved his life on that occasion, and Williamson remained persistent, winning another appeal in 1998. This time, before convening a third trial, prosecutors agreed to DNA testing of evidence found at the Carter crime scene. Fritz's lawyers, including BARRY SCHECK from the CARDOZO INNOCENCE PROJECT, joined that effort, and the tests exonerated both men of involvement in the crime. They were released from prison on April 15, 1999. Prosecution witness Glen Gore, meanwhile, was implicated by DNA testing as Carter's actual slayer, a disclosure that prompted him to stage a jailbreak from the Lexington Correctional Center one day before Fritz and Williamson were liberated. Gore surrendered to police on April 20, 1999.

On June 12, 2000, Dennis Fritz appeared before the U.S. Senate Judiciary Committee in Washington, D.C., to describe his ordeal. Appearing in support of proposed legislation to mandate DNA testing in relevant cases, Fritz told his audience:

At the time of my conviction in 1988, DNA testing had just been accepted by the scientific community. For years while in prison, I repeatedly petitioned the courts to allow me to get my DNA tested. I was flat out denied by one court after another. By the time I got in touch with Barry Scheck and Peter Neufeld, I had lost seven court decisions, and I had just about lost hope. . . .

The refusal of the state of Oklahoma to compare my DNA with the crime scene evidence was only one of the reasons why I lost all those years of my life. The other reason was my trial attorney's ineffectiveness. First, he had no real incentive to defend me since he had only received $500 for representing me in a capital murder case. And besides that, he had never handled a murder case in his life. In fact, he had never handled any type of criminal case whatsoever, due to the fact that he was a civil liabilities lawyer. . . .

It is more than past time to put an end to these unmerciful travesties of injustice that occur when the truth is hidden or disregarded. I appeal to you, the members of this committee, to enact the necessary laws to fully assure that no human being will ever have to suffer unjustly for something of which they are totally innocent.

G

GALL, Franz Joseph (1758–1828)

German neuroanatomist Franz Gall was born at Tiefenbronn, Baden, in what is now south Germany, on March 9, 1758. Defying parental expectations that he join the priesthood, Gall studied medicine in Vienna, Austria, and established private practice in that city after graduation. While compiling a practice of wealthy patients, Gall specialized in study of the brain and its localized mental functions. In 1800, teamed with colleague Johann Spurzheim, Gall developed *cranioscopy,* a proposed technique for determining an individual's personality, intelligence, and moral development based on the shape of his or her skull. Spurred by complaints from the Catholic Church, Austrian emperor Francis I ordered Gall and Spurzheim to cease their lectures and writing in 1801, claiming that cranioscopy challenged the divine nature of human intelligence. Gall moved to France in 1805, but found no warmer reception from Napoleon Bonaparte or the Institute of France, which ruled his theories invalid.

Despite the ongoing controversy over cranioscopy, Gall maintained a lucrative medical practice and contributed to hard science with his groundbreaking discovery that the brain's gray matter contained cell bodies (called neurons), while the white matter contained fibers (dubbed axions). Ironically, a stroke claimed his life in Paris on August 22, 1828, and leaders of the Catholic Church refused to permit his burial in consecrated ground. Cranios-copy—renamed *phrenology* by Spurzheim—found a greater degree of acceptance in Britain (where racists used Gall's theories to explain the "inferiority" of Irishmen and other targets of discrimination) and in the United States, where it enjoyed a 30-year vogue ending around 1850. Pseudoscience aside, many of Gall's theories on localization of brain function were validated years after his death, thus laying the early groundwork of forensic PSYCHIATRY.

GALTON, Francis (1822–1911)

A half cousin of Charles Darwin, Francis Galton was born near Sparkbrook, England, on February 16, 1822. His forebears included various renowned bankers, gun makers, inventors, and scientists, perhaps accounting for his life as anthropologist, eugenicist, explorer, geographer, inventor, meteorologist, and statistician. A child prodigy, Galton read by age two, tackled Greek, Latin, and long division at five, and read Shakespeare for pleasure at age six. Frequent changes in schools and curricula drove Galton to a nervous breakdown at age 22, while his father's death in the same year left him independently wealthy. He abandoned his formal studies after receiving a B.A. degree, which he later supplemented with an M.A. In 1847, Galton roamed the world from 1845 to 1852, leading expeditions for the Royal Geographical Society and publishing a critically acclaimed book on South Africa, followed by a best-selling tourist's handbook, *The Art of Travel.*

In middle age, as a member of the British Association for the Advancement of Science, Galton presented groundbreaking papers in various fields including ANTHROPOLOGY, BIOLOGY, eugenics, geography, heredity, historiometry, and statistics. Publication of his cousin's *On the Origin of Species* (1859) prompted Galton to focus on the various traits of humankind, ranging from mental attributes to FINGERPRINTS and facial features. In 1869, he published *Hereditary Genius,* discoursing at length on patterns of inherited intelligence while debating the roles of heredity versus environment in human development. Further study in that area, including interviews with 190 Fellows of the Royal Society, produced Galton's next work—*English Men of Science: Their Nature and Nurture*—in 1874. Thereafter, he produced *The History of Twins* (1875) and *Inquiries in Human Faculty and Its Development* (1883). Anticipating ALPHONSE BERTILLON, Galton also devised a technique of "composite PHOTOGRAPHY" through which he proposed to identify various human "types"— including criminals—by their superficial appearance. His volume *Fingerprints* (1893) helped spark a bitter feud between HENRY FAULDS and WILLIAM HERSCHEL, both of whom claimed credit as pioneers in the field. Galton's foray into fiction, a utopian novel titled *Kantsaywhere,* was aborted when a niece took offense at the graphic love scenes and burned most of the manuscript. Galton was knighted for his contributions to science in 1909 and died in Surrey on January 17, 1911.

GENERAL Knowledge Exam

Soon after its creation in 1989, the AMERICAN BOARD OF CRIMINALISTICS (ABC) began preparation of a General Knowledge Exam (GKE) to help elevate and standardize forensic science practices throughout the United States. In 1991, the ABC Examinations Committee purchased rights to a test written by the older CALIFORNIA ASSOCIATION OF CRIMINALISTS, then revised that exam by removing questions focused specifically on California statutes and those deemed "too specialized" for a general examination. Other questions were added or modified following a comprehensive evaluation by the Educational Testing Service (widely regarded as America's premier test development organization). The GKE constantly evolves to keep pace with new developments and discoveries in forensic science, presently including some 200 questions involving forensic procedures and the ABC Code of Professional Conduct. (All questions are drawn from a GKE Study Guide published by the ABC.) Various specialty examinations are also offered with their own study guides, ranging from 150 to 300 questions each, while the ABC's Technical Specialist Exams include 150 to 350 questions. Candidates for ABC certification must correctly answer 80 percent of the questions for any given test.

GEOGRAPHIC Profiling

Geographical profiling of unknown criminal offenders differs fundamentally from PSYCHOLOGICAL PROFILING, in that it seeks to pinpoint a subject's location rather than his/her gender, race, occupation, or mental state. It is effective only in a case of serial offenses, be they ARSON, bombing, HOMICIDE, ROBBERY, or SEX CRIMES. Assisted by computer software programs, practitioners of geographic profiling chart the locations of various crime scenes, producing a three-dimensional probability (or "jeopardy") surface suggesting where the offender is most likely based. Depending on the nature of the offense and the number of subjects involved, that base may be an individual's residence, his/her workplace, the headquarters of some organization, and so forth. All certified geographic profilers are presently members of the International Criminal Investigative Analysis Fellowship (ICIAF), a professional organization launched by the FBI in the 1980s.

Dr. Kim Rossmo, a 21-year veteran of the Vancouver (British Columbia) Police Department with a Ph.D. in criminology, is widely recognized as the pioneer of geographic profiling. His groundbreaking efforts sprang from research conducted at British Columbia's Simon Frasier University—where Rossmo also serves as an adjunct professor—in 1989. While the resultant software works best in cases involving five or more separate offenses, it may be applied in more limited instances. Geographic profilers offer the following services to law enforcement agencies:

1. Identifying *catchment areas,* defined as the geographic area served by a particular business, institution or other facility, particularly useful in cases of serial THEFT, FRAUD, robbery, or where

offenders target employees of a particular business chain.

2. Producing distance, speed, and time calculations for subjects or victims moving on foot (walking vs. running, etc.), or by means of different vehicles. This function helps determine if the unknown subject owns a car or travels to nearby crime scenes on foot, using public transportation, etc.

3. Producing maps of a crime scene or series of crimes, for use by investigators in court, during task force presentations, and in reconstruction of "cold" cases.

4. Completion of a geographical profile, which—if accurate—helps field investigators focus their search for a suspect or missing person. The same profile also illustrates possible routes of travel used by an offender passing to and from crime scenes. Coordination of geographic and psychological profiling may suggest possible locations of employment for the unknown subject(s) within a probability surface. As an example, if the psychological profile suggests a blue-collar industrial worker, detectives may concentrate on employees of factories or foundries located within the "jeopardy" surface.

GEOLOGY, Forensic

Geology and its subdiscipline mineralogy encompass the physical study of Earth's component rocks, minerals, and soils. Their application to forensic science includes the identification of various geologic materials and determination of their source. From his debut in 1887, fictional detective Sherlock Holmes was a keen observer of soil and mud, frequently charting a suspect's movements through London and beyond by the variety of stains on his or her shoes and clothing. In his *Handbook for Examining Magistrates* (1893), Austrian criminologist HANS GROSS suggested that "the dirt on someone's shoes could tell more about where a person had last been than toilsome inquiries."

Modern laboratories apply those same principles today, analyzing soil and mineral traces found at crime scenes and elsewhere. Geologic material found on clothing, shoes, or in the tread of automobile tires may place a suspect at a far-distant crime scene, despite denials. Trace evidence found on a corpse may prove that the victim was killed at one loca-

tion, then transported to another for disposal. Expert knowledge of geology is also critical to determining the age or authenticity of jewelry, paintings, sculpture, and precious metals or other minerals (as in cases of mining fraud). According to an article in *Geotimes* (February 2002), geologist John Shroder identified the region of Afghanistan where fugitive terrorist Osama bin Laden sought refuge in 2001, by examining photos of bin Laden with distinctive rocky outcrops in the background. Nonetheless, bin Laden eluded capture.

One case with a more gratifying outcome was the murder of John Bruce Dodson, in October 1995. While hunting with his wife of three months in western Colorado's Uncompahgre Mountains, Dodson suffered a gunshot wound some 200 yards from their camp. A Texas police officer, camped nearby, heard Janice Dodson's cries for help and rushed to the scene, where he found John Dodson dead. Investigators found a .308-caliber cartridge case 60 yards from Dodson's corpse and subsequently located the slug that had passed through his body. At Dodson's camp, they also found a set of coveralls belonging to Janice, coated in mud from the knees down. (Janice claimed that she had stepped into a bog near camp.) Suspicion focused on Janice's ex-husband, J. C. Lee, another hunter who was camped nearby, but Lee presented an alibi witness and told police that his .308 rifle had been stolen from his camp with a box of ammunition. Early snow prevented further gathering of evidence, but local investigators searched the area exhaustively over the next three summers, vainly attempting to locate the murder weapon. During their final search, in 1998, the officers noted a cattle pond lined with bentonite clay, located between Dodson's camp and the site where J. C. Lee had camped on the day of the shooting. Comparison of mud from the pond with that found on Janice Dodson's coveralls convinced a jury that she had stolen Lee's rifle and killed her new husband, while trying to frame Lee for the crime. Although the gun was never found, Janice Dodson received a life sentence.

GEORGIA Innocence Project

Founded in August 2002, the Georgia Innocence Project is a nonprofit organization created to assist persons wrongfully convicted of crimes they did not commit. Its members work primarily to secure post-conviction DNA testing for Georgia prison inmates in cases where such testing may prove innocence or guilt and was unavailable at trial. As noted by GIP president and founding member Jill Polster, "Innocent people are serving a significant portion of their lives in prison for crimes they did not commit. These innocent people need someone to care about justice and to assist them in gaining their freedom." The group achieved a major victory in August 2004, when its work liberated CLARENCE HARRISON, 18 years after his wrongful conviction on charges of kidnapping, rape, and robbery.

GETTLER, Alexander Oscar (1884–1968)

A native of Austria, born in 1884, Alexander Gettler immigrated with his family to the United States in 1889. The Gettlers settled in Brooklyn, New York, and Alexander received his Ph.D. in CHEMISTRY from Columbia University at age 28. Six years later, New York City abandoned its corrupt and inefficient coroner's service, employing Dr. CHARLES NORRIS as the city's first MEDICAL EXAMINER. Norris in turn recruited Gettler from his post as a biochemist at Bellevue Hospital, to furnish expertise in TOXICOLOGY. Over the next four decades, until his retirement in 1959, Gettler served as the Big Apple's primary "blood detective," doubling as a professor of chemistry at New York University and providing future generations of toxicologists with priceless on-the-job training. His aides and protégés included Ray Abernathy, Leo Dal Cortivo, Lester Ellerbrook, Milton Feldstein, Henry Freimuth, Abe Freireich, Leo Goldbaum, Rollo Harger, Clarence Muehlberger, Fred Rieders, Harry Schwartz, Henry Siegel, Abe Stolman, Irving Sunshine, Joe Umberger, and Louis Weiss—all later well known in the field. The "Gettler boys," as they were known, went on to solve thousands of crimes and train new generations in turn, while Gettler himself examined more than 100,000 corpses in the course of his career. He retired in 1959 and died nine years later, at age 84.

GILCHRIST, Joyce forensic chemist linked to frauds

An African-American native of Oklahoma City, Joyce Gilchrist was drawn to the mysteries of police work while still a student at the University of Central Oklahoma. By 1980, when she obtained her degree in forensic CHEMISTRY, Gilchrist was already employed in the Oklahoma City Police Department's crime

lab, working on some 3,000 cases between 1980 and 1993. In 1985, she was named the Oklahoma City Police Department's "civilian employee of the year." Gilchrist made a compelling witness at trial, invariably supporting prosecution theories with the kind of scientific evidence guaranteed to make a jury sit up and take notice. Legendary Oklahoma City district attorney Bob Macy was especially enamored of Gilchrist's technique, and police dubbed her "Black Magic" for her startling conviction rate. "It was in reference to a homicide case," Gilchrist later told *60 Minutes II*, "where the defense attorney referred to me in his closing argument as a sorcerer . . . and stated that I seemed to be able to do things with evidence that nobody else was able to do."

And that, in fact, was the problem.

In 1987, another forensic chemist, John T. Wilson of Kansas City, wrote an angry letter to the Southwestern Association of Forensic Scientists (SAFS), asserting that Gilchrist offered "scientific opinions from the witness stand which in effect positively identify the defendant based on the slightest bit of circumstantial evidence." Wilson took the unusual step of criticizing a colleague after several Oklahoma defense attorneys asked him to review Gilchrist's testimony from preliminary hearings. Convinced that Gilchrist had presented false evidence in court, Wilson ultimately testified against her in three separate murder cases. Although he "got major heat" for siding with the defense in those cases, Wilson told interviewers that he "felt I had an ethical obligation" to do so. "When I read the transcripts and saw what she was saying, I was really shocked. She was positively identifying hair, and there's no way in the world you can do that without DNA." (See FIBER AND HAIR EVIDENCE.)

As a result of Wilson's letter, the SAFS conducted its own investigation and determined that Gilchrist had violated the group's code of ethics, resulting in a formal censure. In 1988, the Oklahoma Criminal Court of Appeals overturned Curtis Edward McCarty's murder conviction, based on the fact that Joyce Gilchrist gave the court "personal opinions beyond the scope of scientific capabilities." (A new trial was ordered, resulting in a second conviction and death sentence for McCarty, but the evidence from his case remained under scientific review in 2001.) In 1989, the same appellate court overturned another murder conviction, finding that Gilchrist had improperly used hair analysis to testify that James Lucas Abels had been "in very close and possibly even violent contact" with the victim.

Such disclosures notwithstanding, Gilchrist was promoted to supervisor of the Oklahoma City crime lab in 1994 and continued to testify in criminal cases through the remainder of the decade. It was only in August 1999, after her rebuke by federal judge Ralph Thompson, that her career began to implode. At issue was the rape-murder conviction of ALFRED BRIAN MITCHELL, sentenced to death largely on the strength of Gilchrist's scientific testimony. Specifically, Gilchrist had testified that tests performed on semen samples in the case were "inconclusive," when she knew defendant Mitchell should have been excluded as a suspect by the test results. Judge Thompson bluntly labeled her testimony "untrue" and overturned Mitchell's rape conviction. (The murder conviction was allowed to stand, but Mitchell's death sentence was later overturned by the 10th Circuit Court of Appeals.)

As a result of Judge Thompson's ruling and criticism arising from similar cases, police removed Gilchrist from the crime lab in March 2000 and assigned her to an administrative post. Seven months later, the Association for Crime Scene Reconstruction expelled Gilchrist for offering sworn testimony that misrepresented evidence. On April 25, 2001, Oklahoma Attorney General Drew Edmondson announced that his office would review several death penalty cases that hinged on Gilchrist's testimony, further requesting that the Oklahoma State Bureau of Investigation review Gilchrist's work in search of possible criminal violations. An FBI report, published on the same date, alleged that Gilchrist misidentified hairs and fibers or gave testimony "beyond the limits of forensic science" in at least eight felony cases. Most ominous was the reported fact that Gilchrist's testimony had sent 23 defendants to death row, with 11 of those inmates subsequently executed.

Defense attorney David Autry, counsel for several defendants convicted with help from Gilchrist, told reporters, "It was common knowledge within the defense bar and should have been to the DA's office that she was incompetent and malicious. She survived because she made close cases for the prosecutors and secured convictions in particularly heinous crimes." One of those she convicted, alleged rapist Jeffrey Todd Pierce, was released from prison on May 7, 2001, after serving 15 years, when DNA tests proved him innocent of the crime. Following that reversal,

Governor Frank Keating ordered a sweeping review of some 1,200 cases involving Gilchrist. On September 25, 2001, Gilchrist was formally dismissed from her job, Police Chief M. T. Berry citing "laboratory mismanagement, criticism from court challenges and flawed casework analysis." Gilchrist's attorney tried to put a bold face on the situation, claiming that his client was "totally and completely a scapegoat" for other, unnamed wrongdoers.

In October 2001, a federal grand jury subpoenaed all evidence from 10 of Gilchrist's murder cases, including nine wherein defendants had been executed and one in which the accused was serving life without parole. By November 2001, Oklahoma investigators had isolated 165 Gilchrist cases that they deemed deserving of further study in depth, reporting that another year or more would be required to complete that review. The Oklahoma Indigent Defense System (OIDS), spearheading renewed DNA testing in various Gilchrist cases, issued a statement that, "whether it was intentional or just negligence, the fact is that her testimony was used to secure death sentences in cases where these people might have been sentenced to life. If just one of these people would have been sentenced to life without her testimony, the entire criminal justice system has been undermined."

Despite the insistence of Oklahoma attorney general Edmondson that "I am personally satisfied that no innocent person was executed," grave doubts remain. An example of the danger posed by Gilchrist's malfeasance is demonstrated in the case of Malcolm Rent Johnson, executed in January 2000 for the 1981 rape-murder of a woman in Oklahoma City. Johnson proclaimed his innocence to the end, despite Gilchrist's testimony that semen found on the victim's bed was "consistent" with Johnson's blood type. Police and prosecutors blocked all attempts at DNA testing while Johnson was alive, but a July 2001 memo obtained by the media seems to indicate that Gilchrist lied under oath at Johnson's trial: specifically, the document states that no sperm was found in semen samples from the crime scene, while Gilchrist testified to the opposite result. In his summation at the 1981 proceedings, D.A. Bob Macy called Gilchrist's testimony "damning, it's condemning, it's conclusive." Today, the state has done a curious turnabout, claiming that Johnson would have been convicted and condemned on the basis of eyewitness testimony alone, without Gilchrist's contribution to the case.

One version or the other must be false.

To date, no charges have been filed against Joyce Gilchrist for perjury or any other criminal offense. A review of her various cases continues, with all sides pledged to the pursuit of truth (although authorities in Oklahoma doggedly resist new DNA testing in any case where inmates have been executed on the basis of Gilchrist's "scientific" testimony). Regardless of whether she faces prosecution at some future date, cases like that of Joyce Gilchrist, RALPH ERDMANN, and FRED ZAIN have shaken the faith of many Americans in the modern system of capital punishment.

GLAISTER, John, Sr., and Jr. (1856–1932) (1892–1971)

Two John Glaisters, father and son, served as Regius Professor of Forensic Medicine at Scotland's Glasgow University between 1899 and 1962. John senior was born at Lanark in 1856 and completed his elementary schooling there before proceeding to Glasgow University, where he graduated with honors, intent on pursuing a legal career. Law school failed to hold his attention, however, and Glaister soon switched to medicine, with emphasis on public health and forensic PATHOLOGY. Glaister enjoyed a 17-year career as a divisional police surgeon attached to the Royal Infirmary and St. Mungo's College, before returning to his alma mater in 1898. Throughout his high-profile career, John senior served as an expert witness in numerous trials, delivering testimony dramatic enough to rate a dedication from author Erle Stanley Gardner in his Perry Mason novel *The Case of the Horrified Heirs* (1964). John senior died in 1932.

John junior, Glasgow-born in 1892, studied both law and medicine before spending three years in Egypt with the Royal Army Medical Corps (1916–19). Back in Glasgow after World War I, he served as an assistant in his father's university department and won admittance to the bar in 1926, before returning to Egypt as a teacher and forensic medical consultant to the government in Cairo (swapping positions with Sir SYDNEY SMITH). Glaister's subsequent experiments with comparison microscopes, examining FIBERS and hairs, prompted him to write the epic reference work *Hairs of Mammalia from the Medico-Legal Aspect* in 1931, followed in due course by other volumes including *Medical Jurisprudence and Toxicology* and *The Power of Poison*. In 1937, he replaced Sydney Smith as chairman of Glasgow University's forensic medical department, filling the post once held by his late father until 1962. Glaister retired from teaching after completing his autobiography, *Final Diagnosis* (1964), and died in 1971.

GLASS

Glass is a uniform amorphous solid material, produced when certain viscous molten materials cool rapidly into solid form. Melted table sugar may produce a crude form of glass, while elements for commercially manufactured glass normally include silica, lime, and soda or potash. Glass takes its name from the Latin *glacies* ("ice"), corresponding to similar terms in German, Middle English, and Anglo-Saxon. Naturally occurring glass (obsidian, etc.) was used for cutting tools during the Stone Age, while Egyptians apparently pioneered the manufacture of glass around 1500 B.C.E. The invention of a glass pressing machine in 1827 permitted mass manufacture, while William Blenko revealed his cylinder method in the early 1900s. Today, glass is so common in daily life that it often features as part of the evidence at crime scenes—as a surface bearing FINGERPRINTS, TRACE EVIDENCE or IMPRESSION EVIDENCE; in broken shards it is useful for reconstruction of a crime, even as a possible weapon.

The most obvious value of broken glass at a crime scene is its utility in physical matching. Criminalists can examine the smallest shards of glass and match them to their original source—a window, vase, etc.—by their color and ingredients. Fragments of the same glass, recovered elsewhere, may also link suspects and/or victims to the crime scene. Glass recovered from the clothing of a corpse found in the desert may prove that the victim was murdered in a particular building or room, far from the body dump site. Likewise, glass shards found in a suspect's vehicle, on his person, clothing or other personal articles may prove that he/she was present at a given crime scene after glass was broken. That evidence may not prove guilt, but at the very least it suggests a need for further investigation of the suspect's alibi and movements, while probably winning approval for search warrants of the subject's home, vehicle and/or workplace.

The evidentiary value of glass is not restricted to physical matching. *Laminated* glass, formed by pressing a sheet of plastic polymer between two layers of safety glass (as in auto windshields) may retain the shape of an object that strikes the glass, thereby

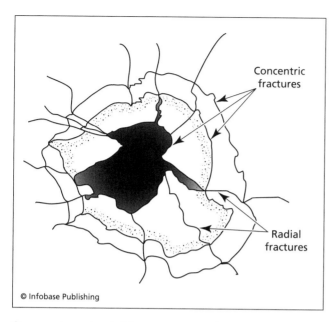

Concentric and radial fractures around an impact site in glass.

assisting in the object's identification. When a bullet or other missile penetrates glass, the impact creates both *concentric* and *radial* fractures. Concentric fractures surround the point of impact like rings on the cross-cut section of a tree trunk, while radial fractures branch outward from the impact point like strands in a spider's web. In a case of multiple impacts, as where several shots are fired through a windowpane, the cracking pattern may determine the order of impacts in time. Specifically, cracks from the first impact arrest passage of cracks from the second, and so on. Shards of glass found on one side of a window or the other also reveal the direction of impact.

Even melted glass at a crime scene provides forensic scientists with clues. ARSON investigators may judge the heat of a fire by the known melting temperature of certain glass and other materials, thereby determining if an accelerant was used and if so, what kind it may have been. Molten glass acts much like any other liquid, in terms of spatter and flow patterns, allowing crime scene analysts to chart the directions in which melted glass dripped, ran, or was flung. In automobile collisions, melted glass found adhering to headlight filaments proves that the headlights were lit at the time of collision—thus proving, for example, that a hit-and-run driver should have seen and avoided the victim on an otherwise darkened street.

GODDARD, Calvin Hooker (1891–1955)

A Baltimore native, born in 1891, Calvin Goddard earned his B.A. from Johns Hopkins University in 1911, followed by his M.D. four years later. He joined the U.S. Army in 1916 and served at various billets in Alabama, Massachusetts, New York, France, Belgium, Germany, and Poland. While rising to the rank of lieutenant colonel, Goddard served as assistant director of Johns Hopkins Hospital, as professor of clinical medicine at Cornell University, and as director of America's first outpatient clinic (in New York City). Meanwhile, Goddard nurtured a lifelong fascination with FIREARMS, which prompted him to quit Cornell in 1925 and join the fledgling Bureau of Forensic Ballistics, founded by colleagues PHILIP GRAVELLE and CHARLES WAITE. Together, those partners invented a new comparison microscope for examination of bullets and adapted a medical cytoscope to study the internal workings of guns.

Goddard's most controversial testimony was delivered in the SACCO-VANZETTI CASE, where he spoke for the prosecution and helped send two immigrant anarchists to the electric chair in Massachusetts. His ballistics findings in that case remain controversial today, in light of declassified FBI documents describing the evidence as "fabricated" and an unindicted felon's subsequent confession to the slayings. Two years after Sacco and Vanzetti were executed, in 1929, Goddard identified one of the submachine guns used in Chicago's notorious St. Valentine's Day massacre. Police seized the weapon from notorious mobster Fred "Killer" Burke, but authorities never charged Burke in that case. Instead, he received a life prison term for the murder of a Michigan policeman. Following a three-month tour of scientific facilities in Europe, Goddard returned to establish and direct a new Scientific Crime Detection Laboratory in Evanston, Illinois, attached to Northwestern University's law school. Goddard also served on the Northwestern faculty, while simultaneously editing the *American Journal of Police Science*.

Recalled to active duty with the U.S. Army during World War II, Goddard served as chief historian of the Ordnance Department in Washington, D.C., then transferred to Japan in 1947 as an officer of the Military Police. There, he trained Japanese law enforcement officers and personally investigated cases throughout the Far East, until failing health forced his return to the United States in 1951. Back on duty with the army's Historical Section, Goddard launched his most ambitious project yet, editing a 40-volume medical history of the recent world war and doubling as an American editor of the *Encyclopedia Britannica*. The army project was still ongoing when Goddard died in 1955, at age 64.

GODSCHALK, Bruce exonerated by DNA evidence

In July and September 1986, two women were raped at the Kingswood Apartments in King of Prussia, Pennsylvania. One victim was unable to describe her attacker, but the other glimpsed his face reflected in a bedroom mirror and gave police a vague description, including a reference to his distinctive shirt and sneakers. Bruce Godschalk, a 26-year-old unemployed landscaper from Radnor, was later arrested for the crimes. Police found no clothing similar to the rapist's in Godschalk's apartment, but one victim identified him as her attacker and a fellow inmate claimed Godschalk had talked about the rapes in jail. More to the point, Godschalk himself confessed in custody, but soon recanted, claiming that his statements were coerced by police. Convicted of rape in 1987, he received a 10- to 20-year prison sentence.

In 1993, Godschalk filed a motion for DNA testing of forensic evidence in the case, but two state courts rejected the bid. Seven years later, supported by attorneys from the CARDOZO INNOCENCE PROJECT, Godschalk filed a federal lawsuit to compel DNA testing on March 22, 2000. Montgomery County prosecutors again resisted the effort, but on March 27, 2001, a federal judge overruled state objections, finding that Godschalk was not constitutionally barred from seeking new tests of the evidence. Those tests, financed by money from his late mother's estate, excluded Godschalk as a source of the semen recovered from the crime scenes. He was released on February 14, 2002, after serving 15 years of his sentence.

Montgomery County District Attorney Bruce Castor Jr. still appeared to have his doubts about the case as Godschalk was released, although he agreed to dismiss all charges in the case. "This is one of those situations where I can't tell you what the truth is," Castor told reporters. "As a prosecutor, I have to be sure. And we're not sure. It's frustrating because I think the evidence is compelling that he's guilty, and the evidence is compelling that he's innocent. I don't like uncertainty. We can't prove it beyond a reasonable doubt, so we let him go. I am not convinced that

Bruce Godschalk was innocent. What I am convinced of is that he cannot be proven innocent [*sic*] beyond a reasonable doubt. And in this business, a tie goes to the defendant."

Godschalk's reaction to that strange declaration was terse and direct: "He's insane."

GRANT, Julius (1901–1991)

A British subject, born in 1901, Dr. Julius Grant was a forensics expert specializing in the field of QUESTIONED DOCUMENTS. During World War II he served MI6—Britain's Secret Intelligence Service—by developing invisible inks and edible paper for spies in Nazi-occupied Europe. On the home front, he also created ration books for civilians that resisted FORGERY and undermined black-marketeering. With the demise of the Axis, Grant entered private practice as an expert witness for hire, testifying in a range of cases that included England's Great Train Robbery. In 1959, he was among the founders of a new Forensic Science Society, serving official and civilian clients throughout the United Kingdom. In 1967, Grant debunked the alleged diary of Italian dictator Benito Mussolini, and two decades later he repeated the performance with the Führer himself, proving that the "Hitler diaries" published in Germany by *Stern* magazine were faked. His last headline case, in 1987, involved the perplexing matter of Ivan Demjanjuk, tried before Israel's Supreme Court as Nazi-era war criminal "Ivan the Terrible." Grant confirmed the authenticity of Demjanjuk's identity papers, resulting in conviction, but that verdict was subsequently overturned on appeal in 1993. Grant had died in the meantime—in 1991—and did not witness that reversal. In 2005, an American court ordered Demjanjuk's deportation to his native Ukraine, ruling that he was in fact a war criminal, though not the "Ivan" charged in his original indictment.

GRAVELLE, Philip O. (1877–1955)

Philip Gravelle was a native of San Francisco, born in 1877. He subsequently settled in New York, studying CHEMISTRY at Columbia University while employed as a textile designer. Gravelle's profession involved use of MICROSCOPY to study FIBERS, and he soon developed a technique for photographing microscopic objects. That work earned him the London Photomicrographic Society's prestigious Barnard

Gold Medal in 1923 and prompted overtures from CHARLES WAITE, who enlisted Gravelle in 1925 as a charter member of his new Bureau of Forensic Ballistics. Working with Waite, CALVIN GODDARD, and John Fisher, Gravelle invented a comparison microscope for bullets and adapted a medical cytoscope—a thin tube with telescopic lenses, used for internal examinations—to explore the interior of FIREARMS. Gravelle participated in many criminal investigations, including the notorious SACCO-VANZETTI CASE and Chicago's gruesome St. Valentine's Day Massacre. He died in Newark, New Jersey, on February 3, 1955.

GRAY, Anthony exonerated by DNA evidence

Maryland native Anthony Gray was arrested in 1991, accused of raping and murdering a woman at Chesapeake Beach. Although innocent of the crime, he was intimidated by police into confessing. Gray pleaded guilty in October 1991, convinced that he would be convicted and executed if he went to trial before a jury. As part of the plea bargain, Gray received a double life sentence, and subsequent appeals based on his limited intellect were rejected. DNA tests finally identified the true killer, but despite that suspect's guilty plea in 1997, Gray remained in prison. More testing proved that Gray had not been present at the crime scene, resulting in his belated release on February 9, 1999.

GREEN, Anthony Michael exonerated by DNA

In spring 1988, a female cancer patient was raped in her room at the Cleveland Clinic Inn, adjacent to the Cleveland, Ohio, hospital where her treatments were performed. She told police that the rapist knocked on her door, identified himself as "Tony," then grabbed her by the throat, brandished a knife, and demanded money before raping her on the bed. After the assault, the rapist wiped his penis on a washcloth, which he dropped on the bathroom floor. After he left, the victim urinated twice and scrubbed her genitals with soap, delaying 90 minutes before she contacted clinic security officers. They in turn called Cleveland police, who collected the washcloth and drove the victim to Mount Sinai Medical Center, where a rape kit was prepared and suspect pubic hairs were collected.

The victim described her assailant as a black male around 23 years old, five feet eight inches tall, with a short Afro hair style and a face scarred by acne. Suspicion focused on clinic employee Anthony Green, who matched the description, but the victim failed to pick his employee ID photo from a selection displayed by police, remarking that he "resembled the attacker, but just not enough." A second photo lineup included Green's booking mug shot with a placard including his height, weight, and age. The victim identified Green—the only person whose photo appeared in both lineups—from the second array. One week after the crime, Green learned that he was a suspect and voluntarily surrendered for questioning. A Cuyahoga County grand jury indicted him for rape and aggravated robbery on June 22, 1988. At trial four months later, the victim identified Green in court, while a civilian criminalist testified that Green and the rapist were both type B secretors. Jurors convicted Green on October 21, 1988, resulting in consecutive sentences of 10–25 years for rape and 10–25 years for aggravated robbery.

In 1997, Green contacted the OHIO INNOCENCE PROJECT for help in challenging his conviction. Project staffers located the crime-scene evidence and finally negotiated its release for DNA testing in May 2001. Dr. Edward Blake of Forensic Science Associates received the washcloth on July 9, 2001, and performed tests that excluded Green as the donor of semen found thereon. Green was released from prison on October 9, 2001, after serving 13 years, and was officially cleared of all charges nine days later. The actual rapist subsequently confessed to police, pled guilty in court, and was sentenced to prison. Green, meanwhile, sued the city of Cleveland for his wrongful conviction. In June 2004, he settled that case with a financial payment and official agreement to conduct an "Anthony Michael Green Forensic Laboratory Audit," reviewing other convictions obtained in similar cases over the past 16 years.

GREEN, Edward exonerated by DNA evidence

In July and August 1987, a serial rapist terrorized women in Washington, D.C. The predator claimed his first victim on July 3, near a local high school; a second woman, attacked at the same place on August 5, fought her way clear without being raped. Based on physical descriptions offered by the two victims, Washington police later arrested suspect Edward Green in the vicinity of the attacks. The first victim picked his photograph from among several others displayed by police; both women also selected Green from lineups at police headquarters and identified him as their assailant at trial. Forensic experts testified that Green's blood type was "consistent" with the rapist's, based on semen samples recovered from the first victim. Jurors deliberated three hours before convicting Green of rape but acquitting him of assault on the second victim.

Prior to sentencing, Green's lawyer filed a motion for postponement pending completion of a DNA test on the state's forensic evidence. Prosecutors opposed several delays, but time was granted by the judge. A final report, issued in February 1990, excluded Edward Green as a source of the semen found on the first victim's clothing. Green's attorney used that finding as the basis for a motion for a new trial, granted at a special hearing on March 19, 1990. The U.S. attorney's office agreed to dismissal of the rape charge, while Green remained incarcerated for an unrelated drug violation.

GREEN, Kevin Lee exonerated by DNA evidence

A Marine Corps corporal stationed in Southern California, Kevin Green went out for a late-night cheeseburger on September 30, 1979, and returned to find that his 20-year-old pregnant wife had been assaulted in their home, raped, and severely beaten. Dianna Green survived the beating but her unborn child, already two weeks overdue, did not. Emerging from a coma in October, with brain damage and memory loss, Dianna named her husband as her attacker, and he was arrested on March 25, 1980, later convicted of sexual assault, attempted murder (of his wife), and second degree murder (of their child). He received a prison term of 15 years to life.

DNA testing was unknown at the time Green went to prison, and by the time he learned about it in the early 1990s he could not afford the $10,000 required for tests on the prosecution's evidence from his case. As luck would have it, in 1996 a DNA test performed on serial killer Gerald Parker linked him to the rape of Dianna Green, and Parker later confessed to the crime. Kevin Green by then had survived inmate attacks and suicide attempts in prison and gone on to earn a college degree in social sciences. Upon his release after DNA testing exonerated him, state legislators discovered that California had no legal mechanism for compensating wrongfully convicted persons. A special bill, passed in 1999, awarded Green $100

for each day he was incarcerated. Today he lives in Missouri and travels widely as a public speaker.

"GREEN River Killer" cold case solved via DNA

Beginning in January 1982, an unknown predator killed at least 40 women around Seattle and Tacoma, Washington; nine more listed as missing are also presumed to be dead. Many of the victims were prostitutes, working along the infamous "Sea-Tac Strip." A few were runaways or hitchhikers. While skeletal remains were found as late as 1988, authorities have not confirmed another slaying in the series since October 1984. The killer's favorite dumping ground led journalists to christen him the Green River Killer.

While theories and suspects abounded in the haunting case, police were unable to solve it. Public interest waned and funds ran out. Nearly two decades after the last confirmed murder, it seemed the case would remain an eternal mystery—like the identity of London's Jack the Ripper or the elusive New Orleans Ax Man—but modern science intervened to shed new light on the murky affair.

DNA evidence lay beyond the reach of American police in 1984. Its first use in a murder trial, against British serial slayer COLIN PITCHFORK, would not make headlines until 1986. The trail in Washington was cold by then, but DNA has an advantage over witnesses and other transitory evidence: if undisturbed by man or nature, it remains to tell its story years, decades, even centuries after the fact.

So it was in the Green River case. One of the original manhunters, King County sheriff Dave Reichert, announced formation of a new task force in June 2001, to test skin cells recovered from materials used to strangle some of the murderer's victims. Most, predictably, would belong to the victims—but Reichert hoped some might be traced to the killer himself. As detective Tom Jensen told reporters, "It's too bad we didn't have this technology back when it was going on, because the case would have been better handled, probably solved."

The best hope for working with 19-year-old evidence lay in the polymerase chain reaction (PCR) process, described by Dr. Beverly Himick of the Washington State Patrol Crime Lab as "a chemical photocopier." In essence, PCR processing takes a microscopic DNA sample and generates multiple copies at high speed, thereby providing forensic scientists with sufficient material to complete their varied tests. Semen recovered from three of the Green River victims was tested, the DNA compared with evidence collected over time from various suspects and known sex offenders in Washington state. In early October 2001, Detective Jensen presented Sheriff Reichert with three DNA printouts: two samples were obtained from victims Marcia Chapman and Opal Mills, murdered in 1982; the third—a saliva sample—had been taken from a suspect by police in 1987.

All three matched.

On November 30, 2001, King County detectives arrested 52-year-old truck painter Gary Lee Ridgway at his place of business, charging him with first-degree murder in four of the 49 Green River cases. According to prosecution press releases, DNA samples obtained from the corpse of 21-year-old Carol Christensen (killed in May 1983) matched Ridgway's DNA so precisely that "it can be estimated that not more than one individual (excluding identical twins) in the world's population would exhibit this DNA profile." Semen retrieved from 31-year-old Marcia Chapman's body was degraded, displaying only nine of 13 possible DNA markers, but all nine matched Ridgway's. Experts placed the odds of another white male matching all nine markers at one in 645 million—more than double the entire U.S. population. Sperm from at least two men was found with the body of 16-year-old Opal Mills, and while DNA results were inconclusive, tests did not exclude Ridgway as a possible donor. No foreign DNA was found on 17-year-old Cynthia Hinds, but Ridgway was charged in her case because Hinds was discovered with Chapman and Mills on August 15, 1982. Both she and Chapman were pinned underwater with heavy rocks, and small stones were inserted by the killer into their vaginas.

With Ridgway in custody, police revealed that they had considered him a suspect in the Green River murders since February 1983, when a Seattle prostitute accused him of violent behavior. Two months later, a pimp watched hooker Marie Malvar climb into a pickup truck with her "trick." When she failed to turn up the next day, her pimp traced the pickup to Ridgway's house and alerted police, but Ridgway denied any knowledge of the incident. Questioned again in April 1984, Ridgway admitted frequent contact with prostitutes—a fact confirmed by sporadic surveillance—but again denied any other wrongdoing. In November 1984, a prostitute informed detec-

DNA evidence directly linked Gary Ridgway to numerous murders in the Green River killings that haunted Washington State in the 1980s. (Reuters NewMedia Inc./ CORBIS)

tives that Ridgway had tried to strangle her during sex, before she broke free and escaped. Ridgway acknowledged that attack but claimed the woman bit him first, and no charges were filed. In 1985, Ridgway allegedly told detectives that he was obsessed with prostitutes and that they "affect him as strongly as alcohol does an alcoholic." A saliva sample was obtained from Ridgway in 1987, then routinely filed away for 14 years, until Sheriff Reichert launched a fresh investigation of the case.

Authorities seemed confident of Ridgway's guilt. "DNA is sort of the physical last link," one investigator told reporters on December 5, 2001, "but it does nothing more than verify what our circumstantial evidence has said before. It's nowhere close to the sole evidence in this case." Indeed, for some that raised a question as to why Ridgway was not arrested earlier. Harold Coleman, chief executive officer for a Seattle-based DNA testing firm, told journalists that

PCR testing "has been widely available since 1996," performed by his own lab under contract for the Indiana State Police and other law enforcement agencies. The Washington State Patrol's crime lab remained "woefully underfunded," unable to perform PCR tests before mid-1999, and Green River fell through the cracks, with new cases assigned top priority. As Coleman suggests, "The DNA was just sitting there in the evidence locker. I think they just didn't think to send it out for somebody else to do it."

On November 30, 2001, using DNA evidence collected for a 1997 sexual assault investigation, Seattle police charged 52-year-old Gary Leon Ridgway with four of the Green River murders. PAINT samples from his factory workplace linked Ridgway to three more slayings in the series. After two years of legal delays, Ridgway confessed to 48 counts of aggravated murder and received a sentence of life imprisonment without parole.

GROSS, Hans (1847–1915)

A native of Graz, Austria, born in 1847, Hans Gross studied law and became an examining magistrate at age 22. Although ostensibly a judge, he soon became Graz's chief investigator of crime, operating on behalf of a police force that lacked the experience and temperament for anything beyond preserving public order. His studies and field experience subsequently earned Gross a position as professor of criminology at the University of Graz. Publication of his classic *Handbuch für Untersuchungsrichter als System der Kriminalistik* (1893) established Gross as an authority in the field. That work saw publication in English during 1907, as *Criminal Investigation,* and established Gross as the "founder of scientific criminology." In 1912, three years before his death, Gross established the Imperial Criminological Museum at the University of Graz, which remains open to tourists to the present day. His son Otto Gross, born in 1877, became a psychiatrist but rejected most of his father's viewpoints on law enforcement, writing in 1913: "I have only mixed with anarchists and declare myself to be an anarchist. I am a psychoanalyst and from my experience I have gained the insight that the existing order . . . is a bad one . . . and since I want everything changed, I am an anarchist."

HAMMOND, Ricky exonerated by DNA evidence

In the early evening of November 20, 1987, a female resident of Hartford, Connecticut, was snatched from a city sidewalk, forced into a waiting car by a stranger who drove her to a rural area outside of town and there sexually assaulted her. After the attack, the kidnapper drove his victim to an unfamiliar neighborhood and left her with a warning that she would be killed if she reported the incident. She told police nonetheless, but arrest of a suspect was delayed since the victim had no clue to her rapist's identity.

Ricky Hammond was subsequently charged with the attack, after the victim identified his photograph and accurately described certain details of his car, including the make and model, scratches in the paint, a torn child's seat, and a wristwatch hanging from the gearshift. Forensic tests on hair retrieved from Hammond's car found it consistent with the victim's hair. (See FIBER AND HAIR EVIDENCE.) Prosecutors hit an apparent snag when tests performed on semen from the victim's clothes excluded Hammond, as to both blood type and DNA, but a court accepted the district attorney's argument that the evidence must have been "contaminated," since the victim's testimony was so detailed and persuasive. Jurors bought the same story, convicting Hammond of KIDNAPPING and sexual assault in March 1990, whereupon he received a 25-year prison sentence. Hammond's motions for a new trial and more detailed forensic testing on available evidence were routinely denied.

Hammond appealed his conviction on three grounds: (1) that the trial court erred in denying his motion for a new trial based on exculpatory blood and DNA analysis; (2) that the court also erred in rejecting his motion for further DNA testing; and (3) that the prosecution made improper statements to the jury, thus infringing on his right to a fair trial. On February 25, 1992, Connecticut's Supreme Court overturned his conviction and remanded the case for further proceedings, noting that the trial judge had ignored or misunderstood "the logical inconsistencies in the prosecution's case, the evidence suggesting that the chemical alteration of the assailant's DNA was physically impossible, or the absence of any evidence that the defendant's scientific tests were unreliable." After serving two years of his sentence, Hammond was acquitted at his second trial and released from custody.

HARRIS, William exonerated by DNA evidence

A state champion athlete from Rand, West Virginia, 17-year-old William Harris was looking forward to college with scholarships in hand when a neighbor was raped near her home in December 1984. Jailed on the basis of a shaky eyewitness identification, Harris was later convicted after state serologist FRED ZAIN testified that his blood type matched that of the rapist. Harris received a 10- to 20-year prison sentence and was still incarcerated a decade later, when

West Virginia authorities discovered that Zain had presented false evidence in various felony cases. DNA tests were performed on the semen smears recovered by police in Rand, and Harris was cleared of all charges. The exoneration came too late to salvage his athletic and scholastic careers, however. It was small consolation when Zain, disgraced, was charged with perjury in West Virginia and Texas.

HARRISON, Clarence exonerated by DNA

At 6 A.M. on October 25, 1986, while waiting at a bus stop in Atlanta, Georgia, a 25-year-old employee of Grady Memorial Hospital found herself confronted by a man who struck her in the face, knocking out two of her teeth, and threatened, "If you scream, I'll kill you right here." The man then walked her to a nearby wooded area where he robbed her of money and a watch, then repeatedly raped and sodomized her. The victim subsequently identified 26-year-old Clarence Harrison from a photo lineup and later named him as her rapist at trial, in 1987. Convicted on multiple felony charges, Harrison received a life prison term. Still protesting his innocence, Harrison saw all of his appeals rejected until February 2003, when the GEORGIA INNOCENCE PROJECT accepted his case for review. In August 2004, DNA testing excluded Harrison as a donor of semen collected from the victim. He was released soon thereafter, having served 17 years in prison for a crime he did not commit.

HARRISON, Harold Charles (1907–1970)

Harold Harrison came to forensic science relatively late in life, but nonetheless scored impressive achievements. A banker's son from Vermont, born in February 1907, Harrison earned his B.S. in GEOLOGY from Virginia's Washington and Lee University (1931), followed by a Ph.D. in CHEMISTRY from Cornell University (1938). While pursuing postdoctoral studies at the Massachusetts Institute of Technology (1939), Harrison served as an assistant professor of chemistry and SPECTROSCOPY at the New York State College of Ceramics (1938–41), then as a chemist and spectroscopist for the Oregon State Crime Detection Bureau and the Oregon State Department of Geology and Mineral Studies (1941–44). He joined the U.S. Navy in 1944 and served with the Bureau of Ordnance until 1946, when he resumed postdoctoral study at Harvard University (1946–49).

Harrison finally found his permanent niche in 1949, when he joined the University of Rhode Island's faculty as an assistant professor of chemistry, promoted to a full professorship seven years later. In 1953 he founded the university's Laboratory for Scientific Crime Detection (LSCD), serving as the lab's director and maintaining a full teaching schedule until his death in 1970. Under Harrison's leadership, the LSCD was nationally recognized for its analysis of forensic TRACE EVIDENCE. Harrison also pioneered investigation of drunk-driving cases and developed Rhode Island's first "breathalyzer" test for alcohol.

HAYES, Robert exonerated by DNA evidence

A 35-year-old resident of Broward County, Florida, Robert Hayes was employed as a groom at the Pompano Harness Track when a female coworker, Pamela Albertson, was raped and strangled to death in 1990. Albertson was found clutching several hairs in her hand, believed to come from her assailant, and prosecutors claimed that DNA tests performed on the hairs proved they belonged to Hayes. Convicted of murder in 1991, he was sentenced to a term of life imprisonment. (See FIBER AND HAIR EVIDENCE.)

On appeal, Hayes's lawyers demonstrated that while Hayes is an African American, the hairs retrieved from Albertson's hand in 1990 belonged to a white man. They also provided expert testimony that DNA extracted from the suspect hairs had been contaminated during testing and did not in fact link Hayes to the crime. Florida's Supreme Court overturned the conviction in 1995 and remanded the case to Broward County for retrial, where Hayes was acquitted of all charges in July 1997. Leaving prison penniless, Hayes returned to his native Canton, Mississippi, and was hired to drive a city dump truck, caring for horses at a local amusement park in his spare time. The rape-murder of Pamela Albertson remains unsolved today.

HAZELWOOD, Robert R. FBI profiler

Robert "Roy" Hazelwood spent 11 years in the U.S. Army, rising to the rank of major in the military police before retiring to join the FBI. For 16 of his 22 years in the bureau, Hazelwood served as a profiler with the Behavioral Science Unit (later Investigative Support Services) under Agents Robert Ressler and JOHN DOUGLAS. In that capacity, some sources credit him with developing the FBI's distinction between "organized" and "unorganized" offenders, broad categories utilized in the PSYCHOLOGICAL PROFILING of unknown subjects. Hazelwood's education includes an M.S. from NOVA University and graduate studies in forensic medicine at the Armed Forces Institute of Pathology in Washington, D.C. While with the bureau, he taught courses at the FBI Academy and for the U.S. Army's Criminal Investigation Division. Since his retirement, Hazelwood has followed in the footsteps of Ressler and Douglas, pursuing a busy schedule of lectures, seminars, and writing for profit. He has coauthored books including *Autoerotic Fatalities* (1983), *Practical Aspects of Rape Investigation* (1987), *The Evil That Men Do: FBI Profiler Roy Hazelwood's Journey into the Minds of Sexual Predators* (1999), and *Dark Dreams: Sexual Violence, Homicide and the Criminal Mind* (2001).

HEINRICH, Edward Oscar (1881–1953)

Wisconsin native Edward Heinrich was born at Clintonville in April 1881, and earned a degree in CHEMISTRY from the University of California. Settling in Tacoma, Washington, he pioneered in the field of forensic science and became a favorite expert witness at criminal trials. As his fame spread, Heinrich was lured from Washington to fill other posts—as police chief in Alameda, California (1917–18), and as city manager in Boulder, Colorado (1918–19). After World War I, he lectured at UC Berkeley on his recent discoveries in the field of ballistics.

While Heinrich participated in more than 2,000 criminal cases, his best-known achievement was the solution of a 1923 robbery and mass murder in Oregon. On October 11, bandits stopped a Southern Pacific train in a mountain tunnel near Siskiyou Station, fatally shooting four railroad employees in a fruitless effort to steal $40,000 from the train's baggage car. Dozens of suspects were interrogated, but Heinrich broke the case after examining a pair of overalls abandoned near the scene by one bandit.

Heinrich told police that their man was a left-handed lumberjack approximately 25 years old, with brown hair and a fair complexion, five feet eight and 165 pounds, and a man of fastidious habits. Detectives were incredulous until Heinrich explained his conclusions. Strands of hair had been recovered from the overalls, along with Douglas fir needles and fresh pitch from pine trees; furthermore, the garment was worn along the right side only, as where a southpaw might lean against trees while swinging his axe left-handed. If this was not enough, a slip of paper found inside one pocket proved to be a receipt for a registered letter. Further investigation identified the sender as Roy DeAutremont, mailing $50 to brother Hugh in New Mexico on September 14. Authorities visited Paul DeAutremont in Eugene, Oregon, and he confirmed that his three sons were all lumberjacks, Roy being the left-handed one.

Capture of the globe-trotting fugitives was delayed until 1927, but no one questioned Dr. Heinrich's key role in solving the crime. Heinrich continued his work in forensic science for decades after his most famous case, and died on September 28, 1953.

HELPERN, Milton (1902–1977)

New Yorker Milton Helpern earned a medical degree from Cornell University in 1926, at age 24. After five years in private practice, he teamed with premier New York City medical examiner CHARLES NORRIS and spent the next four decades building a reputation as the American dean of forensic science. Helpern replaced Dr. Norris as New York's chief MEDICAL EXAMINER in 1954 and held that post until his retirement in 1973. During his tenure with the city, Helpern performed some 80,000 autopsies and coauthored (with Thomas Gonzales and Morgan Vance) a classic text on the subject, *Legal Medicine and Toxicology* (1937). His public statements were sometimes controversial, as when he remarked of the Dallas autopsy performed on President John Kennedy in 1963: "Selecting a hospital pathologist to perform a medico-legal autopsy . . . and evaluate gunshot wounds is like sending a seven-year-old boy who has taken three lessons on the violin over to the New York Philharmonic and expect[ing] him to perform a Tchaikovsky symphony. He knows how to hold the violin and the bow, but he has a long way to go before he can make music." Dr. Helpern died in 1977.

HENRY, Edward Richard (1850–1931)

A child of Irish immigrants, born in London on July 26, 1850, Edward Henry studied at St. Edmund's College and joined Lloyds of London as a clerk in 1866, while pursuing night classes at University College. In 1873, he passed the Indian Civil Service test and was posted to the Bengal Taxation Service as an assistant magistrate-collector, subsequently winning promotion to magistrate collector (1888), joint secretary to the Board of Revenue of Bengal (1890), and inspector-general of police for Bengal (1891). In the process, Henry became fluent in Hindi and Urdu, skills that aided him in his law enforcement duties. He also studied FINGERPRINTS, preferring them as a means of criminal identification over the ANTHROPOMETRY practiced by disciples of ALPHONSE BERTILLON. During 1896–97, Henry developed a system for organizing and searching fingerprint records with relative ease, described in his monograph titled *Classification and Uses of Fingerprints* (1897).

In 1900, three years after India's government adopted the "Henry method" of fingerprinting as its official means of personal identification, Henry was dispatched from India to organize police in South Africa. A year later, he was recalled to London as assistant commissioner for crime of Scotland Yard, commanding the Criminal Investigation Department. Henry created the Metropolitan Police Fingerprint Bureau on July 1, 1901, and the unit secured its first conviction based on fingerprints—of career burglar Henry Jackson—in 1902. Three years later, the bureau secured its first murder convictions, sending brothers Albert and Alfred Stratton to the gallows. In 1903, Henry replaced Sir Edward Bradford as London's police commissioner, holding that post until 1918. Knighted in 1910, Henry survived an assassination attempt two years later, when disgruntled cabdriver Alfred Bowes invaded Henry's Kensington home and shot him as a protest against the suspension of Bowes's license. Plagued with chronic pain from his wounds, Henry hoped to retire in 1914 but remained in his post for the duration of World War I. A strike by 11,000 underpaid constables finally prompted him to resign on August 31, 1918.

Henry subsequently moved to Berkshire, where he served as a justice of the peace and joined the National Society for the Prevention of Cruelty to Children. His only son died in 1930, and Henry followed a few months later, stricken by a massive heart attack on February 19, 1931. His grave lay unattended for six decades, in the cemetery beside All Souls Church, until the Fingerprint Society sponsored its renovation in 1994.

HERNANDEZ, Alejandro See CRUZ, ROLANDO.

HERSCHEL, William James (1833–1917)
A British subject, born in 1833, William James Herschel represented a distinguished lineage. His grandfather and namesake, Sir William Herschel, was a German-born musician and pioneer in the field of stellar astronomy who discovered the planet Uranus. His father, Sir John F. W. Herschel, was an astronomer, physicist, and chemist best known for discovering the use of thiosulphate (or hypo) as a fixing agent in PHOTOGRAPHY. (He also coined the photographic terms *negative* and *positive*.) Herschel entered public life as an officer of the Indian Civil Service, posted to Calcutta, and developed a lifelong interest in FINGERPRINTS from the Indian habit of signing important documents with an inked handprint. Herschel himself used a palm print to seal a government contract with a local contractor, one Raj Konai, in 1858, and continued the practice thereafter on deeds and other legal documents. Herschel later claimed that he used fingerprints as a means of identifying prisoners from 1860 onward, but some latter-day critics dispute that assertion, noting that he used prints primarily as a means of enforcing contracts and never suggested that fingerprints could be lifted from crime scenes for comparison with suspects. In 1880, after HENRY FAULDS penned an article for *Nature* describing his systematic collection of fingerprints in Japan, Herschel responded with a letter trumping Faulds by two decades and launching a feud that lasted until Herschel's death in 1917. Controversy endures to the present day over which man deserves primary credit for adoption of systematic fingerprint records in Britain.

HICKS, Anthony exonerated by DNA evidence
In November 1990, a female resident of Madison, Wisconsin, told police she had been raped by an unknown black man who knocked on her apartment door, then forced his way inside, twice assaulting her before he fled the scene. The 26-year-old victim saw her attacker's face briefly, when he barged into the flat, but was not permitted to see him again for the duration of her ordeal. Anthony Hicks was subsequently jailed for a traffic offense in Madison, whereupon a police dispatcher examined a composite sketch of the rape suspect and told detectives, "That looks like that black guy we just brought in." Hicks was placed in a lineup, whereupon the victim identified him as her assailant. Hicks passed two

polygraph tests, suggesting he was innocent, but the test results were inadmissible in court.

At trial, prosecutors introduced certain pubic hairs found at the crime scene, identified as "consistent" with samples taken from Hicks. The Wisconsin state crime lab had no DNA testing facility at the time, and while defense attorney Willie Nunnery employed a private analyst to test the hairs, the samples proved too small for conclusive testing under the restricted fragment length polymorphism (RFLP) analysis system most commonly used. Nunnery learned that a more efficient method of DNA testing—the polymerase chain reaction (PCR) method—was available from a lab in California, but he elected to skip those tests and used a Chicago expert to contest the prosecution's findings of "consistency" between the hairs. Jurors convicted Hicks in December 1991 and he received a 19-year prison term.

More advanced DNA testing, under the PCR system, was performed on the evidence in 1993,

whereupon Hicks was excluded as a suspect in the rape. Wisconsin's Court of Appeals reversed Hicks's conviction and ordered a new trial, that decision affirmed by the state supreme court "in the interest of justice" when prosecutors appealed. Hicks was released in 1996, after spending four and a half years in prison. (His alleged victim, meanwhile, stands by her identification to the present day, insisting she picked the right man.)

Upon his release, Hicks sued attorney Nunnery for malpractice in failing to pursue the PCR tests in 1991. Jurors in that civil case believed the test would almost certainly have resulted in acquittal for Hicks. They found Nunnery negligent and ordered him to pay Hicks $2.6 million for the time that he was wrongfully imprisoned. Nunnery, outraged, told reporters, "I think it was totally unfair and unprecedented. I was doing all I could to provide aid and assistance to my client. I think I will be vindicated. This, too, shall pass."

The "bump from behind" method of carjacking is demonstrated during an anti-carjacking course. (CORBIS)

HIJACKING

"Hijacking" is a type of ROBBERY, generally understood to mean THEFT of cargo or other valuable items from commercial carriers. The vehicle itself may not be stolen, if the bandits have their own means of transportation, but in some cases—as with hijacking of oil tankers at sea by modern-day pirates—it is easier to steal the vehicle than to offload desired items. Armed theft of automobiles from their owners is widely referred to as *carjacking*, punished since the early 1990s as a federal offense in the United States. Armed commandeering of commercial airliners, sometimes known as *skyjacking*, began in 1931 and hit its "golden age" during the early 1970s, when dozens of airliners were hijacked for ransom or for diversion to some unintended destination. (Many of the flights hijacked in the United States were diverted to Cuba, before Fidel Castro closed his nation's doors to self-styled political refugees from the United States.) The term *hijacking* apparently derives from "highlanding," used in the 19th century to describe armed robbery of stagecoaches, while the modern term was popularized during Prohibition, referring to the theft of bootleg liquor shipments.

Police and forensic scientists identify hijackers by various means, including FINGERPRINTS (often left on rearview or sideview mirrors), IMPRESSION EVIDENCE (such as toolmarks and footprints left on cardboard cartons while unloading cargo), any TRACE EVIDENCE left by the thieves (hairs or fibers [see FIBER AND HAIR EVIDENCE], cigarette butts, etc.), and calculation of distance traveled by a hijacked vehicle between the times when it was stolen and recovered. In some cities, such as New York, trucks have special identification numbers painted on the roof of their cabs, permitting stolen vehicles to be seen from the air. Informants also play a key role in tracking down hijackers, while stolen items are traced (whenever possible) through serial numbers and other unique features.

HILTON, Ordway (1913–1998)

Born in 1913, Ordway Hilton established an international reputation as a handwriting analyst and examiner of QUESTIONED DOCUMENTS. At age 25, he joined the Chicago Police Department's Scientific Crime Detection Laboratory, doubling throughout World War II as a document analyst for U.S. Naval Intelligence. Hilton's war work briefly interrupted his service to the *Journal of Criminal Law, Criminol-*ogy and Police Science, which he served as editor during 1941–43 and 1948–72. Hilton published his masterwork, *Scientific Examination of Questioned Documents,* in 1956 and produced a revised edition in 1982. His 1991 monograph *Detecting and Deciphering Erased Pencil Writing* is also considered a classic in the field. Hilton's famous cases include a review of documents allegedly signed by reclusive billionaire Howard Hughes in the early 1970s and a survey of Adolf Hitler's supposed diaries, purchased by the German magazine *Stern* a decade later. In the first instance, Hilton authenticated a signature from Hughes, thus tentatively proving that the recluse was still living. In the latter case, Hilton agreed with Swiss expert Max Frei-Sultzer that the diary was a FORGERY. Hilton died in May 1998, at age 84.

HOLDREN, Larry   exonerated by DNA evidence

In December 1982 a female resident of Charleston, West Virginia, was attacked while jogging, dragged into a highway culvert, and there repeatedly raped. Charleston resident Larry Holdren was identified by both the victim and an off-duty FBI agent, who testified under oath that he observed Holdren walking near the crime scene on the day of the attack. Convicted at trial on six counts of sexual assault, Holdren received a sentence of 30 to 60 years in state prison. He served 15 years of that term before DNA testing—unavailable at the time of his trial—conclusively excluded him as the source of semen recovered from the victim and the crime scene.

HOMICIDE

Homicide is the killing of one human being by another. Legally, it may be deemed accidental, justifiable (as in self-defense), or wrongful. Purely accidental deaths—often termed "deaths by misadventure"—are rarely the subjects of criminal sanctions, though civil litigation may proceed in some cases, filed by relatives of the deceased against some plaintiff whom they deem responsible for creating fatally unsafe conditions. Wrongful homicides are legally subdivided as *murder* (where death was intended and deliberately inflicted) and *manslaughter* (where fatal consequences, though not planned, could be foreseen as the result of some other negligent or criminal behavior, such as driving while intoxicated or discharging firearms in a populated area).

Both murder and manslaughter are commonly characterized in law by degrees of culpability and malice. *First-degree murder* is any premeditated slaying "with malice aforethought," where the killer has privately planned or conspired with others to commit homicide. Under Supreme Court rulings issued in the 1970s, *capital murder* requires proof of "special circumstances"—including elements such as torture, sexual assault, murder for hire, KIDNAPPING, murder of a law enforcement officer, etc.—to invoke the death penalty. *Second-degree murder* is generally defined as deliberate killing without premeditation, as with homicides committed in the heat of argument or passion. Most American jurisdictions also penalize *felony murders*, broadly defined as any slayings committed during or resulting from commission of another felony such as kidnapping, robbery, or sexual assault. Since felony murder generally includes *any* death resulting from an offender's premeditated crime, a defendant may be charged with murder even if he/she had no personal hand in the slaying or the death was accidental (e.g., a car swerving to avoid a shootout between robbers and police strikes a pedestrian). In rare cases, defendants have even been charged with the "murders" of their own accomplices shot by police officers.

Since manslaughter does not include premeditation, its legal degrees are generally based on the offender's recklessness or culpability in lesser offenses. *Voluntary manslaughter* commonly results from cases of assault (as in a mugging) or mutual combat (as in barroom brawls), where the defendant should have known that his illegal behavior could produce life-threatening injury. *Involuntary manslaughter* typically results from drunken driving or reckless handling of firearms (though some courts impose more severe penalties for habitual drunk drivers). The same charge may be filed in some jurisdictions against owners of vicious or venomous animals that fatally injure humans. *Negligent homicide* suggests that the offender created or maintained unsafe conditions—such as dilapidated premises or abandoned refrigerators with their doors illegally intact—that result in preventable deaths.

Legal penalties for homicide depend on its degree and circumstances of the particular case, which are frequently determined by forensic scientists. Crime scene evidence may indicate premeditation (if the killer lay in wait and brought a weapon with him to the scene, etc.), define parameters of the attack, and demonstrate if steps were taken to conceal the body or obscure incriminating evidence. Examination of the suspect, ranging from his/her physical and psychological condition to evidence of intoxication from alcohol or drugs, may also help a judge and jury to decide the case.

HONAKER, Edward exonerated by DNA evidence

In the predawn hours of June 23, 1984, Samuel Dempsey and his girlfriend, Angela Nichols, were sleeping in their car, parked beside a rural Virginia highway, when a stranger woke them, brandishing a pistol and identifying himself as a police officer. The man ordered Dempsey out of his car and into the nearby woods. He then dragged Nichols to a nearby pickup truck and drove her to a more secluded area, where she was raped and sodomized repeatedly. Authorities prepared a sketch of the suspect from descriptions offered by Dempsey and Nichols, including his military-style camouflage fatigues.

Authorities still had no leads in the case when a second woman was raped, 100 miles from the scene of the original crime. That victim said her rapist resembled a neighbor, 40-year-old Edward Honaker, but Honaker had an airtight alibi and was never charged with the crime. He was photographed by detectives, however, and that photo made its way to Nelson County, where Dempsey and Nichols identified Honaker as their assailant of June 23. Honaker owned a pickup resembling the kidnapper's vehicle, and a search of his home turned up camouflage clothing similar to the rapist's.

There were problems with the prosecution's case from the beginning. First, Honaker once again had an alibi corroborated by four witnesses. Nichols described her rapist as left-handed, whereas Honaker was not. The rapist's semen contained motile sperm, while Honaker had undergone a vasectomy eight years earlier. Although the rapist had disrobed and forced Nichols to perform oral sex, she did not recall a large surgical scar across Honaker's stomach. Finally, while the kidnapper had ranted at length about his Vietnam war experience, Honaker had no such military record.

Nelson County prosecutors forged ahead despite those stumbling blocks. At trial, they dismissed the corroboration of Honaker's alibi as "a put-up job" concocted by friends and relatives to deceive the court. Honaker's vasectomy was dismissed with a claim that sperm found on vaginal swabs came from Sam Dempsey. Dempsey and Nichols testified against Honaker, identifying him under oath as their assailant. Finally, a state forensic expert told jurors that hair found on Nichols's clothing after the rape "was unlikely to match anyone" other than Honaker. Convicted on seven counts of rape, sodomy and sexual assault, Honaker received three life terms in prison plus 34 years.

In the wake of that crushing verdict, Honaker contacted CENTURION MINISTRIES for help in appealing his conviction. Investigators soon discovered that Nichols's first description of the rapist was inconsistent with Honaker and that some of Dempsey's testimony was induced via hypnosis. Centurion Ministries then joined forces with the CARDOZO INNOCENCE PROJECT to pursue DNA testing of evidence collected by police. Prosecutors reluctantly furnished the evidence, and a lab report of January 13, 1994, identified two different seminal deposits in the samples preserved, mismatched between the vaginal swab and a stain found on Nichols's shorts. DNA results positively excluded Edward Honaker as a source

of either sample. A second report, dated March 15, 1994, concluded that while Samuel Dempsey could not be excluded as a source of the clothing stain, he likewise had not produced the semen swabbed from Nichols's vagina. In June 1994 Nichols admitted an affair with a third party unknown to Dempsey, but the secret lover was also excluded by DNA tests as a source for the vaginal samples. The June 1984 rapist remains unidentified.

Virginia statutes forbid introduction of new evidence more than 21 days after trial, regardless of the circumstances, so Honaker was forced to seek a pardon from Governor George Allen. Lawyers filed a clemency petition on June 29, 1994, and Allen officially pardoned Honaker on October 21, 1994, freeing him after he had served 10 years in prison. "It's mind-boggling what our system can do," Honaker told reporters at the prison gates. "What happened to me can happen to any man alive. DNA was my salvation." Governor Allen refused financial compensation on grounds that all officials involved in the case "acted in complete accordance with the law."

I

IDENTI-KIT

Originally developed in the 1950s, Identi-Kits assist law enforcement agencies in preparing sketches of unknown offenders. The early kits included numerous templates of hair styles, eyes, noses, ears, mouths, mustaches, beards, and so forth, used as overlays to create a composite portrait matching (or at least approximating) a suspect's appearance. When completed, the "sketch" could then be photocopied for distribution to detectives, uniformed patrol officers, and the news media. Modern Identi-Kits are computerized and commonly include software permitting adjustment or manipulation of the features selected, thereby (probably) producing more accurate suspect sketches.

IDENTITY Theft

Identity theft is the blanket term for any type of crime wherein the offender uses another individual's legitimate personal information to commit acts of fraud or deception, typically (though not exclusively) for illicit financial gain. The criminal activity extends beyond mere credit card fraud, for example, since offenders literally assume the victim's identity, often using the assumed name to purchase cars and houses, rent apartments, take out loans, book travel reservations. The assumed identity may also be employed for outright criminal activity and furnished to authorities when the offender is arrested, posts bond, and so

forth. If unchecked, the impact on a victim may be devastating, both emotionally and financially.

Unlike DNA or FINGERPRINTS, personal data in modern society consists mainly of numbers—particularly Social Security, credit card, bank account, and telephone calling card numbers. Any or all of those numbers may be obtained by thieves in a variety of ways, ranging from purse-snatching, "dumpster diving," and "shoulder surfing" at pay phones or automatic teller machines to purchase through illegal channels. And in today's world, the vendors of stolen personal data operate primarily on the Internet. Experts on identify theft warn consumers against responding to "spam" e-mail that requests personal information in return for some illusory prize or reward. Likewise, circumspection must be used when making online credit card purchases or when relaying personal data on the telephone. Cellular phones are more risky than traditional land lines, since conversations can be intercepted—literally plucked from the air—without resort to clumsy (and illegal) wire-tapping equipment.

Identity theft became a federal crime in 1998, with passage of the Identity Theft and Assumption Deterrence Act, imposing a maximum sentence of 15 years' imprisonment, plus a fine and forfeiture of any personal property used to commit the offense. Separate federal statutes impose additional penalties for various collateral offenses, including identification fraud, credit card fraud, computer fraud, mail fraud, wire fraud, or financial institution fraud.

Each of these federal offenses are felonies that carry substantial penalties, in some cases as high as 30 years' imprisonment, fines, and criminal forfeiture of property. The U.S. Justice Department accepts online complaints via its Internet Fraud Complaint Center, at http://www1.ifccfbi.gov/index.asp.

Examples of identity theft range from the trivial to the fantastic. A nursing home employee in Elkhart, Indiana, was arrested on March 9, 2002, for stealing an 87-year-old Alzheimer's patient's Social Security number. The object: to restore the offender's telephone service after she fell behind on her monthly payments. In Oregon, meanwhile, police raiders seized 85 computer disks from a fraud suspect's home, revealing personal data collected on every holder of a state driver's license. The disk labeled "B" contained names, home addresses, birth dates, and driver's license numbers for 269,889 individuals. Also recovered in the raid were credit cards, death certificates, Social Security cards, and applications for medical residency at Oregon Health and Science University Hospital. The suspect was initially held on a $1,000 bond, then released a day later due to overcrowding at the local jail.

Prosecutors and financial institutions offer the following tips for self-defense in the new age of rampant identity theft:

1. *Keep personal information on a strict "need to know" basis.* Banks and credit card companies already have your information on file. They do not telephone to request or "verify" such data. When unknown callers offer prizes, "major credit cards," and so forth in return for personal information, demand a written application form—or better still, hang up. Keep your Social Security card in a safe place; do not carry it with you or have the number printed on checks. Defeat "dumpster divers" by shredding or burning crucial documents before they are discarded. Abstain from posting personal information on the Internet—to genealogical or class reunion sites, chat rooms, or questionable vendors. When traveling, have mail held at your local post office until you return, thus preventing theft of credit card statements and other critical documents from your mailbox. When using public telephones or ATMs, be wary of eavesdroppers and "shoulder surfers." Give out no vital information on a cell phone anywhere, at any time.

2. *Check financial information regularly and thoroughly.* Bank and credit card accounts issue monthly statements. If yours do not arrive on time, call the institution(s) and inquire. If statements have been mailed to an unauthorized address, report the fraud immediately and demand copies of all missing statements. Examine monthly statements in detail, confirming all charges and/or debits as legitimate. Report immediately any unauthorized activity on the accounts.

3. *Periodically request copies of credit reports.* These should list all bank and financial accounts under a subject's name, including loans and mortgages. Report any unauthorized activity to the proper authorities.

4. *Maintain detailed records of banking and financial accounts for at least one year.* Financial institutions are required by law to maintain copies of checks, debits and other transactions for five years, but customers without records of their own may have no way to dispute unauthorized charges or signatures.

If, despite these precautions, you still become a victim of identity theft, swift action is required to minimize financial loss and to preserve your reputation. The following contacts can provide assistance:

1. *The Federal Trade Commission.* Report violations by telephone (toll-free) at 1-877-ID THEFT (877-438-4338) or by mail to Consumer Response Center, FTC, 600 Pennsylvania Avenue, N.W., Washington, DC 20580.

2. *The Postal Inspection Service.* For cases of suspected mail fraud or illicit misdirection of mail, contact the nearest post office for telephone numbers and complaint forms.

3. *The Social Security Administration.* Report misuse of Social Security numbers by telephone to 1-800-269-0271.

4. *The Internal Revenue Service.* Report theft of information from tax records or misuse of personal data to commit tax violations by telephone to 1-800-829-0433.

5. *The three principal credit reporting agencies.* Their fraud units may be contacted at the following numbers and addresses:
   a. *Equifax:* call 1-800-525-6285 or write to P.O. Box 740250, Atlanta, GA 30374-0250.

b. *Experian* (formerly TRW): call 1-888-397-3742 or write to P.O. Box 1017, Allen, TX 75013.

c. *Trans Union:* call 1-800-525-6285 or write to P.O. Box 6790, Fullerton, CA 92634.

6. *All creditors with whom your name or personal data has been fraudulently used.* This may include long-distance telephone companies, as well as banks, credit card companies, automobile dealerships, etc.

7. *All financial institutions where you have accounts.* Whether an identity thief has tampered with the accounts or not, the institutions must be warned of a fraud in progress to prevent further losses and assist in apprehending the offenders.

For sheer audacity—or comic relief—23-year-old identity thief Thomas Seitz takes the prize. A New Jersey computer buff, Seitz blamed the U.S. Security and Exchange Commission (SEC) for seducing him into a life of CYBERCRIME. After all, he told authorities, if the SEC did not post thousands of names and Social Security numbers on its public Web site, Seitz would not have taken out car loans in 14 of the listed names—and he would not stand convicted of bank fraud today. It was simply too tempting, Seitz maintained. Granted, his first 12 online loan applications under various pseudonyms were rejected, but he received $15,000 on his 13th attempt. Next, using the stolen identity of a 57-year-old electronics executive in Salt Lake City, Seitz obtained a $44,000 auto loan, an online insurance quote and two credit cards to pay for the policy. When it came to obtaining fake ID in his victim's name, Seitz found that he had 300 Web sites to choose from. "I knew I did something illegal," Seitz admitted, "but I always came out of a situation pretty much better than I anticipated." That is, until a car dealer tried to register his newly purchased vehicle and Seitz was arrested for using a counterfeit driver's license. At that point, he admitted, "I had no defense."

IMMUNOLOGY, Forensic

Immunology is the study of immune systems various living organisms, and the means by which they combat disease. Healthy immune systems resist *pathogens* (disease-causing organisms) by producing *antigens* (substances that stimulate production of *antibodies*). Throughout the 19th century a similar reaction was observed in many cases of blood transfusion, with fatal results for the patients, but physicians did not understand its cause. Finally, KARL LANDSTEINER undertook a series of experiments in 1900–01 that revealed four classes or "types" of blood, which he labeled A, B, AB, and O, after the isoantigens contained in their red cells (determined by heredity). Blood type is determined by applying specific antigens to a sample and observing the *immunoprecipitate*, a solid material formed as antibodies are synthesized. Landsteiner's discovery earned him a Nobel Prize three decades later, and A-B-O blood typing remained the standard method of identifying BLOODSTAINS in forensic science until DNA profiling was introduced in the late 1980s. Unfortunately, as demonstrated over the past two decades by belated exonerations of numerous wrongfully convicted defendants, the more basic blood-typing system is not specific enough to identify a particular offender beyond reasonable doubt.

IMPRESSION Evidence

Impression (or *imprint*) evidence includes all markings left behind by contact between one object or surface and another. The vast range of impression evidence includes (but is not limited to) bite marks, fabric impressions, some FINGERPRINTS, footprints, glove prints, scuff and skid marks, sticking marks, striations, and wear patterns on various objects. *Two-dimensional* impressions are those such as footprints in blood, which lack depth, while *three-dimensional* impressions are those that have depth as well as pattern, thus affecting the manner of collection and storage. Impressions of *dry origin* are those found in substances such as dust or powder, while *wet origin* impressions result from touching or stepping in some liquid (blood, water, etc.) and subsequently leaving marks on another surface. While fingerprints are considered more fully elsewhere, other common types of impression evidence include:

Fabric impressions result when some fabric makes contact with a surface capable of retaining pattern marks, such as clay, paint, or putty. *Glove prints* generally qualify as fabric impressions, and while gloves conceal fingerprints, they may also leave markings that allow a particular pair of gloves to be specifically identified.

Footprints, with or without shoes, constitute an important part of impression evidence. Dermal ridges found on bare feet may be as unique as fingerprints, and in certain cases—e.g., where a subject steps in paint or ink—may be matched in the same way. Shoe prints are less distinctive, since most footwear is mass-produced, but the type and make of shoe can be ascertained from footwear databases maintained by the FBI and some large police departments, while unique wear patterns or damage to the sole may identify a specific shoe.

Plastic deformation is a lasting three-dimensional impression made by some object on a nonelastic surface, as with fingerprints in clay or bite marks on a block of cheese.

Scuff and *skid marks* result from a rubbing, sliding contact between two surfaces. Scuff marks generally refer to traces left by shoes, while skid marks are left by rubber tires on pavement. In the latter case, measurement and mathematical calculation may determine how fast a vehicle was moving when its driver applied the brakes.

Sticking marks are the small impressions sometimes found on medicinal tablets during manufacture, when mechanical punches are used to create the tablets. Sticking marks may be used to identify tablets produced in outlaw labs and other settings where no manufacturer's name, logo or lot number appears on the suspect tablets.

Striations are scratches and other marks resulting from one surface sliding along another. In many cases, as when one car sideswipes another, striations are left on both surfaces. The "lands" and "grooves" found on bullets fired through rifled barrels are a common form of striation.

Tire impressions may be two- or three-dimensional, depending on the contact surface. In either case, tread patterns may determine the type or model of tire, while *track width* (measured on cars and trucks from one end of an axle to the other) reveals the size of the vehicle itself. As with shoes, wear patterns on tires may permit more specific identification beyond mere size and model numbers.

Toolmarks result when any metal tool or mechanism makes contact with softer metals or other surfaces including glass, plastic, or wood. Common examples include marks left by saws or other cutting tools and the marks made on car-

Skid mark next to highway stripe. Skid marks can indicate the speed, direction, and other characteristics of a vehicle involved in an accident or crime scene. (CORBIS)

tridge primers or casings by a particular FIRE-ARM's firing pin and extractor.

Wear patterns occur from normal use of various items and appear in different forms. A loss of pigment may be seen, as when the bluing on a gun barrel wears thin from repeated contact with a holster. Wear patterns often facilitate identification of specific shoes or tires, as when a suspect's shoes with worn-down heels are compared to footprints from a crime scene.

Impression evidence is collected and preserved in various ways, depending on the nature of the evidence and ambient conditions. PHOTOGRAPHY is the first step in preserving impression evidence and may be the only means available in some cases of two-dimensional impressions. Dry impressions may sometimes be preserved by means of an *electrostatic lift*, wherein a high-voltage source creates a charge in the dust or other medium, permitting its transfer to a contrasting background material. Three-dimensional impressions are often preserved by *casting* with various pliant materials—such as plaster, resin, or wax—that harden to retain an image of the imprint. A special spray-on material called Snow Print Wax casts impressions in snow, which would be crushed, distorted, or melted by application of more traditional casting materials.

Once an impression is collected, it remains for investigators to obtain suspect shoes, tires, tools, or other objects for comparison. When a suspect object is obtained, examiners make test impressions and compare them with impressions found at the crime scene. Matches may indicate the same *type* of shoe or other object, while distinctive wear marks or other damage discussed above may indicate a specific match.

As with other types of evidence, impressions may be fabricated or manipulated by unscrupulous persons in pursuit of a FRAME-UP. A classic example is seen in Florida's notorious Groveland rape case. Four young African-American men were accused of raping a white woman in July 1949. Three suspects were arrested, while a vigilante "posse" killed the fourth. Sheriff Willis McCall, a reputed member of the Ku Klux Klan, obtained confessions from the three jailed suspects by means of torture, while Deputy James Yates claimed that impressions from one suspect's shoes matched footprints found at the rape scene. Jurors convicted all three defendants, resulting in two death sentences and one term of life imprisonment (for a 16-year-old defendant). The U.S. Supreme Court ordered a new trial in 1950, whereupon Sheriff McCall shot the two adult defendants "in self-defense," killing one and leaving the other critically injured. A second jury convicted the survivor once again, based on the same evidence. Twelve years later, in 1962, Deputy Yates and a colleague were indicted on charges of faking footprint casts to convict another pair of black defendants on rape charges. Those indictments were later dismissed, because the statute of limitations had elapsed, and Sheriff McCall reinstated both deputies.

INNOCENCE Institute

Pennsylvania's Innocence Institute was founded in 2001 by Bill Moushey, an investigative reporter for the Pittsburgh *Post-Gazette* and professor at Point Park University's Department of Journalism and Mass Communication. The organization began as a class project, with Moushey's students probing real-world claims of wrongful conviction and actual innocence, and it remains the only U.S. innocence project primarily geared toward journalistic investigation. Student reporters examine initial claims of innocence, then study trial transcripts before carrying their research to the streets, visiting crime scenes, locating witnesses, and interviewing law enforcement officers involved in the original case work. If satisfied that a miscarriage of justice has occurred, the students then write detailed accounts of each case for the *Post-Gazette* and various Internet forums, seeking to reverse wrongful convictions in a public forum. Proof of innocence in court remains to be secured by attorneys and forensic scientists working in tandem to review case evidence.

INNOCENCE Project New Orleans

The IPNO was established in 2000 to represent wrongfully convicted inmates in Louisiana and Mississippi, further assisting with their transition from prison to the free world after release. At press time for this work, the group was responsible for liberating six innocent prisoners. The cases of inmates DENNIS BROWN and RYAN MATTHEWS, exonerated by DNA evidence, are fully discussed elsewhere in the text. Dan Bright, convicted of a 1996 New Orleans holdup-murder, won freedom after IPNO members proved that his attorney was intoxicated at his trial and that FBI agents illegally suppressed the true killer's identity. Codefendants Greg Bright and Earl Truvia, sentenced to life without parole for second-degree murder in 1975, were released in June 2003 after IPNO attorneys revealed that the state's sole witness was a schizophrenic heroin addict, testifying under a false name to conceal her own criminal record (all facts concealed from the jury at trial). Dwight Labran, a black defendant with no criminal record, was convicted of a 1997 murder in New Orleans based solely on testimony from the owner of a car in which police found the victim's body. IPNO investigators learned that the "witness" had lied about his identity to conceal outstanding warrants on drug and FIREARMS charges, fingering Labran to spare himself from a potential murder charge. Labran was freed from prison in December 2001.

INNOCENCE Project Northwest

Organized in 1997 as a nonprofit coalition of attorneys, professors, and students at the University of Washington Law School, the Innocence Project Northwest provides free legal aid to Washington inmates who (1) were wrongfully convicted, (2) cannot afford counsel and no longer have a right to appointed counsel, (3) have completed the normal appeals process, (4) have a substantial period of prison time remaining to be served, and (5) have a reasonable claim of actual innocence provable through DNA testing or other newly discovered evidence. During its first eight years of operation, the IPNW liberated 11 inmates from Washington state prisons.

INORGANIC Compound Analysis

Chemical compounds are dubbed "inorganic" if their molecules do not include atoms of carbon bound to hydrogen. Scientists once believed that inorganic compounds were always synthetic, while ORGANIC COMPOUNDS always appeared in living organisms, but the truth is very different. Thousands of organic compounds appear in synthetic materials (drugs, plastics, etc.), while some inorganic compounds—carbonic acid, phosphate ions, sodium chloride, etc.—appear in living organisms and are actually essential to life. The study of inorganic compounds is *inorganic chemistry*. The related study of metal compounds found in living systems is *bioinorganic chemistry*. NEUTRON ACTIVATION ANALYSIS and various other tests are used to identify inorganic compounds in the laboratory. A partial list of inorganic compounds may be found in Appendix 1.

INTEGRATED Ballistics Identification System

IBIS is a ballistics computer database created by the Bureau of Alcohol, Tobacco, Firearms and Explosives (ATF) to facilitate matching of evidence recovered from shooting scenes throughout the United States and the world at large. Its subdivisions, dubbed "Bulletproof" and "Brasscatcher," respectively include digital images of bullets and cartridge cases linked to various shootings. In each case, markings left on bullets and "brass" by specific weapons may be compared to evidence from new crime scenes, thus confirming or refuting links to other unsolved crimes. IBIS parallels the FBI's Drugfire program and performs essentially the same function, without Drugfire's more specific focus on drug-related shootings.

INTERNATIONAL Association of Bloodstain Pattern Analysts

Created in 1983, the IABPA was founded to promote education and encourage research in the field of BLOODSTAIN pattern analysis. With some 600 active members worldwide at press time for this work, the group also promotes standardization of bloodstain pattern analysis training and terminology.

INTERNATIONAL Association of Forensic Nurses

In summer 1992, a group of 74 registered nurses—mostly sexual assault nurse examiners, convened to organize the IAFN. A year later, the group held its first formal scientific assembly in Sacramento, California, with 160 delegates in attendance. By 1999, the IAFN boasted more than 1,800 members, and its membership increases every year. Members include nurses employed as correctional nurse specialists, death investigators, forensic clinical specialists, forensic geriatric specialists, forensic gynecology nurses, forensic psychiatric nurses, legal nurse consultants, nurse attorneys, and those in other specialties. At press time for this volume, the IAFN was the only international organization of registered nurses existing solely to develop, promote, and disseminate information about the field of forensic NURSING.

INTERNATIONAL Association of Identification

In August 1915, Inspector Harry Caldwell of California's Oakland Police Department mailed letters to various criminal identification specialists throughout the United States, asking them to meet in Oakland two months later, to create a professional association. Twenty-two officers answered the call in October, founding the International Association of Criminal Identification with Caldwell as its first president. By 1916, when the IACI held its second annual meeting in Leavenworth, Kansas, its membership had grown to 119. Two years later, recognizing the amount of noncriminal work performed by police identification bureaus, IACI members voted to drop the word "Criminal" from their organization's title. President Warren Harding received an IAI delegation at the White House in 1921, donating a set of his own

FINGERPRINTS to the group's growing files. In 1924, the IAI organized a new Science and Practice Committee to furnish its members with technical assistance. By 1929 the group had eight more committees in place, including Auditing, Compliments, Credentials, Ethics, Legislative, Membership, Press, and Resolutions. Membership dwindled during the Great Depression of the 1930s, but the IAI survived by forging a close relationship with J. Edgar Hoover's FBI. In 1958 the group inaugurated its JOHN A. DONDERO Memorial Award to recognize achievements of its members in the field. (Hoover became the first recipient.) The IAI established its rigorous Latent Print Certification Program in 1977, followed by a Crime Scene Certification Program in 1990. Other IAI certification programs today include Bloodstain Pattern Analysis, Footwear and Tiretrack Analysis, Forensic Art, and Forensic Photography/Imaging. At press time for this volume, the association had 45 divisions representing 50 U.S. states and territories plus 69 foreign countries.

ISOZYME Systems

Enzymes are complex organic substances originating from living cells, which catalyze various chemical changes in organic substances (as in digestion of food). Isozymes (or *isoenzymes*) are enzymes found on the surface of red blood cells that differ in amino acid sequence but catalyze the same chemical reactions. Heredity determines which variant isozymes a particular individual possesses in his/her red blood cells. Initially discovered in 1957, six isozyme systems are presently recognized as genetic markers. They are labeled acid phosphatase (ACP), adenosine deaminase (ADA), adenylate kinase (AK), esterase D (ESD), glyoxalase I (GLO I), and phosphoglucomutase (PGM). ELECTROPHORESIS is generally used to identify the isozymes in a particular blood sample. Prior to the discovery of DNA profiling, isozyme techniques were the best available refinement for blood typing, but today the method is only used with blood samples too small or degraded for DNA typing.

J

JEFFREYS, Alec John (1950–)

Born at Luton, Bedfordshire, on January 9, 1950, Alec Jeffreys graduated from Oxford University in 1977 and pursued graduate research at Leicester University, where he pioneered techniques for DNA profiling and "fingerprinting" in 1985. His method found its first forensic application in the case of serial rape-slayer COLIN PITCHFORK, convicted of murder and sentenced to life imprisonment after his DNA was matched to that of semen samples found on two female victims.

Defense attorneys wasted no time in challenging DNA evidence, but Jeffreys refined his methods as new technology was developed, focusing on highly variable minisatellites in the human genome. Jeffreys developed digital DNA profiling in 1991, used four years later as the basis for Britain's National DNA Database (NDNAD). Current British law requires all persons arrested to submit DNA for storage in the database, but Jeffreys opposes that development, complaining that the database is too restrictive and that access is limited to government agents. Instead, he supports a database of DNA drawn from all British subjects, with access controlled by neutral third parties. Knighted for his discoveries in 1994, Jeffreys received the Albert Einstein World Award of Science in 1996 and the Australia Prize in 1998. The University of Leicester awarded him a D.Sc. in 2004, and in 2005 Jeffreys shared the Lasker Award for clinical medical research with Edwin Southern of Oxford University.

JENKINS, Vincent H. exonerated by DNA evidence

An African-American resident of Buffalo, New York, born in 1939, Vincent Jenkins had a long record of arrests and convictions. By age 43, he had already spent a total of 28 years behind bars for various offenses. He was, in short, one of the "usual suspects" questioned often by Buffalo police when they had crimes to solve, his photo displayed in mug books for victims who did not recognize their assailants.

One such incident occurred in 1982, when a woman strolling through the Tiffts Farm nature preserve was assaulted and raped. Before fleeing, her attacker said, "The liquor made me do it." Vaginal and cervical swabs, taken at a local hospital, revealed semen traces from two different donors. The victim told police that she had performed consensual sex with her husband several hours before the rape. She scanned mug books in vain, unable to identify her assailant, but provided police with a vague description.

Four weeks after the attack, Vincent Jenkins was arrested and exhibited to the victim. Despite watching him for 25 minutes, she refused to name Jenkins as the rapist. Police next ordered Jenkins to speak, but the victim also failed to identify his voice. She changed her mind only after detectives and agents of the prosecutor's office convinced her that Jenkins "must be" the rapist, because of his criminal record. Jenkins was convicted at trial and received a life sentence.

Attorney BARRY SCHECK and the CARDOZO INNOCENCE PROJECT finally rescued Jenkins from prison, after he had served more than 16 years on his latest conviction. DNA tests performed in 1999 conclusively excluded Jenkins as the source of either semen sample recovered from the alleged rape victim in 1982. Oddly, the woman's husband was also excluded as a donor of both samples, which placed the prosecution in a precarious position. Barry Scheck described what happened next, in a televised interview.

When the testing was completed, [the victim] had indicated at the time of the sexual assault that her husband had had prior consensual sex with her 24 hours earlier. The DNA testing showed, very interestingly—it was done blindly—that Jenkins did not match either of the two DNA patterns, either the predominant pattern that was found on the vaginal swab and on the cervical swab, and a trace amount of male DNA that was found on the cervical swab, which is exactly ... what you would expect from prior consensual sex. That would be the trace presumably of her husband. She is still married to that gentleman. And when the knowns were tested, it turned out that the trace amount of DNA did not come back and match her husband. At that point, despite ... requests to the prosecutor that they really didn't want to do it to these people, because going back and saying to her, well, you know, of course she was insisting the tests were wrong, but ... I think that is highly unlikely, because it was cross validated with victim samples and everything else. We have prosecutors coming into court and saying, well, what really happened in this case is that there were three rapists, you know, there was this defendant, who didn't ejaculate, and she didn't notice that two other people raped her in the park that afternoon.

With results of the DNA tests in hand, Buffalo prosecutors agreed not to oppose a motion in state court to vacate Jenkins's conviction, but they fought Scheck's efforts to have a federal court declare Jenkins innocent. Vincent Jenkins, a prison convert to Islam now known as Warith Habib Abdal, was finally released from custody on September 11, 1999.

JIMERSON, Verneal See "FORD HEIGHTS FOUR."

JOHNSON, Calvin Crawford, Jr. exonerated by DNA evidence

One night in early 1983, a female resident of Clayton County, Georgia, woke to find a prowler straddling her back as she lay facedown in bed. The man choked her unconscious with a belt, then waited for her to revive before he wrapped a towel around her head, raping and sodomizing her before he fled the scene. The victim, a white woman, had briefly glimpsed her African-American attacker's face and subsequently viewed police mug books. She identified Calvin Johnson Jr., a 25-year-old mail carrier with a 1981 burglary conviction, as her assailant and Johnson was arrested, charged with both the rape in question and another sexual assault committed two days earlier.

Calvin Johnson Jr., right, and his attorney Peter Neufeld leave the courtroom after a judge freed him from prison. Johnson, who spent 16 years behind bars for a brutal rape, was cleared after DNA evidence proved another man was responsible for the crime. (AP)

At trial, in November 1983, jurors acquitted him of the first assault but convicted him of rape and burglary in the later case. On the day he was sentenced to life imprisonment, Johnson told the court, "With God as my witness, I have been falsely accused of these crimes. I'm an innocent man, and I pray in the name of Jesus Christ that the truth will eventually be brought out."

Legal appeals proved fruitless, but Johnson finally received assistance from the CARDOZO INNOCENCE PROJECT, committed to reexamining cases where DNA evidence may cast new light on dubious convictions. Semen samples preserved from the original case were tested in November 1998 and proved conclusively that Johnson was innocent of the crime for which he stood convicted. After various administrative delays, Judge Matthew Simmons ordered a new trial for Johnson, and he was released from custody in June 1999, after District Attorney Bob Keller formally dropped the charges. Keller, who had prosecuted Johnson 16 years earlier, told reporters, "I didn't feel he should spend one more day in prison." Still, despite shaking Johnson's hand for the news cameras, Keller insisted, "I don't think this was a miscarriage or a failure of the system. It points out the tremendous advantages of new testing that we didn't have in 1983. It is a tragedy when a person spends so much time in prison, and I'm sorry for that."

Johnson, for his part, told the press, "I had faith that in some way, some day, the truth would come out, and I kept the faith." Johnson's 70-year-old father, meanwhile, saw no cause for celebration in his son's belated release. "I don't celebrate tragedies," he declared. "It's something that should've happened 16 years ago, so I'm not going to celebrate now. It's as simple as that."

JONES, Joe C. exonerated by DNA evidence

In the early morning hours of August 24, 1985, three women left a Topeka, Kansas, nightclub and walked to their cars in the parking lot. Instead of leaving at once, they sat talking between the two vehicles for several minutes and were thus engaged when a man armed with a pistol suddenly appeared, moving between the cars and ordering one woman to step out. He dragged the woman to another vehicle nearby, forced her inside, and drove to a different part of town where she was raped.

Joe Jones, a homosexual, was present at the nightclub on the date of the attack. The two eyewitnesses identified him as the kidnapper, and while his alleged victim initially picked another assailant from police mug shots, she later changed her story and likewise fingered Jones. When police searched Jones's home, they found a pair of pants resembling those the rapist wore. At trial, a Topeka shopkeeper testified that Jones was in his store at the time of the assault, dressed in different clothing, but jurors disregarded the statement. Evidence of Jones's homosexuality was deemed inadmissible by the court. On February 13, 1986, he was convicted of rape, aggravated KIDNAPPING, and aggravated assault, sentenced to life imprisonment on the kidnapping charge with shorter concurrent prison terms on the other two counts.

On February 2, 1987 Jones filed a motion of remand with the Kansas Supreme Court, seeking a new trial on the basis of ineffective legal counsel and newly discovered evidence. Since his conviction, Jones had learned of another defendant's conviction for sexual assaults with an identical MODUS OPERANDI, and psychologists were called to testify that Jones was a victim of "unconscious transference," the victim and witnesses recalling his face after previously glimpsing him at the nightclub. The motion for remand was granted on February 13, 1987, but only for the purpose of examining the other suspect. A hearing was convened, at which the other inmate naturally denied committing any additional assaults, and prosecutors noted that the second suspect's photograph had been examined by the witnesses before they identified Jones. The motion for a new trial was denied.

Next, Jones's attorney filed another appeal to the state supreme court, on grounds that Jones's sexual orientation should have been allowed as evidence at trial, and that the trial court wrongfully excluded evidence pointing to another suspect. That motion was denied on March 3, 1989.

In 1991, as news of DNA testing reached the defense team, Jones's lawyers were granted permission to test forensic evidence recovered in the case. After some difficulty and the transfer of the evidence to a second laboratory, test results determined on October 25, 1991, that Jones could not have produced semen samples recovered from the victim in 1985. Jones's attorneys moved for a new trial on December 18, 1991, but the prosecution stalled, demanding repetition of the DNA tests. A second round of testing produced identical results on April 13, 1992, and the DNA evidence was ruled admissible on June 17, 1992. Jones's conviction was vacated, with an order for a new trial, but the prosecution declined to refile charges and Jones was released from prison the same day, after serving six and one-half years of his undeserved sentence.

JONES, Ronald exonerated by DNA evidence

An African-American native of Chicago, born July 6, 1950, Ronald Jones provides another example of the grave injustice that has prompted many Illinois residents to demand an overview of the state's justice system and application of capital punishment statutes. His wrongful conviction and death sentence is scarcely more alarming than the malicious attitude of prosecutors who blocked his release from prison for nearly two years after Jones was proved innocent of any crime.

On March 10, 1985, a 28-year-old mother of three was raped and murdered at an abandoned motel on Chicago's South Side. Seven months elapsed before police detectives extracted a confession from Jones, a 34-year-old alcoholic who lived in the same neighborhood. Authorities insisted the confession was voluntary, but Jones claimed he had signed it only after he was beaten by Detectives Steven Hood and John Markham. According to Jones's sworn testimony, Hood struck him several times across the head with a blackjack, before Markham said, "Don't hit him like this because he will bruise," and then proceeded to punch Jones repeatedly in the stomach.

Voluntary or otherwise, the confession was dubious. Jones described the murder victim as a prostitute, when in fact she had no record of prostitution. Still, Judge John Morrissey admitted the confession as evidence and disregarded Jones's testimony of police brutality. At trial in 1989, prosecutors argued that semen recovered from the victim belonged to Jones, even though the samples were too small for a conclusive blood test using then-current technology. Jones was convicted by a jury and Judge Morrissey sentenced him to die.

Five years later, in 1994, attorney Richard Cunningham asked Judge Morrissey to permit DNA testing on the forensic evidence, but Morrissey twice refused. Reminded that prosecutors had claimed the semen was Jones's, Morrissey sneered from the bench, "Save arguments like that for the press. They love it. I don't." On appeal of those decisions, the Illinois Supreme Court overruled Morrissey and ordered the DNA tests to proceed in 1997. The results conclusively excluded Ronald Jones as a source of the semen, but prosecutors still refused to acknowledge his innocence. More tests were ordered by the state, with the same result. Finally, after 22 months of "reinvestigating the case," state's attorneys dropped all charges when confronted with an order for a retrial. He was released from custody, belatedly, on May 17, 1999. The murder case remains unsolved today.

KERSTA, Lawrence George (1907–)

New Jersey native Lawrence Kersta, born December 22, 1907, studied electrical engineering and physics at New York's Columbia University. In 1962–63, while employed by Bell Laboratories, he began experiments with a sound spectrograph invented by Bell technicians in 1944. That study convinced Kersta that spectrographic tracings of human voices—which he dubbed "voiceprints"—could match known subjects to recordings of unknown persons, as with anonymous telephone calls. Excited by the potential applications of his discovery, Kersta left Bell in 1966, patented the term *voiceprint,* and founded his own International Association of Voice Identification (IAVI). His colleagues included Ernest Nash (who helped create the Michigan State Police crime lab) and Oscar Tosi (a founder of the Michigan State University forensic science program).

For the best part of a decade, Kersta, Nash, and Tosi dominated voiceprint technology in the United States, testifying as expert witnesses in many criminal cases. With some 50,000 individual voice samples on file, IAVI claimed 99.6 percent accuracy in matching anonymous recordings to known subjects. Kersta's technology and methods were adopted by the FBI and are today employed by law enforcement agencies around the world. In 1980, the IAVI was absorbed by the INTERNATIONAL ASSOCIATION OF IDENTIFICATION, previously concerned for the most part with FINGERPRINTS.

KIDNAPPING

Legal definitions of kidnapping vary broadly over time and from one jurisdiction to another, incorporating what one scholar describes as "a wide and ill-defined range of behavior." Essentially, kidnapping involves the taking or detention of a person against his/her will and without such legal authority as lawful arrest, extradition, or imprisonment by order of a court. *Abduction,* though commonly used as a synonym for kidnapping, may be a separate offense in some jurisdictions, referring primarily to disruption of a family unit by taking a child away from his/her parents (even with the child's express consent). Historically, American kidnappings have run the full gamut from "manstealing" (including theft or unlawful liberation of slaves in antebellum days) to the modern practice of divorced parents' absconding with children in violation of a custody decree.

The earliest recorded cases of kidnapping, mostly fictional, were handed down in Greco-Roman and Judeo-Christian myths. In the latter case, biblical kidnappings are treated ambiguously, sometimes presented as heinous acts, at other times portrayed as deeds commanded by God. In few (if any) cases are the crimes themselves subject to independent historical documentation.

More substantial reports of kidnapping proliferated in the ancient world. Vikings abducted countless victims in their raids against the British Isles and western Europe, holding some for ransom and selling others into slavery. Kidnapping also was a staple in the repertoire of pirates, from the Barbary Coast to the Caribbean and the South China Sea. European discovery of a New World in the 15th century opened fresh vistas for abduction. Amerindian tribesmen were no strangers to wartime kidnapping; now, snatched themselves by white invaders for ransom or as slaves, they repaid the European newcomers in kind. Later, Africans were kidnapped en masse to serve white masters in the Western Hemisphere, their value as chattel creating an insidious traffic in free blacks kidnapped from northern U.S. states to serve as slaves below the Mason-Dixon Line. The Civil War eradicated slavery, but peonage remained (enduring to the present day), while racist vigilantes of the Ku Klux Klan abducted countless victims in their war to preserve southern white supremacy.

Researcher Ernest Alix, in his 1978 history of American kidnappings, asserts that no case was reported prior to 1868, but the scope of his study is severely limited by near-total reliance on the *New York Times Index*, with its built-in limitations. (The *Index* began publication in 1852; for many years thereafter it consisted of handwritten volumes focused chiefly on New York, with very sparse coverage of crime.) Most accounts describe America's first "classic" ransom abduction as the still-unsolved kidnapping of young Charles Ross in Philadelphia, during 1874. That case was notorious enough that journalists and ransom notes alike still referred to Ross and his presumed murder as late as the turn of the 19th century. The "first successful" ransom kidnapping in the United States is generally listed as the 1900 case of Edward Cudahy, wherein $25,000 was collected and the kidnappers, although identified, won acquittal at trial. Prosecution of kidnappers remained a state problem until 1932, when passage of the LINDBERGH Law by Congress made interstate abduction a federal crime.

The Alix study of American kidnapping previously mentioned identifies 15 categories of abduction commonly labeled as "kidnapping" in the popular media. Considered with their motives, they include:

1. *"White slavery,"* wherein victims (regardless of race) are compelled to perform as prostitutes for the financial benefit of their captors. Victims of such sexual slavery (lately dubbed "human trafficking") are typically female but may also include younger males. The commercial aspect distinguishes their plight from victims in the fifth category, below.

2. *Hostage situations,* which involve victims taken in the course of another crime (armed ROBBERY, etc.) to protect the offender or to facilitate his/her escape.

3. *Child stealing,* considered the unlawful abduction of a child from parents or legal guardians for some motive not included in the other categories listed here. (Conversion of a minor to a religious cult or fringe political movement might be one example.)

4. *Domestic relations kidnapping,* wherein a child is taken from his/her custodial parent without legal authority, normally by the divorced or separated parent who does not have custody. Infrequent cases may involve removal of an adult family member to gain some advantage (normally financial, as in the collection of a pension or other benefits).

5. *Kidnapping for rape or other sexual assault,* distinguished from "white slavery" by the absence of any financial consideration.

6. *Kidnapping for murder or other nonsexual assault,* a broad category that may include (but is not limited to) the activities of serial murderers, contract killers, terrorists, and vigilantes, or personal enemies of the victim.

7. *Kidnapping for robbery,* wherein the victim is abducted and deprived of money or other valuable property aside from ransom payments. The value of property stolen varies immensely from one case to the next.

8. *Romantic kidnapping,* typically involving a minor "victim" who willingly accompanies the offender against parental wishes, as in cases of elopement.

9. *Ransom skyjacking,* wherein one or more kidnappers seize control of an aircraft, its passengers, and crew. Demands typically include cash or other valuables, a free ride to some unscheduled destination, and/or (in the case of organized terrorists) the liberation of imprisoned comrades.

10. *Ransom kidnapping hoaxes deliberately staged to conceal some other act,* including homicide, financial extortion of the "victim's" family, minors running away from home, or (in the case of celebrities) a desire for free publicity.

11. *Abortive ransom kidnapping,* including plots that die on the drawing board (in which case no

actual kidnapping occurs) and abductions that stop short of ransom demands being made.

12. *Ransom threats for coercion,* wherein kidnapping is threatened but not carried out. "Black Hand" extortionists were known for such threats in the early 1900s, and Third World terrorists such as the Tupamaros guerrillas of Uruguay are notorious for threatening the officers of multinational corporations.

13. *Developmental ransom kidnapping,* a variation of item number 2 above, where hostages are taken during the course of some other crime and ransom is demanded, in lieu of simply using the captives as human shields to facilitate escape.

14. *Classic ransom kidnapping,* in which collection of the ransom payment for a kidnapped victim is the sole or primary motive. Murder may result—and may indeed be planned from the beginning—but collection of ransom remains uppermost in the offender's mind.

15. *Miscellaneous kidnappings,* a catch-all category that includes any motives omitted by the other 14 definitions. Examples might include interrogation (as of political hostages), detention of the victim to forestall some specific event or act, or abduction with intent to swap the victim for some other person (outside the skyjacking venue from item number 9 above).

KING, Amos Lee controversial DNA case

At 2:35 A.M. on March 18, 1977, prison inmate Amos King returned from a work-release assignment to the Tarpon Springs (Florida) Community Correctional Center, where he was serving time for theft of a FIREARM. An hour later, prison counselor James McDonough performed a routine bed check and noted King missing. He subsequently found King outside the prison building with blood on his pants, whereupon King drew a knife and stabbed McDonough 25 times before fleeing. Police responding to that call saw flames leaping from the home of 68-year-old Natalie Brady, located 1,500 feet from the correctional center, and found Brady dying from injuries inflicted by a home invader who had raped, stabbed, and beaten her. Based on scientific testimony from Medical Examiner Joan Wood, jurors convicted King of Brady's murder, and he was sentenced to death on July 8, 1977. Over the next quarter-century, King's execution date was set five times and he received six stays, ranking as the longest-serving death row inmate from Pinellas County.

In 2002, investigative reporters for a local television station reported that former medical examiner Wood had made "big mistakes" in some of her autopsy reports, resulting in wrongful convictions of defendants David Long and John Peel on charges of shaking their own infant children to death. (Both were later exonerated and released.) Two independent pathologists also found "problems" with Wood's work in the Brady case, including "convenient loss of physical evidence" such as King's bloody pants and two ambulance sheets used to wrap Brady's body at the crime scene. Defense attorney Peter Cannon subsequently hired BARRY SCHECK, head of the CARDOZO INNOCENCE PROJECT, to review King's case. The missing sheets surfaced in a police evidence locker and were submitted for DNA testing, while Governor Jeb Bush granted King his latest stay of execution. Unfortunately for King, the tests on those aged BLOODSTAINS proved inconclusive. King was executed by lethal injection on February 26, 2003, while relatives and friends continued to protest his innocence.

KIRK, Paul Leland (1902–1970)

A native of Colorado Springs, Colorado, born on May 9, 1902, Paul Kirk earned his B.S. from Ohio State University in 1924, his M.S. from the University of Pittsburgh in 1925, and his Ph.D. in biochemistry from the University of California (Berkeley) in 1927. While pursuing his doctoral studies at Berkeley, he served as a teaching assistant, then a research fellow, and—following a wartime interruption when he served with the Manhattan Project developing America's first nuclear weapons—as full professor (1945–67). His research in microchemistry found practical applications in both criminology and tissue culture studies, but forensic science was his true academic forte and the subject he taught with most enthusiasm. In 1950, Kirk established UC Berkeley's School of Criminology and served as its chairman until his retirement 17 years later.

Kirk's vaunted expertise often involved him as an expert witness in criminal trials, none more celebrated (or notorious) than the Sheppard murder case. In July 1954, Dr. Sam Sheppard summoned police to his Cleveland, Ohio, home, where officers found his wife bludgeoned to death in the blood-spattered master bedroom. Sheppard claimed that he awoke from a nap on the living room couch to hear his wife screaming, then met a stranger and was knocked unconscious as he rushed upstairs to her aid. Tales of marital infidelity cast doubt on Sheppard's story, and prosecutors charged Sheppard with murder. At trial, longtime coroner Samuel Gerber described BLOOD-STAIN EVIDENCE from the crime scene, including the supposed bloody imprint of an unspecified surgical instrument on a pillow. Jurors took the hint and convicted Dr. Sheppard of second-degree murder, whereupon he received a life prison term. After that verdict was rendered, Sheppard's defense team hired Paul Kirk to reevaluate the crime scene evidence. Kirk's review of the blood-spatter pattern, including a total absence of stains on the bedroom ceiling, convinced him that the fatal blows were struck horizontally, by a left-handed assailant. (Dr. Sheppard was right-handed.) Kirk also opined that the killer should have been covered with blood, while police found only one small bloodstain on the knee of Sheppard's pants. Those opinions, coupled with Sheppard's persistent claims of innocence, spawned a TV series and a later film, *The Fugitive*, about a doctor falsely accused of killing his wife.

Dr. Gerber reacted to Kirk's opinions with a series of vindictive personal attacks and a successful campaign to bar Kirk from membership in the American Academy of Forensic Sciences. Author Cynthia Cooper, in her book *Mockery of Justice* (1995), reports that Gerber also had a personal grudge against Sam Sheppard and his family, repeatedly opposing Sheppard's efforts to start a new hospital in Cleveland. Still, Gerber could not prevent an appellate court from overturning Sheppard's conviction, and a second jury acquitted him of all charges in 1966. Marilyn Sheppard's murder remains officially unsolved today, though two suspects have been named in print. Cynthia Kirk and James Neff (author of *The Wrong Man*, 2001) blame the crime on suspected serial killer Richard Eberling, while ex-FBI agent Bernard Conners names an alternative suspect. In 2002 Conners published *Tailspin*, the case study of Major James Call, who deserted from the U.S. Air Force in 1954 and embarked on a nationwide BURGLARY spree—allegedly including a raid on the Sheppard home in Cleveland. Paul Kirk never learned of those alternate theories, having died in Berkeley on June 5, 1970.

KNOTS

Knots may be critical pieces of evidence in cases of hanging, strangulation, or whenever victims have been bound by their killers or kidnappers. Study of knots is also useful in determining whether some deaths (including those resulting from autoerotic asphyxiation) are accidents, suicides, or homicides. Where unique or elaborate knots appear at multiple crime scenes, as in the 1960s "BOSTON STRANGLER" case, they may suggest a serial offender—and may also help identify the subject if he/she ties shoelaces or other cords in the same way. Knots may also cause bruises, leaving identifiable marks on a victim's flesh after bindings are removed. If the binding cord is recovered, microscopic study of its surface and the victim's bruises may confirm its use in the crime. An offender's choice of knots may also help narrow the search to suspects with experience of sailing or other pursuits where specific knots are commonly employed.

KOEHLER, Arthur (1885–1967)

Born in 1885, Arthur Koehler translated a fascination with wood into a career as head of the U.S. Agriculture Department's Forest Service Laboratory in Madison, Wisconsin. During the late 1920s and 1930s, police frequently sought Koehler's expert opinion on wooden bits of evidence from various criminal cases. During 1932–34, Koehler applied himself single-mindedly to the LINDBERGH KIDNAPPING case, and thereby helped to perpetrate a great injustice.

Soon after the ransom kidnapping of Charles Lindbergh Jr., on March 1, 1932, police found a crude homemade ladder and a 3/4-inch chisel outside the Lindbergh home. Norman Schwarzkopf, commander of the New Jersey State Police, submitted the ladder to Koehler for study, whereupon Koehler identified its various mismatched woods and launched an epic search for their point of origin. Before he finished, Koehler sent inquiries to 1,598 lumber mills and visited 30 East Coast lumberyards, later claiming that yellow pine cut at the same South Carolina mill that produced one rung of the kidnap ladder had been sent to a New York lumberyard where suspect Bruno Hauptmann purchased wood. Granted, Koehler could never prove that Hauptmann bought the planks in question, but that was the least of his failings.

In his original findings, Koehler claimed that no tests could determine the size of chisel used to make the kidnap ladder. An FBI report from May 1932 agreed, stating more specifically that "no conclusion that the chisel [found at Lindbergh's home] was used in building the ladder is warranted." Two years later, at Hauptmann's murder trial, Koehler reversed himself, claiming that tool marks on the ladder were made by a 3/4-inch chisel. Under prosecution coaching, he also claimed that Hauptmann's tool kit contained no 3/4-inch chisel—thus implying that Hauptmann had dropped his outside Lindbergh's house. In fact, however, a suppressed police report uncovered decades later by author Anthony Scaduto reveals that *two* 3/4-inch chisels were found in Hauptmann's garage (and later concealed from the jury).

In respect to the ladder itself, Koehler claimed that one rung was made from wood previously used as attic flooring. Police searched Hauptmann's attic nine times between September 19 and 25, 1934, but found no evidence of missing floorboards. New Jersey state trooper Lewis Bornmann searched the attic twice more on September 26. After his first search, he noted that "nothing of value was found." During a second search that afternoon, however, Bornmann claimed to notice for the first time that a plank of yellow pine was missing from the floor. Koehler arrived on October 10—after Bornmann rented the apartment and barred defense attorneys from the premises—to examine the flooring with Bornmann. Together, they decided that nail holes in the small ladder rung "exactly matched" those in the other floorboards—but they kept the secret to themselves. On December 8, 1934, Koehler "emphatically denied" that any wood from the ladder had been traced to Hauptmann's home. "There is absolutely no truth in the matter at all," he told reporters.

Koehler sang a different tune at Hauptmann's trial, persuading jurors that Hauptmann had torn one plank from his attic, for reasons unknown, ignoring his stockpile of scrap wood, to furnish one rung of the kidnap ladder. That "evidence" and other perjured testimony sent Hauptmann to the electric chair, but FBI agents were not so easily deceived. Their classified report of May 26, 1936, kept secret long after Hauptmann's execution, read in part:

The identification of the wood in the ladder, resulting in the opinion that the wood in the attic of Hauptmann's residence was identical to that of the ladder, was developed subsequent to the withdrawal of the Bureau from an active part in the investigation, and occurred after

the New Jersey State Police had rented the Hauptmann residence.

You will also recall that at one stage in the trial of Hauptmann it was indicated that efforts would be made by the defense counsel to subpoena records of this department relative to Arthur Koehler, with the thought in mind that the defense could establish and check that Arthur Koehler's story concerning the wood identification could be proved as having been fabricated by the joint efforts of the New Jersey State Police and the New Jersey Prosecutor's Office in co-operation with Arthur Koehler. However this request was not received by the Bureau from the defense attorneys.

Koehler spent the rest of his life writing and lecturing about his pivotal role in the Lindbergh case. He died in 1967.

KOTLER, Kerry exonerated and convicted by DNA evidence

A resident of Suffolk County, New York, Kerry Kotler was accused in 1981 of raping a female neighbor on two occasions, the first allegedly occurring in 1978 and the second in 1981. In the first instance, the victim said she arrived home to find a ski-masked stranger at her home who raped her at knifepoint and robbed her of some jewelry. Unable to identify her assailant, the victim reported a simple BURGLARY and told police nothing of the rape. Three years later, she said, a masked man waylaid her outside her back door and again raped her while holding a knife to her throat, then stole $343 in cash. Before fleeing that time, the rapist warned that he might "come back for another visit" in the near future.

After the second rape, the victim scanned police mug books and reportedly selected Kerry Kotler from among 500 other photographs; she later picked him from a police lineup as well, claiming to recognize both his face and his voice. The Suffolk County crime lab analyzed semen stains from the victim's underpants and reported that three non-DNA genetic markers matched suspect Kotler's blood. At trial in 1983, jurors deliberated for two days before convicting Kotler on two counts of first-degree rape, two counts of first-degree burglary, two counts of second-degree burglary, and one count of first-degree robbery. Kotler received a prison term of 25 to 50 years.

Kotler's initial appeal, seeking reversal of the verdict prior to sentencing, alleged prosecutorial misconduct and deficiencies in the court's charge to the jury.

It was denied on December 2, 1983. His next effort, before the state Appellate Division, sought reversal based on erroneous admission of testimony, insufficient evidence to convict and excessive sentencing, but his conviction was affirmed on March 3, 1986. A year later, on March 10, 1987, Kotler brought another motion to set aside his conviction, this one based on false testimony by a police officer, concealment of evidence and improper cross-examination of Kotler regarding his prior criminal record. That motion was also denied, on July 7, 1988, but the appellate court ordered a hearing on whether certain documents had been improperly concealed from the defense before trial. Subsequent to that hearing, on January 8, 1990, Kotler's motion was again denied.

Meanwhile, Kotler had begun to educate himself on the science of DNA testing. He contacted the Legal Aid Society for help in September 1988 and obtained the necessary funds from relatives. Forensic evidence from the case was submitted for testing on February 15, 1989, but the laboratory found an insufficient amount of DNA present for reliable analysis. Kotler's legal aid attorney then suggested a second lab and the tests were repeated in February 1990. Those tests excluded Kotler as a source of semen found on the victim's clothing, but prosecutors rejected the findings. Since DNA from Kotler *and* the suspect stains revealed a "similar" allele (gene), the state hypothesized that part of the semen had come from a consensual sex partner, and another part from Kotler.

To resolve the argument, a third battery of tests was scheduled at yet another laboratory, with the same results. Blood samples were also obtained from the victim's husband (and only reported consensual sex partner), with test results excluding both Kotler and the husband as sources of the suspect semen. Technicians from two laboratories signed a joint statement attesting to that fact on November 24, 1992. The Suffolk County court vacated Kotler's conviction on December 1, 1992, and released him on his own recognizance, after serving 11 years of his sentence. Prosecutors dismissed all charges against him on December 14, 1992.

There is an ironic postscript to Kotler's story of exoneration. On April 8, 1996, one month after winning a $1.5 million legal judgment for wrongful imprisonment, Kotler was arrested for another rape, this one committed on August 12, 1995. DNA tests performed on semen from the latest victim's clothing matched Kotler's samples, already on file from his previous case. The victim reported that Kotler carried a water bottle and tried to wash away evidence after the rape, but new collection methods frustrated the attempt. Convicted of first-degree rape and second-degree KIDNAPPING, Kotler was sentenced to a prison term of seven to 21 years.

KROGMAN, Wilton (1903–1987)

Born in 1903, "bone detective" Wilton Krogman was an American pioneer in the field of forensic ANTHROPOLOGY whose career spanned nearly six decades. While serving as a full-time professor of physical anthropology at the University of Pennsylvania Medical School, Krogman published a series of papers and books that remain classics in their field. His initial publication, in 1927, was the first comprehensive review of prior research on primate dentition. Krogman's "Guide to the Identification of Human Skeletal Material," published during 1939 in the FBI's *Law Enforcement Bulletin,* was followed in 1962 by his masterwork, *The Human Skeleton in Forensic Medicine* (revised and updated in 1986).

Between those publications, Krogman encountered two of his strangest cases. The first, in July 1951, involved the death of 67-year-old Mary Reeser, a widow in St. Petersburg, Florida. Neighbors found Reeser incinerated in her living room easy chair, nothing left of her corpse but part of her left foot, several vertebrae, and her skull shrunken "to the size of a teacup." Krogman examined the remains and photos of the scene, which showed little or no fire damage beyond a black ring surrounding Reeser's favorite chair. Baffled, Krogman called the case "the most amazing thing I have ever seen. As I review it, the short hairs on my neck bristle with vague fear. Were I living in the Middle Ages I'd mutter something about black magic." Police in St. Petersburg closed the case with a claim that Reeser had fallen asleep while smoking and thus ignited her rayon-acetate nightgown, while skeptics list the case as an example of "spontaneous human combustion."

Krogman's second classic puzzler, in February 1957, involved Philadelphia's "boy in the box." Pedestrians in the city's Fox Chase region found a naked blond Caucasian boy, four to six years old, bludgeoned to death inside a furniture box, wrapped in an Indian-style blanket. In addition to the fatal beating, officers found evidence of malnutrition, but the child's hair and fingernails had been recently trimmed. Krogman and an aide examined the remains, but could offer no clues to the identity of either the young victim or his slayer. In June 2002, 15 years after Krogman's own death, detectives interviewed an elderly woman who claimed to have known the boy and his mother, but both still remain unidentified.

KWON, Il Hyung exonerated by DNA evidence

A student at the University of Tennessee in Knoxville, 26-year-old Il Hyung Kwon was arrested for assault and public exposure on April 10, 1997, following an attack on a female student in the school's library. He faced a six-month jail sentence and a $1,000 fine, in addition to expulsion from the university, until July 9, when a Tennessee Bureau of Investigation laboratory completed DNA testing on semen traces left from the assault and cleared him of all charges. Detective D. R. Cook, employed by the University of Tennessee Police Department, told reporters, "I'm pleased with the results, that he has been exonerated. I'm sorry for any embarrassment and inconvenience he has suffered." The school's associate general counsel, Ron Leadbetter, confirmed that no disciplinary measures would be pursued, saying, "It's a really unfortunate situation. Everybody acted in good faith. The hearing process worked. It allowed us to find out what happened; it exonerated someone who was innocent."

Il Kwon's attorney, Samuel King Lee, was less charitable in his description of the incident. His client, Lee declared, "was wrongfully accused, made a victim, and labeled the perpetrator of a heinous sexual crime. Aside from exposing Mr. Kwon to public ridicule and causing upheaval in his life and new marriage, these wrongfully brought charges put Mr. Kwon in jeopardy of criminal sanctions, including six months' incarceration and a $1,000 fine. Albeit, Mr. Kwon's most significant concern was the likelihood of permanent expulsion from the university and preclusion from employment as an engineer."

Lee noted that in cases filed by scholastic authorities, "guilt does not have to be proved beyond a reasonable doubt. In Mr. Kwon's case, since he was present in the library at the time the alleged assault occurred, and since only his wife could corroborate his alibi, but for the DNA evidence that excluded him as a suspect, it is more than probable that he would have been permanently expelled."

L

LaBATTE, Beth controversial DNA case

On November 16, 1991, elderly sisters Ann and Ceil Cadigan were beaten and stabbed to death by an intruder at their home in Kewaunee County, Wisconsin. Five years elapsed before police charged suspect Beth LaBatte with killing the two retired school-teachers. Although there were no witnesses and little physical evidence to place her at the crime scene, jailhouse informants claimed that LaBatte confessed to committing the murders. Jurors convicted LaBatte in 1996 and Judge Dennis Luebke sentenced her to life in prison. Fourteen years later, members of the WISCONSIN INNOCENCE PROJECT sponsored DNA testing of certain crime scene evidence, including bloody socks, a hair recovered from the body of one victim, and genetic material found on a supposed murder weapon. The test results excluded LaBatte as a DNA donor while placing an unknown third party at the murder scene. A Wisconsin appellate court granted LaBatte's motion for a new trial and released her from custody on November 10, 2005. Assistant District Attorney Elma Anderson dismissed the DNA test results as "not particularly relevant," telling reporters that her office would retry LaBatte for murder, even though locating the original trial witnesses would represent "a major undertaking." No date for the new trial had been set at press time for this work.

LABORATORY Information Management System

"Laboratory Information Management System" is a generic name for computer software programs that facilitate administrative tasks (record keeping, reporting, etc.) and permit creation of databases integrating laboratory data. Systems commercially available at press time for this work included those produced by Bika Lab Systems, CACI, Clinigene, Honeywell, Lab-Soft, LabVantage, LIMSource, Microsoft, Nuvotec, and several others.

LACASSAGNE, Jean Alexandre Eugène (1844–1921)

A native of France, born in 1844, Jean Lacassagne enrolled at Strasbourg's military academy and subsequently served in the French army as a surgeon, seeing action in West Africa against Tukulor tribesmen of the Senegal River valley. Returning to civilian life with his hard-earned knowledge of ballistics and battle wounds, Lacassagne embarked on a career in forensic medicine that ultimately made him famous throughout France and western Europe. He performed numerous autopsies and published a ground-breaking article on the use of tattoos in criminal identification, followed in 1878 by his *Précis de medicine*. Administrators at the University of Lyons were impressed with that work and created a new chair for Lacassagne as professor of forensic medicine.

His research on corpses included documentation of the rate at which human bodies cool, the onset and passage of rigor mortis, and the posthumous skin blotching known as livor mortis. In 1889, Lacassagne was the first researcher to suggest that longitudinal grooves on a bullet were caused by rifling inside the murder weapon's barrel. Ten years later, he was the first to publish photos of Jack the Ripper's victims in his case study of French serial killer Joseph Vacher (*Vacher l'Eventreur et les Crimes Sadiques*). Lacassagne's testimony in that case, based on five months of personal study, deflated Vacher's insanity defense and sent him to the guillotine. Lacassagne remained active virtually until his death in 1921.

LaGUER, Benjamin controversial forensics case

In 1983, police in Leominster, Massachusetts, were summoned to investigate the rape of a 59-year-old woman whose home was also robbed. The victim, a diagnosed schizophrenic, described her attacker as "black-skinned," prompting officers to arrest Benjamin LaGuer, the victim's next-door neighbor and the only African-American resident of the their apartment complex. LaGuer volunteered to have a mug shot taken for display in a photo lineup, and he seemed sincerely shocked when the victim fingered him as her attacker. At trial an all-white jury convicted LaGuer despite his protestations of innocence, based on the victim's eyewitness identification, and LaGuer received a sentence of 15 years to life.

From the day of his arrest, LaGuer enjoyed support from various defenders who believed his claims of innocence. Historian Elie Wiesel and former Boston University president John Silber joined the crusade for a new trial, spearheaded by attorney James Rehnquist (son of then-U.S. Supreme Court justice William Rehnquist). In 2001, LaGuer's defenders discovered a contradiction in the prosecution's evidence from 1983. At trial, a state police expert told jurors that one partial FINGERPRINT was recovered from the victim's telephone (whose cord was used to bind her hands) and that it did not match LaGuer's. In fact, as Rehnquist learned in 2001, a state police report indicated that four *full* prints were found on the phone, none matching LaGuer's. Assistant District Attorney Sandra Hautanen resisted LaGuer's appeal, reporting that the fingerprint evidence had "disappeared," while claiming that it was irrelevant in any case. Rehnquist soon learned that other vital pieces of

forensic evidence had "vanished" from police files, and Hautanen herself gave a hint as to what may have happened. Addressing Judge Timothy Hillman in Worcester County Superior Court, Hautanen said, "My understanding is that three to five state troopers spent more than a day going through every piece of paper that were [*sic*] about to be shredded."

Since the rape victim died in 1999, her identification of LaGuer could no longer be challenged. Still, Rehnquist and company pressed for reexamination of surviving forensic evidence in the case. That evidence includes several foreign pubic hairs and a "minimal" amount of semen collected from the victim in 1983. After two years of resistance from county prosecutors, in 2002, LaGuer's team submitted the items for DNA testing at a California laboratory—which reported that the DNA matched LaGuer's profile. While LaGuer's supporters recoiled in embarrassment, LaGuer himself suggested that police might have stolen underwear from his apartment in 1983 to obtain and plant the rape kit evidence. Allen Fletcher, a journalist who wrote several supportive articles on LaGuer for the *Worcester Telegram and Gazette*, spoke for most of the inmate's defenders when he told the *Boston Globe*, "I was brutally disappointed. There is no way he is not innocent."

LANDSTEINER, Karl (1868–1943)

Viennese native Karl Landsteiner was born on June 14, 1868. His father—an attorney and newspaper editor—died in 1874, leaving Landsteiner in sole care of his mother. Landsteiner earned his M.D. from the University of Vienna at age 23, and applied his skills to work in serology. In 1901, he discovered the ABO blood grouping system and thus saved countless lives by refining the previous hit-or-miss technique of transfusion. In 1908, Landsteiner returned to his alma mater as a professor of PATHOLOGY, where his studies established the viral nature of poliomyelitis. He left Vienna after World War I, lived briefly in the Netherlands, then immigrated to New York in 1922. There he joined the Rockefeller Institute for Medical Research and remained a fixture at the institute's laboratory even after his formal retirement in 1939. Landsteiner received the Nobel Prize in medicine in 1930 for his blood-typing research, and 10 years later collaborated with A. S. Weiner to identify the Rh factor in human blood. Landsteiner died in New York on June 26, 1943.

LARSON, John A. (1892–1965)

Born in 1892, Dr. John Larson worked as a police officer and teacher before devoting himself to scientific criminology in Berkeley, California. Collaborating with legendary police chief AUGUST VOLLMER, Larson invented the polygraph—a supposed "lie detector"—in 1921. Testing hinged upon Larson's R/I (relevant/irrelevant) interrogation technique, which intersperses questions relevant to the crime ("Do you own an ax?") with questions entirely divorced from the case ("Are you 40 years old?"). Larson theorized that innocent persons would display similar reactions to both types of questions, while the guilty would react to relevant questions with elevated pulse rate, higher blood pressure, faster breathing, and increased perspiration.

Expert testimony on the results of the polygraph faced a telling challenge in the case of *Frye v. United States* (1923), but Larson kept striving to perfect his device. With colleague Leonarde Keeler, Larson refined the polygraph through the 1930s and published a book on the subject, *Lying and Its Detection* (1932), with coauthors Keeler and George Harry. Most published sources credit Keeler with developing the polygraph in common use today. Larson, meanwhile, retired from crime-fighting to practice psychiatry. He died in 1965.

LATTES, Leone (1887–1954)

A native of Germany, born in 1887, Leone Lattes earned his M.D. in 1905 and pursued postgraduate studies in serology at the University of Munich, with particular emphasis on blood typing as performed by KARL LANDSTEINER. His work in that field earned Lattes a professor's post in Italy, at the University of Turin's Institute of Forensic Medicine. There, on September 7, 1915, he encountered a peculiar case that ultimately revolutionized the science of blood typing.

On that date, Lattes met a local man whose wife was hounding him about two small, unexplained BLOODSTAINS found on the tail of his shirt. She suspected the blood belonged to another woman, while the husband could not account for its presence. Amused and intrigued, Lattes accepted the "case" and developed a new method of rehydrating dried bloodstains with saline solution for typing. He thus proved that the small blood traces came from the shirt's owner—representing anal discharge from a

prostate condition—and so saved the subject's marriage. The same method subsequently exonerated a murder defendant by proving that bloodstains on his clothing did not belong to the victim. Years later, in 1932, Lattes developed a more advanced procedure—known today as the "Lattes crust test"—that permits typing of dried blood flakes by exposure to antibodies. Lattes died in 1954, at the age of 67.

LAVATER, Johann Casper (1741–1801)

A Swiss clergyman, born on November 15, 1741, Johann Lavater rebelled against the 18th-century "Age of Reason" with complaints that the divine nature of man had been diminished by scientific inquiry. To counteract that trend, he pioneered the study of physiognomy, a pseudoscience whose practitioners claimed that an individual's character could be determined by examination of his/her facial features. That practice included "earology," which differed from latter-day OTOSCOPY in that it was not considered a means of personal identification. A German publisher first released Lavater's *Essays on Physiognomy, Designed to Promote the Knowledge and Love of Mankind* in 1772, and he won a convert in England's King George III—an ironic disciple, considering descriptions of his own unlovely features. Lavater's theories enjoyed a certain vogue in Europe, and encouraged artists whose work ran primarily to silhouettes, while paving the way for the theories of ALPHONSE BERTILLON, FRANZ GALL, and JOHANN SPURZHEIM. Lavater died in 1801, before his work fell out of fashion and became subject to ridicule.

LEVIN, Vladimir first Internet bank robber

A 26-year-old mathematics graduate of St. Petersburg's Teknologichesky University, employed at the Russian computer firm AO Saturn, Vladimir Levin led a group of Russian hackers in the first reported Internet bank robbery. The looting began in 1994, when Levin (a.k.a. "Vova") used an obsolete 286 computer to penetrate Citibank's Cash Manager system, illegally obtaining a list of customer passwords and codes. Thereafter, he and others logged onto the system 18 times between June and August, intercepting electronic money transfers and arranging for large sums to be deposited in international accounts. A minimum of $3.7 million (one report claims $11.6 million) was eventually funneled into bank accounts his gang controlled in the United States, Finland, the Netherlands, Germany, and Israel.

Citibank customers began complaining of large losses in July 1994, and bank officials contacted the FBI. Computer tracking of the bandits required collaboration with Scotland Yard's Computer Crime Unit in London, where the Levin gang maintained one of its larger bank accounts. Levin was arrested at London's Heathrow Airport in March 1995, as he entered the country from Russia, and was held on a U.S. federal warrant charging him with bank fraud and wire fraud. He stalled extradition for 30 months with various legal arguments, first claiming that extradition was unwarranted since no U.S. computers were used to access Citibank's accounts (rejected), then opposing trial in New York on grounds that Citibank's computer was located in New Jersey (ditto). Levin's extradition fight was not assisted by the guilty plea of an accomplice, 28-year-old Russian hacker Alexei Lashmanov. Another St. Petersburg native, Lashmanov admitted transferring U.S. funds to an account he had in Israel. An attempt to withdraw $940,000 in cash from the account was foiled, leading to Lashmanov's arrest, extradition and 1995 guilty plea in New York.

As for Levin, after his arrival in New York he devoted his energy to striking a plea bargain with prosecutors. He finally pleaded guilty to one count of wire fraud, admitting the theft of $3.7 million, and was sentenced on February 24, 1998, to three years in prison, with an order to pay Citibank $240,015 in restitution. (Levin later claimed that one of the lawyers assigned to defend him was actually an undercover FBI agent sent to sabotage his case. The guilty plea was not withdrawn.)

Citibank, meanwhile, tried to put a happy face on what could have been a public relations disaster. Bank spokesmen announced that all but $400,000 of the stolen money had been recovered by federal investigators and was safely back in the original accounts. More to the point, press agents claimed, most of the illicit transfers had been accomplished with Citibank's cooperation, as part of the ongoing manhunt for Levin and company. No Citibank employees in the United States or abroad were found to be involved in the conspiracy. At that, the cyber-looting still damaged the public image of a major bank whose advertising boasted that "the Citi never sleeps."

LEVINE, Lowell J. (1937–)

Born in 1937, New York native Lowell Levine earned his B.A. from Hobart College and his D.D.S. from New York University. After a period of private practice in New York City, beginning in 1963, Levine joined his alma mater's medical school as an associate professor in forensic ODONTOLOGY. In an effort to facilitate preservation of evidence, Levine invented a process for taking bite-mark impressions from human flesh and other substances, thereby creating a three-dimensional cast of an assailant's teeth for comparison with any identified suspects. In the 1973 case of *People v. Milone*, Lowell matched bite marks from a victim's thigh to the teeth of her alleged rape-slayer. Jurors accepted that evidence over the contradictory arguments of Dr. Lester Luntz and convicted the defendant on all counts, a judgment upheld on appeal. In 1985, Levine was a member of the scientific team that identified Brazilian drowning victim "Wolfgang Gerhard" as longtime Nazi fugitive Josef Mengele (although final confirmation awaited DNA testing in 1992). A year later, Levine became embroiled in the controversy over American soldiers missing in Southeast Asia, when he disputed the Air Force identification of Capt. George D. McDonald from a single tooth. Levine concluded that "[w]hile it is possible that the original identification of the dental evidence is correct there is no scientific basis for such an identification."

LEVY, Jeffrey Gerard first convicted U.S. software pirate

A 22-year-old senior at the University of Oregon in Eugene, Jeff Levy apparently misunderstood the point of his studies for a major in public policy management. When not occupied with class work, he was busy bootlegging computer software programs, musical recordings, computer games, and digitally recorded movies, posting the various items to a Web site where members of the general public could illegally download them free of charge. University officials blew the whistle on Levy after they noted an unusual volume of bandwidth traffic generated from a Web page on the school's server. FBI agents and Oregon State Police then launched an investigation, confirming that thousands of pirated software programs, movies, and music recordings were featured on Levy's Web site. Following a search of Levy's apartment, with seizure of various hardware, Levy became the first defendant charged under the No Electronic Theft (NET) Act of 1997.

If convicted on all counts, Levy might have faced three years in prison and a $250,000 fine, but he avoided any meaningful punishment with a plea bargain on August 20, 1999. Three months later, on November 24, 1999, he was sentenced to two years' probation, with a waiver of the court's original ban on further Internet activity. Even so, spokesmen for the government and software industry tried to put a bold face on the wrist-slap. According to Mike Flynn, antipiracy manager for the Software & Information Industry Association, "Today's sentencing represents a modest victory for all software companies large and small. Software piracy, and even online piracy by persons not intending to make a profit, can threaten the survival of a software company. . . . SIIA is confident that this conviction and sentence will spur other U.S. Attorneys to aggressively pursue cases of online piracy under the auspices of the NET Act, and send a clear message that online piracy will be vigorously prosecuted."

U.S. Attorney Kristine Olson agreed that Levy's prosecution "represents the latest step in a major initiative of federal and state law enforcement representatives working together to prosecute electronic crimes." She applauded the collaborative efforts of the FBI and state police in Oregon, predicting further operations of the same sort nationwide. From Washington, James Robertson, assistant attorney general for the criminal division, proclaimed that "Mr. Levy's case should serve as a notice that the Justice Department has made prosecution of Internet piracy one of its priorities. Those who engage in this activity, whether or not for profit, should take heed that we will bring federal resources to bear to prosecute these cases. This is theft, pure and simple."

LIMNOLOGY, Forensic

Limnology is a subdiscipline of BIOLOGY, involving the study of life forms found in freshwater bodies including lakes, ponds, rivers, streams, and swamps. Its forensic applications include identification of TRACE EVIDENCE collected from corpses or other objects (clothing, weapons, vehicles, etc.) that have been submerged in freshwater. For objects long submerged, examination of plant material and microorganisms may determine the time of year when submersion occurred. As in the case of forensic GEOLOGY, trace evidence may also link suspects or victims to a particular freshwater body. A case in point involves a brutal attack on two young boys in Connecticut, in July 1991. Three offenders confronted the children with knives, then bound them with duct tape, beat them with a baseball bat, and left them in a nearby pond to drown. Almost miraculously, one boy freed himself and then rescued his friend, then summoned help. Police soon arrested three suspects, who denied involvement in the crime, but examination of their muddy shoes revealed diatoms and algae matching those from the pond and the victims' clothing. Jurors found the evidence compelling and convicted all three suspects of attempted murder.

LINDBERGH Kidnapping miscarriage of justice

Arguably the most famous American of the late 1920s, "Lone Eagle" Charles Lindbergh earned global fame (and fortune) with his solo transatlantic flight in 1927. His son, born on June 22, 1930, was inevitably dubbed "the eaglet" and sometimes described as "America's child." The boy's kidnapping and apparent murder at the tender age of 18 months, described by journalist H. L. Mencken as "the biggest story since the resurrection," launched an investigation fraught with forensic mishaps and malfeasance.

The case began at 10 P.M. on March 1, 1932, when a nursemaid found Charles junior missing from his second-floor nursery in the Lindbergh home near Hopewell, New Jersey. A semiliterate ransom note demanded $50,000 for the boy's safe return. Outside, a crude homemade ladder with a broken step suggested the kidnapper's means of access to the house. It also bore FINGERPRINTS, which remain unidentified today.

News of the abduction provoked national outrage. President Herbert Hoover ordered creation of a special FBI "Lindbergh squad" to offer "unofficial assistance" on the case, but their overtures were rejected by Colonel H. Norman Schwarzkopf, commanding the New Jersey State Police. Disdainful of the "federal glory hunters," Schwarzkopf proceeded to manage the case, while the Lindberghs were swamped with crank calls and letters, including multiple ransom demands. A stranger to the family, 72-year-old Dr. John F. Condon, volunteered to serve as a go-between in contacting the kidnappers, and the Lindberghs accepted his bumbling aid for reasons that remain incomprehensible. Using the code name "Jafsie" (for his initials), Condon placed an ad in the *Bronx Home News* which led to contact with a purported member of the kidnap gang, known only as "John." A late-night cemetery meeting saw the ransom demand increased to $70,000 since Lindbergh had alerted police and the press, but Condon demanded proof that John had the child. Three days later, on March 15, a package arrived at Condon's home, containing a child's sleeping suit that Lindbergh identified as his son's.

The ransom drop was set for April 2 at St. Raymond's Cemetery, in the Bronx. FBI Director J. Edgar Hoover vetoed a plan to stake out the graveyard and catch the kidnapper red-handed. IRS agent Elmer Irey suggested that the ransom be paid in distinctive U.S. gold certificates, with the serial numbers recorded. On the night of April 2, Charles Lindbergh waited in the car while Dr. Condon entered the graveyard with two bundles of cash, one containing $50,000 and the other $20,000. When "John" called out to him from the shadows, Condon gave him the $50,000 parcel but strangely withheld its companion. In return, he got a note with directions to the child's alleged location, aboard a boat off the Massachusetts coast. An exhaustive search proved fruitless, with the baby nowhere to be found. Meanwhile, the first ransom bill surfaced at a New York bank on April 4, with others popping up around the city in subsequent months.

The search for Lindbergh's son apparently ended on May 12, 1932, when a child's mutilated corpse was found in a wooded area four and a half miles from the family estate. Police had searched the forest thoroughly in March, but if one accepts the prosecution's case, they had somehow missed the body. The child's skull was fractured and its left arm was missing, along with its left leg below the knee and most of the internal organs. Decomposition was so far advanced that even the victim's gender could not be determined. Lindbergh and a governess identified the body, but the family's pediatrician refused to do so. If offered $10 million for a positive ID, the doctor said, "I'd have to refuse the money."

Congress passed the "Lindbergh Law" in June 1932, making interstate kidnapping a federal offense, and while the statute had no legal bearing on the present case, President Franklin Roosevelt granted

the FBI "principal jurisdiction" in October 1933. The gesture made no difference. Despite recovery of 97 ransom bills between January and August 1934, G-men remained clueless in their search for the kidnappers. Finally, on September 15, 1934, a New York gas station attendant identified one of the gold certificates and recorded his customer's license number, thereby leading police to the Bronx apartment of Bruno Richard Hauptmann, a 35-year-old carpenter who had emigrated from Germany in 1924.

According to author Ronald Kessler (in *The Bureau*, 2002), FBI agents rushed to Hauptmann's flat but found no one home. Without a warrant, they broke in and searched the place, discovering more than $14,000 of the Lindbergh ransom money stashed in Hauptmann's garage. Realizing that the money would be inadmissible at trial, they replaced it and came back later with New York City police, obtaining permission for a search from Hauptmann's wife and thus "discovering" the cash. In custody, Hauptmann explained that a friend, one Isidor Fisch, had left the shoebox filled with money in his care when he (Fisch) returned to Germany and subsequently died there. Upon discovering the cash inside, Hauptmann took enough to satisfy a debt Fisch owed him, then stored the rest for safekeeping in case Fisch's heirs came looking for it.

Authorities were naturally skeptical of Hauptmann's "Fisch story," and New York detectives beat Hauptmann repeatedly (a fact confirmed by jailhouse doctor Thurston Dexter on September 20, 1934) in a vain effort to make him confess. J. Edgar Hoover suggested that Hauptmann might crack if forced to copy the ransom notes over and over, but local police had already pursued that avenue, compelling him to make seven copies (including misspellings) with three different pens, slanting his writing at various angles in an attempt to match the originals.

When Hauptmann's trial opened at Flemington, New Jersey, on January 2, 1935, he confronted a staggering array of evidence. Eight handwriting experts swore that he had written the Lindbergh ransom notes and other correspondence. A neighbor of the Lindberghs testified that he had seen Hauptmann scouting the estate before the kidnapping. A New York taxi driver, hired to drop a letter at Dr. Condon's house, identified Hauptmann as the man who paid him. Police described finding Condon's address and telephone number, along with the serial numbers of two ransom bills, written inside Hauptmann's closet. A wood expert testified that the kidnap ladder included a plank from the floor of Hauptmann's attic. Finally, Dr. Condon and Lindbergh himself swore under oath that Hauptmann was the "cemetery John" who accepted $50,000 in ransom money on April 2, 1932. Hauptmann was duly convicted on April 13, 1935; his various appeals were denied and he was executed on April 3, 1936.

But was he guilty?

A review of the evidence, coupled with FBI documents declassified long after the fact, suggests a blatant FRAME-UP in the Lindbergh case and proves that G-men were cognizant of the fact. Glaring examples of prosecutorial misconduct include:

Perjured testimony: In 1932, impoverished Lindbergh neighbor Millard Whited twice told police that he had seen no strangers in the area before the kidnapping; by 1934, with reward money in hand and promised more, he changed his story and "positively identified Hauptmann as the man he had seen twice in the vicinity of the Lindbergh estate." Colonel Schwarzkopf also lied, falsely stating that Whited had described the lurking man on March 2, 1932. New York cabbie Joseph Perrone told police in 1932 that he could not identify the stranger who gave him a note for delivery to Dr. Condon, since "I didn't pay attention to anything." Schwarzkopf branded Perrone "a totally unreliable witness," but New Jersey prosecutors used him at trial to finger Hauptmann as the note-passer. Dr. Condon spent two years denying any glimpse of "cemetery John's" face and refused to identify Hauptmann's voice at their first jailhouse meeting, where an FBI agent described Condon as being "in a sort of daze." Later, faced with threats of prosecution as an accomplice to murder, Condon reversed himself and made a "positive" ID under oath. Charles Lindbergh heard only two words from "John"—"Hey, Doc!"—in April 1932, and that from 80 yards away. He later told a grand jury, "It would be very difficult for me to sit here and say that I could pick a man by that voice," yet he did exactly that at trial, naming Hauptmann as the speaker.

Handwriting evidence: FBI expert Charles Appel Jr. told reporters that the odds against anyone but Hauptmann writing the Lindbergh ransom note were "one in a hundred million million," but his grandiose exaggeration flew in the face of logic and the available evidence. Another prosecution expert, 70-year-old Albert Osborn, initially told Schwarzkopf that he was "convinced [Hauptmann] did not write the ransom notes"; at trial, however, he joined seven other experts in stating the exact opposite. Another of the prosecution's expert witnesses was Osborn's son, who in 1971 erroneously certified as genuine alleged writings of billionaire Howard Hughes that were forged by celebrity hoaxer Clifford Irving. Still, 67 years later, FBI historian Ronald Kessler would insist that "nothing undercut the fact that Hauptmann's handwriting matched the ransom note's."

The closet writing: According to coworkers and friends, New York tabloid reporter Tom Cassidy "bragged all over town" that he wrote Dr. Condon's address and telephone number, with the serial numbers of two ransom bills, inside Hauptmann's closet, then reported the "discovery" to police for an exclusive front-page story. Prosecutors accepted the fraudulent writing as evidence, while Cassidy and friends considered it a minor indiscretion in light of Hauptmann's "obvious" guilt.

The kidnap ladder: Crudely made with none of a carpenter's skill, the ladder found at Lindbergh's home bore several latent fingerprints, but they did not match Bruno Hauptmann's. Ignoring that discrepancy, the state called Wisconsin "wood detective" ARTHUR KOEHLER to prove that Hauptmann built the ladder. Koehler initially reported, based on nail holes in the ladder, that its planks had not been previously used for flooring, but he changed his story when a lone plank was discovered missing from the floor of Hauptmann's attic. (That "discovery" was made by two state troopers on September 26, 1934, a week after three dozen officers searched every inch of the flat and saw no gaps in any of the floors.) Because the attic plank was two inches wider than any other board used to build the ladder, Koehler surmised that Hauptmann had laboriously planed it down to fit. Declassified FBI documents bluntly describe Koehler's trial exhibits as "fabricated evidence," but the bureau made no effort to prevent Hauptmann's wrongful conviction.

If there was any doubt of Hauptmann's innocence, it should have been resolved by Colonel Schwarzkopf's own behavior. On the day before Hauptmann's execution, another Lindbergh ransom bill surfaced in the Bronx. Schwarzkopf contacted J. Edgar Hoover, urgently requesting that if any further ransom bills were found they should be secretly destroyed. Hoover's response to that suggestion is unknown, but he made no attempt to interfere with Hauptmann's execution.

LINGUISTICS, Forensic

Linguistics—the study of language—has numerous forensic applications. Broadly speaking, it encompasses review of any text or spoken words that have some relevance to legal cases or the language of the law itself. Documents commonly examined by forensic linguists include contracts, treaties, patent applications, wills, suicide notes, ransom demands, threats of various kinds, and alleged confessions to police by criminal suspects. "Voice prints" from audio tapes may also be used to identify subjects who make anonymous telephone calls or recorded threats. Some practitioners of PSYCHOLOGICAL PROFILING utilize controversial "threat dictionaries" in an effort to determine whether specific threats are serious or if they simply represent some irate person "blowing off steam."

Forensic linguists serve the courts in a variety of ways. Accents in spoken language—sometimes carried over into written words—may suggest the speaker's race or national origin. (In the LINDBERGH KIDNAPPING case, the word *boat* misspelled "boad" in a ransom note persuaded some experts that the kidnapper was German.) Examination of the language used in a confession may reveal if the suspect was coached or coerced by police into using phrases unique to law enforcement personnel, or terms beyond the suspect's education level. The language of a supposed suicide note, coupled with the subject's personal history, may help determine if the death is in fact a suicide, or perhaps a homicide staged to appear so. Study of defamatory or threatening messages may determine authorship, along with the legitimacy of any factual claims included therein. The phrasing of a ransom or extortion note (as in Colorado's notorious JonBenét Ramsey murder) may suggest "inside" knowledge of the victim's private life or financial affairs, thus suggesting a suspect.

Grammar may indicate or exclude specific subjects as the authors of QUESTIONED DOCUMENTS.

One aspect of forensic linguistics, termed discourse analysis, is particularly useful in resolving disputes over spoken language and the testimony of "earwitnesses." At a shooting scene, was the shouted phrase, "Drop it!" a demand to drop a weapon or to change the topic of a heated conversation? When two interpreters present different translations for a foreign-language conversation, which (if either) is correct? Are apparently threatening comments serious, in the context of a conversation between two specific persons? In such cases, linguists may be called upon to analyze not only context of the conversations in question, but the personalities and cultural backgrounds of specific subjects.

Voiceprint technology was pioneered in 1941, by LAWRENCE KERSTA, based on the proposition that all human beings have different and unique vocal structures. While the sound spectrograms produced from audio recordings are used by many law enforcement agencies to identify persons suspected of making anonymous threats or harassing phone calls, the process remains controversial and voiceprints are not generally accepted as evidence in American courts. Likewise, the process of voice stress analysis pioneered in the 1960s remains under a cloud of judicial suspicion and is not generally admissible as a means of DECEPTION ANALYSIS. Legal qualms, of course, do not prevent its use by various law enforcement and intelligence agencies throughout the United States and worldwide.

LINSCOTT, Steven exonerated by DNA evidence

On October 4, 1980, Chicago police found a woman murdered in her apartment. The victim was nude, lying facedown on the floor, with a nightgown wrapped around her neck. She had been beaten and stabbed repeatedly; an autopsy found evidence of sexual assault. One of the victim's neighbors, Steven Linscott, was routinely questioned as police canvassed the area. Although he claimed no knowledge of the crime at first, Linscott later contacted authorities to report memories of a dream he had on the night of the murder, which paralleled the actual event. Specifically, Linscott dreamed of a woman being beaten with a long, thin object while she lay on the ground. (Authorities confirmed the murder weapon was a tire iron.) Linscott also saw his dream-victim dying passively, without resistance, while investigators noted that the dead woman had been found with her hands forming the Hindu "ommudra" sign for placid acceptance of death.

Suspicious now, police recorded further interviews with Linscott, requesting blood, hair, and saliva samples which he willingly supplied. Testing of semen from the crime scene showed that Linscott and the killer had the same blood type. Likewise, analysis of head and pubic hairs left by the unknown suspect were tested and judged "consistent" with Linscott's samples. With that evidence in hand, police arrested Linscott for rape and murder on November 25, 1980. At trial, a Cook County jury deliberated for 10 hours before convicting him of murder and acquitting him on the rape charge. Linscott received a 40-year prison term.

Linscott appealed the conviction, and it was overturned by the Appellate Court of Illinois on August 7, 1985, on grounds that the state had produced no direct evidence of Linscott's guilt and that his dream "confession" contained no admission of guilt. Prosecutors appealed that ruling to the Illinois Supreme Court, which on October 31, 1985, ordered Linscott released on bond, pending a resolution of his case. A year later, on October 17, 1986, the court found sufficient evidence for conviction and reversed the appellate court's decision, but it also noted issues of physical evidence from the trial that had not been addressed on appeal. The case was thereby remanded to the appellate court for further review.

A prosecution expert told the appellate court that only one person in 4,500 could possess "consistent" hairs when tested for 40 different characteristics, but he in fact had tested fewer than a dozen and could not recall which ones they were. On July 29, 1987, the court ruled that the expert's invalid testimony, coupled with prosecution use of it in closing arguments, effectively denied Steven Linscott a fair trial. His conviction was thus overturned once again, but prosecutors appealed to the state supreme court once more, and the appellate court was again overruled on January 31, 1991. A new trial was ordered, to begin on July 22, 1992.

In preparation for that second trial, prosecutors sought to strengthen their case by performing DNA tests that were unavailable in the early 1980s. Forensic evidence was submitted to a laboratory in Boston, which reported that semen recovered from the crime scene could not have come from Linscott. Charges were dismissed on July 15, 1992, after Linscott had served three years in prison and spent seven more under bond.

LLOYD, Eddie Joe exonerated by DNA

In 1984, while confined in the psychiatric ward at Michigan's Herman Kiefer Hospital, 36-year-old Eddie Lloyd penned a letter to the Detroit Police Department, suggesting methods of solving various local homicides. Included on his list was the brutal rape-slaying of 16-year-old Michelle Jackson. Detectives visited Lloyd several times, persuading him that he could help "smoke out" the killer if he confessed to the killing himself. Coached by the officers, who furnished details of the crime scene and the victim's clothing, Lloyd obliged with a written confession and a statement recorded on videotape. Instead of searching for the killer, though, authorities indicted Lloyd and brought him to trial in May 1985. Hamstrung by Lloyd's refusal to file an insanity plea, his attorney watched helplessly as jurors convicted Lloyd after less than an hour's deliberation. At sentencing, Judge Leonard Townsend lamented that state law prohibited him from imposing a death sentence.

Lloyd protested his innocence at sentencing and through a series of appeals, which were uniformly denied. The CARDOZO INNOCENCE PROJECT accepted his case for review in 2002, commissioning DNA tests on crime scene evidence that included semen stains on a bottle used to penetrate the victim's genitals and on the "long john" underwear used as a ligature to strangle her. In August 2002, those test results excluded Lloyd as a possible source of the semen, and he was freed after serving 18 years in prison for a crime that he did not commit. As lawyer BARRY SCHECK told reporters, "This cop had to know, he had to know, that he was feeding a paranoid schizophrenic guy, a guy with a mental disorder, in a mental institution, facts in order to clear a major homicide so everybody could look good. If you permit this kind of questioning, you're going to end up not just with innocent people in jail but the real perpetrators still out there." Ex-detective Thomas De Galan, who obtained Lloyd's false confession, declined any comment, while Sgt. William Rice—who oversaw the case— referred journalists to Deputy Chief Tara Dunlop for comment on the apparent FRAME-UP. Dunlop in turn told the reporters, "I'm sure if something unjust happened it will be discovered." Ex-prosecutor Timothy

Kenny, now a chief judge of the Wayne County Circuit Court, asserted, "There was certainly no withholding of any evidence by any means. Certainly it is appropriate to find out exactly what happened in regards to the death of this particular woman and in terms of the investigation that took place." At press time for this work, no further action had been undertaken on Lloyd's case, and the murder remains officially unsolved.

LOCARD, Edmond (1877–?)

A native of France, born in 1877, Edmond Locard graduated from the Dominican College at Ouillins before proceeding to the University of Lyons, where he earned dual degrees in law and medicine. There, contact with Professor JEAN LACASSAGNE inspired a lifelong interest in forensic science. Following a period of apprenticeship with Lacassagne, Locard established his own laboratory in Lyon, serving the police prefecture of the Rhône. In 1912, an examination of murder suspect Emile Gourbin's fingernails persuaded Locard that Gourbin had indeed strangled his lover. Confronted with the physical evidence, Gourbin confessed his crime and was duly convicted. Before year's end, Locard published the first volume of his epic *Traité de criminalistique,* expounding what soon became known as "Locard's exchange principle"—i.e., the observation that whenever two persons or objects make contact, each leaves some TRACE EVIDENCE behind.

Locard's forensic contributions were not limited to that theory, however. He also did extensive work with FINGERPRINTS, expanding on the research of predecessor FRANCIS GALTON. Locard insisted that study of fingerprints must go beyond the mapping of friction ridges ("ridgeology") to include examination of skin pores ("poreoscopy"). In 1914, Locard published new guidelines asserting that fingerprints with 12 or more concurring points were indisputably identical, while those with 8 to 11 concurring points were "borderline," and prints with fewer matching features could not be considered a match.

Locard's other wide-ranging fields of interest included art, BOTANY, graphology, MATHEMATICS, music and stamp-collecting. His fascination with cryptography proved useful during World War I, when he served as a lieutenant with the French army's Code Section in Paris. One afternoon in 1915, a local priest challenged the unit to crack a code he had developed over a span of decades, using it to encode a famous passage from French literature. While the unit's commander agreed to study the code overnight, Locard cracked it before the priest could exit the building, leaving the clergyman despondent.

LOVITT, Robin controversial DNA case

In 1999, 38-year-old Virginia resident Robin Lovitt was charged with the stabbing death of victim Clayton Dicks at an Arlington pool hall. Prosecutors theorized that Dicks caught Lovitt prying open the establishment's cash box with a pair of scissors, which became the murder weapon as they struggled. Police found the bloody scissors discarded midway between the pool hall and a house occupied by Lovitt's cousin. At trial, Lovitt admitted stealing the cash box but claimed that someone else had stabbed Dicks. Jurors discounted his story and convicted him of murder. Since the slaying occurred during a robbery, Lovitt received a death sentence.

DNA tests performed on the scissors in 1999 proved inconclusive, but Lovitt's defenders staked their hopes on new technology to prove him innocent. In 2001, Virginia state legislators enacted a statute requiring preservation of DNA evidence in all death row cases, but an Arlington court clerk nonetheless destroyed the scissors and other critical evidence several weeks after the law took effect. That illegal action prompted an appeal for clemency to Governor Mark Warner, who commuted Lovitt's death sentence to life imprisonment on November 30, 2005. As Warner told reporters in announcing this decision, "The commonwealth must ensure that every time this ultimate sanction is carried out, it is done fairly." Lovitt's attorneys predictably hailed the decision, while relatives of Dicks and death penalty supporters were highly critical. Michael Paranzino, president of a group called Throw Away the Key, told journalists, "The governor has sided with a killer against the working people of America. Lovitt's a cold-blooded killer and he's just been given an early Christmas gift by Warner."

LYNCH, Gerald Roche (1889–1957)

A British physician, born in 1889, Gerald Lynch spent most of his career immersed in the field of forensic PATHOLOGY. He served as the chief of pathological chemistry at St. Mary's Hospital in London

(1926–54), while simultaneously conducting investigative work for Scotland Yard and the Home Office (Britain's equivalent of the U.S. State Department). In his marginal free time, Lynch also served as president of the Medico-Legal Society of Great Britain and the Society of Public Analytical Chemists. One of Lynch's most famous cases was the "wigwam murder" of October 1942, wherein a woman's badly decomposed remains were found near Godalming, in Surrey. Police recovered crime scene evidence that identified the victim as Joan Wolfe, while Lynch and two colleagues—Eric Gardner and Keith Simpson—determined that her corpse had lain exposed to the elements for at least five weeks after she was fatally beaten and stabbed. Four hundred yards from the body, detectives found a tree branch stained with blood, bearing nine human hairs that matched the victim's. Further investigation revealed that a French-Canadian deserter from the Royal Army, one August Sangret, had lived with Wolfe in a crude "wigwam" for several months. Sangret denied any part in Wolfe's murder, but TRACE EVIDENCE sealed his fate and he was subsequently hanged at Wandsworth prison. Lynch remained active in the field and in academia until his death in 1957, at age 68.

MacDONALD, Jeffrey Robert justice mishandled

Shortly after 3:30 A.M. on February 17, 1970, military police at Fort Bragg, North Carolina, were summoned to the on-post residence of Dr. Jeffrey McDonald, a Green Beret captain and licensed physician. They found the house ransacked, MacDonald bleeding from a stab wound to his chest. The other members of MacDonald's family—26-year-old wife Colette, five-year-old Kimberly, and two-year-old Kristen—had been beaten and stabbed to death in their bedrooms. Dr. MacDonald told investigators that he had awakened in the predawn hours to find four strangers in his home. Three men—two white, one black—attacked MacDonald and his family while a "hippie-type" woman with long blond hair watched from the sidelines, holding a candle, and chanting, "Acid is groovy. Kill the pigs."

Despite the recent Charles Manson murders in Los Angeles and Dr. MacDonald's extensive work with drug addicts in nearby Fayetteville, army investigators quickly dismissed his story and focused on MacDonald as a suspect. FBI agents, responsible for any crimes committed by civilians on a U.S. military reservation, found themselves excluded from the crime scene, relegated to questioning local drug dealers and users. One who volunteered to "help" was part-time police informant Helena Stoeckley, herself an addict with alleged involvement in occult religious practices. (Despite her strong resemblance to the female intruder described by MacDonald, Stoeckley was never presented to MacDonald as a possible suspect.) The FBI's turf war with military police produced curious results, but bureau documents on the case were suppressed until 1990, when they were finally released under the Freedom of Information Act.

In July 1970, Dr. MacDonald was charged with killing his wife and daughters, but a three-month military hearing revealed so many clumsy errors by army investigators that the charges were dismissed on October 27. A memo from FBI Director J. Edgar Hoover, dated one day later, declared that he would resist any efforts to involve the bureau in MacDonald's case because "the Army handled the case poorly from its inception."

MacDonald subsequently left the army and entered private practice in California. In 1974, the FBI reversed Hoover's decision and agreed to examine evidence from the MacDonald case, although that evidence had previously been examined in various army laboratories. (The FBI LABORATORY had a standing rule against accepting previously tested evidence because it might be altered or contaminated; the waiver of that rule in MacDonald's case remains unexplained.) FBI involvement in the case scarcely improved matters, though. In fact, a review of the FBI's records long after the fact revealed no less than 53 items of potentially exculpatory evidence that were either misrepresented or illegally concealed from the defense during MacDonald's 1979 murder trial, which resulted in a conviction and three life sentences for MacDonald. As detailed by authors Jerry Potter and Fred Bost in 1995, those items included:

1. Unidentified candle wax on the living room coffee table.
2. Unidentified wax on a washing machine in the kitchen.
3. BLOODSTAINS on two sides of the washing machine.
4. FINGERPRINTS noted on the washing machine but never collected.
5. Unidentified pink wax on the kitchen floor, near the refrigerator.
6. Blood on the refrigerator door.
7. Three bloody gloves in the kitchen.
8. Blond wig hairs up to 22 inches long, found on a chair beside the kitchen telephone.
9. Unidentified wax and an unidentified human hair, found on a wall in the hallway.
10. A bloody syringe containing unidentified fluid, found in the hall closet.
11. An unidentified hair, covered with a tarlike substance, found in the bathroom sink.
12. Two unmatched blue cotton fibers and a crumpled pink facial tissue in the bathroom sink.
13. An unidentified hair with root intact, found under one of Kimberly's fingernails.
14. Unidentified candle wax on Kimberly's bedding.
15. An unidentified hair on Kimberly's bed.
16. An unmatched black thread on Kimberly's bottom sheet, near a bloody wood splinter.
17. Unmatched blue and pink nylon fibers on Kimberly's bottom sheet.
18. Unmatched black and purple nylon fibers on Kimberly's quilt.
19. Unidentified candle wax on the arm of a chair in Kimberly's bedroom.
20. Unidentified blue and red wax on Kimberly's window curtain.
21. An unidentified red wool fiber and a speck of Type O blood on Dr. MacDonald's reading glasses.
22. Human blood of unknown type from the living room floor near Dr. MacDonald's glasses.
23. An unidentified fingerprint from a drinking glass on the living room end table.
24. An unmatched blue acrylic fiber found in the living room, where Dr. MacDonald claimed to have lain unconscious.
25. Two unmatched black wool fibers found on the murder club.
26. Two hairs that allegedly shook loose from the murder club inside an evidence bag. In 1970, the army called them "human pubic or body hairs"; in 1974, the FBI Laboratory identified them as "animal hairs."
27. An unidentified bloody palm print on the footboard of the master bed.
28. An unmatched pink fiber from the bed's footboard.
29. Two unidentified human hairs from the footboard.
30. Two unidentified hairs from the master bedspread.
31. An unidentified hair found on a fragment of rubber glove, inside a crumpled blue sheet from the master bedroom.
32. A piece of skin tissue from the same sheet, "lost" after it was cataloged (but reportedly before analysis).
33. An unidentified piece of skin found under one of Colette's fingernails and subsequently "lost."
34. An unmatched blue acrylic fiber found in Colette's right hand.
35. An unidentified hair found in Colette's left hand.
36. An unmatched black wool fiber found near Colette's mouth.
37. An unmatched pink fiber from Colette's mouth.
38. An unmatched purple fiber from Colette's mouth.
39. An unmatched black wool fiber on Colette's right biceps.
40. Two unidentified body hairs found on the bedroom floor near Colette's left arm, with three bloody wood splinters.
41. An unidentified hair found beneath Colette's body.
42. An unmatched green cotton fiber found under Colette's body.
43. An unmatched gold nylon fiber stained with blood, found under Colette's body.
44. Two pieces of facial tissue found beneath Colette's body.
45. A clump of FIBERS, all but one unmatched, found stuck to a bloody hair from Colette's scalp.
46. An unmatched clear nylon fiber stuck to a splinter from the murder club, found on the bedroom floor near the crumpled blue sheet.
47. An unidentified hair with root intact, found under one of Kristen's fingernails.
48. Two unidentified hairs found on Kristen's bed, near her body.

49. An unmatched blue nylon fiber found on Kristen's blanket.
50. Several unmatched clear nylon fibers from the same blanket.
51. A clump of unmatched purple nylon fibers on Kristen's bedspread.
52. Unmatched cotton fibers from Kristen's bedspread.
53. An unmatched yellow nylon fiber stained with blood, found on Kristen's bedspread.

In addition to suppressing physical evidence at trial, the FBI also misrepresented statements from critical witnesses during MacDonald's appeals. Forensic pathologist Robin Wright reported that Colette MacDonald was clubbed by a left-handed assailant standing in front of her, whereas her husband was right-handed. In 1984, FBI Agent James Reed prepared an affidavit falsely stating that Dr. Wright had "retracted" his opinion. Wright contradicted that claim, but MacDonald's attorneys did not learn of Reed's false statement until October 1989. G-men also tinkered with the statements of witness Norma Lane, who claimed that suspect Greg Mitchell (a left-handed soldier and drug addict) had confessed to the MacDonald murders in her presence, during 1982. An FBI affidavit claimed that Lane was uncertain whether Mitchell referred to events at Fort Bragg or in Vietnam, a falsehood Lane flatly denies.

Greg Mitchell was not the only suspect who confessed to the MacDonald murders. Mitchell's friend and fellow addict, Helena Stoeckley, offered multiple confessions to military police, the FBI, and retired G-man Ted Gunderson, both before and after Dr. MacDonald's murder trial. She denied involvement on the witness stand, however, and FBI agents buttressed her denial with reports that she "appeared to be under the influence of drugs" when she made an earlier confession (a claim refuted by hospital blood tests performed the same day). Unfortunately for MacDonald, Mitchell and Stoeckley both died from apparent liver disease (in 1981 and 1982, respectively) before their stories could be verified.

Suggestions of official misconduct continue to surface in the MacDonald case. Prosecutor Jim Blackburn received a three-year prison term in December 1993, after pleading guilty to felony counts that included fabricating a lawsuit, forging various court documents (including judges' signatures) and embezzling $234,000 from his law firm. In 1997, MacDon-

ald's attorneys discovered that FBI Lab technician Michael Malone, accused of offering false testimony in other cases, had misrepresented fiber evidence in MacDonald's case. (Specifically, Malone testified that the FBI's "standard sources" revealed that saran fibers could not be used in human wigs; in fact, two of the leading source books in the bureau's lab stated the exact opposite.) Despite such revelations, however, all appeals in MacDonald's case thus far have been denied. The effort to secure a new trial for MacDonald continues.

"MAGIC Bullet Theory" the Kennedy assassination

On November 22, 1963, President John F. Kennedy died from wounds inflicted by a sniper in Dallas, Texas. Governor John Connally, riding in the presidential limousine with Kennedy, suffered multiple wounds in the same incident. Two days later, alleged sniper Lee Harvey Oswald was murdered by gunman Jack Ruby in the basement of Dallas police headquarters. More than four decades after those shocking events, no other facts of the JFK assassination and ensuing events are firmly settled in the public mind.

President Lyndon Johnson appointed a blue-ribbon commission led by U.S. Chief Justice Earl Warren to investigate the murders of Kennedy and Oswald, and while the Warren Commission's final report dismissed all notions of conspiracy in either slaying, the panel's convoluted reasoning and manipulation (some say fabrication and suppression) of physical evidence to support the two-lone-nuts scenario raised more questions than it answered. Forty-three years after the fact, no single aspect of the Warren Report is more controversial today than the "magic bullet theory."

Simply stated, the commission found that Oswald alone fired three shots at Kennedy's limousine from an antique bolt-action rifle, striking Kennedy twice and missing entirely with one shot. One of the bullets that struck JFK also allegedly passed through his body to strike Governor Connally, inflicting all of Connally's various wounds, then popped out of Connally's body and was subsequently found on a stretcher at Parkland Hospital. That theory, as critics soon revealed, was full of gaping holes.

First came the timing of the rifle shots. Eyewitness testimony, coupled with audio recordings and motion picture films of the shooting in progress, confirmed that roughly five seconds elapsed between the first shot striking Kennedy and the last shattering his

President and Mrs. John F. Kennedy smile at the crowds lining their motorcade route in Dallas, Texas, on November 22, 1963. Minutes later, the president was assassinated as his car passed through Dealey Plaza. (Bettmann/CORBIS)

skull. Unfortunately for the lone-gunman scenario, tests performed with Oswald's bolt-action rifle by FBI marksmen and other experts confirmed that a minimum of 2.3 seconds was required to eject a spent cartridge and chamber the next round for firing. (FBI experts also found themselves unable to focus the rifle's telescopic sight on any target until they repaired it, a fact ignored in the *Warren Report*.) That speed was fine if Oswald fired only two shots, but a third shot had been fired as well, missing Kennedy's car and ricocheting from a curbstone to strike bystander James Tague in the face. Other witnesses, ignored by the commission, reported hearing *four* shots at the murder scene, which meant a second gunman firing at the motorcade.

If that discrepancy was not bad enough, Warren Commission members had to cope with the problem of Kennedy's wounds. Surgeons at Parkland Hospital initially described an "entrance" in the front of President Kennedy's throat (manifestly impossible if Oswald was the only shooter, firing from behind), but they later recanted after a fruitless tracheotomy obliterated the wound and made judgment impossible. FBI agents Francis O'Neill Jr. and James Sibert, present at JFK's autopsy, described another mysterious wound in Kennedy's back. As detailed in their report to bureau headquarters:

This opening was probed by Dr. [James] Humes with the finger, at which time it was determined that the tra-

jectory of the missile entering at this point had entered at a downward position of 45 to 60 degrees. Further probing determined that the distance traveled by this missile was a short distance inasmuch as the end of the opening could be felt with the finger. Inasmuch as no complete bullet of any size could be located in the brain area and likewise no bullet could be located in the back or any other area of the body as determined by total body X rays and inspection revealing that there was no point of exit, the individuals performing the autopsy were at a loss to explain why they could find no bullets

That riddle was solved after a fashion by the convenient discovery of a rifle bullet—later dubbed Commission Exhibit 399—on a stretcher at Parkland Hospital. Investigators first believed that the virtually unmarked bullet had worked its way out of Kennedy's back wound while he lay on the stretcher. In that scenario, the back wound represented Oswald's first shot, while Governor Connally was wounded by the second, and JFK's fatal head wound resulted from the third. That scenario collapsed with the discovery that one shot had missed Kennedy's limousine entirely, and since *four* shots within five seconds meant at least two snipers, a new explanation was needed.

That explanation was the "magic bullet theory."

As finally described in the *Warren Report,* JFK was struck by only two shots. The first entered his back and exited through his throat near the Adam's apple, then flew on to wound Governor Connally. Oswald's second shot missed the limousine, wounding James Tague on the sidelines, while his third shot shattered JFK's skull. It was a tidy explanation—which flew in the face of every known fact.

First, Parkland Hospital physicians and Kennedy's autopsy team had to change their descriptions of the throat entrance wound and the shallow back wound with no exit. Next, the back wound's reported downward angle of 45° to 60° was radically altered after engineers determined that the angle from Oswald's sixth-floor sniper's nest was only 17° 43' 30". Governor Connally's physicians reported that the slug which wounded him entered his back at a downward angle of 27° (misstated as 25° in the *Warren Report*), so the bullet must have dropped 10° after exiting Kennedy's throat to find the governor.

But its magic trick was not yet finished.

The slug that entered Governor Connally's back smashed a rib, emerged from his chest to break his right wrist, then buried itself in his thigh. At each point of impact with bone along the way, it left fragments of metal behind, some of which were extracted while others remained in the governor's body (visible on X-rays). Somehow, the slug then vanished from Connally's thigh, leaving the Warren Commission to conclude that C.E. 399 had actually been found at Parkland Hospital on Connally's stretcher, rather than Kennedy's. Unfortunately for that theory, C.E. 399 appeared virtually unscarred, leaving no explanation for the many bullet fragments found inside Connally's chest, wrist, and leg. Dr. Humes, who changed his original autopsy findings to fit the commission's single-bullet theory, still deemed it "most unlikely" that C.E. 399 had inflicted Governor Connally's wounds. The specimen bullet, he said, was "basically intact; its jacket appears to me to be intact, and I do not understand how it could possibly have left fragments in the wrist." As for the fragments extracted from Connally, Humes said, "I can't conceive of where they came from this missile."

Indeed, Governor Connally—and his wife, who rode beside him in the limousine—steadfastly maintained that he was wounded by the sniper's *second* shot, after President Kennedy visibly reacted to his own first wound. The *Warren Report* contradicted Connally, explaining his "mistake" as a bizarre "delayed reaction" to the bullet's impact, but the Connallys refused to accept that conclusion. Dismissing Connally's testimony and all other evidence that suggested multiple snipers, the Warren Commission declared: "Although it is not necessary to any essential findings of the Commission to determine just which shot hit Governor Connally, there is very persuasive evidence from the experts to indicate that the same bullet which pierced the President's throat also caused Governor Connally's wounds."

In fact, there was no such expert evidence—and the "magic bullet theory" was critical to all of the commission's other findings. If one bullet did not wound both victims, then there was a second gunman. There can be no third alternative. The cynicism of the Warren Commission's decision is clearly revealed in the declassified transcript of a conversation between commission member Allen Dulles (former director of the CIA) and commission counsel Albert Jenner:

Dulles: Don't believe people read in this country. There will be a few professors who will read the record. . . .

Jenner: And a few newspaper reporters who will read parts of it.

Dulles: The public will read very little.

MALPIGHI, Marcello (1628–1694)

A son of Italian farmers, born at Cavalcuore on March 10, 1628, Marcello Malpighi entered the University of Bologna at age 17, majoring in Aristotelian philosophy. The subsequent deaths of his parents and maternal grandmother forced Malpighi to leave school temporarily, but he returned in 1647 and earned his M.D. six years later. He received a chair of medical practice at the University of Bologna in 1656, followed by a chair of theoretical medicine at the University of Pisa that same year and a post at the University of Messina in 1661. His first article on human anatomy appeared in the Royal Society of England's journal during 1661, quickly expanding into regular correspondence and culminating with Malpighi's acceptance as the society's first Italian member in 1667. Malpighi's applications of MICROSCOPY included studies in BOTANY, human anatomy, and the formation of FINGERPRINTS—all of which marked him as a pioneer of forensic science. He was the first anatomist to see human capillaries, and several anatomical features today bear his name, including the Malpighi layer of human skin, Malpighian corpuscles found in human kidneys and spleens, plus the Malpighian tubules located in the excretory system of many insects. Pope Innocent XII named Malpighi his papal physician in 1691, and Malpighi taught at the Papal Medical School until a stroke claimed his life on September 29, 1694.

MARSH, James (1794–1846)

British subject James Marsh was born on September 2, 1794, but most details of his early life and education remain obscure today. We know that he joined the British army, serving as a chemist at the Royal Arsenal in Woolwich. There, around 1830, he developed a new timing fuse for mortar shells and a percussion tube for ship's artillery, used for the first time aboard HMS *Castor* in 1832—though final approval for use in coastal artillery was delayed until 1845. Meanwhile, Marsh doubled as an assistant to Commander Michael Faraday at the Royal Military Academy (1829–46) and applied his talents to forensic CHEMISTRY. Called to testify for the prosecution in the 1832 murder trial of defendant John Bodle, Marsh performed the standard test for arsenic on powders found in Bodle's possession, and while those test results were positive, degradation of the samples prior to trial resulted in Bodle's acquittal. (Three years later, he was convicted on unrelated charges of blackmail and FRAUD.)

Angry and frustrated over that outcome, Marsh devised a new test for arsenic—the "Marsh test"—which proved more reliable. In practice, zinc is added to a powerful acid, followed by tissue or body fluids from the alleged poison victim. When arsenic is present in the sample, it reacts with the solution to produce arsine gas. Subsequent heating of the gas causes arsenic to plate in metallic form inside a glass or ceramic container. Marsh published his findings in 1838, in the *Edinburgh Philosophical Journal*, and it saw practical application two years later, in the trial of French poisoner Marie Lafarge. Marsh retained his posts at the Royal Military Academy and the Woolwich arsenal until his death, on June 21, 1846.

MATHEMATICS, Forensic

Mathematics–defined as "the systematic treatment of magnitude, relationships between figures and forms, and relationships between quantities expressed symbolically"—has various applications in the realm of forensic science. Its simplest form, basic arithmetic, lies at the heart of forensic ACCOUNTING, while other branches of science depend on more complex mathematical forms of expression. DNA evidence hinges as much on mathematics as upon BIOLOGY, requiring statistical analysis to express the probability of a suspect's guilt or innocence. Mathematics also figures prominently in ACCIDENT RECONSTRUCTION, in ARSON investigations, in analysis of ballistics evidence, in forensic BIOMECHANICS, ENGINEERING, METALLURGY, SURVEYING, and many other fields. Presenting mathematical calculations and data to "average" jurors is a constant challenge for expert witnesses (who sometimes fail, as in the ORENTHAL JAMES (O. J.) SIMPSON murder case).

MATTHEWS, Ryan exonerated by DNA

In April 1997, grocer Tommy Vanhoose was shot and killed at his store, Comeaux's Grocery, in Bridge City, Louisiana. Police soon arrested two teenagers, Travis Hayes and Ryan Matthews, on suspicion of robbing and killing Vanhoose. While no physical evidence placed either suspect at the crime scene, Hayes admitted hearing gunshots from outside the grocery and driving away with Matthews. After prosecutors filed capital murder charges, Hayes accused Matthews of shooting Vanhoose and testified for the state, thereby sparing himself from death row with a sentence of life imprisonment. Jurors convicted Matthews of first-degree murder during the course of a ROBBERY, resulting in a death sentence. Matthews, meanwhile, continued to protest his innocence.

In 2003, members of the INNOCENCE PROJECT NEW ORLEANS (IPNO) agreed to review the evidence in Matthews's case. Specifically, a ski mask found at the crime scene was submitted for DNA testing of skin cells found inside the mask. Results of those tests excluded both Matthews and Hayes as owners of the mask, while matching a DNA profile for one Rondell Love, already serving 20 years for manslaughter in the 1998 stabbing death of a Bridge City woman. Prison inmates told Matthews's attorneys that Love had boasted of killing Vanhoose and letting two innocent men take the blame. Matthews was released from prison in April 2004, held under house arrest on $105,000 bond until August 10, when Judge Henry Sullivan granted a request from Jefferson County District Attorney Paul Connick to dismiss all charges. A spokesperson for IPNO anticipated that Travis Hayes will also soon be liberated since "the only evidence against [him] is his statement that Ryan Matthews did it, which DNA proves is false." Investigation of Rondell Love's role in the 1997 murder was ongoing at press time for this work.

MAYES, Larry 100th U.S. inmate exonerated by DNA evidence
Late in 1980, the female clerk at a Hammond, Indiana, filling station was kidnapped and raped by a bandit who first cleaned out the till. Police suspected 31-year-old Larry Mayes of the crime, but the victim failed to pick him out of two successive lineups. She finally selected his photo from an array of police mug shots, but only after first being hypnotized (a fact concealed by authorities for two decades). Mayes was arrested in January 1981, and the victim repeated her identification at trial the following year, whereupon Mayes was convicted of ROBBERY, rape, and criminal deviant conduct. He received an 80-year prison sentence, and all his appeals were denied.

Members of the CARDOZO INNOCENCE PROJECT agreed to represent Mayes in 1999, seeking DNA tests of semen traces preserved in the case, but court clerks insisted that the original rape kit was lost. A two-year stalemate ensued, finally broken by Cardozo associate Fran Hardy, an Indiana University law professor, and four of her students. A clerk in Gary was finally persuaded to search the courthouse basement, and the "lost" rape kit was found. Professor Hardy filed a petition for DNA testing of the evidence on July 9, 2001, and Lake County prosecutors agreed. The test results excluded Mayes as a suspect, and he was released from prison, with all charges dropped, on December 21, 2001. He was the 100th U.S. prison inmate exonerated by DNA evidence since regular testing began in the early 1990s. The 1980 rape and robbery remains unsolved today.

McCRONE, Walter (1916–2002)

A native of Wilmington, Delaware, born in 1916, McCrone attended Cornell University, where he earned a B.A. in CHEMISTRY (1938) and a Ph.D. in organic chemistry (1942). After two years' postdoctoral work at Cornell, McCrone worked as a microscopist and materials analyst at the Illinois Institute of Technology (1944–56), then founded McCrone Associates in Chicago, succeeded in 1960 by the nonprofit McCrone Research Institute. There, over the next three decades, McCrone focused primarily on MICROSCOPY and crystallography, simultaneously penning 16 books and some 600 technical articles, while editing *The Microscope* (a quarterly international journal).

McCrone's most famous project involved the so-called Shroud of Turin, a piece of aged linen touted by some as the burial shroud of Jesus, dismissed by others as a hoax fabricated in medieval times to buttress claims of divine authority made by the Catholic Church. (Hence, its presence in Italy, rather than the Middle East.) In 1977, McCrone was one of several scientists selected for the Shroud of Turin Research Project (STURP) by the Holy Shroud Guild, to examine the relic and offer opinions on its authenticity. McCrone specifically examined red stains said to be BLOODSTAINS and determined that they were actually flecks of PAINT. Two other team members—neither one a serologist or expert on pigments—disagreed with McCrone, insisting that the stains were blood. McCrone left STURP in June 1980, complaining that he was "drummed out" for opposing a religious interpretation of the evidence, but his opinion of the hoax remained steadfast. McCrone published his findings in a book, *Judgment Day for the Shroud of Turin,* in 1999. One year later, the American Chemical Society presented McCrone with its National Award in Analytical Chemistry. He died in 2002.

McDONALD, Hugh Chisholm (1913–)

A native of Hopkins, Minnesota, born in 1913, Hugh McDonald attended various universities in his home state and in California before joining the Los Angeles County Sheriff's Department in 1940. Before year's end, though still a rookie, McDonald asserts that he was dispatched to Europe as an undercover agent, penetrating black-market networks and using his artistic skills to sketch various ringleaders when PHOTOGRAPHY was impractical. To make the process easier, McDonald developed numerous templates of common facial features, to assist crime witnesses in sketching likenesses of felons they had seen.

America's entry into World War II cut short McDonald's police work, but not his cloak-and-dagger adventures. As a self-described agent of U.S. Army Intelligence or the Office of Strategic Services (reports differ), he allegedly infiltrated various spy rings throughout Europe during 1942–46. McDonald later recounted—some say fabricated—his wartime exploits in a book titled *Hour of the Blue Fox* (1975), which blamed Russia for annual outbreaks of influenza in the United States during the cold war. Subsequent alleged involvement with the Central Intelligence Agency fueled McDonald's conspiracy theories surrounding the murder of President John Kennedy, explored in his books *Appointment in Dallas* (1975), *Five Signs from Ruby* (1976), and *LBJ and the JFK Conspiracy* (1979).

McDonald ultimately returned to the L.A. County Sheriff's Department, where his European sketchbook became the world-famous IDENTI-KIT tool for preparing sketches of unknown subjects, but his career remained hectic and disjointed. According to various published reports, McDonald served as second-in-command of California's Fort McArthur Military Intelligence School from 1946 to 1954, and served as a major in U.S. Army Intelligence until May 1957. He also reportedly took time off in 1964 to serve as chief of security for Senator Barry Goldwater's ill-fated presidential campaign. McDonald retired from the L.A. County Sheriff's Department in 1967 or 1968 (again, reports vary), and subsequently founded World Associates, a private investigation firm that he led until 1973. Semi-retired at age 60, McDonald still found time for writing and to serve as director of security for the Hollywood Turf Club. His groundbreaking Identi-Kit has been replaced in recent years by various computer software programs.

McGILL, RAYMOND indicted by DNA evidence

Twenty-three-year-old Raymond McGill was serving time for robbery at New York's Clinton Correctional Facility, near Plattsburgh, when DNA evidence resulted in his July 2005 indictment as a possible serial killer. According to authorities, McGill cut his hand and left blood drops in the Albany apartment where 50-year-old Martha Montalvo was murdered in March 2000. DNA evidence also reportedly linked McGill to the rape of an 83-year-old Albany woman in early 2000 and the beating death of a 68-year-old man in January 2004. No trial dates had been set for any of those charges when this volume went to press, and McGill is legally presumed innocent until convicted in court.

McGINN, Rickey Nolen controversial DNA case

On May 22, 1993, 12-year-old Stephanie Rae Flanery vanished from the home she shared with her mother and stepfather, Rickey McGinn, in Brownwood, Texas. Her mother was in Arlington, Texas, that day and had left the girl with her husband. McGinn told police that he drank beer with Stephanie until she vomited and lost consciousness, but claimed that she later awoke and "went for a walk," never returning to the house. Three days later, police found Stephanie's corpse in a rural highway culvert near McGinn's home. She had been raped and bludgeoned with the blunt end of an ax blade, fracturing her skull. Police found blood matching Stephanie's type in McGinn's pickup truck and on an ax hidden beneath the pickup's seat. Forensic tests also linked McGinn to semen and a pubic hair recovered from Stephanie's body. At trial in 1995, three female witnesses testified that McGinn had sexually abused them. One, his own 12-year-old daughter, said under oath that McGinn began molesting her when she was three. Jurors convicted McGinn of rape and murder, whereupon he was sentenced to die.

Despite the varied accusations, some relatives still believed McGinn was innocent. Brother Mikel claimed that while Stephanie disappeared on Saturday evening and Rickey was jailed the next morning, police found her body on Tuesday "lying in fresh blood." Mikel McGinn also claimed that the spot where her corpse was found had been previously searched without result, and that the officer who found the body "changed his story three times." Those claims were insufficient to support appeals, but a new team of attorneys petitioned for DNA testing of the original evidence in June 2000. Governor George W. Bush, known for his callous attitude toward Texas death row inmates, granted his first stay of execution in McGinn's case, but it ultimately made no difference. Test results confirmed Rickey McGinn as the source of semen and hair found on Stephanie's body, while the blood from his pickup and ax was identified beyond question as hers. McGinn died by lethal injection at Huntsville state prison on September 27, 2000, still protesting innocence. "I still want the world to know I'm not guilty," McGinn told reporters. "Somebody else put that there. I know they did it and they know they did it." Nonetheless, he was resigned to death. "I'm ready to go," he said. "I'm tired of living the way I'm living. Any way I leave here, I'm going to be better off."

McMILLAN, Clark exonerated by DNA evidence

A pair of Memphis teenagers were parked on a lover's lane in Overton Park, one night in 1979, when an armed stranger approached their car, robbed the boy, and then raped his girlfriend. Although they seemed initially uncertain, both victims finally identified 23-year-old Clark McMillan as their attacker. McMillan insisted he was innocent, despite a recent conviction on federal FIREARMS charges and police suspicion that he may have committed several similar holdup rapes around Memphis. Conviction on the federal charge earned him a two-year prison sentence, but U.S. authorities left his final disposition to the Memphis court. Convicted of aggravated rape and ROBBERY in 1980, McMillan was sentenced to 119 years in state prison. His several appeals were rejected.

In 1997, McMillan contacted members of the CARDOZO INNOCENCE PROJECT and persuaded them to take his case. Four years of legal maneuvers ensued, before DNA tests were finally performed on semen stains recovered from the rape victim's clothing in 1979. Those tests eliminated McMillan as a possible source of the semen, and his state sentence was vacated on May 2, 2001. Prosecutor William Gibbons told reporters on that day, "The system worked. Someone who did not commit a particular crime is going to be released from our state prisons, so I think the system has worked very well." Gibbons offered no suggestions as to how McMillan should be compensated—if at all—for the 22 years he spent in custody for a crime he did not commit.

Exoneration on the rape and robbery charges was not the end of McMillan's troubles, however. Even before his release from Tennessee's state prison was confirmed, federal authorities announced that McMillan still owed them two years in jail for the ancient firearms conviction. Attorney Peter Neufeld, speaking for the Innocence Project, announced his intention to fight that decision. "If he spent 22 [years] in prison for a crime he didn't commit," Neufeld told journalists, "they should at least give him two years' credit for a case that he would have started serving in 1979."

MEDICAL Examiners

Medical examiners (MEs) are physicians trained in forensic PATHOLOGY, appointed by various jurisdictions—city, county, or state—to scientifically investigate suspicious or unexplained deaths. Prior to 1877, when Massachusetts hired the first American medical examiners, all U.S. jurisdictions relied on *coroners* to certify deaths and determine their cause. Since most coroners were elected officials with no medical training, their investigations were often limited to collecting testimony from witnesses or friends and relatives of the deceased. Many cases were left with cause of death undetermined (or chosen by guesswork), while even HOMICIDES were frequently attributed to "persons unknown." By the time Jack the Ripper terrorized London in autumn 1888, Scotland Yard employed *police surgeons* to examine murder victims and render professional opinions, but final judgment on the cause of death and other vital questions was still left to the coroner or a coroner's jury.

In the latter 19th and early 20th centuries, various American jurisdictions took their cue from Massachusetts and hired full- or part-time pathologists. Each state now has its own medical examiner's office, designed to investigate deaths on state property and to assist those towns or counties that cannot afford their own MEs. Most large cities also retain medical examiners, commonly assisted by a staff of investigators who may or may not be licensed physicians and nurses. The office of coroner persists in many states, and while some (such as Louisiana) require that all coroners be trained forensic pathologists, other jurisdictions recognize a distinction between the two jobs. Coroners without medical training are not authorized to perform autopsies, and they are generally untutored in the rules of collecting and preserving evidence. At a murder scene, the medical examiner's office normally has jurisdiction over any corpses, while police detectives process the rest of the scene. The risk of losing or contaminating vital evidence is thereby minimized and a strict chain of custody preserved.

METALLURGY, Forensic

Metallurgy—the science or study of metals—plays a role in forensic science whenever criminologists examine any metal object. Various events requiring metallurgical analysis include explosions, certain auto accidents, airplane crashes, and the collapse of bridges or buildings. When the fuel tank on TWA Flight 800 exploded in 1996, several witnesses reported a bright object like a missile streaking toward the aircraft from the ground, but metallurgical analysis reported an explosion from within. (That finding and the FBI's handling of the whole investigation fueled ongoing allegations of conspiracy and cover-up.) In other airline crashes, train derailments and the like, metallurgists serving the NATIONAL TRANSPORTATION SAFETY BOARD search for evidence of metal fatigue and similar problems, while other investigators probe the possibility of human error or sabotage. Forensic metallurgists may also assist in ARSON investigations (by determining temperatures at which various metals melt), with examination of bombs and FIREARMS, or other aspects of forensic ENGINEERING.

MICROSCOPY, Forensic

Microscopy involves the use of various magnification devices to study objects smaller than the naked eye can see. In some cases, simple magnifying glasses are sufficient to permit observation, while other cases require microscopes. The simplest of these employ graduated lenses, often with a supplemental light source, to make tiny objects visible. The common *compound microscope* consists of two lenses—the *ocular* (eyepiece) and the *objective* (closer to the object being studied)—mounted in a barrel above a *stage* where slides or other objects are placed for examination. Microscopes may be either *monocular* or *binocular,* depending on whether they have one or two eyepieces. Variations on the basic process include the following:

Comparison or *stereoscopic* microscopes mount two compound microscopes side by side, permitting simultaneous study of two objects such as bullets or FIBERS.

Phase contrast microscopy, pioneered by Dutch physicist Frits Zernike in 1934, employs specialized components to increase the contrast between transparent specimens such as GLASS fragments, certain fibers, and thin tissue slices.

Polarized light microscopy, best known for application to GEOLOGY, permits detailed examination of *anisotropic* materials—that is, the 90 of all solid substances whose optical qualities vary with the orientation of light to their crystallographic axes. Those objects include minerals, compounds, fibers, wood, and various biological molecules (including DNA).

Magnetic resonance microscopy employs medical MR technology to study microscopic details of WOUNDS and other injuries.

Electron microscopy, pioneered by German scientists Max Knoll and Ernst Ruska in 1931, greatly expands the magnification permitted by normal light microscopes—limited by physics to about 1,000 times an object's actual size. That magnification, while impressive, left the fine details of organic cells and other materials invisible to human eyes, since they require magnification of 10,000x or more. In place of light, electron microscopes use focused beams of electrons to "image" an object, thereby revealing its morphology (shape and size), topography (surface features and texture), composition (elements and compounds), and its crystallographic information (how its atoms are arranged). Two kinds of electron microscope presently exist. They are:

Transmission electron microscopes, which operate much like a common slide projector, beaming electrons *through* a specimen to produce an enlarged image on a fluorescent screen or pho-

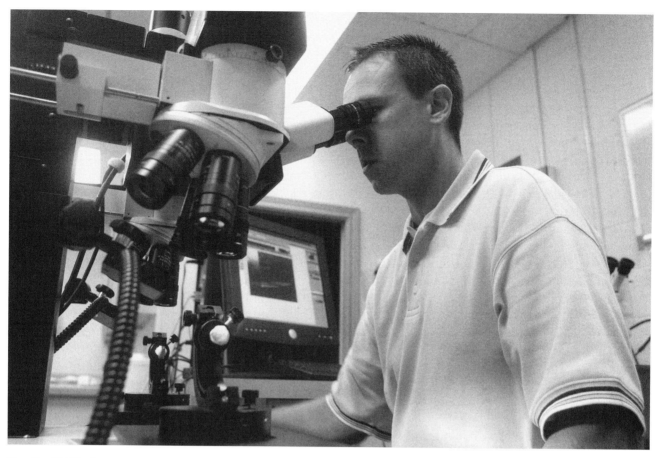

Sgt. Ray Wolfenberger uses a microscope to compare the markings on two different bullets and determine whether the bullet under examination matches the gun involved in the crime. (Kohl Threlkeld/AP)

tographic film. James Hillier and Albert Prebus built the first practical model in 1938, at the University of Toronto, using concepts developed by Knoll and Ruska. Specimens must be specially prepared, shaved to a thickness that permits electrons to pass through the object. Magnifications of 350,000x are routinely obtained with this process, while magnifications exceeding 15 million are reported in certain cases.

Scanning electron microscopes premiered in 1942, but the first commercial instruments were not available until 1965. The delay in production was occasioned by refinement of the electronics needed to "scan" a moving beam of electrons across a specimen (whereas the beam remains static in transmission electron microscopy). In this process, an electron gun (the "virtual source") produces a stream of monochromatic electrons, which is condensed by a series of lenses, after which a set of coils sweep the beam

across the sample in a grid pattern similar to that of a television tube. At each point of fleeting contact between beam and sample, pixels are displayed on a cathode ray tube where the final image is revealed.

MID-ATLANTIC Innocence Project

Organized in 2000 as the Innocence Project of the National Capital Region, the MAIP changed its name the following year and was chartered as a nonprofit organization in Washington, D.C. Its stated mission is "to seek the exoneration and release of persons who have been convicted of crimes that they did not commit in Maryland, Virginia, and the District of Columbia." Research on those cases is performed by student groups at American University's Washington College of Law, Catholic University's Columbus School of Law, Georgetown University's Law Center, the University of the District of Columbia's

David A. Clarke School of Law, and the University of Virginia's School of Law. Since its creation, the MAIP has received more than 1,800 requests for assistance from prison inmates. Each case is initially screened, with those presenting a substantial likelihood of actual innocence referred to pro bono attorneys. As with other innocence projects nationwide, the primary vehicle for proof of innocence is DNA testing of evidence found at crime scenes.

MILGAARD, David exonerated by DNA evidence

Gail Miller, a nursing student in Saskatoon, Saskatchewan, left her apartment for work at 6:45 A.M. on January 31, 1969. Before reaching her usual bus stop, she was ambushed, dragged into an alley, raped, and stabbed repeatedly. A child walking to school found her body at 8:30 A.M. and police were summoned. They found a bloodstained kitchen knife at the scene and retrieved Miller's empty purse from a nearby garbage can. Detectives theoretically linked the rape-slaying with two other recent sexual assaults in the neighborhood, but they had no suspects or conclusive evidence with which to identify the stalker. A $2,000 reward for information finally led to a break in the case—or so it seemed.

David Milgaard, a 16-year-old "hippie" and drifter possessed of a long police record for theft and drug-dealing, had arrived in Saskatoon the same morning Miller was killed, traveling with friends Ron Wilson and Nichol John to visit another acquaintance, one Albert Cadrain. They reached Cadrain's home, close to the Miller crime scene, at 8:30 A.M., Cadrain noting that Milgaard's pants were torn. Milgaard and company explained that they had helped another motorist dislodge his car from a snow bank, with Milgaard ripping his pants in the process. Around 4:30 P.M., the four embarked on a trip to Alberta, then drove on to Wilson's home in Regina, arriving on February 5, 1969.

Cadrain was jailed for vagrancy in Regina a few days later and spent a week in jail. Detectives visited his cell to grill Cadrain about reports that a group of youths had gathered at his Saskatoon flat the day Gail Miller died, but he denied any knowledge of the crime. Back in Saskatoon by early March, Cadrain learned of the $2,000 reward in Miller's case and approached police with a startling new account of January 31. In his revised story, Cadrain said Milgaard had been wearing bloodstained clothes when

he arrived at Cadrain's apartment, and that Milgaard seemed in a rush to leave town. While driving to Alberta, Cadrain now claimed, Milgaard had thrown a woman's cosmetics case out the car window, telling Cadrain that he had to get rid of John and Wilson because they "knew too much."

Police interrogated John and Wilson, both reporting that Milgaard had never been out of their sight long enough to commit a murder on January 31, and that his clothes were not bloodstained. As the relentless grilling continued, detectives apparently fed Wilson bits and pieces of information about the Miller crime scene, with Wilson finally deducing that he would not be released until he told police the story they wanted to hear. Nichol John, a 16-year-old drug addict, was subjected to similar pressure, once left alone in a police interrogation room with Albert Cadrain and ordered by detectives to "discuss" her statement with the Crown's star witness. By the time authorities traced Milgaard to Prince George, British Columbia, and took him into custody, John and Wilson had caved under pressure, both producing statements that incriminated Milgaard. Wilson embellished his tale to the point where Milgaard allegedly confessed that he "got the girl" in Saskatoon. John went even further, claiming she had seen Milgaard stab Gail Miller.

David Milgaard's murder trial consumed two weeks in January 1970, with Cadrain and Wilson appearing as prosecution witnesses. (Cadrain, by then, had collected his $2,000 reward. He had also been briefly confined to a psychiatric hospital, diagnosed as a paranoid schizophrenic after suffering hallucinations wherein Milgaard appeared to him in serpent form.) Nichol John faltered on the witness stand, claiming she could remember nothing of the fatal morning, whereupon Prosecutor T. D. R. Caldwell introduced her previous statement incriminating Milgaard. Two more witnesses from Regina, 18-year-old George Lapchuk and 17-year-old Craig Melnick, testified that they were watching television with Milgaard and two girls, Ute Frank and Deborah Hall, in May 1969, when a news report on the Miller slaying was broadcast. Lapchuk and Melnick (both later identified as longtime police narcotics informants) described Milgaard grabbing a pillow and demonstrating how he had murdered Miller, several times proclaiming, "I killed her!" Judge Alfred Bence criticized the Crown's witnesses, informing jurors that their testimony should be treated skeptically, but the panel convicted Milgaard on January 31, 1970. Bence sentenced Milgaard to life imprisonment and the Saskatchewan appellate court rejected his appeal in 1971. The Supreme Court of Canada subsequently declined to review his case.

Milgaard's 1979 parole bid was rejected on grounds that he still claimed to be innocent, but authorities later allowed him limited, escorted furloughs to visit his family in Winnipeg. On one such excursion, in 1980, Milgaard escaped and fled to Toronto, remaining at large for 77 days before he was cornered and shot in the back—while standing unarmed, with hands raised—by Toronto police. Milgaard survived his WOUND and was returned to prison, while his mother offered a $10,000 reward for information leading to Gail Miller's actual killer. Working with freelance writer Peter Carlyle-Gordge, Joyce Milgaard found Nichol John and Ron Wilson, both of whom admitted that their final statements to police (and Wilson's testimony under oath) were false. Deborah Hall refuted the testimony of George Lapchuk and Craig Melnick, asserting that Milgaard had merely fluffed up his pillow and made no admissions of guilt.

Milgaard's attorneys retained Dr. James Ferris, a forensic pathologist, to review the blood and semen evidence used against Milgaard at trial, Ferris concluding that some of the samples excluded Milgaard as a suspect, while the others were contaminated and yielded inconclusive results. While awaiting a formal review of the case in 1988, the lawyers also learned that Albert Cadrain's next-door neighbor, Larry Fisher, had been convicted and imprisoned for a series of brutal rapes in Saskatoon and Winnipeg, committed around the time of Gail Miller's slaying. Fisher's ex-wife was located with help from CENTURION MINISTRIES, and she admitted suspecting her husband of murdering Miller. She had told police as much in 1980, after learning of the Milgaard family's $10,000 reward, but detectives ignored her statement. Interviews with Larry Fisher's victims revealed that his style of attack was similar to that used by Miller's assailant. Finally, in 1991, Justice Minister Kim Campbell asked the Supreme Court of Canada to review Milgaard's case.

The high court's ruling, issued on April 14, 1992, began with a blanket statement that Milgaard had received a "fair trial" in 1970, with no evidence of police or prosecutorial misconduct, but Ron Wilson's recantation and new evidence concerning Larry Fisher prompted a reversal of the jury's verdict, with a new trial ordered. Milgaard was released from prison three days later, after spending 23 years behind bars. Saskatchewan prosecutors declined to pursue another trial, and the province refused to compensate Milgaard for his years in prison, since he had had no opportunity to prove his innocence in court. Only in 1997, after new DNA tests provided conclusive proof of his innocence, was Milgaard finally compensated for his wrongful conviction. Larry Fisher was charged with Gail Miller's slaying in July 1997 and convicted at trial in 1999.

MILLER, Robert Lee, Jr. exonerated by DNA evidence

In the mid-1980s, Oklahoma City was terrorized by the serial rape-murders of several elderly women. Police, seemingly helpless as the death toll mounted, were severely criticized for their failure to capture the unknown predator. They saw a way to clear the slate in 1987 and jumped at the chance, resulting in a classic case of justice betrayed.

Robert Miller Jr. was 29 years old, an unemployed heating and air-conditioning repairman, when he approached detectives in 1987, offering a strange solution to their frustrating dilemma. Some published accounts describe Miller as a "regular drug user," but all agree that he had no prior criminal record. Miller explained to police that he had experienced "visions" of the recent slayings and believed he had some kind of "psychic link" to the killer. As they listened to his detailed descriptions of crime scenes, questioning Miller over a span of 12 hours, detectives became convinced that *he* was to blame for the murders. Calling his videotaped ramblings a "confession," authorities charged Miller with the 1986 murders of 92-year-old Zelma Cutter and 83-year-old Anna Laura Fowler.

Apparently stunned by the accusation, Miller denied any personal role in the crimes and repeated his odd story of "seeing through the killer's eyes" in trancelike states. Police dismissed the psychic angle and enlisted forensic chemist JOYCE GILCHRIST to match Miller's hair (see FIBER AND HAIR EVIDENCE) with strands recovered from the crime scenes. Gilchrist confirmed the match, and Miller was convicted on all counts at trial, in 1988, receiving two death sentences plus a total of 725 years in prison.

Police and prosecutors evinced no concern when assaults on elderly victims continued in Oklahoma

City. Another suspect, one Ronald Lott, was arrested and confessed to the assaults. When critics of the Miller prosecution pointed out the near-identical MODUS OPERANDI between Lott's crimes and the 1986 murders, police turned again to Joyce Gilchrist, who promptly denied any possible match between Lott and hairs recovered from the Cutter and Fowler crime scenes. Prosecutor Ray Elliott, in charge of both cases (and later an Oklahoma judge), cheerfully assured his friends, "We're going to give Robert Miller the needle. He's just blowfish."

With assistance from attorneys of the CARDOZO INNOCENCE PROJECT, evidence from Miller's case was submitted for DNA testing in 1991 and again in 1993. Results were the same in both instances, positively excluding Miller as the source of hair and semen found at either crime scene while implicating Raymond Lott. Undeterred by mere science, Ray Elliott changed his theory of the crime to claim that even if Lott *was* the rapist, Robert Miller must still have been present at both crimes in order to offer his detailed "confessions." The Oklahoma Court of Criminal Appeals disagreed in 1994, ordering a new trial for Miller on the basis of irrefutable DNA evidence. District Attorney Robert Macy, renowned for placing 60 inmates on death row, announced his intent to handle the new trial himself, but legal delays postponed the event until February 1997, when charges were finally dismissed. A contributing factor to that move was the revelation of "expert" Joyce Gilchrist's false testimony in dozens of cases throughout Oklahoma.

MISSING Persons

This broad category includes an uncertain number of adults and minors who have vanished from their normal settings, either voluntarily or otherwise, in circumstances often undefined. A sampling of typical missing persons includes young runaways, kidnap or murder victims, fugitives from justice or from custody, debtors, amnesiacs, and other victims of mental illness—anyone, in short, who for whatever reason disappears without prior explanation to family, coworkers, or friends.

It is a chilling fact of life in the United States that no group collects comprehensive data on missing persons, and that no two agencies agree on how many are missing at any given time. In 1984, the U.S. Department of Health and Human Resources estimated that 1.8 million minors vanish from home

every years. Ninety-five percent are listed as runaways, and 90 percent of those return home within two weeks, leaving a "mere" 171,000 children at large on the streets. Five percent of the missing—some 90,000—are identified as abductees, with 72,000 reportedly kidnapped by parents involved in custody disputes. The other 18,000 are simply gone.

FBI spokesmen cast doubt on those figures in 1987, reporting that the bureau investigated only 150 "stranger abductions" of children between 1984 and 1986, but what does that disclaimer really prove? G-men normally remain aloof from kidnap cases in the absence of ransom demands or concrete proof of interstate flight, and they take no notice whatever of runaways. Indeed, the statistics themselves are suspect, since different FBI spokesmen radically changed the tune in 1995, admitting reports of some 300 stranger abductions of children *per year,* for an average of one every 29 hours across the nation. Likewise, the "runaway" designation may conceal a multitude of sins. Serial killer Dean Corll and his two teenage accomplices murdered at least 27 boys in Houston, Texas, between 1971 and 1973, while police listed all of the missing as runaways. John Wayne Gacy spent the better part of seven years planting corpses beneath his home in a Chicago suburb, claiming 32 "runaways" before abduction of a final victim aroused official interest.

The case of vanishing adults is even more obscure, with no statistics readily available from any source. A published estimate from 1970, probably conservative, suggested that at least 100,000 adults disappear in the United States each year. Again, the vast majority are tagged as runaways—from debt or legal complications, with increasing numbers of the homeless traveling in search of jobs or warmer climates—but some undoubtedly fall victim to foul play. While people disappear, others are found—sometimes alive, with no idea of their identity; more often dead and decomposed, with no clues to suggest their true identity. Crime historian Carl Sifakis suggests that America's actual murder rate may be double that announced each year by Justice Department spokespersons, if we include unidentified corpses with a sampling of shady "accidents" and "suicides."

The main contribution of forensic science to a missing persons investigation occurs after the subject or his/her remains are discovered. Where subjects are alive or recently deceased, FINGERPRINTS are generally used to establish their identity. Forensic ODONTOL-

OGY is used in other cases, if the subjects have dental records on file. Practitioners of forensic ANTHROPOLOGY meld art and science, reconstructing faces from skeletal remains with uncanny accuracy. When all else fails, DNA profiling—with known samples from the missing person, or via comparison with DNA from relatives—provides the last word in identity.

MITCHELL, Alfred Brian exonerated by DNA evidence

Another Oklahoma prisoner condemned on the basis of false testimony from state forensic "expert" JOYCE GILCHRIST, Alfred Mitchell was accused of murder, rape, and sodomy in the 1991 slaying of college student Elaine Scott. Gilchrist told the trial court that "Mr. Mitchell's sperm had been found on the victim through anal and vaginal swabs," the prosecutor contending that after Mitchell "had his way with her . . . he murdered her, he beat her to death, because she was the only living witness to the crime that he had committed." Impressed by those statements, jurors convicted Mitchell on all counts, and he was sentenced to die. His various appeals in Oklahoma were denied.

U.S. District Judge Ralph Thompson reversed Mitchell's rape and sodomy convictions on August 27, 1999, after discovering that Joyce Gilchrist had lied on the witness stand, while the prosecution withheld exculpatory evidence in Mitchell's case. Specifically, a review of case files had uncovered Gilchrist's handwritten notes of a conversation with FBI laboratory analysts, reporting DNA test results that excluded Mitchell as a donor of semen found at the crime scene. Branding the state's actions as "absolutely indefensible," Judge Thompson noted that:

Gilchrist's trial testimony that the DNA analysis performed by the FBI was 'inconclusive' as to petitioner was, without question, untrue. Over a year before petitioner was tried and convicted of rape and anal sodomy, [FBI] Agent Vick's DNA testing revealed that petitioner's DNA was not present on the samples tested. Petitioner's trial counsel did not receive copies of the autoradiographs developed by Agent Vick. . . . Petitioner's trial counsel did not receive copies of Gilchrist's notes, which demonstrate that she, too, was confident that only Ms. Scott's DNA was present on the vaginal swab and that only Ms. Scott and [her boyfriend's] DNA was present on the panties. Instead, the prosecution turned over only the formal FBI report discussed above which, at best, is unclear and ambiguous.

For that gross violation of judicial ethics, Thompson vacated Mitchell's rape and sodomy convictions, but allowed his death sentence for murder to stand. It remained for the 10th Circuit Court of Appeals to correct the remaining injustice in August 2001. According to that court:

Mr. Mitchell requested and received permission to conduct discovery in this habeas proceeding. As a result, he obtained hand-written notes taken by Ms. Gilchrist during telephone conversations with [FBI] Agent Vick indicating that the agent had conducted two DNA probes on the samples. These probes showed that the semen on the panties matched that of [her boyfriend] only, that no DNA was present on the rectal swab, and that the only DNA on the vaginal swab was consistent with the victim. The results thus completely undermined Ms. Gilchrist's testimony.

The district court held an evidentiary hearing, at which Agent Vick admitted there was no way to tell from his report that he had obtained no DNA results from the rectal swab, no DNA profile other than that of the victim on the vaginal swab, and no DNA profile other than that of the victim and [her boyfriend] on the panties. An expert testified at the evidentiary hearing that the DNA testing performed by Agent Vick unquestionably eliminated Mr. Mitchell as a source of the sperm. This expert reviewed Ms. Gilchrist's trial testimony implicating Mr. Mitchell through her testing . . . and stated that the testimony was based on the use of test methods Ms. Gilchrist knew were less precise than the DNA tests which eliminated Mr. Mitchell. Moreover, he pointed out that one of the tests she performed in fact excluded Mr. Mitchell. Mr. Mitchell was not provided the actual test results developed by Agent Vick or the notes taken by Ms. Gilchrist indicating her knowledge that Mr. Mitchell had been excluded by the FBI's DNA testing.

Ms. Gilchrist thus provided the jury with evidence implicating Mr. Mitchell in the sexual assault of the victim which she knew was rendered false and misleading by evidence withheld from the defense. Compounding this improper conduct was that of the prosecutor, whom the district court found had "labored extensively at trial to obscure the true DNA test results and to highlight Gilchrist's test results," and whose characterization of the FBI report in his closing argument was "entirely unsupported by evidence and . . . misleading." As a result, the jury convicted Mr. Mitchell of rape and forcible anal sodomy despite evidence it did not hear indicating that no such assault had taken place.

We are compelled to address the obvious by pointing out that the state's conduct in this case strikes a heavy blow to the public's "trust in the prosecutor as 'the representative . . . of a sovereignty . . . whose interest . . . in a criminal prosecution is not that it shall win a case, but that justice shall be done.'" The Supreme Court has cautioned that proper disclosure . . . is required in order "to preserve the criminal trial, as distinct from the prosecutor's private deliberations, as the chosen forum for ascertaining the truth about criminal accusations." Nonetheless, as the state takes pains to point out on appeal, our task is not to impose punishment for improper behavior but to assess whether the improperly withheld evidence raises a reasonable probability that, had it been disclosed to the jury, the result of the sentencing proceeding would have been different. . . .

Mitchell's death sentence was accordingly reversed, and charges were subsequently dropped. The murder of Elaine Scott remains unsolved today.

MITNICK, Kevin David convicted hacker

Described by admirers as "the most notorious hacker ever captured," Kevin Mitnick boasts a series of arrests dating from his teenage years, in the 1970s. The early charges were relatively minor, including theft of Pacific Bell Telephone operators' manuals and digital alteration of connections to receive free long-distance telephone service, resulting in stern reprimands and probation. In 1983 Mitnick was convicted of hacking into a Pentagon computer system, then ordered to spend six months at the California Youth Authority's Karl Holton Training School in Stockton.

Confinement failed to curb Mitnick's reckless behavior, and he continued to commit infractions that his friends describe as "crimes of curiosity." A 1989 conviction for computer FRAUD earned him a one-year sentence in federal prison, followed by six months of court-ordered therapy to relieve his computer "addiction." The treatment seemed to help, as Mitnick went to work as a legitimate computer programmer, but the lure of forbidden systems proved irresistible. Arrested in 1992 for violating his 1989 federal probation, Mitnick posted bond and fled California, spending the next three years as America's first cyberspace fugitive.

The long run began to unravel on December 25, 1994, when Mitnick penetrated the computers of Tsutomu Shimomura, a computer security specialist based in San Diego, California. Shimomura's clients included the FBI, the National Security Agency, and the U.S. Air Force, ensuring that any compromise of his work would produce a swift and severe official reaction. Shimomura and his colleagues were still searching for the culprit on January 27, 1995, when Berkeley software designer Bruce Koball found data stolen from Shimomura's computer stashed in one of the designer's Internet accounts on The Well, a local service provider. By February 7, further investigation had revealed that an unknown hacker was using The Well as a launching pad for raids on various corporate and university computer systems. Two days later, the phantom was traced to Netcom Online Communications Services, an Internet service provider in San Jose, California.

Shimomura flew to San Jose and persuaded Netcom administrators to cooperate in shadowing the hacker's activities. Together, they watched him copy files from Apple Computer and other "secure" systems, deprogram telephone circuits, and steal more than 20,000 credit card numbers from an online database. The pirate's cover was blown on February 10, 1995, when he revealed himself as Kevin Mitnick, writing to an Israeli e-mail correspondent with complaints about his photo being published in the *New York Times*. By then, Shimomura had identified Mitnick's apparent base of operations as Raleigh, North Carolina, and enlisted Sprint cellular phone engineers to help trace the hacker's address. Flying to Raleigh on February 12, Shimomura joined technicians armed with diagnostic gear to trace Mitnick's calls and pin down his location. FBI agents toured the apartment complex two days later, tracking Mitnick's telephone signals with a hand-held meter, and he was arrested on February 14, 1995, charged with 23 counts of computer and telecommunications fraud, for a maximum potential prison term of 345 years.

Mitnick pleaded guilty to one count of cellular telephone fraud in North Carolina and received an eight-month prison sentence. Thereafter, he was transferred to Los Angeles for trial on additional charges, denied bond or access to computers, and further barred from unsupervised access to telephones. Additional charges filed in California included federal probation violations plus 27 counts of illegal access, and computer and telephone fraud. Mitnick resolved both state and federal cases with another plea bargain on March 26, 1999, this time pleading guilty to five felony counts. Five months later he received a 60-month prison sentence with three years' probation and a $4,125 fine, the term to run consecutively with his sentence in North Carolina (for a total of 68 months inside). Although his plea agreement was sealed by the court, reports indicate that the court barred Mitnick from selling his story for profit and forbade any use of computers for four years after his release from prison. Mitnick served five years of his sentence and was released on January 21, 2000.

Mitnick's admirers continue to insist that he was persecuted or "framed" by authorities for displaying too much "curiosity" about modern computer technology. In the words of one sympathetic Web site:

The greatest injustice in the prosecution of Kevin Mitnick is revealed when one examines the actual harm to society (or lack thereof) which resulted from Kevin's actions. To the extent that Kevin is a "hacker" he must be considered a purist. The simple truth is that Kevin never sought monetary gain from his hacking, though it could have proven extremely profitable. Nor did he hack with the malicious intent to damage or destroy other people's property. Rather, Kevin pursued his hacking as a means of satisfying his intellectual curiosity and applying Yankee ingenuity. These attributes are more frequently promoted rather than punished by society.

Mitnick's fans overlook his persistent telephone frauds and theft of credit card numbers by the thousands, as well as his personal harassment of Tsutomu Shimomura, including a series of telephone death threats between December 1994 and February 1995. "Purist" or not, such aberrant behavior strains the definition of "curiosity," and no amount of denial erases the mercenary motive evident in theft of credit card numbers and telephone service. Shimomura himself may have come closest to the truth, when he told the *Minneapolis Tribune,* "I'm curious to know what's broken in him, why he feels compelled to do this."

MODUS Operandi

An offender's modus operandi (MO) includes all physical aspects of the criminal act, while excluding motives. A repeat offender's MO commonly changes over time, with an eye toward improving efficiency, gaining greater rewards (or inflicting greater damage), and avoiding detection. A thief, for example, may progress from shoplifting to BURGLARY or armed

ROBBERY, adding various tools or weapons to his repertoire, incorporating disguises, and graduating to more lucrative targets. Sex offenders, likewise, often progress from voyeurism to theft of fetish objects, then actual rape, some extending their crimes to murder as a means of silencing victims. While a criminal's MO may vary radically from one crime to the next, "signature" elements help investigators link crimes that may otherwise seem unrelated. The search for the elusive "BOSTON STRANGLER" is a case in point, where use of flamboyant KNOTS linked victims of disparate ages and races. If investigators are lucky, an MO may allow them to anticipate an unknown offender's next move or bait a trap resulting in his capture. Following an arrest, such evidence may also support charges in other unsolved cases, though broad "pattern" evidence is sometimes unreliable.

MONEY Laundering

In broad terms, money laundering involves the "cleaning" of income derived from illegitimate sources such as drug-running or illicit gambling, whereby criminal income is disguised as revenue from some legitimate enterprise. Another type of laundering involves concealment of income from a legitimate source to evade taxation, while converting the same money into "loans" from second parties or financial institutions. SMUGGLING of cash is often involved in money-laundering operations, as where drug money from foreign countries enters the United States to be funneled through banks or other businesses; and where unreported cash leaves the country bound for foreign banks, which then "lend" the same amount to its original owner (thus incurring a tax deduction, rather than taxable income).

Since money laundering is a covert, illegal activity, no comprehensive tally of amounts "cleaned" in a given year is available. One estimate, published by authors Mauro Corvasce and Joseph Paglino in 1995, claimed that $110 billion was laundered yearly in the United States, with some $300 billion laundered worldwide. Subsequent reports on the wealth of particular foreign drug lords make those figures seem conservative, however, and the same report also cites claims that $900 billion to $1 trillion in drug money moves through New York City alone in any given year. Participants in WHITE-COLLAR CRIME, like the leaders of Houston-based Enron Corporation, conceal much of their revenue each year, often while claiming losses on their state and federal tax returns.

Money laundering occurs in various ways, assisted in our time by computer transfers and other types of CYBERCRIME, but authors Corvasce and Paglino describe the classic laundering scheme as a three-stage process. In the first stage, termed *placement,* illicit funds are used directly to found some legitimate business, ranging in size from a local shop or restaurant to an international bank. The next step, dubbed *layering,* involves collection and storage of illicit cash until it can be placed in public circulation. That occurs during the *integration* phase, when "dirty" money is commingled with "clean" and distributed as salaries, loans, dividends, and so on. Since federal law requires banks to report all cash deposits of $10,000 or more, those involved in laundering money commonly make smaller deposits in a system dubbed *structuring.* While drug money is the most common object of laundering operations, the same techniques are used for cash "skimmed" from legal casinos or obtained from any other outlawed source.

MOON, Brandon exonerated by DNA

While DNA evidence is widely considered definitive in many criminal cases, verdicts in those cases still depend on jury verdicts influenced by testimony of expert witnesses. One case where erroneous scientific testimony resulted in wrongful conviction is that of Texas prison inmate Brandon Moon. Moon was a 25-year-old air force veteran and a sophomore at the University of Texas in El Paso during April 1987, when police charged him with raping a local woman at her home. He had no criminal convictions but was once accused of BURGLARY in a case that was later dismissed. Police included his old mug shot in a photo lineup displayed to the 1987 rape victim, whereupon she named him as her attacker. The woman repeated her identification at trial in 1988, while serologist Glen David Adams (then employed at the Texas state crime lab in Lubbock) testified for the prosecution, stating that DNA testing of semen found at the crime scene included Moon (and 15 percent of the state population at large) as the possible rapist. Impressed with that finding, jurors convicted Moon, and he received a 75-year prison term.

From prison, Moon kept track of new advances in DNA technology and filed numerous motions for retesting of the crime scene evidence. In 1989, rep-

resenting himself, Moon obtained a court-ordered DNA test that seemed to exclude him as a suspect, but the test results were deemed inconclusive since the lab had no DNA samples from the victim for comparison. Seven years later, with other motions still pending, Moon's prosecutors resubmitted their evidence to the state crime lab, but once again technicians failed to obtain DNA samples from the rape victim. Finally, in 2004, attorney Nina Morrison enlisted BARRY SCHECK and the CARDOZO INNOCENCE PROJECT to examine Moon's case. The final round of testing, finally including samples from the victim, excluded Moon as a donor of the crime scene samples and prompted his release from prison in December 2004.

As for Glen Adams, no longer employed at the Lubbock crime lab, Scheck told reporters that "tests performed by Mr. Adams . . . were far from 'reliable'—indeed, they appear to be marred by incompetence, fraud, or both." While El Paso district attorney Jaime Esparza apologized to Moon for his wrongful conviction and 17 years in prison, Scheck pressed his case against Adams. "We have to do an audit of this guy," Scheck told journalists in December 2004. "This is a huge mistake here." Lewis Maddox and Mark Stolorow, spokesmen for Orchid Cellmark Inc. (which tested Moon's evidence free of charge), told the press that "a properly conducted serological analysis may have excluded Mr. Moon at the time of trial."

MOORE, Clarence McKinley exonerated by DNA evidence

Around 1:20 A.M. on January 14, 1986, a female resident of Somers Point, New Jersey, was wakened in her bed by a stranger who demanded money. The woman—known in court records as "M.A."—produced eight dollars from her purse, but the man grew angry when she told him she had no more cash. He ordered M.A. to undress, then raped and sodomized her before compelling her to perform oral sex. Finally, preparing to leave, the rapist ordered her to kneel on the bed and "shake her ass" for an alleged accomplice outside her bedroom window. If she failed to comply, the rapist threatened, he would return and kill her. Four hours thus elapsed before M.A. felt safe enough to leave her bed and summon the police.

Authorities noted that M.A.'s description of her attacker was "vague": a man who "may have been black," five feet eight to five feet 11 inches tall, in his late 20s or early 30s, muscular and strong, wearing blue jeans. Initially unable to describe her rapist further, M.A. suggested to police that hypnosis "might help her remember, in more detail, his face." Hypnosis was performed by a clinical psychologist, Dr. Samuel Babcock, whereupon M.A. professed to see the rapist's face "much clearer" in her mind, with "the features . . . more detailed," and recalled that he had worn a tan suede coat with a zipper and dirt stains around one of the pockets. M.A. then collaborated with an artist to prepare a suspect sketch of her short-haired, bearded assailant. "You could tell he was black," she told police, because of his "tough street talk."

Working from M.A.'s description, Somers Point police prepared a photo lineup of possible suspects. They included a mug shot of Clarence Moore because he had a record of felony convictions spanning 18 years. The various charges included carnal abuse (1968), BURGLARY (eight counts in 1970), marijuana trafficking (1976), robbery, and aggravated sexual assault (three counts). If that were not enough, Moore was awaiting trial for sexual assault in nearby Cape May County, suspected of two other rapes in Somers Point. Police were hardly surprised, therefore, when M.A. picked Moore's photo from the lineup she was shown on February 5, 1986.

That identification secured a search warrant for Moore's residence, where officers found several pairs of blue jeans and a suede-front jacket with sleeves, back and collar made of "sweater material." While the jacket failed to match M.A.'s description, it did have some stains on the front. Eight months after the initial photo lineup, on October 9, 1986, M.A. was shown two more sets of pictures, and selected Moore's photo from each set in turn. According to detectives, M.A. told them at that time, "I'm sure that's him. I'll never forget his face. I see it every time I close my eyes." Police collected blood and saliva samples from Moore, for comparison with crime scene evidence, but the results were not helpful. As the lab report declared: "An insufficient amount of high molecular weight human DNA [deoxyribonucleic acid] was isolated from the vaginal swabs, fitted sheet, beige blanket, yellow blanket and the light blue comforter, therefore no comparisons could be made with blood from Clarence Moore."

A pretrial hearing was convened to determine the admissibility of M.A.'s testimony induced by hypnosis, New Jersey law dictating that such testimony is allowable "if the trial court finds that the use of hypnosis in the particular case was reasonably likely to result in recall comparable in accuracy to normal human memory." In Moore's case, the trial judge found (and an appellate court agreed) that use of hypnosis "was appropriate for the victim's fear-induced traumatic neurosis" and that M.A.'s testimony therefore was admissible.

The main issue at Moore's trial, therefore, was the reliability of M.A.'s identification. Her initial statements to police noted that she had only a "very fleeting opportunity" to glimpse the rapist's face while she was "scared to death," her attacker demanding that M.A. keep her eyes closed under fear of death. Furthermore, M.A. said, she had not worn the contact lenses required to correct her myopia, and the rapist's face was "close enough to see, but not in detail." Hypnosis had apparently corrected all those shortcomings, and M.A. once again identified Moore in court. Moore's wife disputed the identification, testifying that they lived 45 minutes away from M.A.'s home, and that Moore could not have left the house for any length of time without her knowledge. She knew this, Cheryl Moore maintained, because a painful breast infection and frequent nursing of a sickly newborn infant kept her awake throughout much of each night.

The prosecutor, in his three-hour summation, told jurors that Mrs. Moore's testimony made the state's case "stronger than ever." Noting that both Moore's wife and M.A. were Caucasian, the prosecutor then sought to explain his reasoning as follows:

Here's where I ask you to really concentrate on my words because if you misunderstand what I'm saying right now, I am going to feel real bad and foolish, and you are too. So let's all understand it like adults.

Race has nothing whatsoever to do with this case, right? Right. We all know that the race of the people involved does not at all dictate whether he's guilty or anything like that. I mean, let's hope that we all feel that way, whether we are white or black or anything. Okay? So let's clear the air that the statement that I'm about to make has nothing whatsoever to do—and I hope this machine hears this—has nothing whatsoever to do with race.

This has to do with selection, okay? Here's what I mean. All of us select people in life to be with based on whatever reason, whether it's people to marry, whether it's friends, whether it's people to associate with, whether it's business people. We all make choices in life that lead us to relationships with others, and those choices may or may not be significant. . . .

Well, that can be seen, can't it, because maybe the people that you choose to date or marry or be with all appear to be blondes or it might be redheads or it might be green hair. You know, nowadays I guess green is one of the popular colors. It could be anything. You could substitute any color hair or you could substitute any particular trait. Right? . . .

You see my point? It's not a statement of race; it's a question of choice, selection of who you might want to be with, whether it is as a mate or a boyfriend or girlfriend or victim. How about that? How about that some people might choose a victim according to the way they look, whether they be blonde or blue or anything else?

So I ask you this: What did we learn when we found out that Cheryl Moore was the wife of the defendant? I suggest to you in a nonracist way that what we found out was that Clarence McKinley Moore made a choice to be with a Caucasian woman. . . .

Moore's lawyer finally objected at that point, calling for a mistrial, and while the judge denied that motion, he instructed jurors to disregard the prosecutor's comments on race as "an unfair and unreasonable inference to be drawn from the testimony and I'm convinced that it's not proper argument to the jury." Thus rebuffed on his racist appeal, the prosecutor tried another tack:

I say to you that there are two other reasons why you should find that the State's case gets stronger with the testimony of Cheryl Moore. We learned that on December 4, 1985, the defendant's wife gives birth to a child. She further tells you that from that time on up until the time he's arrested, she's disabled. I mean, she has bleeding breasts.

I ask you to consider that and infer that that would give believability to the fact that during that period of time, that is, on January 14, 1986, right in the middle of the time after the birth of the child and the disability of the wife, I ask you to infer that that is a period of time when this individual would have his greatest need for sexual release.

Again, Moore's attorney objected, noting the total absence of evidence "to even suggest that [Moore] couldn't have had sexual relations" with his wife

during January 1986. The objection was sustained, and jurors were instructed once again to ignore the prosecutor's "improper inference." Undeterred, the prosecutor launched into his third and final argument, telling the jury that "if you don't believe [M.A.] and you think she's lying, then you've probably perpetrated a worse assault on her" than had her rapist. Yet again, the judge commanded jurors to ignore the inappropriate remark, but it was already too late. On March 5, 1987, Clarence Moore was convicted on three counts of aggravated sexual assault, plus one count each of second-degree burglary, second-degree ROBBERY, and robbery with intent to commit aggravated sexual assault. Because his prior convictions classified him as a "persistent offender," Moore was sentenced to life imprisonment, with a 25-year minimum to serve before parole.

Moore appealed his conviction, and while a state appellate court found the prosecutor's "outrageous conduct violated ethical principles" and "showed a disregard of the obligation of a prosecutor to play fair and see that justice is done," still Moore's appeal was rejected on grounds that the judge's "forceful" action had "cured" any harm caused by the prosecutor's misconduct. A second appeal was rejected in 1992, and the New Jersey Supreme Court declined to review Moore's case.

By 1997, Moore had discharged his public defender and received assistance from CENTURION MINISTRIES in pursuing a federal appeal. A U.S. district judge found the prosecutor's conduct "offensive and unprofessional," but declined to overturn the state appellate court's finding that evidence produced at trial supported Moore's conviction. Finally on June 22, 2001, the Third Circuit Court of Appeals reversed Moore's conviction, declaring that the New Jersey trial "was so infected with unfairness that it was constitutionally infirm." A new trial was ordered, with Moore released from Trenton State Prison on July 25. New DNA tests were performed on semen samples gathered from the crime scene, and when these excluded Moore as a suspect in the case, the charges were dismissed.

MORGAGNI, Giovanni Battista (1682–1771)

Giovanni Morgagni was born to an affluent family at Forli, Italy, on February 25, 1682. Commencing study of medicine and philosophy at Bologna in 1698, he earned doctorates in both subjects three years later.

In 1704, soon after helping anatomist Antonio Valsalva produce his celebrated volume *Anatomy and Diseases of the Ear,* Morgagni was picked to head the Italian Academy of Investigation—a scientific, rather than forensic, body, which he modeled on the French Royal Academy of Sciences. His work in that post inspired his book *Adversaria Anatomica,* hailed throughout Europe for its "Observations on the Larynx, the Lachrymal Apparatus, and the Pelvic Organs in the Female."

After two years studying CHEMISTRY in Venice (1707–09) and two more of private practice in Forli, Morgagni joined the University of Padua's faculty in 1711 or 1712 (reports differ). Five years later, he won promotion to serve as that school's first professor of anatomy, a post he held until his death on December 6, 1771. At Padua, Morgagni developed his groundbreaking theory of pathological anatomy, surmising that various diseases attacked specific organs. In 1761, Morgagni published his masterwork on PATHOLOGY, *De Sedibus et causis morborum per anatomem indagatis,* subsequently translated from the original Latin into French (1765), English (1769), and German (1771). Morgagni died then, at age 89.

MORIN, Guy Paul exonerated by DNA evidence

At 3:45 P.M. on October 3, 1984, nine-year-old Christine Jessop arrived home from school in Queensville, Ontario, a community 40 miles north of Toronto. Moments later, she left on her bicycle to meet a friend at a nearby park, stopping en route to buy gum at a neighborhood convenience store. Christine never reached the park, and in fact was never again seen alive. Three months later, on December 31, 1984, her decomposed remains were found near a rural home site, 30 miles away from Queensville. Autopsy results indicated that Christine was raped, then bludgeoned, drowned, and dismembered after death.

Evidence recovered from the crime scene appeared to confuse inexperienced detectives of the Durham Regional Police who investigated the slaying. Christine was dressed in underwear when found, the underpants stained with semen, but her parents did not recognize a sweater found near the body, and buttons recovered from the dump site failed to match those ripped from Christine's blouse. A single dark hair, recovered from the victim's necklace, may have belonged to her killer.

Authorities still had no suspect six weeks later, when Detectives John Shephard and Bernie Fitzpatrick focused on Christine's next-door neighbor, identified in Fitzpatrick's notes as "Guy Paul Morin, clarinet player, weird type guy." A 24-year-old "eccentric" who preferred beekeeping and jazz records to dating young women, Morin was marked by neighbors as "strange" for his personal habits and peculiar speech patterns. Detectives Shephard and Fitzpatrick secretly recorded an interview with Morin, and while the tape recorder unaccountably "stopped" in the midst of the interrogation, both officers later claimed Morin had made the cryptic (unrecorded) comment that "innocent little girls grow up to be corrupt." Several other suspects were identified in the Queensville vicinity, including three men with records of sexual violence toward children, but police focused on Morin (who had no criminal record) with an intensity that one critic later described as "tunnel vision."

Police obtained a sample of Morin's hair via subterfuge, and laboratory tests pronounced it "consistent" with the hair recovered from Christine Jessop's necklace. (No positive "match" between hairs is scientifically possible.) With no motive in hand, police theorized that Catherine had come home to an empty house and decided to show her musician neighbor the new recorder she had received at school. Morin, they postulated, then impulsively kidnapped and raped her, afterward killing Christine in a fit of rage or panic. An FBI profile of Christine's killer—"a night owl," "solitary," etc.—appeared to match Morin, but he denied any knowledge of the crime, expressing shock when he was charged with the murder. Police reported that carpet FIBERS from Morin's car were "similar" to several found on Christine's clothing, but again, no positive match could be made. Finally, detectives transferred Morin to a cell wired with microphones, shared by a policeman posing as an inmate. No confession was forthcoming, but Morin once remarked that "no one would ever know" his true relationship to Christine Jessop. Two other inmates subsequently claimed Morin had confessed the slaying in their presence, but efforts to make him repeat the alleged confession on tape were fruitless.

At trial, Morin's attorney revealed a discrepancy in the testimony of Christine Jessop's mother. Janet Jessop initially told police she arrived home from shopping and a trip to her son Kenny's dentist around 4:10 P.M. on October 3, 1984, by which time

Christine had already vanished. Morin's employer, meanwhile, confirmed that Morin left work in Toronto at 3:32 P.M., making it impossible for him to reach home and kidnap Christine before Janet and Kenny returned. Under coaxing from police, Janet Jessop later adjusted her time estimate, stating that she arrived home between 4:30 and 4:40 P.M., thus allowing Morin a few moments within which to kidnap her daughter. Even with the switch, however, the timing was highly suspect, since Morin had returned home with groceries for his family at 5:30 P.M., leaving a maximum time span of 75 minutes for Morin to rape and dismember Christine, complete a 60-mile round trip to the site where her body was dumped, remove all traces of evidence from himself and his vehicle, then finish his grocery shopping and return home. Jurors noted the discrepancy and acquitted Morin of all charges, but his prosecutors appealed that verdict to the Supreme Court of Canada, which ordered a new trial.

Legal delays postponed Morin's second trial until November 1991, by which time Christine's remains had been exhumed for a second autopsy. Amazingly, the new examination revealed gross injuries overlooked in 1985, including a bisected sternum, broken vertebrae, knife-scarred ribs, and a fractured skull (the latter directly contradicting prosecution testimony from 1985). More disturbing still was the volume of "lost" evidence: 150 slides of hair and fiber samples allegedly matched to Morin or his car, shards of plastic found on Christine's clothes, leaves and debris collected at the crime scene, a swatch of carpet and a milk carton found near the body, and so forth—all denied to Morin's defenders. One investigator "lost" his original notes on the case, then "found" a revised set more incriminating toward defendant Morin. The same detective had unaccountably stored various pieces of case evidence at his home and falsified the date on which soil samples were submitted for laboratory analysis (apparently to disguise a 12-month delay in submission of critical evidence).

Morin's attorney sought dismissal of the case on grounds of suppressed evidence, but Judge James Donnelly rejected that motion, instead praising police for their handling of the case thus far. Morin's second trial opened on November 5, 1991, and initially seemed to go well for the defense. Expert witnesses for Morin's side dismissed the hair and fiber evidence as scientifically inconclusive. Police witnesses

did poorly under cross-examination, while Kenny Jessop confessed under oath that he and several other boys had repeatedly molested Christine between the ages of five and eight years, thus presenting a bevy of alternative suspects.

Surprisingly, the tide began to turn when Morin's former cellmates took the stand again, repeating their dubious claims that he had confessed the murder in jail. Strangely, where the first trial jury had dismissed these same witnesses as self-serving liars, the new panel found their testimony "very credible." Morin also took the stand in his own defense, but damaged the case with a halting, nervous performance that smacked of evasion, rather than pure innocence. Finally, in a summation heavily biased in favor of the prosecution, Judge Donnelly urged jurors to accept the most dubious Crown evidence, while ordering the panel to ignore various points scored by the defense. Morin was thereafter convicted and sentenced to life imprisonment, ordered to serve a minimum of 25 years before parole.

Public outcry over the conviction prompted authorities to release Morin on bail, in February 1993, while he pursued his appeal. That hearing was scheduled for January 23, 1995, but it never occurred. Seeking to silence public criticism, prosecutors meanwhile ordered DNA testing on the semen stains from Christine's underwear, the results proving once and for all that Morin had no part in the crime. Charges were finally dismissed on January 22, 1995, and the case remains unsolved today.

MORITZ, Alan Richards (1899–1981)

Born in 1899, Dr. Alan Moritz joined the staff of Harvard University's medical school in the late 1930s, there promoting a new curriculum in forensic PATHOLOGY which elevated medicolegal studies to a position of equality with "normal" medicine. In 1950, the University of Nebraska granted Moritz an honorary doctorate of science, and two decades later he received the American Society for Investigative Pathology's gold-headed cane, awarded annually to a physician who "represents the highest ideals in pathology and medicine." Moritz's book-length publications include *The Pathology of Trauma* (1954), *Handbook of Legal Medicine* (1964), and *Doctor and Patient and the Law* (1971). Moritz died in 1981, at age 82.

NATIONAL Academy of Forensic Engineers

Founded in 1982, the NAFE is a professional organization with a stated goal "to advance the art and skill of engineers who serve as engineering consultants to members of the legal profession and as expert witnesses in courts of law, arbitration proceedings, and administrative adjudication proceedings." Qualified members must have appropriate education in engineering, coupled with practical field experience in forensic engineering. Candidates for membership must furthermore provide detailed references from active NAFE members, attorneys, or senior claims managers who have personal knowledge of the applicant's experience and forensic practice. Formally affiliated with the larger National Society of Professional Engineers, the NAFE has adopted the NSPE's exacting code of ethics.

NATIONAL Institute of Justice

The NIJ was created in 1969, under provisions of the 1968 Omnibus Crime Control and Safe Streets Act, reorganized in January 2003 to be more effective, efficient, and flexible under terms of the 2002 Homeland Security Act. As described on its Web site, the agency "provides objective, independent, evidence-based knowledge and tools to meet the challenges of crime and justice, particularly at the State and local levels." Active in support of modern DNA technology since 1986, the NIJ established its own Commission on the Future of DNA Evidence 12 years later. It also maintains an Office of Science and Technology that "manages technology research and development, development of technical standards, testing, forensic sciences capacity building, and technology assistance to State and local law enforcement and corrections agencies."

NATIONAL Institute of Standards and Technology

Founded in 1901, the NIST is a nonregulatory agency of the U.S. Commerce Department's Technology Administration. Its stated purpose is "to promote U.S. innovation and industrial competitiveness by advancing measurement science, standards, and technology in ways that enhance economic security and improve our quality of life." That mission is accomplished (at least in theory) via four collaborative programs that include the following:

1. The Advanced Technology Program, encouraging accelerated development of innovative technologies for broad national benefit by subsidizing research in the private sector.
2. The Baldrige National Quality Program, designed to promote "performance excellence among U.S. manufacturers, service companies, educational institutions, and health care providers."
3. The Manufacturing Extension Partnership, a nationwide network of local centers offering

technical and business assistance to smaller manufacturers.

4. (4) The NIST Laboratories, conducting research
that advances the nation's technology infrastructure and aids U.S. industry in improving products and services.

Operating from dual headquarters in Gaithers-
burg, Maryland, and Boulder, Colorado, the NIST
claims a role in developing or improving various
devices ranging from automated teller machines and
atomic clocks to mammograms and semiconduc-
tors, plus countless others. Its efforts in standardization also give rise to various instruments and
processes employed in the forensic sciences. Critics
regard much of the NIST's activity as awarding
unjustified hand-outs to billionaire industrialists,
while supporters of the program claim that its eradication would retard vital research and development
nationwide.

NATIONAL Transportation Safety Board

Created in 1967, the NTSB is an independent federal agency charged by Congress with investigating
all U.S. civil aviation accidents and certain public-
use aircraft accidents; railroad accidents involving
passenger trains or any train accident that results
in at least one fatality or major property damage;
major marine accidents and any marine accident
involving a public and a nonpublic vessel; pipe-
line accidents involving a fatality or substantial
property damage; releases of hazardous materials
in all forms of transportation; selected highway
accidents; and selected transportation accidents
that involve problems of a recurring nature. In
addition to its field investigations, the board also
issues safety recommendations aimed at preventing future accidents, maintains a federal database
of civil aviation accidents, conducts special studies
of transportation safety issues of national signifi-
cance, and serves as the "court of appeals" for any
airman, mechanic, or mariner whenever certificate
action is taken by the Federal Aviation Administration or the U.S. Coast Guard Commandant,
or when civil penalties are assessed by the FAA.
Since its creation, the NTSB has investigated more
than 124,000 aviation accidents and more than
10,000 surface transportation accidents, while issu-
ing some 12,000 safety recommendations.

NELSON, Bruce exonerated by DNA evidence

Another case of false accusation belatedly resolved
by science comes from Allegheny County, Pennsylvania, where Bruce Nelson was accused of rape
and murder in 1980. According to Terrence Moore,
Nelson's alleged accomplice and sole living witness,
the crime began when Moore and Nelson stole a
van and drove it to a Pittsburgh parking garage,
in hopes of using it to commit a robbery. In the
garage, they allegedly kidnapped a woman and
forced her into the van, raping her repeatedly at
knifepoint before they strangled her to death with
a piece of cloth. Moore was subsequently arrested
and admitted his role in the slaying, but he named
Bruce Nelson as the instigator and their victim's
actual slayer.

Nelson was by then imprisoned on another, unrelated charge. Authorities indicted him for the rape-
murder and police arranged a confrontation with
Moore. At that meeting, Nelson reportedly asked
Moore, "What did you tell them?" Moore allegedly
replied, "I told them everything." Nelson denied any
part in the crime, but prosecutors introduced his
question—"What did you tell them?"—as a "confession" when he faced trial in 1982. Other evidence
included Moore's FINGERPRINTS, allegedly found on
the victim's purse, plus saliva "consistent" with Nelson's, found on the victim's breast, brassiere, and a
cigarette butt from the crime scene. Jurors convicted
Nelson of rape and murder, whereupon he received a
life sentence with a concurrent 10-to-20-year prison
term on the lesser charge.

Nelson's initial appeal was a habeas corpus petition, asserting that use of his "confession" to Moore
violated Nelson's Fifth Amendment right to stand
silent during interrogation and his Sixth Amendment
right to have counsel present during questioning.
The district court rejected his petition, and the
Pennsylvania Supreme Court refused to review
Nelson's case. On August 17, 1990, the Third Circuit Court of Appeals affirmed the state's ruling on
Nelson's Sixth Amendment plea, but it overturned
the Fifth Amendment ruling and remanded the case
for further review by the state district court. By that
time, DNA testing procedures had been discovered and
recognized as evidence in court, permitting Nelson's
attorney to test the saliva samples used as evidence
at trial. The test excluded Nelson as a source of the
saliva, and his charges were dismissed on August 28,
1991.

NEUTRON Activation Analysis

Pioneered in 1936, neutron activation analysis (NAA) ranks among the most sensitive techniques presently available for qualitative and quantitative analysis of multiple trace elements including solids, liquids, and gases. Also known as gamma ray SPECTROSCOPY, NAA is a nondestructive testing method whose applications to forensic science and other fields are described by proponents as "virtually limitless." In a typical NAA test, samples are placed inside a nuclear reactor and bombarded with neutrons, thus producing radioactive isotopes that decay through the emission of a beta particle and gamma rays with a unique half-life. Calculation of that half-life decay rate identifies the elements within the sample and their relative quantities. Thus, for example, bullet fragments extracted from a corpse can be analyzed and matched to unfired bullets found in the possession of a shooting suspect, and to trace elements found within the barrel of the suspect's gun. Such tests *do not* reveal who pulled the trigger, however, and may indicate only that fragments match a particular lot of bullets manufactured by the thousands at a particular factory during a given time frame.

One of NAA's most controversial applications was seen in the 1963 assassination of President John F. Kennedy. Conflicting evidence from witnesses and autopsy physicians, coupled with exposure of inaccuracies in the 1964 *Warren Report*—which declared JFK's murder the work of lone assassin Lee Harvey Oswald—have spawned multiple conspiracy theories over the past four decades. By 2001, a Gallup poll revealed that 81 percent of all Americans believe that Kennedy died as the result of a conspiracy—a verdict affirmed by the House Select Committee on Assassinations. Three years later, Prof. Kenneth Rahn (University of Rhode Island) and Larry Sturdivan (retired wound ballistics specialist for the U.S. Army) announced that they had proved Oswald's lone guilt by means of NAA. Specifically, they cited analysis of "[f]ive bullet fragments, two large ones, and three small ones [that] were recovered from the limousine, Connally's stretcher in Parkland Hospital and from the men's bodies," reporting that the large fragments "perfectly matched Oswald's rifle," while the smaller ones matched Oswald's ammunition in their constituent amounts of antimony and lead. Unfortunately, Rahn and Sturdivan neglected to mention that the first "large fragment" was in fact a whole bullet—Commission Exhibit 399, star

of the *Warren Report*'s notorious "MAGIC BULLET THEORY"—virtually unmarked by its alleged passage through two human bodies. The analysts also failed to acknowledge reports from various autopsy surgeons that the weight of bullet fragments found in Governor John Connally alone exceeded the microscopic traces missing from C.E. 399. With those glaring omissions in mind, the Rahn-Sturdivan analysis predictably failed to demolish prevailing conspiracy theories in JFK's death.

NEW England Innocence Project

The NEIP was launched in early 2000 by founders Stanley Fisher, Daniel Givelber, Joseph Savage Jr., and David Siegel. Its mission, as stated on the group's Web site, is "to identify, investigate and exonerate wrongfully convicted individuals who are currently incarcerated in New England." Cosponsored by the Massachusetts Association of Criminal Defense Lawyers, the NEIP provides pro bono legal assistance to inmates in cases where actual innocence can be proved by DNA testing or other new evidence previously unavailable at trial. Applications for case review and representation are accepted from prisoners in Connecticut, Maine, Massachusetts, New Hampshire, Rhode Island, and Vermont. Aside from specific case work, the NEIP also supports legal reform to hasten the identification and liberation of innocent inmates while ensuring prevention of future wrongful convictions.

NONLETHAL Weapons

While the primary goal of armed combat remains the permanent incapacitation of enemies, many other situations involving military or law enforcement personnel demand weapons and tactics that do not result in loss of human life or crippling injury. Prevailing laws in the United States likewise restrict civilian ownership or use of deadly weapons and may dictate resort to nonlethal means of self-defense, particularly in a public setting. Whether fending off a solitary mugger on the street, defusing a volatile hostage situation, controlling prison inmates, or dispersing riotous protesters, alternative methods are needed in situations where use of deadly force is counterproductive or prohibited by law.

Nonlethal weapons, in the broadest terms, are any instruments designed for use in combat situations that do not *predictably* result in death. There are occasional exceptions to the rule, of course: asthmatics and the like may suffocate under prolonged exposure to nonlethal gas; electric stun guns may interfere with pacemakers; "flash-bang" concussion grenades might induce a heart attack or cause a subject to fall down with fatal results; rubber bullets and other "baton" rounds may kill in rare cases, if they strike a target's skull or chest with sufficient force. In general, though, nonlethal weapons are not expected to kill.

Nevertheless, there is still room for heated debate over the types, the proper design, and the use of nonlethal weapons, and that debate continues from corporate boardrooms to the Internet. Some critics stand aghast at the prospect of fielding "worse than lethal" weapons, namely those that leave their victims alive but physically or psychologically maimed (as in blinding with lasers, or scarring flesh and lungs with caustic gas). For purposes of this essay, "nonlethal" weapons are presumed to be those that neither kill nor permanently injure when used as intended, against reasonably healthy targets.

In that context, nonlethal weapons are available in many forms. Their usefulness likewise varies, arising in situations where the law forbids use of deadly force, where hostages or innocent bystanders are at equal risk with the intended targets, or when use of deadly force (though legally excused) may only make a volatile situation that much worse. With those limitations in mind, nonlethal weapons fall into several broad categories, including:

1. *Hand-held impact weapons.* The options here include a variety of clubs, flails, blackjacks, and similar weapons. Most U.S. jurisdictions limit a civilian's right to carry such instruments, and mere possession of some (brass knuckles, for example) may be criminal in itself. Law enforcement officers make extensive use of clubs and batons, but their employment is sometimes inflammatory, and they have little value against large groups of adversaries.

2. *Nonpenetrating projectiles.* Typically launched from special guns, the various wooden or rubber bullets, bean-bag projectiles, and so forth deliver a painful or stunning blow at long range, thereby keeping safe distance between combatants. Some concussion grenades also discharge hard-rubber pellets as "stingers," for use in confined spaces. As with clubs, above, most U.S. jurisdictions

limit ownership of these devices to police or military personnel.

3. *High-pressure liquids.* Although southern police were reviled for turning fire hoses against civil rights protesters in the 1960s, high-pressure hoses and "water cannons" remain a fixture of many police and military riot squads. Mounted on trucks or armored vehicles, they have seen frequent use against rowdy mobs in Europe and Asia. Serious injury may result in some cases, due to falls or violent impact with solid objects, but normal damage is limited to drenching and occasional bruises.

4. *Sprays and gases.* Great advances have been made in this field from the early days of bulky tear gas canisters (which still sometimes grow hot enough to set a house on fire). Today a wide variety of nonlethal gases and chemical sprays are available to law enforcement and military personnel. Most are designed to irritate a subject's eyes and/or respiratory system, producing disorientation, temporary blindness, and occasional nausea or unconsciousness. Most U.S. jurisdictions permit civilian ownership of milder forms, in small amounts (Chemical Mace, and so forth). Some states require a rudimentary training course before civilians are authorized to purchase and carry such weapons.

5. *Electric stun guns.* These weapons operate by transmitting a nonlethal electric charge through the target's body, creating electronic "riffles" that disrupt synaptic pathways and result in temporary incapacitation. High on voltage but low on amperage, they are not designed to kill even with prolonged contact, but they may produce small contact burns. Physical contact with the target is required for all such weapons. Many require the stun gun itself to be pressed against an assailant's body, while others (like the Taser) fire barbed darts with slender wires attached to complete the circuit from a distance. Stun guns are widely available in the United States by mail order and on the Internet, but purchasers should consult their local statutes to avoid placing themselves in violation of the law.

6. *Optical weapons.* As suggested by the title, these weapons interfere with vision, in order to confuse, disorient, or temporarily incapacitate the subjects. "Flash-bang" grenades produce a blinding burst of light, coupled with a concussive

The Advanced M-26 model TASER gun. (AP)

shock wave, to stun their targets. (Some, as noted above, also contain rubber "shrapnel" to add an element of pain without serious physical injury.) Pulsing strobe lights use the same principle to disrupt vision. Low-energy lasers may produce temporary blindness, and military technicians have reportedly studied lasers that would make the damage permanent. Obscurants, such as smoke in varied colors, can be used to disorient crowds or individuals, while masking the approach of troops or law enforcement officers.

7. *Acoustic weapons.* As with a subject's eyes, the ears may be assaulted in various ways without inflicting permanent harm. Loud music or similar sound effects are sometimes used as a means of psychological warfare, as when American troops played blaring rock-and-roll outside the besieged headquarters of Manuel Noriega, during the most recent U.S. invasion of Panama. Concussion grenades are designed to stun their targets with a thunderclap of sound. Various lev-

els of either high- or low-pitched sound may be used to disperse crowds. Infrasound broadcasts (the nonlinear superposition of two ultrasound beams) are said to produce "intolerable sensations" including disorientation, nausea and vomiting, and involuntary defecation.

8. *Chemical weapons.* A number of tools are available here, treated separately from the sprays and gases described above. Adhesive agents include a variety of sticky, quick-drying polymer foams that can be removed only with special solvents. Chemical "barriers" consist of dense, rapidly expanding foam or bubbles that inhibit movement and obscure vision, sometimes producing foul odors and/or using dyes to mark subjects for later apprehension. Calmative agents include various sedatives, while hallucinogens confuse and disorient their targets. Lubricants, ranging from simple oil slicks to agents that turn dirt into slippery "chemical mud," impede both attackers and subjects trying to escape. Taggants, while

not technically weapons, employ chemical dyes to identify subjects (as in the explosive dye packs sometimes used to foil bank robberies).

9. *Biological weapons.* Various living organisms, including germs, bacteria, and viruses, have been used as weapons for centuries. Most of those stockpiled or custom-designed by military scientists are lethal, but countless others also exist that cause discomfort, disorientation, or temporary incapacitation without killing their victims. Rumors also persist of military experimentation with various biodeteriorative microbes—i.e., those that devour, break down, or otherwise compromise various inanimate substances, including rubber, metal, concrete, and/or petroleum products. The obvious drawback with any such agent is its relatively slow reaction time, making it a poor choice for use in short-term emergencies. The deteriorants, furthermore, would impartially attack both "friendly" and "hostile" property if carelessly dispensed.

10. *"Entanglement munitions."* Rarely used today, and having no significant value against crowds, this category involved use of nets or similar objects to snare and subdue targets. As implied by the title, the nets are fired from various specialized guns, unfurling in midair to drop over the subject. Nets may also be hand-thrown, laid as snares, or dropped from aircraft, but they would not then be described as "munitions."

Increasing emphasis on human rights throughout society and the world at large, though often honored more in the breach than by observance, will doubtless fuel new research into modes and methods of nonlethal combat. It remains to be seen whether their development and use will decrease violent conflict or cause explosive confrontations to proliferate, as fear of death or maiming injury decreases.

NORRIS, Charles (1867 or 1868–1935)

Born in 1867 or 1868 (reports differ), Charles Norris graduated from New York's Columbia Medical School and continued his studies in Europe, including a valuable internship with German pathologist Eduard von Hofmann. Between 1904 and 1918, Norris was a professor of PATHOLOGY at Bellevue Hospital, in New York City. In the latter year, he was chosen to serve as the city's first chief MEDICAL EXAMINER,

replacing the elected (and often unqualified) coroners who previously ruled on cause of death.

Norris and chief assistant Thomas Gonzales were instrumental in developing forensic pathology as a subspecialty of clinical medicine. Supported by toxicologist Alexander Gettler, Norris and Gonzales revolutionized forensic medicine, eliminating the muddled and corrupt system wherein cadavers were often shuffled around New York's five boroughs, generating fees for multiple coroners but yielding no significant medical findings. In 1934, Dr. Norris established a department of forensic medicine at the New York University College of Medicine. He died the following year, leaving Dr. Gonzales in charge of the medical examiner's office until 1954.

NORTH Carolina Center on Actual Innocence

The NCCAI was created in 2000 to coordinate activities of separate innocence projects at Duke University School of Law and the University of North Carolina School of Law. Since its creation, the center has also been instrumental in launching new innocence projects at the law schools of Campbell University and North Carolina Central University, with collaboration from students at UNC-Chapel Hill's School of Journalism and Mass Communication. The NCCAI's stated mission is "to identify, investigate and advance credible claims of innocence made by inmates convicted of felonies in North Carolina." Its secondary mission is "to educate policymakers, law and journalism students, the public, the media, and the legal/law enforcement communities about systemic problems in the criminal justice system that lead to wrongful convictions, as well as the emerging solutions to those problems." An average of 200 students per year participate in the center's various activities, while income is derived primarily from grants and private contributions. A noteworthy NCCAI success story is the case of Darryl Hunt, liberated by DNA evidence in December 2003, after spending 18 years in prison for a crime he did not commit.

NORTHWESTERN University Center on Wrongful Convictions

Operating in conjunction with the CARDOZO INNOCENCE PROJECT and similar groups around the United States, the Center on Wrongful Convictions declares itself "dedicated to identifying and rectifying wrongful convictions and other serious miscarriages of justice." Center faculty, staff, and collaborating attorneys in private practice investigate cases of alleged wrongful prosecution and provide free legal representation to inmates whose cases include one or more of the following elements:

1. A claim of actual innocence—i.e., a defendant who had no involvement whatsoever in the crime(s) of which he stands convicted, as opposed to cases resting on procedural irregularities or some abusive process used to convict a suspect who is nonetheless guilty as charged.
2. DNA cases, wherein the claim of innocence is scientifically supported by testable biological evidence.
3. For cases not involving DNA, a minimum of 10 years remaining to be served on the defendant's original sentence. (This requirement presumably would be moot in capital cases, where no prison term is specified.)

Prison inmates whose cases meet those criteria are invited to submit inquiries at the following address:

Center on Wrongful Convictions
Northwestern University School of Law
357 East Chicago Avenue
Chicago, Illinois 60611

NUCLEAR Emergency Search Team

It sounds like the plot from any one of several dozen thrillers, from Ian Fleming's *Thunderball* to James Cameron's *True Lies* and Tom Clancy's *The Sum of All Fears*. In 1974, an extortionist threatened to destroy Boston with an improvised nuclear bomb if government officials did not pay a rather modest $200,000 ransom. To encourage prompt payment, the terrorist provided diagrams that appeared to be authentic. State and federal authorities had no response plan in place for such an emergency, so they delivered the cash as ordered—but Mr. X never picked up his payoff. He remains unidentified today, and his weapon of mass destruction—if in fact it ever existed—has never been found.

That near-miss (or cruel hoax) prompted U.S. officials to create a new swift-response team to cope with future emergencies. Dubbed the Nuclear Emergency Search Team (NEST), it comprises more than 1,000 volunteer scientists, engineers, and technicians employed at America's nuclear laboratories and regulatory agencies, collaborating in deployment with the U.S. Army's 52nd Ordnance Group (specialized in disarming nuclear weapons). NEST regional headquarters are located at Nellis Air Force Base (outside Las Vegas, Nevada) and at Andrews Air Force Base (near Washington, D.C.).

While its existence has been publicly acknowledged since 1975, NEST operates for the most part behind a screen of secrecy. Its members are reported to have trained in emergency-response procedures with police and fire departments from New York City, Chicago, Los Angeles, San Francisco, and other large cities, but confirmation remains elusive, with details closely guarded by the Departments of Defense and Energy (controlling nuclear materials). It is known that NEST nuke-hunters employ sophisticated laptop computers (like those reported missing from the Los Alamos Nuclear Weapons Laboratory in May 2000) to detect weapons and determine their probable source via analysis of their design and materials used in construction. Other NEST tools include portable X-ray machines, sophisticated robots used to search dangerous areas, various state-of-the-art radiation detectors, and special nonmagnetic cutting tools to breach a weapon's outer shell. In their laboratories, a rotating staff of 15 to 20 NEST scientists practice constructing crude nuclear weapons with readily available technology, preparing themselves for the day when they may face such a bomb constructed by others.

In the event of a nuclear threat, NEST's reaction proceeds through seven clearly defined phases. They include:

1. *Intelligence collection.* NEST draws information from the FBI, CIA, and other agencies, collated and evaluated at the Department of Energy's (DOE) Nonproliferation Program at Lawrence Livermore National Laboratory (LLNL) in Livermore, California. Threats are reported by outside agencies and assessed by the DOE's Office of Emergency Response.
2. *Standby alert.* Receipt of a threat activates an Operational Emergency Management Team (OEMT), essentially alerting all NEST members to prepare for action.
3. *Credibility assessment.* Any available data (such as the Boston extortionist's diagrams) is processed

through LLNL's exhaustive computer database (containing "every last published word" about nuclear weapons). If the threat is deemed credible, NEST deployment proceeds to the next phase.

4. *Searching for the weapon.* NEST nuke-hunters deploy with members of the FBI's Hostage Rescue Team and/or military personnel from various elite "special mission" units. Sophisticated scanning gear is used to detect either gamma or neutron radiation. If a specific facility is threatened, the search may proceed on foot. Otherwise, roving teams may operate from land vehicles, boats, or aircraft with a variety of larger scanners. (NEST maintains its own air force and volunteer pilots, as well as specialized armored vehicles.) Within an urban setting, false alarms may be triggered by a wide variety of common objects, including medical X-ray machines and security devices, pacemakers, fresh asphalt, the dye that colors certain tiles, and even the granite used in some civic monuments. If a weapon is found, the next phase proceeds.

5. *Recovery.* Any and all necessary force may be employed to retrieve nuclear weapons before they are detonated. Killing the offenders without warning may be authorized.

6. *Ordnance disposal.* When any human threat has been neutralized, special diagnostic and assessment teams examine the suspect device. Deactivation takes priority. Proposed methods range from manual disarmament (by human hands or high-tech robots) to disabling portions of the bomb with pinpoint gunfire. Liquid nitrogen or other freezing agents may be introduced to render the mechanism inoperative. Radiation dispersal devices, consisting of a 35-foot nylon tent filled with thick, quick-drying foam may contain the threat from a ruptured canister, but they have not been tested with an actual nuclear bomb. Should these efforts fail, survivors are left to cope with the last phase of the process.

7. *Consequence management.* NEST has no direct responsibility for disaster relief, and its volunteer members have no particular expertise in this area. Given the secrecy surrounding NEST deployment, it is probable that a failed mission—i.e., detonation of a nuclear device in some populated area—would occur with little or no warning to local officials or civilians. "Consequence man-

agement" thus becomes the task of those who survive the blast and the outsiders who are eventually sent to deal with casualties and the resultant physical damage from a nuclear blast.

Federal authorities admit that NEST has evaluated "more than 110" nuclear threats since 1975, with volunteers actively mobilized to respond in "about 30" of those cases. Thus far, all threats received have been officially deemed hoaxes. Sketchy details have leaked to the media in six of those cases, although the solution in five of the cases remains "unknown"—meaning no information is available on any suspects who may have been identified or apprehended. The known cases of NEST activation include:

January 31, 1975 Los Angeles, California: A letter allegedly written by anonymous members of the radical Weather Underground organization, including a schematic drawing of a one-megaton hydrogen bomb, claimed that nuclear devices had been placed in three separate build-

ings. No bombs were recovered, and no suspects have been publicly identified.

November 23, 1976 Spokane, Washington: Police received a ransom demand for $500,000 in small bills, threatening detonation of 10 explosive charges, each with 10 pounds of radioactive waste material. No bombs were recovered, and no suspects have been publicly identified.

January 30, 1979 Wilmington, North Carolina: The manager of a General Electric nuclear plant received an extortion letter containing a sample of uranium dioxide powder. The letter claimed that 10 gallons of enriched uranium dioxide had been stolen from the plant and would be scattered at random in an unnamed U.S. city if a $100,000 ransom payment was not forthcoming. An employee of a GE subcontractor was arrested, convicted, and sentenced to 15 years in prison for extortion. Officially, no other radioactive material was recovered.

April 9, 1979 Sacramento, California: Governor Jerry Brown received a postcard claiming that a small amount of plutonium had been released in the Capitol building to demonstrate the folly of nuclear energy development. No contaminant was found, and no suspect has been publicly identified.

November 27, 1987 Indianapolis, Indiana: An anonymous telephone caller, claiming affiliation with a Cuban political faction, warned that a homemade nuclear bomb would be detonated in a local bank overnight. No bombs were recovered, and no suspects have been publicly identified.

April 13, 1990 El Paso, Texas: Mayor Suzanne Azar received a telephone threat that a nuclear weapon built with uranium had been set to destroy a three-square-mile area of the city. No bombs were recovered, and no suspects have been publicly identified.

NEST was not involved in the Chicago arrest of Jose Padilla (a.k.a. Abdullah Al Mujahir) on May 8, 2002, allegedly for plotting with Middle Eastern terrorists to build and detonate a "dirty" nuclear bomb at some unspecified point in the United States. Attorney General John Ashcroft announced Padilla's arrest a month after the fact, on June 10, 2002, claiming the suspect was seized at O'Hare International Airport upon returning from Pakistan, where

he reportedly spent time with members of Osama bin Laden's al-Qaeda terrorist network. Although a native-born citizen of the United States, unarmed at the time of his capture, Padilla was held in military custody at a U.S. Navy brig in Charleston, South Carolina. Ashcroft, speaking to the nation on a satellite hook-up from Russia, declared that warnings of Padilla's plot had been received from "multiple, independent, corroborating sources." As with previous arrests and federal warnings broadcast since the terrorist attacks of September 11, 2001, no further information was provided to support the accusation. Attorney General Ashcroft, ignoring the fact that no declared state of war exists in America, told reporters, "We have acted with legal authority both under the laws of war and clear Supreme Court precedent, which establishes that the military may detain a United States citizen who has joined the enemy and has entered our country to carry out hostile acts." A Pentagon spokesman, Lieutenant Colonel Rivers Johnson, seemed less certain, telling the press that "military officials have not decided whether to charge Mujahir or what charges to file." Regardless of charges, suspect Padilla is considered innocent under American law until proven guilty at trial.

NUCLEAR Magnetic Resonance

Nuclear magnetic resonance (NMR) is a physical phenomenon based on the magnetic properties of nuclei found in some (but not all) atoms. The process analyzes a magnetic nucleus by aligning it with an external magnetic field, then disrupting that alignment with radio waves of varying frequency and observing the result. The "wobble" produced in different nuclei by various frequencies permit observers to determine the molecule's structure and thus identify it. Physicists Felix Bloch and Edward Purcell independently described the process in 1946, sharing a Nobel Prize for their discovery six years later. During its early phase, NMR technology used a method called continuous-wave SPECTROSCOPY, which examined one frequency at a time and thus proved too slow for practical applications. An improved method pioneered by Richard Ernst, dubbed Fourier transform NMR spectroscopy, permitted the examination of multiple frequencies at once, a method improved still further with Fourier transform spectroscopy and multidimensional nuclear magnetic resonance spectroscopy.

Today, NMR spectroscopy ranks among the primary techniques for obtaining information about specific molecules, and it is the only method available for detailing the three-dimensional structure of biological molecules in solution. The best-known application of NMR technology lies in the field of medical diagnosis, where it is commonly called magnetic resonance imaging (MRI). Forensic scientists use NMR to determine the composition of various molecules during ORGANIC COMPOUND ANALYSIS. NMR is particularly useful in the analysis of small soluble proteins.

NURSING, Forensic

Forensic nursing is the branch of nursing concerned with treating victims of traumatic injuries and catastrophic accidents, as well as the assessment and treatment of criminal offenders and the families of both. The American Nurses Association officially recognized forensic nursing as a specialty in 1995, though nurses have long been involved in various aspects of forensic medicine, including preservation of physical evidence that may be presented in court. Specific job descriptions in the field include (but are not limited to) the following:

Forensic nurse examiners: Nurses who examine and evaluate trauma related to crimes of violence, accidents, or disasters, while serving as liaisons between health care institutions, legal agencies, and courts of law.

Sexual assault nurse examiners: Forensic nurses specially trained to collect evidence in sexual assault cases and to counsel the victims of sex crimes.

Forensic pediatric nurses: Nurses who apply their skills and knowledge primarily to minors in cases of abuse or neglect, and where legal or human rights issues pertain.

Forensic psychiatric nurses: Nurses specializing in the care and treatment of psychiatric patients in legal custody and/or those facing court-ordered psychiatric evaluations. Their expertise also extends to institutional personnel who have suffered or witnessed violent assaults, those who have lost patients to suicide, and so forth.

Forensic nurse investigators: Also dubbed *nurse death investigators* and *medical examiner nurse investigators,* these registered nurses assist physicians and police in their investigation of any violent or unexpected death. Specialists in this field are employed by public or private agencies, nursing homes, and insurance companies to verify information surrounding suspect deaths and document evidence pertaining to abuse, neglect, or fraud.

Forensic nurse attorneys: Registered nurses who also obtain law degrees and become practicing attorneys in the field of nursing jurisprudence (the equivalent of physicians who are also lawyers).

Legal nurse consultants: Registered nurses who may not possess degrees in law, but who assist attorneys with their cases in any context where law and medicine overlap. Some definitions limit the role of these nurses to civil (rather than criminal) cases.

O

OCHOA, Christopher exonerated by DNA evidence

A native of El Paso, Texas, born in 1967, Christopher Ochoa graduated from high school with honors in 1984. Friends knew him as a quiet, soulful poet and songwriter who served as an editor for Riverside High School's literary magazine. In 1988, at age 21, he lived in Austin and worked at one of several Pizza Hut restaurants scattered around the state capital. Ochoa's roommate and close friend, Richard Danziger, worked at the same restaurant. In November 1988, the manager of another Pizza Hut in Austin, 20-year-old Nancy DePriest, was attacked in her own restaurant after hours, repeatedly raped and sodomized, then murdered execution style by close-range gunshots to the head. Coworkers reported Ochoa and Danziger to police as possible suspects in the slaying on November 10, after the pair toasted DePriest's memory at work. Detectives agreed such behavior was "odd" and picked the pair up for questioning on November 11.

Ochoa would later report that one of the arresting officers, Sgt. Hector Polanco, hurled chairs around the interview room while questioning Ochoa and threatened that "if he didn't confess they'd crush his head." Donna Angstadt, manager of the restaurant where the two suspects worked and Danziger's girlfriend at the time of his arrest, recalled her own interrogation by Polanco and Sgt. Bruce Boardman as "the most horrific, the most horrible experience I've ever been through in my life." According to Angstadt, the police-

men initially accused her of supplying the murder weapon, threatening to remove Angstadt's two young children from her custody. "Your boyfriend's holding [DePriest's] head," Polanco said at one juncture, "and you're the one who pulled the trigger for your little love interest." When that approach failed, the officers told Angstadt that "if Richard gets out, he's going to hunt me down and kill me like he did Nancy DePriest."

After three days of relentless grilling, all conducted without legal counsel, Ochoa confessed to the murder in an effort to save himself from execution. The catch: in order to earn his plea bargain and confirm a life sentence, Ochoa had to help the state convict Danziger. Legal maneuvers delayed Danziger's trial until 1990, the defendant protesting his innocence at every opportunity. Ochoa, meanwhile, told relatives he, too, was innocent, but that he feared death if he recanted his statement. "They made me confess," Ochoa insisted, "and how am I going to prove my innocence now? It's my word against theirs." At trial, Ochoa described the crime in terms that judge and jury alike found "very compelling," including details of the scene only the killers (or investigating officers) should logically have known. Ochoa's testimony persuaded jurors that he and Danziger had bound and gagged DePriest, then raped and sodomized her eight different times, including two assaults after she had been shot. Danziger was convicted and sentenced to 99 years' imprisonment, with his subsequent appeals rejected.

On February 27, 1991, Danziger was attacked in prison by another inmate, Armando Gutierrez, serving 18 years for assaulting a police officer. Gutierrez knocked Danziger to the ground and kicked him repeatedly in the head with steel-toed boots, inflicting permanent brain damage. Gutierrez received an additional 25-year sentence for the assault, while Danziger was confined to Skyview psychiatric prison, thereafter sporadically unable to identify close relatives or carry on coherent conversations.

A year after Danziger's assault, in 1992, Sgt. Polanco was dismissed from the Austin Police Department for lying under oath in another murder case. An arbitrator subsequently attributed Polanco's perjury to a "memory lapse," and he was reinstated with the department. Unsatisfied with merely getting his job back, Polanco sued the department and won a $350,000 jury award for wrongful termination. Investigation of Polanco's alleged official misconduct did not extend to the DePriest murder case, but new evidence soon cast doubt on the investigation.

In early 1996, while serving a life sentence for aggravated robbery and other crimes, Texas inmate Achim Josef Marino "found Jesus" and felt himself morally obligated to clear the books on other crimes he had committed. On February 5, 1996, Marino sent a six-page letter to the Austin *American-Statesman*, confessing that he alone was responsible for DePriest's murder. Local police began investigating Marino's confession in March 1996, but they had reached no conclusion by 1998, when Marino sent additional letters to the American Civil Liberties Union and Governor George Bush. Neither responded, and word of Marino's confession leaked to the public only in February 2000, after members of the REMINGTON CENTER INNOCENCE PROJECT took over Chris Ochoa's defense. Belated DNA test results confirmed that Marino was the sole rapist of Nancy DePriest, and Ochoa was released from prison on January 17, 2001. Danziger's release was delayed for another two months, while transfer to a managed care facility was arranged. Austin police reported that no action could be taken against the officers who secured Ochoa's false confession, since the statute of limitations had run out on their crimes.

ODONTOLOGY, Forensic crime scene dentistry

Forensic odontology is the application of dentistry and/or dental records to police work for the purpose of identifying unknown persons, living or deceased, who may be either criminals or victims of a crime. In dealing with deceased subjects, the same techniques are also used to identify remains in accidental deaths or cases where the cause of death may be unknown.

Identification via forensic odontology proceeds in different ways, depending on whether or not the procedure involves establishment of identity or determination of guilt. In the former circumstance, technicians normally compare known dental charts and X-rays with the teeth of a deceased subject whose identity is unknown. (The same methods could be used to identify living subjects, as in cases of amnesia or where a criminal suspect refuses to identify himself.) By matching the shape, size, and configuration of teeth, along with any injuries or distinctive dental work, identity may be established with a certainty equivalent to that of FINGERPRINTS or DNA testing. This technique is used hundreds of times each year in the United States, to identify mutilated victims of homicide, fires, explosions, airplane crashes, or natural disasters, and in cases where advanced decomposition rules out fingerprints or other common means of identification.

Forensic odontology may also be used to identify criminals, though in a rather different way than it is used on unknown corpses. In this application, a suspect's teeth are compared with bite marks left behind during commission of a crime. The bite marks may be found on human flesh (as from a fight or sexual assault) or on any other object that retains observable bite marks (as where a burglar stops to raid a victim's refrigerator and bites into a piece of cheese). In one midwestern case, a rape victim had the presence of mind to bite the rubber window molding of her attacker's car, while she was being assaulted in the front seat. The bite marks, as proof of her presence in the rapist's vehicle, supported the victim's story and sent her attacker to prison.

The most famous bite-mark case in history is that of cross-country serial killer Theodore Robert Bundy. A sexual sadist and necrophile, Bundy killed at least 30 girls and young women between January 1974 and February 1978. He claimed victims in at least four states, starting in Washington and ending his run in Florida, after a nocturnal rampage left two women dead and one gravely injured in a college sorority house. Bite marks on the buttocks of one lifeless victim were a critical piece of prosecu-

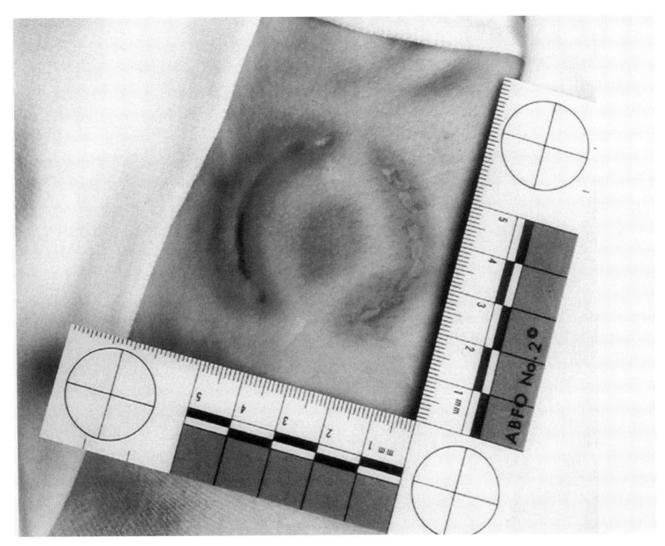

Forensic odontology can be used to identify a criminal, in which case a suspect's teeth are compared to bite marks left behind during commission of a crime. (Courtesy of C. Michael Bowers D.D.S., J.D.)

tion evidence, securing Bundy's first-degree murder conviction in July 1979. He was executed for his crimes on January 24, 1989, 11 years and nine days after inflicting the wounds that sent him to death row.

OHIO Innocence Project

The OHP is one of 30-odd innocent projects across the United States, based at the University of Cincinnati College of Law. Its stated goal is "to identify and assist those prison inmates who claim to be actually innocent of the crimes for which they were convicted." To that end, OIP members review and investigate claims from Ohio prison inmates, accept-

ing only those cases where newly discovered evidence supports a claim of innocence. As noted on the OIP's Web site, "The best type of new evidence is physical evidence (DNA evidence) that was not tested prior to the inmate's trial." Once a case is accepted, the OIP provides free investigative services and arranges legal representation on a pro bono basis. OIP participants include members of the Lois and Richard Rosenthal Institute for Justice (RIJ), founded at the University of Cincinnati College of Law following local race riots in April 2001. As stated on its Web site, the RIJ "seeks to harness the idealism, energy and intellect of law students and turn those qualities into a vehicle for positive social and legal change in Cincinnati, the state of Ohio, and beyond."

OLLINS, Calvin, et al. exonerated by DNA evidence
On the night of October 18, 1986, medical student Lori Roscetti was returning to her home on Chicago's West Side, after a late study session at Rush University, when several men forced their way into her car. Driven to a lonely railway access road, Roscetti was gang-raped and murdered, her body found the next morning. Police considered several suspects before settling on four black teenagers, including Marcellius Bradford, cousins Calvin and Larry Ollins, and Omar Saunders. Arrested some three months after the crime, the suspects were subjected to marathon grilling without legal counsel. After 24 hours of threats and alleged beatings, Bradford confessed to the crime, claiming the four ambushed Roscetti for bus fare back to Chicago's infamous Cabrini-Green housing project. Calvin Ollins, a 14-year-old described in court records as "mildly retarded," also confessed to the slaying, later claiming he was tricked by police who told him a confession would allow him to go free.

The defendants were tried separately. Bradford pleaded guilty to a reduced charge and received a 12-year prison term in return for his testimony against Larry Ollins. Three successive trials sent the other suspects to prison for life, under highly suspect circumstances. Two key prosecution witnesses later recanted in interviews with the *Chicago Tribune*, one claiming he lied under oath to secure a $35,000 reward for information in the case, another telling reporters he testified against the four defendants to divert suspicion from himself. Police crime scene analyst Pamela Fish testified that semen stains found on the victim's body and clothing were "consistent" with the defendants' blood types, but subsequent findings cast doubt on both her judgment and veracity.

The convictions and life prison terms were upheld on appeal. (Bradford served half of his 12-year sentence and was later sent back to prison on a BURGLARY conviction.) Saunders and the Ollins cousins languished in prison until 2001, when a series of articles in the *Chicago Tribune* began poking holes in the prosecution's case and new attorney Kathleen Zellner submitted various pieces of crime scene evidence to an independent DNA expert, Dr. Edward Blake, for testing that was unavailable in 1987. Dr. Blake's report, submitted in November 2001, excluded all of the four accused defendants as donors of the semen recovered from Lori Roscetti's corpse and underpants. At the same time, Dr. Blake examined Roscetti's coat and jogging pants, discovering 22 more semen stains on garments which, according to Pamela Fish's sworn testimony, bore no stains at all. Those 22 stains likewise excluded the four defendants as donors, the aggregate weight of the evidence prompting Dr. Blake to brand Fish's testimony "a scientific fraud." In December 2001, Cook County prosecutors dismissed all charges against the three defendants still in prison, and they were released after serving more than 14 years.

Assistant State's Attorney Celeste Stack assured the court and the public that the original Roscetti investigation was "done in good faith, based on the best evidence we had at the time," but attorney Zellner seemed closer to the truth when she told reporters, "I cannot overstate the official misconduct, the abuse of power, the activities that went on that I believe were criminal in nature." The Illinois statute of limitations prohibits any charges being filed against investigators or witnesses who may have committed perjury in 1987, and Pamela Fish—reassigned since 1987 to an administrative post at the Forensic Science Center in Chicago—declines to comment on the case. On January 18, 2002, Zellner filed litigation seeking compensation for her clients, blaming Fish and others for submitting false evidence that resulted in imprisonment of four innocent men. Lora Roscetti, meanwhile, was further traumatized by the new revelations in her daughter's case. "It's 15 years," she said. "How are they going to find them now?" Thus far, DNA comparison with 30 additional suspects has proved fruitless, and the case remains unsolved.

ORFILA, Mathieu Joseph Bonaventure (1787–1853)
Mathieu Orfila was born in Spain to French parents on April 24, 1787. Following his father's lead, he went to sea at age 15 but subsequently rejected a sailor's life to study medicine in Barcelona, Valencia, Madrid, and Paris. Upon completing his studies in 1811, Orfila became a private lecturer in CHEMISTRY, persisting in that trade until 1819, when he was named professor of medical jurisprudence in Paris. Four years later, he assumed duties as a professor of chemistry at the Parisian faculty of medicine, and Orfila was promoted to dean of that institution in 1830. Orfila's special field of interest was TOXICOLOGY, wherein he published volumes including *Traité*

des poisons ou toxicologie generale (1813), *Elements de chimie medicale* (1817), *Leons de médecine legale* (1823), *Traité des exhumations juridiques* (1830), and *Recherches sur l'empoisonnement par l'acide arsenieux* (1841). While arsenic was the main poison used by murderers in Orfila's day, his various works classified all known poisons and described contemporary methods for discovering the type and quantity of poisons present in corpses or living humans.

French king Louis-Philippe bestowed various honors on Mathieu Orfila, appointing him to serve on the council of education for France and the general council of the department of the Seine, while also naming Orfila a commander of the Legion of Honor. Those accolades failed to impress leaders of the Republic in 1848, and some observers contend that the indignities Orfila suffered under postmonarchist regimes hastened his end. He died in Paris following a short illness, on March 12, 1853.

ORGANIC Compound Analysis

Chemical compounds are deemed "organic" if their molecules include carbon bonded to hydrogen. The scientific study of organic compounds is *organic chemistry,* but since this vast array of compounds includes all carbohydrates, fats, and proteins, it also dominates the field of *biochemistry.* Organic compounds may be natural or synthetic, including many drugs. As an example, opium and its natural derivatives (codeine and morphine) are organic compounds, along with heroin (synthetically derived from opium). Many PRESUMPTIVE TESTS are used in forensic science to identify organic compounds, in addition to techniques including CHROMATOGRAPHY and SPECTROSCOPY. For a list of common organic compounds, see Appendix 2.

OSBORN, Albert Sherman (1858–1946)

Born in 1858, Albert S. Osborn was an American pioneer in the field of QUESTIONED DOCUMENTS. His textbook of the same title, initially published in 1910 and reprinted many times with additional material from the several sons who followed in his footsteps, is still widely regarded as a classic in the field. During the course of his career, Osborn designed a comparison microscope that was later manufactured by Bausch & Lomb. He also founded the American Society of Questioned Document Examiners on Sep-

tember 2, 1942, and served as its president until his death in 1946.

Without question, Osborn's most famous and most controversial case was the LINDBERGH KIDNAPPING of 1932, climaxed three years later with the trial and execution of defendant Bruno Hauptmann. After examining the ransom notes, Osborn noted certain consistent misspellings and inferred from phraseology that the author was probably German. Osborn prepared a paragraph of text for police to use when testing suspect handwriting, instructing detectives that the sample must be dictated aloud and not simply copied by sight (to compare the misspellings). Following Hauptmann's arrest, police delivered nine pages of dictated writings to Osborn's eldest son, Albert D. Osborn, for comparison with the Lindbergh ransom notes. While police initially claimed that Hauptmann tried to "disguise" his handwriting, independent researchers learned that he was instructed to write in various slants and styles with three different pens, while officers dictated misspellings of critical words (spelled correctly in other examples of Hauptmann's correspondence, written before his arrest). Even with that "help" from the police, Albert junior found no similarity between Hauptmann's handwriting and that of the ransom notes. When offered further samples, he told authorities that they would not change his opinion.

Both Alberts, father and son, resumed study of the ransom notes and Hauptmann samples on the day after Hauptmann's arrest. Two hours into their review, neither expert had found anything more than scattered, superficial similarities between the originals and Hauptmann's dictated writings. Then word arrived that police had found quantities of Lindbergh ransom money at Hauptmann's residence. Remarkably, an hour later, both Osborns positively identified Hauptmann as the author of the ransom notes. Both testified for the prosecution at trial and were instrumental in persuading jurors to convict Hauptmann of murder.

After the elder Osborn's death in 1946, his sons—Albert, Paul, and Russell—continued in the family trade as professional analysts of questioned documents. Their next world-famous case arrived in 1971, when they were retained to examine an alleged autobiography of reclusive billionaire Howard Hughes, sold to *Life* magazine by supposed middleman Clifford Irving. Paul and Russell Osborn scrutinized the document, comparing it with known samples written by Hughes, and told *Life*'s editors:

Both the specimen and questioned documents reveal great speed and fluency of writing. Yet the questioned documents accurately reflect in every detail the genuine forms and habit variations thereof which make up the basic handwriting identity of the author of the specimen documents. Moreover, in spite of the prodigious quantity of writing contained in the questioned documents, careful study has failed to reveal any features which raise the slightest question as to the common identity of all the specimens and questioned signatures and continuous writing. These basic factors . . . make it impossible . . . that anyone other than the writer of the specimens could have written the questioned signatures and continuous writing.

In fact, however, the Hughes "autobiography" was a FORGERY, as Irving admitted following his indictment for FRAUD. Historians who regard the Lindbergh trial as a FRAME-UP point to the results of Irving's case as proof that even the most respected experts sometimes make glaring (or tragic) mistakes.

OTOSCOPY

Otoscopy is the process of attempting to identify a person by the shape of his or her ears. While most often practiced by comparing an unknown subject's ears with photographs of a known individual (as where other facial features are destroyed or decomposed), otoscopy may also include study of "ear prints" (if, for instance, a person eavesdropped at a window with his ear against the glass). As with CHEILOSCOPY—the study of "lip prints"—American courts thus far have failed to recognize otoscopy as a unique and reliable means of personal identification.

P

PAINT

"Paint," when used as a noun, is the generic term for a wide range of products used to decorate and/or protect various surfaces by covering them with layers of pigmented coating. The three components of most paints are the *binder* (usually natural or synthetic resins such as acrylics, latex, melamines, oils, polyesters, or polyurethanes), the *diluent* (typically water and/or organic solvents such as alcohols, esters, glycol ethers, or ketones), and various *additives* (including but not limited to adhesion promoters, catalysts, dyes, emulsifiers, flatteners, stabilizers, texturizers, and thickeners). Following application, paint solidifies by cooling, curing, or evaporation, depending upon the binder employed. Paint may be applied in gaseous, liquid, or solid form. Gaseous paint is applied with a spraying device; liquid paints are applied with a variety of brushes, rollers, even human body parts (as in finger-paint); solid paint is applied as fine powder and baked at high temperatures (usually in automotive or industrial applications). Common variants include *enamel* (which dries to a hard, glossy finish); *lacquer* (a solvent-based paint that dries quickly with a durable finish); *varnish* or *shellac* (clear paints that provide protective coatings without adding color); and *wood stain* (a paint with low viscosity, designed to penetrate wood surfaces rather than coating them). A relatively new development for security purposes is *anti-climb paint,* which renders coated surfaces unusually slick to deter would-be intruders.

Study of paint has various applications to forensic science. Many paints were once manufactured with INORGANIC COMPOUNDS, principally lead and other metals, which have now been discontinued due to their toxicity. Still, many structures retain their old coatings of toxic paint (sometimes in defiance of prevailing safety statutes), and their identification may have bearing on legal cases where children or others are harmed by contact with outlawed substances. Paint chips or smears may also be important as TRACE EVIDENCE in various cases, including hit-and-run auto collisions or any instance where victims or offenders have contact with paint. One classic case in point was the series of murders committed by London's "Jack the Stripper" between 1959 and 1964. "Jack" strangled eight prostitutes, dumping their bodies in close proximity to the Thames River. Multicolored spray paint found on two of the corpses led police to theorize that they had been stored after death in an industrial paint shop. Detectives later claimed that the shop had been identified, but the killer was never publicly named, the case being "solved" instead with reports of an unnamed suspect's suicide.

PASSWORD "Sniffers" covert rip-off software

Password "sniffers" are computer programs that monitor and record the name and password of computer users as they log on, delivering the critical information to a hacker who has already penetrated the

209

system and put the sniffer to work. With passwords in hand, the intruder is free to roam at will through the violated system, downloading classified information, altering or deleting files, transferring funds in the case of financial institutions, or impersonating rightful system users in a variety of other ways. As the case of KEVIN MITNICK amply illustrated, data may not only be removed, but also added and concealed without the knowledge of a system's normal user. A report in the *Wall Street Journal* suggested that hackers may have sniffed out passwords used by members of America Online, an Internet service with more than 35 million subscribers.

Another hazard for legitimate users whose passwords are stolen lies in the possibility that they may be held responsible, either inadvertently or through a deliberate FRAME-UP, for the unlawful actions of a hacker who has hijacked their accounts. One possible scenario might involve theft of credit card numbers, stored in a hacked account without the legitimate user's knowledge, later traced by law enforcement officers who come calling with search warrants. In similar fashion, many other forms of cyber-contraband, from stolen files to CHILD PORNOGRAPHY, may be loaded into an innocent user's computer, either for the hacker's momentary convenience or as a deliberate form of harassment.

Passwords are "sniffed" when users log onto their local area networks (LANs) and their computers are briefly vulnerable to every other computer using the same network. While the login process cannot be avoided and present PC technology sounds no alert when a password is monitored, analysts recommend frequent changes in passwords to limit the time when a stolen code may be used to the thief's advantage.

PATHOLOGY, Forensic

Pathology—from the Greek *pathos* (pain, feeling) and *logos* (study)—is the study of processes underlying abnormality, disease, dysfunction, and/or death. In biological terms, it involves the study of functional and structural changes that damage cells, tissues, and organs. A *pathologist* is a medical doctor specializing in diagnosis of disease. *Anatomical pathology* involves diagnosis based on examination of cells and tissues, while *clinical pathology* involves study of bodily fluids (blood, semen, urine, etc.). *Forensic pathology* concerns itself with determining cause of death, examining injuries or WOUNDS, and

studying fluids or tissues that are relevant to criminal cases.

Regardless of their specialty, pathologists rarely meet living patients, working instead from specimens (obtained via *biopsy* from patients still living) or via *autopsy*—a postmortem examination (or *obduction*) of a corpse, its name derived from the Greek, "to see for oneself." Postmortem examinations performed on animals are called *necropsies* (from the Greek, "seeing a dead body"). Autopsies may be either *clinical* (normally performed in hospitals or medical schools for research purposes) or *forensic* (related to a legal matter, whether criminal or civil). The primary goal of a forensic autopsy is to determine cause of death. American law recognizes five categories of human death, including: natural (from disease or old age), accidental (sometimes called "death by misadventure," including fatal attacks by animals), HOMICIDE (death inflicted by another human being), suicide (self-inflicted), and undetermined (where no cause is apparent).

A normal autopsy begins with delivery of the corpse to a hospital or MEDICAL EXAMINER's office. An *external* examination is performed, including collection of any TRACE EVIDENCE found on the clothing or body, which is disrobed in the process. X-rays may be taken at this stage, depending on the nature of the injuries observed (gunshot wounds, apparent fractures, etc.) or if examiners suspect that foreign objects may be found inside the corpse (as where drugs or other items have been swallowed to conceal them). Following a thorough external survey, the body is washed, weighed, and measured. Blood may be extracted at this point, for TOXICOLOGY testing. The *internal* examination comes next, normally beginning with a large "Y" incision that opens the thorax and abdomen. Internal organs are removed, weighed, and examined individually for damage or disease. Tissue samples may be excised for subsequent testing, and wound channels (if any) are measured to determine the angle of gunshots or the size and shape of stabbing WEAPONS. Frequently, the skull is also opened and the brain removed for study.

Following completion of an autopsy, the corpse is *reconstituted* insofar as may be possible, for viewing by mourners prior to burial or cremation. Some medical examiners replace organs within the body (unless they have been preserved as evidence), while others leave morticians to insert artificial padding material. Clothing covers the primary "Y" incision, while the severed skull "cap" is replaced and covered with the corpse's scalp stitched back in place. Some religions forbid or discourage autopsies, but their tenets have no authority where prevailing statutes require postmortem examination to resolve the cause of death.

PATRICK, Jesse Joe controversial DNA case

On July 8, 1989, a prowler invaded the home of 80-year-old Nina Rutherford Redd in Pleasant Grove, Texas. The intruder beat and raped Redd, then slashed her throat with a rusty butcher knife. Police found the knife at the scene, as well as a bathroom screen that had been pried loose from outside. Early that same morning Jesse Patrick had called police to report a BURGLARY at his house, two doors away from Redd's home. Responding officers found no one home but noted the back door kicked in, and a large bloody rock lying nearby. A search of Patrick's home revealed a sock and wadded toilet tissues stained with Redd's blood, plus a pair of men's jeans bearing "suspicious stains." Patrick's live-in girlfriend subsequently identified the murder weapon as Patrick's knife, and DNA tests linked Patrick to three hairs found at the crime scene. Police arrested Patrick at a relative's home in Mississippi, on July 22, 1989. Jurors convicted Patrick of capital murder, and he was condemned on April 16, 1990. Various state and federal appellate courts rejected Patrick's appeals during 1995–2002.

With his execution scheduled for September 17, 2002, Patrick made a last-ditch effort to save himself via DNA testing. While previous analysis of blood evidence already linked him to the victim and the crime scene, Patrick petitioned for genetic testing of the semen recovered from Redd's corpse (but never tested) in 1998. The trial court ruled that Patrick was not entitled to further scientific tests under Texas law because there was no reasonable probability that favorable DNA results would have led to an acquittal. The same judge granted Patrick permission to pursue the tests at his own expense, but prosecutors appealed that judgment to the Texas Court of Criminal Appeals. That court, in turn, ruled on September 11, 2002, that Patrick was not legally entitled to new DNA tests regardless of who paid the bill. While opponents of the death penalty condemned that "egregious" ruling, Patrick's time ran out, and he was executed by lethal injection as scheduled, on September 17.

PATTERSON, James Earl first "cold hit" on DNA evidence

A Virginia native, born January 31, 1967, James Earl Patterson was approaching his 20th birthday on January 11, 1987, when a night of "partying" on drugs and liquor turned to brutal murder. Running short of money for cocaine, Patterson decided to burglarize the home of a recent acquaintance in Prince Georges County, 56-year-old Joyce Snead Aldridge. Shortly before midnight, Patterson broke into Aldridge's home, confronting the woman with a demand for cash. Enraged when he learned that she had only a handful of coins in her purse, Patterson raped Aldridge, then stabbed her three times with one of her own kitchen knives and left her for dead. Aldridge had strength enough to call police, and she was attempting to dial her son's home number when Patterson returned, stabbing her 14 more times and leaving her dead on the floor. The crime was still unsolved a year later, when Patterson raped an 18-year-old woman he met at a party. Convicted on that charge, he was sentenced to 25 years in prison, eligible for parole in the year 2005.

Incarceration changed Patterson's life, according to later reports. He "found Jesus" in the Big House and was "born again," but repentance somehow stopped short of confessing his undisclosed crimes. A born-again reader as well as a religious convert, Patterson studied the modern advances in DNA testing, harboring fears that it might prove to be his undoing. As he later told reporters, "It always played out in the back of my mind that [the evidence] could be put together . . . that it could come back to haunt me." His own DNA had been added to Virginia's ever-growing databank in 1990, following the rape conviction, but despite his newfound religious zeal—"The crimes really tear at my heart. My prayers constantly go out to the family members of the victims."—Patterson still made no effort to wipe the slate clean. In March 1999, Prince Georges County investigators scored a first-ever "cold hit" in the Aldridge case, comparing a genetic profile of her unknown killer to samples in the state database, and they went to visit Patterson in prison. "When I saw the badges come out, it literally took my breath away," he told the press. "The day of judgment had met me."

And still he lied to authorities, denying any role in Aldridge's murder. Only when confronted with irrefutable scientific proof of guilt did Patterson change his tune and confess to the crime. In June 2000,

Patterson pleaded guilty to murder, rape, forcible sodomy, and abduction with intent to defile, asking Judge James D'Alton Jr. to impose the ultimate penalty. "As I look around this courtroom, I see lives that I've wrecked," Patterson told the court. "Saying I'm sorry to these people is a hollow statement. These families were touched by me because, in some instances, they befriended me. In befriending me, it turned into their worst nightmare. . . . Your honor, I've thought about the death sentence, and I beg you to give me the death sentence. I pray today that it will be some type of closure for these families. I'm deeply sorry. . . . I just pray the Lord touches their lives and take away the pain I brought upon them." Judge D'Alton granted the request, based on the vile nature of Patterson's crime and his potential for future mayhem.

While passing his final months on death row, rejecting all appeals of his sentence, Patterson waxed philosophical on the marvels of DNA testing. "I applaud the science," he told one interviewer. "It's become a good thing. It has condemned people who needed to be condemned and released people who needed to be released." As for himself, Patterson insisted, "I feel at peace with my decision. It's either going slow or dying quickly. I'm ready to go. I could be running my head against the wall, bawling my eyes out, but it's not that way. I'm getting ready for the big transformation." That transformation came at 9:10 P.M. on March 14, 2002. Before his execution by lethal injection, Patterson told the small audience of court-appointed witnesses, "My heart goes out to the Aldridge family. God bless each and every one of you who is here tonight."

Virginia has been a persistent leader in the use of DNA science to solve criminal cases. The state's 1994 execution of serial killer TIMOTHY SPENCER was the first of a U.S. defendant convicted on the basis of genetic evidence. Statewide, a database of DNA material collected from some 180,000 convicted felons enabled Virginia police to score 300 "cold hits" in 2001, with another 92 between January 1, 2002 and the date of Patterson's execution. In the wake of that event, Virginia's state legislature passed a new law permitting collection of DNA samples from persons awaiting trial for violent crimes, rather than waiting for the outcome of their trials.

PEPPER, Augustus Joseph (1849–1935)

A British subject, born in April 1849, Augustus Pepper studied medicine at London's University College Hospital and subsequently found employment at St. Mary's Hospital, where he teamed with WILLIAM WILLCOX and Bernard Spillsbury in the concentrated study of PATHOLOGY. Together, the three forensic practitioners gained a solid reputation with Scotland Yard, but their names remained unknown to the public at large until they became embroiled in the case of Dr. Hawley Harvey Crippen.

An American physician, born in 1862, Crippen was married to a former theatrical singer named Cora who preferred her stage name of "Belle Elmore." The couple met and married in New York, then moved to England in the early 1900s where Cora's nagging, heavy drinking, and expensive tastes soon soured the relationship. Dr. Crippen took comfort from his 28-year-old secretary, Ethel Clara Le Nerve, which in turn prompted Cora to threaten a costly divorce. In February 1910, Crippen poisoned Cora, then shot her for good measure, dismembered her corpse, and buried its parts in the cellar of their home. Ethel moved in the following month, Crippen telling friends that Cora had deserted him. Crippen subsequently announced that Cora had fallen ill in the United States, followed shortly by news of her death in a small town near San Francisco. Suspicious friends of Cora's sounded the alarm at Scotland Yard, and Crippen changed his story under official questioning. Cora was alive, he now declared, and living with her lover—a boxer named Bruce Miller—in Chicago. The truth was so embarrassing, said Crippen, that he had manufactured the tale of her death to save face. A search of Crippen's home revealed no evidence of foul play, and police went away satisfied.

When officers returned a short time later, to clear up some minor details of the case, they found Crippen's house abandoned. A second search then revealed Cora Crippen's remains, whereupon arrest warrants were issued for Dr. Crippen and Ethel Le Nerve. While gross mutilation of Cora's remains left even the victim's gender in doubt, Pepper, Willcox, and Spilsbury pinned their hopes on microscopic examination of a small piece of skin from Cora's abdomen, retaining pubic hairs and microscopic fragments of the abdominal muscles. Police traced Crippen and his mistress aboard the Canadian Pacific steamer *Montrose,* where they posed as father and son while sailing from Antwerp to Canada. Detectives traveling aboard a faster ocean liner beat Crippen and Le Nerve to Canada, arresting both for extradition to London. Scientific testimony from Pepper and his colleagues prompted jurors to convict Crippen of murder, followed by his execution on November 28, 1910. Ethel Le Nerve was acquitted of all charges and released. Augustus Pepper died at Sidcup, England, in 1935.

PERSONAL Tracking Units individual surveillance devices

Personal tracking units (PTUs) are electronic devices used to monitor the whereabouts and movements of specific individuals, most commonly criminal defendants who have been sentenced to a term of house arrest as an alternative to prison. PTUs are worn by the surveillance subjects, typically on a locked ankle strap that emits a silent alarm if the device is removed or damaged in some way. The cheaper, more common type of PTU operates with a "tamper-proof" base set installed in the subject's home, sounding an alarm (to the police, the subject's probation officer, etc.) if the subject moves outside an established perimeter (generally one's home or the adjacent property). A more advanced (and more expensive) form of PTU incorporates global positioning satellite (GPS) technology to chart the subject's actual movements with near-pinpoint accuracy. The latter devices, in various forms, may also be used for covert surveillance of individuals or specific vehicles, if they can be attached without the subject's or driver's knowledge.

PHARMACOLOGY, Forensic

Pharmacology is the study of drugs and their effects on living organisms. Subdisciplines include *pharmacodynamics* (the study of how drugs and their metabolites affect organisms) and *pharmacokinetics* (the study of how drugs move through the body). Forensic pharmacology overlaps the disciplines of PATHOLOGY and TOXICOLOGY, seeking answers to such questions as: What drugs were taken? What quantity of each drug was ingested? When were the drugs ingested? And what effects (if any) did the drugs produce? Pharmacokinetic studies demonstrate that various drugs are absorbed and eliminated at different rates, with their known half-lives permitting estimates of original dosage and approximate time of ingestion. Some drugs metabolize into different drugs—as with heroin, internally converted to morphine—which thus extend half-lives and slow the process of absorption/elimination.

PHONETICS, Forensic

Phonetics is a subdiscipline of LINGUISTICS, involving the study of various sounds that constitute human speech. Its forensic application generally focuses on the analysis of recorded comments—threats, obscenities, etc.—from some unknown person in an effort to identify the speaker. Regional accents, pitch, tone, speed of talking, and various other factors contribute to the isolation of a likely suspect. Sound spectrographs are often used to compare and match "voiceprints" in various cases, but while those results may satisfy forensic linguists (or solve sundry fictional crimes), the results are not generally admissible as evidence in American courts.

PHOTOGRAPHY, Forensic

Initially developed in the 19th century, photography—literally "light writing" in Greek—has multiple applications in the field of forensic science. As used today, the term generally includes use of any camera (still, motion picture, video, or digital) to produce accurate visual records of persons, objects, places, or events. Photography is an essential part of modern crime scene documentation, recording the placement of bodies and other critical objects without the confusion that may spring from sketches or notes. Items of TRACE EVIDENCE are normally photographed in situ, commonly with rulers or other objects included to indicate size, distance from a corpse, and other pertinent spatial relationships. Infrared photography is often used with QUESTIONED DOCUMENTS to study inks, reveal indented writing or other impressions, and to reveal writing that the naked eye cannot observe (invisible inks, erasures, writing on charred paper, etc.). At the crime lab, *photomicrography* involves taking pictures through various microscopes, thus preserving visual records of evidence including blood and other body fluids, DNA test results, ballistics markings on bullets, and countless other examples. Digitized photos permit comparison of specific evidentiary items with vast databases such as AUTOMATED FINGERPRINT IDENTIFICATION SYSTEM (AFIS), COMBINED DNA INDEX SYSTEM (CODIS), and INTEGRATED BALLISTICS IDENTIFICATION SYSTEM (IBIS). The X-rays produced during autopsies represent another aspect of forensic photography, as does the use of various cameras and BIOMETRIC devices in security and surveillance applications. Finally, photos constitute a vital part of the

Grant Lee of the Montgomery County Police Department Forensic Services photographs part of the crime scene outside a Maryland Target store where four teenagers were stabbed. (Hans Ericsson/AP)

criminal records system, although they are no longer used to calculate bodily measurements as in the days of ALPHONSE BERTILLON.

Unfortunately, photographs may also be fabricated or manipulated to portray events that never occurred. The modern high-tech age provides numerous tools for the potential hoaxer, such as Photoshop software and others. With those relatively simple programs, one may appear in photos of Paris without leaving one's Brooklyn apartment, transplant a celebrity's face onto one's own body, and perform myriad other tricks for whatever motive. Many "famous" photos on the Internet have been revealed as hoaxes, including a dramatic snapshot of a huge shark leaping toward a helicopter and a scene supposedly shot on the roof of New York's World Trade Center on September 11, 2001, depicting a clueless tourist smiling for the camera while one of al-Qaeda's hijacked airliners approaches from behind him.

Trick photography, with or without digital technology, has played a central role in certain alleged FRAME-UPS throughout recent history. Easily the most famous case of modern times is that of President John Kennedy's assassination on November 22, 1963. Amateur photographer Abraham Zapruder captured the fatal shots on film, revealing in graphic frames the death shot that shattered JFK's skull. Curiously, when selected frames were published in the 1964 *Warren Report*, they were printed out of order in a way that seemed to alter the movement of Kennedy's body on impact—and thus, said conspiracists, obscure the presence of an unknown sniper on the infamous "grassy knoll." Another photo from the same case depicts alleged assassin Lee Harvey Oswald posing with a rifle and a communist newspaper in his backyard. Some analysts note discrepancies between the shadows on Oswald's face and those cast by his body, suggesting that a picture of the suspect's head was superimposed on an impostor's body to cast Oswald as a gun-happy subversive. Other photos—snapped by the CIA in September 1963, depicting a still-unknown man who used Oswald's name at the Russian embassy in Mexico City—remain unexplained today.

PHYSICAL Evidence

The vast realm of physical evidence—distinguished from the *testimonial evidence* offered by witnesses to some event—includes any substantial object, regardless of size, that may be tested, weighed, or measured, and presented in a court of law. Whether collected at a crime scene or during an autopsy performed by a MEDICAL EXAMINER, physical evidence must be subject to observation and quantification. It may be observed and preserved by a staggering variety of methods, including (but not limited to) CHROMATOGRAPHY, ELECTROPHORESIS, MICROSCOPY, NEUTRON ACTIVATION ANALYSIS, PHOTOGRAPHY, RADIOLOGY, SEISMOLOGY, SPECTROSCOPY, or various SURVEILLANCE DEVICES. The items collected may include human remains or parts thereof, vehicles, WEAPONS,

IMPRESSION EVIDENCE, QUESTIONED DOCUMENTS, and any manner of TRACE EVIDENCE conceivable, from BLOODSTAINS or FINGERPRINTS to FIBERS and hairs, flecks of PAINT, shards of GLASS, or the KNOTS used to bind a victim. Much evidence that was useless or unknown to investigators through the first half of the 20th century—including DNA—now speaks volumes to skilled technicians. In each case, however, courts must rule on the ADMISSIBILITY OF EVIDENCE, an aspect determined in equal parts by its perceived relevance to the case at hand and the manner of collection—including proper search warrants, where required, and maintenance of a verified chain of custody to forestall allegations of contamination, loss, or a deliberate FRAME-UP. Even the most conclusive evidence may fail to win convictions when, as in the ORENTHAL JAMES (O. J.) SIMPSON case, jurors either fail to grasp its import or chart a deliberate course of "jury nullification" against the prosecution. Evidence discovered after a case has been adjudicated may or may not be considered by the courts. Acquittal terminates prosecution of defendants for specific crimes, under the U.S. Constitution's ban on *double jeopardy,* but even wrongfully convicted inmates may not benefit from new evidence, if statutory deadlines for appeals have elapsed in their respective states.

PIERCE, Jeffrey Todd exonerated by DNA evidence

At noon on May 8, 1985, a female Oklahoma City resident returned home from work to find a window of her apartment broken, the flat ransacked. While she was examining the damage, a knife-wielding stranger emerged from another room, overpowered the woman, and raped her. In her statement to police, the victim speculated that her attacker may have been the same man she briefly observed while leaving for work that morning. On that occasion, the unidentified man had been standing in some nearby shrubbery, holding what appeared to be a garden tool.

Police initially suspected that the rapist might be a groundskeeper employed by the apartment complex, one of whom was 23-year-old Jeffrey Pierce. On the day of the rape, however, a patrol officer pointed Pierce out to the victim and asked her if he was the assailant, whereupon she answered, "I don't think so." Another 10 months passed before Pierce was arrested and charged with the crime, in March 1986, after the victim changed her mind. At trial, in October 1986, the victim who initially dismissed Pierce as a suspect told the jury, "I will never forget his face." Pierce countered with two alibi witnesses who said he was eating lunch with them at the time of the rape. Jurors were finally swayed by testimony from police chemist JOYCE GILCHRIST, who declared that 28 scalp hairs and three pubic hairs recovered from the crime scene were "microscopically consistent" with Pierce's hair. (See FIBER AND HAIR EVIDENCE.) Prosecutor Barry Albert told the court that the odds of Gilchrist being mistaken were "totally astronomical." Upon conviction, Pierce received a 65-year prison term.

On appeal, Pierce's attorney noted that Gilchrist had ignored a court order to provide suspect hair samples for independent testing. The Oklahoma Appeals Court agreed that her conduct was illegal but refused to order a new trial, stating that the defense had an "equal obligation" to enforce the judge's order (although what means they might have used was not explained). Gilchrist's mishandling and falsification of evidence was eventually exposed, an FBI lab report noting that she "went beyond the acceptable limits of forensic science or misidentified hair and fibers in at least six criminal cases," including that of Jeffrey Pierce.

As that scandal unfolded in May 2001, the Oklahoma State Bureau of Investigation announced the results of DNA testing on hairs from the 1985 crime scene. Those tests exonerated Pierce, and three months later identified the actual rapist as a prison inmate already serving 45 years for another sexual assault. Because the statute of limitations had expired, no further charges could be filed against the guilty party. Upon hearing the announcement, original trial juror Roy Orr told reporters, "I feel like I was part of a scam. The evidence wasn't correct, and we counted on the police department and forensic specialists to be honest and truthful, and that wasn't the case." Joyce Gilchrist, promoted to an administrative post in 1993 and placed on leave of absence when the scandal broke, told the television program *60 Minutes II,* "I've never lied in court. I've always told the truth. I've never lied to anyone about anything. If you don't want to know the truth, don't ask me because I'm not going to sugarcoat anything for you. I'm going to tell it to you. . . . I'll tell it to you just the way it is."

Legislation to financially compensate wrongfully imprisoned inmates was introduced in the Oklahoma State Senate on May 9, 2001, two days after Pierce was freed from prison. Despite initial optimism, the bill was defeated 11 days later. Rather than settle for the state's apology, Pierce's attorneys filed a $75 million federal lawsuit on April 1, 2002, against Joyce Gilchrist, former District Attorney Bob Macy, and the Oklahoma City Police Department, charging the defendants with false imprisonment and violation of Pierce's civil rights. The lawsuit remains unresolved at this writing.

PISZCZEK, Brian   exonerated by DNA evidence

In the early morning hours of July 29, 1990, a female resident of Cleveland, Ohio, was drawn to her apartment door by unexpected knocking. Looking through the security peephole, she saw a stranger standing on her doorstep. When she asked the man to identify himself, he gave the name of a mutual friend, and claimed that friend was parking his car outside. The woman later told police she thought the man's voice was familiar, believing him to be an acquaintance named Tom or Tim, who had visited her home once before. She opened the door to admit him, whereupon the stranger drew a knife, slashing the victim's neck, breast, and stomach before he raped her on the floor.

Two months after the attack, the victim identified suspect Brian Piszczek from a police photo lineup, and later repeated that identification in court. Piszczek acknowledged visiting the woman's home on one prior occasion, with the same mutual friend whose name was mentioned by the rapist in July 1990. Piszczek's alibi, in turn, was corroborated only by his girlfriend, whom jurors found unconvincing. On June 25, 1991, Piszczek was convicted of rape, felonious assault, and BURGLARY, receiving a sentence of 15 to 25 years in prison.

On appeal, with a new attorney from the public defender's office, Piszczek challenged the police photo identification process and complained of ineffective trial counsel, noting that his first attorney had not requested DNA testing of semen recovered from the crime scene. That appeal was rejected, prompting attorneys from the CARDOZO INNOCENCE PROJECT to take Piszczek's case. The new team filed a release-of-evidence motion with the Cuyahoga County Court of Common Pleas, which was granted on March 11, 1994. Test results delivered on July 6, 1994, excluded Piszczek as a donor of the semen found at the crime scene, and one day later the prosecutor's office asked a judge to overturn Piszczek's conviction. Even then, Piszczek remained in custody for another three months, until a judge declared him innocent and ordered his release on October 6, 1994. The case remains officially unsolved today.

PITCHFORK, Colin first killer convicted by DNA evidence

On November 22, 1983, 15-year-old Lynda Mann was raped and strangled in the English village of Enderby, Leicestershire. Police were still hunting for suspects on July 31, 1986, when 15-year-old Dawn Ashworth was killed in identical fashion, in neighboring Narborough. Convinced that a local man was responsible for both crimes, authorities requested blood samples from all area males between the ages of 16 and 34, for purposes of comparing their DNA "fingerprints" with semen samples recovered from the victims. By July 1987, 3,556 individuals had been cleared of involvement in the crimes, including a 17-year-old Narborough youth already booked on suspicion of committing the Ashworth homicide.

Of 4,196 men in the area, only two refused to submit blood samples when asked. One provided authorities with an undisclosed "legitimate excuse" for refusing, while the other—Colin Pitchfork, a 27-year-old bakery worker from Littlethorpe—seemed curiously evasive. Pitchfork had skipped three appointments with police in January 1987, then finally paid coworker Ian Kelly £200 to donate blood in his name. Kelly complied and Pitchfork was "cleared," until Kelly had a change of heart and informed police of the ruse in August 1987. Pitchfork was thereafter arrested, and detectives got their blood sample, which positively linked Pitchfork to both murders. (The helpful coworker was charged with conspiracy to pervert the course of justice, convicted, and sentenced to 18 months in prison.)

A review of Pitchfork's police record turned up prior convictions for indecent exposure, and Pitchfork confessed to the slayings when confronted with scientific proof of his guilt. At the same time, he was also positively linked to the rapes of two more women who survived his attacks. On January 22, 1988, he pleaded guilty on two counts of murder and two counts of indecent assault, receiving a double life sentence on the murder charges and two concurrent 10-year sentences for the attacks on surviving victims.

PRATT, Juneal controversial DNA case

In 1975, a black intruder raped and robbed two white sisters in their room at an Omaha, Nebraska, motel. The victims subsequently picked Juneal Pratt from a police lineup and jurors convicted him on the basis of their courtroom testimony. Pratt, still protesting his innocence, received a prison term of 32 to 90 years for multiple counts of rape, sexual assault, and ROBBERY. Three decades later, members of the CARDOZO INNOCENCE PROJECT petitioned for DNA testing of semen samples recovered from the Omaha victims in 1975. Such testing did not exist at the time of Pratt's trial, but it is now considered nearly foolproof in resolving such cases. Eyewitness testimony, by contrast, was responsible for the wrongful conviction of some 125 inmates exonerated by DNA evidence since the mid-1990s. At press time for this work, Douglas County District Judge Richard Spethman had not issued a ruling on Pratt's motion for DNA testing, but his defenders remain hopeful that the new technology will succeed in liberating him from prison.

PRESUMPTIVE Tests

In forensic science, presumptive tests are preliminary examinations performed on unknown substances, generally at a crime scene, to determine the presence of various substances including blood, drugs, EXPLOSIVES, gunshot residue, or semen. Such tests normally involve application of some chemical that produces a marked color change if the sought-after substance is present. (Other common terms include *color tests, screening tests* and *spot tests.*) Presumptive tests are not conclusive, and require more detailed laboratory follow-up procedures (called *specific tests*) to confirm their preliminary findings. Common presumptive tests used by forensic scientists include the following:

Benzidene: A presumptive test for blood involves application of benzidene to suspect stains. If blood is present, a chemical reaction with hemoglobin turns the clear liquid blue. This method has fallen out of favor with most criminalists since benzidene's carcinogenic properties were identified.
Cobalt thiocyanate: This chemical reagent is used in a presumptive tests for cocaine. After being dissolved in distilled water (sometimes with

other additives), the reagent is poured over unidentified powder. If cocaine is present, the mixture should produce a blue precipitate.

Crystal (or microcrystal) tests: Variously used to identify blood, certain drugs, and explosives, crystal tests involve placing suspect samples on a microscope slide, to which specific chemical reagents are then added. Microscopic examination of the resultant crystals may identify the substance present in the sample.

Dermal nitrate (paraffin) test: This presumptive test for gunshot residue, abandoned due to the high number of false positive results obtained, involved painting a suspect's hands with hot wax, then treating the resultant cast with a mixture of diphenylamine and sulfuric acid, whereupon the nitrates found in gunpowder turn blue. The test proved unreliable because nitrates are also found in many other common substances, including (but not limited to) cosmetics, fertilizers, tobacco, and urine.

Dillie-Koppanyi test: A presumptive test for barbiturates, this two-phase procedure includes application of a methanol-cobalt acetate solution to suspect powders, followed by addition of a methanol-isopropylamine solution. If barbiturates are present, the sample should present a reddish-purple hue.

Diphenylamine test: This presumptive test for gunshot residue involves treating the suspect residue with a solution of diphenylamine in sulfuric acid. Any nitrates present in the sample should produce a blue color, but their common occurrence in various everyday items raises the same objections previously posed against dermal nitrate testing.

Duquenois-Levine test: A presumptive test for hashish or marijuana, this procedure uses three chemical reagents to identify tetrahydrocannabinol (THC), the active substance found in both plants. The reagents used include chloroform, concentrated hydrochloric acid, and an ethanol solution containing 1 percent acetaldehyde and 2 percent vanillin. When mixed with the suspect plant matter in a test tube, THC is indicated by a purple shade in the separate chloroform layer.

Ehrlich's test: Used to detect LSD and related ergot alkaloids with hallucinogenic properties, this test involves combination of the suspect sample with *p*-dimethylaminobenzaldehye in a solution of hydrochloric and sulfuric acid. Positive results are indicated by appearance of a blue-violet color.

Fehling's solution: This solution of copper sulfate, potassium tartrate, and sodium hydroxide is normally blue in color but turns red when exposed to simple sugars such as glucose and fructose (often used as cutting agents in drugs). It is frequently used to check for drug traces in urine but may return false positive results in many cases.

Ferric chloride: Another presumptive test for drugs, this one involves a 10-percent solution of ferric chloride in water, which turns green when exposed to morphine.

Fluorescein: This reagent causes BLOODSTAINS normally invisible to the naked eye to fluoresce when exposed to ultraviolet light.

Froehde's reagent: This versatile solution of molybdic acid and sulfuric acid serves forensic science in presumptive tests for three different drugs. Heroin causes the reagent to turn olive green or purple, while LSD produces a blue-green color and mescaline turns the solution yellowish green.

Griess test: This presumptive test for the nitrates and nitrites found in explosives and gunshot residue uses a solution of acetic acid, napthylamine and sulfanilic acid. Mixture of gunpowder with the solution produces a red dye whose brightness roughly indicates the quantity of nitrates or nitrites present.

Guaiacum test: One of the first presumptive tests for blood, now obsolete, this method employed a solution of guaiacum resin extracted from trees (family Zygophyllaceae) and hydrogen peroxide, which turns bloodstains blue.

Jaffe test: Yet another presumptive test for drugs, this procedure uses picric acid to produce a red hue when reacting with creatinine in human urine.

Kastel Meyer (KM) test: This uses phenolphthalin and hydrogen peroxide to test suspected bloodstains. Hemoglobin turns pink when treated with the solution, but the test is not specific and may yield false positive results with other substances (including horseradish, leather, and various plant extracts).

Leucomalachite green: Another presumptive test for blood, less frequently used than the Kastel

Meyer test or luminol, this procedure employs a solution of leucomalachite green, glacial acetic acid, methyl alcohol, sodium perborate, and Vertrel XF. The proteins found in blood turn green when treated with the reagent.

Luminol: Luminol is a chemical reagent containing sodium carbonate, sodium perborate, and 3-aminophthalhydrazide, which causes bloodstains to fluoresce when exposed to ultraviolet light. While it cannot be used in sunlit areas, it remains the most popular presumptive test for blood among modern criminalists, favored because it can be sprayed over large areas, it does not cause samples to change color, and it does not interfere with subsequent DNA testing.

Mandelin test: This versatile presumptive test for drugs requires a solution of ammonia vetavanadate and sulfuric acid. Depending on the drug encountered, it produces different colors: brown for heroin, bluish green for amphetamines, olive green for codeine, and orange for cocaine. As with similar procedures, the Mandelin test is not specific.

Marquis test: As with the Mandelin test, this presumptive test for drugs produces various colors for different CONTROLLED SUBSTANCES, employing a 40-percent solution of formaldehyde in sulfuric acid. Amphetamines and methamphetamine produce an orange color; LSD turns the solution black; mescaline produces a reddish orange hue; methadone turns the liquid pinkish yellow; while the alkaloids found in various opiates and opium derivatives produce a purple color.

Mecke's test: Yet another presumptive test for drugs, Mecke's procedure uses a solution of selenious acid and sulfuric acid to test for heroin (a yellow color, fading into green), LSD (olive green, turning black), and psilocybin (yellow-green, turning brown). Specific tests are required to confirm the presence of drugs in any suspect sample.

Nessler's reagent: Also called Channing's solution, this solution of mercuric potassium iodide is used to detect traces of ammonia (commonly found in urine). Small traces of ammonia cause the solution to turn yellow, while higher concentrations may produce a brown precipitate. Extreme care is required when handling Nessler's reagent, since it is corrosive (causing burns) and toxic if swallowed, inhaled, or absorbed through the skin. The solution is also carcinogenic, presents a neurological hazard, and may cause sterility in humans.

Nitric acid: When used as a presumptive test for drugs, nitric acid reacts with heroin (producing a yellow color, fading to green) and with morphine (red changing to yellow).

Orthotolidine (Tolidine) test: This presumptive test for blood employs orthotolidine and hydrogen peroxide, which cause hemoglobin to turn bluish green. Unfortunately, the reagent also produces false positives when applied to the same substances that frustrate users of the Kastel Meyer test (see above).

Reinsch test: This presumptive test is used to detect heavy metals—antimony, arsenic, bismuth, mercury, selenium, or thalium—in human bodily fluids or tissue. To perform the test, dissolve the fluid or tissue sample in a hydrochloric acid solution, then insert a clean copper strip into the solution. Mercury produces a silvery coating on the copper, while other heavy metals produce a dark gray coating. Findings are then confirmed by means of absorption or emission SPECTROSCOPY, X-ray diffraction, or other methods suitable for analysis of INORGANIC COMPOUNDS.

Ruybal test: A more complicated variation on the cobalt thiocyanate test (see above), this procedure also identifies cocaine. It involves three separate solutions: cobalt thiocyanate and glycerin in distilled water, a hydrochloric acid solution, and chloroform. As in the previous test, application of the cobalt thiocyanate to cocaine powder produces a blue precipitate. Addition of the hydrochloric acid changes the blue precipitate to pink, while addition of the chloroform produces two layers, one clear and one blue.

Schiff test (PAS): Named for Hugo Schiff, this test employs a colorless reagent (fuchsine and sodium hydrogen sulfite) to detect aldehydes, which turn the solution magenta or purple. Since human skin cells contain aldehydes, and are shed in large numbers with vaginal secretions, the Schiff test is employed by criminalists to detect human vaginal material (as at suspected rape scenes). The skin cells, once detected, may then be subjected to DNA testing.

Urobilinogen: A colorless compound formed in the intestines by the reduction of bilirubin, urobilinogen is excreted in the feces where it oxidizes to urobilin. Application of appropriate reagents—including Ehrlich's reagent (see above) or 4-Methoxybenzene diazoniurn salt—detect urobilinogen as part of a presumptive test for feces. The forensic application includes use of penile swabs to document sodomy charges. DNA may be revealed on the same swabs, and thus identify the victim.

Van Urk test: An obsolete name for Ehrlich's test (see above).

Vitali's test: Named for Italian physician Dioscoride Vitali (1832–1917), this presumptive test examines suspect substances for mydriatic vegetable alkaloids found in some drugs. The test is performed by adding a microdrop of fuming nitric acid to the sample and observing any color change, then allowing the sample to dry before adding alcoholic potassium hydroxide to produce another color change. Specific color reactions include brownish purple for LSD, reddish brown for mescaline, and yellow shades for heroine and morphine.

Walker test: This procedure is used primarily to test for gunshot residue on clothing. In the Walker test, suspect samples are collected and transferred to inactivated photographic paper treated with 2-napthylamine and sulfanilic acid. Any nitrites present in the sample, such as those found in propellant charges of FIREARMS ammunition, should produce a reddish orange stain on the paper.

PSYCHIATRY/PSYCHOLOGY, Forensic

Both psychiatry and psychology involve study of the human mind and human behavior. *Psychiatrists* are medical doctors who specialize in treating mental or behavioral disorders and who are legally authorized to prescribe medication. *Psychologists* are not physicians and may not prescribe drugs, since their training is normally limited to a master's degree or a Ph.D. Psychiatrists and psychologists play dual roles in forensic science. Before an offender is identified, they may analyze crime scene evidence as a means of PSYCHOLOGICAL PROFILING, to focus investigation on suspects of a particular age, race, gender, occupation, educational level, and so on. Once a suspect is identified and charged, professionals are often employed to judge his/her mental state. The result of those

examinations may determine whether a defendant is deemed competent for trial, and may affect a jury's verdict in cases where an insanity plea has been filed. As noted elsewhere in this work, profiling rarely (if ever) leads directly to a suspect's arrest, while insanity pleas remain a topic of heated controversy nationwide.

PSYCHOLOGICAL Profiling

As an investigative tool, psychological "profiling" of unknown subjects at large—UNSUBS in law enforcement jargon—is a relatively new technique, used for the first time in the mid-1950s. It is also one of the most controversial methods used by detectives to track down their prey. In fictional portrayals, such as television's *Millennium* and *Profiler* series, profilers are often depicted as near-psychic, receiving "flashes" from an unknown criminal's mind with every visit to a crime scene, pursuing their quarry with intuitive leaps akin to divine revelation.

Unfortunately, such is not the case.

When hyperbole and hype are stripped away, profiling remains nothing more nor less than educated guesswork, based on crime scene evidence and statistical probability. At its best, the guesswork may be highly educated, drawing on experience from previous cases and assisted by computer analysis, refining a fugitive's portrait into fine detail. On the other hand, a bungled profile may be worse than useless, leading investigators down a false trail while the object of their pursuit escapes scot-free. In most cases, the reality of profiling falls somewhere between the two extremes: experts are able to prepare a fair likeness of their UNSUB without providing the essential details of identity required for an arrest.

Ironically, the first application of psychological profiling in modern criminology is also the only case to date wherein a profiler contributed directly to the subject's capture. In 1956, forensic psychiatrist JAMES BRUSSEL prepared an astoundingly accurate profile of New York City's elusive "Mad Bomber," deducing the subject's impotence from the phallic shape of his pipe bombs, generating a sketch that could have passed for the bomber's mug shot, even predicting correctly that the subject would be wearing a double-breasted suit (with the jacket buttoned) on the day of his arrest. More important, however, Dr. Brussel advised police on a means of provoking the bomber to reveal himself by writing to the press, a ploy that led manhunters to his doorstep. No other profiler to date has rivaled Brussel's triumph, and even where specific profiles have proved accurate in the wake of apprehension, the capture is always effected by routine police work.

Two cases often cited as profiling "success stories" demonstrate the gap between hype and reality. In Sacramento, California, sheriff's deputies and FBI agents prepared a profile of an UNSUB blamed for six gruesome murders during January 1978. At his arrest, defendant Richard Trenton Chase was found to match the profile in every respect, yet psychological analysis played no role in his capture. Rather, Chase was seen by a former high-school classmate wandering the streets in bloodstained clothing after the last murder, and was turned in to police, who then found copious evidence in his car and home. Six years later, Florida serial killer Bobby Joe Long was the subject of another FBI profile, which again proved remarkably accurate once police had him in custody. Retired G-men hail their achievement as if they had caught Long themselves, but in fact Long sealed his own fate by leaving his penultimate victim alive, to provide authorities with a description of Long and his car.

When profilers miss their target, meanwhile, the results are sometimes truly bizarre. In 1963, a panel of psychiatrists—including the aforementioned Dr. Brussel—was convened to stalk the "BOSTON STRANGLER." The experts concluded that Boston was plagued by *two* serial killers, one who killed elderly women, and another—thought to be homosexual—who preferred younger females. (In fact, no gay male in history has ever been identified as a serial slayer of women.) Beyond the divergence in victim selection, many similarities were postulated, including the suggestion that both men were teachers, living alone and killing on seasonal school holidays. Both UNSUBS were diagnosed as sexually inhibited, the products of traumatic childhoods featuring weak, distant fathers and cruel yet seductive mothers. In fact, confessed strangler Albert DeSalvo was a construction worker, living with his wife and two children, an insatiable heterosexual. Examination of his background showed a brutal, domineering father and a mother who was weak and ineffectual. DeSalvo was in his 30s, as projected for the two hypothetical teachers, but there the resemblance ended. Recent DNA testing has cast doubt on DeSalvo's guilt in the Boston murders, his confession notwithstanding, but it should be

noted that none of the alternative suspects identified thus far bear any resemblance to the pair of homicidal teachers profiled in 1963.

An even more dramatic failure comes from Los Angeles, where another "expert panel" gathered to profile the brutal "Skid Row Slasher," a serial killer of homeless men. On January 30, 1975, the media broadcast descriptions of the killer as a "sexually impotent coward, venting his own feelings of worthlessness on hapless drifters and down-and-outers." Profilers described the slasher as a friendless loner, probably a homosexual and possibly deformed, "driven to a frenzy to commit these murders as a substitute for normal heterosexual relations." His bloodlust was probably "spurred by an unresolved rage he feels toward his father, who could have been a brutal alcoholic." Sketches drawn to fit the profile showed a white male in his late 20s or early 30s, six feet tall, 190 pounds, with shoulder-length stringy blond hair framing a gaunt face. At his arrest, two days later, slayer Vaughn Greenwood was revealed to be a stocky African American with no apparent deformities, whose crimes were the product of ritual occultism, complete with blood-drinking and salt sprinkled around the corpses of his victims.

It is worth noting that profilers themselves disagree on the value of their contribution to crimefighting. Dr. Norman Barr, one of the Skid Row Slasher panelists in California, belatedly told reporters, "I don't think my statements would make any more sense than those of the average housewife." Across the continent, at Boston University, psychologist Russell Boxley agreed, declaring, "I think the people who do profiles are bastardizing their discipline with a lot of mumbo-jumbo, without really knowing what they're doing. You know, it's a mystical thing, and people are very impressed. It's also a media thing." Boxley concluded that forensic psychiatrists tracking an unknown felon "can't do any better than a college student with the same materials in front of him."

FBI "mindhunters," meanwhile, stand by their record and tactics, with several retired G-men finding new careers as authors of memoirs that relate (and inflate) their achievements. In print, every case appears to hinge upon a brilliant profile, but in fact some of their conclusions are vague, at best. Following extensive interviews with various convicted felons in the 1980s, members of the bureau's Behavioral

Science Unit (later Investigative Support Services) divided murderers into two broad categories, "organized" and "disorganized."

Organized killers typically possess good intelligence and are socially competent, tending toward skilled occupations. A review of the subject's childhood, if and when he is arrested, normally reveals a high birth-order status (the oldest or the only child), a father with stable employment, and a home life marked by inconsistent discipline, alternately harsh and lax. In adulthood, the organized killer often lives with a partner, frequently a legal spouse, and is sexually active. Violence is precipitated by "stressors," including marital discord or loss of employment, and is often fueled by alcohol. The killer is mobile, maintaining one or more vehicles in good repair. His mood is controlled on the hunt, and he normally follows the progress of police investigations through the media. Crime scene characteristics of the organized offender betray a crime planned well in advance, reflecting the killer's overall control of his environment. The organized offender typically conceals the bodies of his victims and takes care to leave no evidence behind. If pressed by police, he may flee the area to avoid apprehension.

Disorganized offenders, by contrast, are possessed of average intelligence at best, sometimes mentally retarded, and nearly always socially inept. The subject mirrors his father's unstable work record by quitting or losing one job after another, rarely qualifying for a skilled occupation. The UNSUB's social life is equally barren: the offender typically lives alone and is sexually incompetent, sometimes virginal in adulthood. Disorganized killers rarely drink to bolster their courage, since their crimes are impulsive and unplanned. No serious precipitating stress is seen; rather, the killer strikes at random, almost whimsically, without thinking through his actions. He often lives and/or works near the crime scene, perhaps attacking a neighbor, and displays little interest in media coverage of the case. Crime scenes are sloppy, often rife with forensic evidence. Too distracted or dim-witted to recognize danger, the disorganized offender seldom makes any dramatic lifestyle changes to avoid arrest.

The FBI's profiling categories are deliberately broad, and while fictional slayer Hannibal Lecter may have been unduly harsh in blaming "a real bottom feeder" for the system's conception, federal profilers have admitted its deficiency by creating an intermediate "mixed" category for troublesome cases.

Q

QUALITATIVE and Quantitative Analysis

Qualitative analysis determines the contents or constituent parts of an evidentiary sample, while quantitative analysis determines the amount of each component present. In forensic science both aspects of testing are generally required to complete analysis and identification of evidence recovered from a victim or a crime scene. As an example, qualitative analysis of FIBERS found on a body may determine that they are composed of nylon and rayon. Quantitative analysis of the same fibers reveals the proportion of nylon and rayon present, thus potentially linking the fiber to a particular source where such fibers are used to make clothing, blankets, and so on. The same methods are applied to many other substances, ranging from accelerants found by ARSON investigators to bullets extracted from murder victims. In each case, identification of specific components and their relative quantities may point investigators toward known manufacturers or suppliers. Various processes used in qualitative and quantitative analysis include CHROMATOGRAPHY, MICROSCOPY, NEUTRON ACTIVATION ANALYSIS and SPECTROSCOPY.

QUALITY Assurance Techniques

Evidence means nothing if its integrity is compromised at any point during collection, analysis, or storage. During each step of a forensic investigation, certain protocols must be observed to satisfy both the law and professional ethics. The process begins—or *should* begin—with proper training of forensic personnel, ensuring that everyone who handles evidence possesses the requisite education, technical training, and experience to maintain an ironclad chain of custody while avoiding loss or contamination of samples. Accreditation procedures for law enforcement agencies, crime labs, and individual criminalists are now available throughout the United States, though some agencies fail to pursue certification. Persons involved in testing or analysis of evidence must follow good laboratory practice (GLP) and exercise suitable standards of care in handling all samples, including use of standardized equipment and testing procedures. Periodic testing of lab personnel with "blind" samples—submitted as if they belonged to an active case in progress, as a means of spot-testing—helps ensure consistent quality of performance. During actual investigations, known *control* samples should be employed for comparison purposes wherever feasible. In courtroom presentations, expert witnesses should be precise and accurate, avoiding vague or misleading remarks described by forensic professionals as "weasel words." When criminalists fail to observe standard ethics, as in the cases of JOYCE GILCHRIST, FRED ZAIN and some operators at the FBI LABORATORY, scandal and tragedy result. Even when those standards *are* observed, an implication of impropriety—as in the ORENTHAL JAMES (O. J.) SIMPSON murder case, may result in miscarriage of justice.

QUESTIONED Documents

In forensic science, questioned documents are those requiring investigation to establish their authenticity or to determine their legitimate contents after some damage or alteration has occurred. Any document may be questioned if it is pertinent to some legal matter and/or is submitted as evidence. Examiners strive to detect COUNTERFEITING and FORGERY in a wide range of questioned documents including checks, contracts, deeds, promissory notes, securities, wills, and various historical items (diaries, letters, etc.) that may be valuable to collectors.

While forensic experts place little or no faith in *graphology* (study of handwriting to determine personality traits), handwriting analysis plays a critical role in questioned document analysis. Signatures on checks and other legal documents rank among the most common types of forgery. Analysts examine known exemplars of a subject's handwriting, including both *request* and *nonrequest standards*. The former are prepared at an examiner's request, after a given document has aroused suspicion, while the latter are samples written before the controversy arose. Analysis includes close study of such features as the writer's *beginning strokes* (which start a word or sentence), *sequence strokes* (used to create individual letters), *connecting strokes* (which link letters within a word), and *pen lift* (breaks between letters or words). Other factors considered include the writer's normal *slant, line quality* (the smoothness and darkness of individual lines on paper), and any *tremors* in his/her handwriting caused by age, illness, or other impairment. Where multiple documents of unknown origin are involved—as with ransom notes or terrorist threats—samples may be compared to items catalogued in the FISH (*Forensic Information System for Handwriting*) database, created and maintained by the U.S. Secret Service.

Handwritten forgeries take various forms. Forged signatures may be produced either by *tracing* known exemplars of a subject's handwriting or by *freehand simulation,* wherein the forger uses no template. *Normal hand forgery* occurs when the forger crafts a false document—such as a letter or promissory note penned under a false name—without attempting to alter one's normal handwriting. *Disguised writing,* by contrast, attempts to mask the forger's normal penmanship by various means, including altered slant and writing styles or holding a pen in the forger's weaker hand. Examination of a suspect document may also detect erasures or obliterations, determine the normal *pen pressure* applied by an individual writer, and even identify specific pens by measuring *striae grooves*—the marks created on paper by a pen that contains no ink. *Indented writing*—the impressions left on a surface underneath a handwritten document—may be detected by various means including an electrostatic detection apparatus (ESDA), thus demonstrating that the document was written on a notepad or desk blotter owned by the suspect.

Printed or typewritten documents pose a different range of challenges for questioned document examiners. Specific typewriters may be identified by unique imperfections in their fonts, as where a particular letter is chipped or fouled with ink. If *carbon paper* is used to make copies and is thereafter found in a suspect's possession, it may bear an impression of the questioned document. Computer printers are more problematical, since fonts can readily be changed, but major brands may be identified by the number of lines per inch they produce in a particular font. Photocopied documents may also reveal *trash marks*—specks or lines imaged on a document that reflect imperfections in the copier's glass plate—thereby linking various documents printed on one copier or tying specific documents to one machine.

Another aspect of questioned document analysis, employed with both modern and alleged historical items, is analysis of paper itself. Regardless of its quality, all paper contains a variety of wood and/or cotton fibers, with various binders, bleaches or dyes, coatings, and preservatives. Cotton (or "rag") content increases with the quality and cost of paper, so that cheap "pulp" paper may have none at all. Many brands of paper include *watermarks,* which identify the manufacturer and may assist in dating a document. Some inks also contain *taggants,* which identify their manufacturers. In some factories, paper is marked by imperfections in the large *dandy roll* used to produce it, permitting experts to trace a particular sheet of paper from a crime scene to the paper mill, if necessary. Both paper and ink may also be dated by chemical means to determine whether a supposed historical document was produced within the proper time frame.

R

RADAR/LIDAR Law Enforcement Applications

Radar—from *R*adio *D*irection *a*nd *R*anging—was initially developed as a military tool and later utilized in civilian capacities, primarily for tracking aircraft on their approach to airports. It is used in the same way by U.S. Customs Service agents and members of the Drug Enforcement Administration to track smugglers approaching America's borders with narcotics and other contraband. The police application most familiar to the average citizen, however, is probably the use of radar to monitor ground traffic speeds and apprehend drivers who exceed the maximum posted speed limit.

In essence, radar uses radio waves to detect and monitor various objects. Its original (and simplest) function is to determine distance between two objects by emitting a concentrated radio wave and recording the echoes of any objects that block its passage. Since radio waves move through air at a constant speed, radar devices calculate the distance between the transmitter and its target based on how long it takes the "bounced" signal to return. Radar can also measure an object's speed, by means of a phenomenon called "Doppler shift." When a radar transmitter and its target are both stationary, the echo has the same wave frequency as the original signal. When the target is moving, however, wave patterns are changed. Vehicles moving away from the transmitter "stretch" the waves, while objects approaching the transmitter "compress" the waves, increasing the fre-

quency. Based on the frequency changes, a radar gun calculates how quickly the target (normally but not necessarily a vehicle) is moving toward or away from the transmitter. Further calculations allow for movement of the radar gun itself, as when mounted inside a police car. If the cruiser is traveling at 50 miles per hour and the target vehicle is moving away from it at 30 miles per hour, then the target must be traveling at 80 miles per hour. (If both vehicles hold a constant speed, there is no deviation in the pattern.)

A newer variation of this tracking system is Lidar—for *L*ight *D*etection *a*nd *R*anging. As suggested by the name, lidar guns use concentrated infrared light (laser) beams in place of radio waves. Calculations are performed on the same basis as with radar, but using the speed of light, rather than the speed of sound. In place of constant, oscillating radio waves, the lidar gun emits rapid-fire pulses of light to track moving objects over a protracted distance. Many police departments use hand-held or dashboard-mounted lidar guns, but the devices may also be mounted beside highways, continuously operating to monitor the speed of each passing vehicle. Such stationary emplacements frequently include high-speed cameras, employed to snap pictures of the license plates (and sometimes drivers' faces) any time a passing car registers excessive speed. Speeders may thus be traced through computer data banks and receive their citations by mail, without involving officers in time-consuming (and often hazardous) traffic stops.

225

Lawbreakers normally outdo law enforcement agencies in adopting new technology, and while police initially had the edge in using radar and lidar devices, there is today no shortage of high-tech instruments designed to frustrate their efforts. The simplest evasion devices are radar detectors, basic radio receivers tuned to police frequencies, which (the speeder hopes) will pick up radar signals in time to slow down and avoid a citation. Simple detectors are most effective when traffic officers leave their radar guns constantly turned on, without sighting a particular target, thus beaming detectable signals throughout their patrol shift. The detector is useless, though, if an officer turns off his gun until a target is sighted. In that case, the driver's warning comes too late, since the speed has already been recorded.

More sophisticated radar-jamming devices are also available, operating on the same principle used for years by military aircraft to avoid detection by their enemies. Jammers, unlike simple radar detectors, are not passive devices. They register incoming, then transmit their own signal, replicating the original radar gun's signal but mixing it up with additional radio noise, thus preventing an accurate reading. Many U.S. jurisdictions have outlawed radar detectors or jammers, making their possession a separate offense. In those areas, police are often equipped with "VG2" devices—simple high-powered radio receivers tuned to the signal frequency commonly used by radar detectors and jammers. Ironically, a driver with an active radar detector in the car may then be stopped and cited for illegal possession, even if not speeding at the time.

Scofflaws have not been lacking in response to lidar technology, either. Many modern radar detectors include a light-sensitive panel to register beams from police lidar guns, but their effectiveness is limited, since lidar guns are best used over short distances and focus strictly on a single target. Thus, again, by the time a detector alerts the speeding driver, he or she has already been "painted" by the lidar beam, with the illicit speed recorded. Some dedicated speeders try to defeat lidar by decreasing the reflectivity of their vehicles. Black paint may be help-

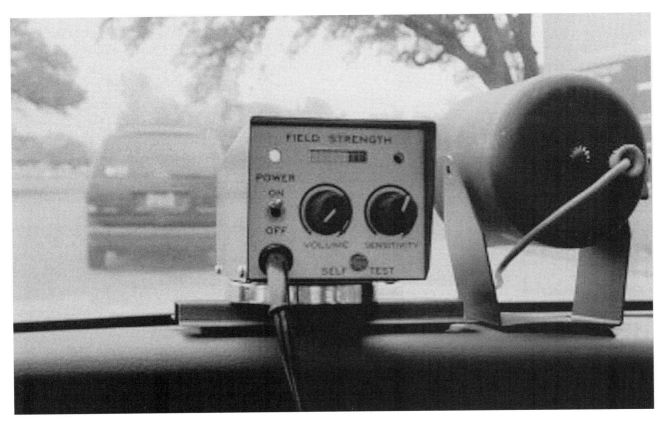

Police and state troopers use "radar detector detectors" to pull over drivers operating illegal radar detectors during travel. (AP/TDPS)

ful, since it absorbs more light and reflects less than other hues, while certain plastic covers reduce the reflective properties of metal license plates. At best, however, such tricks buy the speeder a few seconds to slow down between the time one's car is sighted and the speed is registered by the lidar gun. Lidar jammers are more effective, equipped with their own light-emitting diodes (LEDs) that blind a lidar gun to reflected light.

The prevalence of radar guns in modern traffic enforcement has fostered a number of myths. It is not true, for instance, that inclement weather disables radar guns, although their sensitivity may be somewhat diminished by extremely heavy rain, snow, or dust storms. Radar and lidar do not "prefer" one type or color of vehicle—red sports cars, for instance—over any other (although, as a psychological matter, it may be true that drivers of bright-colored sports cars are more likely to speed and/or draw attention to themselves). Likewise, with the exception of black paint (discussed above), no particular color of vehicle makes detection by lidar less likely (and color has no effect whatsoever on radar). By the same token, radar and lidar guns are not infallible. Their readings may be challenged and occasionally proved inaccurate. Various publications detail means of fighting radar/lidar citations in court, and further discussion of the subject may be found at www.CopRadar.com.

RADIOLOGY, Forensic

Radiology is the use of X-rays for dental or medical purposes. Its forensic application applies various uses of X-rays to cases involving the civil or criminal law. Forensic PATHOLOGY makes frequent use of X-rays to identify unknown corpses (via dental records, unique skeletal injuries, etc.) and to search for foreign objects in a body—such as bullets, broken blades, or items swallowed by an individual. *Fluoroscopy,* a kind of "live" or real-time X-ray examination (versus *plain film*), is used in AIRPORT SECURITY and in other cases where the contents of a package, envelope, or other object must be examined for contraband. An X-ray image known as an *autoradiograph* reveals DNA fragments produced during certain kinds of genetic profiling or testing. X-rays are also used in certain kinds of SPECTROSCOPY.

RAINGER, William See "FORD HEIGHTS FOUR."

RAY, Isaac (1807–1881)

A native of Beverly, Massachusetts, born on January 16, 1807, Isaac Ray earned his M.D. from Maine's Bowdoin College at age 20, subsequently practicing in Eastport and Portland, Maine. A devotee of psychiatric study, Ray published his volume *Medical Jurisprudence of Insanity* in 1838, thus prompting Maine authorities to make him superintendent of the state asylum at Augusta three years later. He subsequently transferred to Rhode Island's Butler Hospital for the Insane, where he served as superintendent from 1845 to 1866. During that period, Ray published two more classic works on psychiatry, *Education in Relation to the Health of the Brain* (1851) and *Mental Hygiene* (1863). Following retirement from the Butler Hospital, Ray settled in Philadelphia. Brown University granted him an LL.D. in 1879, but Ray had little time remaining to pursue the law. He died in Philadelphia on March 31, 1881.

Ray's primary importance was his conceptualization in 1838 of the "irresistible impulses" caused by mental disease or disorder, during which "the affective as well as the intellectual faculties are subject to derangement." Ray also considered the problem of lucid intervals that mask insanity—itself a legal term, devoid of medical or scientific meaning—and recognized the difficulty jurors have in retaining objectivity about violent crimes. Ray's views strongly influenced the judicial handling of Daniel M'Naughten, a deranged Scotsman whose bungled attempt to kill British prime minister Sir Robert Peel claimed the life of Peel's secretary instead. At trial in 1843, Presiding Judge Tindell found Ray's theories so persuasive that he ordered M'Naughten's acquittal on grounds of insanity. Thus was established the "M'Naughten Rule," still prevailing in some American jurisdictions, which measures insanity on the basis of a defendant's ability to tell right from wrong (or to recognize a specific act as illegal) at the moment a crime is committed.

REMINGTON Center Innocence Project

Affiliated with the Frank J. Remington Center at the University of Wisconsin Law School, the Remington Center Innocence Project (RCIP) is yet another group committed to the legal defense of incarcerated inmates who claim actual innocence of the crimes for which they stand convicted. Founded in 1998, codirected by Professors Keith Findley and John Pray,the RCIP "is interested in cases in which some type of new evidence can be found to prove innocence." As defined on the group's Web site, "'New' means evidence that was not presented at trial because it did not exist, was inadvertently overlooked by the defense or withheld by the prosecution." The center makes its selection of cases once a year, in August, utilizing a staff of 20 law students to investigate and litigate claims under the supervision of professors. The center takes cases "only after a person has been convicted and all direct appeals have ended or the time for filing a direct appeal has passed." While "nearly all" cases litigated by the RCIP involve Wisconsin inmates, an exception to the rule was CHRISTOPHER OCHOA, liberated from a Texas prison by DNA evidence in 2001. Prisoners seeking assistance on cases within the RCIP's guidelines should address inquiries to:

Innocence Project of Frank J. Remington Center
University of Wisconsin Law School
975 Bascom Mall
Madison, WI 53706

RIGGS, Sterling convicted by DNA evidence

On April 15, 1985, 15-year-old Tracey Poindexter was found by Indianapolis police officers, bound, gagged, and drowned in Fall Creek. Semen traces were recovered from her body, but authorities had no suspect in the case for more than 15 years, until the latter part of 2000. At that time, Sgt. Michael Crooke of the Indianapolis Police Department used DNA technology—unknown at the time of the slaying—to compare the crime scene evidence with DNA profiles of 25,000 convicted felons (violent criminals and burglars) maintained in a data bank by the Indiana State Police. In that manner, Sgt. Crooke identified defendant Sterling Riggs, then on parole for his prior conviction in a kidnapping and rape committed nine days after Tracey Poindexter's body was found in 1985. Riggs—who lived in a house adjacent to that of Poindexter's aunt and three blocks from the crime scene—denied any part in the murder, but the scientific evidence was irrefutable. A jury convicted him of first-degree murder on October 31, 2001, and four weeks later he was sentenced to 115 years in prison, assuring that he will never walk the streets again.

ROBBERY

The term *robbery* generally applies to any THEFT accomplished by means of immediate coercion or violence. If weapons are used in the crime, it becomes *armed robbery* and incurs additional penalties. *Extortion*, though involving threats and sometimes force, is commonly distinguished from robbery because payment is demanded at some future date (as in the classic underworld "protection" rackets). Armed theft of a vehicle from its owner is called *carjacking*, punishable since the early 1990s as a federal offense in the United States. Capture of commercial vehicles and their cargo or passengers is often dubbed HIJACKING. Strong-arm robbery of victims selected at random in public is often called *mugging*. In many jurisdictions, any death occurring in the course of a robbery makes the robbers liable to prosecution for *felony murder*, a charge equivalent to premeditated HOMICIDE (even if the bandits themselves did not slay the victim).

As with theft in general, robbery is commonly motivated by greed, although some terrorist (see TERRORISM) groups support themselves by "liberating" cash at gunpoint from their perceived enemies. Since the 1960s, extremist groups of both right and left have staged political holdups throughout western Europe, North and South America. Cash is the most common goal in armed robberies, although bandits also steal jewelry, precious metals, furs and designer clothing, works of art, stocks, bonds, and other negotiable instruments. Except in the case of currency, stolen objects must generally be sold to provide robbers with a profit. As with BURGLARY and other forms of theft, illegal dealers known as fences purchase stolen merchandise at a fraction of its normal value, then mark it up for a profit on resale. The same middlemen may arrange for a discounted purchase of cash, in cases where stolen currency is marked by the authorities or the serial numbers of specific bills are recorded.

Forensic scientists examine a robbery scene for any evidence the bandits may have left behind, including FINGERPRINTS, IMPRESSION EVIDENCE, or any kind of TRACE EVIDENCE. Violent incidents may leave BLOODSTAINS at the scene for DNA profiling. If shots are fired, ballistics experts have an opportunity to match bullets and spent cartridge cases to specific suspect FIREARMS, and to link the shooting with others through access to the federal Drugfire or INTEGRATED BALLISTICS IDENTIFICATION SYSTEM databases. Stolen cash may be identified by serial numbers, chemical markers (called *taggants*), or in the event that a defensive dye pack has been planted with the money. Identification of other stolen property relies primarily on serial numbers, manufacturer's marks, and similar means.

ROBINSON, John Edward Sr. first "Internet serial killer"

A native of Cicero, Illinois, born in 1943, John Robinson was well known in his community by age 13, an honor student at Quigley Preparatory Seminary and an Eagle Scout who led a troop of 120 other scouts in a command performance for Queen Elizabeth II. By 1961 he was enrolled at a local junior college, studying to become an X-ray technician. Three years later, he married Nancy Jo Lynch in Kansas City, Missouri.

Robinson was on the path to a solid middle-class life, but he somehow went astray. In June 1967, while working as a lab technician for a Kansas City doctor, he embezzled $33,000 and was placed on three years' probation. At his next job, as manager of a television rental company, Robinson stole merchandise and was fired, but his boss declined to prosecute. In 1969, he began work as a systems analyst for Mobil Oil. On August 27, 1970, exactly two weeks after his probation officer wrote that Robinson was "responding extremely well to probation supervision," Robinson stole 6,200 postage stamps from the company. This time, he was fired *and* charged with THEFT.

Moving on to Chicago in September 1970, Robinson embezzled $5,500 from yet another employer. He was fired again, but the victim waived prosecution when Robinson's father repaid the loss. Drifting back to Kansas City, Robinson was jailed for violating his probation and his term of supervised release was extended another five years, until 1976. A probation report from April 1973 records his "good prognosis," unaware that Robinson had recently swindled an elderly neighbor out of $30,000. His probation officer was so impressed with Robinson's improvement, in fact, that Robinson was discharged in 1974, two years ahead of schedule.

It was not the system's first mistake with Robinson, nor would it be the last.

A free man once more, Robinson promptly created the Professional Service Association (PSA), ostensibly formed to provide Kansas City physicians financial counseling. More embezzlement followed, prompting a federal grand jury to indict Robinson on four

Missouri authorities describe John Robinson as the "first Internet serial killer." (Getty Images)

counts of securities and mail FRAUD. In June 1976 he was fined $2,500 and placed on three years' probation—another wrist-slap that taught him precisely nothing.

In 1977, with his wife and four children, Robinson moved to Johnson County, Kansas, and took a fling at hydroponic farming behind the corporate front of Hydro-Gro Inc. A community activist who tackled multiple projects, Robinson was voted local "Man of the Year" in 1977 for his work with the handicapped. By 1980, Robinson had taken on a second job as personnel director for a local branch of Borden Foods—where he promptly embezzled $40,000, financing a love nest for kinky liaisons with female bondage enthusiasts. Arrested in that case, he faced a seven-year prison term but spent only two months in jail, with five years' probation added to his tab.

The first of Robinson's suspected murder victims, Paula Godfrey, was employed by Robinson when she vanished in 1984. Police later received a letter, purportedly signed by Godfrey, insisting that she was "O.K." and that she did not wish to see her family. She remains among the missing to this day.

In December 1984, Robinson approached a Kansas City hospital and adoption agency, introducing himself as the spokesman for "Kansas City Outreach," allegedly a firm created to provide housing and job training for young unwed mothers. The hospital sent Robinson his first client, 19-year-old Lisa Stasi, in January 1985. Stasi promptly vanished, leaving behind a typed letter explaining her urge to leave Missouri for parts unknown. Robinson's childless brother and sister-in-law took custody of Stasi's newborn daughter, paying Robinson $5,500 for a set of forged adoption papers.

Robinson's next brainstorm was the formation of a sado-masochistic prostitution ring, for fun and profit. FBI agents learned of his venture and sent a female decoy around for a job interview, but the initial conversation was so disturbing that G-men backed out, citing fear for their undercover agent's safety. Robinson's first known S&M employee was 21-year-old Theresa Williams, for whom he rented an apartment and arranged transportation on "dates." In May 1985, after less than one month on the job, Williams woke one morning to find Robinson raging through her apartment with a pistol, furious because she had invited a boyfriend to the flat. FBI agents relocated Williams, while Robinson faced assault charges. His probation was revoked for unauthorized FIREARMS possession, but that decision was reversed on appeal, a higher court finding that the FBI denied Robinson's constitutional right to confront his accuser in court.

The agents found some consolation in January 1986, when Kansas jurors convicted Robinson of another investment scam. Sentenced as a habitual offender, Robinson drew a prison term of six to 19 years, but appeals stalled his incarceration until May 1987. In the meantime, 27-year-old Catherine Clampitt moved from Texas to Kansas, drawn by Robinson's promise of "a great job, a lot of traveling and a new wardrobe." She was never seen again.

In prison, Robinson quickly earned a reputation as a model inmate, using his time to develop a computer program that saved the Kansas penal system $100,000 yearly on administrative tasks. The cooperative attitude and a series of mild strokes earned Robinson the sympathy of prison psychologists. In November 1990, they described him as a "devoted family man" and a "non-violent person [who] does not present a threat to society." Kansas paroled Robinson in January 1991, but he still owed time in Missouri, where he remained incarcerated until spring 1993.

Kansas prison librarian Beverly Bonner admired Robinson so much that she divorced her husband in 1993 and moved to Kansas City as the "president" of Hydro-Gro. She vanished in January 1994, after sending her family a letter explaining that her new job required extensive travel. Six months later, after prolonged correspondence, Sheila Faith left Colorado to join Robinson—her "dream man"—in Kansas City. Faith brought along her teenage daughter Debbie, confined to a wheelchair, and both soon disappeared.

By that time Robinson had discovered the Internet, trolling for fresh victims in cyberspace. One who survived told journalist David McClintock that she lost $17,000 to Robinson on a fraudulent investment scheme, arranged through e-mail correspondence. She was lucky, compared to Izabel Lewicka, a Polish immigrant and freshman at Indiana's Purdue University. Lewicka met Robinson online in early 1997, and that June she left home to serve an "internship" with Robinson in Kansas. Communication with her parents ceased abruptly, and they went looking for Izabel in August 1997, leaving Kansas empty-handed, without contacting police. Unknown to Izabel's family, Robinson had coerced her into signing a six-page "slave contract," convincing her the document was legal, while he kept her at an apartment in Olathe, Kansas. Lewicka survived in Robinson's clutches until August 1999, then dropped from sight. He told acquaintances that she had been deported for smoking marijuana.

Robinson's last known victim was 27-year-old Suzette Trouten, a Detroit nurse to whom Robinson offered a job in September 1999. The package was attractive: a $60,000 yearly salary, a company car, and wide-ranging travel. Trouten moved to Kansas City on February 13, 2000, and was last seen alive on March 1.

Kansas authorities, meanwhile, had been building a case against Robinson for sexual assault on yet another victim. They arrested Robinson on June 2, 2000, and searched his Olathe home, seizing five computers and a host of other evidence, including a blank piece of stationery signed by Lisa Stasi 15 years earlier and her last motel receipt, dated January 10, 1985. Searchers visited a storage facility rented by Robinson and found a cache of S&M toys, along with various items related to Izabel Lewicka and Suzette Trouten: more blank stationery with signatures affixed, a birth certificate and Social Security card, Lewicka's slave contract, and sundry photographs (including bondage shots).

On June 3, 2000, police searched Robinson's 16-acre farm near La Cygne, Kansas, recovering two 55-gallon drums with women's corpses packed inside. The victims, both beaten to death with a hammer, were identified as Lewicka and Trouten. Two days later, another raiding party scoured another storage facility rented by Robinson, this one in Cass County, Missouri. They found three more oil drums, sealed with duct tape and planted on mounds of cat litter to mask death's sickly odor. Inside the drums lay Betty Bonner, Sheila Faith, and Sheila's daughter Debbie. Like the rest, they had been hammered lifeless and entombed.

Robinson was charged in Kansas with two counts of capital murder, one count of first-degree murder, and various lesser charges. He was convicted and, in 2003, received two death sentences and one life sentence. That left him facing three murder charges in Missouri that were resolved later in 2003 when prosecutors accepted Robinson's guilty plea in each case in return for three sentences of life without parole. Robinson's execution, scheduled for 2005, was delayed when the Kansas Supreme Court declared the death penalty statute unconstitutional.

RODRIGUEZ, George exonerated by DNA

In February 1987, two Hispanic men snatched a 14-year-old girl from a public street in Houston, Texas, drove her to a house where she was raped repeatedly, then placed her in their car once more and dropped her off beside a local highway. The victim initially described her attackers as "the skinny one and the fat one." One had called the other "George," but she believed it was a pseudonym, since they openly discussed the need to avoid using their real names in her presence. Her description of the CRIME SCENE led officers to a house owned by brothers Manuel and Uvaldo Beltran, whose friends included one George Rodriguez. When questioned by police, Rodriguez

said that he was working when the rape occurred, a claim confirmed by several coworkers. Meanwhile, Uvaldo Beltran told authorities that he was watching television at home when brother Manuel and another man, Isidro Yanez, arrived with the victim and took her into a bedroom. Manuel confessed the crime, naming Yanez as his accomplice, and police subsequently confirmed that the girl had been kidnapped in Yanez's car.

That should have solved the case, but officers had already shown the victim a photo lineup prior to Uvaldo Beltran's statement, and she picked a photograph of George Rodriguez from that array. Despite the overwhelming evidence against Isidro Yanez, and the victim's admission that she had glimpsed her attacker's face for only three to four seconds, prosecutors indicted Rodriguez and Manuel Beltran for the rape. Two months after the attack, detectives showed the victim another group of photos, including both Rodriguez and Yanez. She selected both pictures, noting their similarities, but finally settled again on Rodriguez as the second rapist. At trial in October 1987, a technician from the Houston Police Department's crime lab linked Manuel Beltran to semen found on the victim's clothing, while claiming that a hair found in her underwear was "microscopically similar" to that of Rodriguez. The same witness testified that testing of the semen samples "definitely" excluded Yanez as a possible donor (a claim refuted by the state's own test results, concealed from the court and jury). Both defendants were convicted, Rodriguez receiving a 60-year prison term for aggravated kidnapping and aggravated sexual assault on a child. His various appeals were uniformly denied.

In 2002, the CARDOZO INNOCENCE PROJECT accepted Rodriguez's case for review. Police had already destroyed most of the relevant biological evidence, while purging their files in 1995, but the new defense team obtained the lone hair allegedly matched to Rodriguez. After a year of legal wrangling, permission was granted for DNA testing, and those results, obtained in 2004, excluded Rodriguez as a possible source of the hair. The test *did not* exclude Isidro Yanez. New serological tests further revealed that Yanez had been mistyped in 1987 and should not have been excluded from the suspect pool. Based on those findings, the Texas Court of Criminal Appeals vacated Rodriguez's conviction in August 2005, and prosecutors dismissed all charges against him the following month. At press time for this work, no charges had been filed against Yanez.

ROSS, Johnny exonerated by blood analysis

For many years, rape was a capital crime in states of the southern United States, but critics of the death penalty noted that those defendants condemned for nonfatal sexual assaults were nearly always African Americans accused of attacking white victims. Prior to 1960, many of those so accused were lynched without trial, while countless others were convicted and sentenced to prison or death after "confessing" under what amounted to police torture. A modern case in point is that of 16-year-old Johnny Ross, accused of rape and condemned by Louisiana authorities in proceedings that made a mockery of justice.

Ross was 16 years old in 1975, when police in New Orleans accused him of raping a white woman. Ross was beaten by detectives until he admitted the crime, and with that false confession in hand, his capital trial was completed within a few hours. The death sentence was a foregone conclusion, and appeals seemed hopeless until 1981, when Alabama lawyer Morris Dees and his Southern Poverty Law Center took an interest in the case. DNA testing had yet to be discovered, but it hardly mattered, since neither prosecutors nor Ross's original defense counsel had even bothered to check his blood type against semen recovered from the crime scene. When those rudimentary tests were performed, Ross was positively excluded as a suspect, and the New Orleans district attorney's office dismissed all charges, freeing Ross after he had spent six years on death row for a crime he did not commit. The case remains unsolved today.

While Ross was imprisoned, the U.S. Supreme Court addressed the issue of capital punishment for rapists in the case of *Coker v. Georgia* (1977), ruling that execution for rape (or, by extension, any other crime not resulting in death of the victim) constituted grossly disproportional punishment and therefore violated the Eighth Amendment of the U.S. Constitution.

RUNNION, Samantha murder case solved by DNA evidence

Five-year-old Samantha Runnion was kidnapped outside her Stanton, California, apartment on July 15, 2002, by a man who asked her to help him find a missing dog. Witnesses described the kidnapper as Hispanic, driving a light-green sedan. A massive Orange County search for Samantha and the suspect was in progress, heralded by national publicity, when Runnion's nude corpse was found on July 16, in neighboring Riverside County. Evidence collected at the crime scene proved that she had been sexually assaulted, then asphyxiated.

Relentless broadcasts of a composite sketch and descriptions of the kidnapper's car paid off for police on July 17, when Lake Elsinore neighbors of 27-year-old Alejandro Avila fingered him as a suspect. Authorities placed Avila under surveillance, then arrested him on July 19, 2002. Blood samples were drawn under court order and DNA comparison with the CRIME SCENE evidence was completed in near-record time, producing an announcement on July 21 that Avila's genetic profile matched the semen recovered from Runnion's corpse. Avila's sister told police that he had abruptly canceled a family dinner on the night Runnion was kidnapped, and a background check revealed that Avila had faced child-molesting charges two years earlier. He was acquitted by a jury in that case, apparently due to a lack of forensic evidence, but prosecutors in Orange County declared themselves "confident" of his guilt in the Runnion case.

"The evidence is very, very compelling," District Attorney Tony Rackauckas told reporters on July 23. "We are satisfied we have the right person and will be able to bring in a guilty verdict in this case." Avila was charged with murder, KIDNAPPING, and two counts of forcible lewd acts on a child, the latter charges ranked as "special circumstances" that allow prosecutors to seek a death penalty under California's penal code. Prosecutorial confidence notwithstanding, indictments are merely accusations of criminal activity, and all defendants are presumed innocent until they are convicted at trial.

RYAN, Edward James (1899–1978)

Born in 1899, Edward Ryan studied dentistry and established a private practice in Chicago during the early 1920s. His first foray into the realm of forensic ODONTOLOGY came in 1937, when Ryan published an article in the *Journal of Criminal Law and Criminology,* suggesting that dental charts might prove as effective as FINGERPRINTS or photographs in terms of personal identification. That article included Ryan's prototypical standardized chart. A year later, writing for *Scientific American,* Ryan expanded his theory with a claim that each human tooth bears unique markings imposed by a subject's manner of eating and such peripheral habits as chewing on pencils or biting fingernails. While Ryan did not extend his theory to casting of bite marks from crime scenes, by the time of his death in 1978 dental identification was standard practice in cases where fingerprints and other external features are lost due to mutilation or decomposition.

S

SACCO-VANZETTI Case miscarriage of justice

America's most controversial holdup-murder of the 20th century occurred in South Braintree, Massachusetts, on April 15, 1920. At three o'clock that afternoon, a paymaster and armed guard for the Slater & Morrill shoe factory were shot and killed by two bandits, the gunmen escaping with $15,776.51. The robbers, seen by multiple witnesses, tossed their loot into a car occupied by several other men and fled the scene. Their vehicle was found abandoned two days later, in some nearby woods.

Police in Bridgewater, 10 miles to the south, were already investigating a similar holdup, committed without loss of life on December 24, 1919. In both cases the thieves were described as probable Italians. Authorities suspected anarchist roommates Mario Boda (or Buda) and Ferrucio Coacci in the Bridgewater case, further noting that Coacci—jailed as an "enemy alien" during a series of recent "Red raids" had failed to report for his scheduled deportation hearing on the day of the South Braintree heist. Police questioned Boda on April 20, then released him in hopes that he would lead them to his accomplices. Officers lay in wait at a garage, springing their trap on May 5, when Boda, Coacci, and three other men came to retrieve the car. Boda escaped in the confusion, while police arrested Coacci, Riccardo Orciani, Nicola Sacco and Bartolomeo Vanzetti. Boda was never caught. Coacci was belatedly deported without further charges, while Orciani provided an ironclad alibi for both ROBBERY dates, leaving Sacco and Vanzetti to face trial alone.

Sacco and Vanzetti had arrived in the United States from their native Italy in 1908, when Sacco was 17 years old and Vanzetti was 20. Both were avid readers of the anarchist newspaper *Cronaca Sovversiva*, and by 1916 they were active in support of "radical" labor unions. Vanzetti logged his first arrest that year, for joining a rally in support of striking miners. Both fled to Mexico in 1917, thereby avoiding military conscription when the United States entered World War I. By 1919, they were listed in FBI files as "radicals to watch," but there was insufficient evidence to justify their deportation. On April 25, 1920, Vanzetti visited New York City in an effort to see fellow anarchist Andrea Salsedo, illegally confined at the FBI's Manhattan office on suspicion of participation in terrorist bombings. Salsedo plunged to his death from a 14th-story window on May 3, in what G-men described as a suicide. Sacco procured passports for Salsedo's family on the day after Salsedo's death, but his arrest on May 5 spoiled their plans for a return to Italy.

Spokesmen for the FBI's Boston office had initially described the Braintree holdup as a professional job, but they changed their tune overnight after Sacco and Vanzetti were arrested. Instead of searching for hardened criminals, G-men delivered their files on Sacco and Vanzetti to state prosecutors and infiltrated the Sacco-Vanzetti Defense Committee with informants who reportedly looted its treasury. Another spy was planted in jail with Sacco and Vanzetti, eavesdropping in vain for admissions of guilt. Vanzetti was indicted for the Bridgewater holdup on June 11, 1920, convicted on July 1 and sentenced on August 16 to a prison term of 12–15 years.

The main event began in Dedham, Massachusetts, on May 21, 1921, before Judge Webster Thayer—a bitter enemy of radicals, who deemed anarchism "cognate with the crime." Prosecutor Frederick Katzmann cast ethics to the wind in his pursuit of a conviction, while defense attorney John Vahey proved so inept that he was later accused of collusion with the state. (Coincidentally or otherwise, Vahey became Katzmann's legal partner in 1924.) Judge Thayer, for his part, welcomed prosecution arguments alluding to the defendants' nationality, their religious and political beliefs, overruling Vahey's few objections.

The resultant trial was a travesty. Witnesses who had refused to identify either defendant in 1920 had changed their minds in the meantime, naming both in court as the South Braintree bandits. One who glimpsed the getaway car for three seconds or less described Sacco in detail, including "a good-sized [left] hand . . . that denoted strength." Ballistics experts agreed that five of the seven fatal bullets came from pistols other than those confiscated from Sacco and Vanzetti, but State Police Captain William Proctor found one .32-caliber slug "consistent" with Sacco's gun, while a second expert witness—Charles Van Amburgh—agreed with that nebulous finding. Jurors convicted both defendants of murder on July 14, 1921, and Judge Thayer sentenced them to die, afterward crowing to his friends, "Did you see what I did to those anarchist bastards?"

Protests against the verdict and sentence were immediate, both in the United States and Europe. While FBI agents mounted surveillance on the protesters, the state's case began to unravel. Captain Proctor recanted his ballistics testimony in 1923, blaming the "confusion" on Prosecutor Katzmann. It was all a matter of semantics, Proctor said: "Had I been asked the direct question, whether I had found any affirmative evidence whatever that this so-called mortal bullet had passed through this particular Sacco's pistol, I should have answered then, as I do now without hesitation, in the negative." Judge Thayer declined to reopen the case, and he stood firm again

in 1924, when Charles Van Amburgh was exposed as a perjurer who frequently lied under oath to please prosecutors. Next, in November 1925, career criminal Celestine Madeiros confessed to driving the South Braintree getaway car for Joe Morelli's holdup gang, confirming that "Sacco and Vanzetti was not in said crime." Six months later, on May 12, 1926, the Massachusetts Supreme Court upheld the original verdict and Judge Thayer's sentence.

Disturbed by the ongoing protests, Governor Alvan Fuller appointed a special commission to review the case in June 1927. Despite noting Judge Thayer's "grave breach of official decorum" at trial, the commission found no reason to recommend clemency. On August 15, Justice Department spokesmen refused to open FBI files for the Sacco-Vanzetti Defense Committee, insisting that no proof of guilt or innocence was found therein, much less evidence of collusion between federal agents and the prosecution. Sacco and Vanzetti were executed eight days later. Another 45 years would pass before the redacted files were finally opened, in 1974. Three years later, on the 50th anniversary of their deaths, Sacco and Vanzetti were officially exonerated by proclamation of Massachusetts governor Michael Dukakis.

SALAZAR, Ben exonerated by DNA evidence

A resident of Travis County, Texas, Ben Salazar was 28 years old in 1991, when police arrested him on suspicion of forcible rape. Although Salazar denied involvement in the crime, prosecutors felt they had enough evidence to proceed with the case. Their suspect smoked the same brand of cigarettes as the rapist, had a tattoo in the same place described by the victim, and possessed a blood profile shared by only one in every 200 Hispanic-American men. Based on that circumstantial evidence and a tentative identification from the victim, jurors convicted Salazar in 1992, and he was sentenced to serve 30 years in prison. Five years later, a new defense attorney submitted semen traces from the crime scene for advanced DNA testing, and the results excluded Salazar as a possible donor. He was pardoned by Governor George Bush and released from prison on November 20, 1997. The state of Texas subsequently paid Salazar $25,000 in compensation for his five years of unjust confinement. The rape case remains unsolved today.

SCHECK, Barry C. (1949–)

A native of Queens, New York, born in September 1949, Barry Scheck earned his B.S. from Yale University (1971) and his J.D. from the University of California at Berkeley (1974). He subsequently spent three years as an attorney with New York's Legal Aid Society. Later, in private practice, Scheck earned a reputation for defending clients in criminal cases with DNA evidence. That experience convinced him that many prison inmates have been wrongfully convicted, whereupon he joined colleague Peter Neufeld to found the CARDOZO INNOCENCE PROJECT in 1992. Two years later, Scheck joined the so-called "dream team" employed by celebrity murder defendant ORENTHAL JAMES (O. J.) SIMPSON in Los Angeles, challenging forensic evidence while cocounsel Johnny Cochran promoted theories of a FRAME-UP by racist police. That combination punch won acquittal for Simpson in September 1995 (although a civil jury later found him responsible for the murders of both victims in that case). One journalistic observer dubbed Scheck's grilling of Los Angeles Police Department criminalist Dennis Fung "the greatest cross-examination since the Scopes trial" (wherein Clarence Darrow challenged William Jennings Bryan on the legal points of creationism versus evolution). Critics of Scheck's approach to Fung and other witnesses adopted the phrase "to Scheck" as a synonym for melodramatic bullying, but the National Association of Criminal Defense Lawyers named Scheck America's Most Outstanding Criminal Defense Lawyer in 1996. Aside from serving as the NACDL's president, Scheck is also a professor at the Benjamin N. Cardozo School of Law (home of the Innocence Project), director of the Clinical Education for the Trial Advocacy Program and director of the Center for the Study of Law and Ethics. With Peter Neufeld, Scheck is the coauthor of *Actual Innocence*, published in 2000.

SCHNEIDER, Albert (1863–1928)

Born in 1863, Albert Schneider earned his M.D. from Chicago's College of Physicians and Surgeons in 1887 and his Ph.D. from Columbia University 10 years later. At various times, he taught bacteriology and pharmacology at Northwestern University, the University of California (Berkeley), and the University of Nebraska. At Berkeley he collaborated with AUGUST VOLLMER on various forensic science research projects and in the establishment of Berkeley's first police academy. In 1916, Schneider pioneered the use of a vacuum apparatus to collect TRACE EVIDENCE at crime scenes. He was also the first to theorize a link between physical stress and electric activity in the human brain, inventing a device for DECEPTION ANALYSIS that anticipated the modern polygraph. Schneider died in Portland, Oregon, from a cerebral hemorrhage, in late October 1928.

SCRUGGS, Dwayne exonerated by DNA evidence

On the night of February 1, 1986, a woman walking home from a bus station in Indianapolis, Indiana, was stopped on the street by a man who approached her from behind, held a knife to her throat, and forced her toward a grassy area beneath a highway overpass. There, while trying to conceal his face, the attacker robbed his victim of six dollars, then raped her and fled the scene on foot. The victim viewed 200 mug shots of convicted sex offenders before identifying suspect Dwayne Scruggs as her assailant "with 98 percent certainty." She later picked Scruggs from a second photograph and repeated her identification in open court. Scruggs denied involvement in the crime, but he acknowledged familiarity with the area and owned a pair of boots resembling those worn by the rapist. Jurors convicted Scruggs of rape and ROBBERY on May 13, 1986, whereupon he received concurrent prison terms of 40 years and 20 years on the respective charges.

Scruggs appealed the conviction on dual grounds, including a lack of sufficient evidence to convict and an "evidentiary harpoon" consisting of a detective's testimony that the victim had selected Scruggs's photo from a group of "individuals who have all been arrested for rape or a sexual assault." The court had warned jurors to ignore that comment, but the defense's motion for a mistrial was denied. The Supreme Court of Indiana rejected Scruggs's appeal in August 1987.

Five years and four months later, on December 18, 1992, Scruggs's public defender petitioned for release of prosecution evidence that included semen traces and a BLOODSTAIN from the rapist gathered by Indianapolis police in February 1986. Subsequent motions, filed on February 24 and April 26, 1993, sought DNA testing (unavailable in 1986) on the

SEISMOLOGY, Forensic

CRIME SCENE evidence and a sample of Scruggs's blood. Permission for the tests was granted on April 27, 1993, and the results excluded Scruggs as a possible donor of either the semen or blood. Prosecutors verified the test results, then joined Scruggs's defender in a motion to vacate his conviction. That motion was granted on December 17, 1993, and Scruggs was released from prison. His record was expunged by court order on March 29, 1994. The rape remains unsolved today.

SEISMOLOGY, Forensic

Seismology is the study of earthquakes and seismic waves—waves of energy that move through or around Earth, caused by sudden breaking of rock or by explosions. Several different types of seismic waves are recognized, broadly divided into body waves (traveling through the planet's inner layers) and surface waves (confined to Earth's surface like ripples on water). Body waves are further divided into P (primary) and S (secondary) waves: P waves from an earthquake push and pull the rock or water through which they move, while S waves cause their medium to rock up and down or side to side. Surface waves are divided into Love waves (named for British mathematician A. E. H. Love) and Rayleigh waves (named for another British mathematician, John William Strutt, Lord Rayleigh). Love waves are the faster surface waves, moving ground or water from side to side. The slower and larger Rayleigh waves produce most of the sensation experienced during earthquakes, moving their medium up and down or from side to side.

Scientists around the world constantly monitor seismic activity with devices called seismographs. Their vigilance records not only natural events, but also significant explosions caused by human agency. That forensic application of seismology permits long-distance detection of nations that violate nuclear test-ban treaties, as well as charting major accidents. A case in point involved the Russian nuclear submarine *Kursk*, which exploded during a routine torpedo-testing exercise on August 12, 2000, and sank to a depth of 350 feet in the Kara Sea, off the coast of Severomorsk. The initial explosion measured 1.5 on the Richter scale (used to quantify earthquakes) and killed all 118 personnel aboard the *Kursk*. Officially, the disaster was blamed on a chemical chain reaction.

SEX Crimes

Sexual offenses are a controversial topic in America, with varied definitions and emphasis on enforcement creating wide gaps in perception from one jurisdiction to another. Broadly speaking, "sex crimes" include any offense including recognized sexual behavior such as heterosexual intercourse, sodomy, child molestation and a range of other activities ranging from voyeurism and exhibitionism to production of child pornography. Religious principles enshrined as law in the United States also impose Judeo-Christian ethics on sexual behavior in some jurisdictions. In the last decade of the 20th century, 49 states banned prostitution, 28 named various kinds of vaguely defined pornography, 27 (and the U.S. military) criminalized adultery, 26 and the District of Columbia outlawed bestiality, 18 banned some form of sodomy (variously defined as anal or oral sex, between heterosexual or same-sex couples), 10 outlawed heterosexual intercourse between unmarried persons, and 10 banned cohabitation between unmarried lovers, regardless of gender. At press time for this volume, nine states still punished premarital sex, seven banned cohabitation, and two—Michigan and Missouri—clung to their antisodomy statutes despite pending challenges in federal court.

In general, however, when "sex crimes" are discussed today, the term commonly refers to sexual acts inflicted upon unwilling participants or minors legally incapable of granting consent. (The age of consent in the United States ranges from 13 years in New Mexico to 19 in Wyoming.) An argument advanced since the 1980s, contending that "rape is a crime of violence, not sex," seems to miss the point that virtually *any* criminal offense—from ARSON, BURGLARY, and THEFT to multiple HOMICIDE—may spring from sexual motives. Some of the *paraphilias* (formerly known as "perversions") that are known to motive criminal activity include:

Anthropophagy: Sexual fixation on eating human flesh in acts of cannibalism. When applied specifically to corpses, often in advanced stages of decomposition, the proper term is *necrophagia*. Cannibalism of young girls, as practiced by serial killer Albert Fish in the 1930s, is termed *parthenophagy*.
Bondage: The use of restraints in sexual activity may be harmless between consenting adults, or deadly when applied by a violent offender.

While not punished as a sexual offense, nonconsensual restraint may classify as the offense of unlawful confinement.

Exhibitionism: Compulsive nudity is generally punished as a misdemeanor throughout the United States under statutes defining "indecent exposure." The same laws are frequently applied to acts with no sexual motive, as when drunken persons are caught urinating in public places.

Hematophilia/hematomania: Sexual fixation on blood, while not illegal in itself, has inspired various sadists and killers to indulge in acts of vampirism with unwilling victims. In those cases, where death does not result, the attack would normally be prosecuted as a form of aggravated battery.

Mutilation: Often seen in sadistic or sexually motivated crimes, mutilation of living victims may be legally classified as aggravated battery or *mayhem,* depending on the nature and extent of injuries inflicted. In psychiatric terms, *colobosis* refers specifically to mutilation of male genitalia, *mazoperosis* to the female breasts, and *perogynia* to mutilation of women (primarily their genitals).

Necrophilia: Sexual fixation on corpses is not criminalized in all U.S. jurisdictions, although several states passed new statutes in the closing decades of the 20th century. Where illegal, necrophilia is generally covered under laws banning abuse or mishandling of corpses.

Pedophilia: The proclivity for sex with children—variously defined under different age-of-consent statutes—arouses some of the most heated reactions in American jurisprudence and the media. Specific fixation on young boys is termed *pederasty.*

Sadism: Arousal dependent on the suffering of others, criminalized in all U.S. jurisdictions when unwilling partners are subjected to physical abuse or torture. *Necrosadism* involves abuse or mutilation of corpses, criminally punished in some (but not all) American jurisdictions. Bestial *sadism,* the sexually motivated torture of animals, is also punished in most states, though often as a misdemeanor. Only California presently mandates psychiatric counseling for those convicted of abusing animals.

Voyeurism: Generally the passive act of watching others undress or have sex, commonly accompanied by masturbation, voyeurism is usually punished as a misdemeanor under various statutes concerning disorderly conduct or indecent exposure. Conviction may result in the offender's listing as a registered sex offender.

Zoophilia: Sexual attraction to animals, regardless of species, is classified as a misdemeanor or felony in 26 states and the District of Columbia.

The FBI's *Crime Classification Manual* (1992) broadly defines "sexual assault" as including any "criminal offenses in which victims are forced to participate in sexual activity. Physical violence may or may not be involved." Bureau profilers recognize four kinds of rapists, based on underlying motivations. They include:

Power-reassurance rapists, for whom the attack is primarily an expression of rape fantasies wherein victims enjoy the experience and may even fall in love with their assailants.

Exploitative rapists, craving submissive victims, for whom most sexual behavior is expressed as impulsive predatory acts.

Anger rapists, misogynists expressing rage at a specific female or women in general through violent sexual acts.

Sadistic rapists, who realize their fantasies of pain and domination with unwilling partners but without the specific anger seen in the previous category.

One or more motives may be involved in what the FBI terms *criminal enterprise rape,* defined as "sexual coercion, abuse, or assault that is committed for material gain." *Felony rape* is defined as sexual assault committed during the commission of some other felony, such as burglary or robbery. A further breakdown includes designations for *primary felony rape* (wherein a nonsexual crime is the offender's main intention) and *secondary felony rape* (where the offender plans a rape and adds some other crime, such as robbery, for additional gain).

Forensic scientists collect evidence of sex crimes from victims, from crime scenes, and from the persons or surroundings of suspects (including their homes and workplaces). Semen is collected on swabs, as well as from clothing or other objects, and additional TRACE EVIDENCE may also link the offender to a specific victim or crime scene. DNA profiling today permits positive identification or exclusion of specific offenders, whereas simple use of blood typing prior to the late 1980s resulted in many cases of wrongful conviction.

SHEPHARD, David exonerated by DNA evidence

On December 24, 1983, while engaged in some last-minute Christmas shopping, a female resident of Union County, New Jersey, was accosted by two men in the parking lot of a shopping mall. The strangers forced their victim into the backseat of her own car, one man holding her immobile while the other drove them to a nearby residential neighborhood. There, both men raped the woman repeatedly, one calling his companion "Dave" during the prolonged attack. Tiring at last, the rapists shoved the woman from her car and drove away. The victim's car and handbag were later found near a building at Newark International Airport, where David Shephard was employed.

The victim subsequently identified Shephard by sight and the sound of his voice as one of her attackers. A blood test revealed that Shephard's antigens and secretor type matched those of one rapist. Shephard's alibi was uncorroborated and collapsed under cross-examination at trial, in September 1984. Jurors deliberated for a day before convicting Shephard of rape, robbery, terrorist threats, and weapons violations. Following conviction, he received a 30-year prison term. The second rapist was never identified, as Shephard continued to protest his innocence and refused to name an accomplice.

Shephard's appeals had been exhausted by 1992, when he filed a motion for DNA testing of all semen samples collected by police in 1983 (before such tests were recognized). Prosecutors agreed, and the test results excluded Shephard as the donor of one semen sample recovered from a vaginal swab. Shephard was not exonerated, however, since two rapists were involved and the genetic material found on a second swab produced inconclusive results. Shepard's attorney next sought test results for semen stains on the victim's underpants, where two distinct genetic profiles failed to match Shephard's. Prosecutors theorized that one donor of the underwear stains might be the victim's boyfriend, but further tests excluded him as well. The Union County Superior Court ordered a new trial for Shephard, whereupon prosecutors declined to pursue the case. Shephard was

freed on May 18, 1994, after serving nearly 10 years for a crime he did not commit. New Jersey statutes barred financial compensation of defendants wrongfully convicted, but the law was soon changed on the basis of Shephard's case.

"SHOT Spotter" Microphones audio surveillance technology

Invented by Triton Technology of Los Altos, California, as a means of focusing police response to gunshots fired in urban areas, "Shot Spotter" microphones made their public debut in the high-crime Willowbrook district of Los Angeles in March 2000. Two months later, the devices had produced only one arrest, but law enforcement spokesmen remained hopeful that the system would be useful in the future.

Organized as a privately funded experiment, Shot Spotter microphones were installed atop utility poles and selected rooftops throughout a one-square-mile area of the Willowbrook neighborhood. Each microphone in turn is linked to a computer system that can pinpoint the origin of a gunshot or other similar sounds within a radius of 20 feet, in seven seconds. A parallel system, if activated, places telephone calls to residents in the immediate area of the gunfire, to seek out witnesses and additional information. Willowbrook was selected as a testing ground because its streets had witnessed 120 unsolved homicides in the preceding 30 months. During the first two months of operation, police were startled to note how few gunfire incidents were reported by local residents: of 124 shootings recorded by Shot Spotter, authorities received phone calls on only eight, leaving 94 percent of local shootings unreported.

Reactions to the new technology were mixed. James Pasco, executive director of the Fraternal Order of Police, told *USA Today*, "Any technology that provides police and citizens with more notice of a potentially deadly situation has tremendous public safety implications." Jeff Chester, a spokesman for the privacy-conscious Center for Media Education, took an opposite view, regarding Shot Spotter as the opening wedge of a potential police state. "This is a first visible example that we're creating an infrastructure of surveillance," Chester said. "We want a rapid response to protect public safety, but I think this kind of intrusive technology goes beyond prudent police work. This community eavesdropping is a very dangerous concept." Thus far, local authorities contend, they have received no complaints of privacy invasion from Willowbrook's residents.

SIMPSON, Cedric Keith (1907–1985)

A physician's son, born at Brighton, England, in 1907, Cedric Smith enrolled at Guy's Hospital Medical School in 1924 and received his D.D.S. with honors in 1930, followed by a second degree in PATHOLOGY two years later. The school's administration valued Simpson enough to offer him a teaching post, and he remained at his alma mater as a professor of pathology until 1937. He then moved on to the London University, where he became that institution's first full professor of forensic medicine in 1962, a post he retained for another decade. Simpson's textbook, *Forensic Medicine,* was published in 1947. Four years after he retired, in 1976, the University of Edinburgh granted Simpson an honorary LL.D. His autobiography, *Forty Years of Murder* (1978), was a British best seller. In addition to his other duties, Simpson served as president of England's Medico-Legal Society (1961–63) and as founding president of the British Association in Forensic Medicine (1966–67).

Simpson once told an interviewer that he specialized in forensic pathology and ODONTOLOGY to minimize his own contact with suffering patients. Still, during the course of his career Simpson encountered more violence (albeit posthumously) than most physicians ever see outside of wartime or an urban trauma center. Simpson's nefarious subjects included serial killer John Haigh, who dissolved his victims in acid as a means of avoiding detection, and a rape-slayer hanged in 1948 after Simpson matched his teeth to a bite mark on the victim's breast. Equally interested in forensic ENTOMOLOGY, Simpson used the maggots of a blue bottle fly to pinpoint another murder victim's time of death in 1964—and thus sent another killer to prison for life. His refusal to autopsy an AIDS victim in 1983 sparked controversy in Britain, although the Department of Health sided with Simpson. A brain tumor claimed Simpson's life in July 1985, at age 78.

SIMPSON, Orenthal James acquitted despite DNA evidence

Since the early 1990s, prosecutors and defense attorneys alike have hailed DNA evidence as the "Rosetta

O. J. Simpson was acquitted of murder despite overwhelming DNA evidence. (PACHA/CORBIS)

stone" of guilt or innocence in criminal cases. Analysis of a suspect's "genetic fingerprint," compared to biological evidence found at a crime scene, may now identify a specific individual to the virtual exclusion of any other person on the planet (except an identical twin). And yet, the strongest evidence is only as good as the prosecutors who present it and the jurors who consider it. The murder case of athlete/actor O. J. Simpson is a perfect case in point.

On the night of June 12, 1994, Simpson's estranged wife, Nicole Brown Simpson, and her male friend Ronald Goldman were attacked outside a private residence in the Los Angeles suburb of Brentwood. Both were slashed to death with a knife, in what appeared to be a frenzied assault. Police responding to the scene found a size-12 shoe print in the victims' blood, and scattered to its left, four drops of blood belonging to neither victim, as if the killer had himself been injured on the left side of his body during the attack. A knitted wool cap lay beside the mutilated bodies. Nearby, a gate revealed more blood, ultimately matched to the four "alien" drops found beside the killer's footprint.

Mindful of the history surrounding O. J. Simpson and Nicole, including several police reports of wife-beating and death threats, officers proceeded to Simpson's home to question him. There, they found spots of blood inside his Ford Bronco, in the driveway, and inside the house on one of Simpson's socks. A bloody leather glove was also found behind the house, lying in some shrubbery. Simpson sported a fresh, deep cut on the middle finger of his left hand, but told investigators he had no idea how it had happened.

DNA analysis was rapidly performed on the various blood samples found at the crime scene and around Simpson's home. The blood drops found beside the killer's size-12 shoe print (O. J.'s shoe size) and the stain on the gate near the crime scene proved to match Simpson's DNA—in the case of the gate stain, narrowing the search to one unique person in 57 billion (roughly 10 times the population of planet Earth). Bloodstains from Simpson's car included his own DNA, along with that of Nicole and Ron Goldman. Likewise, the glove found behind Simpson's house bore his own blood, plus blood from both victims. DNA from the blood found on Simpson's sock, inside his house, was a positive match for Nicole.

In addition to DNA evidence, the case also furnished a number of hairs and FIBERS that helped put the crime in perspective. From the knit cap found in Brentwood, police recovered nine hairs microscopically identical to O. J. Simpson's. A 10th matching hair was recovered from Ron Goldman's shirt. The bloody glove outside Simpson's mansion also carried hair matching O. J.'s and synthetic fibers microscopically identical to the carpet of his Ford Bronco.

Police issued an arrest warrant for Simpson on June 17, 1994, finally taking him into custody after the now-famous "slow-speed chase" that featured Simpson holding a gun to his own head and threatening suicide. In court, Simpson denied any role in the murders, enlisting a so-called "dream team" of high-priced lawyers to defend him. Ironically, the defense team's DNA experts were BARRY SCHECK and Peter Neufeld, later renowned for their work with the CARDOZO INNOCENCE PROJECT, using DNA

evidence to liberate wrongfully convicted inmates. In Simpson's case, their role would be somewhat different.

Former prosecutor Vincent Bugliosi, in his book *Outrage* (1996), noted that there were only three possible explanations for O. J. Simpson's blood being found at the Brentwood crime scene: (1) He somehow cut himself at the scene, while the crime was in progress; (2) he coincidentally spilled blood at the scene on some previous occasion; or (3) samples of his blood were deliberately planted as part of a FRAME-UP. When blood from both victims was found in his car and at his home, the second possibility—sheer coincidence—was effectively eliminated.

Simpson's defenders never offered the court a satisfactory explanation for the fresh cut on his hand. Instead, they devoted their efforts to a two-pronged attack on the prosecution. Simpson had been framed, they said, by racist police who planted the bloody glove at his house, furthermore dribbling blood from the murdered victims on Simpson's sock and the interior of his car. As for his own blood at the CRIME SCENE, if it was not planted by authorities to frame Simpson, then the test results were simply wrong, a result of "cross-contamination" in the police crime lab. Barry Scheck branded the L.A. crime lab a "black hole" of contamination, where blood samples were allegedly mixed and mingled indiscriminately. A forensic expert for the defense, Dr. Henry Lee, appeared to testify that "something is wrong" with the state's DNA evidence. (FBI experts refuted that claim, and they also pointed out that marks that Dr. Lee identified as probably footprints of the "real killer" were actually imbedded in the crime scene's concrete pavement, laid years before the murders.)

The "contamination" argument was disingenuous at best. Bugliosi notes, and DNA experts universally agree, that all crime scene evidence samples are contaminated, to some extent, by contact with other physical objects, but such contamination never results in a "false positive" reading. At worst, the results of a test on contaminated blood would be inconclusive, identifying no one. Simply stated, it is physically impossible to take a blood sample from Suspect "A" and mix it with any combination of elements on earth to produce a positive DNA match with Suspect "B." The blood of an unknown killer cannot be altered, transmuted, or transformed into the blood of O. J. Simpson by any method known to earthly science. It simply cannot be done.

Simpson's marathon trial in Los Angeles lasted from January to October 1995, including weeks of scientific testimony, but jurors seemed to have reached their decision far in advance. The panel finally deliberated less than four hours, precluding any real discussion of the evidence, and acquitted Simpson on all charges. One juror, a 72-year-old woman who admitted during pretrial questioning that she never read anything but daily racing forms and "didn't really understand" those, told reporters after the fact, "I didn't understand the DNA stuff at all. To me, it was a waste of time. It was way out there and carried absolutely no weight with me." A second juror found Dr. Lee's discredited testimony the "most impressive" evidence presented—because he had paused to smile at the jury before he testified. Small wonder, then, that journalists described the verdict as a case of "jury nullification," unrelated to logic or evidence. (Lead prosecutor Marcia Clark later described the trial jurors as "moon rocks.")

A second jury listened to the same evidence in 1996, at the trial of a civil lawsuit filed against Simpson by survivors of the two murdered victims, and that panel reached a very different conclusion. In the civil case, Simpson was judged legally responsible for the murders ("wrongful death," outside the venue of a criminal court) and was ordered to pay substantial damages. To date, the winners in that case have reportedly collected nothing.

"SMART" Guns attempts to improve firearm security

With the exception of religious questions such as legalized abortion and prayer in schools, few public issues raise quite so much heated controversy in America as the issue of "gun control." On one side, proponents of unlimited civilian firepower argue that the U.S. Constitution's Second Amendment guarantee of a "right to keep and bear arms" is sacrosanct, and any legislative effort to abridge that freedom smacks of seditious conspiracy. At the other extreme, proponents of a total FIREARMS ban quote, misquote, and sometimes fabricate statistics to portray guns as a lethal blight on the nation at large. Between those polar opposites lies a body of judicial rulings and some 20,000 federal, state, and local statutes regulating the "right to bear arms" in various U.S. jurisdictions.

One proposed solution to the controversy is development of personalized (or "smart") guns that incorporate technology designed to prevent use of a weapon by anyone other than its rightful owner. Typically employing BIOMETRICS—palm or FINGERPRINTS—to identify a firearm's legitimate user, such weapons would theoretically be inoperable in the hands of a stranger, be it a neighbor, a thief, or a curious child. Proponents of "smart" gun technology include Physicians for Social Responsibility (PSR), who deem gun violence "a public health emergency" and view the new technology as critical "in order to reduce the use of firearms in unintentional, homicidal, and suicidal deaths and injuries." Executives of the Colt Manufacturing Company, a leading U.S. handgun producer, announced efforts to produce a "smart" pistol in 1996, declaring that it would save lives in American homes and on city streets, where felons could no longer hope to arm themselves by looting stores or wrestling weapons away from police officers. At the same time, Colt spokesmen declared, the new weapons should make it "less likely that our 2nd Amendment rights will be legislatively reduced or limited." On May 1, 1999, Philadelphia's city council proposed legislation (never enacted) that would penalize buyers, sellers, and shooters alike for any injury inflicted by guns unequipped with "smart" technology.

Critics of the smart-gun concept (and of gun control in general) point out certain built-in problems with the plan that has become a panacea in some quarters. Those problems include:

Unproven technology Today, none is commercially available or found in general use. Critics cite this fact as evidence that the concept is faulty and perhaps unworkable. If smart guns work, where are they?

Combat limitations Police and others required to carry weapons might be placed in jeopardy by smart-gun technology. Since current systems allow programming for only one hand, a right-handed officer wounded in a gunfight could find himself unable to fire his own weapon left-handed in self-defense, with potentially fatal results. It is also theoretically possible that while grappling for a weapon, the officer might retain sufficient contact to let his assailant trigger a shot as if he were the authorized shooter.

Feasibility Americans presently own more than 190 million firearms, including some 65 million pistols. None of them are "personalized," and there is no reason to suppose that gun owners will trade in their weapons, much less spend billions of dollars on new ones to replace the old.

Increased civilian firepower While a majority of smart-gun advocates are drawn from the ranks of those whose agenda includes the reduction of civilian armament, civilian firepower might actually increase if present gun owners "traded up" to replace their existing weapons with personalized handguns. The reason: a "Guns in America" survey from the 1990s revealed that some three-quarters of all civilian-owned pistols had an ammunition capacity below 10 rounds (reflecting the fact that most were revolvers or older semiautomatics manufactured before the invention of high-capacity magazines). Newer pistols generally accommodate the legal maximum 10-round magazine, thus meaning that legitimate shooters who "go bad" would have increased lethal firepower at their disposal.

Disarming minors Critics argue that smart-gun technology would have no effect on minors who commit acts of violence with firearms, since persons below age 21 are already barred by law from purchasing pistols, while a 1998 *New York Times* poll revealed that 15 percent of Americans aged 13 to 17 already own other types of firearms. Various arguments that smart guns would thus reduce juvenile violence or suicide are thereby rendered virtually meaningless.

Suicide Speaking of self-destruction, protestations from the PSR and others notwithstanding, there is no good reason to believe smart guns would prevent suicides. An individual intent on ending his life would simply be required to purchase a weapon and have it programmed to fit his hand.

Accidental shootings Advocates of smart-gun technology assert that it would eliminate "virtually all" accidental firearms injuries and deaths. They refer specifically to deaths of children,

The "smart gun" uses technology that recognizes the gun's owner and prevents anyone else from firing the weapon. (AP)

who in fact account for barely 15 percent of accidental shooting deaths in any given year. (In 1995, an average year, 181 out of 1,225 accidental firearms deaths involved victims under 15 years of age.) In any case, new technology would do nothing to prevent an accidental shooting by the weapon's "authorized" user, regardless of his or her age.

Black-market sales Smart-gun advocates suggest that the new technology would eliminate many illegal (or "straw") sales, but critics vehemently disagree. Prospective manufacturers such as Colt admit that "smart" firearms could be reprogrammed for new users at will—i.e., no sale is "forever." Nothing would prevent black-market dealers or buyers from adapting the weapons to fit a new user's hand with minimal effort (the equivalent of encoding a new combination on a safe, for example).

Firearms theft While smart-gun proponents claim advancing technology would somehow reduce theft of weapons, critics note that ease of reprogramming would not discourage any thief with access to a cooperative technician. Likewise, circulation of smart guns would do nothing to prevent theft of the 190 million firearms already at large in the country.

At present the arguments for and against smart-gun technology remain strictly academic. Until such time as personalized weapons are physically available—and then at competitive prices—the theoretical advance in technology will have no real-world impact on crime in the United States.

SMITH, Frank Lee posthumously exonerated by DNA

In 1985, a prowler invaded the Florida home of eight-year-old Shandra Whitehead, raping and fatally beating the child in her bed. Police arrested suspect Frank Lee Smith, then on parole for two previous killings. No physical evidence linked Smith to the CRIME SCENE, but jurors convicted him in 1986 after witness Chiquita Lowe described Smith lurking in darkness outside Whitehead's house. Smith received a death sentence, but Lowe recanted her testimony in 1989, less than a month before his scheduled execution. She had only fingered Smith, Lowe said, because police assured her he was dangerous. In fact, the man she *really* saw at Whitehead's home

on the night of the murder was Eddie Lee Mosley, a deranged serial killer suspected of several other rape-slayings in the same area. With one week left to live, Smith won a stay of execution from Florida's supreme court, but a Broward County judge refused his bid for a new trial after prosecutors portrayed Lowe as a liar. In 1998 Smith's attorneys petitioned for DNA testing of semen found at the crime scene, but Broward County prosecutors objected on grounds that the bid came too late under standing court rules—even if testing proved that the semen belonged to another suspect.

While his case dragged through the courts, Smith developed cancer. His lawyers subsequently claimed that jailers ignored Smith's declining health until the disease was too advanced for successful treatment (a claim denied by state authorities). Smith died in January 2000, but his attorneys pressed on with their plan for DNA testing, and the results proved their case in December, finally exonerating Smith of involvement in Whitehead's murder. Attorney Martin McClain told the *St. Petersburg Times*, "We knew he was innocent in December of 1989. We told the courts, and we told them who was the real killer, but no one cared, and they kept Frank Lee Smith on death row for another 10 years until he died." In McClain's view, Smith's case was "just a snapshot of how unreliable the system is. If you were grading the system, this case shows it flunked."

SMITH, Sydney Alfred (1883–1969)

A child of British immigrants and the youngest son of a large family, Sydney Smith was born in Roxburgh, New Zealand, on August 4, 1883. Viewing a medical career as a passport to travel, he apprenticed with a local pharmacist, then worked at a dispensary in Dunedin, subsequently studying CHEMISTRY and physics at Victoria College while working at Wellington Hospital. Bankrolled by forays in gold speculation, Smith struck off for Scotland, where he won a scholarship in botany and zoology to Edinburgh University. Smith graduated with honors in 1912 but abandoned general practice after one month and returned to Edinburgh University as an aide to Sir Harvey Littlejohn, the dean of medicine and chief police surgeon, working in forensic PATHOLOGY. Smith assisted Littlejohn on various murder cases while earning a diploma in public health (1913) and taking honors for his M.D. thesis on examination of BLOODSTAINS (1914).

With that experience behind him, Smith returned to New Zealand as a public health officer in 1914, then joined the army as a sanitation officer in 1915, with the rank of major. Two years later, when the British forensic expert in Egypt died, Smith was sent to replace him. In Cairo, Smith found himself responsible for investigating all murders committed nationwide, while simultaneously lecturing on forensic medicine at the national university. His other forensic duties included consultation on cases of livestock poisoning and various injuries (often self-inflicted) that produced legal claims against the government. As if his schedule was not crowded enough, Smith also provided medicolegal advice to British authorities in Palestine and the Sudan. In 1924, his study of FIREARMS and ballistics helped convict the assassins of Egypt's military commander in chief (for which Smith received the Order of the Nile in 1925).

Smith's classic text, *Forensic Medicine,* first saw publication in Arabic (1924), then was translated into English (1925) and won the Swiney Prize—jointly bestowed by the Royal College of Physicians and the Royal Society for the encouragement of Arts, Manufactures and Commerce—in 1929. (Its seventh edition appeared in 1940.) In 1927, while vacationing in Edinburgh, Smith collaborated with Dr. Littlejohn on ballistics experiments that accused defendant Donald Merrett of killing his mother. Sir Bernard Spilsbury contested those findings in court and secured Merrett's acquittal, but Smith's side was later vindicated when Merrett murdered his wife and mother-in-law, then committed suicide to escape a second trial. Littlejohn died before year's end, whereupon the University of Edinburgh offered his chair to Smith. Smith accepted and remained as a professor at his alma mater from 1928 until 1953. He also served from 1931 until his retirement as the university's dean of medicine. Smith's work with the General Medical Council earned him a Commander of the British Empire honor (CBE) in 1944 and a knighthood five years later. The same year brought him an honorary M.D. from the University of Louvain, while the Law-Sciences Institute of Texas established a scholarship in Smith's name, in 1956. Three years later, his autobiography—*Mostly Murder*—topped British best-seller charts. Smith died at home in Edinburgh, on May 8, 1969.

SMITH, Walter D. exonerated by DNA
In 1984, while struggling with a cocaine addiction, Walter Smith attempted to rob a Columbus, Ohio, gas station. Police jailed him for that crime, which he freely admitted, but prior to sentencing they also slapped him with charges of raping three women on the city's North Side. All three victims identified Smith, and jurors ignored his protestations of innocence, convicting him on multiple felony counts. Smith's sentence, 78 to 190 years, ensured that he would die in prison.

Twelve years later, attorney Daniel Marinik convinced Franklin County prosecutor Michael Miller to reopen Smith's case and permit DNA testing of the crime scene evidence. Smith's family raised $2,000 to finance the tests, which excluded Smith as a possible donor of semen found on the victims in 1984. Miller confirmed those results with a second round of testing, and Smith was freed from prison on December 6, 1996. Just over four years later, in January 2001, Ohio's Court of Claims awarded Smith $249,989.05 for his wrongful conviction.

SMUGGLING
Smuggling is broadly defined as the surreptitious and illegal transportation of any object(s) or substance(s) with intent to evade detection, confiscation, and/or taxation. The item smuggled may not be illegal, but its covert transportation may constitute an offense in itself (as when large amounts of cash are smuggled in aid of MONEY LAUNDERING or taxable items purchased abroad are hidden from customs inspectors to avoid paying duties). Depending on a given jurisdiction's laws, nearly any object may be subject to smuggling. Federal statutes in the United States once banned interstate shipment of films depicting prize fights, and smuggling of untaxed tea was a trigger of the American revolution against British rule. Today, commonly smuggled objects include drugs and other CONTROLLED SUBSTANCES, WEAPONS, endangered species, or products derived from their slaughter, all kinds of stolen property, currency (in excess of $10,000, when leaving the United States), and human beings (including fugitives, illegal immigrants, and slaves).

Motives for smuggling are diverse. As noted previously, many smugglers are profit-motivated to deliver contraband or trade in untaxed merchandise, transport stolen property, and so forth. Smuggling may

An Indonesian prosecutor holds a pack of heroin confiscated from the "Bali Nine," a drug-trafficking ring. (Firdia Lisnawati/AP)

also be politicized, as when income from the crime is used to finance a specific cause or where it serves the cause more directly (as in smuggling of runaway slaves along the 19th-century Underground Railroad). Other acts of smuggling—as when medical supplies are infiltrated into nations known for the corruption of their governments, thus diverting treatment from the needy—may even be viewed in some quarters as altruistic. Most smuggling occurs across national or state borders, but smuggling of contraband is also common in prison and other restrictive environments. Forensic scientists crack smuggling cases first by identifying contraband products (where their identity is not already obvious), and by using any evidence available to identify the smugglers or their customers. Since much modern smuggling is carried out by organized gangs or syndicates, prosecution for conspiracy and racketeering is common in these cases.

SNYDER, LeMoyne (1899–1975)

A Lansing, Michigan, native, born in 1899, Le-Moyne Snyder earned his M.D. from Harvard Medical School and served his internship at New York City's Fifth Avenue Hospital, where his frequent contact with crime victims sparked a fascination with forensic PATHOLOGY. Snyder subsequently returned to Lansing, earning an LL.B. from Michigan State University to aid him in his courtroom presentation of forensic evidence. Snyder abandoned private practice when his work with the Michigan State Police demanded too much time, although his busy schedule of investigations and expert testimony still permitted Snyder to lead occasional seminars on forensic medicine. One such, at Harvard, lured mystery novelist Erle Stanley Gardner as a student, and he soon became fast friends with Snyder. Gardner's novel *The D.A. Breaks an Egg* is dedicated to Snyder.

Three years before that story's publication, in 1946, Snyder joined Gardner to create the "Court of Last Resort," a private panel of experts gathered to investigate apparent miscarriages of justice. The group's first case involved Clarence Boggie, a lumberjack serving a life term for murder in Washington State. The panel proved him innocent with such persuasive evidence that Tom Smith, former warden of Walla Walla Penitentiary, joined the panel himself. The group's most famous case was that of William Marvin Lindley, a homeless defendant accused of rape and murder in Los Angeles, based on circumstantial evidence and an alleged deathbed statement from his victim. Lindley was first pronounced insane, then certified competent for trial after nearly a year in a state institution, whereupon jurors convicted him, and he received a death sentence. Defense attorney Alfred Matthews enlisted the Court of Last Resort, whose members satisfied themselves that Lindley's alibi was solid. Correspondence from Gardner's panel convinced Governor Earl Warren to commute Lindley's capital sentence, and Lindley was later exonerated of all charges. Gardner's "court" also reviewed the case of Cleveland murder defendant Sam Sheppard but abandoned it after polygraph tests proved inconclusive.

The Court of Last Resort dissolved in the early 1960s, soon after Gardner's retirement from the panel, but Dr. Snyder continued his forensic work without fear of controversy. In 1958, he told delegates to a medical conference that 20 percent of all deaths recorded in the United States might be

HOMICIDES, imploring his colleagues to demand autopsies in any case where the cause of death was not readily apparent. Snyder remained active in the field until his death at age 76, in 1975.

SNYDER, Walter exonerated by DNA evidence

In the early morning hours of October 28, 1985, a female resident of Alexandria, Virginia, was attacked, raped, and sodomized by a stranger who broke through the door of her apartment. The victim, a Caucasian, was initially unable to describe her attacker beyond the fact that he was African American and wore red shorts. Police prepared a photo array, including a picture of Walter Snyder, a 19-year-old black man who lived across the street from the crime scene. The victim passed over his photo at first, but officers then marched her past a bench in police headquarters where Snyder sat alone. She subsequently selected his photo and picked Snyder from a lineup, declaring herself "100 percent sure" that he was the rapist. A search of Snyder's apartment revealed a pair of red shorts, and his Type A blood matched that of the attacker.

At trial, the victim once again named Snyder as her rapist, while prosecutors introduced the shorts and basic blood evidence. Snyder's alibi—that he was home, asleep, when the attack occurred—was corroborated by his mother, but jurors chose to disregard her testimony. On June 25, 1986, they convicted Snyder of rape, sodomy, and BURGLARY, recommending a 45-year sentence, which the trial judge confirmed and imposed. Snyder's appeal of the conviction was rejected, but he subsequently learned of new advances in the field of DNA testing and "genetic fingerprints." Convinced that such a test would prove him innocent, he sought a lawyer to pursue the case and finally contacted members of the CARDOZO INNOCENCE PROJECT. Staff attorneys agreed to handle Snyder's case on a pro bono basis (free of charge) if his family could raise the money to pay for expensive DNA testing. Virginia prosecutors agreed to release their forensic evidence in May 1992, and a Boston laboratory eliminated Snyder as a suspect seven months later. Prosecutors insisted on repeating the tests, with identical results from the FBI's crime lab.

Snyder should have been released immediately, but Virginia statutes require that any motion for a new trial based on newly discovered evidence must be filed within 21 days of a defendant's conviction. Since

more than six years had elapsed from Snyder's trial to the conclusive demonstration of his innocence, state courts rejected any further arguments. The only recourse lay in a request for executive clemency from Governor L. Douglas Wilder. Snyder's prosecutor joined defense attorneys in requesting a pardon for Snyder, but Governor Wilder delayed his decision until public outcry from the press made his position untenable. Wilder finally granted the overdue pardon on April 23, 1993, and Snyder was released after serving nearly seven years for a crime he did not commit. The Alexandria Circuit Court granted Snyder's petition to expunge his criminal record on January 11, 1994. The rape remains unsolved today.

SOPHONOW, Thomas exonerated by DNA evidence

Shortly before 9:00 P.M. on December 23, 1981, 16-year-old Barbara Gayle Stoppel was found strangled and near death in the women's restroom of a Winnipeg, Manitoba, doughnut shop where she worked after school. Rushed to St. Boniface Hospital, Stoppel was placed on life support, but she was later declared brain-dead, and mechanical support was discontinued later in the week by mutual agreement of her family and physicians. Back at the CRIME SCENE, several witnesses described a man seen leaving the ladies' room shortly before Stoppel's body was found. They described the murder suspect as a white male, 21 to 30 years old, with brown hair and mustache, a "scruffy" appearance, and acne-scarred complexion, wearing prescription glasses and a dark-colored cowboy hat. One witness had pursued the suspect and confronted him, but the man escaped after tossing a box, a pair of gloves, and some twine used in the murder off Norwood Bridge. Composite sketches were prepared and circulated to the media.

Police suspected that the killer was a local resident, who may have killed Stoppel in revenge for some previous altercation. That theory was abandoned, though, when detectives mistakenly traced the "unique" nylon twine discarded by their suspect to a manufacturer in Washington state, thereafter focusing their manhunt along the West Coast. (In fact, later analysis proved the twine had been manufactured at Portage la Prairie, 50 miles west of Winnipeg.) While scouring the wrong location, authorities focused their attention on Thomas Sophonow, a 28-year-old Vancouver resident who frequently visited Winnipeg and who vaguely resembled the composite drawing of Stoppel's killer. Sophonow was arrested and charged with the crime on March 12, 1982, but convicting him would be no easy task. The first trial ended with a hung jury, but Sophonow was tried twice more, convicted on both occasions, only to have his convictions reversed by the Manitoba Court of Appeal. He was released in December 1985, after spending three years and nine months in jail, suffering multiple assaults by other inmates. When prosecutors expressed their intent to try him again, that move was blocked by Canada's Supreme Court.

Still, Sophonow remained a prime murder suspect in the public eye, guilty as charged to many casual observers of the case. Another five years passed before Winnipeg police admitted their mistake, with a June 2000 announcement that DNA test results on evidence found at the crime scene had finally exonerated Sophonow of any role in the murder. At the same time, detectives announced their location of an unnamed "new suspect," but that lead proved ephemeral. The slaying remains open today, ranking high among Canada's unsolved mysteries.

As for Thomas Sophonow, falsely accused of murder, robbed of nearly four years' time, his reputation ruined, the road to meager compensation has been long and fraught with frustration. On November 5, 2001, Manitoba justice minister Gird Mackintosh released a report by retired Supreme Court justice Peter Cory, recommending payment of $2.6 million to Sophonow, with 50 percent to be paid by the City of Winnipeg, 40 percent by Manitoba's provincial government, and 10 percent from Canada's federal government. Manitoba officials countered with an offer of $1 million for Sophonow and $75,000 to the Stoppel family. Ultimately, in 2003, Sophonow received the full $2.6 million in compensation.

SPECTROSCOPY

Spectroscopy (or *spectrophotometry*) is the study of light's interaction with matter. Its forensic application involves varied means of ELEMENTAL ANALYSIS. Basic spectrometers are instruments that include a light source, a filter for selecting wavelengths, a device to hold the sample being tested, and a detector that converts light into measurable electric current. The spectrometer thus identifies a questioned sample by recording its absorption of light, with those results compared to known absorption standards for vari-

ous elements. Varieties of spectroscopy presently in use include:

Atomic absorption spectroscopy, used to detect metals such as arsenic, antimony, barium, copper, and lead in samples vaporized by a *nebulizer.*

Atomic emission spectroscopy, performing a similar function with metals but using a plasma torch to produce more extreme temperatures.

Auger spectrophotometry, employing X-rays in a manner similar to that of X-ray photoelectron spectroscopy. X-rays interact with atoms, causing ejection of inner-shell electrons and subsequent absorption of outer-shell electrons to replace them.

Colorimetry is a type of spectroscopy used on colored samples—that is, the range of light visible to naked human eyes. Modern instruments such as the Spectronic 20 and Spectronic 21 convert the colored light to electrical current, which may be displayed in alternate ways, analyzing the concentration of various chemicals in a solution.

Energy dispersive spectroscopy is the technique utilized in scanning electron MICROSCOPY, using beams of ions in place of light to achieve much greater magnification of microscopic samples than a normal light microscope can produce. Results are checked against a database called SLICE—*s*pectral *li*brary for *i*dentification and *c*lassification *e*ngine—developed by the FBI.

Infrared spectroscopy, as suggested by its name, uses infrared light, which has unique absorption rates for different molecules. Most infrared spectrophotometers sold in the past two decades include a device called a Michelson intergerometer, which allows multiple infrared wavelengths to bombard a sample simultaneously.

Ion mobility spectrometry, originally known as plasma CHROMATOGRAPHY, mimics the process of ELECTROPHORESIS to detect drugs, EXPLOSIVES, and various chemical weapons. Instead of using a gel medium, however, the process tests samples that are vaporized into gas. In expert hands, an ion mobility spectrometer can detect drugs or explosives inside closed containers.

Mass spectrometry determines the mass-to-charge ratio of ions and separates them accordingly.

It is most commonly used to find the composition of a vaporized sample by generating a *mass spectrum* displaying the masses of various compounds found in the sample. Molecules are thus identified by their known, constant masses. In essence, samples are vaporized and ionized (broken down into ions), then are sent into an ion acceleration chamber and pass through a vent in a metal sheet while under the influence of a magnetic field. That field causes lighter ions to deflect farther than heavy ones, producing a curved display on the instruments detector. MATHEMATICS does the rest, with calculation of the sample's mass-to-charge ratio. Five variant forms of the process are *gas chromatography/mass spectrometry* (employing a gas chromatography to separate compounds), *liquid chromatography/mass spectrometry* (replacing gas with a mixture of water and organic solvents), *ion mobility spectrometry/mass spectrometry* (incorporating IMS techniques discussed above), *quadrupole mass spectrometry* (with a filter composed of four parallel metal rods, used as a detector in gas chromatography), and *tandem mass spectrometry* (involving multiple steps in mass selection or analysis of molecules fragmented by one of five methods: blackbody infrared radiative dissociation, collision-induced dissociation, electron capture dissociation, electron transfer dissociation, or infrared multiphoton dissociation.

Microspectrometry combines spectrometry and MICROSCOPY to analyze a variety of substances including drugs, dyes, FIBERS, inks, and PAINT with infrared or ultraviolet light. In 2005, the Arizona Department of Public Safety and California-based CRAIC Technologies announced a new application of microspectrometry for the identification of stolen jewels, measuring the spectra of visible and ultraviolet light created by known imperfections in various gems. Such flaws in famous stones are currently "mapped" by the Gemological Institute of America, with the results collected in a computerized database.

Raman spectrometry, a technique that identifies both the materials used to construct an object and those used to decorate its surface. The process operates by shining a laser beam onto an object's surface, where a small percentage of the light interacts with molecules and scatters (the "Raman effect"). That scattered light is collected to create a spectrum, from which the target material is then identified. Because the Raman effect is very small, practical forensic applications of the process were limited until recently by hardware considerations, but new advances in laser technology permit use of Raman spectrometry to identify materials ranging from plastics and rust to precious gems.

Ultraviolet spectroscopy employs ultraviolet light, invisible to naked eyes, which causes various substances to fluoresce. When applied to QUESTIONED DOCUMENTS, ultraviolet spectroscopy may reveal inks and erasures that might otherwise be overlooked.

X-ray photoelectron spectroscopy is a process in which atoms are bombarded with X-rays, causing them to eject photoelectrons which thus identify the sample's surface composition.

SPENCER, Timothy Wilson serial killer convicted by DNA

A Virginia native, born in 1962, Timothy Spencer was on parole from a BURGLARY conviction, living in a Richmond halfway house and working at a local furniture factory, when he launched a spree of brutal rape-slayings. His first victim, Carol Hamm, was assaulted and strangled at her Arlington home in January 1984. An innocent suspect confessed to that slaying under police pressure and was sentenced to prison, while Spencer managed to restrain himself from committing another attack for three years and eight months. His second victim, in September 1987, was Richmond resident Debby Davis. Two weeks later, again in Richmond, he raped and murdered Dr. Susan Hellams. November 1987 witnessed the identical murder of teenager Diane Cho, in a Richmond suburb. Returning to Arlington for his final murder, Spencer raped and strangled Susan Tucker in December 1987.

Thus far, Virginia's elusive "South Side Strangler" had been careful to leave no fingerprints behind at any of his crime scenes. The only evidence available to the police, therefore, was semen recovered from the bodies and clothing of his victims. Arlington detective Joe Horgas, mindful of recent developments in DNA technology and the British conviction of rape-slayer COLIN PITCHFORK based on such evidence, staked his hopes on snaring the strangler via "genetic fingerprints." He was successful in 1988, linking Spencer to three of the five local murders with DNA evidence. Convicted at trial and sentenced to die for his crimes, Spencer became the first U.S. defendant condemned on the basis of DNA evidence. Virginia's Supreme Court upheld that conviction, and Spencer was executed on April 27, 1994. The innocent suspect who had been coerced into confessing Carol Hamm's murder was belatedly exonerated and released after serving nearly five years in prison for Spencer's crime.

SPURZHEIM, Johann Gaspar (1776–1832)

German native Johann Spurzheim was born outside Trier on December 3, 1776. He studied medicine at the University of Vienna and there met FRANZ JOSEPH GALL, who hired Spurzheim as an assistant in 1800. Together, over the next dozen years, the two men pioneered theories of ANTHROPOMETRY and published their findings with joint bylines. A falling out in 1812 left Spurzheim on his own, traveling and lecturing widely on the system of identification by skull shape that he dubbed *phrenology,* otherwise known as "Drs. Gall and Spurzheim's physiognomical system." During his first American lecture tour, in 1832, Spurzheim contracted typhus and died in Boston. Following a public autopsy, his organs were preserved in jars of alcohol, while admirers erected a monument for Spurzheim in Cambridge's Mount Auburn Cemetery. Phrenology was soon supplanted by ALPHONSE BERTILLON's system of criminal identification, which in turn gave way to use of FINGERPRINTS in the early 20th century.

STAS, Jean Servais (1813–1891)

A native of Louvain, Belgium, born on August 21, 1813, Jean Stas enrolled at the local university in 1832 and earned his M.D. three years later, at age 22. He then joined the university staff and focused on CHEMISTRY, devising innovative experiments that challenged standard methods for calculating the atomic weight of different elements. In 1837, Stas transferred to the École Polytechnique in Paris, teaming with Jean-Baptiste Dumas to establish the atomic weight of carbon. Three years later, after being named a professor at the Royal Military School in Brussels, Stas undertook a series of experi-

ments that won him international acclaim for determining the atomic weights of various elements with unprecedented accuracy. His work disproved the earlier hypothesis of British physicist William Prout that all atomic weights must be integral multiples of hydrogen's atomic weight. Stas used oxygen as his standard instead, thereby laying the groundwork for the periodic table of elements completed by Dmitri Mendeleev. When not engaged in elemental analysis, Stas also contributed to TOXICOLOGY by developing a new technique for detection of vegetable alkaloid poisons in corpses. Failing health prompted Stas to retire in 1869, followed by a brief stint as commissioner of the Belgian mint (1869–72). He died in Brussels on December 13, 1891.

STEIN, Robert J. (1912–1994)

A Russian native, born in 1912, Robert Stein immigrated to the United States with his family before the Bolshevik revolution of 1917 and settled in Brooklyn, New York. As an adult, he studied medicine at Austria's University of Innsbruck, receiving his M.D. in 1950, then completed graduate studies in PATHOLOGY at Northwestern University, in Evanston, Illinois. From there, it was a short step to employment as a forensic pathologist in Chicago. When Cook County finally abandoned its coroner's office, long a tool of political patronage, Stein was retained on personal merit as a MEDICAL EXAMINER. In 1976, he won promotion to serve as the county's chief medical examiner, a post that he held for 17 years.

During his tenure, Stein supervised investigations of some 20,000 deaths around Chicago and environs. His famous cases included the 1978 exploration of serial killer John Wayne Gacy's crawl-space graveyard and a 1979 airplane crash at O'Hare International Airport that claimed 279 lives. With so many investigations ongoing at any one time, controversy was inevitable. One such case involved the January 1976 rape-murder of Lisa Cabassa. Dr. Stein opined that two assailants were involved, assuming that one man would need to control the struggling victim, and police used that opinion to build their case against suspects Michael Evans and Paul Terry (both later exonerated when DNA evidence proved their innocence and linked the murder to a single offender). Twelve years later, Stein issued a verdict of SUICIDE in the death of police captain Michael O'Mara—a finding hotly disputed by O'Mara's family and their attorney. Asked later whether he had any doubts about the O'Mara diagnosis, Dr. Stein replied: "Well, the very fact that I put pending further investigation, perhaps there was. But if the information that I got, the information was they have nobody in custody, they have no suspects, nothing like that, so I just made it suicide." Dr. Vincent DiMaio, chief medical examiner for Bexar County, Texas, was summoned to Chicago to testify as an expert and subsequently declared O'Mara's death a HOMICIDE.

Stein died in 1994, soon after his retirement. In addition to his long career as a pathologist, he was remembered as a founding member of the Medical Council on Handgun Violence. The Cook County Institute of Forensic Medicine, completed under his supervision in 1983, was renamed the Robert J. Stein Institute of Forensic Medicine in February 1994.

STRINGHAM, James S. (1775–1817)

James Stringham was a native of New York City, born in 1775. He earned a B.A. in theology from Columbia University (1793), but soon forsook the pulpit in favor of medicine, studying first in New York, under renowned physicians Samuel Bard and Davis Hosack, then at the University of Edinburgh, where Stringham obtained his M.D. in 1799. Returning to his native shore, Stringham joined the Columbia faculty as a professor of CHEMISTRY in 1802. The post offered no salary, but Stringham was supported by yearly payments of four dollars from each junior and senior. In 1804, he joined the New York State Medical Society and was elected president of the Physical Society in New York City. Stringham taught chemistry until 1813, when he transferred to the university's College of Physicians and Surgeons as a professor of medical jurisprudence. As such, he was America's first lecturer on that subject, and is widely regarded as the field's founder in the United States. In 1814, he published a syllabus of his lectures in the *American Medical and Philosophical Register*. Stringham died on June 28, 1817, during a holiday visit to St. Croix, Wisconsin.

STYLISTICS, Forensic

In LINGUISTICS, stylistic analysis involves the identification of patterns in speech or writing. As with PHONETICS, its forensic application focuses on iden-

tifying the unknown source of oral or written communications (e.g., threats, ransom demands, etc.). Regional accents and similar factors are useful in stylistic analysis, but their admissibility is often challenged in court. In the New Jersey case of *United States v. Van Wyk* (2000), the defense challenged linguistic reports concerning questioned documents on grounds that the stylistic testimony was "subjective, unreliable, and lack[ed] measurable standards." The appellate court agreed in part, ruling that expert testimony should be "limited to the comparison of characteristics or 'markers' between writings known to have been authored by Defendant and the writings in which authorship is 'questioned' or unknown." However, state experts were barred from offering opinions "regarding any 'external' or extrinsic factors . . . [or] . . . conclusion[s] regarding the identity of the author of the 'questioned' writings."

SURVEILLANCE Devices

Electronic surveillance—"ELSUR" in FBI parlance—has long been a staple of intelligence agencies throughout the world. In addition to court-ordered surveillance conducted by various law enforcement agencies, the manufacture, sale, and installation of surveillance devices has become a huge covert industry in the United States. A State Department report from the mid-1990s estimated that some $800 million in illegal eavesdropping equipment is imported from foreign sources and installed into U.S. corporate settings each year. Another $6 million per day is spent with domestic suppliers, while any would-be secret agent with a minimal knowledge of electronics can easily construct his own gear from components readily available at stores such as Radio Shack. In New York City alone, more than 85 firms advertise the sale, installation, and monitoring of surveillance devices.

In broad terms, surveillance devices are built to provide audio transmissions, video transmissions, or a combination of both. Audio surveillance is divided into bugs and wiretaps. A "bug" is any listening device installed in a target location to intercept conversation or other sounds and transmit them to a listening post. Depending on the equipment employed, the monitor may be located in an adjacent room or miles away from the scene. The five primary types of bugs are:

Surveillance cameras help police identify and track down criminals. (Steve McDonough/CORBIS)

Acoustic The simplest and cheapest method, this technique involves capture of sounds with the naked ear, by means of a stethoscope, water glass, or other primitive listening device inserted into the target area or placed against a common wall, eavesdropping through air vents, and so forth.

Ultrasonic This method involves conversion of sound into an audio signal beyond the range of human hearing, whereupon the ultrasonic signal is transmitted to a receiver and converted back to audio.

Radio frequency (RF) The best-known kind of bugging device is a radio transmitter concealed in the target area. Cheap and disposable, such bugs are relatively easy to detect with electronic scanners, but they are near-impossible to trace.

Optical Optical bugs convert sound or data into a beam of light (optical pulse), which is transmitted to a receiver and there decoded. Expensive and thus uncommon, this variety includes active and passive laser listening devices.

Wiretaps, unlike bugs, specifically involve the interception of communications carried via wires or cables. Taps are most commonly applied to telephones, but in recent years they have also been used to bleed information from PBX cables, local area networks (LANs), closed-circuit television systems, coded alarms systems, and other communications media. The four main categories of wiretaps include:

Hardwired After gaining physical access to the line of communication, an eavesdropper attaches secondary wires and bridges the signal to a secure location, where it may be overheard and/ or recorded. If discovered, this method is the easiest to trace back to a remote listening post, since the wire itself provides a trail.

Record Similar to a hardwired wiretap, this method simply involves a tape recorder wired into the line of communication. Popular with private investigators and amateur spies, the record wiretap is easily detected by sophisticated scanners and is relatively dangerous to operate because the tapes must be changed frequently. A stakeout on the listening post is virtually guaranteed to catch the wiretapper within a 24-hour period.

Soft This technique, sometimes called REMOBS (*rem*ote *obs*ervation), involves modification of the software used to run a telephone system, thus permitting interception of messages transmitted. The task may be accomplished at the telephone company (where it would be difficult for surveillance subjects to trace) or through the on-site PBX switchboard (where it can be uncovered more easily). If discovered, the soft wiretap is difficult to trace.

Transmit This hybrid technique involves attachment of a radio frequency (RF) "bug" to a communications line, which intercepts conversations and transmits them to a remote listening post. The bug's emission of RF energy makes it easy for professional "sweepers" to locate.

Bugs and wiretaps are so well known today that some perennial surveillance targets—members of organized crime, political extremists, intelligence agents, and the like—now routinely avoid any sensitive conversations via telephone or in their homes, offices and automobiles. Open-air conversations may be monitored by a variety of directional (or "shotgun") microphones, designed to pick up sounds from a distance, and lip-readers have been employed (with mixed success) to monitor subjects in various cases.

Video surveillance, unlike certain forms of wiretapping, requires the physical insertion of a camera into the target location. Once unwieldy and obvious, video cameras have been dramatically reduced in size by fiber-optic technology that permits transmission of an image via narrow wires. Such cameras are used not only for stationary surveillance, but also by SWAT officers to "case" a scene before entry to resolve hostage situations. Closed-circuit television and video recorders are widely used for security purposes in banks, schools, airports, hospitals and nursing homes, shopping malls, convenience stores, public transportation centers, parking lots, and in any other location where crimes are likely to occur without an official witness being present. Increasingly, civilians also make use of surveillance cameras (sometimes dubbed "nanny cams") to moni-

tor suspect activity by spouses, children, neighbors, baby-sitters, and employees. Photos or videotape of a crime in progress may be submitted to police and to the courts as evidence, as in the Rodney King and Reginald Hill cases from Los Angeles.

Video technology is so advanced today that cameras mounted on satellites in outer space may be used for surveillance missions, transmitting pictures so detailed that individual persons can often be recognized, while viewers are able to make out addresses, license plate numbers, and other key objects crucial to tracking and identification. Another means of surveillance from beyond the atmosphere involves GPS (*global positioning satellite*) technology, initially developed for the military but now available for a wide variety of civilian applications. GPS equipment transmits no pictures, but it can determine the location of a targeted person or object precisely, within a matter of inches, at any point on earth. In one notorious U.S. case, officials of Acme Rent-a-Car used GPS systems to track their hired cars and illegally fine customers for speeding. Another case, reported in September 2001, saw a judge order Florida defendant Joseph Nichols to be monitored by GPS technology for up to 15 years, following his release from prison on a conviction for squirting young girls with a semen-filled water pistol. Nichols was required to wear a PERSONAL TRACKING UNIT that reports his location via satellite at 10-minute intervals.

Various warning signs may serve as an alert to ongoing covert surveillance. Some of the tip-offs include:

- Revelations that unauthorized persons have knowledge of confidential business activities, or trade secrets;
- Unusual sounds, interference, or changes in volume on telephone lines;
- Peculiar sounds emanating from a telephone when it is not in use (suggesting the presence of a hidden transmitter);
- Frequent "hang-up" calls when no one speaks or a faint, high-pitched sound is heard on the line;
- Unusual interference on a television or radio (either inside a building or in a vehicle);
- Evidence of break-ins where nothing is stolen;
- Obvious (or subtle) damage or alterations to locks, including sticky tumblers, scratches around keyholes, etc.;

- Small circular discolorations on a wall or ceiling (perhaps indicative of a microphone or camera recently installed;
- Electrical wall plates scratched, smudged, or found slightly askew;
- Crooked or displaced electrical devices (clocks, illuminated signs, smoke detectors, etc.), sprinkler heads, picture frames, posters, furniture, etc.;
- New lumps or ridges under carpets, vinyl floors, or baseboards;
- Traces of dust, sawdust or other debris near the base of walls (suggesting recent drilling);
- The continued, unusual presence of utility trucks, delivery vans, and similar vehicles parked near a potential target location (which may be mobile listening posts).

It is even theoretically possible, with modern technology, to mount surveillance on a subject's silent thoughts. Dr. Lawrence Pinneo, a neurophysiologist and electronic engineer at Stanford University, pioneered this field in 1974, with the development of a computer system that correlated brain waves on an electroencephalograph (EEG) with specific verbal commands. Twenty years later, neurophysiologist Donald York and speech pathologist Thomas Hensen identified 27 words or syllables in brain wave patterns produced by computer software containing a "brain wave vocabulary." Critics of covert surveillance suggest that intelligence agencies are capable of decoding human thoughts "from a considerable distance" by scanning the magnetic field around a subject's head via satellite, then feeding the data to computers, which in turn decode the target's internal "conversation." While that scenario may sound fanciful—and no proof of such surveillance presently exists—concerned civil libertarians dread the day when Big Brother may indeed be watching from the inside of our skulls.

SURVEYING, Forensic

Surveying is the measuring and mapping of physical objects, whether natural or man-made. Forensic applications include any survey involved in legal matters, whether criminal or civil. Examples include the precise determination of disputed property lines, surveys of CRIME SCENES to chart the location of bodies or other evidentiary items in relation to surrounding features (buildings, cliffs, etc.), and studies to identify the source of long-range gunfire. Surveyors participated in the investigation of President John Kennedy's assassination, in 1963, and in the sniper-slaying case of Dr. Martin Luther King five years later. In both cases, while the source of gunfire was reportedly determined and linked to lone gunmen, other evidence—ballistics, eyewitness testimony, audio recordings, films, and photographs—dispute the official findings and fuel diverse conspiracy theories. In Kennedy's case, surveyors reported that shots fired from Lee Harvey Oswald's supposed sixth-floor sniper's nest should have struck JFK at a downward angle slightly less than 18°, while surgeons found the wound in question to have an angle of 45° to 60°. Likewise, surveyors in King's case allegedly traced the fatal shot to a nearby rooming house bathroom, where James Earl Ray supposedly stood in the bathtub and fired through a window. Physical examination of the rooming house disclosed that firing from the tub, against an angle of the wall, required an awkward aiming posture—and that trees outside obscured the sniper's view of King's motel. (Witnesses also reported a gunman fleeing from bushes behind the rooming house, below the bathroom window.) Neither case saw the evidence tested in court, since Oswald was murdered prior to trial and Ray pleaded guilty.

TAYLOR, Alfred Swaine (1806–1880)

A child of affluent parents, born at Hounslow, England, in 1806, Alfred Taylor was educated in his youth by private tutors, then served for a year as a physician's apprentice (1822), before enrolling as a student at Guy's Hospital. Taylor received his M.D. five years later, in 1828, dividing the next two years between internship and continental travel. The Royal College of Surgeons accepted Taylor as a member in 1830, and he spent that summer in Paris, as a spectator to the latest outbreak of revolutionary violence. Back in London after the excitement faded, he joined the Guy's Hospital staff as that institution's first professor of medical jurisprudence—a post he retained for nearly half a century. As a specialist in TOXICOLOGY, Taylor was called to testify in various poisoning trials, including the first known British case of murder for life insurance. (Taylor was fond of saying, "A poison in a small dose is a medicine, and a medicine in a large dose is a poison.") Defense attorneys frequently employed William Herapath (1796–1868), a founder of the Bristol Medical School and the Chemical Society of London, to contradict Taylor's testimony at trial, through which experience the men became renowned enemies. Taylor's book-length publications on forensic medicine include *Medical Jurisprudence* (1845), *A Manual of Medical Jurisprudence* (1873), and *On Poisons in Relation to Medical Jurisprudence and Medicine* (1875). Taylor retired from Guy's Hospital in 1877 and died three years later, at age 74.

TEARE, Robert Donald (1911–1979)

Robert Teare was born on the Isle of Man, in July 1911, and earned his bachelor's degree from King William's College there, before pursuing medical studies at Cambridge and at St. George's Hospital. Upon qualifying as a physician, he remained at St. George's to specialize in PATHOLOGY. During World War II, with London under constant bombardment by the German Luftwaffe, Teare had ample opportunity to examine trauma victims. In an age when autopsies were still unusual, Teare campaigned tirelessly to make them routine. In the early 1950s, he joined the staff of St. Bartholomew's Hospital Medical School as a professor of forensic medicine, transferring to Charing Cross Medical School in 1963. There Teare remained until his retirement from teaching in 1975. He received an honorary LL.D. from the University of Sheffield in 1977 and died in 1979, at age 68.

TELECOMMUNICATIONS Fraud

This criminal activity is broadly defined as including any theft or fraud involving the use of telecommunications service or equipment. Such activities are subdivided into two main categories: (1) the THEFT of service from commercial providers and (2) use of telecommunications services to defraud third parties.

Theft of telephone service is the province of "phreaks"—the designation self-applied to individuals who swindle telephone companies for fun and profit. Prior to the advent of computer modems, dedicated phreaks constructed homemade devices like the "BLUE BOX" to mimic the 2600-hertz tone sounded by telephone switching systems, thereby granting access to long-distance lines free of charge. Enterprising phreaks thus saved money on telephone calls and also earned income by selling their illicit devices to others. (Author Steve Ditli reports that the founders of Apple Computers, Steve Wozniak and Steven Jobs, manufactured blue boxes during their undergraduate days in college, selling them off to classmates for $80 each with an unconditional guarantee of satisfactory performance.) By the mid-1970s, AT&T spokesmen reported yearly losses of $30 million due to telephone fraud. In February 1998, estimated yearly loss to long-distance fraud ranged from $4 billion to $8 billion.

The advent of wireless telephones opened a whole new world of telecommunications fraud to zealous phreaks. In the 1990s, CELL PHONE CLONING was all the rage, with transmitter codes snatched from thin air and transferred to computer chips inside one or more "clones" of the original phone, off-loading astronomical bills to the accounts of legitimate service subscribers. Cities hardest hit were those with large concentrations of narcotics dealers, since the pushers found a double benefit in cloned cell phones: aside from saving money on their calls, any discussions of their outlaw business intercepted by police would lead investigators not to the dealer himself, but to the innocent user of the telephone whose code had been hijacked. In 1994, the mayor and police commissioner of New York City both fell prey to cell phone pirates, proving that the crime wave recognized no barriers of rank or privilege.

Other forms of telecommunications fraud include:

Modem fraud In the simplest method, hackers penetrate a computer system and gain access to its local area network (LAN), thereafter routing free long-distance calls through that circuit instead of using their home telephones.

Toll-free fraud In a variation on the previous scenario, computer-savvy phreaks penetrate a legitimate company's toll-free system, find an outside line monitored by another computer, and proceed to make long-distance calls at the corporate victim's expense.

Subscriber fraud This technique involves registration for telephone service under a false name, either an alias plucked from thin air or (more commonly today) the name of an actual person acquired by means of IDENTITY THEFT. Use of real identities is preferable, since many customers pay their phone bills without checking specific calls, and thieves can spread the cost around by using multiple stolen identities, thus often forestalling detection.

PBX fraud Some hackers take advantage of a private branch-exchange (PBX) system that permits employees of a given firm to place calls through the company's home office (typically on a toll-free line) from locations outside the workplace. By using a personal identification number (PIN), the employees may then bill calls to the company as if they were dialing from work. Hackers who penetrate a company's system sometimes obtain employee PBX passwords and make their own calls, untraceable since the corporate office is billed as the source of the calls.

Credit card fraud Hackers steal credit card numbers on-line, or individuals purchase the stolen numbers (sometimes in bulk, by the hundreds or thousands), then use them to purchase goods and services by telephone or through e-commerce. Federal sources reported 3,721 cases of fraud in the first four months of 2007, with losses of $3.2 billion.

Telemarketing fraud Long-distance swindlers use various fraudulent games, giveaways, and investment scams to milk cash from their victims, often calling internationally. Montreal, Canada, is recognized as a hotbed of telemarketing fraud, targeted since the late 1990s by a collaborative team of Canadian and U.S. authorities in a sting operation dubbed "Project Colt." Elderly persons living on fixed incomes are the favored prey of fraudulent telemarketers, but no one with a telephone is entirely safe.

Consumer advocates and law enforcement agencies advise consumers to use common sense and exercise normal caution to avoid being victimized by some form of telecommunications fraud. The obvious safeguards include:

1. Maintaining strict security over telephone calling cards, PIN numbers, credit card numbers, computer or voicemail passwords, and other personal data that enable unauthorized users to launch an illicit spending spree in an innocent party's name.
2. Exercise caution in any purchase made on-line or on the telephone. Recognize that some avenues of e-commerce are safer than others, and insist on certain minimal security precautions.
3. Verify a telemarketer's credentials before agreeing to any transaction. Again, be extremely cautious when giving out credit card numbers and other important personal information.
4. Immediately report any loss or theft of cell phones, calling cards, credit cards, or similar items that thieves may use to run up bills on your account.
5. Use caution when discussing any personal matters or financial transactions on a cellular telephone. The calls are *not* secure and may be intercepted in various ways.
6. If long-distance or overseas calls are not anticipated, ask your cellular phone provider to remove or disable those functions, thereby barring another party who steals or finds your telephone from running up long-distance bills.
7. Report frequent hang-ups or "wrong number" calls received on a cellular phone, which may indicate unauthorized use of a cloned version by some unknown party.
8. Thoroughly check all telephone bills for unauthorized calls and report any suspicion of fraud to the service provider.

TERRORISM

The terrorist attacks that claimed more than 3,000 American lives on September 11, 2001, were the culmination of a relatively low-tech conspiracy. While several of the airline hijackers were graduates of private U.S. flight schools (available before 9/11 to any literate applicant with sufficient funds to cover the tuition), they commandeered the aircraft using only simple box cutters and made the planes themselves their weapons, avoiding even the need to construct a crude bomb. Even the wave of anthrax mailings that

followed the September 11 assaults seemed poorly conceived, disorganized, their chaotic nature perhaps contributing to the fact that those involved remain at large.

Those facts notwithstanding, U.S. authorities were naturally fearful of further attacks, perhaps involving high-tech weapons or techniques designed to damage the nation's critical communications infrastructure. Likewise, law enforcement spokesmen have stated repeatedly (without supporting evidence thus far) that global terrorists, including 9/11 mastermind Osama bin Laden and others, communicate regularly on the Internet, holding the equivalent of conference calls in cyberspace via e-mail, chat rooms, and encrypted messages posted to various Web sites. Ten days after the September 2001 attacks, a *Washington Post* report claimed that "for at least three years, federal agents had found evidence that bin Laden's group embedded secret missives in mundane e-mails and on Web sites. But efforts to track down and decipher the messages have floundered."

Skeptics are inclined to ask how FBI agents and others know such communications are ongoing, if they have been unable to "track down" a single coded message, but simple logic dictates that some terrorists, somewhere on earth, must by now have exploited the Internet's broad range of possibilities. Encrypted messages are only part of the package, in a realm where even teenage hackers have penetrated corporate and government computer systems, defacing Web sites and deleting vital data, looting bank accounts around the world, paralyzing businesses, and forcing the White House Web site itself to go offline for repairs. What else might terrorists accomplish if they truly set their minds to it? Diverting troops or weapons? Raiding classified files to unmask confidential informants and double-agents? Retrieving the launch codes for nuclear missiles?

The ultimate worst-case scenario for high-tech terrorism involved use of nuclear weapons to spread mass destruction. Prior to 1991 and the collapse of Soviet communism, such incidents were confined to best-selling novels, action films, and sporadic anonymous threats proved groundless by agents of the U.S. NUCLEAR EMERGENCY SEARCH TEAM. Over the past decade, however, persistent reports have suggested that the bankrupt governments of former Soviet states and satellites, confronted with hardship and virtual anarchy in some cases, may be selling off their nuclear warheads at random to the highest bidders.

Hundreds of volunteers participated in rescue efforts at the site of the collapsed World Trade towers. Terrorist hijackers conspired to launch a relatively low-tech attack, commandeering airplanes with knives and using the planes themselves as weapons. (FEMA)

Members of the global "Russian Mafia," likewise, are said to traffic in weapons of mass destruction, though once again, no such cases have been publicly documented so far.

Two months after the 9/11 attacks, in November 2001, reports circulated that Osama bin Laden's al-Qaeda terrorists in Afghanistan had attempted to build a nuclear weapon from scratch, but the "plans" recovered from an abandoned house in Kabul suggested that bin Laden had been duped by an Internet prankster. Cyber-journalist Jason Scott, writing for the Internet newsletter rotten.com, reportedly traced the blueprint to a spoof originally published in 1979, titled "How to Build an Atomic Bomb in 10 Easy Steps." The original article, run in the short-lived *Journal of Irreproducible Results*, suggested that a warhead constructed in the price range of $5,000 to $30,000 "is a great ice-breaker at parties, and in a pinch, can be used for national defence." Bin Laden and his Taliban associates were presumably confounded by "decadent" Western humor, or else received the "plans" without their accompanying satirical text.

The pursuit of terrorists in cyberspace is serious business, however, and thus far the results for American hunters has been disappointing. If terrorists are, in fact, using the World Wide Web to communicate among themselves, they have so far been able to cover their tracks absolutely. Encryption techniques such as steganography make a "cold hit" on any particular message or sequence of code a virtual impossibility, while evasion of physical traces may be as simple as shifting from one Internet café to another between transmissions. David Lang, director of the computer forensics department at the Virginia-based Veridian Corporation, explained the problem to a *New York Times* reporter in March 2002. "The Internet presents two main challenges," Lang said. "One is it's ubiquitous—you can access it from just about anywhere in the world. The other thing is you can be easily hidden."

One of the few known instances wherein terrorists have been tracked down via e-mail was the kidnap-murder of Daniel Pearl, a reporter for the *Wall Street Journal* in Pakistan. The kidnappers used Hotmail, a Microsoft e-mail service, to announce Pearl's kidnapping on January 30, 2002, and their transmission was traced to New Skies, a company based in the Netherlands that provides Internet access to many nations via satellite. From there, investigators were able to identify and locate the computer used in the transmission, resulting in the arrest of Pearl's kidnappers. Four defendants in that case were convicted on July 15, 2002, with one condemned to hang and the other three sentenced to life imprisonment.

Tracing the perpetrators of real-world crimes via computer is one thing, but protecting computers themselves from a cyberattack is even more challenging. Since the 1980s, various government, corporate, and university computers have been penetrated repeatedly by hackers ranging from curious adolescents and disgruntled employees to industrial spies and transnational bank robbers. No system is truly secure, as demonstrated by penetration of every major telephone company, the White House, FBI headquarters, the Justice Department's National Crime Information Center, various Pentagon computers, systems operated by the National Aeronautics and Space Administration, and computers housed at various military bases throughout the United States. Whether the hackers responsible are engaged in childish cybervandalism or downloading of classified information, deleting priceless files or uploading the latest computer viruses, each penetration confirms the inherent weakness of a society dependent on computers and the Internet. As Rep. Jane Harman (D-Calif.) told *USA Today* reporter Tom Squitieri in May 2002, "Cyber terrorism presents a real and growing threat to American security. What I fear is the combination of a cyber attack coordinated with more traditional terrorism, undermining our ability to respond to an attack when lives are in danger."

Various domestic cyberattacks caused a reported $12 billion in damages across the United States during 2001, and while some are clearly pranks—like the July 2002 assault on *USA Today*'s Web site, inserting spurious news items amidst the legitimate reports—other attacks are clearly carried out with the desire to harm (if not destroy) specific corporate targets. President George W. Bush sought $4.5 billion for new computer protection systems in his budget for 2003, but skeptics wondered if any amount of new technology could hold the line for long against determined hackers.

The nearest thing to all-out cyberwar began 11 months before the 9/11 attacks on America, and it came—perhaps predictably—in the strife-torn Middle East. Hackers sympathetic to Palestinian militants fired the first broadside on October 6, 2000, defacing 40-odd Israeli Web sites in a matter of hours. Pro-Israeli hackers swiftly retaliated, bombarding Palestinian Web sites with floods of e-mail from computers based in Israel and the United States. The terrorist group Hezbollah's Web site, featuring appeals for Palestinians to kill as many Israelis as possible, was overwhelmed and crippled by millions of rapid-fire "hits" from abroad, coordinated from a pro-Israeli site called "Attack and Destroy Hizballah" (www.wizel.com). Arab hackers disabled the Israeli government's official Web site and the Web site of its foreign ministry on October 25, 2000, using identical techniques. When Hezbollah established "mirror" sites of its original Web page,

enemies tracked them, adorning each in turn with Stars of David and messages in Hebrew. Palestinian hackers, meanwhile, disabled still more Israeli Web sites, including those maintained by the ministries of defense, immigrant absorption, religious affairs, industry, and trade, along with that of the Tel Aviv Stock Exchange and private organizations including a number of Hebrew schools. Aftahat Ma'Khevim, the military unit charged with maintaining Israeli computer security, reported that most of the attacks were traced to Lebanon and the Persian Gulf states, but also that many originated from Muslim students enrolled at American universities.

Israeli retaliation in the ongoing Mideast cyberwar has thus far been an unofficial project, at least from outward appearances. A group calling itself Israeli Hackers (www.israelhackers.cjb.net) led the charge, ably assisted by members of another group dubbed "m0sad" (presumably unconnected to Israel's Mos= sad intelligence network) and various independent

According to law enforcement officials, global terrorists like Osama bin Laden and his network communicate regularly via the Internet. (Getty Images)

operators. Public calls for an "army of Israeli soldiers on the net" to perform "search and destroy" missions against a list of Arab Web sites have led to further escalation in the so-far bloodless conflict. Pro-Israeli sites in the United States have also come under fire, as when a hacker known as "Dr. Nuker," based in Pakistan, penetrated the American Israel Public Affairs Committee (AIPAC) Web site on November 1, 2000, posting a list of "Israeli massacres" and other derogatory comments. According to investigators, "Dr. Nuker" also accessed credit card numbers and other personal information of recent contributors to AIPAC, and sent the group's 3,500 e-mail subscribers a message proclaiming that "it's a shame Hitler didn't finish what he set out to do" in slaughtering Jews during World War II.

With 70-plus Middle Eastern Web sites vandalized or temporarily disabled in the first month of conflict, James Adams, chairman of the iDefense computer security firm told reporter Carmen Gentile and *Wired News,* "We expect to see more wars like this one being waged out there. Their weapon of choice, the laptop, is easily available, and the ammunition, viruses and hacking programs, is free on the Internet." Arab hacker gangs like Unity, a group with ties to Hezbollah, vow to continue their "e-jihad" against Israel, threatening to expand attacks from government targets into "phase four of the cyber war," attacking Israeli e-commerce to cause "millions of dollars of losses in transactions." An independent hacker known on-line as "dodi," meanwhile, has threatened to shut down NetVision, the Israeli internet service provider (ISP) that hosts nearly 70 percent of Israel's Internet traffic. Groups including m0sad and the Israeli Internet Underground, meanwhile, vow to defend their nation's computer infrastructure and retaliate in kind for any new attacks. One faction ready to face that challenge is Gforce Pakistan, an activist group that recently claimed credit for penetrating the Web site at Jerusalembooks.com, inserting the name "Palestine" in flaming letters, with messages asking Israelis if the Torah teaches them to rape women and murder innocent children. In mid-July 2001, hackers from m0sad struck a stunning 480 Arab Web sites in what Internet reporter James Middleton called "a political hack that probably took less than a minute."

Not unexpectedly, the Arab-Israeli conflict in cyberspace has drawn attention—and unwelcome participation—from hackers around the globe. Ben Venzke, director of intelligence production at iDefense, told reporter Brian Krebs in late November 2000, "We're starting to see groups that have no connection or relationship to anything going on in the region jumping into the fray because they think it's a neat thing, [and they] want to be part of it." That reaction intensified after September 11, 2001, with reports that American hackers planned retaliation against computer systems in Pakistan, Iraq, and other alleged "terrorist states." No actual incursions were reported, but they may well have been lost in the confusion of cyberwar already raging throughout the region. Attacks on Iran's Ministry of Agriculture and Ministry of Foreign Affairs, for example, were reported even before 9/11, presumably conducted by hackers sympathetic to Israel.

No such concerted political attacks have thus far been directed against the U.S. government or e-commerce outlets, though "recreational" hackers have briefly disabled such on-line giants as Yahoo and Amazon.com. Given the state of world affairs and America's continuing involvement in regions fraught with turmoil, it would be naïve to assume that the United States can maintain long-term immunity against attacks in cyberspace. No death or physical destruction may result from such incursions, but victims will experience disruption in their daily lives as cyber-terrorism spreads around the globe.

THEFT

The term *theft* generally covers any unlawful taking or procurement of another's property, regardless of the object's size or intrinsic value. Most jurisdictions distinguish between *petty* and *grand* theft, based on the property's value, and adjust their penalties accordingly. Theft accomplished with weapons or violence is generally termed ROBBERY, and incurs significantly harsher punishment. *Shoplifting* involves theft of merchandise from commercial venues, while theft of cash from an employer is often called *embezzlement*, and theft of large amounts in corporate venues ranked as WHITE-COLLAR CRIME.

Most thefts are motivated by greed, although some compulsive thieves (dubbed *kleptomaniacs*) achieve emotional or sexual release from stealing. Many urban thefts are drug-related, staged by addicts to support their expensive habits. Theft of cash provides immediate rewards, but other objects must be sold unless the thief himself desires to keep them for some reason. Sales of stolen property are often accomplished through middlemen known as "fences," who purchase items at a fraction of their market value from a thief, then turn around and sell the objects at a profit. The more expensive or unique an item is—as with famous works of art or renowned pieces of jewelry—the more difficult disposal may become. Art thieves may be commissioned by an unscrupulous collector to steal a particular masterpiece for his/her private collection, although it may never be displayed.

With theft, as in cases of BURGLARY, forensic scientists must work from evidence recovered at the crime scene. Successful thieves will do their best to avoid leaving FINGERPRINTS, IMPRESSION EVIDENCE, or TRACE EVIDENCE of any kind for the authorities. Some merchandise, if recovered, may be identified by serial numbers or a distinctive jeweler's mark. Paintings may require scientific study to distinguish originals from expert copies. Such tests may determine the age and composition of paint, canvas, and frame, while microscopic examination of brush strokes proves useful in some cases.

TOWNSEND, Jerry Frank exonerated by DNA evidence

In retrospect, the worst anyone could really say about Jerry Townsend was that he seemed eager to please others—including the Florida detectives who falsely accused him of multiple murders and rapes. Diagnosed with an IQ somewhere between 50 and 60, equivalent to the mental capacity of an eight-year-old child, Townsend proved malleable in the hands of police interrogators who fed him information on a series of sex crimes around Miami and Fort Lauderdale, then took down his "confessions" as a way to close outstanding cases with a minimum of effort.

Townsend, age 27 at the time of his arrest for raping a pregnant Miami woman on a public street in 1979, did not initially confess any wrongdoing, but the victim and several bystanders pointed him out to police. Persistent grilling eventually produced statements that led to his indictment for two unsolved Fort Lauderdale murders. Investigators knew there were serious problems with Townsend's confessions, even then. In the case of Terry Cummings, a 20-year-old McDonald's restaurant employee found dead in a burned-out building, still wearing her uniform, Townsend "remembered" killing a woman dressed

in shorts, in her own apartment. (Tape recordings of Townsend's confessions reveal police correcting him and "refreshing his memory" when he offered inaccurate statements.) Nonetheless, prosecutors proceeded to trial and jurors convicted Townsend on both counts of first-degree murder. Once incarcerated, he confessed in 1980 to four more slayings and a nonfatal rape, piling one life sentence upon another. (One published report claims Townsend may have confessed to as many as 23 serial slayings, but the rest were never formally charged against him.)

Townsend sat in prison for 21 years after that spate of false confessions, before DNA evidence finally cleared him on all charges. Broward County prosecutors asked the court to vacate Townsend's convictions in May 2001, after DNA analysis of bodily fluids retrieved from three local crime scenes identified another suspect, one Eddie Lee Mosley, as the actual offender. (Mosley, in fact, had been a suspect at the time of Townsend's confession, but those statements caused police to abandon their search for further evidence.) Broward County Sheriff Ken Jenne visited Townsend's cell to deliver a personal apology on June 8, 2001, and Miami judge Scott Silverman ordered Townsend's release a week later, calling his imprisonment "an enormous tragedy."

Miami Assistant Police Chief James Chambliss explained to the press how such a miscarriage of justice could happen. "He liked the cops," Chambliss said. "He wanted to be with the cops. They were his buddies, and frankly that's a great tool if you get suspects to like you. That's a good thing." Collusion in the imprisonment of an innocent man, however, is itself a criminal offense in every U.S. jurisdiction, though it seems unlikely anyone involved with Townsend's case will ever see the inside of a cell. Still, there are some who feel regret for the way his case was handled. While defense attorneys branded Townsend "a human parrot," willing to confess any crime to please his interrogators, Miami detective Confesor Gonzalez told reporters, "The confessions do not fit the physical evidence. This case was bad."

TOXICOLOGY

Toxicology is the study of the adverse effects of various chemicals on living organisms. *Toxicity* is a measure of the degree to which a particular substance is toxic or poisonous. *Poisons* are substances that cause injury, illness, or death by chemical reaction or other means, usually on a molecular scale. *Toxins* are naturally occurring substances, produced by living cells, such as the bacterial proteins that cause various diseases. Animal toxins delivered via bites or stings, whether during predation or for self-defense, are properly called *venom*. (A subdiscipline, *toxinology*, deals specifically with biological toxins.) *Poisonous* substances cause damage when consumed, while *venom* is injected by a living creature (but may often be consumed with impunity). Some poisonous substances are *indirectly toxic*, as when the human liver converts methanol to deadly formaldehyde. Toxic substances may be ORGANIC or INORGANIC. While MATHIEU ORFILA is widely regarded as the "Father of Toxicology," based on publication of his *Trait des poisons* in 1813, predecessor Auroleus Phillipus Theostratus Bombastus von Hohenheim, a.k.a. "Paracelsus" (1493–1541), fairly summarized the subject when he said, "All things are poison and nothing is without poison. It is the dose that makes a thing poisonous."

Three basic types of toxic entities are chemical, biological, and physical. *Chemicals* include a wide range of inorganic substances (various acids, gases, metals) and organic compounds (drugs and medicines, venoms, etc.). While dosage is critical with chemicals, *biological* toxicity may involve only a single bacterium, parasite, or virus. *Physical* toxins include a variety of things normally excluded from lists of poisons, including extreme temperatures (hot or cold), sounds or other vibrations, various forms of light (visible or infrared), and various types of radiation, whether particulate (alpha rays, beta rays, etc.) or nonparticulate (gamma or X-rays). Toxicity is commonly measured by the effects a substance has on its target, often expressed in population-level terms, since individuals display radically different levels of resistance to various toxins. Thus, for example, an "LD40" toxicity rating indicates a concentrated *lethal dose* expected to kill 40 percent of a target population. On an individual basis, toxicity is affected by various factors including the toxin's physical form (gas, liquid, or solid), path of administration (absorption, ingestion, inhalation, or injection), time of exposure (short- or long-term), number of exposures, and the target's personal condition (genetics, overall health, etc.).

Biotoxins occurring in nature are generally used for predation (as in the bites of spiders or venomous snakes) or for defense (in various plants, amphibians, and insects). *Hemotoxins*, like those found in the venom of most vipers, destroy red blood cells and may produce internal hemorrhaging. *Neurotoxins*, like those found in elapid snakes (cobras, mambas, etc.) and black widow spiders affect the nervous system, frequently producing death by asphyxiation. *Necrotoxins*, like those found in brown recluse spiders and "flesh-eating" bacteria (necrotizing fasciitis) produce necrosis (death) in all types of tissue. Toxins produced by bacteria are properly termed *toxoids*.

Inorganic toxins include various acids and bases (corrosives), plus certain metals and other compounds. Toxic metals include the light metal beryllium and certain light metal oxides (hydroxides and superoxides), plus various heavy metals: antimony, barium, cadmium, chromium, lead, mercury, thallium, and uranium. Other inorganic compounds toxic to humans include arsenic and its various compounds, bleach and other hypochlorates, Fowler's solution, hydrofluoric acid, hydrogen sulfide, phosgene, and phosphine.

Most drugs and medicines, regardless of their intended use, may prove toxic if consumed in abnormal doses or by persons with unusual sensitivity such as allergies. Meanwhile, the following list includes the more significant toxic plants found in nature.

aconite (*Aconitum napellus*)
American wake robin (*Arum triphyllum*)
balsam apple (*Momordica balsamina*)
baneberry (*Actaea spicata*)
bitter apple (*Citrullus colocynthis*)
black bryony (*Tamus communis*)
black hellebore (*Helleborus niger*)
black nightshade (*Solanum nigrum*)
bloodroot (*Sanguinaria candensis*)
Bolivian coca (*Erythroxylon coca*)
cabbage tree (*Andira inermis*)
calabar bean (*Physostigma venenosum*)
calotropis (*Calotropis procera* and *C. gigantea*)
cherry laurel (*Prunus laurocerasus*)
clematis (*Clematis recta*)
deadly nightshade (*Atropa belladonna*)
European white bryony (*Bryonia alba*)
false hellebore (*Adonis autumnalis, Adonis vernalis*)
foxglove (*Digitalis purpurea*)
gelsemium (*Gelsemium nitidum*)
green hellebore (*Veratrum viride*)
hemlock (*Conium maculatum*)

hemlock water dropwort (*Oenanthe crocata*)
Indian hemp (*Cannabis sativa*)
Ignatius beans (*Strychnos Ignatii*)
indicus cocculus (*Anamirta paniculata*)
laburnum (*Cytisus laburnam*)
meadow saffron (*Colchicum autumnale*)
mescal buttons (*Anhalonium Lewinii*)
mountain laurel (*Kalmia latifolia*)
nux vomica (*Strychnos nux-vomica*)
Paris herb (*Paris quadrifolia*)
poison ivy (*Rhus toxicodendron*)
spurges (*Euphorbias*)
stavesacre (*Delphinium staphisagria*)
strophanthus (*Strophanthus Kombé*)
thornapple (*Datura stramonium*)
water hemlock (*Cicuta virosa*)
water lovage (*Cenanthe fistulosa*)
white bryony (*Bryonia dioica*)
white hellebore (*Veratrum album*)
white poppy (*Papaver somniferum*)
yew (*Taxus baccata*)

TRACE Evidence

Trace (or *transfer*) evidence is a vast category including any and all items created or transferred under EDMOND LOCARD's Exchange Principle, which states that some transfer of material occurs whenever two objects make contact. That evidence, used to link persons and objects with specific locations and with each other, may include (but is not limited to) ARSON debris, biological matter (either plant or animal, including blood and other body fluids), EXPLOSIVES and gunshot residue, FIBERS and hairs, GLASS, headlight filaments, IMPRESSION EVIDENCE (including footprints, tire toolmarks, tire tracks, etc.), PAINT, soil samples, and "miscellaneous unknowns" requiring both QUALITATIVE and QUANTITATIVE ANALYSIS.

Federal guidelines for the ADMISSIBILITY OF EVIDENCE require that strict rules of procedure be followed in detection, collection, analysis, and preservation of trace evidence. Documentation must include permanent notes concerning date and time of collection, the name(s) of person(s) involved in collection, a descriptive listing of items collected, a unique identifier for each item (such as case numbers), and the location of each piece collected (documented by notes, measurements, sketches, photographs, videotapes, or some combination of methods). A proper *chain of custody* must be initiated with collection of each item and maintained until its final disposition. Every effort must be made to avoid contamination or loss of trace evidence, which may jeopardize adjudication of the case either by undermining prosecution of the guilty or compromising exculpatory evidence that might acquit an innocent defendant.

Basic practices to avoid contamination or loss of evidence, applied both at crime scenes and in laboratory settings, include limitation of contact between law enforcement personnel and evidentiary items prior to collection of trace evidence, and use of protective clothing (omitted in many Hollywood *CSI*-type productions) to prevent transfer of extraneous items from examiners to the CRIME SCENE and its evidence. Methods of detecting trace evidence include basic visual ("naked eye") searches, visual inspection assisted by alternative light sources (high-intensity, laser, oblique, ultraviolet, etc.), and inspection aided by magnification. Once discovered, trace evidence is collected with minimal handling, by various means that include:

Picking: Separation of evidence such as fibers or glass fragments from their surroundings with clean forceps or similar instruments, whereupon each item is separately packaged and sealed to prevent contamination.

Lifting: Retrieval of FINGERPRINTS and other evidence by means of adhesive objects such as tape, which may be used for both collection and storage. Usually, the "lifts" are then placed on some transparent backing such as clear plastic sheeting or glass slides, which both protect the evidence and permit easy viewing. Caution must be exercised in lifting to (*a*) avoid use of soiled tape, (*b*) refrain from "overloading" tape with multiple evidentiary items, and (*c*) prevent the tape's edges from collecting extraneous material.

Combing: Use of a clean comb or brush to retrieve trace evidence from the hair of a person or animal. Proper handling dictates that the comb or brush be packaged with the evidence collected and it should not be reused.

Scraping: Use of a clean blade, spatula, or other tool to dislodge trace evidence from beneath fingernails or from other surfaces to which it adheres. Risk of contamination dictates that scraping is usually conducted in a laboratory, morgue, or other reasonably sterile setting.

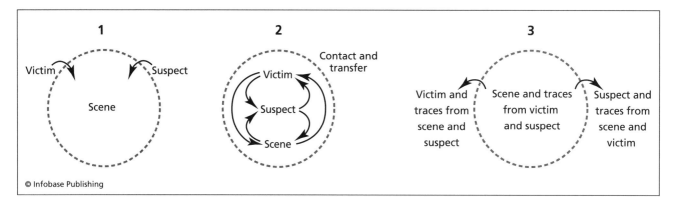

Schematic of Locard's exchange principle, which states that any contact between people or between a person and a place results in the exchange of material. The characteristics of the transferred material are physical evidence of the contact.

Scrapings must be collected in such manner that no contamination occurs before they are stored and sealed.

Clipping: Another method commonly used to obtain evidence from beneath an individual's finger- and toenails. As in combing and scraping, clean instruments should be used and the nail clippings should be packaged in clean paper or plastic envelopes. Typically, clippings from the left and right hands (or feet) are packaged separately. Some examiners package clippings from each finger or toe separately, as a further hedge against confusion or contamination. Nails with obvious damage or other special identifying characteristics should always be packaged separately.

Vacuum sweeping: Commonly practiced at crime scenes and during vehicle searches, this method employs a vacuum cleaner with a filter trap, the filter and its collected evidence being packaged immediately to avoid loss or contamination. Furthermore, the vacuum sweeper and its trap must be thoroughly cleaned between collections, to prevent contamination.

Packaging and storage of trace evidence requires use of containers that prevent tampering (or at least clearly reveal its occurrence), while eliminating loss or contamination—i.e., sealed lids or flaps, no open seams or edges. Small, loose items must be secured in clean containers never previously used, which are then typically secured inside larger envelopes or paper bags. Larger items (clothing, tools, WEAPONS,

etc.) bearing visible and firmly attached trace evidence should be sealed individually in clean, new packaging for transportation to a secure laboratory environment. Wet clothing must be air-dried at the operator's earliest convenience, without exposure to damaging sunlight or heat, in such a manner that any trace evidence will be preserved from loss or contamination.

At the crime lab or other controlled facility, all equipment and work surfaces must be cleaned before and after each examination to prevent contamination. Adequate lighting must be available, while examiners should also have means of controlling such problem features as excessive air currents and static electricity. Examination of various items must be conducted separately, avoiding contact between known and questioned pieces of trace evidence. Any contact or condition that may cause contamination must be documented at the lab, communicated to the relevant law enforcement agency, and ultimately disclosed to defense counsel of any defendants charged in the case. After examination and analysis, all evidence must be properly stored and secured against loss, damage, tampering, or contamination.

TYRRELL, John F. (1861–1955)

Milwaukee native John Tyrrell was born in 1861. He developed a lifelong fascination with penmanship while employed as a clerk with the Northwestern Life Insurance Company, where he encountered numerous cases of FORGERY and FRAUD. Honing his skills, Tyrrell soon left the insurance game to become a professional expert witness in criminal trials. His first headline case was the 1899 trial of Raymond Molineux, charged with sending poisoned patent medicine to an enemy and killing his target's landlady by mistake. Prosecutors called Tyrrell and competing expert ALBERT OSBORN to prove that Molineux addressed the lethal package, a feat accomplished when Tyrrell presented oversized handwriting replicas to the jury. Journalists thereafter dubbed Tyrrell the "Wizard of the Pen," as he pursued a long and sometimes flamboyant career in the field of QUESTIONED DOCUMENTS. Tyrrell's famous trials included Chicago's Leopold-Loeb murder case, wherein he traced a mock ransom note to one defendant's typewriter, and the LINDBERGH KIDNAPPING, where he teamed once again with Albert Osborn. Tyrell and Osborn subsequently joined forces to create the American Society of Questioned Document Examiners on September 2, 1942. Tyrrell died in 1955, after six decades of active investigation.

UHLENHUTH, Paul Theodore (1870–1957)

German immunologist Paul Uhlenhuth was born in Hannover, in 1870. By age 30 he was employed at the University of Greifswald's Institute of Hygiene, performing experiments with the blood of various animal species. After injecting hen's blood into rabbits, Uhlenhuth discovered that the rabbits thus treated precipitated the protein in hen's blood but showed no reaction to the blood of other mammals. Uhlenhuth published his findings in paper titled "A Method for Investigation of Different Types of Blood."

That paper intrigued Otto Beumer, Greifswald's coroner and professor of forensic medicine at the local university, who teamed with Uhlenhuth for further experiments. Together, they developed a precipitin test using animal serums to detect human blood in dried stains, regardless of their age. July 1901 brought the first practical test of that method, when two children were murdered on the Baltic island of Rügen. Prime suspect Ludwig Tessnow had escaped conviction in a nearly identical case, three years ear-

lier, because police could not tell if stains found on his clothing were human or animal blood. In the latest case, Uhlenhuth tested some 100 stains on Tessnow's clothing, locating human BLOODSTAINS on his hat, jacket, vest, shirt, and trousers. Tessnow was thus convicted on two counts of murder and executed at Greifswald prison in 1904.

Uhlenhuth's precipitin test earned him the first-ever Emil von Behring Prize from the University of Marburg, but it was not his sole contribution to medicine. During World War I, he also discovered the cause of the often-fatal Weil's disease (leptospirosis)—also variously known as canicola fever, caver's flu, infectious jaundice, hemorrhagic jaundice, mud fever, sewerman's flu, spirochetal jaundice, swamp fever, or swineherd's disease. Uhlenhuth discovered that the *Leptospira interrogans* bacterium is carried by a water-borne spirochete, commonly found in rat's urine, transmitted to humans by contact with polluted water. Uhlenhuth died in 1957, at age 87, after nearly six decades of medical research.

VASQUEZ, David exonerated by DNA

On January 24, 1984, a prowler invaded the home of a woman in Arlington County, Virginia, raping the victim before he placed a noose around her neck and hanged her. Police suspected David Vasquez, who lacked an alibi and whose pubic hairs were "consistent" with samples found at the CRIME SCENE. Vasquez also proved malleable under questioning, a circumstance that defense lawyers attributed to borderline mental retardation. Transcripts of his interrogation include the following exchange with detectives:

> Detective 1: Did she tell you to tie her hands behind her back?
> Vasquez: Ah, if she did, I did.
> Detective 2: Whatcha use?
> Vasquez: The ropes?
> Detective 2: No, not the ropes. Whatcha use?
> Vasquez: Only my belt.
> Detective 2: No, not your belt. Remember being out in the sunroom, the room that sits out to the back of the house? And what did you cut down to use?
> Vasquez: That, uh, clothesline?
> Detective 2: No, it wasn't a clothesline. It was something like a clothesline. What was it? By the window? Think about the Venetian blinds, David. Remember cutting the Venetian blind cords?

> Vasquez: Ah, it's the same as rope?
> Detective 2: Yeah.
> Detective 1: Okay, now tell us how it went, David—tell us how you did it.
> Vasquez: She told me to grab the knife, and, and, stab her, that's all.
> Detective 2: David, no, David.
> Vasquez: If it did happen, and I did it, and my fingerprints were on it.
> Detective 2: You hung her!
> Vasquez: What?
> Detective 2: You hung her!
> Vasquez: Okay, so I hung her.

Jurors were spared from hearing that "confession," since Vasquez pleaded no contest to burglary and second-degree murder on February 4, 1985, receiving a 35-year prison term. Four years later, after DNA evidence linked serial killer TIMOTHY SPENCER to several similar slayings, Virginia's state laboratory and two private facilities tested evidence collected from the crime scene, but results were inconclusive. Nonetheless, an FBI report concluded that Spencer probably killed Vasquez's alleged victim, in addition to several more. Prosecutors joined Vasquez's attorneys in a petition for executive clemency, and Vasquez was released with an unconditional pardon on January 4, 1989. Timothy Spencer was never charged with the crime in question, but earned death sentences for two other slayings and was executed on April

271

27, 1994. Vasquez received state compensation in an undisclosed amount for his wrongful conviction and incarceration. No police officers were disciplined for extracting his false confession.

VICAP

While Hollywood has wildly exaggerated the role played by FBI agents in pursuing and capturing serial killers, the bureau *does* play a part in tracking such predators. The "chase" is typically a mental exercise of profiling unknown subjects, with most of the work done in basement quarters at the FBI Academy in Quantico, Virginia, by members of the bureau's Investigative Support Unit (formerly Behavioral Science). Accurate profiling requires input from detectives working on the case, wherever they may be, and that information is collected through VICAP—the Violent Criminal Apprehension Program.

VICAP was the brainchild of retired Los Angeles police commander Pierce Brooks, a veteran of serial murder investigations dating from the 1950s who recognized the glaring lack of any information network geared to track nomadic killers on the move. In Brooks's day, the only method of pursuing such cases was exhaustive study of long-distance news reports or steady correspondence with other (sometimes hostile) law enforcement agencies. Computers offered the obvious solution, and Brooks told anyone who would listen of his plans for a nationwide network designed to collect and compare details of unsolved crimes, thus charting patterns that might otherwise be missed.

Retained by the FBI in 1981, Brooks and former Seattle detective Robert Keppel began hammering out VICAP's framework, drafting an investigative questionnaire for local officers, but they still had far to go in terms of winning over the Washington bureaucracy. Best-selling author Ann Rule beat the drum for VICAP with a series of editorials in 1982, joining Brooks and others to plead the FBI's case in July 1983 Senate hearings. A year later, in July 1984, President Ronald Reagan announced the creation of a National Center for Analysis of Violent Crime, charged with the primary goal of tracking repeat killers. The VICAP computer network, based at the FBI Academy, went online in May 1985, accepting reports of murders, MISSING PERSONS, and discarded corpses from across the nation.

Unlike fictional G-men and -women, members of the VICAP team and ISU are paid to analyze crimes rather than to conduct active field investigations. With fewer than a dozen full-time agents, ISU is not equipped for staging manhunts, crashing into suspect hideouts, or gunning down desperate killers. On the rare occasions when VICAP agents *do* visit a CRIME SCENE, their function is purely advisory, reviewing local task force operations and suggesting more efficient means of handling information. The national program's success or failure ultimately hinges on cooperation from local agencies, where jealousy, resentment, or simple fatigue sometimes conspire to frustrate VICAP.

Six months of operation was enough to highlight VICAP's problems in the field. Overworked police considered the 44-page federal questionnaire too cumbersome and time-consuming. If a killer picked off 10 or 15 victims and the FBI required a separate questionnaire for each, some locals opted to ignore the federal team and spare themselves a case of writer's cramp. The current VICAP forms are two-thirds shorter than their predecessors, but reduced paperwork has not solved all the bureau's problems in coordinating manhunts. For many local officers, the FBI is still J. Edgar Hoover once removed, a headline-grabbing agency more interested in claiming credit for cases solved by local police than helping out the average working cop. Some bureau spokesmen are still too quick to shoot from the lip—as when an agent in Atlanta blamed anonymous black parents for the deaths of several murdered children—and many police departments still view the feds as rank interlopers, their very presence a tacit indictment of local methods.

A VICAP case where everything apparently worked out as planned occurred in Wilmington, Delaware, where five prostitutes were tortured to death between November 1987 and October 1988. FBI profilers reviewed the case evidence, sketching a portrait of a suspect who was white, a local resident employed in the construction trade, age 25 to 35, fascinated with police work, and using a van for transport and disposal of his victims. FIBER samples taken from bodies narrowed down the range of carpeting inside the van, and VICAP agents recommended a decoy operation to lure the killer with policewomen disguised as hookers. One such decoy managed to obtain some carpet fibers and a license number for the "creepy" trick whose mannerisms set alarm bells ringing in her mind, and SURVEILLANCE was established on suspect Steven Pennell. A 31-year-old white man, Pennell was a professional electrician with two college semesters of criminology behind him. His applications to local police departments had all been rejected, but he clearly fit the VICAP profile as a "police buff." Scientific analysis of hairs, fibers, and BLOODSTAINS from his van convinced a jury of Pennell's guilt in two murders, and he was executed by lethal injection on March 14, 1992.

VICAP spokesmen often cite Pennell's case as proof positive of their success in profiling killers, but Delaware authorities—while grateful for the FBI's help—are more reserved. The fiber evidence was critical, they grant, but it had no connection to the suspect profile, which local investigators now describe as "mostly general stuff." The decoy operation was standard police work, they say, and would have caught Pennell regardless of his occupation, race, or age.

Sour grapes? A touch of jealousy, perhaps? In any case, while many frontline homicide investigators readily acknowledge VICAP's value in connecting far-flung crimes, some still insist that the program has yet to prove itself capable of identifying a specific predator and bringing him (or her) to justice.

ViCLAS

ViCLAS—the Violent Crime Linkage Analysis System—was the brainchild of Canada's first criminal profiler, Sergeant Ron MacKay. Assigned to the General Investigative Section of the Royal Canadian Mounted Police (RCMP) in North Vancouver, MacKay envisioned a system that would improve on the FBI's VICAP program for linking unsolved homicides and sexual assaults across the country. When MacKay conceived his idea in August 1990, the RCMP already maintained a Major Case File at headquarters in Ottawa, but most local police departments refused to submit the voluminous paperwork required for case submissions. MacKay and colleague Keith Davidson sought to remedy that problem with computers, recruiting two students at Ottawa's Algonquin College—Paul Leury and John Ripley—to write the necessary software programs.

Although actively employed from 1992, ViCLAS was formally unveiled on December 16, 1993, with a press conference held at the Ontario Provincial Police Academy outside Toronto. Present for the system's public launch were various RCMP leaders, together with officers from 23 Canadian law enforcement agencies, the FBI, New York and New Jersey State Police, and members of Iowa's Sex Crimes Analysis Section. Administration of ViCLAS was assigned to a new Canadian Association of Violent Crime Analysts (CAVCA).

Like VICAP, the ViCLAS program requires submission of detailed questionnaires from field investigators. Submission forms consist of a 36-page booklet with 245 questions (cut from an original 262 in 1995) or a shorter eight-page form with 83 questions. Within 18 months of its launch, ViCLAS had drawn 57 links among 584 unsolved cases on file. By the end of 1995, the system permitted MacKay to estimate that Canada hosted 12 to 20 active serial killers at large. While some resistance lingers, voluntary ViCLAS submissions increased from 124 cases in 1992 (the year before its formal launch) to 120,362 cases by September 2001.

Since its inception, interest in ViCLAS has spread rapidly around the world. Authorities in Austria and the Netherlands committed to its use on February 9, 1995, four days before MacKay presented the system at an international conference in China. Since then, ViCLAS has been adopted in Australia, Sweden, and several U.S. states. FBI agent Mike Cryan, assigned to the VICAP program at Quantico, Virginia, described ViCLAS as "the Cadillac system in the world," and VICAP pioneer David Cavanaugh (at Harvard University) was equally impressed. "The Canadians," Cavanaugh said, "have done to automated case linkage what the Japanese did with assembly line auto production. They have taken a good American idea and transformed it into the best in the world." On December 13, 1995, summarizing police failures in the case of Ontario sex-slayers Paul Bernardo and Karla Homolka, Justice Archie Campbell recommended that ViCLAS submissions should be mandatory throughout the province. He wrote:

> *Experience shows that it is not enough merely to encourage ViCLAS reporting by means of the standard policies and procedures of individual forces. Encouragement is not enough. Unless the entry of information into ViCLAS is centrally mandated and enforced throughout Ontario, and its operation supported through training and strong reinforcement of the reporting requirement, its power to link predatory serial crimes is greatly weakened.*

Despite such widespread praise and multiple requests from its own analysts, FBI headquarters remains stubbornly opposed to adoption of ViCLAS in place of VICAP.

VICTIMOLOGY

Victimology is the study of crime victims, designed to yield information concerning the offenders who prey upon them. Practitioners of forensic BEHAVIORAL SCIENCE profess to learn much from such studies, incorporating their suppositions via PSYCHOLOGICAL PROFILING. Thus, the elusive "BOSTON STRANGLER'S" choice of elderly female victims suggested rage against a mother figure—at least, until the still-unidentified slayer began claiming younger victims. In various cases, especially SEX CRIMES and serial offenses, choice of victims may suggest an offender's sexual proclivity, race, even religious or political beliefs (as in hate crimes or extremist activity). High-risk victims, especially favored by serial rapists and killers, include prostitutes and other "sex workers," the homeless, unattended children, and elderly persons living or traveling alone.

Statistically, 90 percent of America's identified killers and 75 percent of all murder victims in any given year are male. Serial killers reverse that trend, claiming 65 percent female and 35 percent male victims. Ninety-odd percent of American murderers claim victims of their own race, while serial slayers again deviate from the norm, claiming 65 percent same-race victims, while 10 percent kill only victims of another race and 11 percent cross the color line impartially. (The race of killers still at large is unknown in the other 14 percent of serial cases.) While most murders remain impulsive crimes, often committed by relatives or acquaintances of the victims, serial stalkers take more care in selection of their prey: 40 percent apparently choose their victims by gender; 7 percent select human prey with an eye toward potential profit (from inheritance, insurance payments, etc.); 6 percent select victims by age (children or seniors); 3 percent—principally murderous doctors and nurses—choose victims on the basis of their health or physical condition; 2 percent select their targets by race; another 2 percent picks victims on the basis of their residence or lack of same (homeless targets, residents of a particular apartment complex, etc.); the basis of selection is unknown in 12 percent of all serial cases, with killers still unidentified; and selection methods change over time in 13 percent of known cases (as with Arthur Shawcross,

who killed two children in the 1970s, then graduated to adult female prostitutes in the late 1980s).

Whatever police and forensic scientists learn about a killer's psychology from the lives or remains of his victims, hard evidence is still required to identify offenders and see them convicted at trial. Careless killers leave that evidence in the form of FINGERPRINTS and footprints, bullets and abandoned WEAPONS, hairs and FIBERS, blood and semen that reveals their DNA profiles to expert eyes, and countless other pieces of TRACE EVIDENCE. Only then may law enforcement officers arrest their suspect, bringing him or her to trial.

VOLLMER, August (1876–1955)

The son of German immigrants, born in New Orleans in 1876, August Vollmer ended his formal education in sixth grade, with a subsequent course in bookkeeping, typing, and shorthand at New Orleans Academy. His family moved to Berkeley, California, in 1891, and Vollmer joined a friend to run a coal and feed store, while serving with the city's volunteer fire department. With the outbreak of the Spanish-American War in 1898, he volunteered for military service and was twice decorated for valor during combat in the Philippines. Back in civilian life, he worked as a Berkeley mail carrier, then won election as city marshal in 1905, on a platform calling for reorganization of the city's police department along military lines. Vollmer held that post (renamed chief of police in 1909) until 1932, and in the process revolutionized American police work.

Vollmer took office at a crucial moment for the Berkeley Police Department. The force was a corrupt and brutal unit, so ineffectual that street gang violence in West Berkeley had forced the Southern Pacific Railroad to abandon its local depot. Instead of hiring more sluggers—the kind of policemen Vollmer labeled "dumbbells"—he publicly denounced both excessive force and capital punishment, calling instead for a concerted attack on the sociological roots of crime. In 1908, Vollmer opened the Berkeley Police School, serving as its chief instructor, expanding over time until 1930s recruits spent 312 hours in the classroom. Vollmer's tactical innovations included use of bicycles, then automobiles, to make his patrolmen more mobile, linked to headquarters by two-way radios. He also pioneered in use of FINGERPRINTS, handwriting classification, and use of "lie detectors" to screen criminal suspects, while leading the nation in employment of female officers. When recruiting, Vollmer gave priority to college graduates and himself taught summer sessions in police science at the University of California from 1916 to 1932.

Vollmer's approach to crime-fighting was outlined in a 1919 article for *Police Journal,* "The Policeman as a Social Worker." He encouraged his officers to intervene in the lives of civilians on their beats, especially where juveniles might be diverted from a life of crime. For detection of felons already at large, Vollmer established the nation's first professional crime lab in 1916, and developed MODUS OPERANDI files as a form of early PSYCHOLOGICAL PROFILING. Vollmer's reputation prompted supervisors of the Los Angeles Police Department to "borrow" him for a year, during 1923–24, and while Vollmer did his best for LAPD—founding the department's police academy, establishing a modern motor pool and commissioning five new precinct houses, schooling his men in Constitutional ethics—LAPD in the 1920s was essentially beyond redemption.

By 1932, when he retired from Berkeley PD, Vollmer had been hired as a consultant by civic leaders in Chicago, Dallas, and Havana, Cuba. Twenty-five of his former subordinates also served as police chiefs in various towns nationwide, while Vollmer himself headed President Herbert Hoover's Commission on Law Enforcement. In retirement, Vollmer served as professor of police administration in the department he had established at UC Berkeley. He also distilled a lifetime of study into one volume, *The Criminal,* published in 1949. In the early 1950s, Vollmer was diagnosed with throat cancer (from a lifetime of smoking) and the onset of Parkinson's disease. After willing his body to the University of California's medical center, he committed suicide on November 4, 1955.

VUČETIĆ, Juan (1858–1925)

Ivan Vučetić was born at Lessina, Dalmatia (now Croatia), on July 20, 1858. A child prodigy in MATHEMATICS and science, he immigrated to Argentina in 1882 and joined the police force in Buenos Aires, quickly rising through the ranks to head its statistical bureau (including criminal records). Argentinean police used ANTHROPOMETRY to identify criminals, following the lead of ALPHONSE BERTILLON, but Vučetić was also fascinated by FRANCIS GALTON's publications on FINGERPRINTS. In 1891, he began collecting fingerprints systematically, and in the following year he used them to obtain the first known conviction based solely on fingerprint evidence. Defendant Francisca Rojas had murdered her two sons, then slashed her own throat in an effort to blame an intruder, but her bloody fingerprints betrayed her, prompting a confession.

With that victory behind him, Vučetić expanded and revised Galton's system of fingerprint classification to make it his own, dubbed "dactyloscopy." By 1896, the system was officially adopted in Argentina and several neighboring countries, where it remains in use to this day. Vučetić published his opus *Comparative Dactyloscopy* in 1904, while traveling to scientific conferences as far away as India and China. He died at home, in Buenos Aires, on January 25, 1925. The La Plata police academy—Escuela de policia Juan Vucetich—is named in his honor, as is the Center for Forensics Examinations (Centar za kriminalistička vještačenja) in Zagreb, Croatia.

WAITE, Charles E. (1874–1926)

A New York native, born in 1874, Charles Waite nurtured a fascination with FIREARMS dating from childhood, but his application of that interest to forensic science dated from 1917 and a near-tragic miscarriage of justice. Defendant Charles Stielow stood condemned for the 1915 murders of his employer and a female housekeeper, based on testimony from self-styled ballistics expert Dr. Albert Hamilton, who told jurors that the fatal bullets had been fired from Stielow's revolver. While Stielow awaited his date with the electric chair at Sing Sing prison, another man confessed to the slayings, whereupon Governor Charles Whitman ordered a full review of the case. Waite, then employed as an investigator with the state attorney general's office, was assigned to study the case.

Waite soon learned that Albert Hamilton was a manufacturer of patent medicines who had bestowed the "doctor" title on himself without benefit of special training in ballistics or any other subject. Waite also observed that test bullets fired through Stielow's pistol bore no real resemblance to the slugs extracted from either victim in 1915. Convinced of the need for a comprehensive firearms database, Waite undertook the Herculean task of compiling technical information on every gun manufactured in the United States and Europe. By the time he completed that odyssey, in 1923, Waite realized that he still had no reliable means of matching slugs to a specific gun. To that

end, he created a new Bureau of Forensic Ballistics in New York City, recruiting physicist John Fisher, microscopist PHILIP GRAVELLE, and military ordnance expert CALVIN GODDARD to join in the effort. Together, Waite's team invented new comparison microscopes and other tools for precise examination of firearms, bullets, and cartridge casings, elevating ballistics testing from haphazard guesswork to the level of true science. Waite died in 1926, leaving his colleagues to carry on the work.

WASHINGTON, Earl, Jr. exonerated by DNA

In 1982, a prowler raped Rebecca Lynn Williams at her home in Culpepper, Virginia, then stabbed her 38 times and left her to die. Police focused their suspicion on 22-year-old Earl Washington after he broke into an elderly woman's home, struck her with a chair, then stole her pistol and used it to shoot his own brother. They further said that Washington, who suffers from borderline mental retardation, confessed the Williams rape-slaying in custody (a claim that Washington steadfastly denied). Convicted of murder with "special circumstances"—rape and BURGLARY—Washington received a death sentence. In 1993, after DNA testing of the crime scene evidence produced inconclusive results, Governor L. Douglas Wilder commuted Washington's capital sentence to a prison term of life without parole. Seven years later, in October 2000, further DNA tests performed using new technology excluded Washington as a possible donor of semen traces found on the 1982 murder victim. Governor Jim Gilmore pardoned Washington on that charge, but Washington remained incarcerated for the unrelated assault and shooting. Defense attorney Eric Freedman denounced that compromise as an example of "bureaucratic buck-passing and governmental cowardice," claiming that any other inmate convicted on similar charges would have been paroled by 1994. "To keep Earl Washington in jail one day longer," Freedman told reporters, "is a desperate attempt to defend the indefensible."

WATERS, Kenneth exonerated by DNA evidence

In 1980, Ayers, Massachusetts, resident Katharina Brow was stabbed and beaten to death in a brutal ROBBERY. Suspect Kenneth Waters was indicted after two ex-girlfriends told police that he had boasted to them of committing the crime. At trial, in 1983, Waters argued that he was in court at the time of the slaying, on an unrelated charge of assaulting a police officer, and thus could not be guilty. Court records confirmed his presence on the day of the murder, but could not pin down specific times. His ex-girlfriends testified for the state, and prosecutors claimed that Waters sold some of the victim's jewelry six weeks after the murder. Jurors convicted Waters of first-degree murder and robbery on May 12, 1983. He subsequently received a sentence of life imprisonment.

Kenneth's younger sister, Betty Ann Waters, devoted her life to proving his innocence. Although a high school dropout and divorced mother of two at the time of his trial, Betty Ann went on to earn her GED, then her bachelor's and master's degrees, finally graduating from law school at Roger Williams University, in Rhode Island. While still at Roger Williams, she began to correspond with attorneys from the CARDOZO INNOCENCE PROJECT concerning her brother's case. Attorney BARRY SCHECK agreed to take the case, after a court clerk directed Betty Ann to a box of old case evidence stored in the courthouse basement. The stash included blood samples from the presumed killer, found at the crime scene, and DNA testing excluded Kenneth Waters as a donor of the evidence. He was released on March 15, 2001, after 18 years in prison, while prosecutors announced their intention to hold a new trial.

Despite the threat of another trial, Waters seemed confident, telling reporters that the true story of his wrongful conviction was "going to come out and it is going to be a shocker." That trial would not take place, however. On September 6, 2001, in Middletown, Rhode Island, Waters fell from a 15-foot wall while taking a short cut to his brother's home for a family dinner. He fractured his skull in the fall and died on September 19, in a local hospital.

WEAPONS

Any object used to inflict pain or injury is a weapon. Fists, feet, and teeth were the first weapons wielded by humans—and in certain circumstances, as with professional boxers or martial arts experts—bodily appendages may still be deemed deadly weapons under law. Sticks and stones came next, followed by more sophisticated instruments designed to cut or hack, then to strike from a distance when thrown or propelled by slings, bows, blowguns, catapults, or FIREARMS. While some degree of violence is implicit in the use of any weapon, lethal objects may not *seem* like weapons at first glance. Any flexible object (or *ligature*) may be used in strangulation, while countless victims have been smothered with pillows and other soft objects. In forcible drowning and assaults with high-pressure hoses, the weapon is water. All poisons, plus many other chemicals and gases, have utility as weapons. So do most vehicles and many biological agents (bacteria, viruses, etc.). In our modern age, the high-tech arsenal includes electricity, light, and sound waves.

Where weapons are missing from a CRIME SCENE or otherwise unknown, criminalists and forensic pathologists strive to identify them by examining wounds or cause of death and collecting IMPRESSION or TRACE EVIDENCE. Firearms leave projectiles, along with gunshot residue (GSR) and spent cartridge casings traceable via toolmarks to a specific gun. The size and type of blade used to stab, slice, or hack a victim may be determined by measurement and examination of WOUNDS. TOXICOLOGY locates traces of poison or drugs in bodily fluids, tissue, and hair. Bruises, broken bones and other evidence of trauma may suggest specific weapons, while impressions left on flesh or bone may pinpoint a specific bludgeon. Forensic ODONTOLOGY reveals when teeth are used as weapons on the human body. Strangulation, asphyxiation, and drowning all leave characteristic traces recognizable by MEDICAL EXAMINERS. Even NONLETHAL WEAPONS may leave identifiable marks, as when electric stun guns inflict small pattern burns on naked flesh.

Discovery of weapons used in crimes of violence opens new doors to forensic examination. With firearms, ballistics and other traits link guns to the bullets they fire and the cartridge cases they eject. Identification of mass-produced knives may be more problematic, but blood and other biological evidence found on a specific cutting tool is often subject to DNA profiling, and thus to matching with specific victims or offenders. GLASS and PAINT help identify vehicles used as weapons, while ACCIDENT RECONSTRUCTION may prove whether or not a specific collision was deliberate. EXPLOSIVES are often traceable through taggants or chemical composition, while timing devices and other components used in homemade bombs may help identify the bomber(s). In cases of beating and manual strangulation, modern technology even permits the retrieval of shoeprints and FINGERPRINTS from human flesh in some cases.

WECHT, Cyril Harrison (1931–)

A child of immigrants from Eastern Europe, born at Bobtown, Pennsylvania, on March 20, 1931, Wecht moved with his family to Pittsburgh as a child. Despite teenage aspirations to become a professional musician, he studied medicine, earning his M.D. from the University of Pittsburgh's medical school and his J.D. from the University of Maryland in Baltimore. After serving in the U.S. Air Force, Wecht specialized in forensic medicine, joining the staff of Pittsburgh's St. Francis Hospital. In 1965, he became Allegheny County's deputy coroner. Four years later, Wecht won election as the county coroner, a post he held until he resigned in 2006. He served additionally as president of the board of trustees of the American Board of Legal Medicine, president of the American College of Legal Medicine Foundation, as a clinical professor at the University of Pittsburgh School of Medicine, and as an adjunct professor of law at Duquesne University. As coroner, he has personally performed more than 14,000 autopsies.

Wecht's outspoken opinions on high-profile cases—including those of ORENTHAL JAMES (O. J.) SIMPSON, Klaus von Bülow, JonBenét Ramsey, Vincent Foster, and both Kennedy assassinations, among others—have sparked controversy throughout his tenure as coroner. Pittsburgh *Post-Gazette* reporter Robert Dvorchak once described Wecht as "a man

who never met a TV camera he didn't like, a man who never had an opinion he didn't share and a man who carries his own local political baggage." While that baggage has never cost him an election, it has kept Wecht in the public eye for decades. In 1978, he testified before the House Select Committee on Assassinations, condemning the Warren Commission's "MAGIC BULLET THEORY," and he subsequently called (unsuccessfully) for exhumation of President Kennedy's corpse. On the local front, in 1979 Wecht faced accusations of depositing autopsy fees into a personal bank account, rather than into the coroner's office account, but he won acquittal at trial on those charges. County officials then sued Wecht to recover $390,000, sparking a nine-year legal fight that ended in 1992 with Wecht paying $200,000 in damages. While maintaining his coroner's post, Wecht lost an electoral bid to become Allegheny County's chief executive in 1999. Five years later, the county grand jury launched a new investigation of Wecht's office, probing charges that Wecht and his staff performed private autopsies-for-profit at county expense, that he aided plaintiffs filing federal lawsuits against Pittsburgh police for wrongful deaths in custody, and that he wrongfully used members of his medical staff as chauffeurs. In 2006, a grand jury indicted Wecht on 84 counts, including mail and wire fraud, but as of 2007, the case had not gone to trial.

Wecht's numerous books include *Microscopic Diagnosis in Forensic Pathology* (1980), *Forensic Sciences* (1981), *Cause of Death* (1983), *United States Medicolegal Autopsy Laws* (1989), *Preparing and Winning Medical Negligence* (1992), *The Search for Lee Harvey Oswald* (1995), *Grave Secrets* (1998), *Who Killed JonBenet Ramsey?* (1998), *November 22, 1963: A Reference Guide to the JFK Assassination* (1999), *Handling Soft Tissue Injury Cases* (1999), *Silent Witness* (2002), *Mortal Evidence* (2003), *Crime Scene Investigation* (2004), *Forensic Aspects of Chemical and Biological Terrorism* (2004), *Forensic Science and the Law* (2005), and *Tales from the Morgue* (2005).

WEST Virginia Innocence Project

In June 2005, faculty and students of West Virginia University's Forensic and Investigative Sciences Program and its College of Law organized the West Virginia Innocence Project to investigate apparent cases of wrongful conviction in the Mountain State. Of

30-odd innocence projects active across the United States, West Virginia's was the first to combine a university's law school and forensic science program. As envisioned by its founders, the WVIP would first screen applications from inmates claiming actual innocence, then members of the forensic science department would review any available evidence in the selected cases to determine whether grounds for an appeal exist. If DNA or other evidence supports the inmate's claim of innocence, it is then submitted to a third-party laboratory for further study. Marjorie McDiarmid, director of the WVU College of Law's Clinical Law Program, expects a warm reception from state prosecutors. "Once a prosecutor is convinced a miscarriage of justice occurred," she told reporters, "we'll get a lot of cooperation with bringing the case back before a court. It's not in the interest of prosecutors or police to keep innocent folks in jail. That frequently means a guilty [person] is walking around." In fact, however, prosecutors in various other states have doggedly resisted admission of DNA evidence to exonerate wrongfully convicted inmates. At press time for this work, the WVIP's expectation of official cooperation remained untested.

WHITE-COLLAR Crime

Sociologist Edwin Sutherland (1893–1950) coined the phrase *white-collar crime* in a speech delivered to the American Sociological Association on December 27, 1939. Ten years later, in a monograph of the same title, Sutherland defined white-collar crime "approximately as a crime committed by a person of respectability and high social status in the course of his occupation." Over the past half-century that basic definition has been altered and refined to include most "business crimes," including various offenses committed via paperwork or by means of computers. White-collar crimes are generally contrasted with "street crime" or violent offenses such as HOMICIDE, ROBBERY, and SEX CRIMES. Despite Sutherland's initial stipulation of respectable defendants, however, modern white-collar offenses often overlap activities of "lower class" organized crime, while some offenses—such as check FRAUD—are committed predominantly by persons of lower income.

Upper-echelon white-collar crimes are often difficult to prosecute, since the offenders are experienced

Enron founder Kenneth Lay leaves the courthouse at the end of day 51 of his fraud and conspiracy trial, May 3, 2006, in a Houston file photo. The Enron scandal embodied corporate corruption and white-collar fraud. Lay was found guilty of 10 charges against him in May 2006, but he died of a heart attack in July 2006, before his sentencing. (Pat Sullivan/AP)

swindlers with substantial wealth and influence at their disposal, protected by expensive lawyers and political connections. When prosecutions *do* occur, resulting in convictions, punishment is generally more lenient than that applied to low-income offenders. (Witness TV maven Martha Stewart's five-month incarceration at "Camp Cupcake," versus the draconian sentences imposed on some offenders for drug possession, THEFT, etc.) Another deviation from the norm of prosecution is the fact that white-collar criminal charges may also be filed against organizations—including corporations, law firms, churches, charities, and so on. Arrests are often based on law enforcement "sting" operations, prompting frequent complaints of entrapment from defendants charged with bribery and similar offenses. Common white-collar crimes include the following:

Antitrust violations—federal offenses related to illegal monopolies, price-fixing, and other outlawed forms of unfair competition in the "free market."

Bankruptcy fraud—practiced by individuals and corporations alike, including concealment or falsification of assets to defraud creditors and evade taxes.

Bribery—any offer of cash or other valuable consideration made with the intent of influencing the recipient's actions. While government officials and law enforcement officers are frequent defendants in bribery prosecutions, no official standing is required to invoke bribery statutes.

COUNTERFEITING—as discussed elsewhere in this volume, any production and/or circulation of spurious currency or other items of value that are fraudulently misrepresented as genuine.

CYBERCRIMES—including all manner of computer and Internet fraud, hacking, computer sabotage, etc.

Credit card fraud—comprising any unauthorized use of actual credit cards or production of counterfeit cards to obtain cash or merchandise.

Economic/industrial espionage—involving any theft of trade secrets from an individual, a company, or an industry, committed either by private parties or agents of some official body.

Embezzlement—occurring whenever a person entrusted with cash or other property of any kind converts it to his/her personal use or benefit without approval from the owner. The most common form of embezzlement involves surreptitious theft of money by employees from their employer.

Environmental violations—including illegal dumping, violation of various statutory restrictions on pollution, falsification of compliance documentation, and traffic in endangered species.

Financial institution fraud—including all types of fraud committed by or within banks, credit unions, savings and loan institutions, and so forth. Common offenses include check fraud, counterfeiting of negotiable instruments, fraudulent loans, money laundering, check kiting, and mortgage fraud.

Government fraud—referring *not* to frauds committed by public officials, but rather frauds perpetrated *against* the government at some level, including offenses by holders of government contracts and participants in various entitlement programs (welfare, Social Security, Medicare, etc.). Curiously, some firms with multiple convictions for defrauding the federal government are still favored with new contracts and various subsidies at taxpayers' expense.

Health care fraud—a broad class of offenses including fraudulent billings; kickbacks; performance of unnecessary tests, treatments or surgeries; sale of adulterated or ineffective medicine, etc.

Insider trading—as defined by the Securities and Exchange Commission, any trading of stocks that occurs when persons privileged with confidential information regarding crucial events use that knowledge either to reap profits or avoid loss in the stock market, to the detriment of the company and/or common investors.

Insurance fraud—a wide gamut of swindles by insurance firms, their policy holders, and third-party claimants that may include sale of invalid policies, unethical cancellation of insurance when claims are made, submission of fraudulent or exaggerated claims, and so on.

Kickbacks—illegal collusion between the buyer and seller of any product, wherein a portion of the purchase price is secretly refunded to encourage sales.

Mail fraud—any fraud perpetrated via the United States Postal Service, as defined by federal law.

MONEY LAUNDERING—as described elsewhere, the concealment and "cleaning" of illicit revenue through various means, either to obscure its source or to avoid taxation.

Public corruption—occurring whenever a public official at any level of government (elected, appointed, or hired) solicits, accepts or agrees to accept anything of value to influence his/her performance in office.

Securities fraud—any illegal manipulation of stocks, bonds, or other securities as defined in federal law, along with theft and counterfeiting of securities.

Tax evasion—including the filing of false returns or failure to file at all, whether by an individual or corporation.

Telephone or telemarketing fraud—involving either fraud against telephone service providers or CONFIDENCE GAMES wherein victims are bilked of cash by high-pressure telephone sales and fraudulent merchandise offers.

WHITEHURST, Frederic (1948–)

Born in 1948, Fred Whitehurst earned four Bronze Stars for bravery in the Vietnam War and displayed special valor on the night he stopped four fellow U.S. soldiers from torturing and raping a female villager. Back in civilian life, he earned a Ph.D. in CHEMISTRY and joined the FBI in 1982. Four years later he was assigned to the bureau's Laboratory Division and spent the next decade as an EXPLOSIVES residue analyst in the Materials Analysis Unit.

Whitehurst encountered problems at the lab almost from the moment he was assigned to supervisor Terry Rudolph for training. It soon became apparent that Rudolph and others cut corners in their work, skipping various tests required or "suggested" by FBI lab protocols, and that they often phrased reports in terms favoring the prosecution. Whitehurst was pressured to do likewise and complained repeatedly, without result. Finally, at the 1989 federal trial of defendant Steve Psinakis (accused of shipping explosives to the Philippines in an effort to topple dictator Ferdinand Marcos), Whitehurst aired his concerns to the defense. Psinakis's attorney first suspected that Whitehurst was "some kind of weirdo," then embraced the G-man as an expert witness. Psinakis was acquitted, whereupon his prosecutors complained to the Justice Department, expressing "serious questions" about "the FBI laboratory's procedures."

Still, slipshod work continued at the lab despite that episode and Whitehurst's ongoing complaints. In February 1993, he met twice with FBI director William Sessions, who promised a full investigation by the bureau's Office of Professional Responsibility (OPR). When nothing came of that, Whitehurst contacted the National Whistleblower Center (NWC) in Washington, sitting for interviews with the group's attorneys in October and December 1993. NWC lawyer Stephen Kohn wrote to FBI headquarters in February 1994, demanding a full investigation of Whitehurst's charges, while Whitehurst personally voiced his complaints to the OPR. Attorneys for the FBI's Office of General Counsel interviewed Whitehurst in May 1994, reporting back to Justice that all of Whitehurst's complaints had been fully investigated and resolved except for charges he leveled against Terry Rudolph.

The falsity of that claim was revealed in 1995, when Whitehurst was subpoenaed as a defense witness in the second trial of defendants charged in the 1993 World Trade Center bombing. Judge Lance Ito refused to permit a similar appearance at the ORENTHAL JAMES (O. J.) SIMPSON murder trial, but Whitehurst's allegations went public in September 1995, with his appearance on ABC-TV's *Prime Time Live*. That broadcast named lab supervisor Roger Martz as "one of the agents who pressured Whitehurst to go along with allegedly altered test results." Lab spokesmen refused to be interviewed on camera, but they faxed ABC a statement claiming the bureau had thoroughly investigated Whitehurst's "concerns about forensic protocols and procedures" and "reviewed more than 250 cases involving work previously done by the Laboratory." The end result of that investigation: "To date, the FBI has found no evidence of tampering, evidence fabrication or failure to report exculpatory evidence."

In fact, ABC's broadcast triggered the first real investigation so far, conducted over the next 18 months by the Inspector General's office. A 517-page draft report was submitted to Justice in January 1997, but its contents were withheld in a seeming effort to avoid further problems with the upcoming trial of Oklahoma City bomber Timothy McVeigh. Whitehurst filed suit to compel publication in March 1997, supported by the NWC and the National Association of Defense Lawyers. Only then was a publication date fixed for April 15, 1997, with the McVeigh trial already in progress.

As a result of the Inspector General's findings, agents Roger Martz and David Williams were removed from their posts at the FBI lab, while two others criticized in the report—James Thurman and Michael Malone—had already retired. Whitehurst was penalized at the same time, suspended and placed on administrative leave in a move that violated terms of the 1989 Whistleblower Protection Act. He sued the FBI again and won his case on February 26, 1998, when the bureau agreed to pay him $1,166,000 for illegal retaliation. Two weeks later, the FBI settled a second lawsuit filed by Whitehurst under the Privacy Act. While most such claims are settled for $5,000 or less, the bureau agreed to pay Whitehurst $300,000 ($258,500 in legal fees plus the equivalent of salary and pension benefits he would have earned if employed by the FBI to retirement age). As part of the March settlement, FBI officials also promised to release 180,000 pages of lab reports prepared by analysts whom Whitehurst had publicly criticized.

WHITFIELD, Arthur exonerated by DNA

Within the space of one hour, on the night of August 14, 1981, a knife-wielding predator raped two women in Norfolk, Virginia. Both victims were accosted while getting out of their cars, then threatened and forced to undress. While the second attack was in progress, the first victim drove to a friend's house and summoned police. Officers showed the first victim an array of seven photographs, including Arthur Whitfield's. She selected him and later chose him from a lineup at police headquarters. The second victim subsequently confirmed that identification, and Whitfield was scheduled for separate trials on multiple felony charges.

At trial for the first case, in 1982, Whitfield's alleged victim repeated her identification, insisting that she had several opportunities to see his face clearly, illuminated by a streetlight and a spotlight on a nearby house. Oddly, both victims stated that their rapist had no facial hair, while Whitfield wore a beard. Whitfield's attorney suggested a case of mistaken identification, calling several relatives of Whitfield to testify that he had spent the evening of the crimes in their company. Jurors nonetheless convicted him of rape, sodomy and ROBBERY, resulting in a 45-year prison term. Soon afterward, Whitfield struck a plea bargain with prosecutors in the second case, pleading guilty to rape and accepting a consecutive 18-year sentence while additional felony counts were dismissed. His initial parole bid was denied in 1991.

Ten years later, Virginia legislators passed a statute permitting prison inmates to present DNA evidence in alleged cases of wrongful conviction. Whitfield filed a motion for testing in October 2003, but authorities reported that the biological evidence from his case had been destroyed. Two months later, in December 2003, a technician at the state crime lab discovered evidentiary samples preserved in a notebook by serologist Mary Jane Burton (in direct violation of laboratory protocol). Testing of those samples proceeded in 2004, and the results exonerated Whitfield of both rapes while pointing the finger at another inmate already serving life for another sexual assault. Whitfield was released from prison on August 23, 2004, after serving 22 years for crimes he did not commit. At press time for this volume, he had not been compensated by the state.

WHITLEY, Drew controversial DNA case

One night in 1988, a bandit lay in wait for 22-year-old Noreen Malloy outside the fast-food restaurant she managed in West Mifflin, Pennsylvania. As Malloy left with the day's receipts, her assailant shot her and fled with the cash. Police found a nylon mask at the murder scene, with 39 pieces of human hair inside. They subsequently arrested small-time hoodlum Drew Whitley and charged him with Malloy's murder. At trial in 1989, forensics experts testified that hair from the mask "closely resembled" Whitley's when viewed under a microscope. Jurors ignored Whitley's pleas of innocence and convicted him across the board, resulting in a life prison term.

DNA profiling was still in its infancy when Whitley received his sentence, but technical advances over the next 16 years prompted him to seek testing of the hairs collected in his case. While a state law passed in 2003 authorized such testing, Allegheny County District Attorney Stephen Zappala opposed all such requests in court, on grounds that DNA tests may cost up to $1,000 per sample. However, following the August 2005 DNA exoneration of inmate THOMAS DOSWELL, Zappala was forced to revise his position. On September 21, 2005, Judge Walter Little granted Whitley's motion for testing of the suspect hairs. Results of those tests had not been published when this volume went to press.

WIENER, Alexander (1906–1976)

A native of Brooklyn, New York, born in 1906, Alexander Wiener earned his B.A. from Columbia University and his M.D. from the State University of New York (1930). His research on human blood groupings, conducted during his collegiate years and afterward, at Brooklyn's Jewish Hospital, built on the ABO classifications discovered by KARL LANDSTEINER in 1901. Landsteiner received the Nobel Prize for that discovery in 1930 and formally retired nine years later, but he remained active in the laboratory, collaborating with Wiener and Philip Levine on new discoveries. In 1940, while experimenting with rhesus monkeys, the trio discovered an antigen they dubbed the "Rh factor" (for *rh*esus). Most human beings are

Rh-positive, meaning that their red blood cells contain the antigen, but a minority are Rh-negative and produce an antibody called anti-Rh which causes Rh-positive blood to agglutinate (clump) on contact. Transfusion of mismatched blood would thus prove fatal, while further complications ensued for Rh-negative mothers who carried Rh-positive fetuses, thereby producing extreme anemia (*erythroblastosis fetalis*) in the unborn child. Having discovered the cause of that ailment, Wiener also developed a procedure for replacing the blood of affected fetuses.

While thus engaged with medical discoveries that saved thousands—perhaps millions—of lives, Wiener also applied himself to numerous criminal cases. In 1935, and again in 1952, Wiener's testimony before New York's state legislature secured passage of statutes upholding the ADMISSIBILITY of serological evidence in both criminal and civil (paternity) cases. Beginning in 1938, Wiener also served as chief of bacteriology and serology for the New York City MEDICAL EXAMINER's office. Hailed in some press reports as a "blood detective," he testified in numerous trials prior to his death in 1976, at age 70.

WILHOIT, Gregory R. exonerated by forensic odontology

In the early morning hours of May 31, 1985, Kathy Wilhoit was found dead in her home at Pawhuska, Oklahoma, the victim of a brutal rape and murder. Investigators determined that she had been strangled with a telephone cord. They found a FINGERPRINT on the telephone receiver and retrieved a lone pubic hair from a pool of blood near the corpse. A bite mark on the victim's breast was photographed and measured by technicians.

Kathy Wilhoit's estranged husband, Gregory, was an immediate suspect. The couple had separated barely two weeks earlier, and Gregory lived in Tulsa, 40 miles southeast of Pawhuska. Gregory kept odd hours and had no alibi for the time of the murder, but he was initially encouraged when his fingerprints failed to match the one on Kathy's phone and microscopic study of the suspect pubic hair revealed no match with his. Still, the prosecution forged ahead, claiming that Wilhoit's teeth matched the bite mark found on his wife.

A competent defense attorney would have challenged that assertion with expert testimony, but Wilhoit had the grave misfortune to be represented by George Briggs, a 78-year-old brain-damaged alcoholic who had been censured by the American Bar Association weeks before he took Wilhoit's case. Constantly intoxicated, Briggs had been known to soil his own trousers in court, and he vomited several times in the judge's chambers during Wilhoit's 1987 trial. Worse yet, from his client's perspective, Briggs was so confused throughout the proceedings that he failed to challenge the bite-mark testimony offered by the prosecution. Wilhoit was convicted of the slaying, so despondent at the outcome of his trial that he requested execution in lieu of a life sentence. The judge obliged him, and Wilhoit was packed off to death row. (George Briggs was disbarred soon after the trial and died a short time later.)

When Wilhoit recovered from the shock of his conviction, he appealed the verdict and death sentence. Attorney Mark Barrett handled the appeal, swiftly recognizing that forensic ODONTOLOGY was the key to Wilhoit's guilt or innocence. Copies of the bite-mark photos and Wilhoit's dental records were sent to 11 recognized experts in the field, including technicians employed by the FBI and the Royal Canadian Mounted Police, as well as dentists who had reviewed evidence in the Ted Bundy and "Hillside Strangler" serial murder cases. The verdict was unanimous: Greg Wilhoit's teeth had not inflicted the bite mark on Kathy's breast.

The appellate court granted Wilhoit a new trial in 1993, on grounds that his original defense counsel had been "ineffective" (to say the least). With the new forensic evidence in hand, he was acquitted by a second jury. The murder of Kathy Wilhoit remains unsolved today.

WILLCOX, William Henry (1870–1941)

British physician William Willcox was born in 1870. While employed at St. Mary's Hospital, in London, he met AUGUSTUS PEPPER, another physician who shared Willcox's interest in forensic medicine. While Pepper focused chiefly on PATHOLOGY, however, Willcox's primary fascination lay with TOXICOLOGY. Murders by poison were fairly common in England during the 19th and early 20th centuries, but arsenic was also found in many common objects—ranging from the obvious pesticides and herbicides to PAINT, wallpaper, and patent medicines. In Victorian times, many women ate arsenic mixed with chalk and vinegar to lighten their weathered complexions. For the Crippen murder case of 1910, Willcox developed a new analytical method of heating alkaloid crystal samples and determining their content by specific melting points. Unfortunately, various alkaloids had similar melting points, which prompted Willcox to conduct further experiments. In 1911, he pioneered a new technique of judging the arsenic content in human tissue based on its crystalline weight. While other tests were still required to isolate arsenic from other materials, Willcox's work paved the way for a new generation of toxicologists to achieve their own breakthroughs. By 1955, 14 years after Willcox's death, 30 specific tests existed for morphine alone.

WILLIAMS, Dennis See "FORD HEIGHTS FOUR."

WILLIAMSON, Ronald See FRITZ, DENNIS.

WINGEART, Jerald Leroy convicted by DNA evidence
A resident of Chesaning, Michigan, 20-year-old Dawn Lee Magyar vanished on a shopping trip to Owosso on January 27, 1973. Her father-in-law found Dawn's car the next morning in a supermarket parking lot, the driver's door open, bags of groceries on the front seat, with Dawn's keys lying on the ground nearby. A two-day search by law enforcement officers and some 4,000 volunteers failed to discover any further traces of the missing young woman. On March 4, 1973, two boys found Magyar's body discarded in a neighboring county. She had been raped and shot three times at close range with a .22-caliber weapon. In 1974, police found a pistol they believed to be the murder weapon, discarded in the Shiawassee River near the scene of Magyar's abduction, and Magyar's wallet was found on a riverbank in the same area two years later, but the clues brought detectives no closer to Dawn's killer.

The advent of DNA testing raised hopes among Michigan State Police investigators, but those hopes were dashed in 1995, when testing cleared an Owosso resident, their only real suspect to date, of any involvement in the crime. Another four years passed before investigators traced the .22 pistol's original owner, and he in turn directed them to 59-year-old Jerald Wingeart, residing in Center Line, Michigan. Wingeart, police discovered, had been convicted of robbing and raping a blind college student in 1961, receiving concurrent sentences of 9–30

years for robbery and 10–30 years for sexual assault. He was paroled in 1968, five years before the Magyar slaying.

Unable to present sufficient evidence to secure a court order for Wingeart's blood, detectives lifted cigarette butts from his household trash (considered public property once garbage is placed outside the home for pickup) and matched DNA from Wingeart's saliva to the semen samples recovered from Magyar's corpse 26 years earlier. Wingeart was arrested on murder charges in March 2001 and tried nine months later. Convicted on November 28, 2001, he received a mandatory life prison term on January 19, 2002. Circuit Judge Gerald Lostracco noted that "a life sentence for someone who's 61 years old has less of an impact," regretting that Wingeart had not been captured in 1973, when life imprisonment might have had "some meaning." Still, Lostracco observed, "I'm convinced if you were still out in the streets that you would strike again, so it's not too late for the protection of society."

WISCONSIN Innocence Project
The Wisconsin Innocence Project, operating from the University of Wisconsin Law School's Frank J. Remington Center in Madison, represents inmates of Wisconsin prisons who profess actual innocence of the crimes for which they are incarcerated. (In "extraordinary circumstances," and as time allows, cases may also be accepted from the upper midwestern states of Illinois, Indiana, Iowa, Michigan, and Minnesota.) In order to qualify for WIP assistance, inmates (a) must be presently incarcerated on a wrongful conviction, (b) must have seven years or more remaining on their sentences, (c) must have exhausted all normal appeals, (d) must assert innocence based on substantial new evidence not previously considered in court, and (e) must not be presently represented by counsel or have the ongoing right to court-appointed counsel. Conclusive scientific evidence of innocence (such as DNA) is preferred but not required. Inmates liberated by the WIP to date include STEVEN AVERY, BETH LABATTE and CHRISTOPHER OCHOA.

WITTHAUS, Rudolph August (1846–1915)
A native of New York City, born in August 1846, Rudolph Witthaus earned his B.S. from Columbia University at age 21, then spent three years abroad at

the Sorbonne before returning to Columbia, where he received an M.S. Further study abroad preceded his enrollment at New York University, where Witthaus obtained his M.D. at age 29. Teaching posts followed, at New York University and at the University of Vermont, where Witthaus served as a professor of CHEMISTRY and TOXICOLOGY. The latter field was his forte, prompting appearances as an expert witness in various criminal trials. The most renowned was that of Raymond Molineux, who mailed poisoned Bromo-Seltzer to an enemy in 1899. Molineux's target spurned the gift, but his landlady took the medicine and subsequently died. Witthaus identified the poison, while another forensic expert, JOHN TYRRELL, proved to jurors that Molineux had addressed the fatal package.

When not engaged in trials or classroom lectures, Witthaus produced a series of books considered classics in their field. His works include *General Medical Chemistry for the Use of Practitioners of Medicine* (1881), *The Medical Student's Manual of Chemistry* (1888), *Essentials of Chemistry and Toxicology* (1894), and *A Laboratory Guide on Urinalysis and Toxicology* (1898). With coauthor T. C. Becker, Witthaus also produced the four-volume *Medical Jurisprudence, Forensic Medicine and Toxicology* (writing the third volume entirely on his own). Witthaus finished his teaching career at Cornell University, where he served as professor from 1900 until his retirement in 1911. He died four years later, at age 69.

WOODALL, Glen Dale exonerated by DNA evidence

In 1986, two female residents of Huntington, West Virginia, were kidnapped in separate incidents from the parking lot of a local shopping mall. In each case, the male offender wore a ski mask and brandished a knife, ordering his victims to keep their eyes shut. In the first attack, he drove around aimlessly in the victim's car, then stopped and raped her repeatedly, stealing a gold watch and $5 in cash before he fled. The victim opened her eyes long enough to see that the rapist wore brown pants and was uncircumcised. The second victim, also raped repeatedly and robbed of a gold watch, glimpsed the attacker's hair and boots, further confirming that he was uncircumcised. Both victims told police that their attacker exuded "a distinctive smell."

Detectives eventually settled on suspect Glen Woodall, a gravedigger from Charleston, West Virginia. Prosecutors based their case on a variety of evidence, including a "partial visual identification" by one victim, another victim's identification of brown pants found in Woodall's home, confirmation from both victims of an odor pervading Woodall's workplace, and the fact that Woodall was uncircumcised. In terms of scientific evidence, hairs recovered from one victim's car were found to be microscopically "consistent" with samples from Woodall's scalp and beard. Finally, state police chemist FRED ZAIN opined that Woodall's blood secretions matched semen evidence recovered from the victims.

In a pretrial hearing, Woodall's attorney asked the court to perform "experimental new" DNA tests on the CRIME SCENE evidence, but the motion was denied in favor of chemist Zain's "more conventional" evidence. On July 8, 1987, jurors convicted Woodall on two counts of KIDNAPPING, two counts of aggravated ROBBERY, one count of first-degree sexual assault, and one count of first-degree sexual abuse. At sentencing he received two life prison terms plus separate terms of 203 and 335 years, the four terms to be served consecutively. The trial court belatedly ordered a DNA test after Woodall was convicted, but ruled the results "inconclusive."

West Virginia's Supreme Court affirmed Woodall's conviction on July 6, 1989, but he continued filing appeals for new DNA testing on the crime scene evidence. Permission for testing was finally granted, and the results excluded Woodall as a donor of the semen found at either crime scene. The trial court vacated his conviction on July 15, 1991, and released him on $150,000 bond, monitored by an electronic PERSONAL TRACKING UNIT while further investigation continued. Research on the case revealed a romantic liaison between one rape victim and a primary investigator, along with the fact that both victims had been secretly hypnotized to "enhance" their memories of the crimes. A second round of DNA tests once again excluded Woodall as the rapist, in April 1992, and all charges were dismissed the following month. Subsequent investigations of chemist Fred Zain in West Virginia and Texas have reopened scores of cases wherein Zain apparently perjured himself to convict various defendants. Glen Woodall was awarded $1 million for his wrongful conviction and false imprisonment in West Virginia.

WOUNDS

Examination of wounds is a critical aspect of forensic PATHOLOGY, whereby a MEDICAL EXAMINER may determine cause of death and the kind of WEAPON used. The nature and positioning of wounds may also furnish information about the attacker's height, his/her relative strength, and whether he/she was right- or left-handed. The wounds commonly observed on victims of violent crime include:

Blunt trauma injuries inflicted by striking with fists or objects that have no sharp edges. Death in such cases normally results from brain damage, injury to the trachea that obstructs breathing, or from other damage to internal organs. The most common visible result of blunt trauma is a *contusion* (bruising). Blows to the head produce *coup* and *countercoup* injuries to the brain. The initial injury (coup) occurs at the point of impact. The countercoup injury occurs directly opposite the impact site, as the brain is propelled away from the point of impact, against the inside of the skull. Analysis of coup/countercoup damage tells pathologists whether head trauma occurred from a fall or assault with a bludgeon.

Bullet wounds come in all shapes and sizes, depending on the weapon used, the ammunition employed, and the distance from which shots are fired. *Contact* wounds are those inflicted with a FIREARM's muzzle pressed against the victim's skin, whereupon expanding gases from the muzzle-blast rupture the flesh in a starlike (*stellate*) pattern. Shots fired from an 18-inch range or less produce *tattooing* (or *stippling*) as particles of gunpowder penetrate the skin. *Distance wounds,* produced by shots fired beyond the 18-inch range, lack tattooing but still display contusion rings around the point of impact and a *bullet wipe* or *smudge ring* pattern where the penetrating projectile shears off cells from the skin's surface. *Entrance* and *exit* wounds are distinguished by their size, with the latter commonly much larger. Smaller-than-normal *shored exit wounds* occur when tight clothing confines the damage of a normal exit wound. *Keyhole* wounds, named for their shape, are entrance wounds inflicted by a tumbling bullet (as where the projectile was destabilized by impact with some intervening object).

Edged weapons inflict either *stab wounds* (punctures) or *incised wounds* (cuts and slices). *Defensive wounds* commonly appear on hands and arms when a victim attempts to ward off an attack. *Hesitation wounds,* by contrast, are the small cuts self-inflicted by a suicidal subject, commonly found at the wrists, elbows, and around the neck. *Excision* (removal) of various internal organs is seen in some cases, chiefly murders with a sadistic motive or those involving morbid religious practices involving human sacrifice. *Disarticulation* or *dismemberment* occurs when head and limbs are separated from the torso. The tools, technique, and skill involved in such operations may provide insight into the killer's motives or level of education—as in Cleveland's still-unsolved "torso murders" of the 1930s, where investigators suspected that the city's "Mad Butcher" might be a doctor or medical student. Unfortunately, PSYCHOLOGICAL PROFILING in such cases is not conclusive, and even if accurate in general terms it cannot pinpoint the offender.

Study of wounds—dubbed *wound ballistics*—permits investigators to reconstruct events of a homicide or assault. Was the victim confronted directly or ambushed and taken by surprise? Did he or she resist the attack? What kind of weapon(s) inflicted the wounds? The angle of impact for a close-range bullet wound may indicate whether the victim was standing, seated, kneeling, or lying down when shot; it may also help determine the shooter's height. In long-distance shootings, the angle of impact—or *triangulation,* in the event of multiple gunshots—may point detectives toward a remote sniper's nest. With blunt trauma or cutting wounds, the angle of impact again suggests the assailant's stature, while revealing whether he/she wielded the weapon right- or left-handed. An absence of defensive wounds or other signs of struggle may suggest that the victim and killer were acquaintances, even friends or relatives. In any case, the evidence must be allowed to speak for itself without imposition of preconceived theories or suppositions.

WYNIEMKO, Kenneth exonerated by DNA

On April 30, 1994, a stranger wearing a nylon stocking mask invaded a home in Clinton, Michigan. He woke the solitary female tenant, handcuffed her, and blindfolded her with her own underwear before raping her several times in different rooms. Before leaving, he also forced the victim to perform fellatio, then ordered her to drink soda and chew a pair of her own panties to remove any traces of semen. The victim described her attacker to police as a white male 20 to 25 years old, between six feet and six feet two inches tall, weighing 200–225 pounds. She also assisted in preparation of a suspect sketch, but told detectives it would not be very useful since she only caught brief glimpses of the rapist's face. When the sketch was completed, the victim rated it 60 percent accurate.

Eleven weeks later, on July 14, officers jailed 43-year-old Kenneth Wyniemko on unrelated misdemeanor charges. Although he was 20 years older than the rapist, five feet 11 inches tall and 198 pounds, police displayed him in a lineup to the victim and she named Wyniemko as her attacker. Semen from the victim's underwear was never analyzed, but police serologists found stains from her sheets consistent with a type A donor. That finding matched the victim's husband but excluded Wyniemko and the victim, who were both type O. At trial, the victim's testimony alone secured Wyniemko's conviction on 15 counts of sexual assault, plus charges of ROBBERY and breaking and entering. He received a sentence of 40–60 years in prison.

Members of the COOLEY INNOCENCE PROJECT accepted Wyniemko's case for review in 2002. In June 2003, Michigan's State Police Forensic Science Division performed DNA tests on numerous pieces of CRIME SCENE evidence, confirming that semen from her sheets came from the victim's husband. Stains found on her underwear, however, included semen from the husband and an unknown male contributor. Those tests excluded Kenneth Wyniemko as a donor, and his conviction was dismissed on June 17, 2003. Authorities settled Wyniemko's claim of wrongful conviction and imprisonment on November 29, 2005, with a lump-sum payment of $3.7 million. The rape remains officially unsolved today.

Z

ZACCHIA, Paolo (1584–?)

An Italian doctor, born in 1584, Paolo Zacchia served as the personal physician to Popes Innocent X and Alexander VII, as legal adviser to the Rota Romana, and as head of health systems for the Papal States. His contribution to forensic science lies in his series of books collectively entitled *Questiones Medicina-Legales*, published in nine volumes between 1621 and 1651. Zacchia's work covered a wide range of medicolegal subjects including questions of age, bodily fluids, death in childbirth, dementia, feigned diseases, impotence, legitimacy, malpractice, medical ethics, miracles, mutilation, parent-child resemblance, poisoning, pregnancy, public health matters, rape, and WOUNDS. Despite some errors occasioned by limits in contemporary anatomical knowledge, Zacchia's work stands as a milestone in the evolution of forensic medicine.

ZAIN, Fred Salem (?–2002) police chemist accused of fraud

A troubling case of apparent official malfeasance, reminiscent of the JOYCE GILCHRIST scandal in Oklahoma, involves serologist Fred Zain, employed for 13 years at the West Virginia State Police crime laboratory, and afterward in Texas. Like Gilchrist, Zain stood accused of faking test results and testifying falsely under oath in numerous felony cases, sending numerous innocent defendants to prison. Once revered as "a god" by West Virginia prosecutors,

Zain was totally discredited in 1993, when West Virginia's Supreme Court ordered a review of every case on which he worked, ruling that "as a matter of law, any testimonial or documentary evidence offered by Zain at any time should be deemed invalid, unreliable and inadmissible."

Zain began his tenure at the West Virginia crime lab in 1977, at age 26, quickly building a reputation as an expert who could nail down even the most difficult cases, assuring prosecutors of convictions with a scientific basis. District attorneys who adored Zain were presumably unaware of his curious tactics, but the same cannot be said about his supervisors at the laboratory. In some cases he testified to positive results for tests the crime lab could not even perform, since it lacked the necessary equipment, but none of his superiors came forward to correct him. In 1985, FBI lab director James Greer informed Zain's boss that Zain had lied about his credentials to obtain the West Virginia post—he had, in fact, failed basic courses in forensic serology and biochemical methods of testing BLOODSTAINS—but Zain remained on the job. At least two other crime lab employees also complained to their superiors about Zain's methods, and they likewise were ignored. Zain's public reputation began to unravel in 1991, after alleged rapist GLEN WOODALL—convicted chiefly on Zain's testimony in 1987—was exonerated by DNA evidence.

Fred Zain, meanwhile, had left West Virginia for Bexar County, Texas—coincidentally the scene of

289

numerous false autopsy reports filed by pathologist RALPH ERDMANN—in 1989, where he served as chief of physical evidence for the county's MEDICAL EXAMINER. Alerted by the West Virginia controversy, Texas prosecutors charged Zain with perjury and jury tampering in one of his cases, but the charge was thrown out on grounds that the statute of limitations had expired. Around the same time, in 1994, Zain was indicted for perjury in Marion County, West Virginia, a grand jury concluding that he lied during the 1991 rape and robbery trial of defendant Paul Walker. (West Virginia prosecutors continued to use Zain's testimony even after he left the state for Texas.) One count of the perjury indictment was dismissed prior to trial, jurors acquitted Zain of a second charge, and deadlocked on the third (an accusation that he lied under oath regarding fees he received for a double-murder trial). Another West Virginia grand jury, in Kanawha County, indicted Zain again in March 1998, but Judge Andrew MacQueen dismissed the charges nine months later, on grounds that the state government could not be a legal victim of fraud. The state supreme court reversed that ruling in 1999.

Zain, for his part, denied any wrongdoing in even a single case, much less the hundreds in which he stood accused of falsifying evidence. In a rare 1997 interview with reporter Sandy Wells, Zain claimed that he "would never want anybody put in jail—having been through trial myself—who was innocent of what he is being charged with." Rather than taking personal responsibility for years of false testimony, Zain advanced the novel defense of blaming various prosecutors who put him on the witness stand, as well as his supervisors at the West Virginia crime lab. He was, Zain claimed, an innocent "scapegoat" for the sins of others. Defense attorney Sam Bayless, meanwhile, seemed ready to admit that his client had testified falsely in various cases but told reporters in September 2001, "I think there's no criminal intent."

Zain was facing further legal action, including a $10 million civil lawsuit filed by a defendant falsely convicted of murder on Zain's testimony, when he was diagnosed with cancer. Zain's health delayed further trials, and he died in Florida in December 2002.

ZEIGLER, Tommy controversial DNA case

On Christmas Eve 1975, the quiet town of Winter Garden, Florida, was rocked by news of a mass murder. The victims included 29-year-old Eunice Zeigler, her parents Perry and Virginia Edwards (visiting from Georgia), and 35-year-old Charles Mays. The massacre occurred at a furniture store run by Eunice Zeigler and her husband, Tommy (also wounded by a gunshot), where Charles Mays worked as a handyman. Prosecutors charged that Tommy Zeigler committed the murders to collect $500,000 life insurance on his wife, and shot himself through the side to pose as a victim of unidentified robbers. Jurors accepted that story and convicted Zeigler, resulting in a sentence of life imprisonment without parole. In 2001, Zeigler won a motion for DNA testing of blood evidence recovered from the CRIME SCENE, and his lawyers were encouraged by the results. Specifically, lab reports found blood from only one victim (Mays) on Zeigler's clothing, while Mays had blood from Perry Edwards on his pants. Lawyer John Pope contended that Mays had engaged in a fight with Edwards, first killing him, and then proceeded to slaughter the remaining witnesses before Zeigler killed Mays in self-defense. Circuit Court Judge Reginald Whitehead rejected Zeigler's bid for a new trial in April 2005, declaring that Zeigler "has not shown that the DNA testing results would exonerate him or mitigate his sentence." Furthermore, Judge Whitehead wrote, "The fact that only Mays' blood was found on the left arm of the Defendant's T-shirt does not exonerate Defendant or even tend to exonerate Defendant." As for the blood found on Mays's pants, Whitehead declared that it merely proved Mays was standing near Edwards when Edwards was shot. Spokesmen for the state's attorney's office declined to comment on Judge Whitehead's ruling.

Glossary

ABO   ABO blood group system

abuse   deliberate behavior resulting in significant negative emotional or physical harm

accuracy   the correctness of a measure when compared to a known standard

acquitted   found not guilty in judicial proceedings

actus reus   guilty by act (Latin)

addiction   physiological or psychological dependence on some agent

adjudicated   settled in a civil or criminal court

admissible   legitimate, allowable

adult   arbitrary legal designation for a person who is no longer a child or minor (generally 18 years or older in the United States)

aerosol collector   an instrument that collects aerosols and analyzes their composition

AIDS   acquired immunodeficiency syndrome

amino acid   any of 20 basic building blocks of proteins

anecdotal evidence   oral or written descriptions of events not made under oath

anoxic   lacking oxygen

antemortem   before death

antigen   any foreign substance, such as a virus, bacterium, or protein, that produces an immune response by stimulating the production of antibodies

aperture   an opening

assassination   murder, usually of a public figure

assault   a physically aggressive act, graduated to battery if contact is made

ATF   Bureau of Alcohol, Tobacco, Firearms and Explosives

AVED   Antivirus Emergency Discussion list: an online mailing list for professional computer anti-virus researchers, designed for rapid notification of a new virus emergency

BAC   blood alcohol concentration

bacterium   a single-celled, microscopic organism without a distinct nucleus

baffle   a device used to deflect light

bait/decoy file   a dummy file written to the drives of a computer to facilitate virus detection

ballistics   the study of projectiles in motion

bolometer   a detector mainly used to measure infra-red radiation

bootlegging   making unauthorized copies of commercial software, prerecorded videocassettes, etc., for illegal resale

CAB   Civil Aeronautics Board

capital crimes   crimes punishable by death

capital punishment   the death penalty

carbonaceous compounds   materials containing carbon or carbon compounds

carcinogen   a substance that induces cancer

catalyst   a substance that promotes a chemical reaction but which itself remains unaltered at the end of the reaction

CDC   Centers for Disease Control

CE   capillary electrophoresis

Celsius   scale of temperature in which water freezes at 0 degrees and boils at 100 degrees (formerly called centigrade)

centrifugation   separating molecules by size or density using centrifugal forces generated by a spinning rotor

CFN   clinical forensic nursing

CGE   capillary gel electrophoresis

charged particles   particles with a positive or negative charge (electrons, protons or ions)

chemical properties properties of matter that cannot be identified without producing chemical reactions that may change the material tested

child an arbitrary legal designation for a person who has not attained the legal age of adulthood (variously defined in different jurisdictions)

chromosome a single DNA molecule

circumstantial evidence nondirect evidence used to draw conclusions, including most of the evidence studied in forensic science

climatology the study of climate: the prevailing atmospheric conditions of humidity, temperature, etc.

cluster virus a DOS computer virus that saves its code to a computer's hard drive, rather than attaching itself directly to infected files

CODIS combined DNA indexing systems

community notification the distribution of information regarding released sex offenders to citizens and community organizations

compos mentis of sound mind (Latin)

concave curved inward (as opposed to convex)

convection transport of heat through movement of a gas or liquid

convex curved outward (as opposed to concave)

convicted found guilty in a judicial proceeding

coroner a public official primarily charged with the duty of determining how and why people die

corporal punishment punishment involving the infliction of pain or physical injury short of death (generally banned in U.S. penal institutions)

corpus delecti in Latin, "the body of the crime," including a criminal act itself and all related evidence

corroborate to confirm or provide supporting evidence

cracker hacker jargon for someone who gains unauthorized access to protected systems; often a pejorative term, contrasting those with criminal motives to "pure hackers"

crime an illegal act committed with malicious intent

criminalistics the study of physical evidence related to crime

criminology the study of crime, criminals, and penology

CSA Controlled Substances Act

culture an organism growing in a laboratory medium

CVS covert video surveillance

cyber-cops police assigned to investigate computer or Internet crimes

cyberethics the ethics of computer use, often honored more in the breach than the observance

CZE capillary zone electrophoresis

DA district attorney

data facts from which other information may be inferred

DEA Drug Enforcement Administration

defendant the party accused of wrongdoing in a civil or criminal case

delinquent offending, usually in a minor way; an offender who is delinquent (often applied to juveniles)

demonstrative evidence physical evidence

denature to induce structural alterations that disrupt the biological activity of a molecule

density mass per unit of volume

density gradient centrifugation high-speed centrifugation in which molecules "float" at a point where their density equals that in a gradient of cesium chloride or sucrose

deposition a sworn statement given under oath outside a courtroom setting

destructive testing tests that consume or destroy the evidentiary samples

diminished capacity mental incapacity that prevents an individual from conforming his/her behavior to legal standards or prevents understanding that specific acts are criminal

direct evidence evidence that requires no interpretation, including DNA typing, fingerprints, contraband found in a suspect's possession, etc.

dispersion scattering of an electromagnetic wave as light is split into its constituent colors by a prism or diffraction grating

DOJ Department of Justice

domestic violence violence within a family or family-type relationship

Doppler shift the change in observed frequency due to relative motion between source and observer

DOS disk operating system: a computer's primary system of operation

DRE drug recognition expert

DRIFTS diffuse reflectance infrared Fourier transformation spectroscopy

dropper any computer program that installs a virus but is not itself infected

Dumpster diving raiding trash cans to obtain data

such as credit card numbers, financial records, etc.

ecology   the study of interactions of organisms with their environment and with each other

EDS   energy dispersive spectroscopy

EDXRF   electron diffraction X-ray fluorescence spectroscopy

electromagnetic radiation   energy composed of particles (photons) or waves, usually described as bands of radiation of similar wavelength (infrared, radio waves, X-rays, etc.)

electron   a fundamental physical particle (and component of an atom) with a negative charge

element   a set of stable atoms from which all known molecules are made

empirical evidence   evidence procured from experiments, analysis and/or observation

EMR   electromagnetic radiation

EMT   emergency medical technician; a paramedic

endemic   peculiar to a specific region

environment   all external factors affecting living things

EPA   Environmental Protection Agency

ethics (professional)   codified guidelines regulating the behavior of professionals in their dealings with clients or patients and with one another

evidence   something legally presented before a court (a statement of a witness, an object etc.) that bears on or establishes the point in question

exclusionary/exculpatory evidence   evidence that excludes specific persons as suspects in a crime

FAA/FAS   flame atomic absorption spectroscopy

Fahrenheit   scale of temperature in which water freezes at 32 degrees and boils at 212 degrees

FBI   Federal Bureau of Investigation

felony   any crime punishable by one or more years in prison, including capital crimes

fetal alcohol syndrome   birth defects related to use of alcohol during pregnancy

filicide   the murder of a child more than 24 hours old by his/her parent

FISH   forensic information system for handwriting

floater   slang term for a drowning victim or body found in water

forensic   related to public debates or the law

FTIR   Fourier transform infrared spectroscopy

fungicide   an agent, such as a chemical, that kills fungi

fungus/fungi   various organisms that lack chlorophyll and subsist on dead or living organic matter (molds, mushrooms, etc.)

garrote   a ligature used in strangulation, formerly a legal means of execution in parts of Europe

GC   gas chromatography

genetic marker   a gene or group of genes used to "mark" or track the action of microbes

GLP   good laboratory practice

GSR   gunshot residue

hearsay   testimonial evidence related to events outside a witness's personal knowledge, told to the witness by others

herbicide   any substance that is toxic to plants

histology tissue   samples of solid organ taken at the time of autopsy to establish or aid in diagnosis

HIV   human immunodeficiency virus, the virus that leads to AIDS

homicide   the killing of one human being by another

HPLC   high performance liquid chromatography

hydrocarbons   a group of chemical compounds composed only of carbon and hydrogen

IAFIS   integrated automatic fingerprint identification system

IC   ion chromatography

ICP-AES   inductively coupled plasma-atomic emission spectroscopy

ICP-MS   inductively coupled plasma-mass spectroscopy

IMS   ion mobility spectrometry

inclusionary evidence   evidence that fails to exclude a potential suspect

inculpatory evidence   evidence suggesting involvement in a crime

indeterminate sentence   confinement to a prison or mental institution for an unspecified period of time

index offense   the offense for which an offender is presently incarcerated

indict   formally charge with a crime

infanticide   the murder of an infant, usually by a parent

inmate   a person confined involuntarily to a jail, prison, mental institution, or similar setting

infrared light   radiation invisible to the unaided human eye, which can be sensed as thermal radiation

insanity   a legal term without medical meaning, describing a person whose mental illness renders the victim incapable of conforming his/her behavior to lawful standards

instrument an apparatus capable of registering information with a precise objective

in situ refers to performing assays or examinations at the original scene or with intact tissues

ion an electrically charged atom

intoxicants any substance which intoxicates, rendering users "drunk," "stoned," etc.

IRS Internal Revenue Service

jail a locally administered penal institution designed to confine individuals awaiting trial or serving misdemeanor sentences

jurisprudence the study of law, legal science, legal practice, and legal precedent

juvenile in the United States, a person under 18 years of age

Kelvin (K) a unit of the absolute temperature scale, in which the temperature of the triple point of water (the temperature at which water can exist simultaneously in solid, liquid, and gaseous form) is 273.16°K

key logger any computer program that records keystrokes, generally used by hackers to steal passwords

kiting use of normal delays in processing financial transactions to make assets appear where none yet exist, employing the bogus assets to secure loans, cover cash withdrawals, etc.

lapping employee diversion of incoming cash to a bogus account, while thefts are covered with funds from other incoming accounts

legalization removal of all statutory penalties for some previously outlawed behavior

lens transparent optical element or assembly with either a concave or convex surface, which refracts light to form an image

ligature an object used to cause strangulation, as a rope or cord

light all electromagnetic radiation can be called light, but the term is commonly used for that radiation visible to the unaided human eye

living forensics that part of forensic science applied to the just resolution of legal issues involving living victims (as opposed to forensic pathology)

locus/loci location(s); in genetics, a specific location or site on a chromosome

logic bomb a computer code that delays execution of a virus payload, typically calling for action on a certain date, at a specific time, or after a predetermined period of time

magnetometer an instrument for measuring the magnitude and the direction of a magnetic field

malignant having the properties of cancerous growth

malware malicious software, generally including all viruses, worms, and Trojans

manslaughter unplanned or unintended homicide

mapping determining physical location; in genetics, plotting the location of a gene or genetic marker on a chromosome

mass the total amount of matter in a body

mass mailer a virus that distributes itself via e-mail to multiple addresses captured from the host computer's address book

matter a physical substance, having mass and occupying space

MECC/MEKC micellular electrokinetic capillary chromatography

mens rea guilty in mind; criminal intent (Latin)

metabolism the biochemical processes that sustain a living cell or organism

methane a colorless and odorless gas, produced by decomposition

micron one-thousandth of a millimeter, often used to measure the wavelength of light

misdemeanor a crime punishable by one year or less (often in county jail) or by a fine

molecular biology the study of the biochemical and molecular interactions within living cells

molecular genetics the study of the flow and regulation of genetic information between DNA, RNA, and protein molecules

MSP microspectrophotometry

MtDNA/mDNA mitochondrial DNA

multipartite virus any virus capable of infecting two or more different types of computer systems

Munchausen's syndrome a mental disorder prompting subjects to claim or fake numerous nonexistent ailments

Munchausen's syndrome by proxy a condition in which a subject feigns or induces illness in children to gain attention or sympathy

NAA neutron activation analysis

NASH natural, accidental, suicidal, homicidal (causes of death)

NCAVC National Center for Analysis of Violent Crime

NCIC National Crime Information Center

neonaticide the murder of an infant on the day of its birth (versus filicide)

NIJ   National Institute of Justice

NMR   nuclear magnetic resonance

nondestructive testing   tests that do not alter or destroy the evidentiary sample

NTSB   National Transportation Safety Board

nucleic acids   deoxyribonucleic acid (DNA) and ribonucleic acid (RNA)

nucleus   the membrane-bound region of a cell that contains the chromosomes

offender   a lawbreaker

optics   instruments used to enhance vision (glasses, microscopes, telescopes, etc.)

organics   carbon-based materials

OTC   over the counter (drugs and medicines sold without prescriptions)

overwriter   the simplest kind of computer virus, one that copies itself on top of existing programs

paleontology   the study of the fossil record of past geological periods and of the relationships between ancient and contemporary plant and animal species

paraphilia   sexual arousal induced by any object or practice outside societally accepted norms (AKA "perversion")

parasitic virus   any computer virus that modifies an existing code within the host computer to achieve replication

parasuicide   an unsuccessful suicide attempt

parole   conditional release from prison prior to expiration of an inmate's statutory sentence

pathogen   an organism that can cause disease in another organism

pathology   the study of diseases and their effects on the body

PCR   polymerase chain reaction (DNA)

PDR   *Physician's Desk Reference*

penology   the branch of criminology concerned with management of prisons and inmates

perimortem   occurring at or very near the time of death

perjury   false statements made while under oath, punishable by law

PERK kit   physical evidence rape kit

person of interest   a criminal suspect

pesticide   a substance that kills harmful organisms

phenotype   the observable characteristics of an organism

pheromone   a hormonelike substance that is secreted into the environment

photochemistry   the study of the effects of light on chemical reactions

physical matching   linking separate pieces of evidence that once belonged to a single item

physical properties   properties of matter measurable by physical (versus chemical) means, without changing the material's chemical composition (color, size, weight, etc.)

pixel   a single picture element of a detection device

plaintiff   the party who files a civil lawsuit

plethysmograph   an instrument for testing sexual response, commonly used with male sex offenders in therapy (the "peter meter")

PLM   polarizing light microscopy

PMI   postmortem interval

polymer   a molecule composed of repeated subunits

pornography   the visual depiction of erotic behavior, more specifically defined in various statutes

prison   a state or federal penal institution housing convicted felons

proton   a positively charged constituent of all atomic nuclei

proximate cause   the action/event nearest to the event in question

postmortem   occurring after death

RCMP   Royal Canadian Mounted Police

race   a people or group of peoples regarded as deriving from a common stock (Caucasoid, Mongoloid, and Negroid)

recidivism   repeated offenses committed by a previously convicted subject

reference collections   sample specimens used for comparison and identification of evidence (fibers, firearms, fingerprints, glass, paints, etc.)

resident virus   any computer virus that remains running and active within an infected system, as opposed to one that delivers its payload and then becomes inactive

RFLP   restricted fragment length polymorphisms (DNA)

RMNE   random man not excluded (by DNA testing)

SANE   sexual assault nurse examiner

SEC   size exclusion chromatography

SEM   scanning electron microscopy

shaken baby syndrome   various internal injuries (often fatal) commonly observed in small children who have been violently shaken by adults

SIDS   Sudden Infant Death Syndrome: a catch-all term for the otherwise inexplicable death of children in the early months of life

social engineering various methods of duping another person into revealing passwords or other sensitive data via conversation

STR short tandem repeats (DNA)

substrate the material on which some other material is deposited or layered (as fabric stained by blood)

suicide self-murder

suspect a person thought to have committed a crime

temperature the physical parameter characterizing the thermal state of a body, measured in units of degrees Celsius, Fahrenheit, or Kelvin

testimony oral description of events given under oath in a courtroom setting

transient evidence evidence that is temporary in nature or subject to change (odor, temperature, impressions, etc.)

Transylvanian effect the alleged impact of lunar cycles on human (and particularly criminal) behavior

trauma physical or mental injury

uxoricide the murder of a wife by her husband

VIN vehicle identification number

violence any overt expression of force intended to cause damage, injury or death

VNTR variable number of tandem repeats (DNA)

war crime any violation of international law or regulations governing military behavior during an international armed conflict

XRD X-ray diffraction spectroscopy

XRF X-ray fluorescence spectroscopy

zero tolerance rigid enforcement of particular laws

Appendix 1
Inorganic Compounds

aluminum oxide
aluminum chloride
aluminum hydroxide
aluminum monostearate
aluminum sulfate
ammonia
ammonium bicarbonate
ammonium cerium(IV) nitrate
ammonium chloride
ammonium nitrate
ammonium sulfate
antimony(III) acetate
antimony hydride
antimony pentachloride
antimony pentafluoride
antimony trioxide
arsine
arsenic trioxide (arsenic(III) oxide)
barium carbonate
barium chloride
barium hydroxide
barium iodide
barium nitrate
barium sulfate
beryllium hydroxide
beryllium oxide
bismuth(III) oxide
bismuth subsalicylate
borane
borax
boric acid
boron carbide
boron nitride
boron oxide
boron trifluoride

bromine pentafluoride
bromine trifluoride
n-butyllithium
sec-butyllithium
tert-butyllithium
cacodylic acid
cadmium chloride
cadmium sulfate hydrate
caesium bicarbonate
caesium carbonate
caesium chloride
caesium fluoride
calcium carbide
calcium carbonate
calcium chloride
calcium fluoride
calcium hydride
calcium hydroxide
calcium sulfate
carbon dioxide
carbonic acid
carbonyl fluoride
carboplatin
cerium(III) chloride
cerium(IV) sulfate
chromic acid
chromium(III) chloride
chromium(II) chloride
chromium(III) oxide
chromium(IV) oxide
chromium(VI) oxide
cobalamin (vitamin B_{12})
cobalt(II) chloride
cobalt(II) carbonate
copper(II) carbonate
copper(I) chloride

copper(II) chloride
copper(I) oxide
copper(II) oxide
copper(II) sulfate
copper(I) sulfide
copper(II) sulfide
cyanogen
cyanogen chloride
cyanuric chloride
decaborane
diborane
dichlorosilane
dimethylmercury
disilane
dysprosium(III) chloride
europium(III) chloride
gadolinium(III) chloride
gallium arsenide
gallium(III) chloride
germanium tetrahydride
gold(III) chloride
hexafluorotitanic acid
hydrazine
hydrazoic acid
hydrobromic acid
hydrochloric acid
hydroiodic acid
hydrogen bromide
hydrogen chloride
hydrogen fluoride
hydrogen peroxide
hypochlorous acid
hypophosphorous acid
indium(I) chloride
indium phosphide
iodic acid

iodine monochloride
iridium(IV) chloride
iron(III) chloride
iron(II) oxide
iron(II,III) oxide
iron(III) oxide
iron-sulfur cluster
iron(III) thiocyanate
lanthanum carbonate
lead(IV) acetate
lead(II) chloride
lead(II) iodide
lead(II) nitrate
lead(II) oxide
lead(IV) oxide
lithium aluminum hydride
lithium bromide
lithium carbonate
lithium chloride
lithium citrate
lithium diisopropylamide
lithium hydride
lithium hydroxide
lithium nitrate
lithium sulfate
magnesium carbonate
magnesium chloride
magnesium oxide
magnesium phosphate
magnesium sulfate
manganese(IV) oxide
manganese(II) acetate
manganese(II) chloride
manganese(IV) fluoride
manganese(II) phosphate
mercury(I) chloride
mercury(II) chloride
mercury fulminate
mercury(II) sulfide
metaphosphoric acid
methylmercury
methylmercury hydroxide
molybdate orange
molybdenum trioxide
molybdenum disulfide
molybdenum hexacarbonyl
molybdic acid
n-butyllithium
neodymium(III) chloride
nessler's reagent

nickel(II) hydroxide
nickelocene
nickel(II) nitrate
niobium pentachloride
nitric acid
nitric oxide
nitrogen dioxide
nitrosylsulfuric acid
nitrous oxide
orthophosphoric acid
osmium tetroxide
oxybis(tributyltin)
oxygen difluoride
ozone
palladium(II) nitrate
pentaborane
pentasulfide antimony
perchloric acid
perchloryl fluoride
phenylarsine oxide
phenyllithium
phenylmercuric acetate
phenylphosphine
phosgene
phosphine
phosphomolybdic acid
phosphoric acid
phosphorus pentabromide
phosphorus pentafluoride
phosphorus tribromide
phosphorus trichloride
phosphorus trifluoride
phosphorus triiodide
phosphotungstic acid
platinum(IV) chloride
platinum(II) chloride
plutonium(IV) oxide
potash alum
potassium bromide
potassium hydrogencarbonate
potassium carbonate
potassium chloride
potassium citrate
potassium hydroxide
potassium iodide
potassium monopersulfate
potassium nitrate
potassium permanganate
potassium sulfate
praseodymium(III) chloride

prussian blue
radium chloride
radon difluoride
rhodium(III) chloride
rubidium hydroxide
ruthenium(VIII) oxide
samarium(II) iodide
samarium(III) chloride
sec-butyllithium
selenium dioxide
silane
silica gel
silicic acid
silicochloroform
silicofluoric acid
silicon dioxide
silver chloride
silver(I) fluoride
silver iodide
silver nitrate
soda lime
sodium acetate
sodium bromide
sodium carbonate
sodium chloride
sodium chlorate
sodium cyanide
sodium hydride
sodium hydrogen carbonate
sodium hydroxide
sodium iodide
sodium nitrate
sodium nitrite
sodium percarbonate
sodium phosphate
sodium silicate
sodium sulfate
sodium sulfide
sodium sulfite
stannous chloride
stibine
strontium chloride
strontium nitrate
sulfamic acid
sulfane
sulfur dioxide
sulfurated potash
sulfuric acid
sulfurous acid
sulfuryl chloride

tantalum carbide
tantalum(V) oxide
tellurium tetrachloride
terbium(III) chloride
tert-butyllithium
tetraborane(10)
tetrabutyltin
tetrachloroauric acid
tetraethyl lead
tetraethyl tin
tetrafluorohydrazine
tetramminecopper(II) sulfate
tetraphenyltin
thallium(III) sulfate
thallium(I) fluoride
thallium(III) oxide
thallium(I) carbonate
thionyl chloride
thiophosgene

thiophosphoryl chloride
thorium dioxide
thulium(III) chloride
tin(II) chloride
tin(II) fluoride
tin(IV) chloride
titanic acid
titanium dioxide
titanium(IV) chloride
titanocene dichloride
triethylaluminium
trimethyltin chloride
triphenylantimony
tripotassium phosphate
trisodium phosphate
tungsten carbide
tungstic acid
uranium hexafluoride
uranyl zinc acetate

uranium oxide (pitch
  blende)
vanadium oxytrichloride
vanadyl sulfate
vanadium(V) oxide
water (H_2O)
xenon difluoride
xenon hexafluoroplatinate
xenon tetrafluoride
xenon tetroxide
ytterbium(III) chloride
ytterbium(III) oxide
yttrium fluoride
zinc chloride
zinc chromate hydroxide
zinc oxide
zirconium(IV) chloride
zirconium(IV) oxide
zirconocene dichloride

Appendix 2
Organic Compounds

abietic acid
acenaphthene
acenaphthoquinone
acenaphthylene
acepromazine
acetaldehyde (ethanal)
acetamide
acetaminophen
acetaminosalol
acetamiprid
acetanilide
acetic acid (ethanoic acid)
acetoguanamine
acetone
acetonitrile
acetylcholine
acetylene
n-acetylglutamate
acetylsalicylic acid (asprin)
acid fuchsin
acridine
acridine orange
acrolein
acrylamide
acrylic acid
acryloyl chloride
acyclovir
adamantane
adenosine
adipamide
adipic acid
adiponitrile
adipoyl dichloride
adonitol
adrenaline (epinephrine)
adrenochrome

aflatoxin
alanine
albumin
alcian blue
aldosterone
aldrin
aliquat 336
alizarin
allantoic acid
allantoin
allethrin
allyl propyl disulfide
allylamine
allyl chloride
ambergris
amido black 10b
p-aminobenzoic acid (PABA)
aminodiacetic acid
aminoethylpiperazine
5-amino-2-hydroxybenzoic acid
aminophylline
5-aminosalicylic acid
aminothiazole
amiodarone
amiton
amobarbital
amoxycillin
amphetamine
amyl nitrate
amyl nitrite
anethole
anilazine
aniline
aniline hydrochloride
anisole
anisoyl chloride

anthanthrene
anthracene
anthramine
anthranilic acid
anthraquinone
anthrone
antipyrine
aprotinin
arabinose
arginine
aroclor
ascorbic acid (vitamin C)
asparagine
aspartame
aspartic acid
astrablue
atrazine
auramine o
aureine
avobenzone
azadirachtin A
azathioprine
azelaic acid
azinphos-methyl
aziridine
azithromycin
azo violet
azobenzene
azulene
azure a
bacillomycin
barbital
barbituric acid
behenic acid
benomyl
benzaldehyde

benzalkonium chloride
benzamide
benzanthrone
benzene
benzethonium chloride
benzidine
benzil
benzilic acid
benzimidazole
benzisoxazole
benzo(a)anthracene
benzo(a)pyrene
benzo(c)phenanthrene
benzo(e)fluoranthene
benzo(e)pyrene
benzo(ghi)perylene
benzo(j)fluoranthene
benzo(k)fluoranthene
benzo(c)thiophene
benzocaine
benzofuran
benzoic acid
benzoin
benzothiazole
benzothiophene
benzoxazole
benzoyl chloride
benzyl alcohol
benzyl chloroformate
benzylamine
benzyldimethylamine
benzylidene acetone
betaine
butylated hydroxytoluene
biotin (vitamin H)
2,2'-bipyridyl
1,8-bis(dimethylamino)
   naphthalene
bis(chloromethyl) (ether)
bismarck brown y
bisphenol A
biuret
borneol
brassinolide
bromacil
bromoacetic acid
bromobenzene
2-bromo-1-chloropropane
bromocresol purple
bromocyclohexane

bromoform
bromomethane
bromophenol blue
2-bromopropane
bromothymol blue
bromotrifluoromethane
brucine
buckminsterfullerene
buspirone
1,3-butadiene
butadiene resin
butane
butene
2-butoxyethanol
butylamine
butyllithium
2-butyne-1,4-diol
butyraldehyde
butyrophenone
butyryl chloride
cacodylic acid
cacotheline
cadaverine ($NH_2(CH_2)5NH_2$)
cadinene
cafestol
caffeine
calcein
calciferol (vitamin D)
calcitonin
calmodulin
calreticulin
camphene
camphor
cannabinol
caprolactam
caprolactone
capsaicin
captan
captopril
carbazole
carbazol-9-yl-methanol
carbofuran
carbon dioxide
carbonic acid
carbonyl fluoride
carboplatin
carboxypolymethylene
carminic acid
carnauba wax
carnitine

cartap
carvacrol
carvone
castor oil
catechol
cedar wood oil
cefazolin
cefotaxime
ceftriaxone
cellulose
cellulose acetate
cetrimide
cetyl alcohol
chloracetyl chloride
chloral
chloral hydrate
chlorambucil
chloramine-T
chloramphenicol
chloranilic acid
chlordane
chlorhexidine gluconate
chloro-m-cresol
chloroacetic acid
chlorobenzene
chlorodifluoromethane
chloroethene
chlorofluoromethane
chloroform
2-chloro-2-methylpropane
chloronitroaniline
chloropentafluoroethane
chloropicrin
chloroquine
chlorostyrene
chlorothiazide
chlorotrifluoromethane
chlorotrimethylsilane
chloroxuron
chlorpyrifos
chlorthiamide
cholesterol
choline
chromotropic acid
cilostazol
cinchonine
cinnamaldehyde
cinnamic acid
cinnamyl alcohol
cinnoline

cis-2-butene
cis-3-hexanal
cis-3-hexen-1-ol
citral
citric acid
citronella oil
citronellal
citrulline
clobetasone
clopidol
cloxacillin
cobalamin (vitamin B$_{12}$)
cocamidopropyl
colchicine
collagen
collodion
congo red
coniine
coomassie blue
coronene
coumarin
creatine
cresol
cresyl violet
crotonaldehyde
18-crown-6
crystal violet
cubane
cumene
cupferron
cuscohygrine
cyanogen
cyanogen chloride
cyanoguanidine
cyanuric acid
cyanuric chloride
cyclodecane
α-cyclodextrin
cyclododecane
cycloheptatriene
1,3-cyclohexadiene
1,4-cyclohexadiene
cyclohexane
cyclohexanol
cyclohexanone
cyclohexene
cyclonite
cyclooctatetraene
cyclopentadiene
cyclopentane

cyclopentanol
cyclopentanone
cyclopentene
cypermethrin
cysteamine
cysteine
cystine
cytosine
DABCO
DDT
decaborane
decahydronaphthalene
decane
dehydroacetic acid
dehydrocholic acid
deltamethrin
demeton
denatonium
dexamethazone
dextran
dextrin
3,3'-diaminobenzidine
di-t-butyl peroxide
diacetylene
diazinon
diazomethane
dibucaine hydrochloride
dichloroacetic acid
p-dichlorobenzene
dichlorodifluoromethane
dichlorodimethylsilane
1,2-dichloroethane
dichlorofluoromethane
dichlorophen
dichlorotrifluoroethane
dichlorvos
diclofenac sodium
dicofol
dicrotophos
dicyclopentadiene
dieldrin
diethanolamine
diethion
diethylamine
diethylene glycol
diethylenetriamine
diethyl ether
difluoromethane
digitonin
dihydrocortisone

diisoheptyl phthalate
diisopropyl ether
diketene
dimethicone
dimethylamine
n,n-dimethylacetamide
n,n-dimethylaniline
1,2-dimethylbenzene (o-xylene)
1,3-dimethylbenzene (m-xylene)
1,4-dimethylbenzene (p-xylene)
n,n-dimethylformamide
dimethyldiethoxysilane
dimethylglyoxime
dimethylmercury
dimethyl sulfoxide
dinoseb
dioctyl phthalate
dioxane
dioxathion
dioxin
diphenylacetylene (tolane)
diphenylmethanol (benzhydrol)
dipyrone
diquat
Direct Blue 1
disulfiram
disulfoton
dithranol
2,6-di-tert-butylphenol
2,6-di-tert-butyl-4-methylphenol
2,6-di-tert-butylpyridine
diuron
divinylbenzene
docosane
dodecane
dodecylbenzene
domperidone
dopamine
doxylamine succinate
EDTA (ethylenediamine-n,n,n',n'-
    tetraacetic acid)
eicosane
endosulfan
endrin
eosin
ephedrine
epibromohydrin
epinephrine
erucic acid
erythritol

estradiol
ethacridine lactate
ethane
ethanol
ethene
ethidium bromide
ethyl acetate
ethylamine
ethylbenzene
ethyl chloride
ethylene
ethylene glycol
ethylene oxide
ethyl formate
2-ethyl-1-hexanol
eugenol
farnesol
fipronil
flunixin
fluoranthene
fluorene
9-fluorenone
fluorescein
fluorobenzene
fluoroethylene
fluoxetine
folic acid (vitamin M)
follicle stimulating hormone
   (FSH)
fonofos
formaldehyde
formamide
formanilide
formic acid
formoterol
fumaric acid
furan (furane)
furfural
furfuryl alcohol
galactose
gamma-aminobutyric acid
gamma-butyrolactone
gamma-hydroxybutyrate (GHB)
geraniol
gibberellic acid
gluconic acid
glucose
glutamic acid (glutamate)
glutamine
glutaraldehyde

glutaric acid
glutathione
glyburide
glycerin
glycerol
glycerophosphoric acid
glycidol
glycine
glycogen
glycolic acid
glyoxal
guaiacol
guanidine
guanine
guanosine
halothane
hematoxylin
hepes
heptadecane
heptane
hexachloropropene
hexadecane
hexafluoro-2-propanol
hexafluoro-2-propanone
hexafluoroethane
hexafluoropropylene
hexamethyldewarbenzene
hexamethyldisilazane
hexamethylenimine
hexamethylolmelamine
hexamine
hexane
hexanitrodiphenylamine
hexanoic acid
cis-3-hexanal
cis-3-hexen-1-ol
hippuric acid
histidine
histamine
homoarginine
homocysteine
homocystine
homotaurine
hydrochlorothiazide
hydrocinnamic acid
hydroquinone
hydroxyproline
5-hydroxytryptamine
hygrine
ibuprofen

imazapyr
imidazole
imiquimod
indazole
indene
indigo
indole
indole-3-acetic acid
inositol
iodoxybenzene
ionone
ipratropium bromide
isatin
isoamyl isobutyrate
isobenzofuran
isoborneol
isobornyl acetate
isoflurane
isoindole
isoleucine
isomelamine
isooctanol
isophthalic acid
isopropanol
isoquinoline
isoxazole
itraconazole
jasmone
Jenner's stain
kanamycin
kepone alcohol
keratin
ketene
kojic acid
lactic acid
lactose
lauric acid
lauryl alcohol
LDA (lithium diisopropylamide)
leucine
levulinic acid
limonene
linalool
linoleic acid
linolenic acid
lipoamide
lithium diisopropylamide
loratadine
LSD
luminol

2,6-lutidine
lycopene
lysine
malachite green
malathion
maleic anhydride
malic acid
maltose
mandelonitrile
mannide monooleate
mannose
mauveine
MDMA
mecoprop
MEK
melatonin
Meldola's blue
meloxicam
menthol
2-mercaptoethanol
2-mercaptopyridine
merocyanine
mesityl oxide
mesitylene
mesotartaric acid
metaldehyde
methane methanesulfonic acid
methanol
methionine
methomyl
4-methoxybenzaldehyde (anisal-
    dehyde)
methoxychlor
methoxyflurane
methyl acetate
methyl-2-cyanoacrylate
methyl isobutyl ketone (MIBK)
methyl isocyanate
methylal
methylamine
4-methylbenzoic acid (p-toluic
    acid)
methyl chloroformate
methylcyclohexane
methylene blue
methylhydrazine
methylmercury
methylmorpholine
2-methylpropene (isobutylene)
n-methylpyrrolidone

methyltriethoxysilane
methyltrimethoxysilane
metoprolol
metronidazole
Michler's ketone
milrinone
monocrotophos
monosodium glutamate
mordant red 19
morpholine
MTBE
murexide
mustard gas
myrcene
n-nonadecane
n-tetradecylbenzene
naphthalene
naphthoquinone (vitamin K)
2-naphthylamine
neomycin
niacin or nicotinic acid (vitamin
    B_3)
nicotine
niflumic acid
nile red
nimesulide
nitrilotriacetic acid
nitrobenzene
nitrocellulose
nitroethane
nitrofen
nitrofurantoin
nitroglycerine
nitromethane
nitron
n-nitroso-n-methylurea
nitrosomethylurethane
nonacosane
nonane
noradrenaline, norepinephrine
norephidrine
norcarane
norleucine
nujol
octane (C_8H_{18})
1-octanethiol
octanoic acid
4-octylphenol
oleic acid
orcin

orcinol
ornithine
orotic acid
oxalic acid
oxalyl chloride
oxamide
oxazole
oxolinic acid
oxymetholone
PABA
paclitaxel
palmitic acid
pantothenic acid (vitamin B_5)
para red
paraformaldehyde
parathion
pelargonic acid
pentachlorobiphenyl
pentachlorophenol
pentadecane
pentaerythritol
pentaethylene glycol
pentafluoroethane
pentane
pentetic acid
perfluorotributylamine
permethrin
peroxyacetic acid
perylene
petroleum ether
phenacetin
phenacyl bromide
phenanthrene
phenanthrenequinone
phencyclidine
phenethylamine
phenobarbital
phenol
phenol red (sodium salt)
phenolphthalein
phenothiazine
phenylacetic acid
phenylacetylene
phenylalanine
p-phenylenediamine
phenylhydrazine
phenyllithium
4-phenyl-4-(1-piperidinyl)
    cyclohexanol (PPC)
phenylthiocarbamide

phloroglucinol
phorate
phosgene
phthalic anhydride
phthalic acid
phytic acid
4-picoline
picric acid
pimelic acid
pinacol
piperazine
piperidine
piperonal
piperylene
pivaloyl chloride
polyacrylonitrile
polyamide 6 (Nylon 6)
polybenzimidazole
polyethylenimine
polygeline
polyisobutylene
polypropylene
polypropylene glycol
polystyrene
polyurethane
polyvinyl acetate
polyvinyl alcohol
polyvinyl chloride
polyvinylidene chloride
polyvinylidene fluoride (PVDF)
polyvinylpyrrolidone
porphyrin
prednisone
primaquine
procaine
progesterone
prolactin
proline
propane
propanoic acid
2-propanone
propargyl alcohol
propiconazole
propiolactone
propiolic acid
propionaldehyde
propionitrile
propoxur
proton-sponge (Aldrich)
purine

putrescine
pyrazine
pyrazole
pyrene
pyrethrin
pyridazine
pyridine
pyridinium tribromide
pyridoxal
pyridoxine or pyridoxamine
  (vitamin B_6)
pyrilamine
pyrimethamine
pyrimidine
pyrocatechol violet
pyroglutamic acid
pyrrole
pyrrolidine
pyruvic acid
quinaldine
quinazoline
quinhydrone
quinoline
quinone
quinoxaline
raffinose
resorcinol
retinene
retinol (vitamin A)
rhodanine
riboflavin (vitamin B_2)
ribofuranose
ribose
ricin
rosolic acid
rotenone
saccharin
safrole
salicin
salicylaldehyde
salicylic acid
salvinorin-A
sarin
sclareol
sebacic acid
sebacoyl chloride
selacholeic acid
selenocysteine
selenomethionine
seratonin

serine
serine kinase
serotonin
sildenafil (Viagra)
skatole
snakeroot oil
sorbic acid
sotolone
spermidine
squalene
stearic acid
strychnine
styrene
succinic anhydride
sucrose (sugar)
sulfanilamide
sulfanilic acid
sulforhodamine b
suxamethonium chloride
tabun
tannic acid
tannin
tartaric acid
tartrazine
taurine
terephthalic acid
terephthalonitrile
p-terphenyl
α-terpineol
testosterone
tetrachlorobiphenyl
tetrachloroethylene
tetrachloromethane (carbon tetrachloride)
tetradecane
tetraethylene glycol
tetrafluoroethene
tetrahedrane
tetrahydrofuran
tetrahydronaphthalene
tetramethrin
tetramethylsilane
tetramethylurea
tetranitromethane
tetrathiafulvalene
tetrazine
tetrodotoxin
tetryl
thalidomide
thiamine (vitamin B_1)

thiazole
thioacetamide
thiolactic acid
thiophene
thiophosgene
thiourea
thiram
thorin
threonine
thrombopoietin
thymidine
thymine
thymol
thymolphthalein
thyroxine (T4)
tiglic acid
tinidazole
tocopherol (vitamin E)
toluene
toluene diisocyanate
p-toluenesulfonic acid
p-toluic acid (4-methylbenzoic acid)
toxaphene
triazole
tributyl phosphate
tributylamine
tributylphosphine
trichloroacetic acid
trichloroacetonitrile
1,1,1-trichloroethane
trichloroethylene
trichlorofluoromethane
2,4,6-trichloroanisole
2,4,6-trichlorophenol
tricine
triclabendazole
triclosan

tricosane
tridecane
tridecanoic acid
triethylaluminium
triethylamine
triethylamine hydrochloride
triethylene glycol
triethylenediamine
trifluoroacetic acid
1,1,1-trifluoroethane
2,2,2-trifluoroethanol
trifluoromethane
trimellitic anhydride
trimethoxyamphetamine
trimethyl phosphite
trimethylamine
trimethylbenzene
2,2,4-trimethylpentane (isooctane)
trinitrotoluene (TNT)
tri-o-cresyl phosphate
triphenyl phosphate
triphenylamine
triphenylantimony
triphenylmethane
triphenylmethanol
triphenylphosphine
tropane
tropinone
trypan blue
tryptophan
tyrosine
umbelliferone
undecanol
uracil
urea
urethane
uric acid
uridine

valine
Valium
vanillin
venlafaxine
vinyl acetate
vinylidene chloride
violanthrone-79
vitamin A (retinol)
vitamin B
vitamin B_1 (thiamine)
vitamin B_2 (riboflavin)
vitamin B_3 (niacin or nicotinic acid)
vitamin B_4 (adenine)
vitamin B_5 (panthothenic acid)
vitamin B_6 (pyridoxine or pyridoxamine)
vitamin B_{12} (cobalamin)
vitamin C (ascorbic acid)
vitamin D (calciferol)
vitamin E (tocopherol)
vitamin F
vitamin H (biotin)
vitamin K (naphthoquinone)
vitamin M (folic acid)
vitamin P (niacin or nicotinic acid)
vitamin S
warfarin
xanthan gum
xanthone
xylene
xylene cyanole ff
xylenol orange
xylose
xylyl bromide
yohimbine hydrochloride
yohimbinic acid monohydrate
zingiberene

Bibliography

Abrahamsen, David. *Confessions of Son of Sam.* New York: Columbia University Press, 1985.

———. *Murder and Madness.* London: Robson Books, 1992.

———. *The Murdering Mind.* New York: Harper & Row, 1973.

Abrams, Stanley. *The Complete Polygraph Handbook.* Lexington, Mass.: Lexington Books, 1989.

Adelson, Lester. The Pathology of Homicide. Springfield, Ill.: Charles C. Thomas, 1974.

Aitken, C. G. G., and D. A. Stoney. *The Use of Statistics in Forensic Science.* Boca Raton, Fla.: CRC Press, 1991.

Almiral, Jose. *Forensic Science Explained.* Boca Raton, Fla.: CRC Press, 2005.

American Chemical Society. *Science in a Technical World: Criminal Forensics.* New York: W. H. Freeman, 2001.

Anderson, William. *Forensic Sciences in Clinical Medicine: A Case Study Approach.* Philadelphia: Lippincott Williams & Wilkins, 1998.

Armed Forces Institute of Pathology. *Autopsy Manual.* Washington, D.C.: U.S. Government Printing Office, 1960.

Arnold, Robert. *Interpretation of Airphotos and Remotely Sensed Imagery.* Englewood Cliffs, N.J.: Prentice Hall, 1996.

Ashraf, Mozayani, and Carla Noziglia, eds. *Handbook of the Real Crime Labs.* Totowa, N.J.: Humana Press, 2005.

ATF, *Arson Investigative Guide.* Washington, D.C.: ATF Publications, 1992.

Babrauskas, Vytenis. *Ignition Handbook: Principles and Applications to Fire Safety Engineering, Fire Investigation, Risk Management and Forensic Science.* Independence, Ky.: Fire Science Publications, 2003.

Banhu, Bir, and Xuejun Tan. *Computational Algorithms for Fingerprint Recognition.* New York: Springer, 2003.

Barber, Jacqueline. *Crime Lab Chemistry: Teacher's Guide.* Berkeley, Calif.: Gems, 1989.

Barnett, Peter. *Ethics in Forensic Science: Professional Standards for the Practice of Criminalistics.* Boca Raton, Fla.: CRC Press, 2001.

Bass, William. *Human Osteology: A Laboratory and Field Manual of Human Skeleton.* Columbia, Mo.: Missouri Archaeological Society, 1995.

Batten, Jack. *Mind over Murder: DNA and Other Forensic Adventures.* Toronto: McClelland & Stewart, 1996.

Bauchner, Elizabeth. *Document Analysis.* Broomall, Pa.: Mason Crest, 2005.

Beavan, Colin. *Fingerprints: The Origins of Crime Detection and the Murder Case That Launched Forensic Science.* New York: Hyperion, 2001.

Becker, Ronald. *Scientific Evidence and Expert Testimony Handbook.* Springfield, Ill.: Charles C. Thomas, 1997.

———. *The Underwater Crime Scene: Underwater Crime Investigative Techniques.* Springfield, Ill.: Charles C. Thomas, 1996.

Bell, Suzanne. *Encyclopedia of Forensic Science.* New York: Facts On File, 2003.

———. *The Facts On File Dictionary of Forensic Science.* New York: Facts On File, 2004.

Berry, Dennis. *Fire Litigation Handbook.* Quincy, Mass.: National Fire Protection Assn., 1984.

Bevel, Tom, and Ross Gardner. *Bloodstain Pattern Analysis: With an Introduction to Crime Scene*

Reconstruction. 2d ed. Boca Raton, Fla.: CRC Press, 2001.

Birks, John. *Chemiluminescence and Photochemical Reaction Detection in Chromatography.* Weinheim, Germany: VCH, 1989.

Blackburn, Ronald. *The Psychology of Criminal Conduct: Theory, Research and Practice.* New York: John Wiley & Sons, 1993.

Bodziak, William. *Footwear Impression Evidence: Detection, Recovery and Examination.* 2d ed. Boca Raton, Fla.: CRC Press, 1999.

Bogusz, Maciej, and M. J. Bogusz. *Forensic Science.* Burlington, Mass.: Elsevier Science Ltd., 2000.

Bohan, Thomas, ed. *Forensic Accident Investigation: Motor Vehicles.* Charlottesville, Va.: The Michie Co., 1994.

Bologna, Jack. *Handbook on Corporate Fraud: Prevention, Detection, and Investigation.* Burlington, Mass.: Butterworth-Heinemann, 1992.

Bologna, G. Jack, and Robert Lindquist. *Fraud Auditing and Forensic Accounting: New Tools and Techniques.* New York: John Wiley & Sons, 1995.

Bolz, Frank. *The Counter-Terrorism Handbook: Tactics, Procedures, and Techniques.* Boca Raton, Fla.: CRC Press, 1996.

Brach, Raymond, and Patrick Dunn. *Uncertainty Analysis for Forensic Science.* Tucson, Ariz.: Lawyers & Judges Publishing, 2004.

Bradford, Russell, and Ralph Bradford. *Introduction to Handwriting Examination and Identification.* McLean, Va.: Nelson-Hall, 1992.

Breger, Dee. *Journeys in Microspace: The Art of the Scanning Electron Microscope.* New York: Columbia University Press, 1995.

Brenner, John. *Forensic Science: An Illustrated Dictionary.* Boca Raton, Fla.: CRC Press, 2004.

———. *Forensic Science Glossary.* Boca Raton, Fla.: CRC Press, 1999.

Brogdon, B. G. *Forensic Radiology.* Boca Raton, Fla.: CRC Press, 1998.

Brown, John, Kenneth Osborn, and Thomas Osborn. *Forensic Engineering: Reconstruction of Accidents.* Springfield, Ill.: Charles C. Thomas, 1990.

Brown, Phyllis, and Richard Hartwick. *High Performance Liquid Chromatography.* New York: John Wiley & Sons, 1989.

Brunnelle, Richard, and Robert Reed. *Forensic Examination of Ink and Paper.* Springfield, Ill.: Charles C. Thomas, 1984.

Brussel, James. *Casebook of a Crime Psychiatrist.* New York: Bernard Geis, 1968.

Buckleton, John, Christopher Triggs, and Simon Walsh, eds. *Forensic DNA Evidence Interpretation.* Boca Raton, Fla.: CRC Press, 2004.

Buckwalter, Art. *Investigative Methods.* Burlington, Mass.: Butterworth-Heinemann, 1984.

Budowle, Bruce. *DNA Typing Protocols: Molecular Biology and Forensic Analysis.* Westborough, Mass.: Eaton Publishing/Biotechniques Books, 2000.

Butler, John. *Forensic DNA Typing: Biology, Technology, and Genetics behind STR Markers.* San Diego, Calif.: Academic Press, 2005.

Byrd, Jason, and James Castner. *Forensic Entomology: The Utility of Arthropods in Legal Investigations.* Boca Raton, Fla.: CRC Press, 2000.

Canter, David. *Fires and Human Behaviour.* London: David Fulton, 1990.

Carper, Kenneth, ed. *Forensic Engineering.* 2d ed. Boca Raton, Fla.: CRC Press, 2001.

Carroll, John. *Physical & Technical Aspects of Fire and Arson Investigation.* Springfield, Ill.: Charles C. Thomas, 1983.

Casey, Eoghan. *Digital Evidence and Computer Crime: Forensic Science, Computers, and the Internet.* London: Cambridge University Press, 2000.

Chadwick, David. *Color Atlas of Child Sexual Abuse.* Chicago: Year Book Medical Publications, 1989.

Chafe, Linda, and Elliott Leyton. *Serial Murder: Modern Scientific Perspectives.* Aldershot, England: Ashgate, 1999.

Chamberlain, Andrew. *Human Remains.* Berkeley: University of California Press, 1994.

Chamelin, Neil, Leonard Territo, and Charles Swanson. *Criminal Investigation.* 5th ed. New York: McGraw-Hill, 1992.

Chaney, Robert, Thomas August, Michael Telepchak and Glynn Chaney, eds. *Forensic and Clinical Applications of Solid Phase Extraction.* Totowa, N.J.: Humana Press, 2004.

Christianson, Scott, and Lowell Levine. *Bodies of Evidence: Forensic Science and Crime.* Guildford, Conn.: Lyons Press, 2006.

Cindrich, Ivan, and Nancy Del Grande. *Aerial Surveillance Sensing Including Obscured and Underground Object Detection.* Bellingham, Wash.: Society of Photo-Optical Instrumentation Engineers, 1994.

Clark, Derek. *Practical Forensic Odontology.* Burlington, Mass.: Butterworth-Heinemann, 1992.

Cole, Lee. *The Investigation of Motor Vehicle Fires.* El Cajon, Calif.: Lee Books, 1985.

Collins, Clarence. *Fingerprint Science.* Belmont, Calif.: Wadsworth Publishing, 2001.

Conklin, Barbara, Robert Gardner, and Dennis Shortelle. *Encyclopedia of Forensic Science: A Compendium of Detective Fact and Fiction.* Westport, Conn.: Oryx Press, 2002.

Connelly, James. *Applications of Signal and Image Processing in Explosives Detection Systems.* Berlin: Springer Verlag, 1992.

Coppock, Craig. *Contrast: An Investigator's Basic Reference Guide to Fingerprint Identification Concepts.* Springfield, Ill.: Charles C. Thomas, 2001.

Corvasce, Mauro, and Joseph Paglino. *Modus Operandi.* Cincinnati: Writer's Digest Books, 1995.

———. *Murder One.* Cincinnati: Writer's Digest Books, 1997.

Cowger, James. *Friction Ridge Skin: Comparison and Identification of Fingerprints.* Boca Raton, Fla.: CRC Press, 1983.

Crippin, James. *Explosives and Chemical Weapons Identification.* Boca Raton, Fla.: CRC Press, 2005.

Cupp, Melanie. *Toxicology and Clinical Pharmacology of Herbal Products.* Totowa, N.J.: Humana Press, 2000.

Cupp, Melanie, and Timothy Tracy, eds. *Dietary Supplements: Toxicology and Clinical Pharmacology.* Totowa, N.J.: Humana Press, 2003.

Curran, William, ed. *Forensic Psychiatry and Psychology: Perspectives and Standards for Interdisciplinary Practice.* Philadelphia: F. A. Davis, 1986.

———. *Modern Legal Medicine: Psychiatry and Forensic Science.* Philadelphia: F. A. Davis, 1980.

Curriden, Mark, Benjamin Wecht, and Cyril Wecht. *Cause of Death.* New York: Onyx Books, 1994.

———. *Grave Secrets.* New York: E. P. Dutton, 1996.

Daeid, Niamh. *Fire Investigation.* Boca Raton, Fla.: CRC Press, 2004.

Damjanov, Ivan, and James Linder. *Anderson's Color Atlas of Pathology.* St. Louis: Mosby-Year Book, 1997.

Davis, Geoffrey, ed. *Forensic Science.* Washington, D.C.: American Chemical Society, 1986.

Davis, J. E. *Introduction to Tool Marks, Firearms and the Striagraph.* Springfield, Ill.: Charles C. Thomas, 1958.

DEA Narcotics Investigator's Manual. Boulder, Colo.: Paladin Press, 1981.

Dean, John. *Analytical Chemistry Handbook.* New York: McGraw Hill, 1995.

DeForest, Peter, R. E. Gaensslen, and Henry Lee. *Forensic Science: An Introduction to Criminalistics.* New York: McGraw-Hill, 1983.

Derelanko, Michael, and Mannfred Hollinger, eds. *CRC Handbook of Toxicology.* Boca Raton, Fla.: CRC Press, 1995.

Descotes, Jacques. *Human Toxicology.* Burlington, Mass.: Elsevier Science Ltd., 1996.

DiMaio, Dominick, and Vincent DiMaio. *Forensic Pathology.* Boca Raton, Fla.: CRC Press, 1993.

DiMaio, Vincent. *Gunshot Wounds: Practical Aspects of Firearms, Ballistics, and Forensic Techniques.* Boca Raton, Fla.: CRC Press, 1992.

Dix, Jay. *Guide to Forensic Pathology.* Boca Raton, Fla.: CRC Press, 1993.

———. *Time of Death, Decomposition, and Identification, An Atlas.* Boca Raton, Fla.: CRC Press, 2000.

Douglas, John, Ann Burgess, Allen Burgess, and Robert Ressler. *Crime Classification Manual.* San Francisco: Jossey-Bass, 1992.

Douglas, John, and Mark Olshaker. *The Cases That Haunt Us.* New York: Scribner, 2000.

———. *Journey into Darkness.* New York: Pocket Books, 1997.

———. *Mind Hunter.* New York: Scribner, 1995.

———. *Obsession.* New York: Scribner, 1998.

Douglas, John, and Stephen Singular. *Anyone You Want Me to Be.* New York: Scribner, 2003.

Douthit, Gretchen, and Paul Deyoub. *A Practical Guide to Forensic Psychology.* New York: Jason Aronson, 1996.

Easteal, Simon, Neil McLeon, and Ken Reed. *DNA Profiling: Principles, Pitfalls, and Potential: A Handbook of DNA-Based Evidence for the Legal, Forensic and Law Enforcement Professionals.* London: Harwood Academic Publishing, 1991.

Eckert, William. *Crime Scene Investigation.* Wichita, Kans.: I.N.F.O.R.M., 1986.

———. *Introduction to Forensic Sciences.* Boca Raton, Fla.: CRC Press, 1997.

Edge, Martin, and Ian Turner, eds. *The Underwater Photographer.* Woburn, Mass.: Focal Press, 1996.

Eiceman, Gary, and Zeev Karpus. *Ion Mobility Spectrometry.* Boca Raton, Fla.: CRC Press, 1995.

Ellen, David. *The Scientific Examination of Documents, Methods and Techniques.* 2d ed. London: Taylor and Francis, 1997.

Eubanks, Jerry. *Pedestrian Accident Reconstruction and Litigation.* Tucson, Ariz.: Lawyers & Judges Publishing, 1996.

Evans, Colin. *The Casebook of Forensic Detection: How Science Solved 100 of the World's Most Baffling Crimes.* Hoboken, N.J.: Wiley, 1998.

Fairgrieve, Scott, ed. *Forensic Odontology Analysis: A Book of Case Studies.* Springfield, Ill.: Charles C. Thomas, 1999.

Faith, Nicholas. *Blaze: The Forensics of Fire.* New York: St. Martin's, 2000.

Faron, Fay. *Missing Persons.* Cincinnati: Writer's Digest Books, 1997.

———. *Rip-Off.* Cincinnati: Writer's Digest Books, 1998.

Fayemi, A. Olusegun. *Pathology.* 10th ed. Englewood Cliffs, N.J.: Prentice Hall, 1993.

Federal Bureau of Investigation. *Handbook of Forensic Sciences.* Washington, D.C.: U.S. Government Printing Office, 1990.

———. *The Science of Fingerprints.* Washington, D.C.: U.S. Government Printing Office, 1984.

Federal Judicial Center. *Reference Manual on Scientific Evidence.* Washington, D.C.: U.S. Government Printing Office, 1995.

Fellenbaum, Charlie, and Donna Jackson. *The Bone Detectives: How Forensic Anthropologists Solve Crimes and Uncover Mysteries of the Dead.* Boston: Little, Brown & Co., 1996.

Fernandes, T.R.C. *Microprobe Analysis of Paint Flakes in Forensic Science.* Salisbury: Institute of Mining Research, University of Rhodesia, 1978.

Ferner, R. E., and Elizabeth Norman. *Forensic Pharmacology: Medicines, Mayhem, and Malpractice.* New York: Oxford University Press, 1996.

Ferry, Ted. *Modern Accident Investigation and Analysis.* New York: John Wiley & Sons, 1988.

Field, Kenneth. *History of the American Academy of Forensic Sciences, 1948–1998.* West Conshohocken, Pa.: ASTM International, 1998.

Fisher, Barry. *Techniques of Crime Scene Investigation.* 7th ed. Boca Raton, Fla.: CRC Press, 2003.

Fisher, David. *Hard Evidence.* New York: Simon & Schuster, 1995.

Fitch, Richard, and Edward Porter. *Accidental or Incendiary.* Springfield, Ill.: Charles C. Thomas, 1997.

Ford, Jean. *Explosives and Arson Investigation.* Boca Raton, Fla.: CRC Press, 2005.

Fowlis, Ian. *Gas Chromatography.* New York: John Wiley & Sons, 1995.

Fritz, James. *Analytical Solid-Phase Extraction.* New York: Wiley-VCH, 1999.

Furst, Arthur. *The Toxicologist as Expert Witness: A Hint Book for Courtroom Procedure.* London: Taylor & Francis, 1996.

Gaensslen, Robert. *Sourcebook in Forensic Serology, Immunology, and Biochemistry.* Washington, D.C.: National Institute of Justice, 1983.

Genge, Ngaire. *The Forensic Casebook: The Science of Crime Scene Investigation.* New York: Ballantine, 2002.

Geradts, Zeno. *Forensic Science Informatics: Improving Investigations through Information Technology.* Boca Raton, Fla.: CRC Press, 2005.

Gerber, Samuel. *Chemistry and Crime: From Sherlock Holmes to Today's Courtroom.* Washington, D.C.: American Chemical Society, 1983.

Geberth, Vernon. *Sex-Related Homicide and Death Investigations.* Boca Raton, Fla.: CRC Publications, 2003.

Grauer, Anne. *Bodies of Evidence: Reconstructing History through Skeletal Analysis.* New York: Wiley-Liss, 1995.

Green, Arthur, and Dian Schetky. *Child Sexual Abuse: A Handbook for Health Care and Legal Professions.* London: Brunner/Mazel, 1988.

Greenberg, Keith. *Bomb Squad Officer: Expert with Explosives.* Woodbridge, Conn.: Blackbirch Marketing, 1995.

Haglund, William, and Marcella Sorg, eds. *Forensic Taphonomy: The Postmortem Fate of Human Remains.* Boca Raton, Fla.: CRC Press, 1997.

Hall, Harold, and David Pritchard. *Detecting Malingering and Deception: Forensic Deception Analysis.* Delray Beach, Fla.: St. Lucie Press, 1996.

Harris, Daniel. *Quantitative Chemical Analysis.* 4th ed. New York: W.H. Freeman, 1995.

Harris, Vivian, ed. *Radiographic Atlas of Child Abuse: A Case Studies Approach.* Tokyo: Igaku-Shoin Medical Publications, 1996.

Hazelwood, Roy, and Ann Burgess. *Practical Aspects of Rape Investigation: A Multidisciplinary Approach.* 2d ed. Boca Raton, Fla.: CRC Press, 1995.

Hazelwood, Roy, and Stephen Michaud. *Dark Dreams.* New York: St. Martin's, 2001.

Heard, Brian. *Handbook of Firearms and Ballistics: Examining and Interpreting Forensic Evidence.* New York: John Wiley & Sons, 1996.

Heger, Astrid, and S. Jean Emans, eds. *Evaluation of the Sexually Abused Child: A Medical Textbook and Photographic Atlas.* New York: Oxford University Press, 1992.

Helmer, Richard, and Mehmet Iscan. *Forensic Analysis of the Skull: Craniofacial Analysis, Reconstruction, and Identification.* New York: Wiley-Liss, 1993.

Henderson, Bruce. *Trace Evidence.* New York: Penguin, 1998.

Hennessee, Judith, and Michael Baden. *Unnatural Death: Confessions of a Medical Examiner.* New York: Ivy Books, 1992.

Henssge, Claus, and Bernard Knight. *The Estimation of Time Since Death in the Early Postmortem Period.* Sydney, Australia: Edward Arnold, 1995.

Herrmann, Bernd, and Susanne Hummel, eds. *Ancient DNA: Recovery and Analysis of Genetic Material from Paleontological, Archaeological, Museum, Medical, and Forensic Specimens.* Berlin: Springer-Verlag, 1993.

Hilton, Ordway. *Detecting and Deciphering Erased Pencil Writing.* Springfield, Ill.: Charles C. Thomas, 1997.

———. *Scientific Examination of Questioned Documents.* Boca Raton, Fla.: CRC Press, 1993.

Hobbs, Christopher, and Jane Wynne. *Physical Signs of Child Abuse: A Colour Atlas.* London: W. B. Saunders, 1996.

Hollien, Harry. *The Acoustics of Crime: The New Science of Forensic Phonetics.* New York: Springer, 1990.

Hoorwitz, Aaron. *Clinical Detective: Techniques in the Evaluation of Sexual Abuse.* New York: W. W. Norton, 1992.

Horgan, John. *Criminal Investigation.* New York: Glencoe/Macmillan, 1979.

Horswell, John. *The Practice of Crime Scene Investigation.* Boca Raton, Fla.: CRC Press, 2004.

Houck, Max. *Mute Witness: Trace Evidence Analysis.* San Diego: Academic Press, 2001.

Howitt, Dennis. *Paedophiles and Sexual Offences against Children.* New York: John Wiley & Sons, 1995.

Hueske, Edward. *Practical Analysis and Reconstruction of Shooting Incidents.* Boca Raton, Fla.: CRC Press, 2005.

Hunter, John, and Margaret Cox. *Forensic Archaeology: Anthropology and the Investigation Of Mass Graves.* New York: Routledge, 2006.

Hunter, William. *Mark and Trace Analysis.* Broomall, Pa.: Mason Crest, 2005.

———. *Solving Crimes with Physics.* Broomall, Pa.: Mason Crest, 2005.

Icove, David, and John DeHaan. *Forensic Fire Scene Reconstruction.* Englewood Cliffs, N.J.: Prentice Hall, 2003.

Icove, David, Vernon Wherry, and J. David Schroeder. *Combating Arson-For-Profit: Advanced Techniques for Investigators.* Columbus, Ohio: Battelle Press, 1997.

Inman, Keith, and Norah Rudin. *An Introduction to Forensic DNA Analysis.* Boca Raton, Fla.: CRC Press, 1997.

Innes, Brian. *Body in Question: Exploring the Cutting Edge in Forensic Science.* Guelph, Ontario: Sterling Creations, 2005.

Iscan, Mehmet. *Age Markers in the Human Skeleton.* Springfield, Ill.: Charles C. Thomas, 1989.

Iscan, Mehmet, and Kenneth Kennedy. *Reconstruction of Life from the Skeleton.* New York: Wiley-Liss, 1989.

Jackson, Andrew, and Julie Jackson. *Forensic Science.* Englewood Cliffs, N.J.: Prentice Hall, 2004.

James, Stuart, ed. *Scientific and Legal Applications of Bloodstain Pattern Interpretation.* Boca Raton, Fla.: CRC Press, 1999.

James, Stuart, and William Eckert, eds. *Interpretation of Bloodstain Evidence at Crime Scenes.* 2d ed. Boca Raton, Fla.: CRC Press, 1999.

James, Stuart, and Jon Nordby. *Forensic Science: An Introduction to Scientific and Investigative Techniques.* Boca Raton, Fla.: CRC Press, 2002.

———. *Instructor's Guide for Forensic Science.* Boca Raton, Fla.: CRC Press, 2005.

Johnson, Thomas, ed. *Forensic Computer Crime Investigation.* Boca Raton, Fla.: CRC Press, 2005.

Jones, Gary. *Introduction to Fingerprint Comparison.* Wildomar, Calif.: Staggs Publishing, 2000.

Karch, Steven. *Pathology of Drug Abuse.* 2d ed. Boca Raton, Fla.: CRC Press, 1996.

Kaye, Brian. *Science and the Detective: Selected Reading in Forensic Science.* Weinheim, Germany: Wiley-VCH, 1995.

Kelly, John, and Phillip Wearne. *Tainting Evidence: Inside the Scandals at the FBI Crime Lab.* New York: Free Press, 1998.

Keppel, Robert. *The Psychology of Serial Killer Investigations.* Amsterdam: Academic Press, 2003.

———. *Signature Killers.* London: Arrow, 1997.

Kiely, Terrence. *Forensic Evidence: Science and the Criminal Law.* 2d ed. Boca Raton, Fla.: CRC Press, 2005.

Kinnee, Kevin. *Practical Gambling Investigation Techniques.* Boca Raton, Fla.: CRC Press, 1992.

———. *Practical Investigation Techniques.* Boca Raton, Fla.: CRC Press, 1994.

Kintz, Pascal, ed. *Drug Testing in Hair.* Boca Raton, Fla.: CRC Press, 1996.

Kirk, Paul, and John DeHaan. *Kirk's Fire Investigation.* 5th ed. Englewood Cliffs, N.J.: Prentice Hall, 2002.

Kitson, Fulton, Barbara Larsen and Charles McEwen. *Gas Chromatography and Mass Spectrometry: A Practical Guide.* San Diego, Calif.: Academic Press, 1996.

Knight, Bernard. *Forensic Pathology.* New York: Oxford University Press, 1996.

———. *Simpson's Forensic Medicine.* 11th ed. London: Edward Arnold, 1996.

Kobilinsky, Lawrence, Thomas Liotti, and Jamel Oeser-Sweat. *DNA: Forensic and Legal Applications.* New York: Wiley-InterScience, 2004.

Komarinski, Peter. *Automated Fingerprint Identification Systems.* San Diego, Calif.: Academic Press, 2004.

Koppenhaver, Katherine. *Attorney's Guide to Document Examination.* Westport, Conn.: Quorum Books, 2002.

Krogman, Wilton, and M. Yasar Iscan. *The Human Skeleton in Forensic Medicine.* Springfield, Ill.: Charles C. Thomas, 1986.

Kruegle, Herman. *CCTV Surveillance: Video Practices and Technology.* Burlington, Mass.: Butterworth-Heinemann, 1996.

Kropowicz, Thomas. *Fingerprints: Innocence or Guilt: The Identity Factors.* Chicago: Terk Books, 2001.

Kurland, Michael. *How to Solve a Murder: The Forensic Handbook.* New York: Macmillan, 1995.

Lampton, Christopher. *DNA Fingerprinting.* New York: Franklin Watts, 1991.

Lane, Brian. *Encyclopedia of Forensic Science.* London: Headline Books, 1993.

Lane, Mark. *Rush to Judgment.* New York: Fawcett, 1967.

Langford, A., ed. *Practical Skills in Forensic Science.* Englewood Cliffs, N.J.: Pearson Prentice Hall, 2005.

Lee, Henry, and R. E. Gaensslen, eds. *Advances in Fingerprint Technology.* 2d ed. Boca Raton, Fla.: CRC Press, 2001.

———. *DNA and Other Polymorphisms in Forensic Science.* Chicago: Year Book Medical Publications, 1990.

Lee, Henry, and Howard Harris. *Physical Evidence in Forensic Science.* Tucson, Ariz.: Lawyers & Judges Publishing Co., 2000.

Lee, Henry, Timothy Palmbach, and Marilyn Miller. *Henry Lee's Crime Scene Handbook.* San Diego, Calif.: Academic Press, 2001.

Lee, Robert. *Scanning Electron Microscopy and X-Ray Microanalysis.* Englewood Cliffs, N.J.: Prentice Hall, 1992.

Lennard, Chris, Pierre Margot, Milutin Stoilovic, and Christophe Champod, eds. *Fingerprints and Other Ridge Skin Impressions.* Boca Raton, Fla.: CRC Press, 2004.

Lentini, John. *Scientific Protocols for Fire Investigation.* Boca Raton, Fla.: CRC Press, 2006.

Lerner, K. Lee, and Brenda Lerner. *World of Forensic Science.* Farmington Hills, Mich.: Thomas Gale, 2005.

Lester, Doug. *Crime Photographers Handbook.* Boulder, Colo.: Paladin Press, 1996.

Levy, Harlan. *And the Blood Cried Out: A Prosecutor's Spellbinding Account of the Power of DNA.* New York: Basic Books, 1996.

Lewis, Peter, Ken Reynolds, and Colin Gagg. *Forensic Materials Engineering: Case Studies.* Boca Raton, Fla.: CRC Press, 2003.

Libal, Angela. *Fingerprints, Bite Marks, Ear Prints: Human Signposts.* Broomall, Pa.: Mason Crest, 2005.

———. *Forensic Anthropology.* Broomall, Pa.: Mason Crest, 2005.

Lide, David, and H. P. R. Frederikse, eds. *CRC Handbook of Chemistry and Physics: A Ready-Reference Book of Chemical and Physical Data.* Boca Raton, Fla.: CRC Press, 1996.

Limburg, Peter. *Deep-Sea Detectives: Maritime Mysteries and Forensic Science.* Toronto: ECW Press, 2004.

Lincoln, Patrick, Jim Thomson, and James Thomas, eds. *Forensic DNA Profiling Protocols.* Totowa, N.J.: Humana Press, 1998.

Lindsay, Sandy. *High Performance Liquid Chromatography*. New York: John Wiley & Sons, 1987.

Liu, Ray, and Daniel Gadzala. *Handbook of Drug Analysis: Applications in Forensic and Clinical Laboratories*. Washington, D.C.: American Chemical Society, 1997.

Liu, Ray, and Bruce Goldberger, eds. *Handbook of Workplace Drug Testing*. Washington, D.C.: American Association for Clinical Chemistry, 1995.

Lloyd, Harvey. *Aerial Photography: Professional Techniques and Commercial Applications*. New York: Amphoto, 1990.

Lynch, Virginia. *Emergency Nursing: Forensics, Protocols, Policies and Guidelines*. New York: Aspen, 1995.

Mactire, Sean. *Malicious Intent*. Cincinnati: Writer's Digest Books, 1995.

Malmquist, Carl. *Homicide: A Psychiatric Perspective*. New York: American Psychiatric Press, 1996.

Maltoni, David, Dario Maio, Anil Jain, and Salil Prabhakar. *Handbook of Fingerprint Recognition*. New York: Springer, 2005.

Maples, William, and Michael Browning. *Dead Men Do Tell Tales: The Strange and Fascinating Cases of a Forensic Anthropologist*. New York: Doubleday, 1994.

Marriner, Brian. *On Death's Bloody Trail: Murder and the Art of Forensic Science*. New York: St. Martin's, 1993.

Marrs, Jim. *Crossfire: The Plot That Killed Kennedy*. New York: Carroll & Graf, 1989.

Marshall, Evan, and Edwin Sanow. *Handgun Stopping Power: The Definitive Study*. Boulder, Colo.: Paladin Press, 1992.

Marx, Gary. *Undercover: Police Surveillance in America*. Berkeley: University of California Press, 1990.

Mason, J. K., ed. *The Pathology of Trauma*. Boston: Little, Brown & Co., 1993.

McCaffrey, Robert, Arthur Williams, and Jerid Fisher, eds. *The Practice of Forensic Neuropsychology: Meeting Challenges in the Courtroom*. New York: Plenum, 1996.

McDonald, Peter. *Tire Imprint Evidence*. Boca Raton, Fla.: CRC Press, 1993.

McEwan, J. Thomas, and David Weisburd. *Crime Mapping*. Monsey, N.Y.: Willow Tree Press, 1997.

Meloan, Richard. *Criminalistics: An Introduction to Forensic Science*. 7th ed. Englewood Cliffs, N.J.: Prentice Hall, 2000.

Melton, Gary. *Psychological Evaluations for the Courts: A Handbook for Mental Health Professionals and Lawyers*. New York: Guilford Press, 1987.

Menzel, E. Roland. *Fingerprint Detection with Lasers*. London: Marcel Dekker, 1980.

———. *An Introduction to Lasers, Forensic Lights and Fluorescent Fingerprint Detection*. Jacksonville, Fla.: Lightning Powder Co., 1991.

Message, Gordon. *Practical Aspects of Gas Chromatography/Mass Spectrometry*. New York: John Wiley & Sons, 1984.

Meyer, Veronika. *Practical High-Performance Liquid Chromatography*. New York: John Wiley & Sons, 1988.

Meyers, Charles. *Silent Evidence: Firearms Forensic Ballistics and Toolmarks—Cases from Forensic Science*. Boone, N.C.: Parkway Publishers, 2004.

Miller, Hugh. *What the Corpse Revealed: Murder and the Science of Forensic Detection*. New York: St. Martin's, 1999.

———. *Traces of Guilt: Forensic Science and the Fight Against Crime*. London: BBC Books, 1998.

Moenssens, Andre. *Fingerprint Techniques*. New York: Chilton, 1971.

———. *Fingerprints and the Law*. New York: Chilton, 1969.

Moenssens, Andre, James Starrs, Carol Henderson, and Fred Inbau. *Scientific Evidence in Civil and Criminal Cases*. 4th ed. Westbury, N.Y.: Foundation Press, 1995.

Morse, Dan, Jack Duncan, and James Stoutamire, eds. *Handbook of Forensic Anthropology*. Tallahassee, Fla.: Rose Printing, 1983.

Murray, Raymond, and J. C. E. Tedrow. *Evidence from the Earth*. Missoula, Mont.: Mountain Press, 2004.

———. *Forensic Geology: Earth Sciences and Criminal Investigation*. Englewood Cliffs, N.J.: Prentice Hall, 1992.

Nafte, Myriam. *Flesh and Bone: An Introduction to Forensic Anthropology*. Durham, N.C.: Carolina Academic Press, 2000.

National Institute of Justice. *Sources in Forensic Serology, Immunology, and Biochemistry*. Washington, D.C.: U.S. Government Printing Office, 1983.

National Research Council. *DNA Technology in Forensic Science*. Washington, D.C.: National Academies Press, 1992.

Nay, Tara. *True and False Allegations of Child Sexual Abuse: Assessment and Case Management.* London: Brunner/Mazel, 1995.

Newton, Michael. *Armed and Dangerous.* Cincinnati: Writer's Digest Books, 1990.

———. *The Encyclopedia of Serial Killers.* New York: Facts On File, 2000.

———. *The Encyclopedia of American Law Enforcement.* New York: Facts On File, 2006.

———. *The FBI Encyclopedia.* Jefferson, N.C.: McFarland, 2004.

Nickell, Joe. *Detecting Forgery: Forensic Investigation of Documents.* Lexington: University Press of Kentucky, 1996.

Nickell, Joe, and John Fischer. *Crime Science: Methods of Forensic Detection.* Lexington: University Press of Kentucky, 1998.

Noon, Randall. *Engineering Analysis of Fires and Explosions.* Boca Raton, Fla.: CRC Press, 1995.

———. *Engineering Analysis of Vehicular Accidents.* Boca Raton, Fla.: CRC Press, 1994.

———. *Introduction to Forensic Engineering.* Boca Raton, Fla.: CRC Press, 1992.

Nordby, Jon. *Dead Reckoning—The Art of Forensic Detection.* Boca Raton, Fla.: CRC Press, 2000.

O'Hara, Charles. *Fundamentals of Criminal Investigation Study Guide.* 6th ed. Philadelphia: F. A. Davis, 1995.

Olson, Paul. *Forensic Aspects of Driver Perception and Response.* Tucson, Ariz.: Lawyers & Judges Publishing, 1996.

Osterburg, James, and Richard Ward. *Criminal Investigation: Methods for Reconstructing the Past.* Cincinnati: Anderson Publishing, 1991.

Owen, David. *Hidden Evidence.* London: Firefly Books, 2000.

———. *Police Lab: How Forensic Science Tracks Down and Convicts Criminals.* London: Firefly Books, 2002.

Page, David. *Body Trauma.* Cincinnati: Writer's Digest Books, 1996.

Patton, Alexander. *Fire Litigation Sourcebook.* 2d ed. New York: John Wiley & Sons, 1994.

Petraco, Nicholas, and Thomas Kubic. *Color Atlas and Manual of Microscopy for Criminalists, Chemists, and Conservators.* Boca Raton, Fla.: CRC Press, 2003.

———. *Forensic Science Laboratory Manual and Workbook.* Boca Raton, Fla.: CRC Press, 2005.

Phillips, A. P. *Hair Sexing in Forensic Science.* London: Home Office Central Research Establishment, 1972.

Physicians Desk Reference. Oradell, N.J.: Medical Economics, 2005.

Physicians Desk Reference for Non-Prescription Drugs. Oradell, N.J.: Medical Economics, 2005.

Pickering, Robert, and David Bachman. *The Use of Forensic Anthropology.* Boca Raton, Fla.: CRC Press, 1996.

Pilant, Lois. *Forensic Science: Bringing New Technology into the Crime Lab.* Washington, D.C.: International Association of Chiefs of Police, 1993.

Platt, Richard. *Crime Scene: The Ultimate Guide to Forensic Science.* New York: DK Publishing, 2003.

Potter, Jerry, and Fred Bost. *Fatal Justice: Reinvestigating the MacDonald Murders.* New York: W. W. Norton, 1997.

Quintiere, James. *Principles of Fire Behavior.* Florence, Ky.: Thomas Delmar Learning, 1997.

Raine, Adrian. *The Psychopathology of Crime: Criminal Behavior as a Clinical Disorder.* San Diego, Calif.: Academic Press, 1993.

Redsicker, David. *The Practical Methodology of Forensic Photography.* 2d ed. Boca Raton, Fla.: CRC Press, 2000.

Redsicker, David, Gurden Gordner, Stuart James, and Anthony Laws. *Practical Methodology of Forensic Photography.* Boca Raton, Fla.: CRC Press, 1996.

Redsicker, David, and John O'Connor. *Practical Fire and Arson Investigation.* Boca Raton, Fla.: CRC Press, 1996.

Reece, Robert. *Child Abuse: Medical Diagnosis and Management.* Philadelphia: Lea & Febiger, 1994.

Reed, S. J. B. *Electron Microprobe Analysis and Scanning Electron Microscopy in Geology.* London: Cambridge University Press, 1996.

Reichs, Kathleen, ed. *Forensic Osteology: Advances in Identification of Human Remains.* Springfield, Ill.: Charles C. Thomas, 1997.

Ressler, Robert, Ann Burgess, and John Douglas. *Sexual Homicide.* Lexington, Mass.: Lexington Books, 1988.

Ressler, Robert, and Tom Schachtman. *I Have Lived in the Monster.* New York: St. Martin's, 1997.

———. *Whoever Fights Monsters.* New York: St. Martin's, 1994.

Robertson, Bernard, and G. A. Vignaux. *Interpreting Evidence: Evaluating Forensic Science in the Courtroom.* New York: John Wiley & Sons, 1995.

Robertson, Edna. *Fundamentals of Document Examination.* McLean, Va.: Nelson-Hall, 1991.

Robertson, James. *Botanical Evidence in Forensic Science.* Boca Raton, Fla.: 2006.

———. *Forensic Examination of Fibers.* London: Ellis Horwood, 1992.

Robertson, James, A. M. Ross and L. A. Burgoyne, eds. *DNA in Forensic Science: Theory, Techniques, and Applications.* Boca Raton, Fla.: CRC Press, 1990.

Rogers, Spencer. *Forensic Identification from Human Remains.* Springfield, Ill.: Charles C. Thomas, 1987.

Sachs, Jessica. *Corpse: Nature, Forensics, and the Struggle to Pinpoint Time of Death—An Exploration of the Haunting Science of Forensic Ecology.* Jackson, Tenn.: Perseus Publishing, 2001.

———. *Time of Death: The Story of Forensic Science and the Search for Death's Stopwatch.* Portsmouth, N.H.: Heinemann, 2002.

Saferstein, Richard. *Criminalistics: An Introduction to Forensic Science.* 8th ed. Englewood Cliffs, N.J.: Prentice Hall, 2003.

Saferstein, Richard, and Samuel Gerber. *More Chemistry and Crime: From Marsh Arsenic Test to DNA Profile.* Washington, D.C.: American Chemical Society, 1997.

Salamone, Salvatore. *Benzodiazepines and Ghb: Detection and Pharmacology.* Totowa, N.J.: Humana Press, 2001.

Schlesinger, Louis. *Sexual Murder: Catathymic and Compulsive Homicides.* Boca Raton, Fla.: CRC Press, 2003.

Schwoeble, A. J., and David Exline. *Current Methods in Forensic Gunshot Residue Analysis.* Boca Raton, Fla.: CRC Press, 2000.

Science of Fingerprints: Classification and Uses. Collingdale, Pa.: DIANE Publishing, 1988.

Scott, Walter. *Scott's Fingerprint Mechanics.* Boca Raton, Fla.: Charles C. Thomas, 1978.

Sellier, K. G., and B. P. Kneubuchi. *Wound Ballistics.* Burlington, Mass.: Elsevier Science, 1994.

Shepherd, Robin, and J. D. Frost, eds. *Failures in Civil Engineering: Structural, Foundation, and Geoenvironmental Case Studies.* Reston, Va.: American Society of Civil Engineers, 1995.

Shiffman, Melvin, ed. *Ethics in Forensic Science and Medicine: Guidelines for the Forensic Expert and the Attorney.* Springfield, Ill.: Charles C. Thomas, 2000.

Siegel, Jay, and Max Houck. *Fundamentals of Forensic Science.* San Diego, Calif.: Academic Press, 2006.

Siegel, Jay, Geoffrey Knupfer, and Pekka Saukko. *Encyclopedia of Forensic Sciences.* 3 vols. San Diego, Calif.: Academic Press, 2000.

Siljander, Raymond, and Darin Frederickson. *Applied Police and Fire Photography.* Springfield, Ill.: Charles C. Thomas, 1997.

Skoog, Douglas. *Analytical Chemistry, An Introduction.* 7th ed. Orlando, Fla.: Harcourt College Publishers, 2000.

Slyter, Steven. *Forensic Signature Examination.* Springfield, Ill.: Charles C. Thomas, 1997.

Spitz, Werner, ed. *Medicolegal Investigation of Death: Guidelines for the Application of Pathology to Crime Investigation.* Springfield, Ill.: Charles C. Thomas, 1993.

———. *Spitz and Fisher's Medicolegal Investigation of Death.* 3d ed. Springfield, Ill.: Charles C. Thomas, 1993.

Stevens, John, and Margaret Stark, eds. *Clinical Forensic Medicine: A Physician's Guide.* 2d ed. Totowa, N.J.: Humana Press, 2005.

Stevens, Serita, and Anne Klarner. *Deadly Doses.* Cincinnati: Writer's Digest Books, 1990.

Swanson, Charles, Neil Chamelin, and Leonard Territo. *Criminal Investigation.* New York: McGraw-Hill, 1995.

Sweet, J. J., ed. *Forensic Neuropsychology Fundamentals and Practice.* Lisse, Netherlands: Swets and Zeitlinger, 1997.

Swenson, Eric, and Howard Coleman. *DNA in the Courtroom: A Trial Watcher's Guide.* Seattle: Genlex Press, 1995.

Taman, A. *Faintest of Clues: Forensic Science Explained.* Boca Raton, Fla.: CRC Press, 2005.

Taylor, Karen. *Forensic Art and Illustration.* Boca Raton, Fla.: CRC Press, 2001.

Tebbett, Ian. *Gas Chromatography in Forensic Science.* Boca Raton, Fla.: CRC Press, 1993.

Thomas, Peggy. *Talking Bones: The Science of Forensic Anthropology.* New York: Facts On File, 1995.

Thornhill, William. *Forensic Accounting: How to Investigate Financial Fraud.* New York: Irwin, 1994.

Tilstone, William. *Forensic Science: An Encyclopedia of History, Methods, and Techniques.* Santa Barbara, Calif.: ABC-CLIO, 2004.

Towl, Graham, and David Crighton. *The Handbook of Psychology for Forensic Practitioners.* New York: Routledge, 1997.

Turvey, Brent. *Criminal Profiling: An Introduction to Behavioral Science Analysis.* San Diego, Calif.: Academic Press, 1999.

Ubelaker, Douglas, and Henry Scammell. *Bones: A Forensic Detective's Casebook.* New York: Harper, 1993.

Ubelaker, Douglas. *Human Skeletal Remains: Excavation, Analysis, Interpretation.* 2d ed. Washington, D.C.: Taraxacum Press, 1989.

Van Dam, Carla. *Identifying Child Molesters: Preventing Child Sexual Abuse by Recognizing the Patterns of the Offenders.* Binghamton, N.Y.: Haworth Press, 2001.

Vanesis, Peter, ed. *Pathology of Neck Injury.* Burlington, Mass.: Butterworth-Heinemann, 1989.

———. *Suspicious Death-Scene Investigation.* New York: Oxford University Press, 1995.

Wang, Xue, and Brian Herman. *Fluorescence Imaging Spectroscopy and Microscopy.* New York: John Wiley & Sons, 1996.

Ward, Jenny. *Crimebusting: Breakthroughs in Forensic Science.* Poole, England: Blandford Press, 1998.

Warlow, T. A. *Firearms, the Law and Forensic Ballistics.* Boca Raton, Fla.: CRC Press, 1996.

Watts, Alan, Dale Atkinson, and Corey Hennessy. *Low Speed Automobile Accidents: Accident Reconstruction and Occupant Kinematics, Dynamics, and Biomechanics.* Tucson, Ariz.: Lawyers & Judges Publishing, 1996.

Wecht, Cyril. *Forensic Sciences.* Albany, N.Y.: Matthew Bender and Co., 1997.

———. *United States Medicolegal Autopsy Laws.* 3d ed. Washington, D.C.: Information Resources Press, 1989.

Wecht, Cyril, and John Rago. *Forensic Science and the Law: Investigative Applications in Criminal, Civil, and Family Justice.* Boca Raton, Fla.: CRC Press, 2006.

Weisburd, David. *Crimes of the Middle Classes: White-Collar Offenders in the Federal Courts.* New Haven, Conn.: Yale University Press, 1991.

Wells, Kenneth, and Paul Weston. *Criminal Investigation: Basic Perspectives.* Englewood Cliffs, N.J.: Prentice-Hall, 1990.

White, Peter. *Crime Scene to Court: The Essentials of Forensic Science.* London: Royal Society of Chemistry, 1998.

William, Edward. *The Detection of Human Remains.* Springfield, Ill.: Charles C. Thomas, 1990.

Williams, Howard. *Investigating White-Collar Crime: Embezzlement and Financial Fraud.* Springfield, Ill.: Charles C. Thomas, 1997.

Wilson, Keith. *Cause of Death.* Cincinnati: Writer's Digest Books, 1992.

Wilson, Paul. *Justice and Nightmares: Success and Failures of Forensic Science in Australia and New Zealand.* Sydney: New South Wales University Press, 1992.

Wingate, Ann. *Scene of the Crime.* Cincinnati: Writer's Digest Books, 1992.

Witzig, Eric. *Observations on the Serial Killer Phenomenon.* Quantico, Va.: FBI Academy, 1999.

Wonder, Anita. *Blood Dynamics.* San Diego, Calif.: Academic Press, 2001.

Wong, Raphael, and Harley Tse. *Drugs Of Abuse: Body Fluid Testing.* Totowa, N.J.: Humana Press, 2005.

Yereance, Robert. *Electrical Fire Analysis.* Springfield, Ill.: Charles C. Thomas, 1997.

Yinon, Jehuda, ed. *Advances in Analysis and Detection of Explosives.* Norwell, Mass.: Kluwer Academic Publishing, 1993.

———. *Analysis of Explosives.* Burlington, Mass.: Pergamon Press, 1981.

———. *Forensic Applications of Mass Spectrometry.* Boca Raton, Fla.: CRC Press, 1995

Yinon, Jehuda, and Shmuel Zitrin. *Modern Methods and Applications in Analysis of Explosives.* New York: John Wiley & Sons, 1993.

Index